FINANCING EDUCATION SYSTEMS

FINANCING EDUCATION SYSTEMS

Bruce D. Baker
University of Kansas

Preston Green
Pennsylvania State University

Craig E. Richards
Teachers College, Columbia University

PEARSON

Merrill
Prentice Hall

Upper Saddle River, New Jersey
Columbus, Ohio

Library of Congress Control Number: 2007924058

Vice President and Executive Publisher: Jeffery W. Johnston
Senior Editor: Darcy Betts Prybella
Editorial Assistant: Nancy Holstein
Production Editor: Kris Roach
Production Coordination: Karen Fortgang, bookworks publishing services
Design Coordinator: Diane C. Lorenzo
Cover Designer: Kellyn E. Donnelley
Cover Image: Jupiter Images
Production Manager: Susan Hannahs
Director of Marketing: David Gesell
Marketing Coordinator: Bryan Mounts

This book was set in 10/12 Galliard by Aptara, Inc. It was printed and bound by Hamilton Printing. The cover was printed by Phoenix Color Corp.

NOTE: Every effort has been made to provide accurate and current Internet information in this book. However, the Internet and information posted on it are constantly changing, so it is inevitable that some of the Internet addresses listed in this textbook will change.

Pearson Education Ltd.   Pearson Education Australia Pty. Limited
Pearson Education Singapore Pte. Ltd.   Pearson Education North Asia Ltd.
Pearson Education Canada, Ltd.   Pearson Educación de Mexico, S.A. de C.V.
Pearson Education—Japan   Pearson Education Malaysia Pte. Ltd.

10 9 8 7 6 5 4 3 2 1
ISBN-13: 978-0-13-098458-6
ISBN-10:   0-13-098458-2

Introduction

This book has been a long time in the making. Much has changed in the field of public school finance even since we set out on this project 5 years ago. Our initial objective, however, has remained constant—to provide a comprehensive, graduate-level overview of the interdisciplinary field of school finance and to do so with a sufficient level of rigor that students acquire a firm understanding of the relationship between school finance systems and the broader economic, political, and sociological context.

Public school finance is, and will be for the foreseeable future, a massive industry both in the United States and around the world. Since 2003, in the United States alone, federal, state, and local governments combined have allocated over $500 billion annually. Currently, our nation's public elementary and secondary schools serve approximately 55 million children, with another 7 million served in private schools. Yet with constant pressure to increase educational outcomes for not just some, but all children, pressure is mounting on state governments in particular to allocate substantially more funding to K–12 public schools. We do not offer any nostrums for the difficult financial picture K–12 education confronts in the coming decades. We each believe very strongly, however, that American public education has the capacity to become more equitable, to ensure adequate levels of funding to make equity mean something, and to be considerably more efficient in the allocation of existing and future resources. Finally, while we recognize the many problems with No Child Left Behind (NCLB) legislation, we are also convinced that the academic performance of American school children can be vastly improved. We are committed to being a part of the solution to these challenges, and we offer you this textbook as only one of our mutual efforts in the direction of these goals.

Organization of This Book

This book is organized into four major sections, each with three to five chapters.

Section I: The Context of School Finance

Chapters 1 through 3 provide background and context for understanding the financing of public schools. Chapter 1 addresses the various lenses through which we will view school finance policy throughout this text, in particular the legal, political, economic, and sociological lenses. We note that this text has a decidedly economic tone, which we feel is necessary for conveying the theoretical and empirical underpinnings of current approaches to financing public services in the United States. However, the economic considerations of school finance cannot be understood as they are implemented in policy without considerable attention to the legal, political, and sociological dimensions of our current challenges. Chapter 2 explains and summarizes the most significant economic theories that drive U.S. public school finance policy. Chapter 2 also describes some important features of the organization and financing of education systems internationally against which we can profitably compare the U.S. system. Chapter 3 begins our more in-depth look at the public finance of education systems in the United States, exploring in some detail the revenue streams that support American elementary and secondary schools from local, state, and federal sources. Together, these first three chapters provide a foundation for Section II and the exploration of equality.

Section II: Equality of Educational Opportunity

Unlike other school finance textbooks, this book is organized around distinct conceptions and applications of educational equity (addressed in Section II) and conceptions and applications of educational adequacy (addressed in Section III). We do not take this perspective because we believe adequacy and equity to be discrete and easily separable. On the contrary, educational equity, equality of opportunity, and educational adequacy are inextricably linked. Rather, we use this approach for pedagogical reasons. Adequacy litigation, policy, and financial modeling largely follow equity. We hope that our readers will first develop a strong understanding of core principles of educational equity, legal frameworks for understanding educational equity (Chapter 4), empirical measures of equity (Chapter 5), and government interventions to promote equity (Chapter 6). This understanding will provide the necessary foundation for tackling the complexly layered questions embedded in the meanings and measures of educational adequacy.

Section III: Educational Adequacy

This section provides a detailed exploration of conceptions of educational adequacy, state constitutional litigation over the adequacy of education funding, methodologies for measuring education costs, and variations in costs from one child to the next and one location to the next. We also provide extensive discussion with numerous applications of how increasingly state governments are building school finance formulas toward input-based and outcome-based educational adequacy goals. Chapter 7 addresses conceptions of adequacy, adequacy litigation, and measurement of education costs. Chapter 8 addresses variations in education costs across children. Chapter 9 addresses variations in education costs from one location to the next. Chapter 10 develops and applies new frameworks for evaluating state school finance formulas, including measures for evaluating the adequacy of those formulas generally, and the adequacy of those formulas as accommodating varied needs and conditions across public school districts within states.

At the end of Section III (in Chapter 10), we provide computer simulations, available on the Companion Website (www.prenhall.com/baker) for students to integrate their theoretical and policy understandings of equity and adequacy and the dynamic relationship between these two pillars of school finance policy.

Section IV: Productivity and Efficiency

Chapters 11 through 15 explore in-depth conceptions and measures of educational productivity and efficiency and school reforms intended to improve educational productivity and efficiency. In Chapter 11, we provide an economically rigorous discussion of conceptions and measurement of educational productivity and efficiency. In Chapter 12, we discuss private-market-oriented reform strategies that have been leveraged by state and local policy makers to improve educational productivity and efficiency, including models of educational choice and for-profit educational management. In Chapter 13, we discuss the intersection of teacher labor market behavior and school finance policy. In Chapter 14, we discuss the role of accountability and incentives, or outcome-based government-intervention strategies. Finally, in Chapter 15, we discuss the role of internal resource allocation decisions and policies for improving educational productivity and efficiency. Throughout these chapters, we attempt to summarize the most recent and rigorous empirical research on each topic. We note, however, that the landscape changes on a daily basis; research, policy, and political opinion have not yet stabilized.

Unique Features

Unique features of this book include (a) its organization of content, (b) its basis in the most up-to-date research on school finance policy and related fields, and (c) the use of computer simulation and sensitivity analysis activities to engage students in school finance policy analysis. The simulations and analysis activities are both text-based and Web-based, with additional materials and exercises available on the book's Companion Website (www.prenhall.com/baker).

- *Organization:* Unlike earlier school finance texts, and new editions based on those texts, this book is organized around (a) context, (b) equity, (c) adequacy, and (d) productivity and efficiency. We adopt an approach that might be considered a *spiraled curriculum;* throughout the text, we revisit basic ideas and build on them until the student has grasped the full range of associated theories, concepts, and skills (Bruner, 1960).[1]

- *Research Base:* The text is based on the best available and most up-to-date empirical research by leading scholars across the various fields related to school finance policy. Embedded within this text is a comprehensive literature review on the field of public education finance.

- *Simulation Activities:* Finally, this textbook includes numerous spreadsheet simulation and data-analysis activities. We present user-friendly

---

[1]Bruner, J. (1960). *The process of education.* Cambridge, MA: Harvard University Press.

simulations with thorough documentation regarding the use and underlying assumptions of the simulation. In addition, we provide activities and problem sets for students. We encourage you to use these simulations to reinforce key concepts, including specific calculation methods as well as political dynamics and tensions in resolving school funding inequities. The problem sets also provide students of school finance the opportunity to develop policy analysis writing and data representation skills.

Companion Website

The text's Companion Website includes up-to-date, downloadable versions of all chapter simulations and sample PowerPoint slides for integration into faculty lectures on key topics addressed in the text (www.prenhall.com/baker).

We encourage readers to contact us directly about any perceived imbalance, significant gaps, or perceived (or actual) misrepresentations of the research literature.

Acknowledgments

Bruce Baker: I thank Craig Richards for recruiting me, along with Preston Green, into this unique field of school finance and thus changing my life from 1994 to the present. I also especially thank the many individuals across the field of school finance who have significantly shaped my thinking and corrected many of my personal misunderstandings of the field in recent years, especially William Duncombe of Syracuse University, Lori Taylor of Texas A&M, Leanna Stiefel of New York University, and Jay Chambers of the American Institutes for Research. Any remaining misconceptions presented in this text are solely my own and not a function of the advisement of these great scholars. Many others, including Kieran Killeen, John Sipple, Tom Downes, Rob Reich, Craig Wood, Larry Picus, Bruce Cooper, Jennifer Imazeki, Harrison Keller, Jesse Levin, Scott Thomas, Chris Morphew, and Andy Tompkins, have been exceptional sounding boards for ideas and analyses pertaining to school finance in particular and education policy more generally. I also thank my two personal tutors on questions pertaining to education law, Mickey Imber (University of Kansas) and co-author Preston Green. Their frequent differences in legal interpretation have been informative. Finally, I thank my wife and my two best little pals in the world.

Preston Green: I thank my wife, Fiona Greaves, for her love and support. I also thank my two children, Noah and Corinna, for making sure my life is never dull. Finally, I thank my mother, Catherine Williams, and my brother, David Green, for believing in me.

Craig Richards: I acknowledge the many outstanding teachers I have benefited from during my career that laid the foundation for this textbook, and the outstanding colleagues in the American Education Finance Association and students at Teachers College, Columbia University, who provided a forum and testing ground for many of the ideas contained herein over a 25-year research career in education finance.

One always hopes that one's students will exceed them, and I am proud to say that my two co-authors and colleagues have succeeded admirably in that respect. It has been my privilege to work with them. Finally, on a personal note, none of this would have been possible without the patient support of my wife, Elizabeth and my son, Michael, who sustain me in more ways than even I can comprehend.

We would also like to thank the reviewers for their thoughtful and insightful comments and suggestions. They are Morris L. Anderson, Wayne State College; John Babel, Cleveland State University; Perry Berkowitz, The College of St. Rose; Rodney Davis, Troy University, Dothan; Saul B. Grossmann, Temple University; Mary F. Hughes, University of Arkansas (Emeritus); Jack Klotz, University of Central Arkansas; Karen B. Lieuallen, Marian College; Carolyn McCreight, Texas A & M International University; Norma J. H. Patterson, Grand Canyon University; Catherine C. Sielke, University of Georgia; Peter Smith, University of Nebraska at Omaha; and Scott R. Sweetland, The Ohio State University.

BRIEF CONTENTS

CONTENTS

Chapter 15   ALLOCATING RESOURCES TO PROMOTE PRODUCTIVITY AND EFFICIENCY
IN SCHOOLS AND SCHOOL DISTRICTS   399

THE CONTEXT OF SCHOOL FINANCE

CHAPTER 1

THE SOCIAL SCIENCE OF SCHOOL FINANCE

Introduction

The study of school finance is an interdisciplinary field, drawing on concepts, research, and analytical methods from the fields of education, economics, public finance, political science, law, and sociology. Take the following examples:

- From a *political* perspective, the determination of both the level and distribution of school funding at the state and local level results from the joint decisions of local voters to tax themselves and from the taxing, budget allocation, and redistribution deliberations of state elected officials. Thus, understanding the design and ultimately the behavioral dynamics of democratic decision making is critical to understanding the evolution of school finance.

- From a *sociological* perspective, government financing of public schooling may seek to reinforce or to reshape the class structure of modern society. As such, decision makers should design policies with both a thorough understanding of the existing class structure, racial, ethnic, and cultural issues in our society as well as explicit goals for resolving them.

- From an *economic* perspective, governments raise funding for public schooling through taxes on the value of properties, on the incomes of individuals and businesses, and on the consumption of goods and services. By allocation to public schooling, governments then invest those tax revenues back into children, who will in turn generate earnings exceeding what they might have earned without schooling, and who will purchase more goods and

own property, yielding tax revenue for the next generation of public school students.

- From a *legal* perspective, state officials are constitutionally obligated to provide some level of public education services, distributed with some degree of equity to the children of each state.

- Again, from an *economic* perspective, schools are not only a vehicle for advancing the learning of children but also a business—often one of the largest employers in many cities and towns across the United States as well as one of the largest consumers of other local goods and services (paper and other office supplies, fuel for buses, food, etc.).

- Finally, from an *educational* perspective, school funding should be adequate to provide appropriate educational programs to students based on their varied individual educational needs.

Understanding the historical context of public schooling in America and the evolution of federal, state, and local governments and laws can significantly enhance one's understanding of modern-day policies governing the financing of public education.

Throughout this text, we present a variety of perspectives on school finance, though our tone and the balance of our research sources decidedly focus on the *economic* principles of school finance. Courses in school finance policy are taught (a) in schools of education to aspiring school and district-level administrators and state policymakers; (b) in departments of economics, within the contexts of public economics and/or the economics of education; and (c) in schools and departments of public administration. Yet educators, economists, and public administrators often see, critique, and evaluate policies through very different lenses. A major objective of this text is to provide multiple lenses for evaluating school finance policy and to draw on the best available information and the most recent research, across fields, for understanding the complexities of this interdisciplinary field.

Three guiding principles of the public financing of education systems follow:

1. Economic value to the public investment in people exists through investment in education.
2. States' constitutions and the U.S. constitution taken together require *equitable* and arguably minimally *adequate* treatment of all school-aged children.
3. Public education policy in general, and school finance–related policies in particular, will continue to be developed and implemented in the political context of a liberal democracy.

In later sections of this chapter, we explore the concept of investment in people, or **human capital theory,** as emerged from the early writings of Adam Smith in the 1700s through those who synthesized the concepts and empirically estimated the value of human capital in the 1960s (Becker, 1962; Mincer, 1958; Schultz, 1961). Under our second principle, you will find throughout this text that *equitable* can mean many things. Further, you will see that the political structure of our democracy can often produce policies that are at odds with this second principle. That is, some may favor unequal treatment that is otherwise unjustifiable, except for political preference. Reconciliation of these second and third principles produces the constant underlying tension of school finance policy.

This chapter begins with overviews of the scope and dimensions of school finance. Among those dimensions, we explore some of the basic economic, political, legal, and organizational and governance issues surrounding modern school finance policies. We conclude this chapter with an overview of the information explosion in school finance. Like many other academic subdisciplines, especially those of political interest, information on school finance policy has proliferated rapidly over the past few decades. That information ranges from empirical research on the effectiveness of policies, documented in academic journals, to sponsored reports, advocacy-oriented publications, and flat-out propaganda.

The Scope of School Finance

In this section, we address briefly the importance of better understanding school finance policy in other countries for gaining insights into relationships between organization and financing of schools and for better understanding present efforts to publicly finance education in the United States. We provide a more in-depth statistical tour of international school finance in Chapter 2. Also in this section, we address the need to look beyond K–12 public schooling when evaluating American education. Organized systems of education and public financing of those systems are not the exclusive domains of American states. Further, organized schooling does not exist solely to serve the educational needs of children roughly between the ages of 5 and 18 whose parents choose to send them to publicly financed elementary and secondary schools. Schooling is a very large business, and it increasingly serves the interests of labor unions, politicians, and private corporations as well as children. Sometimes these interests coincide; sometimes they do not.

International

Exploring international approaches to governing and financing schooling reveals both commonalities and distinct differences in the role of schooling across varied political economies and social contexts of North and South America, Europe, and Asia. Although this book is not a comparative education policy text, we do find it valuable to provide at least some cursory cross-national comparisons of the organization and financing of public schooling.

The organization of schooling across countries is inextricably linked to the financing of schooling. The organization of schooling, approach to financing education, and overall economic commitment to creating an educated public vary according to differences in the individual tastes of a country's citizens, the available technologies, and broader political philosophy on which countries were founded. Evaluation of why systems of education vary so widely across countries may enhance our understanding of why education systems vary as they do across states in the United States and may also provide insights into alternative models of education finance and organization. Are the reasons primarily historical? Are they primarily political? Or do other demographic, sociological, and/or economic features of countries comparably influence the provision of public education?

Economists, including Roland Benabou (1996), have sought theoretical explanations for why each country's approaches to financing schools vary so widely. As we show in Chapter 2, and as Benabou discusses, "Many countries have made financing of education and health insurance the responsibility of the state" while "some, notably the United States, have left it in large part to families, local communities and employers" (2000, p. 96). Benabou's explanation for why some countries have established a stronger *social contract* than others—as expressed by support for public goods and services and progressive taxation—centers on the degree of socioeconomic segregation and inequality in countries. Benabou notes "redistributions which could increase *ex ante* average welfare command less political support in an unequal society than in a more homogeneous one" (2000, p. 119), resulting in lower redistribution and reinforcement of inequality. The converse is true in more homogeneous, less unequal societies, where preferences for redistribution reinforce equality.

Benabou's explanations of the role of inequality and socioeconomic segregation in influencing school finance across countries provide some insights into differences across states and into the political dynamics of state school finance policy in the United States. For example, large, culturally and economically diverse states such as New York and Texas face an uphill battle when attempting to generate political consensus on the financing and redistribution of education quality, regardless of their liberal or conservative political leanings. In contrast, support for highly redistributive policies may be far more politically palatable in homogeneous states such as Wyoming or Vermont. As the size of the inequality and the degree of diversity increase, the need for redistribution may exceed the willingness of the relatively privileged to redistribute. We also suspect that both the level of wealth and the rate of economic expansion affect willingness to redistribute.

Organizational and Institutional Diversity

Most textbooks on school finance policy, including this one, emphasize government financing and regulation of government-operated kindergarten through 12th-grade schools. By narrowing the focus to this extent, we exclude the 1.1 million children who were homeschooled in 2003 (National Center for Education Statistics, 2004), and we also exclude the "27,000 private schools, with 404,000 full-time-equivalent

(FTE) teachers [which] enrolled 5.3 million students [and which] accounted for 24 percent of all schools in the United States, 10 percent of all students, and 12 percent of all FTE teachers" (in 2000–2001) (Alt & Peter, 2002, p. 3). Further, we exclude the millions of children engaging in learning during early childhood, before K–12 enrollment, as well as those who pursue higher learning beyond K–12 schooling in a vocational and technical setting, in 2- and 4-year colleges and universities.

At various points in this text, we draw comparisons across sectors of U.S. schooling, recognizing that—from political, economic, and sociological perspectives—schooling sectors are interdependent. For example, parents and children choose among public and private schools or may choose to homeschool. Public school finance policy may directly address one's choice of schooling through voucher programs or may indirectly influence choice by supporting a public system that either is or is not of adequate quality for parents with the financial means to choose private schooling. The educational market is dynamic, complex, and adaptive.

Scholars of postsecondary schooling have created an entire separate discipline around the comparative study of public and private colleges and universities and other organizational differences within public and private sectors and, further, of how those institutions may change over time—*institutional diversity*. Scholars of postsecondary institutional diversity have explored how organizations have evolved in some cases to become more alike (isomorphism) and in others to become less alike. We argue the need for similar attention to the study of institutional diversity in elementary and secondary education; its relationship to student and parent choices; teacher labor market dynamics; and ultimately local, state, and federal financing of education.

In later chapters of this text, we show how Catholic schools and conventional public schools have evolved to be quite similar, while newly emerging quasi-public charter schools are taking increasingly different organizational forms. In Chapter 13 we discuss similarities in the teacher workforce in these schools, and in Chapter 15, we discuss similarities in structures and internal allocation of resources.

As recent studies in postsecondary education have already validated, these organizational differences and changes over time may have important financial implications, as well as different learning outcomes (see, e.g., Morphew & Baker, 2004).

We also argue for the necessity of understanding the interrelationship between K–12 and postsecondary education financing. At present, K–12 and public postsecondary education systems are arguably *sibling rivals* in the context of state-level budgeting and finance, and K–12 education has been granted special privileges. Yet the very same state judicial mandates that grant those privileges to K–12 implicitly necessitate a high-quality system of public postsecondary institutions to which access is socioeconomically neutral.

Dimensions of School Finance

In this section, we provide a brief overview of various dimensions of school finance policy. We begin with a discussion of two economic lenses for viewing school finance policy: (a) economics of education and human capital theory and (b) public economics and **neoclassical economic theories** of public behavior pertaining to choices based on marginal utility of goods and services. Next, we discuss the political context of public education, direct and representative democratic processes that influence education funding, and the unique role of public schooling in a liberal democracy. We then address the unique legal status of public schooling in American states, and finally, we address the interrelationship between the organization and governance of schooling and the public and private financing of schooling.

Economic

Two economic lenses through which to view school finance policy are (a) human capital theory and (b) public economics.

Human Capital Theory

Human capital theory addresses the question, Why invest in education with public or private resources? Scott R. Sweetland, in an extensive review of literature on the origins of *human capital theory*, summarizes it as follows:

> Human capital theory suggests that individuals and society derive economic benefits from investments in people. The investment feature of this suggestion significantly differentiates human capital expenditures from consumptive expenditures—those providing few benefits beyond immediate gratification. (Sweetland, 1996, p. 1)

Human capital theory allows for such investments to take many forms in addition to formal primary through postsecondary education. Other forms of investment in human capital include (a) informal learning at home and/or work, (b) on-the-job training and apprenticeships, and (c) specialized vocational training at secondary and higher levels. Each can be assigned a monetary value, including the opportunity costs associated with foregoing earnings while advancing learning.

Sweetland notes that the origins of human capital theory date as far back as the 1700s, when Adam Smith began laying groundwork for the notion that an educated public has economic value. Two principal components laid out by Smith that inform all subsequent human capital frameworks follow:

1. Labor inputs are not merely quantitative. They qualitatively include "the acquired useful abilities of all the inhabitants or members of the society" as well as "the state of the skill, dexterity, and judgment with which labor is applied" (Sweetland, 1996, p. 2).
2. Ability acquired through "education, study, or apprenticeship, always costs a real expense, which is a capital fixed and realized, as it were, in . . . person" (Sweetland, 1996, p. 2).

Economists made significant advancements in human capital theory in the mid-20th century. Economists including Theodore Schultz and Gary S. Becker sought to provide empirical estimates of the added value to individuals seeking higher levels of education and more advanced training. In his presidential address to the American Economic Association in 1961, Theodore Schultz opined:

> Although it is obvious that people acquire useful skills and knowledge, it is not obvious that these skills and knowledge are a form of capital, that this capital is in substantial part a product of deliberate investment, that it has grown in Western societies at a much faster rate than conventional (nonhuman) capital, and that its growth may well be the most distinctive feature of the economic system. (p. 1)

> Much of what we call consumption constitutes investment in human capital. Direct expenditures on education, health, and internal migration to take advantage of better job opportunities are clear examples. (p. 1)

Public financing of services that reap only individual rather than collective benefits is less compelling.

That is, the education produced only a *private rate of return*. Schultz (1961) noted:

> Should the returns from public investment in human capital accrue to the individuals in whom it is made? The policy issues implicit in this question run deep and they are full of perplexities pertaining both to resource allocation and welfare. Physical capital that is formed by public investment is not transferred as a rule to particular individuals as a gift. It would greatly simplify the allocative process if public investment in human capital were placed on the same footing. (p. 15)

This argument assumes that not only an economic return results to the private individual who advances his or her education level, but also a potential *social rate of return* results when public expenditure produces a more educated population.

As interest in human capital theory grew, research proliferated, the subdiscipline of economics of education gained legitimacy, and the call for greater public financing of education systems gained momentum. While the human capital theorists provided the intellectual rationale, the powerful social and political momentum of the Civil Rights Era and the landmark *Brown v. Board of Education* (1954) propelled the pace of change and established an era of social and educational reform unprecedented in American history.

Public Economics

Since the mid-20th century, neoclassical economic theorists have endeavored to wrap principles of rational choice, marginal utility, and the behavior of competitive markets around the provision and consumption of public goods and services. Because public schooling had evolved as an enterprise of local towns (financed primarily by local property taxes, with desired services in the early days, agreed upon by consensus of participants in town meetings), public economic theory pertaining to education evolved to fit the existing model of publicly provided education.

Charles Tiebout (1956) and others argued the virtues of locally controlled and financed systems of schooling. As we discuss in Chapter 2, Tiebout asserted that local (town-based) financing of schooling allowed local voters to, as a group, select the level of public services they desired and set their tax rates accordingly. Further, a voter whose preferences were out-of-synch with those of one community could vote with his or her feet, choosing a residence in a community of more-similar preferences. Such a system would result in communities where the level of available services matched each individual's set of preferences. As with neoclassical application to private sector economics, Tiebout and others held that individuals have sufficient information on service quality and the price–quality relationship from which to make rational choices and that choosing to vote with one's feet is analogous to choosing product A or B off the shelf of a convenience store or choosing to shop at a particular store.

These public economic theories have significantly influenced school finance policy throughout history. State policy has often capitalized on the basic behavior and incentive structure of the Tiebout model. Interestingly, this model of local public goods and services simply assumes the town, municipality, or locality to be an ideal level of governance at which real properties are taxed and service quality set. As you will see in later chapters, this conception, based largely on the historical artifact of town-based schooling in Colonial America, conflicts with emerging educational reforms including school choice, where the relationship between residential location and service quality is compromised. Additional research and theoretical developments in public economics address the public economics of choice and competition in education, again stressing the rational behavior of consumers (see, e.g., Brunner & Sonstelie, 2003).

Political

In nearly every state, the state and local financing of public K–12 education make up the largest share of total state expenditures. The size of state education budgets and financial magnitude of the public education enterprise as a whole foster a highly politicized environment surrounding school finance. School finance therefore must be viewed from the lens of political science and political behavior. Because school finance decisions occur at multiple levels of governance—local, state, and federal—and because local decisions often involve direct referenda, state decisions may involve a mix of direct referenda and representative deliberation. Nearly all federal decisions are made via representative processes. Evaluation of school finance policies therefore must involve careful consideration of the underlying political processes and dynamics. Political perspectives often can explain school finance policies that appear entirely illogical or irrational from an economic or educational perspective. For example, empirical analyses by political scientists have shown that the party balance of state legislatures can significantly influence the overall level of education funding and distribution of education funding by race and poverty (Wood & Theobald, 2003; see also Adolph, 2000). More specifically, empirical research has shown that race, in many cases, continues to have an even stronger effect on the within-state distribution of educational resources than does poverty (Adolph, 2000). That is, poor, predominantly minority schools tend to do less well in state school finance policies than do poor schools in general. In some cases, political control over *need-based* state-aid formulas can lead to the allocation of substantially greater need-based aid to districts with fewer actual cost-related needs. Overall, the role of political balance and preferences in state politics is at least as powerful—if not more powerful—in influencing school finance than the rational expectations based on public economic theory and related empirical evidence. As one might expect, politically motivated policies often run in direct opposition to empirical evidence.

School finance in particular and education reform in general are not only political but also highly politicized. Political ideologies overwhelmingly dominate the popular literature on the best ways to finance and fix schools. For example, as this book entered final production, two separate books were released by politicized organizations critiquing the role of courts in state school funding cases (see Green, 2007; Hanushek, 2006; see also West & Peterson, 2007). The politicization of education reform and school finance requires that one view all literature—even that which poses as nonbiased empirical research—with a critical eye on political motivation and ideology. Choice, privatization, accountability, decentralization of control, and the regulation or deregulation of the teaching profession are among the highly politicized issues of the day. Each of these issues relates to school finance policy in one way or another. We attempt to provide a balanced analysis of the research on the equity, productivity, and efficiency effects of these reforms in later chapters, most notably in Chapters 12 through 15, where we discuss teacher policies for improving productivity and efficiency of schools, including teacher labor market issues (Chapter 13), internal resource allocation concerns (Chapter 15), competitive markets and choice models (Chapter 12), and accountability systems and incentives (Chapter 14).

Legal

Public education from the primary to secondary levels holds a privileged place in state constitutions, statutes,

and regulations and has also received significant attention in federal statutes and regulations. As of July 19, 2004, state school finance policies had been legally challenged in 45 of 50 states, and at that time, 24 separate challenges to state school finance policies were in process. The U.S. Constitution, by virtue of its silence on the subject of education, grants states the authority and responsibility for funding public education. In all states, constitutional provisions regarding the provision of K–12 education have been established. Most legal concerns directly related to the financing of public schools are governed by state constitutions. This is not to suggest, however, that federal statutes and regulations neither directly nor indirectly influence state school finance policy.

Increased national emphasis on standards and accountability has led to changes in state accountability polices that are increasing the legal basis and impetus for further reform of the compensatory aspects of school finance policy. Federal legislation regarding children with disabilities has had a profound impact on school funding policy over the past 30 years. Finally, the vestiges of separate and unequal schooling have not yet been mitigated. At numerous points in this text, we discuss how school finance policies, in both origin and effect, remain tied in some states to the history of racial organization of schooling. We discuss pending federal litigation that alleges racial intent in the differential treatment of students through school finance policy.

Entire Websites now provide advocacy information on legal challenges against states' approaches to financing schools. Nationally, the ACCESS Network (www.schoolfunding.info) provides information on the history and current status of school finance litigation across states. In New York State, plaintiffs who sued the state over its school-funding formula and who were ultimately victorious in the summer of 2003 maintain an extensive Website documenting the history of their case and the ongoing search for a solution (www.cfequity.org). In California, plaintiffs have designed a similar Website presenting and summarizing their experts' analyses and testimony against the state (www.decentschools.org). Similar efforts are ongoing in the following states and likely many others:

Texas (www.equitycenter.org)
Kansas (http://www.fundourpublicschools.com/)
Nebraska (http://www.nebraskaschoolstrust.org/
   pages/2/index.htm)

Organization and Governance

An important theme in this book is that the organization, governance, and financing of schooling are inextricably linked (see international comparisons in Chapter 2). In 1974, David Tyack wrote of one best system, arguing that urban education reform in particular was gridlocked by our inability to break free from a single model of providing public education. Recent policy developments—including publicly funded private education, charter schools, and site-based governance—attempt to diversify the delivery of schooling in America, especially in urban areas. In Chapters 12 through 15, we discuss in detail these reform strategies, their relation to school finance policy, and the emerging evidence as to whether our new emphasis on system diversification is improving the productivity and/or efficiency of urban education in America. Finally, a central issue that continues to influence the distribution of schooling quality in America consists of the residual effects of school segregation, especially in but not limited to southern states. More than 50 years after *Brown v. Board of Education* (1954), public schools in America remain separate and unequal. Recent state court decisions and volumes of research literature affirm this (see Chapters 4 and 7).

School Finance Information

School finance policy is an inherently political topic. Sorting through the facts and fiction and effectively filtering the bias embedded in research in the field can be particularly difficult. As you progress through this text, developing your own analytical skills for evaluating school finance policies, we expect that you will also become a more critical reader of the existing literature in the field. Here, we introduce you to available resources on issues pertaining to school finance policy, and we offer some insights into the classification and organization of those resources. Again, because school finance policy is interdisciplinary, resources can be drawn from a variety of fields. We expect that most readers who are new to the field will be quite surprised and perhaps overwhelmed by the volume of information available. We begin this section with an overview of peer-reviewed research, commentary, and policy-analysis journals that publish articles directly and indirectly related to school finance and the economics of education. Next, we review a variety of other available

resources on school finance, attempting to present a balanced view of their content and quality. Note, however, that we are admittedly selective in our presentation of available literature and that we critique or simply omit publications that we perceive to be excessively biased and misleading, theoretically flawed, or methodologically inept. However, not all the resources that we have excluded from this brief discussion necessarily fit into one of these categories, because the volume of work available precludes exhaustive inclusion.

Research Journals

Only one peer-reviewed journal has the central mission of presenting scholarly work specifically on the field of school finance: *The Journal of Education Finance*, published by the University of Illinois and Association of School Business Officials International (www.asbointl. org). (A peer-reviewed journal is one to which articles, before acceptance for publication, are sent blindly—without authorship indicated—to a group of experts in the field for review on the basis of topic importance and relevance, clarity of writing, research design, and methodological rigor. The rigor of the peer-review process varies widely both across and within academic journals. Peer review alone is no guarantee of quality and methodological rigor.)

You will find many citations to articles in the *Journal of Education Finance* throughout this book, simply because it is the main journal of the field and has been for the past three decades. A second interdisciplinary journal, *Education Finance and Policy*, is now available. Because the study of school finance is interdisciplinary, inquiry into any specific topic in the field requires looking beyond the journals of a single discipline. For example, on the topic of providing aid to schools on the basis of student needs, one might find articles in a variety of journals, across fields, spanning several decades. In 1970 Garms and Smith published "Educational Need and its Application to State School Finance" in the *Journal of Human Resources*. In 1994, the *National Tax Journal* published Thomas Downes's (an economist at Tufts University) article with Thomas Pogue, titled "Adjusting School Aid Formulas for the Higher Cost of Educating Disadvantaged Students" (Downes & Pogue, 1994).

Table 1.1 lists a handful of journals containing useful articles on and related to school finance policy. Table 1.1 is not exhaustive but includes journals from the broad fields of education, public administration,

Table 1.1   Useful Academic Journals for the Study of School Finance

Journal Name	Publisher	Field/Audience	Indexed/ Search Engines
Journal of Education Finance	Association of School Business Officials International and The University of Illinois Press	Education	ERIC/Econ Lit
Education Finance and Policy	MIT Press	Interdisciplinary	
Economics of Education Review	Elsevier Science	Economics/ Education	ERIC/Econ Lit
Educational Evaluation and Policy Analysis	American Educational Research Association	Education (Policy)	
Educational Policy	Sage/Corwin Press	Education (Policy)	ERIC
Public Budgeting and Finance	Association for Public Budgeting and Finance	Public Administration/ Public Finance	Econ Lit
Public Administration Review	Blackwell Publishing	Public Administration	Econ Lit
Journal of Policy Analysis and Management	Association for Public Policy Analysis and Management (APPAM) and John Wiley and Sons	Public Policy/ Administration	Econ Lit
National Tax Journal	National Tax Association http://ntj.tax.org/	Economics/ Public Finance	Econ Lit
Journal of Public Economics	Elsevier Science	Economics	Econ Lit
The American Economic Review	American Economic Association	Economics	Econ Lit
Review of Economics and Statistics	MIT Press	Economics	Econ Lit

public policy, and economics. Absent in Table 1.1 but also important to the study of school finance are a variety of journals in political science, public policy, and sociology. Finally, because the courts have played such a significant role in shaping state school finance policies over the past several decades, law reviews (typically searched via LexisNexis) are also useful resources. Unlike academic peer-reviewed journals, law reviews are journals managed at law schools by law students. A review process is involved for articles and commentary but may be handled entirely internally among law review editors.

Other Books on School Finance

Aside from competing textbooks in the field, numerous resources are available for expanding one's understanding of school finance policy. Several recent books on or related to school finance policy have strongly influenced our views and ultimately the organization and content of this text, and we describe them next.

Two National Academy of Sciences (Division of Behavioral and Social Sciences and Education) books (www.nas.edu), were released in 1999. The first, *Making Money Matter: Financing America's Schools,* edited by Helen Ladd and Janet Hansen (National Research

Council, 1999b), presents a synthesis of research in education finance through 1999 on questions of equity, adequacy, and improving the productivity and efficiency of schooling. The second, *Equity and Adequacy in Education Finance: Issues and Perspectives* (National Research Council, 1999a), is a compilation of commentary and empirical analyses on topics ranging from school finance litigation to the statistical measurement of the cost of providing an adequate education.

Most recently, MIT Press published an exceptional collection of research synthesis essays and state-level case analyses, edited by John Yinger (2004) of Syracuse University: *Helping Children Left Behind: State Aid and the Pursuit of Educational Equity.* This book in particular provides an overview of the most current and rigorous theoretical and empirical work in the field, on topics ranging from the relationship between standards and accountability and school finance policy to state-specific analyses of recent reforms in Michigan, Texas, Vermont, and Kansas.

In addition, the broader field of the economics of education has produced several books and edited collections, including *Does Money Matter,* a collection of analyses edited by Gary Burtless (1996) that grapples with the ongoing debate over the strength of the statistical relationship between educational resources and student outcomes. Other similar books include Helen Ladd's (1996) edited collection titled *Holding Schools Accountable,* which covers topics including performance incentives, school choice, the allocation of funds, and the measurement of education costs.

The American Education Finance Association (www.aefa.cc) also publishes a theme-based yearbook. Recent themes include (a) teacher labor markets in school finance policy (Plecki & Monk, 2003); (b) cost-effectiveness analysis in education (Levin & McEwan, 2002); (c) the politics of school finance (DeMoss & Wonk, 2004); (d) special education finance (Parrish, Chambers, & Guarino, 1999); and (e) resource allocation in schools (Picus & Wattenbarger, 1996). Another useful companion book from which we draw extensively for our tax policy chapter is David Monk and Brian Brent's (1997) *Raising Money for Education: A Guide to the Property Tax.* And another is Henry M. Levin's classic, recently revised *Cost Effectiveness Analysis* (Levin & McEwan, 2001). Finally, we would be remiss if we failed to mention Robert Berne and Leanna Stiefel's (1984) seminal work in the field, *The Measurement of Equity in School Finance.*

Government Reports and Data Sources

Data availability for the study of school finance has increased dramatically over the past decade, and much of those data are available on the Web. On this book's Companion Website (www.prenhall.com/baker), we maintain a Web-based index of state department of education Websites. Several other Websites including the Accessed Network (www.accessednetwork.org) and the U.S. Department of Education also maintain state department indexes (http://bcol02.ed.gov/Programs/EROD/org_list.cfm?category_ID=SEA). Next, we briefly address some available federal sources of reports and data on and related to school finance.

National Center for Education Statistics

The National Center for Education Statistics (NCES) is a division of the Institute for Education Sciences of the U.S. Department of Education (http://www.ed.gov/rschstat/landing.jhtml?src=ct). The role of NCES is to collect and analyze education data, including postsecondary as well as elementary and secondary and early childhood education. Within NCES is the Education Finance Statistics Center (www.nces.ed.gov/edfin).

NCES maintains a Web-based catalog of reports and analyses on and related to school finance (among a vast array of education policy issues). Two series of reports produced by NCES relate directly to school finance: (a) *Developments in School Finance* and (b) *Selected Papers in School Finance.* Both are released with some regularity and include current research in the field.

- *Developments in School Finance*

  - 2001–2002
    http://nces.ed.gov/pubs2003/2003403.pdf
  - 1999–2000
    http://nces.ed.gov/pubs2002/2002316.pdf
  - 1998
    http://nces.ed.gov/pubs2000/2000302.pdf
  - 1997
    http://www.nces.ed.gov/pubs98/98212.pdf

- *Selected Papers in School Finance*

  - 2000–2001
    http://nces.ed.gov/pubs2001/2001378_1.pdf
  - 1997–1999
    http://nces.ed.gov/pubs99/1999334.pdf

NCES also produces, every 5 years, a summary description of each state's aid formula for public education under the title *Public School Finance Programs of the U.S.*

and Canada. The 1999 edition is presently posted on the NCES Website.

- *Public School Finance Programs of the U.S. and Canada* (1993–1994 and 1998–1999) http://www.nces.ed.gov/edfin/state_finance/ StateFinancing.asp

Other notable reports available through the NCES Education Finance Statistics Center are

- *Trends in Disparities in District Level Expenditures per Pupil* http://nces.ed.gov/pubs2000/2000020.pdf
- *Inequalities in Public School District Revenues* http://www.nces.ed.gov/pubs98/98210.pdf

In addition to digests and syntheses of data, NCES serves as a repository for extensive data on various aspects of public, private, and early childhood through postsecondary education including financial data. The centerpiece of NCES elementary and secondary data collection efforts is the *Common Core of Data* (http://nces.ed.gov/ccd/search.asp). Among other topics, the NCES *Common Core of Data* includes the following:

- *Local Education Agency Finance (F-33) Survey* http://nces.ed.gov/ccd/f33agency.asp
    - District-level data on the revenues and expenditures of all U.S. public school districts. Also available through the Census Bureau http://www.census.gov/govs/www/school. html
- *Local Education Agency Universe Survey* http://nces.ed.gov/ccd/drpagency.asp
    - District-level data on the organization/classification of all U.S. public school districts, numbers of teachers and administrators, and some basic school district demographics
- *National Public Education Financial Survey* http://nces.ed.gov/ccd/stfis.asp
    - Summary of state-level data on education finance
- *Public Elementary/Secondary School Universe Survey* http://nces.ed.gov/ccd/pubschuniv.asp
    - Summary of school-level enrollment and basic demographic data for all public elementary and secondary schools in the United States

Other related data sources and sites that can be used to fill some of the gaps of the *Common Core* surveys include the NCES/U.S. Census Bureau's School District Demographics site, which allows for compilation of detailed income, housing, and demographic data at the school district level for all U.S. school districts based on U.S. Census Bureau special tabulation data from 1990 and from 2000 (http://nces.ed.gov/surveys/sdds/).

State-Supported Research on School Finance Policy

Increasingly, state governments are sponsoring and disseminating research on school finance policy. Some states, such as New York, maintain ongoing publicly financed research. In New York, the Education Finance Research Consortium, funded by the State's Board of Regents, involves school finance researchers from Syracuse University, New York University, Cornell University, and the Rockefeller School at the State University of New York at Albany (http://www.albany.edu/edfin/). The research consortium has been a source of multiple significant recent contributions to the field of education finance in spite of the fact that the State of New York appears hopelessly mired in political dispute about resolving its own school finance problems, following a recent high court decision in that state (see Chapter 7 for further discussion). In 2004, the state of Texas also engaged in significant state sponsorship of cutting-edge research in school finance policy (http://www.capital. state.tx.us/psf; however, the link no longer works, as the project died). The Texas School Finance Project involved researchers from around the country and a review panel of well-known economists and school finance researchers. As in New York, however, the Texas experience raises some questions as to the extent that cutting-edge research can directly and immediately influence policy.

Contract Research Institutes and Think Tanks

Due to the political nature of the modern-day think tank, we address only a few organizations that produce research on education policy and finance. Three contract-based research institutes that have conducted extensive, empirically rigorous analyses of school finance policy are the RAND Corporation (www.rand.org), the American Institutes for Research (AIR) (www.air.org), and Mathematica Policy Research (http://www. mathematica-mpr.com/). RAND has been extensively involved in the evaluation of education reforms for decades, and numerous reports and books can be found as full text on its Website. AIR runs the Center for Special Education Finance (CSEF) and also conducts other research on education costs and adequacy. While Mathematica has been less involved in school finance research, per se, researchers at Mathematica have produced influential studies on topics related to education policy and more recently teacher quality.

Other organizations classified broadly as think tanks have also produced significant volumes of influential research on education policy. Perhaps most notable are the Brookings Institution (www.brookings.org) and the Economic Policy Institute (www.epinet.org).

Academic Research Centers and Consortia

A handful of academic research centers and research consortia also produce significant policy research related to education finance. Among those are

- Consortium for Policy Research in Education (CPRE)
  http://www.cpre.org/index_js.htm
- National Center for the Study of Privatization in Education (NCSPE)
  www.ncspe.org
- National Bureau of Economic Research (NBER)
  www.nber.org

CPRE, based out of the University of Pennsylvania, includes researchers from that institution as well as Harvard, Stanford, the University of Michigan, and the University of Wisconsin. Wisconsin researchers have headed up school finance analyses for CPRE. The NCSPE is housed at Teachers College of Columbia University in New York and led by noted education economist Henry Levin. NCSPE's Website is an excellent source for current research on education policy in general and on issues related to the economics of education in particular. Finally, the NBER, while focusing broadly on economics issues, involves researchers who have published numerous studies related to the economics of education and school finance policy.

Other Policy Support and Information Sites

Because school finance policy is largely an issue of the states, organizations that provide technical assistance to state legislatures on education policy issues are also useful. Two important sources of information geared toward state policymakers are

- The Education Commission on the States
  www.ecs.org
- The National Conference of State Legislatures
  www.ncsl.org

In addition, an organization called the Access Network, which was spawned by activists in New York state, challenging their state's school finance formula in court (www.cfequity.org), has grown to be an extensive repository of information on state school finance legislation and litigation. The Access Network (formerly available at www.accessednetwork.org, now also at http://www.schoolfunding.info) contains state-specific information on the history of school finance court cases, pending cases, recent policy research, state-commissioned studies of education costs, and much more.

Organizations

Two organizations involving researchers and policymakers involved in school finance are

- American Education Finance Association
  http://www.aefa.cc/
- American Educational Research Association—Special Interest Group on Fiscal Issues and Policy in Education
  http://www.aera.net

SUMMARY

In this chapter, we have conducted a whirlwind tour of the multiple dimensions of the field of school finance and introduced you to a variety of information sources on, and related to, school finance.

Whatever your own field of study, we hope that throughout this text you remain cognizant of these multiple dimensions and use multiple, diverse sources of information as we delve more deeply into specific topics. We especially hope that you will develop technical skills of analyzing school finance data.

We ascribe to a *learning-by-doing* model, and you will find numerous datasets and simulations on this book's Companion Website (www.prenhall.com/Baker), in addition to the simulations throughout the book. We intend those simulations to provide a starting point. As you progress through this book, we encourage you to return repeatedly to the information sources discussed in this chapter and make a concerted effort to balance your use of sources, both in terms of perspective and origin of the source, whether political, economic, or legal. Balance your use of sources by type, including academic articles and analyses and state or federal reports and documents. Finally, explore and analyze state-level data on school finance.

As you conduct your analysis, you may wish to consult Baker and Richards's (2004) *The Ecology of Educational Systems,* which provides detailed instructions on the use of Microsoft Excel for analyzing various types of schooling data, including data on school finance. You may find that book to be a useful companion text—or even better, a useful text for a prerequisite course on data and systems analysis.

KEY TERMS

human capital theory   Human capital itself is the stock of the productive skills and technical knowledge embodied in labor. Human capital theory assumes that society may invest, through such public services as education or directly in workforce training, in the development of human capital, and that doing so may result in measurable returns to investment in the production process (e.g., that the investment improves the productivity of the workforce).

neoclassical economics   An approach (perhaps the most common) in *economics* focusing on the determination of prices, outputs, and income *distributions* in markets through supply and demand.

REFERENCES

Adolph, C. (2000). Party schools: How the GOP skews state aid to education. *American Prospect, 11*(26), 16–17.

Alt, M. N., & Peter, K. (2002). *Findings from the condition of education, 2002. Private schools: a Brief portrait.* National Center for Education Statistics, U.S. Department of Education. Office of Educational Research and Improvement. NCES-2002-013. Retrieved February 22, 2007, from http://nces.gov/pubs2002/2002013.pdf

Baker, B. D., & Richards, C. (2004). *The ecology of educational systems: Data, models and tools for improvisational leading and learning.* Upper Saddle River, NJ: Prentice Hall.

Becker, G. S. (1962). Investment in human capital: A theoretical analysis. *The Journal of Political Economy, 70*(5, Part 2), 9–49.

Benabou, R. (1996). *Unequal societies.* Working paper 5583. Cambridge, MA: National Bureau of Economic Research.

Benabou, R. (2000). Unequal societies: Income distribution and the social contract. *The American Economic Review, 90*(1), 96–129.

Berne, R., & Stiefel. L. (1984). *The measurement of equity in school finance.* Baltimore: Johns Hopkins Press.

Brown v. Board of Educ. of Topeka, 347 US 483, 495 (1954).

Brunner, E., & Sonstelie, J. (2003). Homeowner, property values and the political economy of the school voucher. *Journal of Urban Economics, 54,* 239–257.

Burtless, G. (1996). *Does money matter? The effect of school resources on student achievement and adult success.* Washington, DC: Brookings Institution Press.

DeMoss, K., & Wonk, K. K. (2004). *Money, politics and law: Intersections and conflicts in the provision of educational opportunity. 2004 Yearbook of the American Education Finance Association.* Larchmont, NY: Eye on Education.

Downes, T., & Pogue, T. (1994). Adjusting school aid formulas for the higher cost of educating disadvantaged students. *National Tax Journal, 47*(1), 89–110.

Garms, W. I., & Smith, M. C. (1970). Educational need and its application to state school finance. *Journal of Human Resources, 5*(3), 304–317.

Green, P. C. (2007). Review of courting failure. *Teachers College Record*. Retrieved from http://www.tcrecord.org/Content.asp?ContentID=13382

Hanushek, E. A. (2006). *Courting failure: How school finance lawsuits exploit judges' good intentions and harm our children*. Stanford, CA: Hoover Institution Press.

Ladd, H. (1996). *Holding schools accountable*. Washington, DC: Brookings Institution Press.

Levin, H. M., & McEwan, P. J. (2001). *Cost effectiveness analysis* (2nd ed). Thousand Oaks, CA: Sage Publications.

Levin, H. M., & McEwan, P. J. (2002). *Cost effectiveness and educational policy. 2002 Yearbook of the American Education Finance Association*. Larchmont, NY: Eye on Education.

Mincer, J. (1958). Investment in human capital and personal income distribution. *The Journal of Political Economy, 66*(4), 281–302.

Monk, D. H., & Brent, B. O. (1997). *Raising money for education: A guide to the property tax*. Thousand Oaks, CA: Sage Publications.

Morphew, C. C., & Baker, B. D. (2004). The cost of prestige: Do new research universities incur higher administrative costs? *Review of Higher Education, 27*(3), 365–384.

National Center for Education Statistics. (2004, July). *NCES National Center for Education Statistics issue brief*. 1.1 Million homeschooled students in the United States in 2003. U.S. Department of Education, Institute of Education Science, NCES 2004-115. Retrieved February 22, 2007, from http://www.nces.ed.gov/pubs2004/2004115.pdf

National Research Council. (1999a). *Equity and adequacy in education finance: Issues and perspectives*. Committee on Education Finance, Ladd, H., Chalk. R., & Hansen, J. S., (eds.). Commission on Behavioral and Social Sciences and Education. Washington, DC: National Academy Press.

National Research Council. (1999b). *Making money matter: Financing America's schools*. Committee on Education Finance, Ladd, H., & Hansen, J. D. (eds.). Commission on Behavioral and Social Sciences and Education. Washington, DC: National Academy Press.

Parrish, T. B., Chambers, J. G., & Guarino, C. M. (1999). *Funding special education. 1998 Yearbook of the American Education Finance Association*. Thousand Oaks, CA: Sage Publications.

Picus, L. O., & Wattenbarger, J. L. (1996). *Where does the money go? Resource allocation in elementary and secondary schools*. Thousand Oaks, CA: Sage Publications.

Plecki, M. L., & Monk, D. H. (2003). *School finance and teacher quality: Exploring the connections. 2003 Yearbook of the American Education Finance Association*. Larchmont, NY: Eye on Education.

Rothstein, R. (2004). *Class and schools: Using social, economic, and educational reform to close the Black–White achievement gap*. New York: Teachers College Press.

Schultz, T. W. (1961). Investment in human capital. *American Economic Review, 51*(1), 1–17.

Sweetland, S. R. (1996). *Review of Educational Research, 66* (3), 341–359.

Tiebout, C. (1956). *A pure theory of local public expenditure. Journal of Political Economy, 64*(5), 416–424.

Tyack, D. (1974). *The one best system*. New York: John Wiley and Sons.

Yinger, J. (2004). *Helping children left behind: State aid and the pursuit of educational equity*. Cambridge, MA: MIT Press.

West, M. R., & Peterson, P. E. (2007). *School money trials: The legal pursuit of educational adequacy*. Washington, DC: Brookings Institution Press.

Wood, B. D., & Theobald, N. (2003). Political responsiveness and equity in public education finance. *Journal of Politics, 65*(3), 718–738.

CHAPTER 2

THE CONTEXT OF PUBLIC EDUCATION FINANCE

Introduction

In this chapter, we provide an overview of broad theoretical concepts in public expenditure theory. We then discuss financing of education internationally and the limited federal role in financing public schooling in the United States. Public expenditure theory provides the economic theory for the means by which U.S. policy makers and educators conceive and construct public financing of education. Public expenditure theory attempts to wrap a market-based rationale around the provision and consumption of public goods and services.

We address the international context of financing education systems for a variety of reasons. First, exploration of international and comparative education finance reveals significant variations in the financing and delivery of schooling in terms of the balance of public and private responsibility among consumers and providers of education services, degrees of centralization or decentralization of the governance of education, and relative emphasis of governments on early childhood through tertiary education. Too often, texts on the topic of school finance policy in the United States are narrowly constrained to the state and local financing of K–12 public schooling alone. Further, we address the international context because systems of schooling, and the ways in which they are financed, operate under differing economic theories, in vastly different political and economic environments. We conclude this chapter with a more detailed look at the very limited role of the U.S. federal government in providing direct financial support to K–12 public schools, although its regulatory role seems to be increasing with the passage of No Child Left Behind (NCLB).

Public Expenditure Theory

Public expenditure theory derives from neoclassical economic theory. Other approaches exist, including political theories of the state, and socialist and neo-Marxist theories. In this book, however, we confine our discussion to the neoclassical economic perspective—although from a critical perspective. It's not that we think markets are a figment of economists' imaginations: They are real and powerful. We do question the way in which markets are modeled and understood as they affect the educational system.

Producers and consumers of private goods rely on competitive markets, supply and demand, to establish in their mind a connection between product quality and product price. Knowing the price of the desired quality of public education is a somewhat more difficult task and governed by social, political, and economic processes. Nonetheless, economic models have become quite sophisticated and have incorporated social and political variables into their equations. These are but a few of the complex issues of an area of public economics known as public expenditure theory.

When the voters in a local school district or state legislators set a tax rate to raise a specific amount of revenue, they must do so with some notion of the product they intend to purchase with that revenue. That is, they decide to provide a public education system of quality level y, and ideally, can estimate it will cost x dollars. In this section, we provide a brief snapshot of public expenditure theory, its origins, and its influence on education finance.

Government Intervention

Ultimately, this is a book about government intervention in the market for education. What is government intervention, and why do governments intervene? From a public economic perspective, governments intervene to compensate for the failure of private markets to effectively and efficiently distribute goods or services that governments (or those who elect them) feel are important. Education is one such service. Fire protection, public safety, and health care are others. As we noted in Chapter 1, an overarching theme of this textbook is the economic value of investment in people. And that value ultimately can be measured both individually—in terms of private returns to education—and collectively as *social returns to education*. Governments may choose to intervene in the distribution of education on this basis alone, although other reasons arise—(e.g., social justice) that are equally compelling.

In a practical sense, government intervention in the financing of public schools in the United States typically translates into state and/or federal education policy seeking to increase overall spending or to redistribute the level of education production. The provision of educational services and production of educational outcomes have historically been a function of cities and towns via their local school districts and local boards of education.

Although private schooling has long played a role in serving significant percentages of the U.S. population, particularly in the northeastern United States, the cost of private education has been beyond the means of many families. When the large wave of immigrants into the United States occurred at the beginning of the 20th century, state and local policy makers saw free public education as a critical vehicle for transmitting American culture and assimilating new immigrants into the mainstream of society.

In this section, we review public economic theory in general, beginning with the early work of Paul Samuelson in the 1950s (Samuelson, 1954). We address four types of *market failures* that may result in the under- or overproduction of educational services. Subsequently, drawing on public economic theory, we address basic ways that governments may intervene to mitigate these market failures. We conclude with a discussion of local governments and local voter choices over taxes and educational expenditures or the demand for local public goods and services.

Equity, Efficiency, and Market Failures

In the mid-1950s, economist Paul Samuelson described the basic conditions for an equitable and efficient economy (summarized in Duncombe, 1996; see also Samuelson, 1954):

1. **Efficiency:** The relative prices of goods should equal the marginal costs of their production and the marginal value that consumers attach to their consumption (the relative price of resources should equal the ratio of their marginal productivity).

2. **Equity:** The marginal change in social welfare from consumption of a particular commodity should be equal across all households. Once this equality has been achieved for one commodity, it will be satisfied for all commodities. The only tool available for equalizing income across households without creating inefficiency is lump-sum taxes.

3. **Government Policy:** Despite the interrelationship between consumer satisfaction and social welfare, the conditions for efficiency and equity can be separated. This principle is particularly important for government policy, because it implies that government can divide economic policy into those related to allocation and those related to distribution.

It is important to understand that when economists like Samuelson speak of an *efficient* economy, they are most often referring to **allocative efficiency.** Allocative efficiency exists when goods and services are allocated such that no one person or agent in the system can be made better off by reallocating those goods or services. In this case, the notion of being made *better off* simply refers to each person having generally what he or she wants, at a price each is willing to pay. (We discuss this concept in greater depth later in this section and again, by comparisons with other efficiency concepts, in Chapter 11.)

In these three fundamental conditions—equity, efficiency, and government policy—Samuelson (1954) assumed some rational connection between the price of a good and the value that consumers placed on that good (or service). Further, the price of the good should also be rationally connected to the cost of producing that good. Finally, these conditions require some relation between the value a consumer places on a good and the cost of producing that good. Applying Samuelson's logic to education, consumers of public education should have some notion of the costs of operating public schools of a given level of quality when determining the taxes they are willing to pay for those schools, and the cost of that education should be in line with the kind of education consumers desire, what economists call *preferences.*

Unfortunately, Samuelson's equitable and efficient economy, though theoretically reasonable where competitive market conditions exist, is difficult to achieve in the real world. Such is the case with most pure theories in economics. Several imperfections in the market, such as speculation, hoarding, poor information, geographical isolation, and monopoly, can provoke market failure. *Market failures* erode the rational economic relationships between production costs, supply, demand, and market prices, resulting in inefficient allocation of goods and services. The failure of the market to meet all public welfare needs produced the field of scholarship and research known as public finance, or public expenditure theory. As noted by Duncombe (1996), "The heart of normative public expenditure theory has been the analysis of the conditions under which competitive markets fail to efficiently allocate goods and services" (p. 26). Normative public expenditure theory focuses on three major sources of market failure: (a) externalities, (b) public goods, and (c) natural monopolies. In addition, we address the role of information and asymmetry of information in market failure.

Externalities

Markets generally consist of two classes of players on any given transaction known variously as producers and consumers, sellers and buyers, or suppliers and demanders. Occasionally and often unwittingly, a third party enters that mix and either incurs costs or reaps benefits as a function of the transaction between the first two parties. This diffusion of costs or benefits that are not incorporated into the price of production or cost to the consumer reduces market efficiency. Recall that efficiency means that individuals get pretty much what they desire, given the price they are willing to pay. When externalities become involved, someone gets something he or she didn't ask for or pay for. Although externalities may involve third-party individuals, more common examples involve social costs or social benefits. An **externality** is an action by either a producer or consumer that affects other producers or consumers but is not accounted for in the market price of the good or service (Pindyck & Rubenfeld, 1995, p. 671). When social costs are incurred, we have a *negative externality,* but when social benefits are received, we have a *positive externality.*

Pigou (1932) addressed the problem of inefficiencies that arise when consumers cannot discern the full so-cial costs or benefits associated with the consumption or production of goods (summarized in Duncombe, 1996). When this happens, market prices fail to incorporate true costs or benefits of the good. Education is generally perceived to produce *positive externalities.* The production of an educated citizenry by one or more towns in a system can result in an improvement to welfare across jurisdictions, even where other towns have not directly incurred the costs of educating those citizens.

A common example of a *negative externality* is that of industrial pollution of air or waterways. Market prices for goods produced by polluting industries are unlikely to incorporate costs incurred downstream or downwind. A parallel might be drawn to public education. A collection of towns in a state might be individually responsible for choosing the quality of education services they wish to provide. Citizens of one town may choose to provide educational services in such a way as to produce a subset of highly economically productive, civically involved citizens, but disenfranchise another subset of students unable to conform to or succeed in the education system townspeople have chosen to provide. Members of the disenfranchised group cannot become involved in community affairs or compete in the workforce and instead pursue lives of crime, pillaging nearby towns, and driving up their costs of public safety. Consider it another form of environmental degradation with costs to neighboring towns analogous to costs of cleaning up pollution.

What role might governments play in correcting for the market failure of externalities? A Pigouvian response (Pigouvian tax) to *negative externalities* would be for governments to tax the producer of the negative externality at such a level as to either (a) cover the costs of mitigating the externality, or (b) provide incentive to the producer to reduce or eliminate the negative externality, or (c) both. In our schooling example, the state government might impose a tax on the town producing the negative externality in order to fund the public safety costs incurred by neighboring towns. An alternative response would be for the government to simply allow the third party to sue the polluting party for costs incurred. More positively, the state could create incentive grants that encourage the townspeople to consider changing their education system to reduce the numbers of disenfranchised students.

Private Versus Public Goods

Samuelson (1954) defined one class of goods particularly susceptible to market failure as "pure public goods" or "collective consumption goods." **Pure public goods** are goods from which individuals cannot be excluded and for which there is nonrivalry. A classic example of a private consumption good is a loaf of bread, which "can be parceled out among two or more persons, with one man having a slice less if another gets a slice more." In contrast, a public consumption good is like an outdoor circus, public park, or national defense, "which is provided for each person to enjoy or not, according to his tastes" (Samuelson, 1955, p. 350).

Clearly, the service of education, publicly or privately financed, fits neatly into neither category. Ideally, many wish to think of publicly provided education as a potential collective consumption good or pure public good. That is, any and all children may arrive at a public school of their choosing on any given day, and each shall reap similar marginal benefits. Regardless of how many children choose to participate, the school will have plenty of space, ample teachers, desks, materials, and supplies, and each child shall have comparable opportunity to *learn something new every day.* Unfortunately, one reality of the U.S. system of education is that the system is relatively undersupplied with respect to possible maximized demand. This occurs in part because we allow provision of the service of education through a complex mix of public and private markets and because, collectively, education is undersupplied in some markets and oversupplied in others.

Private markets in particular will tend to undersupply public goods or services. The undersupply of public goods or services may result from suppliers lacking complete information on the demand for the good or service. From the standpoint of public economics, identifying the efficient level of public good requires full disclosure of each individual's demand for that public good. That is, all members of a local town, state, or entire nation would have to be willing to fully disclose just how much "education" they wish to be publicly available. Yet, it is in the interest of some individuals to not disclose their demand, because they may reap the greatest benefits at the least costs from being a **free rider,** benefiting from the demand of others in the community (Samuelson, 1954, p. 389).

The free rider is like the man who attends the village council meeting every week railing against the proposed public park to be built at taxpayer expense. He succeeds in defeating taxpayer financing of the park, but local citizens rally instead to raise private funding for the park. Now you can find this local curmudgeon casually lounging on any given day near the goose pond on the marble bench on which the names of the various private contributors are inscribed.

Similarly, parents of school-aged children in a town may choose to erect a private academy for their children. Nonparents residing in the town may either oppose or be impartial to their efforts. Nonetheless, they don't contribute financially to the school's infrastructure or ongoing operations. Yet, these free riders do receive measurable economic benefits. For example, if the private academy in this town is perceived as superior to schools in other towns, residents of nearby towns may wish to move into the town, increasing property values of all residents, even those without children in the academy. This benefit is referred to as **capitalization.** Further, the products of the academy— a well-educated citizenry—may reap other economic benefits for their local community.

What types of policies might governments use to mitigate the undersupply of education? Government intervention to improve the distribution of education may involve public financing. Public financing of education through taxation offers a partial solution to this free-rider problem. As we discuss at numerous points throughout this text, public financing at the local, state, or federal level spreads the costs of public education across all those who may ultimately reap benefits, either directly through individual educational attainment and eventual earnings, or indirectly through human capital formation and capitalization in housing values.

A major difficulty lies in the government determination of the precise level of education that the public should offer. According to one popular view, the collective preferences of local citizens should determine the level of education through direct referenda on their own taxes. Yet beyond the governance of local towns, few decisions of taxation and public spending in the United States are governed by direct democracy. Determining the level of education that state governments or the federal government should offer therefore requires that representatives understand their constituents' preferences and can express and support those preferences without bias or other influence. As we will show in later chapters, the extent to which state government (state courts and legislatures) should intervene in defining the level of education that the public should provide has become the heated topic of the day and is often referred to in terms of *educational adequacy.*

Few if any goods and services can fully meet the conditions of nonexcludability and nonrivalry set forth by Samuelson (1954). Like most *perceived* public goods, education (like the circus or local park) may eventually suffer congestion when its usage is sufficiently great. Certainly, the marginal benefits that each child obtains in a crowded classroom are less than those that each child obtains in a less crowded one, just as the travel time on a less-congested highway is much shorter. Problems associated with congestion, and related reduction in value to those who consume the good or service, make public education at best an impure public good. To go a step further, however, at finite cost (or finite willingness to fund public education services), larger and larger numbers of potential participants will likely be excluded or congestion will become so significant that returns to education diminish dramatically.

Meeting the nonrivalry and exclusion requirements of public goods and services is perhaps easier when viewing the *educated citizenry* as the public good, rather than the education process itself. Arguably, the economic and social benefits of an educated citizenry are not reduced when consumed simultaneously by larger numbers of consumers. Further, excluding any individual in society from reaping any of those benefits would be quite difficult.

Counterarguments exist, however. For example, because education is so tightly associated with credentials (e.g., high school diploma, college degree, MBA, etc.) and because employers use credentials to screen candidates for jobs, a surplus of credentialed employees can actually depress the average salary for college graduates if the economy cannot expand quickly enough to absorb them. In this sense, overconsumption of education, or more specifically education credentials, made freely available (the high school degree) has simply shifted the sorting mechanism to the next level where race and class reenter into the access equation.

In the United States, we have determined public K–12 education to be, at the very least, in the public interest and to be a *quasi*-public and impure public good. Federal, state, and local governments have made efforts to correct only partially for the expected market failure of underproduction of K–12 schooling, leaving a sizable share of the population to be served by private markets. For example, the New York City Public schools could not possibly meet the demand of the entire school-aged population within its boundaries, if all religious and independent private schools were to simultaneously close their doors.

Keep in mind that public K–12 schools in the United States, the primary emphasis of this text, are but one component of a larger education system and that public K–12 education systems interact with private K–12 education systems—as well as with other private providers of educational goods and services— and interact with public and private higher education systems. The total demand for education in the United States is thus the sum of demand for public K–12 schooling, private K–12 schooling, higher education, home schooling, pre-K–12 schooling, private tutoring, test preparation courses, and any other educational endeavors that citizens might pursue. Changes in the production and consumption of public sector goods influence changes in the production and consumption of private sector goods and vice versa. Americans appear to accept that about 88% of eligible children choose to participate in public schooling.

Natural Monopolies

There are monopolies, and then there are *natural monopolies*. Oligopolies are a slightly relaxed form of monopoly, where a few competitors, rather than a single competitor, dominate a market for a particular good or service for which no real substitute exists. Monopolies, per se, are not market failures. Critics of public education often levy the claim that, because government-operated schools serve such a large portion of all schoolchildren, they hold a monopoly on education, resulting in inefficiencies, underproducing, and overtaxing. The implication is that policy levers might be used to break up the monopoly of government-operated schooling, yielding smaller, more numerous competitors and increasing market efficiency.

Natural monopolies are monopolies that defy this logic. In a natural monopoly, the market has room for only one player, such as a production technologies player; breaking up the monopoly, even if promoting competitive pricing and product quality, would result in increased production costs and consumer prices and in unwanted externalities. That is, the good is produced most efficiently by the monopoly.

According to Duncombe, "Natural monopolies are generally found in industries where capital investments are quite large relative to the marginal costs of production. Theoretically, it is possible in such an industry for the first firm entering the industry to drive out all competition thus assuring a monopoly" (Duncombe, 1996, p. 28). Natural monopolies may then restrict the quantity supplied to below-optimal levels in order to drive up prices or simply to conceal information on true production costs.

In general, education is a human-resource-intensive industry, but capital costs are not insignificant and may create barriers to entry in the provision of educational services. State and local governments and the

Catholic Church (the second largest provider of education) control the majority of schooling infrastructure in the United States. This control over infrastructure has arguably resulted in relatively entrenched monopolies (in regions with few or no private schools) or oligopolies that have now existed for over a century. It has been difficult, in part, for other competitors to raise sufficient resources to acquire facilities to break into a marketplace that has been so dominated by two well-backed providers for over a century.

Government-operated schools probably are *not* natural monopolies. One might, argue, however, that entrenched urban public schooling systems bear some characteristics of natural monopolies. For years, critics of the failures of urban schooling have attempted to introduce school-choice alternatives to break the monopoly of bureaucratic, inefficient, government-operated urban schools (e.g., see Hanushek, 1994). State and local policy makers have used voucher plans to shift students from the largest market competitor (government schools) primarily to the second largest (Catholic schools). More recently, states have created charter schools in an attempt to erode urban education monopolies. As we discuss in later chapters (Chapter 12 in particular), while charter school policies are intended to reduce barriers to entry into the education marketplace, the experience of charter schools over the past 5 years has actually illuminated many of the barriers specifically associated with the costs of market entry and achieving efficient scale. In some cases, private service providers have attempted, with limited success, to achieve economies of scale more rapidly by operating numerous charter schools in several states or markets and relying on private investors to support market entry (venture capital, per se). Historically, however, evidence is mixed as to whether the deconstruction of urban education monopolies can result in lower ongoing production costs (e.g., see Richards, Shore, & Sawicky, 1996; see also Duncombe & Yinger, 1996).

Appropriate state government intervention might involve additional subsidies for start-up costs that exist beyond marginal costs of production at efficient scale and might even involve continued subsidies for the higher operating costs that result from breaking up a natural monopoly.

Asymmetry of Information

Information is at the core of all rational decision making in economics. Of particular importance is information on the quality of goods and/or services being provided or purchased. Yet rarely do consumers and producers have the same, reliable, *perfect* information on the product or service in question. Rather, their information is asymmetric, with the producer or seller typically having more and/or better information on the product than the consumer. The most common example is that of the market for "lemons" among used cars. A used car with only 50 or 100 miles on its odometer will sell for appreciably less than a new car of nearly identical quality, simply because the consumer assumes the probability that the car is a lemon (else, why would someone be selling it with only 100 miles?). The seller has more information about the car than can be effectively conveyed to the buyer. The buyer's skepticism alone (founded or not) influences the market price for used cars regardless of product quality, and an entirely separate market for used cars emerges (Akerlof, 1970).

We argue that it is especially difficult for the parent as consumer of education for his or her child to evaluate the quality of schooling being provided, either in the context of choosing among public and private options through a publicly subsidized voucher program or the context of choosing a neighborhood in which to live. As such, parents use a variety of proxies for quality, based on preferences that may vary widely across consumers and may or may not include academic indicators such as college matriculation or test scores.

Since the 1990s, state governments have attempted to intervene more significantly in the measurement and dissemination of schooling quality through systems of *standards and accountability*. Most recently, the federal government has increased its involvement by requiring that states play a greater role in generating and disseminating information on schooling quality and specifically that parents of children in schools identified as low quality be provided the option to move their children to schools of higher quality.

Tiebout and the Local Provision of Public Goods

Samuelson (1954) wrote primarily of centralized government control, where bureaucrats, through political processes, determine public expenditures according to the perceived preferences of voting constituents. Charles M. Tiebout (1956), among others, noted some skepticism regarding centralized government's ability to discern the "voter-consumers'" true preferences. Tiebout also discusses the central problem that "voter-consumers" have an incentive to conceal their preferences. Tiebout suggests, "in terms of a satisfactory theory of public finance, it would be desirable (1) to force the voter to reveal his preferences; (2) to be able to satisfy them in the same sense that a private goods market does; and (3) to tax him accordingly" (1956, p. 418).

Tiebout proposes that local, rather than centralized, government financing of public services could result in a form of competitive marketplace that would yield more optimal pricing of public goods through local tax policy and more appropriate alignment of consumer preferences and the quality of public goods:

> The consumer-voter may be viewed as picking that community which best satisfies his preference pattern for public goods. This is a major difference between central and local provision of public goods. At the central level the preferences of the consumer-voter are given, and the government tries to adjust to the pattern of these preferences, whereas at the local level various governments have their revenue and expenditure patterns more or less set. Given these revenue and expenditure patterns, the consumer-voter moves to that community whose local government best satisfies his set of preferences. The greater the number of communities and the greater the variance among them, the closer the consumer will come to fully realizing his preference position. (Tiebout, 1956, p. 418)

As we will describe later, in discussion of market-based policies (in Chapter 12), the Tiebout model represents the most basic form of school choice in the United States. Tiebout argued that this process of "voting with your feet" could lead to an optimal allocation of public services where no one person in the system could be made better off without making someone else worse off. Such a market condition is called **Pareto efficiency,** after the Italian economist (Pindyck & Rubenfeld, 1995, p. 674).

Demand for Local Public Goods

How do local voters or state or federal legislators determine the price they are willing to pay for public goods and services? We focus this discussion on the role of local voters, because local voters historically, and still in many states, can exercise direct control over local tax rates to raise revenues for local public schools. The decision to raise a given amount of revenue through taxes for public schools is an expression of the demand of voters for public education. Local voters will have some expectation of the amount of revenues required to produce a given set of student outcomes.

Economists and political scientists most often characterize demand for local public goods and services in terms of the median, or swing voter, in a model referred to as the *median voter model*. (For an application of the median voter model, see Gramlich & Rubinfeld, 1982.) The median voter model assumes that the level of public good chosen by a group of voters will be a function of (a) the capacity of the median voter to pay for the good, usually measured as the income of the median voter; (b) the price, in taxes, that the median voter must pay for an additional unit of the public good; and (c) the median voter's preferences or tastes regarding the public good. This model expects that voters with higher income can pay more for public education services. Where tax prices (discussed in greater detail later in this chapter) are lower, voters will purchase higher levels of the good. Finally, voters' utility or tastes for education will be a major influence on their choice to raise, or not raise, taxes for education.

For example, economists generally assume that members of a community who have no direct stake in public schools, such as elderly voters whose children are no longer in school, will have a lower demand for public schools. Such concerns are not merely academic. Nationally, the proportion of the population represented by retirees has raised concerns among advocates of educational spending that education revenues will be adversely affected. Indeed, most empirical research supports the contention that elderly voters (age 65+) prefer to spend less on public education. Many studies of demand for education compare differences in spending behavior across districts, showing, for example, that districts with higher percentages of elderly voters spend less on education. Studies of the influence of changes in the aging population have produced varied results but point to a generally negative influence on education spending (see, e.g., Poterba, 1997). Harris, Evans, and Schwab (1999) performed an analysis of national data for 1972, 1982, and 1992 to determine the influence of changes in the age of the population on education spending in the United States. Although they found that increases in the elderly population had a negative effect on education spending, they found that effect to be relatively small.

As we state throughout this textbook, however, the broader ecology of the economy and society can alter the pattern of preferences for educational spending. For example, the current growth rates in education's share of household income cannot continue for more than a few years before it will be forced to decline by competing demands from other sectors of the economy. The graying of America and the cost of health care, retirement, and pension stability are all likely to be factors influencing the willingness of senior citizens on fixed income to continue to support real growth in spending.

Questions of differences in tax price and ability to pay for public education become central to our later discussions on equity. Clearly, the income of the median voter varies among communities. If we assume income to be positively associated with education spending, holding price and preferences constant, the communities with the highest income will typically demand more education. In this case, "more" means higher quality in the form of better teachers, smaller classes, newer facilities, technology, more diverse and extensive course offerings, summer school, preschool, and after-school programs. These are typical of the kinds of differences between poorer and wealthier school systems. As a result, where funding of public education is left entirely in the hands of local voters, the quality and quantity of education services available to children in the community will likely be directly associated with the income of the median voter in that community. Similarly, if voters in one community can pay a lower price for the same quality education, their children will be advantaged. As students of school finance, you might wonder whether a just society should allow important differences in education quality and quantity to be determined by local differences in income and price.

Federal, state, and local interactions also affect tax policy. For example, federal allocations to states influence state allocations of aid to local school districts, which in turn influence local voters' choices regarding how much money they wish to raise for their schools with local taxes. Typically, the greater the federal or state aid, the less the local spending. Despite this generalization, each level of government's reaction to assistance from the higher level can vary. In the context of the median voter model, the state aid, depending on how it is allocated, might act as an income supplement, increasing the capacity of voters to pay for education, or might act to reduce the price paid (supplant) by local voters for an additional unit of education. Economists previously assumed that grants that reduced the price of goods, or matching grants, would stimulate greater consumption than grants that supplement income, such as lump-sum grants. More recent literature challenges this notion, finding similar changes in consumption regardless of grant type (see Duncombe, 1996; Gramlich, 1977). One perverse outcome of matching grants is that they shift funds away from other categories of spending that are important to a state or school district but for which there are no strong constituents to protest the funding cuts. Poor and immigrant children are, of course, the most vulnerable of constituents, because they cannot vote and are often poorly represented by their communities at the polls (see, e.g., Siebert & Goff, 2002[1]).

Education as a Positional Good

William Koski and Rob Reich (2007) have described education as a **positional good,** where individuals, families, or even communities use their ability to acquire more and better education to compete against others for a better place or position in a hierarchical society and economy. This seems quite obvious. Parents want the best education for their own children; and in wealthy towns, people collectively want to bestow greater competitive advantage on their children than already exists through the relative power of their families in an unequal society.

What is perhaps less obvious is that the advantages provided to some are necessarily disadvantageous to others, even if the absolute quality (class size, teacher credentials, number of books, etc.) of the education of others does not change. Such is the nature of positional goods. Hirsch (1976) describes positional competition as follows:

> By positional competition is meant competition that is fundamentally for a higher place within some explicit or implicit hierarchy and that thereby yields gains for some only by dint of loss for others. Positional competition, in the language of game theory, is a zero-sum game: what winners win, losers lose. (p. 52)

Viewing education as a positional good has significant policy implications for appropriate government intervention. Throughout this text, you will notice a theme of shifting arguments from achieving equity in education to achieving adequacy in education. In part, the early adequacy movement (see Chapter 7) emerged as a way to engage very wealthy communities concerned that the equity movement would ultimately level down educational opportunities for their children. The early adequacy movement provided for *leveling up* of the valleys, without *harming* the peaks.

---

[1] Siebert and Goff 2002 demonstrate the complex interactions of race and social class and history regarding voter turnout in North Carolina. (North Carolina had the third lowest voter turnout in the United States during the 2000 elections.)

Viewing education as a positional good—when some communities are allowed to provide enriched education and/or advanced credentials—the value of merely adequate education available to others is necessarily diminished. This equity concern exists both in terms of quantity and quality of education. Certainly, the value of a bachelor's degree in a given labor market is diminished as more individuals obtain graduate degrees. Further, consider a major metropolitan area that presently has not one prestigious, highly selective university, leaving the local labor market—including major international companies—dominated by graduates of local, regional, and state open-enrollment colleges and universities. If a top-ranked national private university were to move into the labor market, the value on the local labor market of degrees from the local open-enrollment universities would necessarily be diminished.

International Perspective

In this section, we provide an overview of the financing of education systems using data from the Organisation for Economic Cooperation and Development (OECD). OECD's (2003) *Education at a Glance 2003* provides data on a number of aspects of the financing and educational and economic outcomes of schooling for the 30 OECD countries as well as a handful of non-OECD countries. We present only a limited summary but

encourage you to explore additional information on the OECD Website (www.oecd.org).

Two issues are central to this discussion. First, with public economic theory in mind, consider the relative balance of public and private support for education systems across the grade span. We emphasize again that an education system, including that of the United States, includes more than just publicly financed, government-operated schooling for children between the ages of 5 and 18. A sizable portion of American schoolchildren is educated in Catholic and other religious schools and an increasing portion in quasi-public charter schools. Further, the importance of postsecondary education for an individual's successful participation in the economy has increased dramatically over the past several decades. Finally, increased domestic and international interest in balancing opportunities from the starting gate has led to increased interest and involvement in the financing of early childhood programs.

Organization of Schooling

Organization, governance, and financing of education systems are inextricably linked. How countries organize the delivery of education services is highly related to how they choose to raise funds for, distribute resources to, and perhaps even directly control the spending of institutions providing educational services.

Table 2.1 provides an overview of levels of government control over key educational governance

Table 2.1   Level of Government Control Over Decision Making in Governance and Finance in Elementary and Secondary Schooling in G-7 Nations

G-7 Nation	Curriculum Development	Examination and Certification	Teacher Qualifications	Allocation and Control Over Financing
Canada	Regional	Regional	Regional	Local and regional
France	Central	Central	Central	Central
Germany	Regional	Regional	Regional	Local and regional
Italy	Central	Central	Central	Central
Japan	Central	Regional entrance exams	Regional with national standard	Regional and central
United Kingdom	Central	National exit exams	Central	Local and regional
United States	Regional	Local, with regional standards	Regional	Local and regional

Source: Adapted from Baldi, S., Lewis, J., & Sherman, J. (2001). Washington, DC: American Institutes for Research. *Education Finance in G-7 Nations* (Table 2.1, p. 6, & Figure 2.1, p. 10).

issues for Group of 7 (G-7) nations. Even among these relatively similar, developed economies, significant differences occur in the governance and financing of schooling. For example, France and Italy operate highly centralized systems of primary through secondary schooling, including centralization of curriculum development, student assessment, teacher qualifications, institutional inspection/accreditation, and both the allocation of and control over fiscal resources. In contrast, the other G-7 nations distribute governance across local, regional, and central levels of government: Japan and the United Kingdom operate

Table 2.2 Sources of Funding for Education in OECD and Non-OECD Countries (2000)

Country	Non-Postsecondary (%)			Postsecondary (%)		
	Public Sources	Private Sources	Private: % of which is subsidized	Public Sources	Private Sources	Private: % of which is subsidized
Malaysia	100.0	0.0				
Portugal	99.9	0.1		92.5	7.5	
Sweden	99.9	0.1		88.1	11.9	
Finland	99.5	0.5	0.0	97.2	2.8	0.0
Norway	99.2	0.8		96.2	3.8	
Denmark	97.8	2.2		97.6	2.4	0.0
Italy	97.8	2.2	0.3	77.5	22.5	6.1
Thailand	97.8	2.2		80.4	19.6	
Slovakia	97.6	2.4		91.2	8.8	
Ireland	96.0	4.0		79.2	20.8	
Austria	95.8	4.2	0.9	96.7	3.3	7.7
Iceland	95.1	4.9		94.9	5.1	
Netherlands	94.6	5.4	1.0	77.4	22.6	2.4
Uruguay	94.5	5.5		99.7	0.3	
Israel	94.1	5.9	1.3	56.5	43.5	0.0
Belgium	93.9	6.1	0.1	85.2	14.8	4.5
India	93.6	6.4		99.8	0.2	
Spain	93.0	7.0	0.0	74.4	25.6	2.5
France	93.0	7.0	1.9	85.7	14.3	2.3
Country mean	**92.8**	**7.2**	**0.4**	**78.6**	**21.4**	**1.9**
Hungary	92.7	7.3	0.0	76.7	23.3	0.0
Canada	92.4	7.6		61.0	39.0	1.7
Greece	91.7	8.3		99.7	0.3	
Japan	91.7	8.3		44.9	55.1	
Czech Republic	91.7	8.3	0.0	85.5	14.5	0.0
United States	*90.0*	*10.0*		*33.9*	*66.1*	
Switzerland	89.0	11.0	1.0			
United Kingdom	88.7	11.3	0.0	67.7	32.3	4.6
Argentina	87.9	12.1		66.2	33.8	0.1
Mexico	86.1	13.9	0.5	79.4	20.6	0.6
Australia	84.8	15.2	0.0	51.0	49.0	0.9
Korea	80.8	19.2	0.9	23.3	76.7	1.1
Germany	80.5	19.5		91.8	8.2	
Indonesia	76.5	23.5		43.8	56.2	
Paraguay	71.9	28.1		62.6	37.4	
Chile	70.0	30.0		18.3	81.7	7.0
Philippines	67.9	32.1		34.4	65.6	
Jamaica	63.6	36.4	0.9	71.5	28.5	2.3

Source: Adapted from Organisation for Economic Cooperation and Development (2003). *Education at a glance, 2003.* Table B3.2. Retrieved July 1, 2005, from http://www.oecd.org/document/34/0,2340,en_2649_37455_14152482_1_1_1_37455,00.html

under a mix of central and regional control; Canada and Germany, primarily at the regional level; and the United States, under a mix of regional and local control.

In general, sources of funding and control over spending mirror other features of education governance. Countries that centralize control over curriculum and certification also centralize control over funding. The exception among G-7 nations is the United Kingdom, where 1990s reforms retained centralization over much of the governance of schooling but gave local units significant control over and responsibility for financing. Baldi, Lewis, and Sherman note:

> Although most local funding originates from the central government through general-purpose transfers, under this recently reformed model, the local government generates most of the education-specific funds. In fact, this decentralization of power and authority goes even further: control over spending in many cases goes from the locality down to the individual school level. (2001, p. 9)

As we show throughout this text, similar variation exists across the United States, with some states exercising significant control over curriculum, certification, and financing, and others devolving much of that control to a variety of different more locally controlled institutions, through a variety of policy mechanisms.

Public Financing of Education

Table 2.2 provides a snapshot of the public financing of non-postsecondary (early childhood through the rough equivalent of American secondary and/or vocational schooling) and postsecondary/tertiary education for OECD and non-OECD countries. Note that for non-postsecondary education, the country mean for publicly supported education is 92.8%, with 7.2% of support from private sources (and/or for private schooling). Several countries far exceed the average, financing nearly 100% of non-postsecondary education services through public sources. The United States falls slightly below that average.

Note that the extent of public support for postsecondary education varies more widely, with some nations still financing nearly 100% from public sources, but some nations financing as little as 18% to 25% through public sources. Figure 2.1 presents a scatter plot of the relationship between non-postsecondary and postsecondary public financing of education. In general, those nations that provide significant public support for non-postsecondary education also provide significant public support for postsecondary education. Points above the inserted trend line are those nations that provide greater support for postsecondary education than would be expected, given their level of

Figure 2.1   Cross-Country Relationship Between Non-Postsecondary and Postsecondary Public Financing of Education

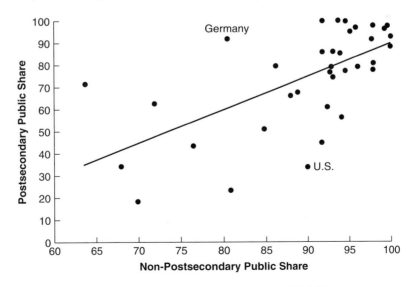

Source: Data from Organisation for Economic Cooperation and Development (2003), Table B3.2.

support for non-postsecondary education. Germany is included in this category. Points below the trend line are those nations providing less support for postsecondary education than would be expected, given their level of support for non-postsecondary education. The United States falls into this category.

Table 2.3 summarizes the degrees of centralization of revenue raising for the support of education systems.

Several countries operate fully centrally funded systems of schooling (primary, secondary, and postsecondary non-tertiary). As indicated in Table 2.1, the United States financially supports education through a blend of regional (state) and local resources, placing the United States near the bottom of Table 2.3 in terms of central support.

Table 2.4 summarizes the relative priority education receives among all public expenditures and the

Table 2.3   Expenditures for Public Education by Government Level (Before Intergovernmental Transfers) (2000)

	Central	Regional	Local	Total
New Zealand	100	0	0	100
Slovakia	100			100
Jamaica	100			100
Paraguay	100	0	0	100
Tunisia	100			100
Uruguay	100			100
Zimbabwe	100			100
Ireland	100		0	100
Chile	95		5	100
Portugal	94	6		100
Thailand	94		6	100
Netherlands	94	0	6	100
Greece	93	7		100
Israel	90		10	100
Philippines	86		14	100
Mexico	82	17	0	100
Italy	81	5	14	100
Czech Republic	80		20	100
France	74	12	14	100
Hungary	71	x	29	100
Austria	70	8	22	100
Country Mean	**49**	**30**	**26**	**100**
Finland	41		59	100
Norway	34		66	100
Denmark	32	10	58	100
Australia	27	73	0	100
United Kingdom	26		74	100
Japan	25	57	18	100
Spain	17	78	5	100
India	10	84	6	100
Argentina	9	91		100
United States	*8*	*51*	*41*	*100*
Germany	8	75	18	100
Russian Federation	7	18	75	100
Poland	5	1	94	100
Brazil	5	58	37	100
Canada	4	70	26	100
Switzerland	3	52	45	100
Belgium	n	94	6	100

Source: Adapted from Organisation for Economic Cooperation and Development (2003). *Education at a glance, 2003.* Table B4.2. Retrieved July 1, 2005, from http://www.oecd.org/document/34/0,2340,en_2649_37455_14152482_1_1_1_37455,00.html

Table 2.4   Education Expenditures as a Percent of Public Expenditure and of Gross Domestic Product (2000)

	Percent Public Expenditure		Percent of Gross Domestic Product	
	2000	**1995**	**2000**	**1995**
Thailand	31.0		5.4	
Malaysia	26.7		6.2	
Mexico	23.6	22.4	4.9	4.6
Tunisia	19.4		7.7	
Korea	17.6		4.3	
Chile	17.5		4.2	
Norway	16.2	18.4	6.7	9.0
United States	*15.5*		*5.0*	
Denmark	15.3	12.2	8.4	7.4
Switzerland	15.1	15.0	5.4	5.5
Slovakia	14.7	14.0	4.1	4.7
Iceland	14.6	12.2	6.0	4.9
Hungary	14.1	12.9	4.9	5.4
Philippines	13.9		3.9	
Australia	13.9	13.3	5.1	5.2
Israel	13.7	13.3	6.8	6.9
Argentina	13.6		4.5	
Ireland	13.5	12.2	4.4	5.1
Sweden	13.4	11.0	7.4	7.2
Canada	13.1	13.1	5.5	6.5
Country mean	**13.0**	**12.1**	**5.2**	**5.4**
India	12.7		4.1	
Portugal	12.7	11.9	5.7	5.4
Poland	12.2	11.5	5.2	5.5
Finland	12.2	11.7	6.0	7.0
Uruguay	11.8		2.8	
United Kingdom	11.8	11.2	4.8	5.1
France	11.4	11.3	5.8	6.0
Paraguay	11.2		5.0	
Spain	11.2	10.6	4.4	4.7
Jamaica	11.1		6.5	
Austria	11.0	10.8	5.8	6.2
Netherlands	10.7	8.9	4.8	5.0
Russian Federation	10.6		3.0	
Belgium	10.6		5.2	
Japan	10.5	11.4	3.6	3.6
Brazil	10.4		4.3	
Italy	10.0	9.2	4.6	4.9
Germany	9.9	8.2	4.5	4.6
Czech Republic	9.7	8.7	4.4	4.9
Indonesia	9.6		1.5	
Greece	8.8	6.2	3.8	2.9

Source: Adapted from Organisation for Economic Cooperation and Development. (2003). *Education at a glance, 2003.* Table B4.1. Retrieved July 1, 2005, from http://www.oecd.org/document/34/0,2340,en_2649_37455_14152482_1_1_1_37455,00.html

relative effort countries put into the funding of education. The first two columns indicate the percentage of all public expenditures allocated to education at all levels. We use this measure as an indicator of public priority. That is, of the money a country spends on public serv-

ices (including national defense, health care, etc.), how much does it spend on education? The second two columns indicate the percentage of a country's gross domestic product (GDP) that is spent on education at all levels. Assuming GDP to be a reasonable indicator of a country's fiscal capacity to support public services, we use this measure as an indicator of a country's *educational effort*. That is, what proportion of its fiscal capacity is a country willing to spend on advancing the education of its citizens?

Figure 2.2 relates the expenditure priorities and educational effort (as a percentage of GDP), with expenditure priority along the horizontal axis and educational effort on the vertical axis. The average educational effort across countries was 5.2%, and average priority was 13.0%. The United States exceeded the average priority, spending 15.5% of all public spending on education. However, the United States fell slightly below average in terms of effort. Thailand spent a very large share of public expenditures on education but spent only an average share of its domestic productivity on education. In contrast, Jamaica spent a sizable portion of its capacity on education and a lower than average share of all public expenditures on education. Indonesia spent little overall on education, either with respect to overall public expenditure or GDP.

Table 2.5 summarizes the expenditures per pupil at various levels of education across countries. Per pupil, expressed in U.S. dollars, the United States outspends other countries on tertiary education and ranks second in secondary, primary, and preprimary education. While public expenditure on tertiary education in the United States is relatively low, the average total expenditure of public and private source dollars on tertiary education is very high when compared with OECD and non-OECD countries. At all levels, the United States expends well in excess of international averages.

Allocation of Resources

Education is human resource intensive, with classroom teachers at the center of service delivery. Table 2.6 summarizes the shares of education expenditures allocated to teaching and to all staffing across countries (primary, secondary, and postsecondary nontertiary). Table 2.6 ranks countries from highest to lowest share of expenditures for total staffing. The United States ranks slightly above the international mean, at 82% allocated to staffing, but well below the international mean for allocation to teaching, at 55.9% compared to a mean of 63%. In only a handful of countries, schools allocated a smaller share of the budget to compensation of teachers. Of course, a variety of explanations may account for this relatively low allocation to teaching, including differences in the organization of schooling and classification of teaching staff to increased investments in other aspects of schooling, including areas such as infrastructure, maintenance, food, and transportation.

Figure 2.2   Public Financing Priorities and Effort

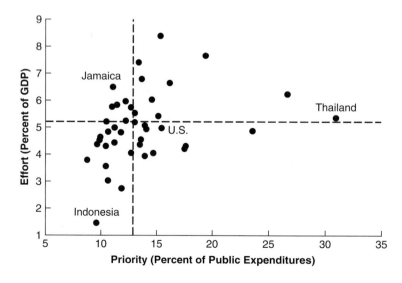

Source: Data from Organisation for Economic Cooperation and Development (2003), Table B4.1.

Table 2.5 Expenditures per Pupil in OECD and Non-OECD Countries (2000)

	Preprimary Education (for Children 3 Years and Older)	Primary Education	All Secondary Education	Postsecondary Nontertiary Education	All Tertiary Education	Expenditure From Primary to Tertiary Education
United States	*$7,980*	*$6,995*	*$8,855*		*$20,358*	*$10,240*
Switzerland	$3,114	$6,631	$9,780	$7,199	$18,450	$9,311
Austria	$5,471	$6.560	$8,578	$10,947	$10,851	$8,430
Norway	$13,170	$6,550	$8,476		$13,353	$8,333
Denmark	$4,255	$7,074	$7,726		$11,981	$8,302
Canada	$6,120		$5,947		$14,983	$7,764
Sweden	$3,343	$6,336	$6,339	$4,452	$15,097	$7,524
Italy	$5,771	$5,973	$7,218		$8,065	$6,928
Australia		$4,967	$6,894	$6,694	$12,854	$6,904
Germany	$5,138	$4,198	$6,826	$10,148	$10,898	$6,849
Japan	$3,376	$5,507	$6,266		$10,914	$6,744
France	$4,119	$4,486	$7,636	$6,207	$8,373	$6,708
Belgium	$3,282	$4,310	$6,889		$10,771	$6,544
Iceland		$5,854	$6,518		$7,994	$6,446
OECD total	**$4,477**	**$4,470**	**$5,501**		**$11,109**	**$6,361**
Netherlands	$3,920	$4,325	$5,912	$5,006	$11,934	$6,125
Finland	$3,944	$4,317	$6,094		$8,244	$6,003
Israel	$3,369	$4,351	$5,518	$4,240	$11,550	$5,837
Country mean	**$4,137**	**$4,381**	**$5,957**	**$4,075**	**$9,571**	**$5,736**
United Kingdom	$6,677	$3,877	$5,991		$9,657	$5,592
Spain	$3,370	$3,941	$5,185		$6,666	$5,037
Ireland	$2,863	$3,385	$4,638	$4,234	$11,083	$5,016
Portugal	$2,237	$3,672	$5,349		$4,766	$4,552
Korea	$1,949	$3,155	$4,069		$6,118	$4,294
Greece		$3,318	$3,859	$1,400	$3,402	$3,494
Czech Republic	$2,435	$1,827	$3,239	$1,624	$5,431	$3,004
Hungary	$2,511	$2,245	$2,446	$3,223	$7,024	$2,956
Chile	$1,563	$1,940	$2,016		$7,483	$2,629
Malaysia	$491	$1,235	$2,238	$8,256	$11,237	$2,219
Poland	$2,278	$2,105			$3,222	$2,149
Slovakia	$1,644	$1,308	$1,927		$4,949	$2,028
Mexico	$1,385	$1,291	$1,615		$4,688	$1,666
Jamaica			$1,327	$3,171	$6,894	$1,426
Uruguay	$1,039	$1,011	$1,219		$2,057	$1,228
Tunisia		$2,280	x(2)			$1,220
Thailand	$848	$1,111	$935		$2,137	$1,173
Brazil	$1,243	$928	$890		$11,946	$1,142
Turkey					$4,121	$1,073
Paraguay		$722	$1,256		$4,012	$1,031
Russian Federation	$1,297		$954	$1,439	$892	$968
Philippines	$93	$573	$587		$1,589	$645
India	$56	$268	$540		$1,831	$446
Indonesia	$85	$137	$416		$1,799	$331

Source: Adapted from Organisation for Economic Cooperation and Development. (2003). *Education at a glance, 2003.* Table B1.1. Retrieved July 1, 2005, from http://www.oecd.org/document/34/0,2340,en_2649_37455_14152482_1_1_1_37455,00.html

Table 2.6   Percent of Education Expenditures Allocated to Teachers and Staffing (2000)

	Compensation of Teachers	Compensation of Other Staff	Compensation of All Staff	Other Current
Mexico	80.6	14.4	95.0	5.0
Portugal			94.3	5.7
Turkey			93.4	6.6
Greece			91.0	9.0
Argentina	61.1	29.5	90.7	9.3
India	78.6	9.6	88.2	11.8
Japan			88.1	11.9
Spain	76.4	9.5	85.9	14.1
Indonesia	78.0	7.7	85.8	14.2
Germany			85.7	14.3
Uruguay	66.7	18.9	85.6	14.4
Philippines	85.6		85.6	14.4
Switzerland	71.9	12.8	84.7	15.3
Korea	75.0	8.5	83.5	16.5
Italy	66.9	15.6	82.5	17.5
Malaysia	69.8	12.4	82.2	17.8
United States	*55.9*	*26.3*	*82.1*	*17.9*
Ireland	76.3	5.5	81.9	18.1
Belgium (Fl.)	68.1	13.7	81.8	18.2
Norway			81.7	18.3
Country mean	**63.0**	**14.9**	**80.3**	**19.7**
France			78.8	21.2
Paraguay	65.6	12.9	78.5	21.5
Denmark	52.3	26.1	78.4	21.6
Austria	69.7	8.5	78.2	21.8
Israel			77.5	22.5
Brazil			77.3	22.7
Poland			77.0	23.0
Netherlands			76.7	23.3
Canada	61.3	15.1	76.4	23.6
Slovakia	58.1	17.9	76.1	23.9
Hungary			74.9	25.1
United Kingdom	53.1	20.5	73.6	26.4
Australia	56.1	16.0	72.2	27.8
Finland	56.3	12.1	68.4	31.6
Czech Republic	46.5	16.4	62.9	37.2
Sweden	46.3	15.0	61.6	38.4
Zimbabwe	60.2		60.2	39.8
Jamaica	48.4	8.8	57.2	42.8

Source: Adapted from Organisation for Economic Cooperation and Development. (2003). *Education at a glance, 2003.* Table B6.3. Retrieved July 1, 2005, from http://www.oecd.org/document/34/0,2340, en_2649_37455_14152482_1_1_1_37455,00.html

Table 2.7 summarizes average salaries of teachers at starting, after 15 years, and at the top of salary schedules in terms of experience, but with minimum required training. At all three levels, teachers in the United States earn above the international average. In addition, salary growth from the first to 15th year for U.S. teachers exceeds average growth (ratio of 1.45 compared to average of 1.39). However, U.S. teachers' salaries fall below international averages when indexed against GDP. Further, because U.S. teachers work more contact hours of teaching than their peers in other countries, their salary per contact hour is relatively low, averaging $37 at 15 years' experience.

Table 2.7   Comparison of Teacher Salaries in OECD and Non-OECD Countries (2001)

	Average Starting Salary/ Minimum Training	Average Salary at 15 Years	Average Salary at Top of Scale/ Minimum Training	Ratio of Salary After 15 years of Experience to GDP per Capita	Ratio of Salary After 15 years of Experience to Starting Salary	Salary per Hour of Net Contact (Teaching) Time After 15 Years' Experience
Japan	$22,800	$43,052	$55,474	1.63	1.89	$78
Korea	$25,089	$42,757	$68,493	2.69	1.70	$70
Germany	$40,455	$49,450	$52,086	1.86	1.22	$68
Denmark	$30,811	$36,871	$37,776	1.23	1.20	$61
Spain	$29,483	$34,357	$42,753	1.64	1.17	$55
Norway	$28,942	$32,621	$35,502	0.88	1.13	$54
Finland	$21,753	$30,183	$31,606	1.14	1.39	$52
Belgium (Fr.)	$25,679	$36,332	$43,969	1.36	1.41	$52
Belgium (Fl.)	$26,594	$37,202	$44,715	1.39	1.40	$51
Austria	$24,126	$32,942	$49,984	1.15	1.36	$50
Ireland	$23,483	$37,101	$41,844	1.24	1.58	$47
Australia	$28,010	$39,684	$39,684	1.44	1.42	$47
Italy	$24,779	$30,504	$37,233	1.15	1.23	$47
Portugal	$19,585	$28,974	$52,199	1.56	1.48	$46
Country mean	**$23,205**	**$32,088**	**$38,862**	**1.36**	**1.39**	**$45**
France	$23,244	$30,735	$44,692	1.20	1.32	$44
Netherlands	$28,245	$38,898	$47,002	1.36	1.37	$44
Scotland	$22,388	$35,872	$35,872	1.42	1.60	$39
Tunisia 2	$17,091	$17,259	$19,464	2.72	1.01	$38
Iceland	$19,016	$22,327	$23,684	0.77	1.16	$37
United States	*$28,727*	*$41,633*	*$50,075*	*1.19*	*1.45*	*$37*
Greece	$20,422	$24,716	$29,798	1.46	1.21	$37
New Zealand	$17,544	$33,941	$33,941	1.61	1.93	$35
Malaysia 1	$12,213	$19,384	$25,559	2.19	1.58	$25
Czech Republic	$11,203	$14,467	$19,301	1.00	1.29	$24
Thailand	$6,057	$14,886	$28,390	2.49	2.46	$22
Turkey	$9,588	$11,606	$16,899	2.04	1.21	$19
Argentina	$9,805	$13,953	$16,825	1.12	1.42	$19
Mexico	$13,348	$17,522	$28,903	1.92	1.31	$18
Hungary	$6,794	$9,725	$13,070	0.75	1.43	$16
Chile	$11,631	$13,097	$17,576	1.39	1.13	$16
Paraguay	$12,560	$12,560	$12,560	2.84	1.00	$14
Philippines	$10,777	$11,896	$12,811	3.06	1.10	$11
Slovakia	$5,319	$6,604	$8,408	0.55	1.24	$11
Peru 1	$5,556	$5,556	$5,556	1.21	1.00	$9
Jamaica	$7,345	$8,751	$8,751	2.38	1.19	$9
Egypt	$2,222	$4,961		1.37	2.23	$8
Indonesia	$1,188	$1,981	$3,535	0.65	1.67	$3
Switzerland	$41,967	$54,931	$64,852	1.81	1.31	
England	$23,297	$36,864	$36,864	1.46	1.58	
Sweden	$22,022	$26,327	$28,877	1.03	1.20	
Brazil	$13,174	$15,245	$16,918	2.07	1.19	
Uruguay 3	$5,903	$7,041	$8,464	0.78	1.19	

Source: Adapted from Organisation for Economic Cooperation and Development. (2003). *Education at a glance, 2003.* Table D5.1. Retrieved July 1, 2005, from http://www.oecd.org/document/34/0,2340,en_2649_37455_14152482_1_1_1_37455,00.html

Table 2.8   Pupil-to-Teacher Ratios in OECD and Non-OECD Countries (2001)

	Primary Education	Lower Secondary Education	Upper Secondary Education	All Secondary Education	Average Primary Through Secondary
Luxembourg	11.0			9.1	10.0
Portugal	11.6	9.9	8.0	8.9	10.2
Norway	11.6	9.3	9.2	9.3	10.4
Italy	10.8	9.9	10.4	10.2	10.5
Denmark	10.0	11.1	13.9	12.4	11.2
Greece	12.7	9.8	9.7	9.7	11.2
Hungary	11.3	11.2	12.5	11.8	11.5
Belgium	13.4			9.8	11.6
Austria	14.3	9.8	9.9	9.8	12.1
Iceland	12.6		10.9		12.6
Spain	14.7			11.0	12.8
Sweden	12.4	12.4	16.6	14.6	13.5
Poland	12.5	13.1	16.8	15.4	14.0
Finland	16.1	10.9	17.0	14.0	15.0
Country mean	**17.0**	**14.5**	**13.8**	**13.9**	**15.5**
France	19.5	13.5	11.2	12.3	15.9
United States	*16.3*	*17.0*	*14.8*	*15.9*	*16.1*
Israel	20.1	12.9	12.7	12.8	16.5
Czech Republic	19.4	14.5	13.1	13.8	16.6
Argentina	22.7	13.2	9.0	11.2	17.0
Australia	17.0				17.0
Netherlands	17.2			17.1	17.2
Russian Federation	17.3				17.3
Slovakia	20.7	14.5	12.9	13.8	17.3
Germany	19.4	15.7	13.7	15.2	17.3
United Kingdom	20.5	17.3	12.3	14.5	17.5
New Zealand	19.6	18.7	12.8	15.7	17.7
Uruguay	20.8	11.8	21.1	14.6	17.7
Japan	20.6	16.6	14.0	15.1	17.9
Canada	18.3	18.4	17.2	17.8	18.0
Malaysia	18.8			18.4	18.6
China	19.9	18.6	20.7	19.1	19.5
Egypt	22.3	21.2	13.2	17.0	19.6
Paraguay	18.8			21.5	20.1
Ireland	20.3	15.2			20.3
Tunisia	22.7	13.3	199.1	21.0	21.8
Indonesia	25.6	19.2	17.0	18.4	22.0
Brazil	24.8	20.7	19.0	20.1	22.4
Thailand	20.4	20.6	33.2	25.4	22.9
Turkey	29.8		17.2	17.2	23.5
Korea	32.1	21.0	19.3	20.1	26.1
Jamaica	33.6	19.4	17.3	19.3	26.5
Mexico	27.0	29.2	23.8	27.3	27.1
Chile	33.4	33.0	28.4	30.1	31.7
Zimbabwe	38.1			31.5	34.8
Philippines	35.2	43.4	22.4	36.4	35.8
India	40.0	36.1	30.4	34.1	37.0

Source: Adapted from Organisation for Economic Cooperation and Development. (2003). *Education at a glance, 2003.* Table D2.2. Retrieved July 1, 2005, from http://www.oecd.org/document/34/0,2340,en_2649_37455_14152482_1_1_1_37455,00.html

Table 2.8 summarizes pupil-to-teacher ratios across countries. Note that in general, the United States has slightly higher than average pupil-to-teacher ratios. Referring back to Table 2.7, one might assert that the United States has chosen to focus on higher salaries in order to improve teaching quality, rather than purchasing more teachers. In Chapter 13, we discuss U.S. teacher labor markets in much greater detail and reach a somewhat different conclusion. Overall, the range of pupil-to-teacher ratios across nations is quite dramatic.

Student Outcomes

Table 2.9 summarizes the performance outcomes of students across countries. In the first two columns,

reading performance is summarized in terms of the percentages of high- and low-scoring 15-year-olds. In some countries, such as Germany, Greece, and Hungary, the percentage of high-scoring students on the 5-point scale is quite similar to the percentage of low-scoring students. Other countries, including Finland, Australia, New Zealand, and Canada, have very high percentages of high-performing students and far fewer low-performing students. Still others, such as Brazil and Mexico, have very high low-performing shares and very few high-performing students.

Figure 2.3 displays the relationship between the percentage of students scoring high on reading tests and students' mean math and science scores. In general, countries with high reading performance also had high

Table 2.9   Performance Outcomes of 15-Year-Olds (2000)

	Reading % Level 1 or Below (335⁻)	Reading % Level 4 or Higher (553⁺)	Math Mean Score	Science Mean Score
Australia	12.5	42.9	533	528
Austria	14.6	33.8	515	519
Belgium	19.0	38.4	520	496
Canada	9.6	44.5	533	529
Czech Republic	17.5	26.8	498	511
Denmark	17.9	30.1	514	481
Finland	7.0	50.1	536	538
France	15.2	32.2	517	500
Germany	22.6	28.2	490	487
Greece	24.4	21.6	447	461
Hungary	22.7	23.5	488	496
Iceland	14.5	32.6	514	496
Ireland	11.0	41.4	503	513
Italy	18.9	24.8	457	478
Japan	10.1	38.6	557	550
Korea	5.8	36.9	547	552
Luxembourg	35.1	12.9	446	443
Mexico	44.1	6.8	387	422
New Zealand	13.7	44.5	537	528
Norway	17.5	34.9	499	500
Poland	23.2	24.4	470	483
Portugal	26.3	21.0	454	459
Spain	16.3	25.3	476	491
Sweden	12.6	36.8	510	512
Switzerland	20.4	30.2	529	496
United Kingdom	12.9	40.0	529	532
United States	*17.9*	*33.7*	*493*	*499*
Country mean	**17.9**	**31.7**	**500**	**500**
Brazil	55.8	3.6	334	375
Latvia	30.6	17.9	463	460
Liechtenstein	22.1	24.6	514	476
Russian Federation	27.4	16.4	478	460

Source: Adapted from Organisation for Economic Cooperation and Development. (2003). *Education at a glance, 2003.* Tables A5.1, A6.1, and A6.2. Retrieved July 1, 2005, from http://www.oecd.org/document/34/0,2340,en_2649_37455_14152482_1_1_1_37455,00.html

Figure 2.3 Relationship Between Reading, Math, and Science Performance

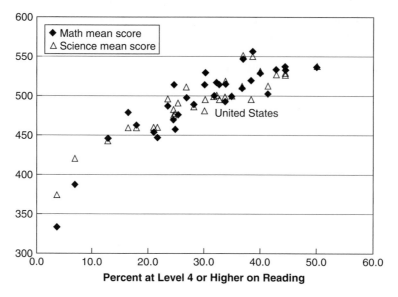

Percent at Level 4 or Higher on Reading

Source: Data from Organisation for Economic Cooperation and Development (2003), Tables A5.1, A6.1, and A6.2.

math and science performance. A higher than average percentage of U.S. children scored above Level 4 on reading. Children in the United States, however, scored slightly below average on both math and science.

We encourage you to explore these international data in greater depth on the OECD Website. For example, how efficient are U.S. schools compared to other countries? That is, how much do we get for what we spend? Preliminary analyses presented in this section suggest that we spend quite a bit in per-pupil terms but that our student outcomes are relatively average. We also encourage you to explore additional relationships among indicators. For example, are pupil-to-teacher ratios associated with higher reading or math performance? Are teacher salaries associated with higher reading or math performance? These are the types of questions we will ask throughout this textbook as we dig deeper into the details of federal, state, and local financing of elementary and secondary education in America.

The Limited Federal Role in American Public Education Finance

You will likely notice throughout this text that we dedicate little space to the federal government's role in funding public education. This may seem at odds with

the amount of time candidates for federal office dedicate to education as a central issue. Recall, however, from earlier in this chapter, that federal revenue for public schools typically amounts to about 8% of direct support to local public schools (8.79% in 2003–2004) (U.S. Census Bureau, 2004b). (This figure is calculated by dividing all federal revenue by total revenue per pupil across all local education agencies in the United States in 2003–2004.) The federal government allocates additional federal funds for the operation of federal education agencies. Educators and policy makers often point to federal funding as a major source for special education; however, the federal funding specifically for special education services, on average, makes up about 8% of special education funding ($7.95 billion in 2003–2004 allocated to local public school districts through states). The other major federal program, Title I of the Elementary and Secondary Education Act (ESEA), provides about $10 billion annually to public schools.

The 2001 reauthorization of ESEA, known as No Child Left Behind (NCLB), allocated approximately $11 billion (approximately $9.9 billion of which is allocated to Title I programs) to local public school districts, but that is still a relatively small share of a nearly $500 billion industry ($401 billion in 2000–2001, up to $473 billion by 2003–2004) (National Center for Education Statistics, 2004). By 2004, local public school districts received a total of $10.2 billion in direct aid through Title I, which constituted approximately 25% of all federal revenue allocated to public school districts. This total was determined by summing local school district revenues under line C14 of the *U.S. Census Bureau Fiscal Survey of Local Governments, Local Education Agency (School District) Finance Survey (F-33)* Data 2004 (U.S. Census Bureau, 2004b).

In this section, we summarize the federal role, with particular emphasis on federal funding that eventually reaches local schools and districts. Certainly, a substantial component of the federal role and of federal funding is the operation of the federal agency and its various responsibilities other than administrating funds that go to states and local districts. In particular, the federal government plays a significant role in stimulating and disseminating educational research through its Office of Educational Research and Improvement and National Center for Education Statistics. We begin this section with a discussion of the two major federal statutes that allocate funds to states and local districts. We conclude this section with a discussion of "schools without a state," or public schools, or students in the United States or abroad that are a direct responsibility of our federal government.

Federal Funding to States and Local School Districts

The two federal statutes that allocate the vast majority of federal funding to local public school districts are the Elementary and Secondary Education Act (ESEA) of 1965 and Individuals with Disabilities in Education Act (IDEA), formerly P.L. 94-142, enacted in the mid-1970s. The intent of funding allocated through the various iterations of ESEA since 1965 generally has been to provide increased opportunities for economically disadvantaged children. Title I of ESEA, "Improving the Academic Achievement of the Disadvantaged," allocated approximately $9.9 billion to local public school districts in 2002. Other ESEA programs include the following:

- Title II, Part D—Enhancing Education Through Technology
- Title II—Preparing, Training, and Recruiting High Quality Teachers and Principals
- Title IV, Part A, Subpart 1—Safe and Drug-Free Schools and Communities

- Title IV, Part A, Section 4126—Community Service Grant Program
- Title IV, Part B—21st Century Community Learning Centers
- Title V, Part A—Promoting Informed Parental Choice and Innovative Programs
- Title V, Part D—Prevention and Information Programs for Children and Youth Who Are Neglected or Delinquent
- Title VI, Part A—Grants for State Assessments and Related Activities
- Title X, Part C, Subtitle B—Education for Homeless Children and Youths

Table 2.10 summarizes Title I funding to states in 2003–2004, based on funds received by local education agencies for Title I programming. Using data from the U.S. Census Bureau's *Small Area Income and Poverty Estimates* (U.S. Census Bureau, 2004a), Table 2.10 shows that on average, local public school districts received from $1,000 to $2,000 per pupil in Title I aid per estimated child in poverty.

In previous iterations of ESEA, Title VII (now Title III) provided funding to support bilingual education programs but was relatively sparsely allocated. In 1995–1996, approximately 112 school districts nationwide out of 15,842 (reporting in the *Common Core of Data*; NCES, 2004) received, on average, about $260 per expected limited-English-proficient (LEP) pupil (as predicted by 1990 census data on the percentage of children aged 5 to 17 who speak English "not well") in direct federal aid for bilingual education (Baker & Markham, 2002). In 2000, 217 districts received on average, about $105 per identified LEP student (Baker & Markham, 2002). However, policy makers never intended Title VII to directly provide services for all LEP students nationwide (Baker & Markham, 2002). Rather, the objective was to serve as a stimulus for state and local districts to take action and as a program of experimentation.

Federal funding for special education is frequently criticized as the federal government's greatest unmet promise. IDEA was originally intended to pay for up to 40% of costs incurred by states and local districts for meeting the needs of children with disabilities. As noted previously, federal funding for IDEA has typically covered about 8% of those costs. Table 2.10 summarizes IDEA allocations to local school districts for 2003–2004. Using data from the NCES (2004) to estimate numbers of special education pupils in each

Table 2.10   Title I Funding to States in 2003–2004

State	Total Enrollment	Estimated Poverty (SAIPE 2004)	Disability Enrollment	Title I Pass-Through Aid	Title I per Poverty Pupil	IDEA Pass-Through Aid	IDEA Aid per Disability Pupil	Total Federal Aid	Total Federal Aid Pupil
Alabama	730,418	146,575	122,213	$203,439,000	$1,388	$133,002,000	$1,088	$625,666,000	$857
Alaska	132,477	14,332	17,723	$38,150,000	$2,662	$24,439,000	$1,379	$286,447,000	$2,162
Arizona	923,190	167,367	105,316	$185,818,000	$1,110	$121,879,000	$1,157	$893,579,000	$968
Arkansas	454,290	84,833	57,562	$104,810,000	$1,235	$83,614,000	$1,453	$423,699,000	$933
California	6,244,644	1,067,857	674,863	$1,884,562,000	$1,765	$1,414,693,000	$2,096	$6,609,513,000	$1,058
Colorado	756,579	83,995	75,581	$121,245,000	$1,443	$98,413,000	$1,302	$435,102,000	$575
Connecticut	560,709	55,199	67,095	$102,413,000	$1,855	$82,723,000	$1,233	$360,967,000	$644
Delaware	117,777	11,865	17,171	$27,269,000	$2,298	$21,104,000	$1,229	$107,492,000	$913
DC	65,099	17,067	11,977	$43,773,000	$2,565	$12,445,000	$1,039	$184,205,557	$2,830
Florida	2,592,997	393,612	399,382	$513,346,000	$1,304	$501,450,000	$1,256	$2,174,314,000	$839
Georgia	1,522,424	269,712	186,318	NR	NR	NR	NR	$1,201,843,000	$789
Hawaii	183,609	16,758	22,533	$35,049,000	$2,091	$34,359,000	$1,525	$236,470,000	$1,288
Idaho	252,037	31,396	28,758	$44,763,000	$1,426	$35,320,000	$1,228	$177,528,000	$704
Illinois	2,084,907	318,303	315,495	$499,917,000	$1,571	$405,500,000	$1,285	$1,747,920,000	$838
Indiana	1,008,546	129,293	170,666	$166,665,000	$1,289	$187,832,000	$1,101	$654,816,000	$649
Iowa	481,226	51,913	63,886	$64,474,000	$1,242	$90,613,000	$1,418	$353,266,000	$734
Kansas	469,622	57,349	64,710	$91,385,000	$1,593	NR	NR	$339,550,000	$723
Kentucky	663,886	129,918	103,573	NR	NR	NR	NR	$607,212,000	$915
Louisiana	721,414	176,916	100,213	$217,524,000	$1,230	$128,485,000	$1,282	$785,967,000	$1,089
Maine	201,056	22,665	33,481	$48,363,000	$2,134	$71,788,000	$2,144	$190,456,000	$947
Maryland	869,113	90,693	108,141	$142,020,000	$1,566	$137,834,000	$1,275	$581,542,000	$669
Massachusetts	962,488	102,904	152,388	$245,354,000	$2,384	$212,373,000	$1,394	$773,841,000	$804
Michigan	1,743,478	230,752	242,877	$412,110,000	$1,786	$305,276,000	$1,257	$1,428,275,000	$819
Minnesota	842,006	74,328	113,478	$115,079,000	$1,548	$148,283,000	$1,307	$523,761,000	$622
Mississippi	492,557	129,261	66,165	$155,755,000	$1,205	$80,257,000	$1,213	$516,520,000	$1,049
Missouri	916,102	144,201	144,752	$172,153,000	$1,194	$139,814,000	$966	$620,282,000	$677
Montana	148,168	21,866	19,267	$40,324,000	$1,844	$29,458,000	$1,529	$191,840,000	$1,295
Nebraska	276,546	28,657	44,448	$52,310,000	$1,825	$51,973,000	$1,169	$240,120,000	$868
Nevada	385,414	52,262	45,161	$48,915,000	$936	$46,566,000	$1,031	$221,488,000	$575
New Hampshire	203,359	15,739	29,390	$25,770,000	$1,637	$22,176,000	$755	$119,354,000	$587
New Jersey	1,450,014	128,946	223,051	$261,223,000	$2,026	$255,431,000	$1,145	$914,067,000	$630
New Mexico	323,066	68,729	63,727	$103,392,000	$1,504	$90,152,000	$1,415	$492,102,000	$1,523
New York	2,827,330	515,880	NR	$1,170,309,000	$2,269	$605,495,000	NR	$3,066,790,000	$1,085
North Carolina	1,354,031	220,269	192,397	NR	NR	NR	NR	$1,032,404,000	$762
North Dakota	101,889	10,639	13,774	$33,175,000	$3,118	$18,406,000	$1,336	$134,759,000	$1,323
Ohio	1,843,423	245,791	257,073	NR	NR	$270,509,000	$1,052	$1,316,783,000	$714
Oklahoma	625,826	104,968	92,895	$161,896,000	$1,542	$97,762,000	$1,052	$593,693,000	$949
Oregon	547,470	76,745	69,643	$128,625,000	$1,676	$95,215,000	$1,367	$460,902,000	$842
Pennsylvania	1,802,381	236,801	252,903	$469,434,000	$1,982	$367,763,000	$1,454	$1,644,032,000	912
Rhode Island	NR	NR	NR	$43,964,000	NR	$28,522,000	NR	$133,415,000	NR
South Carolina	696,376	132,886	109,561	$153,318,000	$1,154	$131,114,000	$1,197	$616,660,000	$886
South Dakota	125,156	16,838	16,944	$30,705,000	$1,824	$22,109,000	$1,305	$156,117,000	$1,247
Tennessee	911,636	154,678	171,594	$167,316,000	$1,082	$173,414,000	$1,011	$692,353,000	$759
Texas	4,327,481	869,418	509,371	$1,021,651,000	$1,175	$566,983,000	$1,113	$3,842,299,000	$888
Utah	490,516	49,907	57,356	$41,465,000	$831	$74,290,000	$1,295	$302,291,000	$616
Vermont	94,929	7,642	14,332	$25,878,000	$3,386	$18,916,000	$1,320	$94,555,000	$996
Virginia	1,191,035	130,214	171,906	$190,096,000	$1,460	$186,512,000	$1,085	$765,353,000	$643
Washington	1,020,877	134,999	110,659	$181,899,000	$1,347	$166,332,000	$1,503	$749,399,000	$734
West Virginia	280,561	56,224	50,176	$79,599,000	$1,416	$0	$0	$290,752,000	$1,036
Wisconsin	874,636	113,017	126,930	$152,503,000	$1,349	$141,241,000	$1,113	$550,729,000	$630
Wyoming	86,925	9,063	13,430	$25,760,000	$2,842	$14,864,000	$1,107	$95,995,000	$1,104

Note: NR, not reported

Sources: Total enrollment and disability enrollment data from the National Center for Education Statistics, *Common Core of Data, Local Education Agency Universe Survey 2003–04* (www.nces.ed.gov/ccd, retrieved April 4, 2007. Title I and IDEA pass-through funds data from the *U.S. Census Bureau Fiscal Survey of Local Governments (F-33) Public Elementary and Secondary Education Finances.* Retrieved April 4, 2007, from www.census.gov. Poverty estimates based on *U.S. Census Bureau Small Area Income and Poverty Estimates for 2004* (SAIPE). Retrieved April 4, 2007, from http://www.census.gov/hhes/www/saipe/school/sd04layout.html. SAIPE poverty rates multiplied times district enrollments.

state, Table 2.10 shows that on average, the federal government allocates approximately $1,000 to $1,500 per special education pupil, an amount quite similar to, though somewhat lower than, the amount for Title 1.

Schools and Children Without a State

In this section, we briefly discuss three groups of children for whom the federal government has a different level of responsibility: (a) children of military personnel living on U.S. installations in other countries; (b) children living and attending school on Indian reservations; and (c) children of military personnel and federal employees, children living on Indian reservations, and children living on other federal property. We focus specifically on the latter two groups in this section.

Table 2.11 summarizes the distribution of federally operated schools. Note that this table includes only those schools directly operated by the federal government. Numerous other schools, including state and locally operated schools serving Native American children and military installations, and tribally governed Indian reservation schools, receive the bulk of their funding from the federal government.

Table 2.11 Federally Operated Schools

State	Number of Schools
Alabama	2
Arizona	7
California	1
Georgia	3
Kentucky	2
Minnesota	1
Montana	1
North Carolina	2
North Dakota	2
New Mexico	4
New York	1
Oklahoma	1
Oregon	1
South Carolina	2
South Dakota	4
Virginia	4
Puerto Rico	1
European Superintendents Offices (DODDS)	7
Pacific Superintendents (DODDS)	5
Total	51

Source: National Center for Education Statistics (2000).

Schools Under Governance of the Bureau of Indian Affairs

The role of the federal government in the affairs of Native American people has long been a source of political and legal conflicts. Nonetheless, most scholars agree that the federal government has a unique trust relationship with Native Americans. Careful consideration of numerous federal treaties and of several U.S. Supreme Court decisions reveals early support for the concept of a federal trust relationship. Nonetheless, the judiciary, which is primarily responsible for the explanation and interpretation of federal treaties when conflict arises, has not specifically included education within the rubric of the trust responsibility.

Despite many obstacles, the Supreme Court has continued to recognize that the federal government has an obligation of honor toward Native American Nations. In *Morton v. Mancari* (1974), Justice Blackmun refers to a letter from President F. D. Roosevelt, which states that the fundamental rights of political liberty, local self-government, *education* and economic assistance must be extended to American Indians in order for them to attain a wholesome American life. As evidenced by recent case law, the judiciary continues to recognize the unique trust relationship between the United States and the American Indians, *County of Oneida v. Oneida Indian Nation* (1985).

As of the late 1990s, approximately 46,500 Native American students were served in 170 Native American elementary and secondary schools and 14 residential facilities (Jordan & Lyons, 1994; National Center for Education Statistics, 1997). Reports of the numbers of schools declined throughout the 1990s from 184 in 1992, to 171 in a 1995 report from the Department of the Interior, to the more recent number of 170. This accounts for 9% of all American Indian students (NCES, 1997). We believe that documented shortfalls of federal government support to Indian reservation schools (Jordan & Lyons, 1994) has rendered education on the reservation a less-viable option over time. As a result, former reservation students are absorbed by the more positively perceived public system. This pattern of migration, in turn, further diminishes the federal responsibility to Native American children, passing the burden primarily over to state and local governments.

Some recent research (e.g., Lawton, 1993), indicates that Indian reservation schools are finding more creative ways to supplement funding that they receive through the Indian Schools Equalization Program.

These efforts have included (a) entrepreneurial ventures such as gaming, (b) lobbying state governments to supplement their federal funding, and (c) seeking additional revenues from branches of the federal government other than the Bureau of Indian Affairs (BIA). Lawton (1993), for example, performed a case study of the benefits of gaming revenue for Native American schools in Minnesota. Lawton's study emphasized the personal side of the benefits of gaming revenue through interviews with officials in Indian schools:

> "Before gaming, this tribe had only one source of on-reserve revenue: that from stripping copper wire for recycling," explained the Indian Education Director. "The tribe's education office consisted of one person: me. The unemployment rate was high; there was not reason for kids to complete school since there were no jobs. Today, there is a staff of nine in the Tribal Education Office. The tribe is building [a] new community center, which will have a pre-school day care open to both Indians and non-Indians. And, there is a post-secondary scholarship fund for tribal members. We even have students in university studying abroad in Europe. As well, we have social services, a psychologist, and a home-school coordinator for kids who don't get involved." (Lawton, 1993, p. 14)

In at least two states, Minnesota and Arizona, extensive lobbying efforts have been successful in obtaining state-provided supplementary aid to Indian schools. Like most states, Minnesota and Arizona have equalization formulas by which they fund what, in theory, should be both an equitable and adequate public education throughout the public schools in the state. In Minnesota, the state legislature has recently included Native American schools under that same umbrella, where Indian Schools Equalization Program (ISEP) funding is considered to be the equivalent of local effort, and the state provides supplementary funds to raise the average per pupil expenditures to a defined level. In Arizona, a similar funding scheme applies to charter schools, now proliferating rapidly throughout the state.

Federal Impact Aid Programs

The original objective of the Federal Impact Aid Program was to compensate states and local school districts for burdens imposed on them by the federal government. For example, the federal designation of land as Indian reservation land or placement of a military institution within a public school district can simultaneously increase enrollments and limit or reduce the taxable property wealth of the district. In the 1950s, when the impact aid program was first passed, most public schools received the majority of their funds from local property taxation. In some isolated cases, more than 95% of students attending local public schools reside on military bases, and the vast majority of property within district boundaries is federal owned; as a result, the local district cannot raise sufficient funding on its own. Zimmer, Buddin, and Gill (2002) note that impact aid reached its peak in the late 1960s at approximately $2 billion annually. Since the mid-1980s, impact aid has stabilized at approximately half that amount (p. 941).

Presently, the following groups qualify to bring impact aid to their local school districts:

- Children of military personnel
- Children of civilian federal employees
- Children living in low-rent housing
- Children living on Native American reservations

Impact aid is allocated to local school districts according to a pupil weighting system that applies different weights based on the category into which students fall. The weighting system is used to create a count of weighted federal student units, or WFSUs. Table 2.12 provides a list of the weights by student type and sample calculation of WFSUs. A district with the pupil distribution shown in Table 2.12 would receive funding for 2,700. Note that the final two categories have a threshold of 1,000 students; the 500 pupils who are children of civilian employees not living on federal property therefore bring no additional funds to the district.

To determine a district's total impact aid, the WFSUs are multiplied times a per-pupil allotment. That allotment is generally defined as 50% of either the state or national average-per-pupil expenditure. For example, in a state with an average-per-pupil expenditure of $8,000 (higher than the national average), the district in Table 2.12 would receive 2,700 × $4,000 = $10.8 million. As one might expect, however, the federal government rarely provides full funding for its impact aid program. As a result, impact aid is prorated using a calculation involving (a) the proportion of students in the district who are "federally connected" and (b) the proportion of the total district budget that would be made up of impact aid, if impact aid were fully funded. (For a more thorough explanation, and an analysis of the effects of this formula, see Zimmer et al., 2002.)

Table 2.13 summarizes the fiscal year 2002–2003 allocations of federal impact aid by state. The largest

Table 2.12   Federal Impact Aid Formula

Type of Student	Weight	Example: No. Eligible Pupils	Funded Pupils
Children of military parents living on base	1	2,000	2,000
Children living on Native American reservations	1.25	200	250
Children of federal civilian employees living on federal property	1	100	100
Children of military parents living off base	0.1	3,000	300
Children living in low-rent housing	0.1	500	50
Children of federal civilian employees not living on federal property	0.05	500	0
Other children living on federal property	0.05		
TOTAL			2,700

Source: Adapted from Zimmer, R., Buddin, R., & Gill, B. (2002), Distributional effects and distorted incentives: Funding policy under the federal impact aid program. *Journal of Education Finance, 27* (4), 943–944.

number of school districts receiving impact aid was in Oklahoma. The second column of the table lists the total enrollment of schools receiving impact aid, not the enrollment of eligible students. The final column of the table lists the total impact aid divided by all pupils. This figure tells us the overall impact of the aid on local districts, as impact aid is not targeted for eligible pupils. Obviously, districts with larger numbers of "high-weight" eligible pupils receive among the highest levels of impact aid per pupil. By state, Alaska districts receiving impact aid receive the highest amount per enrolled pupil. Arizona, Delaware, Montana, and South Dakota each have relatively high levels of impact aid per pupil in districts receiving that aid.

SUMMARY

In this chapter, we have provided an eclectic mix of theoretical background in public economics, followed by a national view of financial support for education. Our discussion of economic theory highlighted the theories of Charles Tiebout (1956) regarding the local provision of public goods and services. We also discussed the role of state government intervention to remediate market failures in the provision of public schooling. Policy makers frequently invoke arguments favoring local control in debates over school finance, and these arguments often coincide with arguments opposing *government* intervention. Yet rarely is the concept of *local* itself questioned, and rarely is *government* clearly defined.

In many conservative states, the word *government* carries negative connotations. In school finance in the United States, the word *government* usually refers to *state-level government*. And in the context of this text

and this chapter more specifically, government intervention most often refers to state-level government intervention in the financing of local school districts. Interestingly, some who most sharply criticize state governments simply accept the appropriate alternative to be *local government schools* (e.g., see Fischel, 2001). That is, local governments such as school districts and/or towns and townships are still *governments*. Many large urban school districts actually enroll more pupils than some small states such as Vermont (approximately 100,000 students) and Wyoming (just over 80,000 students).[2]

In many southern states, school districts are contiguous with counties. In northeastern states many, though certainly not all, school districts are contiguous with city or town boundaries. Town-based financing of public schooling is an artifact of the initial formation of

---

[2] New York City Public Schools, for example, enroll over ten times as many students as the entire state of Vermont. Other local school districts with more students than Vermont include Houston, Dallas, Chicago, Memphis, Philadelphia, and Detroit.

Table 2.13   Distribution of Federal Impact Aid by State 2002–2003

State	Districts	Students	Total Impact Aid (in $1,000s)	Mean per Pupil in Receiving Districts
Alabama	36	288,257	$3,188	$11
Alaska	50	115,409	$103,996	$901
Arizona	27	193,268	$104,801	$542
Arkansas	24	26,542	$956	$36
California	81	1,269,615	$73,969	$58
Colorado	17	122,705	$19,857	$162
Delaware	1	6,665	$8,678	$1,302
District of Columbia	1	67,522	$1,309	$19
Florida	17	1,297,919	$12,776	$10
Georgia	36	502,199	$19,760	$39
Hawaii	1	183,829	$33,235	$181
Idaho	21	37,584	$7,542	$201
Illinois	64	538,146	$20,871	$39
Indiana	14	97,204	$2,381	$24
Iowa	35	28,038	$629	$22
Kansas	27	88,307	$11,062	$125
Kentucky	1		$0	$0
Louisiana	10	159,975	$7,635	$48
Maine	10	27,111	$1,411	$52
Maryland	14	666,127	$10,347	$16
Massachusetts	1		$0	$0
Michigan	21	43,068	$4,982	$116
Minnesota	88	65,581	$11,748	$179
Mississippi	21	85,427	$3,919	$46
Missouri	34	38,760	$19,950	$515
Montana	115	19,472	$15,532	$798
Nebraska	168	112,980	$18,643	$165
Nevada	7	334,200	$4,061	$12
New Hampshire	2		$0	$0
New Jersey	26	180,107	$4,446	$25
New Mexico	29	205,659	$86,754	$422
New York	53	1,171,931	$23,216	$20
North Carolina	47	578,748	$14,237	$25
North Dakota	70	27,411	$8,973	$327
Ohio	5	60,645	$152	$3
Oklahoma	231	282,236	$37,309	$132
Oregon	25	15,866	$3,945	$249
Pennsylvania	54	434,494	$5,591	$13
Rhode Island	7	25,560	$3,525	$138
South Carolina	23	285,792	$4,151	$15
South Dakota	49	39,683	$40,565	$1,022
Tennessee	19	264,550	$3,196	$12
Texas	108	1,153,124	$84,512	$73
Utah	20	274,712	$13,763	$50
Vermont	5	4,753	$27	$6
Virginia	23	626,190	$48,103	$77
Washington	54	328,966	$53,500	$163
Wisconsin	28	32,012	$10,931	$341
Wyoming	10	30,394	$5,018	$165

Sources: Data from National Center for Education Statistics (2000); U.S. Census Bureau (2003).

public schools in colonial times. In current times, and in most of the country, the relationship between current school and school district boundaries and the original colonial conception of *local* government is tenuous at best. Throughout the middle portion of the 20th century, policy makers modified local school district boundaries and merged and consolidated schools and districts by processes no less political than the redrawing of congressional district boundaries in Texas in 2003. Race, poverty, and religion[3] have played and continue to play key roles in redefining *local*. In several metropolitan areas around the country, predominantly white "local school districts" are carefully carved out of the boundaries of predominantly black urban centers.[4] In addition, as recently as the 1960s, many counties consisted entirely of racially restricted housing developments.[5]

Many espouse the virtues of *local control* in public education, assuming that *local* is a meaningful unit of government related to some cohesive group of citizens with common preferences regarding their children's education (Fischel, 2001). Where such cohesiveness does exist, it is highly likely that the cohesiveness is a function of racial, ethnic, and religious separatism endorsed via politicization of school district boundaries and mid-20th-century district reorganization policies. Those who espouse the virtues of local control most vehemently oppose state intervention, in part on assumptions that state governments are too large and inefficient and too far removed from the needs of individual communities.

One important operational difference remains in the way decisions are made, specifically regarding school finance, at the level of state governments versus local governments, including school districts: School funding decisions made at the *local* level are often made by direct voter referenda. That is, registered voters of the town may directly express their opinion and cast their ballot, either at the polls or in a town meeting, regarding the school district's annual budget. Elected state representatives make state-level decisions regarding the financing of public schools. This does not preclude the possibility that state-level officials will choose to offer voters statewide school-funding referenda.

Increasingly, this operational difference—state government as representative democracy, local as direct democracy—has also been reduced, with state governments regulating local spending decisions and with large, urban local governments operating as representative, rather than direct, democracies. The city and state distinctions suffer from problems of scale comparisons. The five largest U.S. cities have more children than the five smallest states!

We hope that you will keep in mind the complexities of the politics, geography, and financing of schools as you read this text. As we noted in Chapter 1, the organization and financing of public schooling are inextricably linked. Many of the most significant problems in improving equity and adequacy of school funding are rooted in organizational complexities of schooling. So, too, may be the solutions.

KEY TERMS

allocative efficiency Where goods and services are allocated such that no one person or agent in the system can be made better off by reallocating those goods or services.

capitalization An increase in the value of one's capital assets that results from investment in public goods or services (context-specific definition). For example, investment

---

[3] For example, in the late 1990s in New York State, the state legislature crafted legislation that would allow a town in Rockland County, dominated by a single Satmar Hasidic Jewish sect, to redraw its boundaries yielding a 100% Satmar Hasidic school district (Kiryas Joel). The U.S. Supreme Court ruled that the state, in crafting legislation so narrowly focused on this one town, had violated the establishment clause of the U.S. Constitution (see *Board of Education of Kiryas Joel v. Grummet*, 1994).

[4] This includes Westside Community Schools, carved out of the city limits of Omaha Nebraska, Center School District, now with significant minority populations, but when formed in 1956, primarily a white middle-class neighborhood in south Kansas City, Missouri.

[5] From 1900 to 1947, 148 of 154 housing subdivisions in Johnson County, a rapidly growing suburb adjacent to Kansas City, Missouri, and Kansas City, Kansas, were racially "restrictive covenants" (Gotham, 2002, p. 39).

through paying higher taxes in quality public schools may lead to capitalization in home values. Market prices are higher for homes in good school districts, all else equal.

efficiency   The relative prices of goods should equal the marginal costs of their production and the marginal value that consumers attach to their consumption.

equity   The marginal change in social welfare from consumption of a particular commodity should be equal across all households.

externality   Action by either a producer or consumer that affects other producers or consumers but is not accounted for in the market price of the good or service.

free rider   A consumer or producer who does not pay for a nonexclusive good (public good/service) but benefits from that good or service.

market failures   Market failures erode the rational economic relationships between production costs, supply, demand, and market prices, resulting in inefficient allocation of goods and services.

pareto efficiency   An allocation of goods in which one person must be made worse off in order to make another person better off.

positional good   A good for which the value of one person's quantity or quality of that good necessarily influences the value of another person's quantity or quality of that good. For example, the labor market value of a bachelor's degree for one individual is contingent upon the numbers of individuals competing for similar jobs who have higher or lower degrees (quantity of education) or bachelor's degrees from more prestigious institutions (quality of education).

pure public good   A good from which individuals cannot be excluded and one for which nonrivalry exists. Public education systems are in relative undersupply and are subject to congestion. Public education systems are not a pure public good.

REFERENCES

Akerlof, G. A. (1970, August). The market for lemons: Quality uncertainty and the market mechanism. *Quarterly Journal of Economics*, pp. 488–500.

Baker, B. D., & Markham, P. (2002). State school funding policies and limited English proficient students. *Bilingual Research Journal, 23*(3), 659–680.

Baldi, S., Lewis, J., & Sherman, J. (2001). *Education finance in G-7 nations.* Washington, DC: American Institutes for Research.

Board of Education of Kiryas Joel Village School District v. Grumet, 512 U.S. 687 (1994).

County of Oneida v. Oneida Indian Nation, 470 U.S. 226 (1985).

Duncombe, W. (1996). Public expenditure research: What have we learned? *Public Budgeting and Finance, 16*(2), 26–58.

Duncombe, W., & Yinger, J. (1996). Why is it so hard to help central city schools? *Journal of Policy Analysis and Management, 16*(1), 85–113.

Fischel, W. A. (2001). *The home voter hypothesis: How home values influence local government taxation, school finance and land use policies.* Cambridge, MA: Harvard University Press.

Gotham, K. F. (2002). *Race, real estate and uneven development: The Kansas City experience 1900 to 2000.* Albany, NY: State University of New York Press.

Gramlich, E. (1977). Intergovernmental grants: A review of the empirical literature and compensation. In W. Oates (ed.), *The Political Economy of Fiscal Federalism.* Lexington, MA: Lexington Books.

Gramlich, E. M., & Rubinfeld, D. (1982). Micro estimates of public spending demand functions and tests of the Tiebout and median-voter hypotheses. *Journal of Political Economy, 90*(3), 536–560.

Hanushek, E. A. (1994). *Making schools work: Improving performance and controlling costs.* Washington, DC: Brookings Institution Press.

Harris, A., Evans, W., & Schwab, R. (1999). *Education spending in an aging America.* Working paper. Department of Economics, University of Maryland, College Park.

Hirsch, F. (1976). *Social limits to growth.* Cambridge, MA: Harvard University Press

Jordan, K. F., & Lyons, T. S. (1994). *Improving educational adequacy and learning opportunities for American Indian youth.* Washington, DC: Office of Indian Education Programs, Bureau of Indian Affairs, U.S. Department of the Interior.

Koski, W., & Reich, R. (2007). When adequate isn't: The retreat from equity in educational law and policy and why it matters. *Emory Law Journal, 56*(3), 545–613.

Lawton, S. B. (1993, March 19–21). *The impact of gaming revenue on American Indian education: A case study.* Paper presented at the Annual Conference of the American Education Finance Association. Albuquerque, NM. Washington, DC: ERIC Clearinghouse: ED396884

Morton v. Mancari, 417 U.S. 535 (1974).

National Center for Education Statistics. (1997). *Characteristics of American Indian and Alaska Native education* (NCES 97-735). Washington, DC: U.S.

Department of Education, Office of Educational Research and Improvement.

National Center for Education Statistics. (2000). *Common core of data, local education agency universe survey.* Washington, DC: National Center for Education Statistics. Retrieved from www.nces.ed.gov/ccd

National Center for Education Statistics. (2003). *Statistics in brief. Revenues and expenditures for public elementary and secondary education: School year 2000-01.* Washington, DC: U.S. Department of Education, Institute of Education Sciences. Retrieved from http://nces.ed.gov/pubs2003/2003362.pdf.

National Center for Education Statistics. (2004). *Common core of data, local education agency universe survey 2003–04.* Retrieved April 4, 2007 from www.nces.ed.gov/ccd

Organisation for Economic Cooperation and Development. (2003). *Education at a glance 2003—tables and charts.* Retrieved July 1, 2005, from http://www.oecd.org/document/34/0,2340,en_2649_37455_14152482_1_1_1_37455,00.html

Pigou, C. (1932). *The economics of welfare* (4th ed.). London: McMillan and Co.

Poterba, J. M. (1997). Demographic structure and the political economy of public education. *Journal of Policy Analysis and Management, 16*(1), 48–66.

Pindyck, R. S., & Rubenfeld, D. L. (1995). *Microeconomics* (3rd ed.). New York: Prentice Hall.

Richards, C. E., Shore, R., & Sawicky, M. (1996). *Risky business: Private management of public schools.* Washington, DC: Economic Policy Institute.

Samuelson, P. A. (1954, November). The pure theory of public expenditure. *Review of Economics and Statistics, 36,* 386–389.

Samuelson, P. A. (1955, November). Diagrammatic exposition of a theory of public expenditure. *Review of Economics and Statistics, 37,* 350–356.

Siebert, M., & Goff, S. (2002). *Risk factors for North Carolina elections: The correlation of low voter turnout with race, wealth and history.* Durham, SC: Institute for Southern Studies.

Tiebout, C. M. (1956, October). A pure theory of local expenditures. *Journal of Political Economy, 64,* 416–424.

U.S. Census Bureau. (2004a). *Small area income and poverty estimates. Model-based estimates for states, counties and school districts.* Retrieved April 12, 2007, from http://www.census.gov/hhes/www/saipe/district.html

U.S. Census Bureau. (2004b). *U.S. Census Bureau fiscal survey of local governments, local education agency (school district) finance survey (F-33).* Retrieved April 4, 2007, from http://nces.ed.gov/ccd/f33agency.asp

Zimmer, R., Buddin, R., & Gill, B. (2002). Distributional effects and distorted incentives: Funding policy under the federal impact aid program. *Journal of Education Finance, 27*(4), 939–964.

RAISING REVENUES FOR PUBLIC SCHOOLS

Introduction

The field of education finance provides several different methods for indexing historical spending patterns. Figure 3.1 shows total growth in federal, state, and local expenditure on public education from 1949 to 2004. The total cost of providing public schooling has increased (in current dollars) tremendously, exceeding $500 billion by 2003–2004. But enrollment in public schooling has also increased quite significantly. Between 1986 and 2004, enrollment grew nationally from 39.7 million to 48.8 million, while total spending grew from about $161.8 billion to $511 billion. Current spending per pupil adjusted for inflation using the consumer price index (CPI) rose from just under $6,000 to nearly $8,000: an increase of about one third (constant 2000 dollars). To assume that this expenditure increase represents real growth, however, is to assume that the CPI is the best possible measure for adjusting for inflation.

Alternatively, Figure 3.1 shows education spending as a percentage of gross domestic product, revealing that while U.S. effort increased in the early half of the 20th century, the share of gross domestic product allocated to public elementary and secondary education in the United States has remained relatively flat for decades. Needless to say, one can paint a variety of different pictures of U.S. education spending over time. Nonetheless, a common perception, supported by many measures, is that education spending has increased steadily over the decades.

A thoughtful analyst would be quick to point out that we have no way of determining whether all students are receiving a better education as a result of this significant increase in spending and effort. We might seek to answer several questions: (a) How has the money been distributed? (b) Did every school share fairly in the increases? (c) How was the money spent once received? (d) Can we find a relationship between the increases in spending and improvements in important student outcomes such as graduation rates, student achievement outcomes, and postsecondary outcomes such as employment, training, and college attendance? These are each critically important questions. The answers tell us something about the equity, efficiency, adequacy, and performance of our educational system. We will address each of these issues in depth in later chapters.

In this chapter, our task is to understand the collection of funds from taxpayers and the consequences of various strategies to collect taxes to pay for schools. Thus far, we have shown that public education systems represent a growing industry and a growing financial commitment. Whether this growth is a sound investment in the future of our children or wasteful spending depends greatly on the effectiveness of our education system in the economy.

The consistent growth in education spending over time relative to per capita income begs the question, "Where does the money come from?" In Chapter 2, we provided an introduction to public expenditure theory, an area within economics that explains how and why local taxpayers and state and federal government officials choose to spend what they do on the provision of public goods and services such as education. The majority of this chapter focuses on taxation and public finance policy at the federal, state, and local levels of government. In particular, we discuss the

Figure 3.1   Growth in Total Education Expenditures and as a Percent of Gross Domestic Product from 1949 to 2003–2004

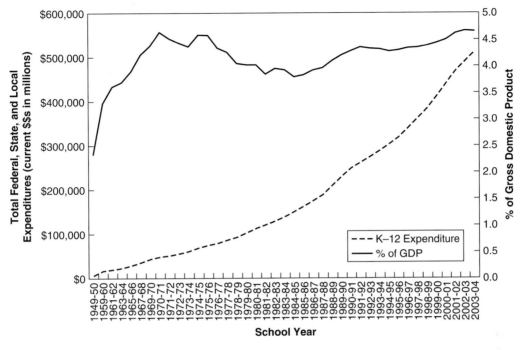

Source: Data from http://nces.ed.gov/programs/digest/d05/tables/dt05_025.asp

changing roles of the federal, state, and local school districts in raising tax dollars to support public schools. We also seek to demonstrate the profoundly different roles states and local school districts in the United States elect to collect taxes for public education—as well as the policy consequences of these differing tax strategies. We explore some of the tensions and value differences that emerge as different states—responding to different local political cultures—seek to address their educational needs. Finally, we also discuss the emerging role of alternative, nontax revenues for supporting public education systems. Increasingly, as states and local school districts reach the upper limit of their tax capacity, they are relying on a combination of fees, entrepreneurial ventures, and private contributions to meet their increasing costs.

Where Do the Dollars Come From?

Figure 3.2 provides a preview of some of the major issues surrounding the locus of control for public education funding. Situated between the extremes of total local control and funding with no state or federal

control and completely national education system with no local or state input are three questions:

1. Who is best able to redistribute tax revenues to achieve greater equity in the quality of schooling?
2. How large can a bureaucracy grow before it becomes an inefficient distributor and regulator of education?
3. Is some mix of autonomy and regulation more effective than either extreme?

Many have argued that the only way that the United States will ever see equally distributed education quality across states and local school districts is if the federal government steps up and plays a much greater role (e.g., Loeb, 2001). Others counter by suggesting that decisions made at the federal level would be insensitive to differences in state and local need (e.g., Loeb, 2001).

Each of the 50 states resolved these tensions through a different solution. Partially the effect of the absence of education in the federal constitution and its explicit and varying provisions in the state constitutions and partially the product of regional economic, political, and cultural differences, the American

Figure 3.2   Where Should the Money Come From?

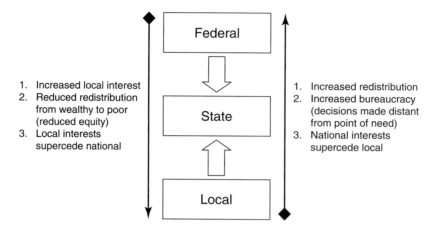

educational system is less of a system than it is a hodge-podge of approaches that has resulted in the following generalizations:

1. American public schools function under a mixed system of school finance.
2. The federal financial role has remained relatively small, while its regulatory role continues to grow.
3. School finance systems continue to vary widely across states. The origins of these variations and potential directions in the near future will be topics of discussion throughout this text.

Table 3.1 provides a summary of the primary tax revenue sources for each level of government and the shares that each level of government provided for public education systems in school year 2002–2003. We discuss each type of tax and the revenues generated by those taxes in much greater detail later in this chapter. In summary, the primary source of revenue for the federal government is the federal income tax. The primary sources of state revenue are income and sales taxes, the balance of which varies substantially from state to

state. The primary source of local revenue has historically been local property taxes. Indeed, there are exceptions, including statewide property taxes and local income and sales taxes. Table 3.1 indicates that states currently provide the largest share of revenues for public education systems. This suggests that the largest share of support for public schools comes from income and/or sales tax receipts.

This national perspective masks wide variation among states. In some states, the local property tax dominates educational spending, while in others state general funds derived from income and/or sales taxes dominate educational spending. What is most telling from Table 3.1 is that the federal government has a small financial investment in public education.

States have not always been the primary source of education funding. In the early 1970s, local governments held primary responsibility for funding public schools, with state governments paying slightly below 40% on average. However, even at this point in time, significant portions of funding raised through "local" property taxes, thus labeled as "local," were actually

Table 3.1   Government Sources of Funding for Education 2002–2003

Level of Government	Primary Tax Revenue Sources	Share of Education Funding
Federal	Income	8%
State	Income and sales	49%
Local	Property and sales	43%

Source: U.S. Census. (2004). Fiscal Survey of local governments, elementary and secondary education finance 2002–03. Retrieved July 1, 2006, from http://www.census.gov/govs/www/school.html

mandated by state governments to ensure some mini-mally adequate level of school funding. Partly as a re-sult of school finance equity litigation, discussed in Chapter 4, the state role in funding public schools in-creased with relative consistency throughout the 1970s and 1980s, until approximately 1990. Since then, state shares have declined slightly. Bear in mind that as state and local roles shift, so do the taxes that provide the revenue for public schools. We will return to this question in more depth shortly.

Numerous perspectives explain why the state role began to level off in the early 1990s. First, the econ-omy began to slow during that period, producing lower income and sales tax receipts for state govern-ments. Second, stimulated in part by *A Nation at Risk* (National Commission on Excellence in Education, 1983), a federal government report highly critical of America's public schools, skepticism regarding the question of whether we were getting our money's worth from public schools increased throughout the mid to late 1980s. Finally, it might be argued that state support had reached its appropriate equilibrium with local support to achieve equitable and adequate educa-tion. The federal role has remained relatively small throughout history, reaching a maximum of about 11% in the late 1970s, following adoption of sweeping federal legislation regarding the education of children with disabilities (PL 92-142). Federal funding stabi-lized in the late 1990s between 6% and 8% but has since increased slightly. Therefore, we pay little atten-tion to federal education funding in this text. At the end of this chapter, we provide a brief overview of fed-eral allocations for children with disabilities through the Individuals with Disabilities in Education Act (IDEA) and allocations for schools with high concen-trations of economically disadvantaged children, or Title I of the Elementary and Secondary Education Act (ESEA). These two sources of revenue are impor-tant to financially strapped urban school systems.

Figure 3.3 displays the differences in federal, state, and local shares of education revenues across the states. Again, note that federal revenues remain rela-tively low across states. The state and local shares, however, vary quite widely. Typically, an inverse rela-tionship exists between state and local resources. For example, in 2000, South Dakota allocated the lowest share of state funding at 34% and Hawaii the highest at 90%. Hawaii has historically functioned as a single-district state, assuming nearly full responsibility for funding education at the state level. Arkansas, New Mexico, and Michigan also provide substantial state support. The level of state involvement in Michigan is primarily a function of major reforms in the mid-1990s intended to eliminate property taxes as the basis of support for public schools and replace those taxes pri-marily with sales taxes. At the other end of the state-aid spectrum, until recently, New Hampshire provided less than 10% (less than 5% in some years) of school aid from state revenue sources. In other states undergoing major changes in their school-funding formulas, like Maryland, we might expect similarly dramatic changes in revenue shares.

An Overview of Taxation

In this section, we provide a broad overview of con-cepts of taxation and review of state and local tax poli-cies. We begin with a framework for evaluating taxes that we will apply as we separately discuss income, con-sumption, property taxes, and lotteries and gambling later in this chapter. Finally, we provide a data snapshot of tax policies across the states.

Evaluating Taxes

Taxes are typically evaluated across the following four dimensions (Monk & Brent, 1997):[1]

- *Equity:* Is the tax fair? To whom?
- *Efficiency:* Does the tax have unintended effects on the economy or create distortions? Is the tax efficient to administer?
- *Responsiveness to Economic Change:* Do revenues provided by the tax grow with the economy? Are revenues provided by the tax stable and pre-dictable?
- *Politically Acceptance:* To what extent does the public like or dislike the tax?

Equity
Tax equity is usually discussed in terms of *horizontal equity* and *vertical equity,* where **horizontal equity**

---

[1]Monk and Brent describe seven attributes of education taxes, including equity, fairness, efficiency, potential for economic growth, stability, administration, compliance, and public acceptance. We choose to collapse these attributes into what we believe to be logical dimensions.

Figure 3.3   Federal, State, and Local Shares Across States 2004–2005

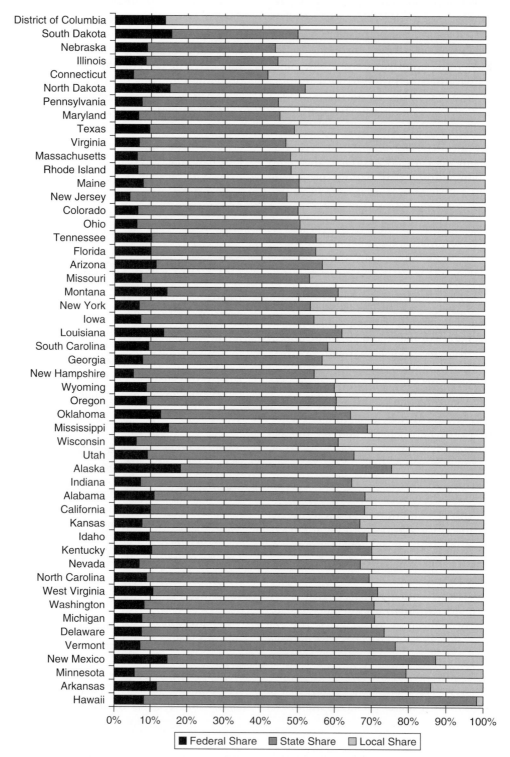

Source: Data from http://nces.ed.gov/pubs2007/expenditures/tables/table_1.asp?referrer=report

refers to the equal treatment of equals, and **vertical equity** refers to the unequal treatment of unequals. For example, a horizontally equitable tax system is one in which similarly situated taxpayers pay either the same amount or the same rate in taxes to support the public good in question. Easier said than done. The difficulty arises when state government has to translate "similarly situated" into tax policy.

Two approaches are typically available for determining "similarly situated" in this particular context. The first is the **benefit standard,** whereby the amount of tax paid is related to the benefits that an individual receives. Using the benefit standard, similarly situated taxpayers are those who stand to reap similar benefits from the public good in question. The amount or rate paid in taxes should be proportionate to the benefits obtained. Applying this standard to evaluating taxpayer equity for local public schools, one might tax the family with two children at twice the rate of the family with one child and not tax the elderly taxpayers who no longer have school-aged children. Of course, one might give a social benefit deduction to the family with two children on the basis that their two children, if educated, will produce more social benefit than another family's one child. The benefit standard does not apply for the majority of education tax dollars. User fees for lab classes, transportation fees, or textbook fees are all based on a benefit standard, as are tolls on roadways and bridges. Taxes and user fees are equivalent in the sense that transfers of income occur from citizens to the government for services rendered.

The more common approach for evaluating tax equity applies the **ability standard:** The amount of tax paid is based on the ability of the taxpayer to pay the tax. The ability standard concerns one's ability to pay for the public good. Applying the ability standard, however, requires first defining ability to pay, and second, setting the rate at which taxpayers must contribute, according to their ability to pay. Setting rates according to one's ability to pay raises the question of **vertical equity**—differential treatment of taxpayers according to some rational basis or reasonable government interest. Should each taxpayer pay the same percentage of his or her income or wealth, thus paying different dollar amounts that reflect ability to pay but the same proportion (e.g., 10%)? Alternatively, should individuals with more wealth and income pay not only a higher dollar amount but also a higher proportion of their wealth or income?

The answers to these questions determine whether a tax is regressive, proportional, or progressive. **Progressive taxation** requires taxpayers with greater ability to pay at a higher rate, typically defined as a percentage of income. An example of a progressive tax is a graduated income tax in which individuals with higher income pay a higher percentage of their income in taxes. In theory, this describes the structure of the federal income tax system. The tax impact of the federal income tax, however, varies widely depending on the wealth class and tax exemptions available to the taxpayer. A proportional tax requires the same rate but not the same amount. **Regressive taxation** requires taxpayers with greater wealth to pay a lower percentage of their income. One example is a flat dollar tax such as a toll bridge. Everyone who crosses in a car, rich or poor, in a Volkswagen or a Rolls Royce, pays the same toll.

The argument for progressive taxation should be understood based on the economic principle of declining marginal utility. In simple terms, for each thousand dollars of additional wealth, one gains less utility (usefulness or benefit) from that wealth. Thus, taxing a billionaire at higher rates than someone making $10,000 per year is justified, because the tax causes the billionaire less pain or loss of utility to pay the tax. A 25% tax rate on a woman who makes $10,000 would leave her near starvation, while a 50% tax on the billionaire still leaves her with $500,000,000. The conservative counter-argument posits that the wealthy will invest their wealth beyond their consumption needs back into the economy. Thus, they have an enduring and critical role to play in stimulating economic growth, which capitalism requires in order to remain viable. High tax rates on capital gains, it is argued, discourage investment and dampen economic growth. Dampening economic growth, in turn, reduces real wages, incomes, and spending, which all reduce the tax base. Thus, the art of tax policy lies in finding rates of taxation that do not dampen investment and economic growth yet provide adequate tax revenue to accomplish social goals such as education.

Efficiency

The efficiency of a tax is also important to its success. In general, questions of tax efficiency focus on whether or not the tax in question distorts economic behavior. For example, sales tax variations within a region on particular goods and services may influence whether individuals choose to purchase those goods and services, how much individuals choose to purchase, and where they purchase. New York residents regularly travel to New Jersey for clothing purchases, because New Jersey exempts clothing from its sales tax while New York does not. As a result, for short periods over recent years, New York City has granted a clothing sales tax amnesty. In some cases, governments rely on, or hope for, distortions of this type. Similarly, in the late 1980s, as income taxes increased in Massachusetts, southern New Hampshire towns experienced a dramatic influx of business and residents, in part because New Hampshire had no income tax at all. Increasingly, governments use taxes with the intent to distort economic behavior. Cigarette taxes might be one example where the government objective is to reduce cigarette consumption by using taxes to increase the price on cigarettes. In this example, how might young persons, poor persons, and wealthy persons react differently to a one-dollar increase in taxes on a pack of cigarettes?

Taxes that create a loss of utility for consumers, above and beyond collected tax dollars, create what economists refer to as *excess burden*. Monk and Brent (1997, p. 25) provide the example of how a property tax might influence a family's decision to build an addition on their home, increasing the home's value, and, as a result, the family's annual tax bill. Indeed, by choosing not to build the addition, the family is able to save the money that would have otherwise been spent. They then suffer the loss of utility of the additional space in their home that they otherwise desired. In fact, the choice to save, rather than build, indicates that the family did not necessarily have other immediate uses for the money in mind. A rational decision to build should see the combined increase in market value plus the consumption utility equal to or greater than the additional property tax per year in present value. Of course, residential property taxes are full of distortions, because tax-assessment levels and rates vary from community to community and even from house to house. All of these effects could be mitigated by statewide assessments that are based on tax equalization formulas.

Administration

Another efficiency issue in taxation is how well taxes are collected and administered. Tax compliance is important for comparing taxes: What percentage of individuals or businesses actually pays the taxes that they are supposed to pay? In addition, the cost of administering a tax is important, including the cost of maintaining high levels of compliance. The administrative costs of income, consumption, and property taxes can vary widely.

Mikesell (1986, cited in Monk & Brent, 1997, p. 33) indicates that tax administration generally involves the following seven steps: (a) maintain and gather records, (b) compute the tax liability, (c) remit tax liability, (d) collect tax, (e) audit, (f) appeal, and (g) enforce. In the case of income taxes, individuals or business are generally responsible for the first three steps, and state or federal governments are responsible for the latter four steps. In the case of sales taxes, the merchant, not the taxpayer or the government, is typically responsible for the first four steps, further reducing costs to government. However, in the case of property taxes, local, county, and/or state governments become more involved in the first two steps, increasing administration costs to them. Of critical importance is the ratio of total cost to the revenue generated by the tax, or the net percentage of tax revenue.

Economic Responsiveness

From the perspective of fiscal planning, a good tax is a tax that produces a stable, predictable flow of revenue and produces more revenue as the economy grows. Of course, a tax that is directly responsive to positive economic changes is likely to be similarly responsive to negative economic changes. Further, a tax for which revenues change in lockstep with economic change is likely to be as unstable or unpredictable as the economy itself. In general, the values of properties fluctuate much less dramatically from year to year than personal and corporate income or personal consumption. Property values also are "sticky" in the downward direction. By sticky, we mean that they do not decrease as rapidly as market prices decrease. This occurs because government has no self-interest in adjusting property values downward, because government is then in the politically unpopular position of having to raise tax rates simply to sustain the previous year's tax revenue. When property tax rates get too far out of alignment with assessments, property owners often appeal for a reassessment. This downward stickiness feature of property taxes, while clearly unfair to taxpayers, provides a compelling reason why state governments are better served by including the property tax as a source of revenue for schools. When recessions occur, property tax states have more ability to withstand them and sustain spending levels.

Economists have devised methods of measuring the revenue-generating behavior of various kinds of taxes. One such measure is *elasticity*. To define this measure, we need to explain a few simple terms first. The **tax yield** is the revenue produced by the tax. The **tax base** is the entity to which the **tax rate** is applied, such as income or property wealth.

$$\text{Rate} \times \text{Base} = \text{Yield}$$

The amount of change in yield that accompanies changes in the tax base is the elasticity of the tax. When a 1% change in the tax base produces a 1% change in yield, the elasticity of the tax is 1.0. Elasticity is typically measured with respect to changes in personal income, for property taxes, sales taxes, and income taxes. Income taxes therefore are most likely to respond to changes in personal income. Progressive income taxes have elasticities greater than 1.0. This occurs because as individual incomes grow, more individuals move into higher tax brackets, paying higher percentages of their income in taxes. Inflation also tends to cause bracket creep, so that the effective tax rate increases even though consumption power has not increased. Sales taxes are also relatively responsive to changes in personal income, because individuals tend to consume more taxable goods as income increases (excluding the very wealthy, whose consumption stabilizes as income increases). The elasticity for sales taxes with respect to personal income is generally assumed to be about 1.0 (Mikesell, 1986). Property taxes tend to be much less responsive to changes in personal income and have elasticities of less than 1.0. One might argue that the elasticity base for property taxes should be market value rather than income, because property in some areas can increase quite rapidly while in other areas of the country the market price is flat or stable.

Political Acceptance

Finally, public perception, or voter perception, of a tax is important because tax policy is determined in a political environment. It may appear quite easy, for example, to raise all of the revenue required for a major reform of public education by implementing an income tax, where one had not previously existed. It might certainly appear that increased income taxes would be a more efficient source of new, statewide revenue than increased, statewide property taxes. Politics and public opinion often dictate otherwise. Gold (1994) provides some general guidelines for tax acceptability:

- Increasing sales taxes are preferred over across-the-board income tax increases.
- Increasing taxes on the wealthy and businesses is popular, as is loophole closing.

Increasing existing taxes are preferred over enactment of new taxes (Gold, 1994, cited in Monk and Brent, 1997, p. 37).

General rules for tax acceptability are unlikely to apply where education revenues are concerned, given the political diversity of states. For example, Vermont and Kansas, two strikingly different states in terms of their politics and geography, are two of the only states in the nation that have chosen to fund public education from a combination of statewide property taxes, supplemented with state sales and income taxes.[2] The Kansas legislature, in the late 1990s, implemented dramatic cuts in property tax rates, shifting the burden of funding education over to income and sales taxes, while the Vermont legislature has chosen to maintain high statewide property taxes. Policy changes in Kansas are largely a result of within-state politics. In Kansas, the majority of income and sales tax revenues are generated in the suburban and urban communities, more or less in the eastern part of the state, while a larger share (though not a majority) of property tax revenues are generated in western Kansas communities with corporate farming, natural gas, and oil deposits. In Kansas, shifting from property tax funding to income and sales tax funding means shifting the burden from west to east. As a result, the balance of tax revenue sources in Kansas is a function of a constant political tug of war between eastern and western legislators.

The Vermont legislature's rationale for initially adopting a high state-wide property tax to fund public education, rather than increasing income taxes, is even more intriguing than the political tug of war in Kansas;

---

[2]The state of Kansas still refers to its statewide property tax for education as a local tax, but the state sets a required rate for raising education revenues. "Excess" revenues that the tax generates in some school districts are remitted to the state to be redistributed to other districts. While county governments carry significant administrative responsibilities, for all intents and purposes, the Kansas school property tax is a statewide tax.

the Vermont legislature *exported* a substantial portion of its tax to residents of other states. Vermont is a state that relies heavily on its quaint, New England charm to attract tourists from around the East Coast, many of whom own properties in the state as second, or vacation, homes. An increase in Vermont's income tax would place the entire burden of raising new revenues on Vermonters, whereas an increase in statewide property taxes places substantial portion of the burden on out-of-state second home and business owners. Using 1999 data on district adjusted gross income per pupil and nonresidential property wealth per pupil, Vermonters would have needed to bear the burden of an additional 1.63% income tax to raise the same revenues as raised by a 1.1% property tax on nonresidential and nonresident-owned properties alone.

Tax Policy Across the States

Table 3.2 presents a summary of tax collections across the states from taxes, including both state and local tax revenue sources for 1994 and 2000. The majority of state tax revenues come from general sales and individual income taxes. That balance, however, varies widely among states. For example, New Hampshire collected no general sales taxes and minimal individual income taxes. The largest share of state-collected tax revenues in New Hampshire was from selective sales, such as taxes on rooms, meals, and liquor. But the largest share of state and local revenues combined in New Hampshire was from property taxes.

In Florida, another state reliant on tourism, general sales taxes produced the largest share of revenue, and the state levied no individual income tax. Other states with no individual income tax include Alaska, Nevada, South Dakota, Texas, Washington, and Wyoming. States with no sales tax include Alaska, Delaware, Montana, New Hampshire, and Oregon. Where no general sales tax exists, it is likely that income taxes make up the majority of state revenues, as in Oregon, and vice versa as in Texas and Washington. The proportions presented in Table 3.2 refer to very different-size total state and local budgets and total state and local budgets per capita. Table 3.3 presents state tax collections per capita for tax years 1994 and 2000. Notice, for example, that New Hampshire collected only $500 per capita in combined sales and income taxes. It is unlikely that New Hampshire, with selective sales tax as its primary revenue-raising tool,

could do much better. Other states with little or no income tax, including Tennessee, Texas, and South Dakota, also rank low in per capita sales and income tax revenue. On state taxes alone, Hawaii ranks first in state tax collections as a percentage of personal income, and New Hampshire ranks 50th.

Table 3.4 presents total state and local taxes as a percentage of median family income, and Table 3.5 presents local property taxes as a percentage of total taxes. Note that in Table 3.4, New Hampshire ranks 50th in total state and local taxes collected as a percentage of personal income in 2000. In Table 3.5, the majority of the tax dollars collected in New Hampshire are local property taxes (over 60%). Property tax collections per capita in New Hampshire are quite high because nearly the entire burden of funding K–12 education is placed on this single source of tax revenue. Recent school finance reforms in New Hampshire have merely reclassified these same dollars. New York ranks first in total state and local taxes as a percentage of median family income in 2000 (Table 3.4) but near the middle of the pack in total state and local revenue generated from property taxes in 2000. While total taxation is high in New York, the share of the burden placed on property taxes is somewhat lower than in New Hampshire. Per-capita property taxes in New York are only modestly lower than in New Hampshire. Note, however, that the per-capita measures and dollar-revenue measures in Table 3.5 do not take into account the good possibility that the costs of providing comparable educational services may vary widely between New York and New Hampshire, or for that matter Nebraska.

Income Taxes

As mentioned previously, income taxes are the primary source of revenue for the federal government and are one of two primary sources of revenue for state governments, along with sales taxes. Personal income taxes made up 40.7% of federal revenue in 1999, with corporate income taxes adding another 8.3%. The federal income tax in the United States has historically been a progressive tax.

The "progressiveness" of the federal tax code has been significantly compressed. Much of the change was the result of major revisions to the federal tax code in 1986, which included dramatic reductions to income adjustments, tax shelters, and deductions, but

Table 3.2   Shares of Total State and Local Revenue by Source

State	Property Tax Share			Sales Tax Share			Income Tax Share		
	1994	2000	Change	1994	2000	Change	1994	2000	Change
Alabama	12%	14%	2.0%	52%	49%	−3.1%	21%	23%	1.8%
Alaska	33%	33%	−0.1%	11%	12%	1.3%	0%	0%	0.0%
Arizona	31%	29%	−1.4%	45%	46%	0.8%	16%	17%	1.3%
Arkansas	15%	16%	1.1%	51%	49%	−1.4%	23%	25%	1.4%
California	27%	22%	−5.5%	36%	33%	−3.4%	23%	33%	9.7%
Colorado	32%	28%	−4.5%	37%	37%	−0.3%	23%	28%	4.1%
Connecticut	39%	35%	−4.3%	29%	32%	2.9%	20%	25%	5.5%
Delaware	15%	15%	−0.3%	12%	11%	−0.7%	33%	30%	−3.1%
Florida	36%	34%	−2.4%	51%	53%	2.1%	0%	0%	0.0%
Georgia	30%	26%	−4.0%	38%	40%	1.7%	24%	27%	3.4%
Hawaii	17%	15%	−1.9%	52%	52%	0.7%	26%	26%	0.3%
Idaho	26%	26%	0.2%	35%	32%	−2.2%	25%	29%	3.9%
Illinois	39%	36%	−2.5%	35%	33%	−1.5%	17%	19%	1.6%
Indiana	35%	34%	−1.0%	28%	31%	3.4%	28%	26%	−1.8%
Iowa	34%	32%	−2.3%	31%	33%	1.9%	24%	24%	0.3%
Kansas	31%	29%	−2.9%	37%	38%	1.1%	20%	24%	4.2%
Kentucky	17%	17%	0.4%	39%	36%	−2.5%	29%	34%	4.8%
Louisiana	17%	16%	−1.3%	54%	57%	3.6%	13%	15%	1.4%
Maine	40%	38%	−2.7%	31%	28%	−2.6%	21%	25%	4.2%
Maryland	27%	26%	−0.9%	26%	25%	−1.1%	37%	39%	2.2%
Massachusetts	35%	32%	−2.9%	21%	21%	0.4%	33%	38%	4.4%
Michigan	41%	30%	−10.9%	25%	31%	6.2%	20%	25%	4.5%
Minnesota	29%	25%	−4.1%	31%	33%	1.0%	28%	31%	2.9%
Mississippi	24%	23%	−0.3%	52%	51%	−1.0%	14%	16%	1.5%
Missouri	23%	24%	0.4%	42%	41%	−1.7%	24%	27%	2.7%
Montana	43%	43%	−0.2%	15%	16%	1.7%	21%	24%	3.5%
Nebraska	37%	31%	−5.7%	35%	34%	−1.0%	19%	24%	4.4%
Nevada	22%	25%	2.9%	63%	62%	−1.5%	0%	0%	0.0%
New Hampshire	66%	62%	−4.0%	19%	17%	−2.5%	1%	2%	0.6%
New Jersey	46%	44%	−2.1%	27%	25%	−2.3%	18%	22%	4.3%
New Mexico	13%	13%	0.4%	52%	51%	−1.8%	17%	18%	1.7%
New York	32%	29%	−3.3%	27%	26%	−0.8%	29%	33%	4.2%
North Carolina	22%	21%	−0.4%	38%	34%	−4.6%	29%	34%	4.9%
North Dakota	29%	30%	1.0%	41%	40%	−0.3%	11%	11%	0.7%
Ohio	29%	28%	−0.6%	32%	30%	−2.3%	30%	33%	3.6%
Oklahoma	16%	16%	−0.6%	44%	39%	−4.4%	22%	26%	4.0%
Oregon	36%	30%	−6.4%	10%	10%	0.1%	37%	44%	6.6%
Pennsylvania	29%	28%	−1.1%	30%	30%	−0.1%	24%	25%	1.7%
Rhode Island	42%	40%	−2.3%	29%	29%	0.4%	21%	24%	3.1%
South Carolina	29%	28%	−0.5%	37%	36%	0.0%	23%	26%	2.4%
South Dakota	40%	36%	−3.4%	47%	50%	3.3%	0%	0%	0.0%
Tennessee	23%	23%	0.5%	62%	59%	−2.9%	1%	1%	0.4%
Texas	37%	38%	0.7%	50%	51%	0.6%	0%	0%	0.0%
Utah	26%	22%	−3.4%	41%	41%	−0.1%	25%	28%	2.9%
Vermont	42%	42%	−0.7%	28%	26%	−2.1%	20%	23%	3.2%
Virginia	31%	28%	−2.6%	31%	28%	−2.9%	27%	32%	5.5%
Washington	30%	29%	−0.7%	61%	61%	0.7%	0%	0%	0.0%
West Virginia	20%	20%	0.1%	42%	42%	−0.3%	20%	22%	2.2%
Wisconsin	37%	31%	−6.6%	28%	29%	0.9%	27%	32%	5.6%
Wyoming	37%	34%	−3.3%	28%	39%	10.8%	0%	0%	0.0%

Source: U.S. Census Bureau. State and local government finances. Retrieved July 1, 2005, from http://www.census.gov/govs/www/estimate.html

Table 3.3   Property, Sales, and Income Tax Revenues (Total State and Local) per Capita

State	Property Tax Revenues per Capita			Sales Tax Revenues per Capita			Income Tax Revenues per Capita		
	1994	2000	% Change	1994	2000	% Change	1994	2000	% Change
Alabama	$196	$301	54.0%	$830	$1,031	24%	$339	$486	43%
Alaska	$1,064	$1,214	14.1%	$354	$452	28%	$0	$0	
Arizona	$669	$761	13.8%	$974	$1,183	21%	$346	$447	29%
Arkansas	$254	$361	42.3%	$853	$1,103	29%	$391	$550	41%
California	$657	$775	17.9%	$877	$1,172	34%	$558	$1,168	109%
Colorado	$726	$856	17.9%	$831	$1,127	36%	$527	$846	61%
Connecticut	$1,337	$1,588	18.7%	$1,012	$1,484	47%	$683	$1,167	71%
Delaware	$371	$488	31.4%	$301	$380	26%	$816	$988	21%
Florida	$788	$882	11.9%	$1,114	$1,393	25%	$0	$0	
Georgia	$624	$725	16.1%	$809	$1,136	40%	$508	$777	53%
Hawaii	$530	$497	−6.2%	$1,642	$1,767	8%	$816	$878	8%
Idaho	$513	$670	30.7%	$680	$827	22%	$498	$746	50%
Illinois	$953	$1,168	22.6%	$860	$1,077	25%	$430	$615	43%
Indiana	$739	$913	23.5%	$590	$841	43%	$590	$702	19%
Iowa	$791	$888	12.4%	$722	$922	28%	$540	$659	22%
Kansas	$725	$809	11.5%	$850	$1,074	26%	$468	$693	48%
Kentucky	$319	$426	33.7%	$747	$912	22%	$562	$853	52%
Louisiana	$298	$390	30.7%	$921	$1,393	51%	$227	$354	56%
Maine	$945	$1,254	32.7%	$719	$937	30%	$496	$845	70%
Maryland	$723	$908	25.6%	$700	$873	25%	$980	$1,351	38%
Massachusetts	$985	$1,204	22.2%	$595	$812	36%	$942	$1,424	51%
Michigan	$1,049	$956	−8.9%	$646	$997	54%	$512	$778	52%
Minnesota	$799	$928	16.2%	$860	$1,201	40%	$755	$1,128	49%
Mississippi	$389	$514	32.1%	$856	$1,126	31%	$239	$354	48%
Missouri	$433	$609	40.4%	$785	$1,042	33%	$448	$688	54%
Montana	$834	$1,007	20.7%	$284	$383	35%	$404	$572	42%
Nebraska	$844	$905	7.3%	$801	$988	23%	$441	$686	56%
Nevada	$514	$719	40.0%	$1,486	$1,795	21%	$0	$0	
New Hampshire	$1,442	$1,641	13.7%	$426	$449	5%	$32	$53	69%
New Jersey	$1,483	$1,717	15.8%	$882	$978	11%	$569	$860	51%
New Mexico	$263	$341	29.6%	$1,104	$1,338	21%	$349	$484	39%
New York	$1,246	$1,328	6.6%	$1,026	$1,184	15%	$1,107	$1,509	36%
North Carolina	$463	$572	23.7%	$806	$895	11%	$607	$896	48%
North Dakota	$585	$821	40.3%	$826	$1,112	35%	$215	$309	44%
Ohio	$629	$841	33.8%	$716	$912	27%	$659	$1,009	53%
Oklahoma	$302	$377	24.9%	$806	$937	16%	$404	$619	53%
Oregon	$816	$815	−0.1%	$216	$267	23%	$837	$1,198	43%
Pennsylvania	$671	$820	22.2%	$695	$882	27%	$556	$756	36%
Rhode Island	$1,052	$1,297	23.3%	$725	$958	32%	$530	$791	49%
South Carolina	$515	$668	29.7%	$657	$867	32%	$418	$610	46%
South Dakota	$725	$838	15.5%	$856	$1,157	35%	$0	$0	−100%
Tennessee	$400	$507	26.8%	$1,086	$1,286	18%	$19	$32	65%
Texas	$755	$950	25.8%	$1,019	$1,275	25%	$0	$0	
Utah	$491	$584	18.7%	$796	$1,088	37%	$485	$740	53%
Vermont	$1,052	$1,284	22.1%	$694	$796	15%	$493	$709	44%
Virginia	$670	$846	26.2%	$674	$843	25%	$582	$965	66%
Washington	$780	$932	19.4%	$1,574	$1,948	24%	$0	$0	
West Virginia	$359	$473	31.6%	$779	$1,016	30%	$368	$534	45%
Wisconsin	$1,005	$1,061	5.6%	$751	$994	32%	$716	$1,110	55%
Wyoming	$940	$1,038	10.5%	$703	$1,181	68%	$0	$0	

Source: U.S. Census Bureau. State and local government finances. Retrieved July 1, 2005, from http://www.census.gov/govs/www/ estimate.html

Table 3.4 Total State and Local Taxes Per Capita and as a Percentage of Median Family Income

	1994		2000	
	Per Capita	% of Median Family Income	Per Capita	% of Median Family Income
New York	$ 3,854	12.08%	$ 4,578	11.24%
Connecticut	$ 3,441	8.37%	$ 4,595	9.16%
Maine	$ 2,351	7.75%	$ 3,343	8.97%
West Virginia	$ 1,839	7.81%	$ 2,413	8.20%
Massachusetts	$ 2,835	7.00%	$ 3,787	8.10%
Louisiana	$ 1,720	6.70%	$ 2,436	7.93%
Vermont	$ 2,482	6.93%	$ 3,080	7.78%
New Jersey	$ 3,216	7.61%	$ 3,903	7.74%
Rhode Island	$ 2,498	7.82%	$ 3,256	7.72%
Wyoming	$ 2,513	7.58%	$ 3,046	7.69%
Wisconsin	$ 2,699	7.63%	$ 3,458	7.67%
North Dakota	$ 2,030	7.18%	$ 2,754	7.65%
California	$ 2,404	6.81%	$ 3,545	7.57%
New Mexico	$ 2,102	7.81%	$ 2,639	7.52%
Arkansas	$ 1,679	6.57%	$ 2,230	7.51%
Washington	$ 2,596	7.74%	$ 3,178	7.47%
Oklahoma	$ 1,846	6.84%	$ 2,391	7.37%
Montana	$ 1,952	7.06%	$ 2,363	7.21%
Pennsylvania	$ 2,342	7.30%	$ 2,979	7.06%
Illinois	$ 2,474	7.05%	$ 3,241	7.04%
Ohio	$ 2,204	6.92%	$ 3,016	7.02%
Alaska	$ 3,225	7.11%	$ 3,687	6.98%
Nebraska	$ 2,290	7.20%	$ 2,906	6.96%
Michigan	$ 2,552	7.23%	$ 3,167	6.96%
North Carolina	$ 2,110	7.01%	$ 2,664	6.95%
Kentucky	$ 1,930	7.26%	$ 2,517	6.94%
Kansas	$ 2,310	8.16%	$ 2,833	6.90%
Minnesota	$ 2,733	8.12%	$ 3,694	6.81%
Georgia	$ 2,115	6.72%	$ 2,841	6.78%
Idaho	$ 1,959	6.21%	$ 2,546	6.77%
Florida	$ 2,186	7.46%	$ 2,624	6.75%
Iowa	$ 2,297	6.94%	$ 2,765	6.75%
Delaware	$ 2,494	6.95%	$ 3,340	6.63%
Indiana	$ 2,119	7.61%	$ 2,691	6.59%
Hawaii	$ 3,185	7.54%	$ 3,384	6.57%
Arizona	$ 2,177	6.96%	$ 2,599	6.53%
Texas	$ 2,027	6.59%	$ 2,505	6.49%
Oregon	$ 2,266	7.20%	$ 2,751	6.47%
Mississippi	$ 1,653	6.51%	$ 2,214	6.46%
Tennessee	$ 1,759	6.14%	$ 2,185	6.41%
Nevada	$ 2,354	6.56%	$ 2,915	6.37%
Colorado	$ 2,245	5.93%	$ 3,073	6.37%
Maryland	$ 2,657	6.78%	$ 3,454	6.33%
South Carolina	$ 1,801	6.03%	$ 2,379	6.33%
Virginia	$ 2,162	5.74%	$ 2,978	6.31%
South Dakota	$ 1,819	6.12%	$ 2,299	6.30%
Alabama	$ 1,601	5.89%	$ 2,117	5.98%
Missouri	$ 1,852	6.13%	$ 2,558	5.67%
Utah	$ 1,920	5.37%	$ 2,630	5.53%
New Hampshire	$ 2,190	6.21%	$ 2,652	5.21%

Source: U.S. Census Bureau. State and local government finances. Retrieved July 1, 2005, from http://www.census.gov/govs/www/estimate.html

Table 3.5   Local Property Taxes per Capita and as a Percentage of Total State and Local Taxes

Description	Total Tax Revenue (in hundreds)	Property Tax Revenue (in hundreds)	Population (April 1, 2000, in thousands)	Property Tax per Capita	Property Tax Share
New Hampshire	$3,598,862	$2,169,494	1,236	$1,755	60.3%
New Jersey	$34,628,804	$16,049,550	8,414	$1,907	46.3%
Maine	$4,541,146	$1,912,158	1,275	$1,500	42.1%
Vermont	$1,965,132	$823,610	609	$1,352	41.9%
Texas	$58,980,508	$24,520,989	20,852	$1,176	41.6%
Rhode Island	$3,622,244	$1,462,064	1,048	$1,395	40.4%
Alaska	$2,069,908	$830,011	627	$1,324	40.1%
Montana	$2,135,182	$852,399	902	$945	39.9%
Connecticut	$15,124,928	$5,995,482	3,406	$1,760	39.6%
Illinois	$41,569,580	$15,872,667	12,419	$1,278	38.2%
Wyoming	$1,818,368	$692,341	494	$1,402	38.1%
Massachusetts	$23,895,436	$8,721,832	6,349	$1,374	36.5%
South Dakota	$1,841,448	$668,048	755	$885	36.3%
Indiana	$16,986,637	$5,976,203	6,080	$983	35.2%
Florida	$44,840,449	$15,754,214	15,982	$986	35.1%
Oregon	$9,003,237	$3,138,875	3,421	$918	34.9%
Wisconsin	$18,609,916	$6,466,173	5,364	$1,205	34.7%
Iowa	$8,330,414	$2,877,921	2,926	$984	34.5%
Nebraska	$5,316,341	$1,748,841	1,711	$1,022	32.9%
Michigan	$30,644,184	$9,793,418	9,938	$985	32.0%
South Carolina	$9,751,701	$3,096,431	4,012	$772	31.8%
Kansas	$7,974,975	$2,524,888	2,688	$939	31.7%
North Dakota	$1,728,755	$532,340	642	$829	30.8%
Virginia	$22,131,246	$6,710,588	7,079	$948	30.3%
New York	$88,878,112	$26,825,697	18,976	$1,414	30.2%
Colorado	$13,900,024	$4,162,161	4,301	$968	29.9%
Washington	$19,513,503	$5,790,556	5,894	$982	29.7%
Arizona	$14,420,322	$4,254,395	5,131	$829	29.5%
Ohio	$36,165,190	$10,643,420	11,353	$937	29.4%
Idaho	$3,291,095	$958,763	1,294	$741	29.1%
Pennsylvania	$37,626,620	$10,910,756	12,281	$888	29.0%
Minnesota	$18,456,409	$5,214,735	4,919	$1,060	28.3%
Georgia	$24,058,380	$6,640,041	8,186	$811	27.6%
Maryland	$19,874,281	$5,412,209	5,296	$1,022	27.2%
Tennessee	$12,973,768	$3,453,047	5,689	$607	26.6%
Nevada	$6,432,564	$1,702,186	1,998	$852	26.5%
Missouri	$15,123,432	$3,880,344	5,595	$694	25.7%
Mississippi	$6,523,722	$1,646,563	2,845	$579	25.2%
California	$120,424,066	$30,242,523	33,872	$893	25.1%
District of Columbia	$3,227,909	$803,389	572	$1,405	24.9%
North Carolina	$22,576,419	$5,421,740	8,049	$674	24.0%
Utah	$6,026,142	$1,419,769	2,233	$636	23.6%
West Virginia	$4,641,349	$900,999	1,808	$498	19.4%
Kentucky	$10,780,757	$1,977,011	4,042	$489	18.3%
Oklahoma	$8,781,889	$1,482,139	3,451	$429	16.9%
Louisiana	$12,182,065	$1,940,420	4,469	$434	15.9%
Arkansas	$6,460,855	$1,003,909	2,673	$376	15.5%
New Mexico	$4,877,614	$755,948	1,819	$416	15.5%
Alabama	$9,718,827	$1,473,554	4,447	$331	15.2%
Delaware	$2,687,098	$399,939	784	$510	14.9%
Hawaii	$4,239,557	$614,930	1,212	$507	14.5%

Source: U.S. Census Bureau. State and local government finances. Retrieved July 1, 2005, from http://www.census.gov/govs/www/estimate.html

also included a significant increase in the available standard deductions.

Anyone who has filed a state or federal income tax return in the United States realizes that defining taxable income is not a simple endeavor. We do not dissect the federal income tax code—or its underlying economic or political rationale—in this text. An awareness of the major issues surrounding taxation and its economic and political rationales is essential, however, to understanding school finance. As with the state tax policies in Vermont and Kansas discussed previously, the existing federal tax code is a result of political tradeoffs and ultimately reflects the values of our federal government (at any given point in time). For example, by granting an exemption for interest paid on home mortgages, the federal government has placed value on home ownership. Similarly, by providing the opportunity to deduct medical expenses, the federal government has placed value on health care. A less straightforward exemption is the exemption of state and local taxes paid. In the case of local property taxes, this exemption reduces the disincentive to increase the value of a property through renovation.

Figure 3.4 displays the distribution of the U.S. population (based on total tax returns filed) by income for 2001. The largest number of tax returns fell between $60 and $200,000. Figure 3.4 also shows the shares of total adjusted gross income earned by individuals in each category. In 2001, individuals with income between $100,000 and $200,000 earned more than 20% of all income. Individuals' whose income exceeded $1 million earned more than 15% of all income. In 2001, the average taxable income was approximately 75% of adjusted gross income (gross income less losses/deficit). Taxable income as a percentage of adjusted gross income, however, ranged from about 3% for individuals with adjusted gross income of less than $10,000 to nearly 90% for individuals with income exceeding $1,000,000. That finding suggests that deductions in the federal income tax code (including standard and itemized deductions) are progressively distributed. That is, individuals with lower income can deduct a larger share of that income to reduce their tax burden. It is important to note, however, that when an individual making $10,000 per year deducts 97% of his or her income, the total deduction is $9,700, whereas when the individual making $1,000,000 deducts only 10% of his/her income, the total deduction is $100,000.

Because the federal role in funding public education is relatively small, our interest in the income tax as

Figure 3.4   Population and Income Distribution 2001

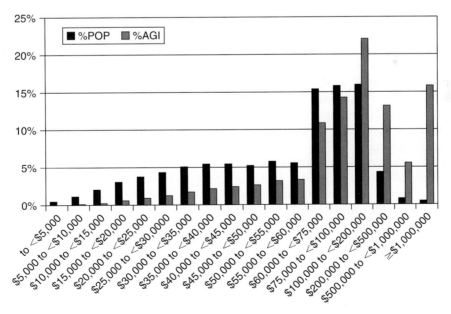

AGI, adjusted grosss income.

Source: Data from U.S. Census Bureau. Current population survey, http://www.census.gov/cps

Table 3.6   Evaluating the Income Tax

	Pros	**Cons**
Equity	Can be structured progressively.	Measurement of income can be difficult. Often results in "flat" tax even where structure is progressive.
Efficiency (Distortions)	Exemptions may be used to reduce (or, for that matter, promote) distortions.	May encourage residential mobility.
Administration	Many compliance costs passed on to taxpayer.	
Economic Responsiveness	Elastic.	Elastic.
Political Acceptance	Can be increased if already in existence.	Difficult to export.

a revenue-raising tool lies mainly at the state level. Seven states have no income tax (Alaska, Florida, Nevada, South Dakota, Texas, Washington, and Wyoming), and two others (Tennessee and New Hampshire) tax only dividend and interest income. Of those states with income tax, six use proportional taxes, or taxes that are neither progressive nor regressive (Colorado, Illinois, Indiana, Massachusetts, Michigan, and Pennsylvania). The largest numbers of brackets exist in Missouri and Montana, each at 10 brackets, with Montana's tax rates ranging from 2% to 11%.

Table 3.6 provides a summary evaluation of the income tax as a state revenue-raising tool. First, from an equity perspective, income tax policies have generally been structured progressively. However, given the distribution of itemized exemptions, differentially taxed income such as capital gains, and recent efforts to compress tax brackets, income taxes have become less progressive at the high end.

Income taxes may create economic distortions, including the possibility that one might choose to live in one state rather than another because of income tax differences. Effects of this type are most likely to occur where significant differentials exist in bordering states. It is important to note, however, that the ability to deduct state and/or local income taxes from federal income tax returns partially mitigates this distortion. Further, income tax codes can be constructed so as to reduce certain distortions, or promote desirable economic behaviors, as in the case of the home mortgage interest deduction.

As noted previously, a major advantage of the income tax is that much of the compliance cost is passed on to individual taxpayers. Also, as noted previously, the elasticity of the income tax is a double-edged sword. Reliance on income taxes is beneficial when incomes are rising but is a detriment to state fiscal planning when incomes recede. Political acceptance of state-level income taxes varies widely by state. One important note about political acceptance and the income tax is that exporting income taxes is difficult, although exceptions exist. For example, New York City does impose an income tax on those who work in but do not live in the city. Other smaller cities along state borders, including Kansas City, Missouri, levy income tax surcharges to those who work in the city but live in the neighboring state.

Sales Taxes

As mentioned previously, consumption or sales taxes are one of two primary sources of state revenue. In many cases, state laws permit the adoption of local- or county-level sales taxes in addition to state sales taxes. In some cases, city- and county-level taxes are limited to specific cities or counties. Sales taxes may apply to some or all retail sales of tangible personal property and/or services. For example, New Hampshire relies primarily on selective sales tax, on meals and alcohol, for state revenues. Several states, including Michigan following its major school funding reform of the mid-

1990s, rely on additional sales taxes on items such as cigarettes. Also, some states exempt certain items from sales taxes. When items such as food and clothing or other basic necessities are taxed, the sales tax is more regressive: Lower-income families tend to spend a much larger share of their income on items such as food and clothing. In some cases, luxury items may be taxed at a higher rate, making sales taxes more progressive in that higher-income individuals are more likely to purchase luxury items. In 1991 the federal government implemented a luxury tax, which, for example, taxed automobiles priced above $30,000. The federal luxury tax began a phase-out in 1997 to be completed by 2002.

Table 3.7 provides a summary evaluation of sales taxes. Sales taxes are perceived as equitable because individuals who benefit directly from purchasing the taxed goods or services incur the costs. Sales taxes, along with user fees such as road tolls and lotteries, are the only major tax revenue source based primarily on the benefit principle. The vertical equity of a sales tax depends entirely on which items are taxed and at what rates. In general, sales taxes are regressive.

Sales taxes, perhaps more than other taxes, are very likely to create easily recognizable economic distortions. This is especially the case where sales taxes differ substantially within a relatively small geographic area, such as from town to town, county to county, or along state borders. Taxes may be higher or lower in one location than another, or different goods may be taxed. For example, significant differences exist among

states in cigarette and gasoline taxes, causing many individuals to purchase cigarettes or gasoline in a neighboring state.

As with income taxes, much of the compliance burden of managing sales taxes is taken out of the hands of government, reducing government administration costs. The majority of the burden for calculating, collecting, and remitting sales tax receipts is passed on to retailers.

Economic stability and responsiveness of sales taxes depend largely on the distribution of the items taxed. Some items, such as food and clothing, for example, consumers purchase with regularity in both good and bad economic times, though the volume of purchases fluctuates somewhat with income. Other types of purchases, such as those tied to tourism, or professional services, such as accounting and architectural fees (Monk & Brent, 1997, p. 31), fluctuate more dramatically with economic changes. As noted previously, the overall elasticity of sales taxes is approximately 1.0.

Sales taxes are generally well liked, as far as taxes go. Their political acceptance may be attributable to (a) the fact that costs are incurred primarily by those who benefit from the purchase of goods and services and (b) the fact that, in many cases, sales taxes can be exported. On the first point, it is perhaps easier for the average taxpayer to measure fairness in his or her own mind via the benefit principle rather than the ability principle. On the second point, it is certainly easier for the taxpayer in a given state to accept the notion of

Table 3.7   Evaluating Sales Taxes

	Pros	Cons
Equity	Based on benefit principle.	Generally regressive.
Efficiency (Distortions)	Necessities easily exempted.	May influence purchasing behavior (quantity, location, etc.).
Administration	Compliance costs passed on to commercial entities.	
Economic Responsiveness	Relatively responsive to consumer sentiment and demand (depends on goods and services taxed).	Relatively responsive to consumer sentiment and demand.
Political Acceptance	High acceptance due to preference for benefit based taxes. Can be exported.	Exportation may reduce economic competitiveness.

taxing visitors from a neighboring state, or around the world. Different types of sales taxes are exported to different degrees. Indeed, while New Jersey residents benefit from the economic stimulus of having New Yorkers purchase clothing in their state, New York residents benefit substantially from the taxes collected on purchases of New Jersey residents while visiting New York. Taxes based on tourism industries, such as taxes on rooms and meals, tend to be more substantially exported than other taxes. For that matter, a larger share of taxes on hotel rooms is exported than on meals, because residents in tourist areas are more likely to take advantage of local dining than local lodging. Exported taxes must be balanced with economic competitiveness. For example, if nearby states have similar tourism opportunities, such as ski tourism in Colorado, Wyoming, and Utah, or in Vermont, New Hampshire, and New York, imposing too-high taxes on tourist-consumed goods may shift consumption to states with lower taxes.

Local Property Taxation

The local property tax is the centerpiece of public education finance. The role of the local property tax in school finance is largely a function of historical origins of public education systems. Public K–12 education remains the largest, most costly public service for which costs are shared, on average about 50/50, by states and local governments. The property tax has long been the primary source, and in many cases the only source, of revenue for local governments. As mentioned previously, in recent years, when states have raised additional revenue to redistribute across local school districts, some have turned to statewide property taxes, perhaps in part due to the tradition of property taxes being used to support public education, despite concerns regarding administrative efficiency.

Property taxes may be levied on (a) real, (b) tangible, or (c) intangible property. **Real property** includes residential, corporate, industrial, and agricultural property. Real property includes both the land and any permanently attached improvements to that land, such as buildings. **Tangible property** may include household or personal property, or motor vehicles, which are often treated separately in property tax codes. Finally, **intangible property** includes assets that do not have physical substance, such as stocks, bonds, or cash.

Recall that, for income taxes, significant differences exist between the income actually earned by an individual, or gross income, and the income that is taxed. Some similar issues occur regarding the valuation of property for taxation. The **fair market value** of a property is the price for which the property could be sold. In the case of residential homes, for example, the market value of a home could be estimated by looking at sale prices of similar homes in the same neighborhood over the past year. Assigning market values to properties is usually the responsibility of someone known as the *assessor*, who in most states, works at the county level. In some states, in particular in New England, assessors work at the city or town level.

Valuation of commercial property may be more difficult than valuation of residential property, because commercial properties are sold less frequently than residential properties. Small businesses are often valued on the basis of net income. Monk and Brent provide this example: "if the profits for a particular business are $20,000 per year and the expected rate of return on this business is 10%, the value of the property is $200,000" (1997, p. 48). They also note that the value of a commercial building might be established by estimating the rent that could be charged for use of the building. Large business properties are often valued on the basis of the cost of replacing the business facility, less depreciation. Other properties, such as utilities and railroads, are often valued using a combination of net income and replacement cost methods.

Rental property is a special case of interest. Most of the cost of the tax on rental property is passed along to the renter except in rent-controlled apartments. Thus, renters pay property taxes for schools proportional to the value of their unit, even though they do not own property!

Valuation of farmland is a particularly tricky endeavor. Like other business properties, estimating what the "typical" farm might sell for on the open market can be difficult. Farmland might, for example, be valued on the basis of net income. Such methods would often produce very low values for farmland. Alternatively, farmland might be valued on the basis of a method known as "best use." Best-use methods consider what the farmland might be worth on the open market, if it were used in other ways, such as residential or corporate development. Best-use methods dramatically increase the values placed on farmland near metropolitan areas. Monk and Brent identify three alternatives to best-use valuation that may be used to reduce the tax burden on farmers:

1. *Preferential use laws:* Property is valued based on its current use.
2. *Deferred taxation provisions:* In general, property is valued based on its current use, but if the owner decides to sell the property for a better use (development that increases value of the property), the owner is responsible for paying back taxes based on best use valuation before the sale.
3. *Provisions for contracts and agreements:* Taxpayers contract, or agree to use, the property in a specific way for a certain period of time. In return, property is valued at less than best use. (Monk & Brent, 1997, p. 50)

Taxes are not necessarily levied against the full market value of a property, for a variety of political and economic reasons. For example, newly constructed housing may be assessed at current market value (the selling price), while homeowners who purchased their home many years ago are still assessed at the old market rate at the time of sale. This bias toward established residents is widespread in many states. The **taxable assessed value** of a home or other property is a percentage of a property's fair market value (sometimes 100%) designated in state policy as the basis for taxation. The taxable assessed value is determined after applying a combination of assessment rates and exemptions. For example, Kansas uses an assessment rate of only 11.5% for residential properties. That is, 11.5% of the value of a residential home is taxable. Next, Kansas provides a deduction of the first $20,000 of the value of a residential home, a measure intended to make property taxes less regressive. As such, the taxable assessed value of a home in Kansas is determined by the following calculation:

$$\text{Taxable Value} = 11.5\% \times (\text{FMV} - \$20,000)$$

Where FMV refers to the *fair market value.* The tax rate is then applied to the taxable value of the property to determine the tax bill, or payment to be made. It is important to understand that when assessment rates are low, tax rates must be higher to create the same yield. Because states vary in their assessment rates, comparison of tax rates can be difficult. Returning for the moment to our two states with statewide education property taxes, Vermont uses a 1.1% statewide property tax rate for education, while Kansas uses a 2.0% rate. Vermont, however, applies the tax to 100% of the fair market value of the home, while Kansas applies the rate to 11.5%, meaning that the Kansas rate is really .23% (11.5% × 2.0) compared to Vermont's 1.1%.

Property tax rates may also be expressed in a number of different ways. Some states refer to property tax rates in terms of "dollars per $100 in assessed valuation," or the equivalent of a percentage rate expressed in dollars. The Vermont rate is typically referred to as a $1.10 rate. In other states, the *mill* rate is used, where a *mill* is 1/1,000. As a result, the Kansas rate of 2.0% is referred to in Kansas as a 20 mill levy. Residential, commercial, utility, and farm properties can also be assessed at different rates, and exemptions may also be applied for purposes ranging from improving equity to stimulating economic development. Different tax burdens therefore are incurred with respect to fair market value, given the same tax rate. Each of these differences in units, valuation methods, and assessment rates increases the complexity of comparing property tax policies across states.

Is the property tax a good tax? Table 3.8 summarizes the property tax according to the attributes we have applied to sales and income taxes thus far. With respect to horizontal equity, property taxes may be evaluated on the basis of both ability and benefit standards. Real property is a measure of ability to pay to the extent that the property may be liquidated in order to pay one's tax bill. Monk and Brent (1997), for example, discuss a method called *reverse equity mortgages,* to allow low-income individuals with significant residential property assets to gradually liquidate those assets in order to pay their tax bill.

The benefit perspective on property taxes is often overlooked. Economic theory suggests (Tiebout, 1956), and empirical research supports, that housing values are directly associated with the quality of public services, including public schooling (Downes & Zabel, 1997; Figlio & Lucas, 2002). As a result, individuals living in more expensive properties, and paying a higher tax bill to support local public schools, benefit from the increased values to their property. If values increase proportionately, individuals living in more expensive homes and paying higher taxes reap greater benefit. Perhaps one reason why the benefit perspective is overlooked is the relative shortsightedness of the average taxpayer, who is more likely to be concerned with his or her annually increasing tax bill than with the potential market value of the home.

Table 3.8   Evaluating the Property Tax

	Pros	**Cons**
Equity		Generally regressive among renters and residential home owners
Efficiency (distortions)	May influence residential selection	May influence purchasing behavior, including improvements to property
Administration		Most compliance costs incurred by government
Economic Responsiveness	Inelastic with respect to income	Inelastic with respect to income
Political Acceptance	Nonresidential tax burdens can be exported	Generally disliked tax

With respect to vertical equity, the property tax is perceived as regressive, especially among renters and residential homeowners. Note that while renters do not pay the tax directly, they do pay the majority of that tax through their rent. Policies may be implemented to reduce the regressiveness of property taxes. One example is the $20,000-exemption approach used in Kansas. Several states use some form of *homestead exemption*, primarily intended to reduce the tax bills of elderly citizens on fixed income who own their own homes. Vermont uses a *circuit breaker* approach that limits the property tax bill to 2% of income when income is less than $75,000. This approach has been referred to as *income-sensitive* property taxation (e.g., see Odden & Picus, 2000).

Variance in property taxes across municipalities does influence economic behavior. Because property taxes are primarily locally adopted, and because property valuations and property types may vary widely from one community to the next, so do property tax rates and average property tax bills paid by residents and corporations. Those differences are likely to influence individuals' or corporations' choices of where to locate. The influence of property tax rates on residential or corporate location decisions is complex, and property tax rates are only one of a plethora of variables that affect such decisions. For example, labor market costs or other geographic and proximity issues may easily outweigh property taxes in corporate choices of where to locate. Further, lower property tax rates are likely to be associated with higher property values.

One might argue that taxes should be levied against land value only and not against the value of structures on that land. Taxes on the structures create distortions that adversely affect the economy, and in some cases create tax burdens illogically associated with benefits. For example, assume that two businesses are on land of similar value in the downtown district of a city. One business is housed in an old structure and another in a new structure, with both structures having similar square footage. The new structure plus its land value, however, is valued at twice that of the old structure, plus its land value. The owner of the new structure therefore pays twice the taxes of the owner of the old structure. From a benefit perspective, the older structure is arguably a greater burden on the community's fire protection and safety resources, as well as a drain on local utilities and potential detriment to economic development. From an economic distortion perspective, there is little incentive for the owner of the older structure to renovate, unless renovations can improve production efficiency enough to offset both the cost of renovations and the cost of future property taxes.

Property taxes are relatively costly and inefficient for state and local governments to administer. As noted previously, property valuation is handled at the county level, but in some cases at the local level. Local and county governments are responsible for estimating the value of all properties and keeping those values up to date. Further, they are responsible for applying each appropriate assessment rate and exemption to each property in order to determine the tax bill. Then, local and county governments are responsible for collecting and managing the tax revenues. Neither income nor sales taxes place similar burden on government.

As states move toward state-level property taxation, state legislators must decide whether each of these processes should remain local and county responsibilities or become state responsibilities. If a state governs tax rates, but county or local officials are responsible for valuation and handing out of abatements, local officials may "game" the system to benefit their local economy and taxpayers. For example, county assessors may value residential properties in their county below actual value to reduce the tax bill of county residents. Under a state property tax, the state would incur the losses, not the county. The same is true where the county or municipality retains the authority to exempt new businesses from property taxes for purposes of economic competition. In statewide property tax systems, either states must assume responsibility for assessment and oversight of exemptions and abatements, or states must play an active role in enforcement, each increasing the costs to the state.

As noted previously, the property tax is relatively inelastic with respect to income, and property tax revenues are relatively stable. This is perhaps the primary advantage of property taxes as a means for supporting public education. Property tax revenues also grow with increased residential development, and increased residential development is tied to increased demand for public schools. In recent years, this has particularly been the case in areas where suburban sprawl has rapidly engulfed farmland, increasing the value of properties recently valued at less than best use. However, property tax revenues also increase with increased nonresidential development, such as the opening or closing of a power plant. Such changes may not be associated with changes in local demand for public schooling but may dramatically influence local revenue-raising ability. Further, while the yield for property taxes is relatively constant in good and bad economic times, compliance rates for property taxes tend to decline in bad economic times.

Finally, property taxes, especially residential property taxes, are generally not well liked (Monk & Brent, 1997, p. 37). As discussed earlier, however, exceptions occur, as in the case of Vermont's ability to use the property tax to export the burden of its new school-funding formula. The local property tax, as a symbol of local control, also continues to have support among individuals favoring a return to, or maintenance of, local control of public education.

Lotteries and Gaming Revenue

We conclude this discussion of local property tax sources by briefly discussing lotteries and gaming. New Hampshire became the first state to partially finance public services with a lottery in 1964 (Monk & Brent, 1997, p. 115). Most other states have since introduced lotteries or gambling, and some, both. Table 3.9 summarizes state-administered lottery revenues and expenses for 2000. Lottery expenses consist primarily of the prizes given out and the administrative costs of operating the lottery system. Note that the percentage of available revenues from lotteries ranged across states from 82% in Delaware and South Dakota to only 15.5% in Minnesota in 2000.

Another frequently expressed concern regarding lotteries is that lottery revenues tend to supplant, rather than supplement, existing state support for public schools, even where lottery revenues are earmarked for schools. Two recent empirical analyses address this question. In a longitudinal analysis of the Ohio lottery from 1958 to 1996, Thomas Garrett (2001) found that new lottery revenues for education were accompanied by a diversion of approximately the same amount of state revenues to other programs and services. That is, increased lottery revenues did not lead directly to any discernable increase in public school revenues. Similarly, in a cross-state analysis of states with and without lotteries, Erekson, DeShano, Platt, and Zeigert (2002) found that the availability of lottery revenues had a negative effect on state expenditures on public schools. That is, as lottery revenues increase, fewer state general funds are spent on public schools.

Using our tax-evaluation framework (see Table 3.10), lotteries are generally perceived as regressive, in that lower-income individuals spend a much larger share of their income on lottery tickets. This occurs because the potential winnings from a lottery have greater utility for lower-income individuals even though the cost is higher, because a dollar has more value to a poor person. Note that several types of lottery games exist, from instant scratch-and-win games, to large-jackpot games, to video lottery terminal games, which resemble casino slot machines (Monk & Brent, 1997, p. 115). Low winnings, high-probability games are particularly regressive in that the lower winnings only have utility for lower-income individuals. In large-jackpot games, some research has shown that as the winnings escalate, more middle- and higher-income individuals

Table 3.9   Income and Apportionment of State-Administered Lottery Funds (2000)

		Apportionment of Funds			
State	Income—Ticket Sales Excluding Commissions	Prizes	Administration	Proceeds Available From Ticket Sales	Percent Available[a]
	1	2	3	4	5
United States	$35,334,448	$20,701,436	$2,235,452	$12,397,560	35.1%
Arizona	$272,351	$140,127	$25,664	$106,560	39.1%
California	$2,419,290	$1,369,435	$163,940	$885,915	36.6%
Colorado	$342,986	$223,575	$31,307	$88,104	25.7%
Connecticut	$840,228	$502,494	$80,379	$257,355	30.6%
Delaware	$328,713	$51,133	$6,883	$270,697	82.4%
Florida	$2,131,285	$1,107,018	$124,910	$899,357	42.2%
Georgia	$2,059,527	$1,260,497	$121,598	$677,432	32.9%
Idaho	$86,508	$50,954	$17,581	$17,973	20.8%
Illinois	$1,369,434	$798,866	$62,205	$508,363	37.1%
Indiana	$530,861	$336,659	$32,430	$161,772	30.5%
Iowa	$158,269	$98,392	$23,088	$36,789	23.2%
Kansas	$175,971	$104,377	$21,078	$50,516	28.7%
Kentucky	$574,671	$410,816	$5,530	$158,325	27.6%
Louisiana	$253,729	$138,748	$17,797	$97,184	38.3%
Maine	$143,134	$84,280	$15,508	$43,346	30.3%
Maryland	$1,172,882	$656,720	$108,572	$407,590	34.8%
Massachusetts	$3,490,861	$2,583,507	$68,386	$838,968	24.0%
Michigan	$1,616,295	$920,800	$81,458	$614,037	38.0%
Minnesota	$370,152	$241,517	$71,385	$57,250	15.5%
Missouri	$475,545	$280,507	$37,608	$157,430	33.1%
Montana	$28,231	$15,575	$6,074	$6,582	23.3%
Nebraska	$68,170	$36,292	$16,222	$15,656	23.0%
New Hampshire	$193,013	$126,148	$6,448	$60,417	31.3%
New Jersey	$1,738,485	$972,799	$52,739	$712,947	41.0%
New Mexico	$110,616	$62,378	$23,414	$24,824	22.4%
New York	$3,313,737	$1,768,155	$99,946	$1,445,636	43.6%
Ohio	$2,155,789	$1,274,979	$95,456	$785,354	36.4%
Oregon	$1,659,542	$841,982	$233,728	$583,832	35.2%
Pennsylvania	$1,589,307	$828,691	$56,502	$704,114	44.3%
Rhode Island	$743,972	$590,679	$6,506	$146,787	19.7%
South Dakota	$121,701	$13,133	$7,979	$100,589	82.7%
Texas	$2,657,290	$1,508,850	$270,886	$877,554	33.0%
Vermont	$75,031	$46,792	$8,999	$19,240	25.6%
Virginia	$981,271	$637,614	$117,109	$226,548	23.1%
Washington	$452,809	$289,608	$62,353	$100,848	22.3%
West Virginia	$252,983	$94,935	$21,599	$136,449	53.9%
Wisconsin	$379,809	$232,404	$32,185	$115,220	30.3%

Source: U.S. Census Bureau. 2000 survey of government finances. Retrieved July 1, 2005, from http://www.census.gov/govs/state/00lottery.html

[a]Column added by authors.

participate, making the lottery somewhat less regressive (Monk & Brent, 1997, p. 116).

Indeed, lotteries influence purchasing behavior. In particular, lotteries result in substitution of goods for many lower income families. For example, lotteries have been shown to reduce spending on alcohol among Florida households (Monk & Brent, 1997, p. 117). While this effect may be desirable, it also may be an important fiscal planning consideration in states relying heavily on both lotteries and alcohol taxes as

Table 3.10   Evaluation of the Lottery as a Tax

	Pros	**Cons**
Equity		Generally regressive
Efficiency (distortions)	"Escalation" of demand as pot increases	Reduction in purchase of other goods
Administration		Expensive to administer
Economic Responsiveness	Initial growth rapid	Revenues reach plateau quickly
Political Acceptance	Generally well accepted (like consumption taxes)	May face moral opposition

revenue sources. Lotteries also result in a pattern of escalation in ticket purchasing as jackpots grow and, as noted previously, changing income distribution of purchasers of lottery tickets. Again, these distortions may be desirable.

Regarding administration and other costs, lotteries are generally perceived to be highly inefficient (Brent, 2000). As mentioned previously and as displayed in Table 3.9, states typically retain about 35% to 40% of ticket sales. Variation in administrative efficiency of lotteries is significant.

With regard to economic responsiveness and potential for growth, lotteries have generated rapid initial increases in revenues, but those revenues generally stabilize after the first few years of implementation (Brent, 2000). States may stimulate additional growth by creating new games and aggressively advertising those games. Doing so, however, necessarily comes at a higher cost.

Finally, lotteries are relatively well accepted by the public as a means for raising state revenues. This follows logically from the assumption that the public, in general, tends to support taxes based on discretionary consumption. As jackpots and games vary from one state to the next, it is conceivable that lotteries may export some tax burden. Lotteries and other forms of gaming, such as video slot machines and legalized gambling, are perhaps more likely to face moral objections than income or sales taxes. The prevalence of state lotteries, however, suggests that these objections are not substantial enough to deter adoption. The same may not be true for legalized gambling.

Later in this chapter, we discuss the federal role in funding schools for indigenous students living on federally designated reservations. These reservations, which have no "taxing authority" per se, have become particularly dependent on gambling revenues to support their public services.

Potential for Tax Reforms

Tax reform is often a hot political topic. Our evaluation frameworks for income, sales, property, and lottery taxes should provide some insight into the types of reforms that would make for a more equitable and efficient tax system. For example, income taxes certainly appear to be more desirable than property taxes for raising state revenues equitably and with relatively low costs to governments. For a variety of reasons, though perhaps most notably public sentiment, the local property tax is one that is often scrutinized as a tax in need of significant reform. We note that public dissatisfaction is the most likely overriding factor driving the call for property tax reform. Lotteries, which are even more administratively costly to operate and less equitable (more regressive), are not scrutinized to the same extent as property taxes.

Interestingly, the commonly proposed "fixes" to the property tax take vastly different forms. The most common proposals include the following:

1. Reduce the role of the property tax.
2. Implement statewide property taxes.
3. Share revenues generated by nonresidential properties.
4. Create or increase state income taxes in lieu of property taxes.
5. Increase sales taxes to supplant property taxes.

Reducing the role of the local property tax in school district funding implies a corresponding reduction in local involvement in the determination of funding levels of public education, because the local property tax is the major source of revenue under local fiscal control. The primary benefit of shifting the burden to the state level is presumably the reduction of funding disparities that occur when school districts have widely varied property values. Some states, most notably Michigan in the early 1990s, have made rather dramatic moves to cut their property taxes and shift the burden of funding education to the state.

Shifting the funding burden to the state means shifting the burden to other tax sources, unless the state wishes to impose statewide property taxes (see proposals 4 and 5 above). Statewide property taxes are rare but are also a legitimate method of equalizing revenues across local school districts. Recall that one of the political benefits of maintaining property taxes is that they are the last bastions of local control. The local property tax empowers local voters to express what they want for their local public schools. Further, the expression of local demand, and resulting variance across communities, is a critical underlying component of the Tiebout process (Tiebout, 1956). When property taxes become statewide taxes, the political advantages of empowering local citizens and promoting competition and sorting among jurisdictions is lost. Statewide property taxes may be politically viable under some circumstances, because the shift from local to statewide property taxation may reduce or eliminate wide variations in tax effort. Tax effort is the relative tax rate required for two different communities to get the same dollar return. Poor communities may have to tax themselves at 200% or 300% the levels of wealthy communities to secure the same amount of funding. Because the differences in the true cost of educating a child within the state are not likely to vary by such a high degree, even though a poor rural community might have lower average costs (e.g., lower salaries and housing costs), that community's property wealth will be even lower. This result produces an unfair tax burden on its local citizens who seek to provide a comparable education to their wealthier neighbors. In all likelihood, however, unless other advantages to the statewide property tax are present (such as with Vermont's ability to export property taxes or the ability to avoid "new" taxes), statewide property taxes are not likely to be broadly adopted, and where they do exist, as in Kansas, they are likely to play a diminished role in state revenue raising due primarily to their unpopularity.

Brian O. Brent (1999) and Helen Ladd (1976) have proposed intermediate solutions to statewide taxes on all properties, called expanded tax base approaches (ETB). One type of ETB approach involves treating nonresidential properties differently from residential properties, taxing those nonresidential properties at either a regional (Brent, 1999) or state level (Ladd & Harris, 1995), while leaving residential property taxation in the hands of local voters. Numerous arguments support this approach. First, nonresidential properties, such as commercial and industrial properties, do not serve the consumption of only those who live in the same town where the shopping mall or electric utility plant happens to be. The value of those properties is largely attributable to the consumption of households throughout the region, state, or even nation. Individuals throughout the region or state therefore should benefit from taxing those properties. Second, spreading the nonresidential wealth in this way can also mitigate losses to any one district that may have a high portion of nonresidential wealth. For example, when a local power plant is closed, losses are spread across all jurisdictions that share revenue from taxing the power plant, rather than just one. Third, maintaining local residential property taxation (a) maintains local control for local voters, which may be politically important, and (b) maintains local voters' ability to capitalize on the value of their homes by promoting public service quality.

Tax and Revenue Limits

Several states impose either statutory or constitutional limitations to taxes that may be implemented by state legislators or local officials. While we introduce the idea of tax and revenue limits in this chapter, we discuss the specific relationship of tax limits to school finance policies in Chapter 6. Monk and Brent (1997, p. 75) list the following approaches to tax limitation:

1. Overall property tax rate limits that set a ceiling that cannot be exceeded without a popular vote: These limits apply to the aggregate rate of tax on all local governments (not just school property taxes).

2. Specific property tax rate limits that set a ceiling that cannot be exceeded without a popular vote: These limits apply to specific types of local jurisdictions.

3. Property tax levy limits that constrain the total revenue that can be raised from the property tax, independent of the rate.

4. Assessment-increase limits that control the ability of local governments to raise revenue by

reassessment of property or through natural or administrative escalation of property values.

5. Full disclosure and truth in taxation provisions that require public discussion and specific legislative vote before enactment of tax rate or levy increases. (Monk & Brent, 1997, p. 75)

One important distinction among limitations on local property taxation is the distinction between those limits that local voters can and cannot override. Such limits are relatively rare, but Kansas, for example, limits local property tax revenues for public education to a specific dollar amount for each district that cannot be exceeded, even by the desires or demands of local voters. In Chapter 6, we will discuss the role of, and rationale for, such policies in the context of state education aid formulas. In the context of this chapter, it is important to understand how limits on local taxing authority may influence alternative revenue-raising behavior of local districts, discussed in the next section.

Other Revenue Sources for Education

For a variety of political and economic reasons, local public school districts in the United States are increasingly seeking ways to raise non-tax revenues to supplement their budgets. Reasons may include (a) the inability to convince local voters to support additional taxes for schools, perhaps due to aging school district populations; (b) statutory or constitutional limits on taxing authority of local districts; and (c) other tax policies that make it less efficient for local districts to raise funds through taxation, and more efficient to use other means. Monk and Brent (1997), and Pijanowski and Monk (1996) identify the following sources of alternative revenue:

1. *User fees:* Busing, food service, textbook and lab fees, and activities fees.
2. *Nonstudent user fees:* Leasing of space (athletic complexes, classrooms, auditorium) or providing services to local community members and groups.
3. *Business partnerships.*
4. *Volunteers:* Though not "revenue" per se, volunteer time is a resource that might be assigned a dollar value.
5. *Investment returns:* Most investment of public tax revenues is typically short term, and restricted to

relatively low-yield, insured accounts. Note, however, that many of the alternative revenues on this list are not so constrained.

6. *Donations:* Donations of money or materials, supplies, and equipment.
7. *Educational foundations:* Independently operated charitable not-for-profit organizations whose primary mission is to raise funds for local public school districts.

We focus our attention in this section on user fees and local education foundations (LEFs). Not all states permit user fees, but Monk and Brent (1997) note that 34 states do. States vary as to the types of fees allowed. If there were a general rule of thumb, it would be that user fees are less likely to be allowed for those services, materials, or supplies deemed essential for participating in public schooling. However, Monk and Brent identify eight states that permit user charges for certain textbooks (Alaska, Illinois, Indiana, Iowa, Kansas, Kentucky, Utah, and Wisconsin). Even in states where fees for required texts and/or required classes are not permitted, fees may be imposed for supplemental texts and workbooks, or elective classes.

User fees generally gain public support because they are based on the benefit principle. However, broad-based user fees on texts, required courses, or transportation are regressive. While some fees for athletics, elective courses, and other activities may in application be more progressive, they may also serve to exclude lower-income individuals from participating.

A rapidly emerging approach to raising alternative revenue is the LEF. Local education foundations are primarily tools of higher-income school districts that have found it necessary or more efficient to raise revenues for local schools by establishing a nonprofit entity, typically governed by local business leaders and other prominent local citizens. Communities establish LEFs with the specific purpose of raising private contributions to supplement local school districts' annual operating budgets.

Local education foundations raise two types of funds: (a) annual gifts and (b) capital or (c) endowment fund-raising campaigns. School districts use annual gifts for specific purposes in the district during the year in which those gifts are raised. Annual gifts are typically raised through annual giving campaigns that solicit donations from local citizens and businesses. Well-organized and more active LEFs also conduct capital fund-raising campaigns as well as campaigns intended to raise much larger sums of money in order to build an endowment. Capital campaigns may have the specific purpose of raising large sums of money to be saved and invested, and eventually used on high-cost major projects, perhaps construction of a new athletic facility. Endowment funds are raised with the specific purpose of investment. Ideally, once endowment funds are invested, the principal of the endowment is not used. Rather, the goal is to build a large enough endowment such that the annual investment returns from that endowment can provide a useful, relatively constant revenue stream for the local public school district.

Table 3.11 displays the LEF revenues of 12 Vermont school districts in 1999 and 2000, relative to their total revenues. In 1998, the state of Vermont implemented a new formula for funding public education. Along with that formula, the state changed tax policy so that wealthy towns would be required to share any additional revenue they might raise with local property taxes. This particular sharing provision infuriated many more wealthy Vermonters, who felt, for a variety of reasons that the new tax policy went too far. An immediate response to the sharing provision was that several school districts established, or dramatically expanded, LEFs. LEFs were stimulated in part by the promised support of a large nonprofit foundation, the Freeman Foundation, based in the state.

Table 3.11 shows that Vermont school districts have been quite successful at raising private revenues. An important organizational note on Vermont school districts is that most are not K–12, comprehensive districts. Foundation funds raised by a foundation established in a particular town might be used, for example, to benefit the K–6 or K–8 school in that town, and the 9–12 Union High School to which that town sends its students. As a result, foundation revenues should be evaluated as a percentage of total expenditures for those districts that are comprehensive K–12 districts. Stowe, Vermont, home to the Freeman Foundation, raised 30% of its annual revenue in 1999 through its foundation, much of which went to the town's endowment fund. However, Stowe derived 9% of its expenditures from foundation funds. In Wilmington, Vermont, which spent its foundation revenues, foundation expenditures were 24% of district expenditures.

If evaluated as a tax, one might argue that gifts to LEFs are somewhat progressive, in that wealthier individuals are likely to give larger gifts and perhaps even larger gifts as a proportion of their income. Note, however, a balancing effect because the gifts of high-income individuals to LEFs result in a reduction of their taxable income. The gift to the LEF therefore benefits the contributor's local school district and, in turn, the contributor, through property capitalization—if that contributor lives in the local school district. Further, the reduction of the contributor's income reduces the state revenue that might be generated and redistributed to other school districts.

As with lotteries, cost–benefit and/or operational efficiency questions are an important concern with local education foundations. That is, what does it cost to operate these independent nonprofit entities, and what is the average return? In the only comprehensive analysis of LEFs, Brian Brent provides some insights. Table 3.12 presents a summary of the average revenues, operating expenses, contributions, and fund balances (per pupil) for LEFs operating in New York and California (Brent, 2002). As Table 3.12 suggests, LEFs are a relatively efficient method for raising additional revenues at the local level.

While LEFs may be operationally efficient and effective means for raising supplemental revenues for relatively wealthy school districts, significant equity consequences result from shifting the burden of funding public schools to private donors. Brian Brent (2002) also provides some evidence of the differences in socioeconomic characteristics of districts with and without LEFs in New York and California. Brent found that districts with local education foundations tend to serve lower percentages of low-income students and have higher median family income or higher property wealth per pupil.

Brent's findings clearly show that districts with LEFs tend to serve lower percentages of low-income students and have higher median family income or higher property wealth per pupil. Zimmer, Crop, and Brewer (2003) of the RAND Corporation, in a pilot study, also find that socioeconomic factors influence the level of support and type of support school districts receive through private contributions.

The issue of private fund-raising for public schools is not new. A 1933 report entitled *Research Problems in School Finance*, prepared as part of the National Survey of School Finance, included an entire chapter on private contributions to public schools, noting:

> It is not to be assumed that these private contributions will reach any large proportion of the total amount of money needed for the support of public education, nor is it to be assumed that such private

Table 3.11 Local Education Foundation Revenues in 12 Vermont School Districts

District[a]	Year[b]	Foundation Revenue	Foundation Expenditures[c]	Pupils	Total Revenue[d]	Total Expenditures	Foundation Revenue %	Foundation Expenditure %
Sherburne (pK–6)	2001	$532,772	$557,272	111	$1,761,000	$1,647,000	30%	34%
Manchester (K–8)	2001	$674,854	$2,272,489	508	$6,801,000	$6,920,000	10%	33%
Weston	2001	$239,667	$195,514		$723,000	$718,000	33%	27%
Plymouth (K–6)	2000	$200,231	$148,628	41	$558,000	$572,000	36%	26%
Ludlow (K–6)	2001	$1,022,813	$908,335	194	$3,372,000	$3,550,000	30%	26%
Peru	2001	$250,720	$162,375		$646,000	$644,000	39%	25%
Wilmington (pK–12)	**2001**	**$967,292**	**$987,633**	**492**	**$4,235,000**	**$4,131,000**	**23%**	**24%**
Warren (pK–6)	2001	$543,389	$578,061	193	$2,421,000	$2,495,000	22%	23%
Stowe (K–12)	**1999**	**$1,896,069**	**$571,333**	**688**	**$6,284,000**	**$6,046,000**	**30%**	**9%**
Shelburne (pK–8)	2000	$978,032	$574,959	876	$9,178,000	$9,118,000	11%	6%
Burlington (K–12)	**1999**	**$981,865**	**$755,869**	**3681**	**$36,079,000**	**$35,560,000**	**3%**	**2%**
Williston (pK–8)	2001	$954,178	$212,300	1114	$11,543,000	$11,542,000	8%	2%

[a]A complicating factor in Vermont is that most of these districts serve either K–6 or K–8 students and send high school students to a Union high school. In this table, pupils and total revenues and expenditures are reported for town school districts, and may, in the case of non-K–12 districts, overstate the influence of foundations.

[b]Year of local education foundation financial data (www.guidestar.org).

[c]Includes all operating, administrative, and other expenditures in fiscal year as reported on IRS 990.

[d]Total revenue as counted in the Census of Local Governments does *not* include local education foundation revenue. As such, percentages presented herein represent the extent to which foundation revenue enhances total revenue, not the extent to which foundation revenue is a portion of total revenue.

Source: Foundation revenue and expenditures retrieved July 1, 2004, from www.guidestar.org. Total revenue and expenditures from Census of Local Governments 2000 (F-33 financial survey).

Table 3.12   Local Education Foundation Revenues and Expenses in New York and California

	New York	California
Revenues per pupil	$31.5	$200.7
Operating expenses per pupil	$2.9	$11.6
Contributions to district	$17.2	$114.2
Operating expense share	9.2%	5.8%

Source: Adapted from Brent B. O. (2002). Expanding support through district education foundations. *Leadership and Policy in Schools: A Tale of Two States,* 1(1), p. 40.

contributions will in any sense make possible the usurpation of the control of education. It is well, however, to acknowledge the assistance which has come to public education from these private sources, to give due publicity to the place which public education has secured in the benefactions of mankind, and to encourage this type of support as a further assistance to education, which is the most significant program of social welfare that mankind has yet advanced. (Cooper, 1933, p. 112)

SUMMARY

In this chapter, we addressed the multitude of ways in which public K–12 schools derive their financial resources. We have discussed the relative equity and efficiency of federal, state, and local taxes. In addition, we addressed emerging revenue sources for public schooling, including private contributions through local education foundations. The economic downturn of the early 21st century put many states in a precarious budgetary situation, raising new concerns as to how states will generate sufficient, stable revenue flow to support public services such as K–12 schools in the future. In most states, elementary and secondary schools are—and will be into the foreseeable future—the largest state budget item.

During the economic boom of the 1990s, which followed 30 years of shifting the burden of funding public schools from local communities to states, few could foresee the potential for such revenue shortfalls. In 2002–2003, for example, Texas was looking at a shortfall in state revenues on the order of $15 billion, while California was looking at a shortfall of as much as $35 billion. Some argue that a major reason why the Texas deficit was so much smaller than the California deficit is due, in part, to the state's continued reliance on property taxation to support a substantial portion of K–12 education spending, while California in particular relies very heavily on income taxes to support state general fund revenues. Income tax revenues have been particularly sensitive to the recent downturn.

Recent events, while creating grim, short-term budgetary situations for many states and school districts across the country, may provide us with some useful insights into ways to stabilize K–12 revenues in the future. In this chapter, we discussed some of the possibilities, including Helen Ladd (1976) and Brian Brent's (1999) arguments for statewide or regional taxation of nonresidential properties. While Brent (1999) in particular points to the equity virtues of such policies, the increased stability of state revenue flow may be a comparable advantage. In any case, we expect to see states paying more attention to balancing their revenue portfolios in future years.

In the next several sections of this book, we focus intensively on the expenditure side of the school-funding equation. Keep in mind, however, that a logical, equitable, and adequate formula for allocating expenditures across school districts can only remain logical, equitable, and adequate if sufficient revenues are available. Further, equitable treatment of students on the expenditure side of the equation should occur in conjunction with, not at the expense of, equitable treatment of taxpayers.

KEY TERMS

ability standard   The amount of tax paid is based on the ability of the taxpayer to pay the tax. Progressive income tax policies that require higher-income taxpayers to pay a higher percentage of income are based on the ability standard.

benefit standard   The amount of tax paid is related to the benefits received by an individual. For example, sales tax functions on the benefit standard. Those who buy more stuff (reaping the benefits of that stuff), pay more tax.

fair market value   The value that a property and the structures on that property would command as a sales price.

horizontal equity (in tax policy)   Comparable treatment of individual taxpayers, such as paying the same tax *rate* across all taxpayers.

intangible property   Intangible personal property includes assets that do not have physical substance, such as stocks, bonds, or cash.

progressive taxation   Progressive taxation requires those of greater ability to pay more in taxes, usually measured by a higher rate (not dollar value) of taxation.

real property   Real property includes both the land and any permanently attached improvements to that land, such as buildings.

regressive taxation   Regressive taxation exists where higher-ability taxpayers pay lower rates of tax.

tangible property   Tangible personal property may include household or personal property, or motor vehicles, which are often treated separately in property tax codes.

tax base   The measure to which the tax rate is applied in order to determine an individual's tax bill.

tax rate   The rate, or percentage, at which taxes are paid on any particular base. Tax rates are expressed in a number of ways, especially for property taxes. In many states, property tax rates are expressed as mills, or mill levies. A mill is 1/1.000, or .1%. In other states, property tax rates are expressed in dollars per $100 in assessed valuation, the equivalent of percent, but expressed in dollars. For example, in Missouri, taxpayers in a given school district might pay a tax rate (school levy) of $3, which is $3/$100 assessed value), or 3%.

tax yield   Rate × Base = Yield.

taxable assessed value   A percentage of a property's fair market value (sometimes 100% of FMV, fair market value) designated in state policy as the basis for taxation. For example, states may choose to apply statewide school property taxes to *x*% of FMV fair market value (11.5% in Kansas, 19% in Missouri).

vertical equity (in tax policy)   Differential treatment of taxpayers according to some rational basis, or reasonable government interest. For example, requiring higher-income taxpayers to pay a higher share of income to support public services, because they can afford to (progressive taxation, based on ability standard). Vertical equity also applies to differential treatment by property type in property taxation.

REFERENCES

Brent, B. O. (1999). An analysis of the influence of regional nonresidential expanded tax base approaches to school finance on measures of student and taxpayer equity. *Journal of Education Finance, 24*(3), 353–378.

Brent, B. O. (2000). Yes, the lottery is a tax, and not a very good one. *School Business Affairs, 66*(5), 22–28.

Brent, B. O. (2002). Expanding support through district education foundations. *Leadership and Policy in Schools: A Tale of Two States, 1*(1), 30–51.

Cooper, J. M. (1933). National survey of school finance: Research problems in school finance. American Council on Education. Washington, DC: United States Department of the Interior, Office of Education.

Downes, T., & Zabel, J. (1997) The impact of school characteristics on house prices: Chicago 1987–1991. Working Paper, Department of Economics, Tufts University, Medford, MA.

Erekson, O. H., DeShano, K. M., Platt, G., & Zeigert, A. L. (2002). Fungibility of lottery revenues and support for public education. *Journal of Education Finance, 28*(2), 301–311.

Figlio, D. N., & Lucas, M. (2002–May). *What's in a grade? School report cards and house prices*. Working Paper, National Bureau of Economic Research. Retrieved April 2007 from www.nber.org

Garrett, T. A. (2001). Earmarked lottery revenues for education: A new test of fungibility. *Journal of Education Finance, 26*(3), 219–238.

Gold, S. (1994.) *Tax options for states needing more school revenues*. Report prepared for the National Education Association. West Haven, CT: National Education Association.

Ladd, H. F. (1976). Statewide taxation of commercial and industrial property for education. *National Tax Journal, 29*, 143–153.

Ladd, H. F., & Harris, E. W. (1995). Statewide taxation of non–residential property for education. *Journal of Education Finance, 21*(1), 103–122.

Loeb, S. (2001). Estimating the effects of a school finance reform: a framework for a federalist system. *Journal of Public Economics, 80,* 225–247.

Mikesell, J. L. (1986). *Fiscal administration: Analysis and application for the public sector.* Homewood, IL. Dorsey.

Monk, D. H., & Brent, B. O. (1997). *Raising money for education: A guide to the property tax.* Thousand Oaks, CA: Corwin Press.

National Commission on Excellence in Education. (1983). *A nation at risk: The imperative for educational reform. A report to the nation and the secretary of education.*

Washington, DC: U.S. Department of Education. Retrieved April 2007 from http://www.ed.gov/pubs/NatAtRisk/index.html

Odden, A. R., & Picus, L. O. (2000). *School finance: A policy perspective.* New York: McGraw-Hill.

Pijanowski, J., & Monk, D. H. (1996). There are many fish in the sea. Alternative revenues for public schools. *School Business Affairs, 62*(7), 4–10.

Tiebout, C. M. (1956, October). A pure theory of local expenditures. *Journal of Political Economy, 64,* 416–424.

Zimmer, R., Crop, K., & Brewer, D. (2003). Private resources in public schools: Evidence from a pilot study. *Journal of Education Finance, 28*(4), 485–522.

CHAPTER 3 SIMULATIONS

TAX EQUITY IN MISSOURI

Background

For this activity, you will need to download the simulations for Chapter 3 from the book's Companion Website (www.prenhall.com/baker). Two versions of the simulation are available. One includes a sample of only 20 Missouri school districts and is useful for demonstration purposes. The other includes all 522 Missouri school districts. The goal of this simulation is to evaluate the equity, or lack thereof, in the ability of Missouri school districts to raise revenue for schools from local property taxes alone. In Chapter 5, we will examine how states apply aid to local school districts to compensate for these inequities. In this simulation, we will explore differing perspectives on those inequities through some relatively simple calculations.

Table 3s.1 shows the data for the 20-district data set. Districts range widely in numbers of enrolled pupils, from under 1,000 in both Wellston and Brentwood to over 30,000 each in both St. Louis and Kansas City. All districts in Table 3s.1 are in either the Kansas City or St. Louis metropolitan areas. Notice that the taxable assessed property value per pupil also varies widely, from under $25,000 in Wellston to nearly $337,000 in Ladue, a few miles away. In addition to taxable assessed value data, Table 3s.1 includes median housing unit value data and median household income data from the 2000 Census, available through the NCES School District Demographics System (http://nces.ed.gov/surveys/sdds/). Other data are from 2002–2003. Tax levies (operating and teacher) represent the actual school-operating revenue property tax levies of these districts. In the late 1990s, the state of Missouri separated out special levies to increase teacher salaries as a political tool for local boards of education.

An important feature of the table is that housing values and income are not necessarily highly correlated with total taxable assessed value per pupil. The total taxable property wealth includes widely varied shares of nonresidential, commercial, and industrial property. Little farm property or natural resource wealth is present in the suburban and urban districts in this sample. However, stereotypical "savage inequalities" are found in Table 3s.1. For example, Wellston, Missouri, is a small, 98% black, 100% poor district on the inner urban fringe of St. Louis, with the lowest income, housing values, and taxable property wealth in the sample. Ladue and Clayton, a few miles to the south, have more than 10 times the taxable property wealth per pupil, 10 times the housing unit values, and 3 to 4 times the income of Wellston.

A district's total operating levy is the sum of the two (teacher and incidental levy), such that in Wellston, the total is 5.10%, expressed in Missouri as $5.10 per $100 assessed valuation. The assessment rate for single-family homes is 19%. So, the median voter/homeowner in Wellston would have a taxable assessed value on his or her home of $.19 \times 29,000 = 5,510$, and the median voter/homeowner in Ladue would have a taxable assessed value of $.19 \times 308,200 = 58,558$. The Wellston homeowner would pay a property tax rate of $5.1\% \times 5,510 = \$281$, while the Ladue homeowner would pay $2.63\% \times 58,558 = \$1,540$.

Table 3s.1   20-District Sample

Name	Enrollment 2003	Operating Levy (Incidental)	Operating Levy (Teacher)	Median Household Income	Median Housing Unit Value	Assessed Value per Pupil
Belton 124	4,573	$1.75	$1.75	$46,678	$87,900	$45,745
Blue Springs R-iv	12,862	$1.62	$2.07	$56,570	$115,700	$69,110
Brentwood	868	$1.00	$1.47	$50,643	$116,500	$253,084
Center 58	2,562	$4.30	$—	$36,905	$93,400	$141,823
Clayton	2,478	$0.79	$1.81	$60,554	$368,200	$319,203
Ferguson-Florissant R-ii	11,949	$1.94	$2.80	$40,500	$71,600	$75,200
Grandview C-4	4,225	$4.93	$—	$42,303	$89,700	$77,670
Hazelwood	19,266	$1.66	$2.67	$48,909	$85,600	$82,824
Independence 30	11,201	$4.23	$—	$38,757	$81,000	$57,868
Jennings	3,131	$2.55	$1.77	$27,134	$49,300	$29,274
Kansas City 33	33,642	$4.95	$—	$29,634	$58,400	$75,186
Ladue	3,272	$1.20	$1.43	$82,889	$308,200	$336,855
Lee's Summit R-vii	14,861	$4.37	$—	$59,944	$129,400	$70,601
Liberty 53	7,428	$2.69	$1.38	$56,481	$125,000	$62,328
Normandy	5,859	$4.30	$—	$30,404	$52,500	$37,270
North Kansas City 74	17,030	$2.30	$1.69	$45,961	$96,500	$98,740
Park Hill	9,343	$4.99	$—	$57,120	$131,100	$96,563
Raymore-Peculiar R-ii	4,627	$3.14	$—	$56,198	$124,800	$57,663
Riverview Gardens	7,778	$3.90	$—	$33,744	$58,900	$29,474
St. Louis City	42,654	$2.73	$1.00	$27,156	$63,500	$73,398
Wellston	747	$2.55	$2.55	$21,458	$29,000	$24,686

Source: Enrollment, operating levy, and assessed value data from the Missouri Department of Elementary and Secondary Education (DESE), 2003 data, accessed in 2005 from http://www.dese.mo.gov/schooldata/ftpdata.html. Income from Census 2000 (NCES School Districts Demographics System). Retrieved from http://nces.ed.gov/surveys/sdds/

The yield per pupil also varies widely. Wellston's 5.1% tax rate generates 5.1% × $24,686 = $1,259 per pupil for Wellston schools. Ladue's 2.63% tax rate generates $8,859.

Table 3s.2 shows the manipulable interface of the 20-district simulation. This interface allows you to replace the current tax rates with a uniform rate. Table 3s.2 also allows you to adjust the assessment rate and add an exemption to the first *x*% of the value of housing units. Lopping off a flat portion of housing unit values is one relatively simple approach to providing tax relief to lower-income families residing in low-value homes. For example, taking the first 20,000 in taxable value off the median home in Wellston reduces the taxable value of that home to .19 × (29,000 − 20,000) = 1,710 and reduces the tax bill to $87.21.

Obviously, this policy would also reduce the revenue generated from local property tax. **This simulation does not adjust accordingly the total taxable property wealth of each district. The exemption adjustment is useful only for evaluating tax impact on homeowners. Total school revenue will appear to be the same but clearly cannot be.**

Table 3s.2 includes three types of output. The first is the yield per pupil, which is simply the product of the uniform tax rate selected times the taxable assessed value per pupil of the district. The second is the median tax bill paid, and the third is the median tax bill paid as a percentage of median income. Note again, that when adding the exemption, the simulation will not appropriately adjust the yield. The median tax bill (tax bill of the median homeowner/voter) of the district is the product of the uniform tax rate times the assessment rate times the median value home. The tax effort is calculated as the median tax bill expressed as a percentage of median household income.

Another perspective on local property taxes is whether the tax bills paid by local residents and/or the tax effort put forth by local residents are proportionate to the revenue generated. One can certainly envision a circumstance where substantial nonresidential property values in one district significantly compromise this relationship. Table 3s.2 includes the correlations across districts between tax bill and yield and tax effort and yield. The accompanying graphs, however, may be more useful.

Figure 3s.1 shows the relationship between median tax bill and yield per pupil at a 100% assessment rate and 1% uniform tax rate. Because this sample includes prima-

Table 3s.2   Manipulable Interface of the 20-District Simulation

Uniform Property Tax Rate	$ 1.00
Assessment Rate on Residential Property	19%
Exemption on first $X of Residential Value	$ —

	Yield per Pupil	Median Tax Bill	Tax Effort (% Income)
95th percentile	$3,192	$585.58	0.71%
Median	$734	$170.43	0.40%
5th percentile	$293	$93.67	0.33%
Correlation with yield		0.86	0.82

Source: Enrollment, operating levy, and assessed value data from the Missouri Department of Elementary and Secondary Education (DESE), 2003 data, accessed in 2005 from http://www.dese.mo.gov/schooldata/ftpdata.html. Income from Census 2000 (NCES School Districts Demographics System). Retrieved from http://nces.ed.gov/surveys/sdds/

rily urban and suburban districts with a high residential concentration, the relationship is relatively strong, with $1 in tax bill associated with $1 increase in revenue per pupil (found in the equation $y = .9523x - 52.51-$).[1]

Clearly, at least a few points don't fall nicely into line. For example, under this scenario, Brentwood has a median tax bill of about $1,165 and yield per pupil over $2,500. Meanwhile, Raymore-Peculiar has a median tax bill over $1,200 and yield per pupil of just over $500.

Figure 3s.2 presents an alternative perspective on tax equity, evaluating each district's median tax bill with respect to median income. That is, property taxes are essentially expressed as income taxes. For some districts, the picture changes little. In Brentwood, the median voter is paying 2.3% of income in property taxes, with a school district yield per pupil over $2,500.

In Figure 3s.1, two districts stood out in the far upper right corner, Ladue and Clayton. In Ladue the median tax bill was $3,082 and yield per pupil was $3,369.

Figure 3s.1   Median Household Tax Bill and Property Tax Revenue per Pupil

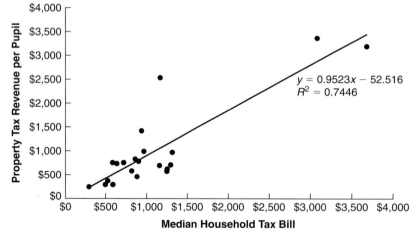

$y = 0.9523x - 52.516$
$R^2 = 0.7446$

Source: Enrollment, operating levy, and assessed value data from the Missouri Department of Elementary and Secondary Education (DESE), 2003 data, accessed in 2005 from http://www.dese.mo.gov/schooldata/ftpdata.html. Income from Census 2000 (NCES School Districts Demographics System). Retrieved from http://nces.ed.gov/surveys/sdds/

---

[1]For those needing a quick refresher on algebra, this equation describes the "slope" and "intercept" of the best-fit trend line. The intercept, -52.516, is relatively meaningless in practical terms but represents where the diagonal line crosses the vertical axis when the tax bill is $0. Theoretically, the intercept should be $0 and certainly not negative. In this case, the value suggests that in a district where homeowners pay, on average, no property tax, the yield per pupil will be slightly less than $0. The more meaningful value is .9523, the slope of the trend line, which indicates that for every 1-unit increase along the horizontal axis, the line increases .9523 (or nearly one unit) up the vertical, or y, axis.

Figure 3s.2 Tax Effort and Yield

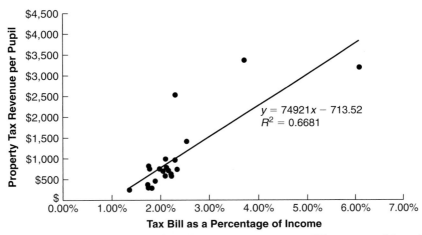

$y = 74921x - 713.52$
$R^2 = 0.6681$

Source: Enrollment, operating levy, and assessed value data from the Missouri Department of Elementary and Secondary Education (DESE), 2003 data, accessed in 2005 from http://www.dese.mo.gov/schooldata/ftpdata.html. Income from Census 2000 (NCES School Districts Demographics System). Retrieved from http://nces.ed.gov/surveys/sdds/

In Clayton, the median tax bill was $3,682 and yield was $3,192. Clearly, Ladue has a slight advantage, producing more than 1 for 1 yield. That advantage is more significant when expressed as a percentage of median income. At a 100% assessment rate on homes, and a 1% uniform tax rate, the median Ladue voter pays 3.72% of income to raise $3,369 and the median Clayton voter pays 6.08% of income to raise slightly less in per-pupil revenue.

Figure 3s.3 evaluates the progressiveness or regressiveness of the uniform tax rate on residential property owners at 100% assessed value and a 1% uniform rate. Figure 3s.3 shows that across most districts, the flat uniform tax rate results in a relatively flat income tax equivalent. Clayton, with its 6% income tax equivalent, is an extreme exception. In Figure 3s.3, a more progressive pattern would be one in which the higher-income communities, along the horizontal axis, are paying higher percentages of their income. Even under the flat tax rate with no exemption, the property tax is slightly progressive in Figure 3s.3, primarily due to the position of Ladue and Clayton.

Figure 3s.3 Progressiveness or Regressiveness of the Uniform Tax Rate on Residential Property Owners

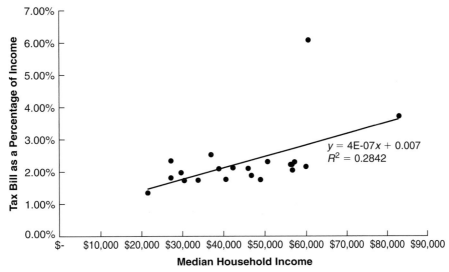

$y = 4E\text{-}07x + 0.007$
$R^2 = 0.2842$

Source: Enrollment, operating levy, and assessed value data from the Missouri Department of Elementary and Secondary Education (DESE), 2003 data, accessed in 2005 from http://www.dese.mo.gov/schooldata/ftpdata.html. Income from Census 2000 (NCES School Districts Demographics System). Retrieved from http://nces.ed.gov/surveys/sdds/

Problem Set Questions

For Question 1, hold constant the assessment rate at 100%, and adjust only the uniform tax rate.

1. How does changing the uniform tax rate affect

   a. Differences in yield per pupil?
   b. Differences in median tax bill per pupil?
   c. Differences in tax effort per pupil?
   d. The relationship between tax bill and yield?
   e. The relationship between tax effort and yield?

For Question 2, hold constant the uniform tax rate at 2.75%, and adjust only the assessment rate.

2. How does changing the assessment rate affect

   a. Differences in yield per pupil?
   b. Differences in median tax bill per pupil?
   c. Differences in tax effort per pupil?
   d. The relationship between tax bill and yield?

For Question 3, hold constant the uniform tax rate and assessment rate, and adjust only the exemption figure.

3. How does changing the exemption amount affect

   a. Differences in median tax bill per pupil across the districts in the sample?
   b. Differences in tax effort across lower and higher income communities and the relationship between tax effort and income?

Additional Questions

4. Which districts in the 20-district sample appear most advantaged in terms of

   a. Their ability to generate revenue for schools, with respect to the tax bill paid by homeowners?
   b. Their ability to generate revenue for schools, with respect to the share of their income that is paid in local property taxes?

5. Which districts in the 20-district sample appear most disadvantaged in terms of

   a. Their ability to generate revenue for schools, with respect to the tax bill paid by homeowners?
   b. Their ability to generate revenue for schools, with respect to the share of their income that they pay in local property taxes?

6. Thinking ahead (but not looking ahead in the book), if the state were to play some role in moderating the disparities in the ability of these 20 districts to raise local property tax revenues, how might you go about it? What factors/measures would you consider in determining how to provide financial support to these districts from a pot of state money (raised from statewide taxes)?

EQUALITY OF EDUCATIONAL OPPORTUNITY

CHAPTER 4

EQUITY APPROACHES TO SCHOOL FINANCE LITIGATION

Introduction

Since the late 1960s, litigants in 45 states have challenged the constitutionality of their school funding systems (Ryan & Saunders, 2004). Legal scholars have divided school finance litigation into three historically consecutive waves, during which one legal theory has dominated (Anker, 1998; Enrich, 1995; Fogle, 2000; Green & Baker, 2002; Heise, 1995; Palfrey, 2002; Thro, 1994). Equity approaches dominated the first two waves. First-wave plaintiffs asserted that disparities in funding and resources violated the equal protection clause of the Fourteenth Amendment. Second-wave plaintiffs argued that such disparities ran afoul of state equal protection and education clauses. Third-wave plaintiffs have alleged that state school finance systems violate state education clauses by failing to provide districts with an adequate education (Green & Baker, 2002). However, "[t]he shift toward adequacy . . . has been neither as sudden nor as complete as the wave metaphor suggests" (Ryan & Saunders, 2004, p. 467). The supreme courts of New Jersey (*Robinson v. Cahill*, 1973) and Washington (*Seattle School District No. 1 of King County v. State*, 1978) struck down their school finance systems on adequacy grounds. Also, equity challenges have endured in the third wave. Nevertheless, since the 1960s, the three waves describe the overall momentum of school finance litigation.

This chapter analyzes equity approaches to school finance litigation. The first section provides an overview of the American legal system. The second section examines equal protection clause litigation. Specifically, we discuss reasons for the advent of first-wave litigation. We also discuss how the Supreme Court appeared to put an end to first-wave litigation in *San Antonio Independent School District v. Rodriguez* (1973), and we analyze attempts to reinvigorate this course of action after the demise of the first wave. The third section focuses on state equal protection and education clause litigation. In particular, we identify the reasons that the courts provided for rejecting equity challenges during the second wave. We also examine equity litigation during the third wave.

Overview of the American Legal System

The American judiciary consists of one federal system and 50 state systems. Figure 4.1 depicts the structure of the federal system. The federal court system consists of district courts, circuit courts of appeals, special federal courts, and the U.S. Supreme Court. The district courts are the general trial courts of the federal system. Each state has at least one federal district court. Most states have more than two, while Texas and California have four district courts each. Decisions may be appealed to the circuit courts of appeals, and on occasion, directly to the Supreme Court (Alexander & Alexander, 2005). The circuit Courts of Appeals are the intermediate appellate courts in the federal system (see Table 4.1). Eleven numbered circuits cover a geographical area, with a Circuit Court for the District of Columbia and a Federal Circuit Court. The U.S. Supreme Court, which is the highest court in the federal system, hears cases by appeal or through its original jurisdiction. The Supreme Court is the final interpreter of federal issues.

Figure 4.1 Federal Court System

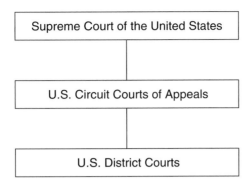

State court systems generally consist of courts of limited jurisdiction, courts of general jurisdiction, intermediate appellate courts, and state high courts. State courts may issue rulings pertaining to federal or state law, and their opinions are final to the extent that they do not conflict with federal court decisions (Alexander & Alexander, 2005). State courts are the final arbiter of state constitutional law and state statutes.

Plaintiffs have challenged the constitutionality of school finance systems in both federal and state courts. Because the federal equal protection clause was the sole basis of most first-wave cases, legal challenges during this period were issued primarily in federal courts. Second- and third-wave school finance litigation has relied primarily on state constitutional provisions. These cases have taken place in state courts.

Table 4.1 Federal Circuit Courts

Circuit	Jurisdiction
First	Maine, Massachusetts, New Hampshire, Rhode Island, and Puerto Rico
Second	Connecticut, New York, Vermont
Third	Delaware, New Jersey, Pennsylvania, Virgin Islands
Fourth	Maryland, North Carolina, South Carolina, Virginia, West Virginia
Fifth	Louisiana, Mississippi, Texas
Sixth	Kentucky, Michigan, Ohio, Tennessee
Seventh	Illinois, Indiana, Wisconsin
Eighth	Arkansas, Iowa, Minnesota, Nebraska, North Dakota, South Dakota
Ninth	Alaska, Arizona, California, Guam, Hawaii, Idaho, Montana, Nevada, Northern Mariana Islands, Oregon, Washington
Tenth	Colorado, Kansas, New Mexico, Oklahoma, Utah, Wyoming
Eleventh	Alabama, Florida, Georgia
District of Columbia	District of Columbia, and cases involving federal government
Federal	U.S. Court of Federal Claims, U.S. Court of International Trade, and cases involving patents

Federal Equal Protection Clause Litigation

Reasons for the Advent of the First Wave

During the first wave of school finance litigation, which lasted from the late 1960s to 1973, plaintiffs argued that disparities in funding between rich and poor districts violated the equal protection clause, which provides that no state "shall deny to any person of its jurisdiction the equal protection of the laws" (U.S. Constitution Amendment XIV, § 1). A variety of factors contributed to the advent of the first wave.

The first factor was the Supreme Court's equal protection clause litigation that appeared to provide support for challenges to disparities based on resources, instead of race (Enrich, 1995, 2003). Under Chief Justice Earl Warren's guidance during the 1950s and 1960s, the Supreme Court employed the equal protection clause to invalidate a number of inequitable governmental practices during this period.

For those interested in challenging school-funding inequality, three strands of Warren Court equal protection clause jurisprudence were particularly appealing. The first strand was the school desegregation cases (Enrich, 1995). In *Brown v. Board of Education* (1954), the Court ruled that *de jure*, or intentional, racial discrimination of the public schools violated the equal protection clause. In reaching this conclusion, the Court spoke of the importance of education in impassioned terms:

> Today, education is perhaps the most important function of state and local governments. Compulsory school attendance laws and the great expenditures for education both demonstrate our recognition of the importance of education to our democratic society. It is required in the performance of our most basic public responsibilities, even service in the armed forces. It is the very foundation of good citizenship. Today it is a principal instrument in awakening the child to cultural values, in preparing him for later professional training, and in helping him to adjust normally to his environment. In these days, it is doubtful that any child may reasonably be expected to succeed in life if he is denied the opportunity of an education. Such an opportunity, where the state has undertaken to provide it, is a right which must be made available to all on equal terms.
> (*Brown v. Board of Education*, 1954, p. 493)

Because of the description of the importance of education, it was reasonable for contemporary observers to assume that the fundamental importance of education was part of the rationale for the Court's decision in *Brown* and that the Court would be open to equal protection clause challenges in educational contexts outside the realm of *de jure* segregation (Enrich, 1995).

The second strand of equal protection clause cases focused on discrimination based on wealth (Enrich, 1995). Enrich observes that the most prominent of these "was the series of cases requiring the states to ensure that criminal defendants could avail themselves of protections offered by the criminal justice system, regardless of their financial resources" (pp. 117–118). These cases were significant to the school finance context because they "made clear that the equal protection clause also limited governmental policies and requirements that, while facially drawing no distinctions among classes, had the effect of denying opportunities to one class that were made available to others" (p. 118). However, Enrich also observes that the wealth discrimination cases differed from the school-funding context in two key aspects. First, in the wealth-discrimination cases, "the deprivations were suffered by individuals based on their personal financial circumstances, whereas in the educational context the variations resulted from the financial circumstances of the larger community in which the student lived" (p. 119). Second, in the wealth-discrimination cases, "lack of financial resources had the effect, for at least some individuals, of working a complete deprivation of the salient opportunity, whereas in the educational context the consequence was only a relative deprivation, a diminution in the quantity or quality of educational services and opportunities" (p. 119).

According to Enrich (1995), this is where the third strand of the Warren Court's equal protection clause jurisprudence, the legislative apportionment cases, came into play. These cases dealt with the proper way in which state legislators should be apportioned or distributed among election districts. Several states had failed to reapportion districts for many years despite shifts in populations. Consequently, a minority of their populations could control state legislatures. In *Baker v. Carr* (1962), the Court held that a plaintiff could challenge the legislative apportionment of a state on equal protection clause grounds. In *Reynolds v. Sims* (1964), the Court held that state legislative apportionment schemes had to be on the basis of population. The legislative apportionment cases were pertinent to the school-funding context because they involved state actions that created differential opportunities for citizens of different political subdivisions of the state. And, as with education funding, no voter was deprived of representation altogether; rather, the states had established structures under which only the amount of representation attaching to each vote varied from district to district. The apportionment cases thus disclosed in the equal protection clause a right of all citizens to mathematically equivalent treatment, regardless of the district in which they resided. They also demonstrated the readiness of the courts to enforce this right, even when the challenged disparities resulted from demographic factors not of the state's making, and even when the effect was a deep intrusion into the state's traditional control over its own internal political structures (Enrich, 1995, p. 120).

Thus, the Warren Court's decisions suggested to civil rights attorneys that the courts would be amenable to an equal protection clause challenge to school finance disparities. As Enrich (1995) explains:

> The same arithmetical calculations that, in the apportionment cases, showed the dilution of voting power due to differences in district population could be deployed in the education funding context to show the dilution of education spending power due to differences in district property wealth. Given the Court's strong intimations in the desegregation cases of the constitutional significance of the right to education, and given the additional presence in the education context of the wealth dimension, which was generally absent from the apportionment cases, extension of the *Reynold*'s equal protection argument to the field of education finance appeared virtually unstoppable. (pp. 120–121)

A second reason for the advent of school finance litigation in the 1960s was the country's focus on eradicating poverty (Enrich, 1995, 2003; Hanushek, 1991; Neuman, 1999). During this period, President Lyndon B. Johnson had initiated his War on Poverty. Also, the Civil Rights Movement had begun to shift its focus away from race toward addressing barriers created by poverty (Enrich, 1995). In conjunction with this change in focus, advocates for the poor attacked governmental discrimination in a variety of areas including educational funding (Neuman, 1999). These advocates attempted to build on the Warren Court's decisions that tentatively recognized wealth as a classification requiring heightened scrutiny under the equal protection clause (Enrich, 1995).

A third reason for the development of school finance litigation was the need to address the limitations of school desegregation litigation (Enrich, 1995, 2003; Rebell, 2001; Wetzler, 2004). "[A]lthough the Supreme Court did not settle the question until [*Keyes v. School District No. 1* (1973)], it was becoming increasingly clear that the constitutional prohibition on segregated schools would be limited to cases of *de jure* . . . segregation, and would provide no relief in the common situations where segregation was the result of housing patterns and municipal or district boundaries" (Enrich, 1995, p. 122). Even where plaintiffs could prove that intentional segregation had been committed, resistance to remedies such as busing and "white flight" from urban areas dramatically limited the success of school desegregation litigation (Enrich, 1995). Thus, desegregation litigation provided little hope for minority students attending underfunded and racially isolated urban schools (Enrich, 1995).

First-Wave Litigation

In spite of the initial promise of equal protection clause litigation, first-wave challenges to school finance disparities were unsuccessful because (a) courts refused to apply heightened scrutiny to classifications based on property wealth, and (b) no measurable standards existed for determining how educational aid should be distributed. In *McInnis v. Shapiro* (1968), plaintiffs alleged that Illinois's school finance system violated the equal protection clause by permitting "wide variations in the expenditures per student from district to district, thereby providing some students with a good education and depriving others, who have equal or greater educational need" (p. 329).

A federal district court dismissed the complaint. It refused to find that school desegregation cases warranted the application of **strict scrutiny,** which is the most difficult level of scrutiny for the government to overcome in equal protection and substantive due process challenges. Courts apply strict scrutiny to equal protection challenges that infringe upon a fundamental right or a suspect class. Courts also apply strict scrutiny in substantive due process challenges to government actions that infringe upon a fundamental right. The school desegregation cases were inapplicable because they were based on the inherently suspect classification of race. The district court concluded that more lenient standards were applicable: (a) "[a] statutory discrimination will not be set aside as the denial of equal protection of the laws if any state of facts reasonably may be conceived to justify it" (p. 332); and

(b) "[t]he constitutional safeguard is offended only if the classification rests on grounds wholly irrelevant to the achievement of the State's objective" (p. 332). Applying these standards, the court concluded that permitting school districts to determine their own tax burden was a reasonable means to encourage local choice and experimentation.

The court also dismissed the complaint because there were "no 'discoverable and manageable standards' by which a court can determine when the Constitution is satisfied and when it is violated" (*McInnis v. Shapiro,* 1968, p. 335). The court found that "the only possible standard is the rigid assumption that each pupil must receive the same dollar expenditures" (p. 336). However, equalizing expenditures failed to account for other factors that had an impact on educational need. For example, the court noted that "[d]eprived pupils need more aid than fortunate ones," and "a dollar spent in a small district may provide less education than one used in a large district" (pp. 335–336). The court further cautioned that "[a]s new teaching methods are devised and as urban growth demands changed patterns of instruction, the only realistic way the state can adjust is through legislative study, discussion and continuing revision of the controlling statutes" (p. 336). Even if guidelines for measuring educational need were available to the judiciary, the *McInnis* court warned that "the courts simply cannot provide the empirical research and consultation necessary for intelligent educational planning" (p. 336).

In *Burruss v. Wilkerson* (1969), a federal district court denied the plaintiffs' claim that Virginia's school finance system violated the equal protection clause by failing to provide for the varying educational needs of school districts. The court refused to grant such relief because it had "neither the knowledge, nor the means, nor the power to tailor the public money to fit the varying needs of these students throughout the State" (p. 574). Instead, the court saw that its sole responsibility was to ensure that "the outlays on one group are not invidiously greater or less than that of another" (p. 574). Applying this rather lenient standard, the court found that the school finance system did not violate the equal protection clause.

Shortly after the *McInnis* and *Burruss* decisions, the California Supreme Court in *Serrano v. Priest* (*Serrano I*) (1971) injected new life into equal protection clause litigation by finding that the state's school finance system violated the equal protection clause.

The *Serrano* court held that strict scrutiny was applicable to the plaintiffs' claims. This was the case because wealth was a suspect classification, and the school finance system's reliance on local property taxation classified districts on the basis of wealth because "districts with small tax bases simply cannot levy taxes at a rate sufficient to produce the revenue that more affluent districts reap with minimal tax efforts" (*Serrano I,* 1971, p. 1250). Citing *Brown*'s declaration that "education is perhaps the most important function of state and local governments," the court also found that strict scrutiny was appropriate because education was a fundamental right under federal and state constitutions (*Serrano I,* 1971, p. 1256). A **fundamental right** is a right that is created by the Constitution. Classifications that impinge on fundamental rights are subject to strict scrutiny. Fundamental rights include interstate travel, voting, marriage, and contraception.

Applying strict scrutiny, the court rejected the assertion that the fiscal scheme was necessary to advance local administrative control because "[n]o matter how the state decides to finance its system of public education, it can still leave this decision-making power in the hands of local districts" (*Serrano I,* p. 1260). The court also rejected the claim that local property taxation was necessary to promote local fiscal choice. In fact, poor districts were deprived of fiscal choice because their low tax bases limited the amount of money they could spend on education.

In *San Antonio Independent School District v. Rodriguez* (1973), the U.S. Supreme Court ended the first wave by ruling that Texas's reliance on local property taxation did not violate the equal protection clause. The Court rejected the claim that the school finance system should be subject to strict scrutiny because the plaintiffs were members of a suspect classification based on wealth. A **suspect class** is a government classification based on race or national origin. Such classifications are subject to strict scrutiny under equal protection analysis. The Court ruled that the school finance system did not discriminate against a suspect class of poor persons because there was no evidence that the state's poor persons were concentrated around the poorest school districts and were completely deprived of an education. Additionally, the Court rejected the contention that the system discriminated against a suspect class of individuals who lived in comparatively poor school districts. It raised doubts about whether such a class could ever be considered "suspect" and observed that, in any event, the plaintiffs failed to establish a direct correlation between family wealth within each district and expenditures for education. Finally, the Court refused to find that district wealth was a suspect classification because this classification "had none of the traditional indicia of suspectness: the class is not saddled with such disabilities, or subjected to such a history of purposeful unequal treatment, or relegated to such a position of political powerlessness as to command extraordinary protection from the majoritarian political process" (*San Antonio Independent School District v. Rodriguez,* 1973, p. 28).

The Court also rejected the notion that strict scrutiny was applicable because education was a fundamental right under the Constitution. As the Court explained: "[T]he key to discovering whether education is 'fundamental' is not to be found in comparisons of the relative societal significance of education. . . . Rather, the answer lies in assessing whether there is a right to education explicitly or implicitly guaranteed by the Constitution" (*San Antonio Independent School District v. Rodriguez,* 1973, p. 33). Employing this test, the Court concluded that education was not "among the rights afforded explicit protection under our Federal Constitution" (*San Antonio Independent School District v. Rodriguez,* 1973, p. 34). Further, the Court refused to find that education was implicitly protected by the Constitution because it was necessary for the effective exercise of constitutional guarantees such as freedom of speech and the right to vote. Although guaranteeing that citizens could speak effectively or vote intelligently were desirable goals, they were "not values to be implemented by judicial intrusion into otherwise legitimate state activities" (*San Antonio Independent School District v. Rodriguez,* 1973, p. 36).

Instead of strict scrutiny, the Court found that the rational basis test was the appropriate form of analysis. The **rational basis test** is the most preferential level of scrutiny that courts use for equal protection challenges. In government actions that do not involve a fundamental right, or a suspect class, a court will uphold a law as long as it is rationally related to a legitimate interest. The Court then concluded that the use of local property taxation was rationally related to encouraging local control of the public schools. By becoming involved in educational decisions at the local level, community members demonstrated their depth of commitment to public education. Local control also provided each locality with the means for participating

"in the decision making process of determining how local tax dollars will be spent" (*San Antonio Independent School District v. Rodriguez,* 1973, p. 50). Moreover, local control enabled school districts "to tailor local plans for local needs" and encouraged "experimentation, innovation, and a healthy competition for educational excellence" (p. 50).

The Court rejected the argument that the use of local taxation was irrational because other policies were available that could have accomplished the goal of local control while achieving greater equality in educational expenditures. As the Court explained, "[w]hile it is no doubt true that reliance on local property taxation for school revenues provides less freedom of choice with respect to expenditures for some districts than for others, the existence of 'some inequality' in the manner in which the State's rationale is achieved is not alone a sufficient basis for striking down the entire system. . . . It may not be condemned simply because it imperfectly effectuates the State's goals" (*San Antonio Independent School District v. Rodriguez,* 1973, p. 51).

The Court also rejected the argument that the state's reliance on local property taxation was irrational because the quality of education was based on "the fortuitous positioning of boundary lines of political subdivisions and the location of valuable commercial and industrial property" (*San Antonio Independent School District v. Rodriguez,* 1973, p. 54). The Court observed that any scheme of local taxation required the establishment of arbitrary jurisdictional boundaries. Furthermore, the availability of taxable resources did not always turn on "happenstance": Local residents could exert some control over the amount of taxable wealth available to their districts. For example, local communities might encourage commercial and industrial enterprises to locate within a school district. Moreover, the Court cautioned that if it struck down local property taxation schemes as a way to raise educational revenue, then similar policies to raise funds for other governmental services, such as police, fire protection, and hospitals, would be placed in jeopardy.

Attempts to Resuscitate Equal Protection Clause Litigation

Plaintiffs have responded to *Rodriguez* by looking for ways to revitalize equal protection clause litigation within school finance challenges. In *Plyler v. Doe* (1982), the Supreme Court appeared to resuscitate the equal protection clause by suggesting that governmental classifications involving education should be subject to a heightened form of rational basis analysis. In *Plyler*, the Court invalidated a Texas statute that withheld funds from school districts for the public education of undocumented children of alien parents. Although the Court agreed with the conclusion of *Rodriguez* that public education is not a fundamental right under the Constitution, it also observed that education was distinguished from other social welfare programs because of its importance "in maintaining our basic institutions, and the lasting impact of its deprivation on the life of the child" (p. 221). The Court then found that the statute "can hardly be considered rational *unless it furthers some substantial goal of the state*" (p. 224) (emphasis added).

The Court identified and rejected three "colorable" interests that might have supported the statute. First, the Court found no evidence that denying an education to undocumented alien children furthered the state's interest in protecting itself from an influx of illegal immigrants. Second, the state failed to present evidence demonstrating that the discriminatory classification furthered the interest of improving the quality of education offered by the state. Finally, the Court rejected the claim that excluding undocumented children furthered the interest of focusing educational resources on those children who would remain in the state. The record clearly showed that many undocumented children stayed in the state and that some would become legal residents or citizens.

It appeared that *Plyler*'s use of heightened rational basis scrutiny might revive school finance litigation under the equal protection clause (Farrell, 1999). The rational basis test traditionally provides a great deal of latitude to governmental entities. Under traditional rational-basis analysis, a classification is constitutional "if there is any reasonably conceivable state of facts that could provide a rational basis for the classification" (*FCC v. Beach Communications*, 1993, p. 312). Moreover, the burden is on the plaintiffs to "negative every conceivable basis which might support [the classification] whether or not the basis has a foundation in the record" (*Heller v. Doe*, 1993, p. 320). Applying this level of analysis, the Supreme Court in *Rodriguez* found that local control is a plausible reason for reliance on local property taxation.

By contrast, heightened rational basis review would be more difficult for the government to over-

come for the following reasons: (a) the requirement that a classification "further" a state interest implies "a more direct connection to purpose than the ordinary 'rational relation'"; and (b) the requirement that the relationship be "substantial" is "clearly a more demanding test than that of 'legitimacy'" (Farrell, 1999, p. 383). Thus, under heightened rational-basis review, a court might conclude that an insufficient connection exists between local property taxation and local control, especially if plaintiffs could establish that local property taxation actually deprived poor districts of fiscal choice.

However, in *Kadrmas v. Dickinson Public Schools* (1988), the Supreme Court appeared to foreclose *Plyler* as a means for subjecting school finance formulas to heightened rational-basis analysis. In *Kadrmas*, the Court ruled that a North Dakota statute that permitted some school districts to charge a user fee for bus transportation did not violate the equal protection clause. Although the Court acknowledged that *Plyler* had applied "a heightened level of Equal Protection Scrutiny," it asserted that it had "not extended this holding beyond the 'unique circumstances' . . . that provoked its 'unique confluence of theories and rationales'" (p. 459). *Plyler* was inapplicable because the plaintiff was not penalized for the parents' illegal conduct and no class of students had been completely deprived of a public education. The court then articulated a very deferential standard of rational basis review: A statute would not be invalidated "unless the varying treatment of different groups or persons is so unrelated to the achievement of any combination of legitimate purposes that we can only conclude that the legislature's actions were irrational" (p. 463, internal quotations omitted). Applying this standard, the Court concluded that encouraging districts to provide bus service is a legitimate purpose, and it was rational for the state to refrain from undermining this objective by passing a rule requiring "that general revenues be used to subsidize an optional service that will benefit a minority of the district's families" (p. 462).

Kadrmas indicates that school-funding disparities are ineligible for heightened rational-basis review because they do not completely deprive children attending poor districts of an education. *Campaign for Fiscal Equity v. State* (1995), a New York school finance case, supports this conclusion. In *Campaign for Fiscal Equity*, the Court of Appeals of New York refused to find that *Plyler* warranted the application of heightened scrutiny to an equal protection clause challenge to the state's failure to provide "a minimum, adequate education." The court rejected this argument because there were "important differences" between the plaintiffs' challenge and *Plyler*: "the educational deprivation was absolute in *Plyler* and was intentionally discriminatory toward a defined subclass" (p. 668).

In *Papasan v. Allain* (1986), the Supreme Court suggested another avenue for resuscitating equal protection clause litigation. In *Papasan*, the Court held that *Rodriguez* did not foreclose equal protection clause challenges to funding disparities caused by state distribution policies. In *Papasan*, plaintiffs alleged that Mississippi's unequal distribution of educational funds from "Sixteenth Section or Lieu Lands" violated the equal protection clause. The Fifth Circuit Court of Appeals held that *Rodriguez* was controlling and dismissed the complaint. The Supreme Court vacated the judgment and remanded the case to the federal district court. While the Supreme Court agreed with the Fifth Circuit's holding that the rational-basis test should be applied to the plaintiffs' claim, it found that the Fifth Circuit incorrectly concluded that *Rodriguez* was controlling. As the Court explained, *Rodriguez* applied only to school-funding disparities that were caused by local property taxation but did not address the constitutionality of state decisions "to divide state resources differently among school districts" (*Papasan v. Allain*, 1986, p. 288).

The prevalence of cost-adjusted two-tier formulas might cause plaintiffs to consider mounting equal protection clause challenges under *Papasan*. Such formulas consist of a first-tier base-aid component provided by the state to local districts (either in the form of a foundation aid-type program or per-pupil block grant), adjusted to reflect varied costs across districts, and a second tier in which local districts are allowed to raise additional local taxes to supplement the first tier. The second tier usually involves state matching aid for low-property-wealth districts, in some cases including an income adjustment as well. A response to the success of third-wave litigation, two-tiered funding formulas are designed to raise the funding of poor districts to a constitutionally adequate level (through the first tier), while permitting wealthy districts to continue to spend on education as they deem appropriate (through the second tier).

Cost-adjusted two-tier formulas might provide affluent districts with an opportunity to perpetuate funding disparities between themselves and their underprivileged counterparts. Green and Baker (2002) observe that first-tier cost adjustments include provisions designed to meet the particular needs of individual school districts. Cost adjustments that are designed to compensate for student characteristics, such as funding for students with disabilities and limited English proficiency, are more likely to benefit urban school districts. On the other hand, adjustments for district characteristics, such as economies of scale and geographic cost adjustments, are more likely to benefit suburban districts, because they tend to be smaller and have more experienced, and thus more expensive, teachers (Green & Baker, 2002). Because of the political power of wealthy suburban districts, it is possible for "legislators representing wealthy school districts to more than offset the compensating effects of poverty adjustments that advantage poor districts by implementing [economies of scale] and geographic cost adjustments that advantage wealthier districts" (Green & Baker, 2002, pp. 153–154).

The major limitation to *Papasan*-based litigation is the Supreme Court's conclusion that rational basis analysis would apply to such claims. As explained previously, the rational-basis test is traditionally a very deferential standard. *Montoy v. State* (2005), a Kansas school finance case, is illustrative. In this case, plaintiffs alleged that the state's funding distribution scheme, which included a number of cost adjustments that disproportionately favored rural and suburban school districts over their urban counterparts, violated the equal protection clause. Applying the rational-basis test, the Kansas Supreme Court upheld the cost adjustments on the ground that they were rationally related to legitimate governmental interests.

State Equal Protection and Education Clauses

Second Wave

After the Supreme Court put an end to first-wave litigation in *Rodriguez (San Antonio Independent School District v. Rodriguez*, 1973), plaintiffs responded by bringing equity challenges under state equal protection and education clauses. This second wave of school finance litigation lasted from 1973 to 1989 (Anker, 1998; Fogle, 2000; Green & Baker, 2002; Palfrey,

2002). This approach had limited success. Six state supreme courts overturned their school finance formulas,[1] while 13 courts upheld their formulas.[2]

Rejection of the *Rodriguez* Test for Determining Fundamental Rights

In a number of second-wave cases, plaintiffs argued that state courts should use the Supreme Court's approach in *Rodriguez* (*San Antonio Independent School District v. Rodriguez,* 1973) for determining whether education is a fundamental right warranting strict scrutiny. Recall that in *Rodriguez,* the Court refused to find that education was a fundamental right for the purpose of equal protection clause litigation, because it was neither explicitly nor implicitly mentioned in the U.S. Constitution. By contrast, every state constitution contains an education clause that defines the state's responsibility for establishing a system of education (McUsic, 1991). Thus, education would be a fundamental right under state constitutions if courts applied the *Rodriguez* test. Indeed, in *Washakie County School District v. Herschler* (1980), the Supreme Court of Wyoming applied the *Rodriguez* test to conclude that education was a fundamental right under the state constitution. As the court explained: "[i]n the light of the emphasis which the Wyoming Constitution places on education, there is no room for any conclusion but that education for the children of Wyoming is a matter of fundamental interest" (p. 333). The court went on to find that the school finance system was unconstitutional.

Nevertheless, most courts found that the *Rodriguez* test was inapplicable for determining whether education is a fundamental right under state constitutions. For example, in *Fair School Finance Council of Oklahoma v. State* (1987), the Oklahoma Supreme Court acknowledged that if it had applied the *Rodriguez* test to the plaintiffs' state equal protection clause challenge, "then educational opportunity would arguably be a fundamental interest in Oklahoma entitled to strict scrutiny" (pp. 1148–1149). The court still found that the *Rodriguez* test was inappropriate because:

> The United States Constitution is one of restricted authority and delegated powers. By contrast our state constitution is not one of limited powers where the State's authority is restricted to the four corners of the document. Rather, the Oklahoma Constitution addresses not only those areas deemed fundamental but also others which could have been left to statutory enactment. While the Congress of the United States may do only what the federal constitution has granted it the power to do, our state Legislature generally may do, as to proper subjects of legislation, all but that which it is prohibited from doing. Thus, under the Oklahoma Constitution, fundamental rights are not necessarily determined by whether they are provided for within the document. (*Fair School Finance Council of Oklahoma v. State,* 1987, p. 1149)

In *Thompson v. Engelking* (1975), the Idaho Supreme Court refused to apply the *Rodriguez* test to a state equal protection clause challenge to the state's school finance system because of the difficulties inherent to distinguishing between "fundamental" and "nonfundamental" rights:

> "But we have not found helpful the concept of a 'fundamental' right. No one has successfully defined the term for this purpose. Even the proposition discussed in *Rodriguez,* that a right is 'fundamental' if it is explicitly or implicitly guaranteed in the Constitution, is immediately vulnerable, for the right to acquire and hold property is guaranteed in the Federal and State Constitutions, and surely that right is not a likely candidate for such preferred treatment. And if a right is somehow found to be 'fundamental,' there remains the question as to what State interest is 'compelling' and there, too,

---

[1]These states are as follows: (1) Arkansas, *DuPree v. Alma School District No. 30 v. Crawford County* (1983); (2) California, *Serrano v. Priest* (1976) ("*Serrano II*"); (3) Connecticut, *Horton v. Meskill* (1977); (4) New Jersey, *Robinson v. Cahill* (1973); (5) Washington, *Seattle School District No. 1 of King County v. State* (1978); and (6) Wyoming, *Washakie County School District No. One v. Herschler* (1980). It is also important to observe that the *Robinson* and *Seattle School District No. 1* cases were decided on adequacy rather than equity grounds.

[2]Those states are as follows: (1) Arizona, *Shofstall v. Hollins* (1973); (2) Colorado, *Lujan v. Colorado State Board of Education* (1982); (3) Georgia, *McDaniel v. Thomas* (1982); (4) Idaho, *Thompson v. Engelking* (1975); (5) Maryland, *Hornbeck v. Somerset County Board of Education* (1983); (6) Michigan, *Milliken v. Green* (1973); (7) New York, *Board of Education, Levittown Union Free School District v. Nyquist* (1982); (8) Ohio, *Board of Education of City School District of City of Cincinnati v. Walter* (1979); (9) Oregon, *Olsen v. State* (1976); (10) Oklahoma, *Fair School Finance Council of Oklahoma, Inc. v. State* (1987); (11) Pennsylvania, *Danson v. Casey* (1979); (12) South Carolina, *Richland County v. Campbell* (1988); (13) Wisconsin, *Kukor v. Grover* (1989).

we find little, if any, light. Mechanical approaches to the delicate problem of judicial intervention under either the equal protection or the due process clauses may only divert a court from the meritorious issue or delay consideration of it. Ultimately, a court must weight the nature of the restraint or the denial against the apparent public justification, and decide whether the State action is arbitrary. In that process, if the circumstances sensibly so require, the court may call upon the State to demonstrate the existence of a sufficient public need for the restraint or the denial." (*Thompson v. Engelking*, 1975, p. 646, quoting *Robinson v. Cahill*, 1973, p. 282)

Applying rational-basis analysis, the Idaho court held that the state's use of local property taxation was rationally related to local control.

Rejection of the *Serrano* Test for Determining Fundamental Rights

During the second wave, plaintiffs also asserted that state equal protection clause challenges to school finance disparities should be subject to strict scrutiny because of the societal importance of education. This argument proved successful in *Serrano v. Priest* (*Serrano II*) (1976). In this case, the Supreme Court of California ruled that *Rodriguez* (*San Antonio Independent School District v. Rodriguez*, 1973) left intact its holding in *Serrano I* that education was a fundamental right under the state constitution because of its importance to society. The court found that *Rodriguez* was inapplicable to the state claim because California's constitutional guarantees "are possessed of an independent vitality which, in any given case, may demand an analysis different from that which would obtain if only the federal standard were applicable" (*Serrano v. Priest*, 1976, p. 950).

Nevertheless, several courts refused to follow the lead of the *Serrano* courts because of the constitutional doctrine of "separation of powers," which refers to the duties assumed by the legislative, executive, and judicial branches of government. These courts found that determining the importance of education is a matter for the legislature instead of the judiciary. For example, in *Lujan v. Colorado State Board of Education* (1982), the Supreme Court of Colorado acknowledged "unequivocally that public education plays a vital role in our free society" (p. 1017). However, the court refused to find that the importance of education made it a fundamental right under the state constitution, because

While our representative form of government and democratic society may benefit to a greater degree from a public school system in which each school district spends the exact dollar amount per student with an eye toward providing identical education for all, these are considerations and goals which properly lie within the legislative domain. Judicial intrusion to weigh such considerations and achieve such goals must be avoided. This is especially so in this case where the controversy, as we perceive it, is essentially directed toward what is the best public policy which can be adopted to attain quality schooling and equal educational opportunity for all children who attend our public schools. (*Lujan v. Colorado State Board of Education*, 1982, p. 1018)

Denial of Wealth as a Suspect Classification

Plaintiffs also failed to convince courts to apply strict scrutiny to their state equal protection clause challenges on the ground that wealth is a suspect classification. In *Lujan*, for example, the Supreme Court of Colorado refused to find that the state had discriminated against a suspect class of low-wealth school districts or low-income persons. The court found that poor school districts could not be a suspect class, because the state's equal protection clause applies only to individuals. No evidence indicated that "poor persons in Colorado are concentrated in low-property wealth districts, or that they uniformly or consistently receive a lower quality education, or that the districts in which they reside uniformly or consistently expend less money on education" (*Lujan v. Colorado State Board of Education*, 1982, p. 1020). Furthermore, the plaintiffs failed to show that the state had intentionally subjected poor persons to unequal treatment.

Acceptance of Local Control Doctrine

Instead of strict scrutiny, state courts during the second wave generally followed the lead of *Rodriguez* and applied rational basis analysis to state equal protection clause claims. As was the case in *Rodriguez*, most plaintiffs found the local control doctrine impossible to overcome. During the second wave, only the Arkansas Supreme Court held that disparities created by local property taxation were not rationally related to the purpose of maintaining local control (*DuPree v. Alma School District No. 30 of Crawford County*, 1983). In *Thompson v. Engelking* (1975), a case upholding Idaho's school finance system against a state equal protection clause challenge, the Supreme Court of Idaho captured the importance of local control in the following passage:

> Traditionally, not only in Idaho but throughout most of the states of the Union, the legislature has left the establishment, control and management of the school to the parents and taxpayers in the community which it serves. The local residents organized the school district pursuant to enabling legislation, imposed taxes upon themselves, built their own school house, elected their own trustees and through them managed their own school. It was under these circumstances that the "Little Red School House" became an American institution, the center of community life, and a pillar in the American conception of freedom in education, and in local control of institutions of local concern. In the American concept, there is no greater right to the supervision of the education of the child than that of the parent. In no other hands could it be safer. The American people made a wise choice early in their history by not only creating [a] forty-eight state system of education, but also by retaining within the community, close to parental observation, the actual direction and control of the educational program. This tradition of community administration is a firmly accepted and deeply rooted policy. (*Thompson v. Engelking*, 1975, p. 645)

Refusal to Find That Education Clauses Require Equality of Resources

During the second wave, plaintiffs asserted that inequality in educational funding violated state education clauses. Such claims most frequently involved provisions that required states to provide "general," "uniform," or "efficient" systems (Patt, 1999). These claims were unsuccessful because courts refused to find that state education clauses required equality of funding. In one representative case, *Olsen v. State* (1976), the Supreme Court of Oregon rejected the assertion that the state education clause, which requires the legislature to "provide by law for the establishment of a uniform and general system of Common schools," mandated equality of funding. Instead, the court found that the constitutional mandate would be met "if the state requires and provides for a minimum of educational opportunities in the district and permits the districts to exercise local control over what they desire, and can furnish, over the minimum" (p. 148). The court went on to find that Oregon's school-funding system satisfied this mandate.

Third Wave

In 1989, the supreme courts of Kentucky, Montana, and Texas held that their school finance systems violated their state education clauses. Numerous commentators (Anker, 1998; Enrich, 1995; Fogle, 2000) have argued that these cases represent the beginning of a third wave of school finance litigation, in which courts have invalidated school finance systems because of their failure to provide students with an adequate education in accordance with state education clauses. However, an analysis of school finance litigation reveals that plaintiffs have also mounted equity challenges to school finance disparities under state equal protection and education clause theories. A discussion of third-wave equity litigation follows.

Equal Protection

Similarly to the second wave, plaintiffs who have challenged school finance disparities under their state equal protection clauses have had to overcome the rational-basis test. The rational basis test has also proved to be a formidable barrier. Two state supreme courts have invalidated their school finance formulas on state equal protection grounds under the rational-basis test. In *Tennessee Small School Systems v. McWherter* (1993), the Supreme Court of Tennessee rejected the notion that reliance on district wealth was rationally related to the purpose of maintaining local control. First, the court observed that poor school districts do not exercise local control, because they are "limited by the economic conditions of the county in which they are located" (p. 155). Furthermore, the legislature could not use the inability or indifference of local governments to provide for their educational needs to excuse the legislature of its constitutional duty to maintain and support a public school system.

In *Brigham v. State* (1997), the Supreme Court of Vermont ruled that a twofold disparity in per-pupil expenditures between the richest and poorest districts in the state violated the state's equal protection provision. In reaching this conclusion, the court concluded that discussions as to what level of judicial scrutiny to apply was irrelevant because "[l]abels aside, we are simply unable to fathom a legitimate governmental purpose to justify the gross inequities in educational opportunities evident from the record" (p. 396). The court rejected the claim that local property taxation was rationally related to local control because "poorer districts cannot realistically choose to spend more for educational excellence than their property wealth will allow, no matter how much sacrifice their voters are willing to make" (p. 396). In another example, the Alabama Supreme Court ruled that a lower court ruling that the state's school finance system violated state and federal equal protection clause provisions was binding unless appealed (*Opinion of the Justices, 338,* 1993).

However, six state supreme courts have rejected state equal protection clause challenges under rational basis analysis.[3] In *City of Pawtucket v. Sundlun* (1995), plaintiffs claimed that Rhode Island's school finance system violated the state equal protection clause because poor school districts did not receive as well funded an education as their more affluent counterparts. The Rhode Island Supreme Court found that rational-basis analysis was appropriate because education was not a fundamental right and wealth was not a suspect classification. The court went on to find that the funding system was rationally related to the preservation of local control.

Even where courts have found that education was a fundamental right to an education under the state constitution, they have found that rational-basis analysis was still applicable to funding disparities. In *Skeen v. State* (1993), for example, the Supreme Court of Minnesota held that the state constitution created a fundamental right to a "general and uniform system of education" for the purpose of equal protection analysis. This fundamental right, however, did not extend to the funding of the educational system beyond the basis-funding requirement. Another constitutional provision required the legislature to provide taxes to "secure a thorough and efficient system." "Thus," the court noted, "a clear reading of the original constitution indicates that the drafters intended to draw a distinction between the fundamental right to a 'general and uniform system of education' and the financing of the education system, which merely must be 'thorough and efficient'" (*Skeen v. State,* p. 315). It fol-

lowed that while strict scrutiny should be applied in determining whether the state had provided a "general and uniform system of education," the rational-basis test applied "to the determination of whether the *financing* of such a system is 'thorough and efficient'" (p. 315, emphasis supplied by the court). The court found that the state had provided students with a "general and uniform system of education": the funding system provided uniform funding to each student in the state sufficient to meet all state standards. Thus, the system of education withstood strict scrutiny analysis. The state's financing of education withstood rational-basis analysis because the state had a legitimate interest in encouraging school districts to supplement the base amount of funding.

Education Clause

Plaintiffs have had limited successes challenging school finance disparities under state education clauses during the third wave. Three state supreme courts have found that disparities in school funding violate education clauses. In *Helena Elementary School District No. 1 v. State* (1989), the Supreme Court of Montana ruled that funding disparities among the state's school districts violated the state education clause, which required all students to receive equal educational opportunity. In *Edgewood Independent School District v. Kirby* (1989), the Supreme Court of Texas held that the school finance system, which generated a 700 to 1 ratio between the taxable property of richest and poorest districts and a ninefold disparity in per-pupil expenditures, violated the state education clause's requirement for an "efficient" public school system. In *Roosevelt Elementary School District No. 66 v. Bishop* (1994), the Supreme Court of Arizona ruled that the state's financing scheme violated the state education clause's requirement for a "general and uniform" public school system by causing gross disparities in school facilities. Five state courts, however, found that

---

[3]These states are as follows: (1) Illinois, *Committee for Education Rights v. Edgar* (1996); (2) Kansas, *Montoy v. State* (2005); (3) Maine, *School Administrative District No. 1 v. Commissioner* (1995); (4) Minnesota, *Skeen v. State* (1993); (5) New York, *Reform Educational Finance Inequities Today v. Cuomo* (1995); (6) Rhode Island, *City of Pawtucket v. Sundlun* (1995); and (6) Wisconsin, *Vincent v. Voight* (2000). Additionally, in *Gould v. Orr* (1993), the Nebraska Supreme Court dismissed a claim that a school-funding scheme denied plaintiffs of equal protection, equal educational opportunity, and uniform and proportionate taxation for failure to state a cause of action upon which relief could be granted. The court held in this manner because petition failed to demonstrate how unequal funding affected the quality of education received by students.

disparities between rich and poor districts did not violate state education clauses.[4] These cases were similar to second-wave education clause litigation in that the courts found that the state education clause did not mandate substantial equality between rich and poor districts.

Department of Education's Title VI Implementing Regulations

For a short time during the third wave, it appeared as though the Department of Education's (DOE) implementing regulations pursuant to Title VI of the Civil Rights Act of 1964 might provide plaintiffs with a powerful tool for mounting equity challenges to school-funding disparities (Baker & Green, 2003; Morgan, 2001). Section 601 of Title VI provides: "No person in the United States shall, on the ground of race, color, or national origin, be excluded from participation in, be denied the benefits of, or be subjected to discrimination under any program or activity receiving Federal financial assistance" (Title VI, 2007). Section 602 authorizes agencies providing financial assistance to issue "rules, regulations, or orders of general applicability which shall be consistent with achievement of the objectives of the statute authorizing the financial assistance" (Title VI, 2007). Pursuant to § 602, the DOE promulgated implementing regulations that forbid organizations that receive federal funding from adopting policies that have a disparate impact on the basis of race (*Code of Federal Regulations*, 2007).

Courts have employed burden-shifting analysis used in Title VII employment cases to analyze Title VI disparate-impact cases (Baker & Green, 2003). The plaintiff bears the initial burden of demonstrating that a facially neutral practice has had an adverse disparate impact upon a protected group. If the plaintiff meets this burden, the burden of persuasion shifts to the defendant to demonstrate that the challenged practice is justified by "educational necessity." If the defendant meets this burden, then the plaintiff must establish the existence of an equally effective alternative with less discriminatory impact, or that the justification is merely a pretext for racial discrimination. Employing this analysis, a New York trial court ruled in *Campaign for Fiscal Equity v. State* (2001) that the state's weighted per-pupil funding system had a disparate impact on New York City's minority students.

From the plaintiffs' perspective, disparate-impact litigation would be more desirable than state and federal equal protection clause challenges to school finance litigation. Under equal protection, plaintiffs could obtain heightened scrutiny for racial disparities only by proving that the disparities were the result of intentional governmental discrimination. Because of the unlikelihood of this endeavor, racial disparities are analyzed under the extremely deferential rational basis test. By contrast, under disparate-impact litigation, plaintiffs could obtain the benefits of heightened scrutiny without having to establish that the funding disparities were the result of intentional discrimination.

It now appears that plaintiffs may not be able to enforce the Title VI implementing regulations. In *Alexander v. Sandoval* (2001), the Supreme Court foreclosed Title VI as a means for plaintiffs to challenge school finance disparities by ruling that Section 602 did not create an implied private right of action to enforce Title VI implementing regulations. This was because the language in that statutory provision failed to demonstrate that Congress intended to create a private remedy. Plaintiffs have responded to *Sandoval* by trying to enforce these regulations under 42 U.S.C. § 1983, which provides:

> Every person who, under color of any statute, ordinance, regulation, custom, or usage, of any State or Territory or the District of Columbia, subjects, or causes to be subjected, any citizen of the United States or other person within the jurisdiction thereof to the deprivation of any rights, privileges, or immunities secured by the Constitution and laws, shall be liable to the party injured in an action at law, suit in equity, or other proper proceeding for redress. (42 U.S.C. § 1983, 2007)

However, in *Gonzaga University v. Doe* (2002), the Supreme Court appears to have foreclosed § 1983 as a means to enforce the Title VI implementing regulations. *Gonzaga University* addressed the question

---

[4]Those states are as follows: (1) Illinois, *Committee for Education Rights v. Edgar* (1996); (2) Minnesota, *Skeen v. State* (1993); (3) New York, *Reform Educational Finance Inequities Today v. Cuomo* (1995); (4) North Dakota, *Bismarck Public School District No. 1 v. State* (1994); (4) Oregon, *Coalition for Equitable School Funding Inc. v. State* (1991); and (5) Virginia, *Scott v. Commonwealth of Virginia* (1994).

of whether a plaintiff may bring a § 1983 action against a private university for violating the Family Educational Rights and Privacy Act of 1974 (FERPA), which prohibit recipients of federal funds from releasing educational records without parental consent. The Supreme Court found that "[a] court's role in discerning whether personal rights exist in the § 1983 context should . . . not differ from its role in discerning whether personal rights exist in the implied right of action context" (*Gonzaga*, 2002, p. 285).

Thus, the correct inquiry was whether Congress intended to create a private right to enforce the statute. The Court held that the plaintiff may not bring a § 1983 action under FERPA, because Congress failed to make clear within the statute that it was creating enforceable rights. Ryan (2002) reasons that "[g]iven that the Court held in *Sandoval* that the [Title VI implementing] regulations do not create [enforceable] rights, *Gonzaga* seems to preclude their being enforced by § 1983" (p. 1698).

SUMMARY

Plaintiffs have attempted to mount equity challenges to disparities caused by school finance formulas. According to one legal theory, school-funding disparities between rich and poor districts violate state and federal constitutional provisions. In the first wave, plaintiffs argued that school finance disparities violated the equal protection clause. The Supreme Court ended this wave in *Rodriguez* (*San Antonio Independent School District v. Rodriguez*, 1973) by finding that local property taxation was rationally related to the interest of promoting local control. Since the *Rodriguez* decision, plaintiffs have tried to resuscitate equal protection clause litigation by arguing that school finance disparities should be subject to heightened rational-basis scrutiny and by challenging school finance disparities that are the direct result of unequal state distributional policies.

In the second wave, plaintiffs asserted that disparities between rich and poor districts violated state equal protection and education clauses. During the second wave, courts rejected such claims because (a) they refused to apply strict scrutiny analysis, (b) they found that local property taxation is rationally related to the interest of promoting local control, and (c) they refused to find that education clauses require equal educational opportunity. Equity claims are still being brought, with some success, in the third wave.

Recently, it appeared as though the Department of Education's implementing regulations to Title VI might enable plaintiffs to mount equity challenges to school-funding disparities. The implementing regulations were superior to equal protection challenges because plaintiffs could obtain the benefits of heightened scrutiny without having to prove that the school finance classifications had been established with racially discriminatory intent. Recent Supreme Court case law, however, appears to have brought an end to this litigation strategy.

KEY TERMS

fundamental right   A right that is created by the Constitution. Classifications that impinge on fundamental rights are subject to strict scrutiny. Fundamental rights include interstate travel, voting, marriage, and contraception.

rational basis test   The most preferential level of scrutiny that courts use for equal protection challenges. In government actions that do not involve a fundamental right, or a suspect class, a court will upheld a law as long as it is rationally related to a legitimate interest.

strict scrutiny   The most difficult level of scrutiny for the government to overcome in equal protection and substantive due process challenges. Courts apply strict scrutiny to equal protection challenges that infringe upon a fundamental right or a suspect class. Courts apply strict scrutiny in substantive due process challenges to government actions that infringe upon a fundamental right.

suspect class   Government classification based on race or national origin. Such classifications are subject to strict scrutiny under equal protection analysis.

REFERENCES

Alexander, K., & Alexander, M. L. (2005). *American public school law* (6th ed.) Belmont, CA: Wadsworth.

Alexander v. Sandoval, 532 U.S. 275 (2001).

Anker, K. K. (1998). Differences and dialogue: School finance in New York State. *New York University Review of Law and Social Change, 24*, 345–381.

Baker, B.D., & Green, P. C. (2003). Can minority plaintiffs use the Department Of Education's implementing regulations to challenge school finance disparities? *West's Education Law Reporter, 173*, 679–696.

Baker v. Carr, 369 U.S. 186 (1962).

Bismarck Pub. Sch. Dist. No. 1 v. State, 511 N.W.2d 247 (N.D. 1994).

Board of Educ., Levittown Union Free Sch. Dist., v. Nyquist, 439 N.E.2d 359 (N.Y. 1982).

Board of Educ. of City School Dist. of City of Cincinnati v. Walter, 390 N.E.2d 813 (Ohio 1979).

Brigham v. State, 692 A.2d 384 (Vt. 1997).

Brown v. Board of Educ., 347 U.S. 483 (1954).

Burruss v. Wilkerson, 310 F. Supp. 572 (W.D. Va. 1969).

Campaign for Fiscal Equity v. State, 665 N.E.2d 661 (N.Y. 1995).

Campaign for Fiscal Equity v. State, 719 N.Y.S.2d 475 (N.Y.Sup. 2001).

City of Pawtucket v. Sundlun, 662 A.2d 40 (R.I. 1995).

Coalition for Equitable School Funding Inc. v. State, 811 P.2d 116 (Or. 1991).

Code of Federal Regulations 34 § 100.3 (2007) (Nondiscrimination Under Programs Receiving Federal Assistance through the Department of Education Effectuation of Title VI of the Civil Rights Act of 1964)

Committee for Educ. Rights v. Edgar, 672 N.E.2d 1178 (Ill. 1996).

Danson v. Casey, 399 A.2d 360 (Pa. 1979).

DuPree v. Alma Sch. Dist. No. 30 of Crawford County, 651 S.W.2d 90 (Ark. 1983).

Edgewood Indep. Sch. Dist. v. Kirby, 777 S.W.2d 391 (Tx. 1989).

Enrich, P. (1995). Leaving equality behind: New directions in school finance reform. *Vanderbilt Law Review, 48*, 101–194.

Enrich, P. (2003). Race and money, courts and schools: Tentative lessons from Connecticut. *Indiana Law Review, 36*, 523–559.

Fair Sch. Fin. Council of Oklahoma, Inc. v. State, 746 P.2d 139 (Okla. 1987).

Farrell, R. (1999). Successful rational basis claims in the Supreme Court from the 1971 term through *Romer v. Evans. Indiana Law Review, 32*, 357–416.

FCC v. Beach Communications, 508 U.S. 307 (1993).

Fogle, J. L. (2000). *Abbeville County School District v. State*: The Right to a Minimally Adequate Education in South Carolina. *South Carolina Law Review, 51*, 781–805.

Gonzaga Univ. v. Doe, 536 U.S. 273 (2002).

Gould v. Orr, 506 N.W.2d 349 (Neb. 1993).

Green, P., & Baker, B. (2002). Circumventing *Rodriguez*: Can plaintiffs use the equal protection clause to challenge school finance disparities caused by inequitable state distribution policies? *Texas Forum on Civil Liberties & Civil Rights, 7*, 141–165.

Hanushek, E. A. (1991). When school finance "reform" may not be good policy. *Harvard Journal on Legislation, 28*, 423–466.

Heise, M. (1994). State constitutions, school finance litigation, and the "third wave": From equity to adequacy. *Temple Law Review, 68*, 1151–1176.

Helena Elem. Sch. Dist. No. 1 v. State, 769 P.2d 684 (Mont. 1989).

Heller v. Doe, 509 U.S. 312 (1993).

Hornbeck v. Somerset County Bd. of Educ., 458 A.2d 758 (Md. 1983).

Horton v. Meskill, 376 A.2d 359 (Ct. 1977).

Kadrmas v. Dickinson Pub. Sch., 487 U.S. 450 (1988).

Keyes v. School Dist. No. 1, Denver, Co., 413 U.S. 189 (1973).

Kukor v. Grover, 436 N.W.2d 568 (Wis. 1989).

Lujan v. Colorado St. Bd. of Educ., 649 P.2d 1005 (Colo. 1982).

McDaniel v. Thomas, 285 S.E.2d 156 (Ga. 1982).

McInnis v. Shapiro, 293 F.Supp. 327 (N.D.Ill. 1968).

McUsic, M. (2001). The use of education clauses in school finance litigation. *Harvard Journal on Legislation, 28*, 307–340.

Milliken v. Green, 212 N.W.2d 711 (Mich. 1973).

Montoy v. State, 102 P.3d 1160 (Kan. 2005).

Morgan, D. (2001). The new school finance litigation: Acknowledging that race discrimination in public education is more than just a tort. *Northwestern University Law Review, 96*, 99–189.

Neuman, G. L. (1999). Equal protection, "general equality" and economic discrimination from a U.S. perspective. *Columbia Journal of European Law, 5*, 281–331.

Olsen v. State, 554 P.2d 139 (Or. 1976).

Palfrey, Q. A. (2002). The state judiciary's role in fulfilling *Brown*'s promise. *Michigan Journal of Race and Law, 8*, 1–61.

Papasan v. Allain, 478 U.S. 265 (1986).

Patt, J. (1999). School finance battles: Survey says? It's all just a change in attitudes. *Harvard Civil Rights-Civil Liberties Law Review, 34*, 547–575.

Plyler v. Doe, 457 U.S. 202 (1982).

Rebell, M. (2001). Educational adequacy, democracy, and the courts. In Ready, T., Edley, C., & Snow, C. (Eds.), *Achieving high educational standards for all* (pp. 218–267). Washington, DC: National Academy Press.

Reform Educ. Fin. Inequities Today v. Cuomo, 655 N.E.2d 647 (N.Y. 1995).

Reynolds v. Sims, 377 U.S. 533 (1964).

Richland County v. Campbell, 364 S.E.2d 470 (S.C. 1988).

Robinson v. Cahill, 303 A.2d 273 (N.J. 1973).

Roosevelt Elem. Sch. Dist. No. 66 v. Bishop, 877 P.2d 806 (Ariz. 1994).

Ryan, J. (2002). What role should courts play in influencing educational policy?: The limited influence of social science evidence in modern desegregation cases. *North Carolina Law Review, 81,* 1659–1702.

Ryan, J. E., & Saunders, T. (2004). Foreword to symposium on school finance litigation: Emerging trends or new dead ends? *Yale Law and Policy Review, 22,* 463–480.

San Antonio Indep. Sch. Dist. v. Rodriguez, 411 U.S. 1 (1973).

Scott v. Commonwealth of Va., 443 S.E.2d 138 (Va. 1994).

Seattle School Dist. No. 1 of King County v. State, 585 P.2d 71 (Wash. 1978).

Serrano v. Priest (Serrano I), 487 P.2d 1241 (1971).

Serrano v. Priest (Serrano II), 557 P.2d 929 (1976).

Shofstall v. Hollins, 515 P.2d 590 (Ariz. 1973).

Skeen v. State, 505 N.W.2d 299 (Minn. 1993).

Tennessee Small Sch. Sys. v. McWherter, 851 S.W.2d 139 (Tenn. 1993).

Thompson v. Engelking, 537 P.2d 635 (Idaho 1975).

Thro, W. (1994). Judicial analysis during the third wave of school finance litigation: The Massachusetts decision as a model. *Boston College Law Review, 35,* 597–616.

Title VI of the Civil Rights Act of 1964, 42 U.S.C. § 2000d (2007).

U.S. Code 42 U.S.C. § 1983 (2007).

U.S. Const. Amend. XIV, § 1.

Vincent v. Voight, 614 N.W.2d 388 (Wis. 2000).

Washakie County Sch. Dist. v. Herschler, 606 P.2d 310 (Wyo. 1980).

Wetzler, L. (2004). Buying equality: How school finance reform and desegregation came to compete in Connecticut. *Yale Law and Policy Review, 22,* 481–524.

UNDERSTANDING AND MEASURING EQUITY

Introduction

Judging the fairness of government policies for allocating funds to public education systems implies a preexisting set of ethical standards as to what constitutes *fairness*. In this chapter, we explore these issues by reviewing existing concepts and frameworks. We then propose additional frameworks of our own. We begin by discussing education policy analysis in general and using that framework as a foundation for the analysis of school-funding equity. Next, we review the most frequently referenced tools and concepts in the field of school finance developed by Robert Berne and Leanna Stiefel in 1984 in their seminal work, *The Measurement of Equity in School Finance*. We then explain how the ecological context of school finance systems influences policy options via the cultural and political context, the resources on which they draw, and features of the broader economic system that produces those resources. We demonstrate the advantages of taking a dynamic rather than static perspective by progressive convergence toward equity objectives while maintaining system stability.

Conceptual Framework for Policy Analysis

Public education policies have evolved over time to involve a delicate balance of local, state, and federal laws and regulations regarding education programs and education funding. States have become increasingly dominant since the 1970s in their governance of educational programs and control over the allocation of revenues, wresting back state authority previously devolved to local districts since colonial times. This section focuses primarily on the evolving nature of the relationship between state policies and local school districts. One can extend similar concepts to the relationship between federal policies and states or the relationship between local districts and schools within districts. Currently, however, the central policy tension in most states is between local school districts and their state governance and finance mechanisms.

Table 5.1 displays a conceptual framework for understanding and evaluating state policies and their relationship to local districts. State legislators draft, deliberate over, and ultimately approve the various written policies that govern everything from school accountability systems, to teacher credentials, to the specific formulas for the allocation of state funds to local school districts. You can find most of these written policies in either their original drafted forms or in digested forms on state legislative and/or state department of education Websites.

An important distinction in Table 5.1 exists between state words and state deeds. State policy processes are the actions of the state in carrying out written policies. Such actions include how funds are actually allocated across local districts and schools and how policies (or which policies) are strictly (or loosely) governed by state agencies.

Baker (2001), for example, conducted a study of how states allocate additional funds to local districts to help support programs for at-risk, gifted, and limited-English-proficient (LEP) students. Using census data to predict expected need (numbers of children who speak English "not well"), Baker found that while written policies in the state of Kansas imply that districts receive an additional 20% per LEP child (which would equal approximately $720 in 1993), in reality, Kansas districts typically received (in 1993) approximately $1 of state aid per expected LEP student (Baker, 2001). Several recent studies dissecting aid allocations for special populations have found similar issues across states (Baker, 2001). More extensive discussion on this topic occurs in Chapter 10.

State policy processes lead to state policy outcomes, which ultimately contribute to local district inputs. State policy outcomes may be assessed either at the macro or micro level. The macro level involves the collective response of school districts, and analyzing the macro level response involves looking for patterns across all schools or districts in a state. For example, one might ask whether a state funding system in general provides for greater *equal opportunity* across school districts. The micro-level response, or unit response, focuses on single schools and seeks answers to parallel questions such as whether the resources available to a given school under given circumstances are equal to those available to similar schools for providing suitable education programs. Another policy approach focuses on the adequacy of the resources available. Some states may be highly equal in per-pupil expenditures, but the level of funding is too low to provide for an adequate education. Again, this analysis might compare resources at the district level or compare similar schools with similar needs, exploring both vertical and horizontal equity questions.

Finally, we must also evaluate the products and outcomes of school and district responses to state poli-cies. What do the students, and ultimately society, gain from our efforts, and are those gains equitably distributed? Some questions we might seek answers for are: Are graduates literate and numerate? Are they prepared for citizenship in a highly complex and interdependent world? Do schools increase earnings potential, and do they do so in an equitable manner? Beyond student achievement scores and postsecondary earnings and other indices of economic growth, measuring the outcomes of our educational system can be quite difficult; less easily measured outcomes, however, are not necessarily less important.

Ex Ante Versus *Ex Poste* Analysis

Ex ante and ex poste analyses are approaches to policy analysis that relate directly to the policy framework presented in Table 5.1. **Ex ante analysis** involves the study of policy inputs, such as review and evaluation of state policy documentation. Such documentation can be highly informative regarding the intent and design of state policies for accomplishing specific objectives. For example, in Chapter 6 we discuss extensively state policies designed to create more equitable revenues across school districts of varied local fiscal capacity. These formulas may be described as equations or presented in tables of district-level allocations by state departments of education so that district officials, policy makers, or policy analysts may better understand the state policies. Ex ante analyses may involve making judgments as to whether the described formula "makes

Table 5.1   Conventional Framework for Policy Analysis

Elements	Examples of Various Research Concerns
1. State Policy Inputs Written policies	• Regulatory policies—statutes and departmental regulations regarding identification and services • Funding policies—Written allocation formulas
2. State Policy Processes Application of state policies	• Distribution of actual state resources • Oversight practices regarding mandates and regulations
3. State Policy Outcomes *District and School Inputs* District implementation response to state policies	• Collective (all schools/districts) response—How response of all lower units generates a pattern of distribution of opportunities • Unit (school/district) response—Types of opportunities offered by individual units
4. District and School Products	• Individual benefit—Benefits of individuals receiving services from a school or district that has responded to state policy in a certain way
5. Outcomes	• Societal benefit

sense," given what we know about school-funding policies and student needs and/or whether the state support prescribed in the policy appears sufficient.

Ex poste analysis involves evaluating state-policy outcomes, most commonly in macro, or distributional terms. Typically, ex poste analysis involves statistical evaluation of the patterns and levels of opportunities and resources available to students across districts as a result of existing state policy inputs. For example, when a state applies a policy of allocating additional aid to help poor districts "catch up," one might analyze the effectiveness of that policy by measuring the extent to which poor district revenues compare with rich district revenues over time. Combining ex ante and ex poste methods may reveal important inconsistencies in state policy inputs and outcomes, revealing unintended and unexpected consequences of certain policy designs or applications and at times revealing subversive political agendas.

Framework and Methods for Evaluating Equity

This section begins with a conceptual overview of Berne and Stiefel's (1984) seminal work on the measurement of equity in school finance. Their work has formed the basis of much expert witness testimony in court litigation around school finance equity. It is also widely used by state departments of education and legislatures to monitor their own educational finance systems.

School Finance Equity Framework

In 1984, Robert Berne and Leanna Stiefel presented the field of school finance with a new framework for understanding and measuring equity. Their framework centered around four key questions:

1. *Who?* What is the makeup of the groups for which school finance systems should be equitable?

2. *What?* What services, resources, or, more generally, objects should we distribute fairly among members of the groups?

3. *How?* What principles should we use to determine whether a particular distribution is equitable?

4. *How much?* What quantitative measures should we use to assess the degree of equity? (Berne & Stiefel, 1984, p. 7)

Next, we examine each of these questions in greater detail.

Who?

The first critical issue in evaluating the fairness of a school finance system is the question of "fair to whom?" Pupils have generally been the center of attention when the question of "who?" is involved. School-funding policies, however, affect other constituents as well, including, for example, taxpayers who provide the revenue for the public good and teachers (and all other employees) who benefit from employment in schools. A state legislative action to raise more revenues and spend more on schools may provide the greatest benefit to teachers, who may receive higher salaries as a result but not to students, because despite higher salaries, teaching practices might remain unchanged. The decision by the legislature to spend more on education also necessarily affects taxpayers and may affect taxpayers differently across communities. Further, parents are a subset of taxpayers who receive different benefits from the public education system than nonparent taxpayers or parents who elect to send their children to private schools. For the latter, one might argue they are paying twice for their children's education.

What?

Identifying "what?" or the object of interest is also important in understanding and measuring equity. That is, what should be available to the constituents in question? Should we focus on efficient, noncumbersome processes for appraising the taxable property wealth of local citizens, or should we focus on equal distribution of fiscal inputs to students? Table 5.2 presents examples of various objects that might be of interest to students, taxpayers, or teachers. Focusing on students, inputs of interest might range from actual dollars allocated to the education of a child, to dollars adjusted for differing prices of educational goods or services across communities, to sizes of classrooms and/or numbers and qualifications of available teachers. Educational processes might include the type and level of curriculum taught and/or the teaching methods applied in the classroom, and educational outputs might include student test scores, including performance on statewide assessments. Student outcomes might include the extent to which students ultimately succeed in the labor force or life in general.

Table 5.2   Identifying Objects of Interest

What/Who	Students	Taxpayers	Teachers
Inputs	Dollars Physical resources Teachers (pupil to teacher ratios, teacher qualifications)	Tax rates, effort, burden	Salaries
Processes (and throughputs)	Curricular opportunities	Appraisal process/appeals	Working conditions
Outputs	Achievement Educational attainment	Direct benefits of public good	Positive academic culture
Outcomes	Earnings/income Satisfaction	Changes in social welfare resulting from tax policy Economic effects of tax policy or education quality	Higher average salaries

Obviously, a substantial time commitment is involved in understanding the extent to which specific school-funding policies influence student outcomes that may take as long as 20 years to be measurable. While policy makers must pay attention to such effects, they cannot always wait years to evaluate the efficacy of policy decisions. As such, policy makers often rely on the premise that educational achievement and attainment are strong predictors of earnings and/or career satisfaction and focus their efforts on the measurement of output rather than outcome differences across students. Output measurement, such as measuring student achievement across specific content areas, is not without problems. For example, it is often extremely difficult to fully understand the plethora of student background and environmental factors that intervene in the relationship between the educational inputs available to students and the outputs produced. We will discuss the economic modeling of this educational production function in more detail in Chapter 11.

The measurement of educational processes such as the delivery of specific content knowledge or the method by which that content is delivered can also be quite difficult. In recent years, federal efforts have been made to increase data availability on teaching practices. The Third International Math and Science Study (TIMSS) conducted by the National Center for Education Statistics (NCES) includes detailed information on student time spent on specific content and activities related to that content as well as videos of teacher practices. It is difficult to conceive, however, how one would present an unbiased evaluation of the equity of content delivery across classrooms, schools, or districts with such information. As such, equity analysis has typically focused on the distribution of fiscal and other resources, or inputs, to students. Speakman and others (1996) delineated between pure fiscal inputs, and resources purchased with those inputs, referring to the purchased resources as "throughputs." Schooling throughputs might include organization features of the school or district, measures of teacher qualifications, or time allocated to specific content.

How?
Equal Opportunity
A series of frameworks for addressing how to measure and understand school equity issues began to emerge in the late 1960s, in the wake of the Civil Rights Movement and the Coleman report (1966). Table 5.3 presents the continuation of Berne and Stiefel's (1984) framework. Legal theorists began to postulate how they might construct challenges to the fairness of school-funding formulas, or identify school-funding formulas as discriminatory policies warranting state or federal court intervention. Two views of equal opportunity emerged at this time:

1. The principle of geographic uniformity (Horowitz, 1966)
2. The theory of fiscal neutrality (Coons, Clune, & Sugarman, 1969)

Geographic uniformity meant that the quality of a child's education, or the quantity of objects received by the child, should not vary simply on the basis of

Table 5.3 Conceptions of Equity

Questions Related to Conceptions of Equity	Alternative for Each Question	Defined as Follows
How? What is the principle to be used to determine fair distribution?	Horizontal equity	Equal treatment of equals
	Vertical equity	Unequal treatment of unequals
	Neutrality/equal opportunity	Lack of relationship between opportunities/objects and unrelated student/district measures
	Effectiveness	Ability to produce student outcomes efficiently Marginal productivity of student?

where that child lived. The principle of **fiscal neutrality** was somewhat less restrictive in that it dictated that the quality of education, or quantity of objects (usually fiscal inputs), received by a child should not be associated with the fiscal capacity (usually property wealth) of the school district in which the child resides. In other words, fiscal neutrality was a lack of relationship between the quality and quantity of schooling available, and the wealth and/or income levels of taxing jurisdictions raising local resources for public schooling. Fiscal neutrality usually was measured as the relationship between taxable property wealth and per-pupil spending across public school districts within a state, where a fiscally neutral system would show no statistical relationship between the two measures. These early theories are consistent with Berne and Stiefel's (1984) later discussions of *equal opportunity*, or that "there should not be differences (in availability of objects) according to characteristics that are considered illegitimate, such as property wealth per pupil, household income, and per-pupil wealth or fiscal capacity" (p. 17).

A neutral system is not necessarily uniform, but a uniform system is necessarily neutral. That is, a uniform system is a system where all constituents have access to exactly the same set of objects. A neutral system is a system where the availability of objects is not associated with objectionable external criteria, such as community wealth. Neutrality does not exclude the possibility of variance.

How Much?
Horizontal and Vertical Equity
Equity concepts, including the horizontal and vertical components presented in Table 5.3, consider only the distribution of the objects in question to the constituents in question, without considering factors such as property wealth or geography.

Horizontal equity is often defined as the equal treatment of equals, in terms of educational inputs provided. *Treatment* refers to the distribution of the object in question, and *equals* refers to a set of constituents with comparable educational needs or under comparable educational circumstances. If, for example, we presume the general population of students in a state to have a uniform set of educational needs, then it should be appropriate to provide those students with the same level of fiscal inputs to their education, or the fiscal inputs required to purchase the same level of educational resources if resource prices vary. This concept applies whether we are considering a uniform group of "regular education" students or uniform group of students with a specific disability.

Vertical equity, superficially, is also a relatively intuitive concept. **Vertical equity** is the differential treatment of individuals or groups of students with identifiably and measurably different educational needs. Not all students are equals. Students have vastly different needs for educational and support service in order to fully participate in educational programs. Meeting these needs often requires additional resources. A component of the equity framework therefore must accept that some "unequal" students should have access to "unequal" levels of resources. While vertical equity provides such a conceptual framework, until recently, little strong empirical evidence suggests just "how much" is needed in terms of supplemental resources, to create vertical equity for students with specific educational needs (Baker, 2005).

The gap between the concept of vertical equity and its measurement remains considerable. Vertical equity is, however, a concept fraught with dilemmas. For example, does giving a special education student a higher per-pupil allocation mean that a gifted student should be given less, because he or she might be able to learn an adequate level of reading or math with fewer resources? Or if we use marginal productivity as the measure, perhaps the gifted student should receive a higher allocation, because his or her net contribution to society will be higher, for example, accomplishing more, paying higher taxes.

Alternative frameworks for analyzing the supplemental or marginal costs of providing comparable services to special needs pupils yield conflicting results. One central unresolved issue is what constitutes comparable opportunities for students of differing educational needs. Some have suggested that comparable opportunities may be measured by student outcomes. For example, one might estimate the cost of providing opportunities such that each child may achieve a state's minimum-competency standards. This approach, however, implies that students exceeding minimum standards at a given point in time have negative marginal costs and total educational costs that may approach $0. The alternative is to suggest that each child should have the opportunity to achieve comparable gains from participation in the public education system. Under this model, students both behind and ahead of the curve, so-to-speak, would require material and/or human resources to supplement the general education program. As we discuss more extensively in Chapter 8, the alternative is also not without conceptual dilemmas.

Alternative Views

Julie Underwood (1995) argues that vertical equity is a form of educational *adequacy*. That is, the cost of an adequate instructional program is differentiable by student need, and the result of differentiated adequacy is vertical equity. We discuss this premise in much greater detail in Chapter 8. Unfortunately, Underwood's conception does little to resolve our previously mentioned dilemmas. Underwood's conception merely shifts emphasis from (a) an illusive goal of identifying how to make one child's education comparable/equitable to that received by a different child with different needs to (b) an emphasis on separately identifying adequacy for each child and therefore differentiation for each child, given specific individual needs.

Imber (1990) constructs a typology of discrimination that provides some parallels to Berne and Stiefel's (1984) equity framework. Michael Imber (1990) discusses *passive* and *active* discrimination, where active discrimination is the differential treatment of individuals on bases not directly associated with educational need. For example, active discrimination might include providing different services to children on the basis of race or different levels of service quality on the basis of local property wealth. Active discrimination is a violation of the principles of horizontal equity and equal opportunity that Berne and Stiefel describe.

Passive discrimination is the failure to treat individuals with measurably different educational needs differently (Imber, 1990). Placement of a learning disabled student in a regular education classroom without supplemental support constitutes passive discrimination. As such, passive discrimination is a violation of vertical equity. In one simple sense, Imber's conception is more easily operationalized. Providing the *same* services to a child with different needs is simply insufficient for at least one of the two children in question.

Other ethical complications exist: How should we treat two students of equal circumstances and abilities, one who works diligently to learn, the other who puts in minimal effort? Under some models, we would ignore the high-effort student and turn even more attention to the low-effort student (the compensatory model). As one can see from the current discussion, given a zero-sum system, who gains and who loses provokes considerable ethical tension. One mechanism for surfacing these tensions is with the following simulation:

> Assume you had 100,000 dollars to divide among 10 students. Further assume that 2 of these students were 2 years below grade level (special ed), 2 were 2 years above grade level (gifted), and the remaining six were average. Now let us add one complication. Half of each group of students consisted of highly motivated and hard-working students; however, the other 50% were very unmotivated and putting very little effort into their work. How would you divide up the resources among these 10 children?

Measuring Equity

In this section, we explore specific measures of school-funding equity. We focus predominantly on the measurement of horizontal equity and fiscal neutrality, because these have been the most applied and are the least problematic areas of equity analysis. We discuss

Table 5.4   Measurement of Equity

Questions Related to Conceptions of Equity	Alternative for Each Question	Defined as Follows
How much? What summary statistics are used to assess the degree of equity?	Dispersion statistics (horizontal equity)	Range and federal range ratio Standard deviation Coefficient of variation Gini coefficient
	Relationship statistics (fiscal neutrality)	Elasticity and slope correlation

the measurement of vertical equity in this section but offer few viable statistical solutions. We also present a new set of ecological and dynamic indicators.

Table 5.4 continues Berne and Stiefel's (1984) equity framework. The measurement of horizontal equity generally involves measures of the ranges and distribution of available resources across constituents. Again, the most common application is to measure the distribution of fiscal inputs to schooling across pupils. The measurement of fiscal neutrality generally involves relationship measures, such as correlations, between available objects and local fiscal capacity measures such as assessed property valuation per pupil.

Units of Analysis

An important prerequisite to performing equity analyses is an understanding of alternative units of analysis. Typically, state school finance data are available by district, or perhaps by school. Often, however, the goal is to estimate the distribution of objects not to the school or district but to the pupil. Consider the four districts in Table 5.5, where district A is a very small district with very high per-pupil revenues, and district D is a larger district with much lower revenues per pupil. We have two options for calculating the average per-pupil revenue. First, we can simply add the per-pupil revenues to a sum of $28,000 and divide them by 4 (number of districts) to get an average of $7,000 per pupil. This approach is called a *district unit of analysis* approach. Where pupils are concerned, however, reporting that the average per-pupil revenue is $7,000 seems somewhat inappropriate when 1,500 pupils receive less than $7,000 and only 110 receive more.

An alternative is to calculate the pupil-weighted mean, or use the pupil unit of analysis. To do so, we multiply the pupils times their revenue and sum the total revenue in the school-funding system across the four districts. That is, 10 pupils had $10,000, giving us $100,000, 100 pupils had $8,000, giving us another $800,000, and so on. We then divide the total dollars in the system by the total number of students for an average of $4,907, a much more reasonable estimate of the distribution of resources to students. Note that this type of calculation can be set up manually in a spreadsheet, or calculated in some statistical programs by using pupil counts as *frequency weights*.[1]

In the following sections, and in the Microsoft Excel template (Chapter5.xls) that accompanies this chapter on the Companion Website (www.prenhall.com/baker), we calculate several indices by both district and pupil unit of analysis. Often, differences in findings resulting from alternative units can be revealing regarding availability of opportunities in smaller versus larger districts in a state. At a later point in this text, we discuss pupil weights and weighted pupils in relation to the concept of vertical equity. It is important to understand the difference between the weighted analyses performed here and the concept of applying a weight, or creating a weighted pupil, for allocating additional funds to students, schools, or districts with additional resource needs.

---

[1]For those students who are more statistically advanced, it is important to understand that frequency weighting assumes that all students in a given district receive precisely the average resources per pupil available in that district. There is assumed to be no variance at all in within district resources. As such, use of frequency weights often overstates statistical significance in differences between group averages. A better weighting approach is to use what are called *analytical weights* in some software, including STATA (www.stata.com). Analytical weighting assumes district aggregate per-pupil expenditure (or whatever is being measured) values to represent means, with normally distributed variance, and treats the district, rather than the student, as the primary sampling unit in the analysis.

Table 5.5   Comparison of Direct and Pupil-Weighted Mean

District	Pupils	Per-Pupil Revenue	Pupils × Revenue (total revenue)
A	10	$10,000	$100,000
B	100	$8,000	$800,000
C	500	$6,000	$3,000,000
D	1,000	$4,000	$4,000,000
Sum	1,610	$28,000	$7,900,000
Average District		$7,000	
Average Pupil			$4,907

Horizontal Equity Tools

Each of the following examples draws from the Microsoft Excel template (Chapter5.xls) that accompanies this chapter on the Companion Website (www.prenhall.com/baker). Table 5.6 presents a sample of 20 school districts from the state of Missouri in 2003. Welcome to middle America. Data included in the table are the enrollments of each district, ranging from only 277 pupils to over 40,000 pupils, the assessed property value per pupil, the income per pupil (district aggregate income based on state tax returns divided by enrolled pupils), the property tax rate, the local revenue per pupil resulting from applying the local tax rate to local assessed valuation per pupil, the state aid

Table 5.6   20-District Sample of School Finance Data in Missouri (2003)

Name	Number	Enrollment	Assessed Value per Pupil	Median Household Income	General Levy ($/100)	Local Revenue per Pupil	State Revenue per Pupil
Festus R-VI	50,006	2,672	$56,179	$40,964	$2.87	$1,612	$2,505
Hillsboro R-III	50,003	3,592	$44,725	$48,548	$2.94	$1,315	$2,881
Ozark R-VI	22,093	3,925	$50,363	$40,352	$2.75	$1,385	$2,878
Sedalia 200	80,125	4,191	$60,485	$31,267	$2.75	$1,663	$2,638
Branson R-IV	106,004	3,143	$145,745	$32,098	$2.31	$3,367	$945
Bolivar R-I	84,001	2,350	$45,392	$29,257	$2.75	$1,248	$3,148
Waynesville R-VI	85,046	5,147	$21,799	$36,724	$2.70	$589	$3,822
Hannibal 60	64,075	3,645	$53,855	$31,962	$2.86	$1,540	$2,945
Jefferson City	26,006	8,263	$105,067	$41,924	$3.23	$3,394	$1,688
Raymore-Peculiar R-II	19,142	4,627	$57,663	$56,198	$3.14	$1,811	$3,302
Warrensburg R-VI	51,159	3,167	$58,619	$32,477	$3.70	$2,169	$3,135
Mehlville R-IX	96,094	11,799	$108,448	$53,741	$3.01	$3,264	$2,073
Cooter R-IV	78,004	277	$19,918	$31,094	$2.75	$548	$4,861
Lee's Summit R-VII	48,071	14,861	$70,601	$59,944	$4.37	$3,085	$2,866
Columbia 93	10,093	16,076	$83,170	$36,516	$3.93	$3,269	$3,122
Ferguson-Florissant R-II	96,089	11,949	$75,200	$40,500	$4.74	$3,564	$3,575
St. Louis City	115,115	42,654	$73,398	$27,156	$3.73	$2,738	$4,911
Kansas City 33	48,078	33,642	$75,186	$29,634	$4.95	$3,722	$4,360
Wellston	96,115	747	$24,686	$21,458	$5.10	$1,259	$7,094
Ladue	96,106	3,272	$336,855	$82,889	$2.63	$8,859	$1,966

Source: Data from Missouri Department of Elementary and Secondary Education. Retrieved June 1, 2005, from http://www.dese.mo.gov/schooldata/ftpdata.html

per pupil allocated by the state funding formula and the total revenue per pupil, which combines local with state revenue. The districts are in no particular rank order.

Table 5.7 displays selected horizontal equity statistics for the districts in Table 5.6, using both district and pupil units of analysis. For example, we find that the mean property value per pupil using district unit of analysis is approximately $78,368, whereas the mean property value per pupil using pupil unit of analysis is $79,481. This tells us that in general, the larger districts in the sample have slightly higher property wealth per pupil, or that more pupils are in districts with slightly higher property wealth per pupil. In contrast, weighting the analysis by pupils decreases the mean income per pupil, suggesting that districts enrolling more pupils tend to have lower income. We created this effect by our choice to include the state's two very large, poor urban districts: Kansas City and St. Louis.

Several other equity statistics are presented in the table, including:

1. Range = High − Low
2. Range Ratio = (High − Low)/Low
3. Federal Range Ratio (FRR) = (95th percentile − 5th percentile)/5th percentile
4. Coefficient of Variation (CV) = Standard Deviation/Mean

Each dispersion measure characterizes the differences in available resources across students or districts in a state and can be calculated using either district or pupil units of analysis. However, we include only pupil unit analyses for coefficients of variation in the table. Range statistics simply compare differences between high and low values, such as high and low local revenues per pupil. Range statistics remain the same whether we use district or pupil units.

Ratios are useful for standardizing the scale of equity indicators. For example, Table 5.8 presents a comparison of two states, where State A has a high-spending district with $8,000 per pupil and a low-spending district with $6,000 per pupil, and State B has a high-spending district with $4,000 per pupil and a low-spending district with $3,000 per pupil. Using range to compare only equity across the two states, we conclude that State A is less equitable than state B. However, if we calculate the disparity (range) as a percentage of the minimum, we find that the disparity is 33% for both states. Just as ratios allow comparisons across states with varied levels of resources, ratios can also allow comparison of conditions in a given state over time, where inflation has changed the overall level of resources. Often, ranges of expenditures will grow over time, while range ratios will decline due to increases in average or base levels of spending.

It may be useful and more representative to restrict the range for analysis, or remove extreme dis-

Table 5.7   Selected Horizontal Equity Statistics

Unit = District	Enrollment	Assessed Valuation per Pupil	Income per Pupil	Property Tax Rate	Local Revenue per Pupil	State Aid per Pupil
Mean	8,999.95	$78,368	$40,235	3.36	$2,520	$3,236
Standard deviation	11,030.33	$67,992	$14,252	0.84	$1,812	$1,339
Range	42,377.00	$316,937	$61,431	2.79	$8,312	$6,149
Range Ratio	152.99	15.91	2.86	1.21	15.17	6.51
Federal range ratio	46.12	6.16	1.27	0.9	5.78	2.04
Coefficient of variation	1.23	0.87	0.35	0.25	0.72	0.41

Unit = Pupil	Enrollment	Assessed Valuation per Pupil	Income per Pupil	Property Tax Rate	Local Revenue per Pupil	State Aid per Pupil
Mean		$79,481	$37,804	3.84	$2,991	$3,603
Standard deviation		$40,094	$12,289	0.79	$1,133	$1,098
Coefficient of variation		0.5	0.33	0.2	0.38	0.3

Source: Calculation based on data in Table 5.6.

Table 5.8 Summary of Equity Statistics for Two Hypothetical States

	State A	State B
High	$8,000	$4,000
Low	$6,000	$3,000
Range	$2,000	$1,000
Range ratio	33%	33%
Mean	$7,000	$3,500
Standard deviation	$500	$250
Coefficient of variation	7.1%	7.1%

tricts at each end of the distribution. For example, notice that the property wealth per pupil in Ladue is $336,855 compared to an average of $78,368 (district unit). A common approach to restricting the range is to identify the 95th percentile and 5th percentile districts, removing 5% of the districts (district unit), or districts enrolling 5% of the pupils (pupil unit) at each end of the distribution and recalculating the range. The federal range ratio (FRR) is simply a range ratio where the top and bottom 5% have been removed. Note that the variance in assessed valuation per pupil is cut nearly in half (from 5.9 to 3.0) when restrict range analysis is applied.

The coefficient of variation is perhaps the most commonly applied measure of school finance equity. It, too, is a ratio, allowing comparisons across data of differing scale. The coefficient of variation is based on the standard deviation of the distribution of the object around the mean level of the object in question. Again, consider states A and B in Table 5.8, where the mean expenditures per pupil of State A are $7,000 and State B are $3,500 and the standard deviations are $500 and $250, respectively. Assuming a normal distribution (which is rarely if ever the case with school finance data), we can expect that approximately two thirds of the districts in either state fall within 1 standard deviation of the mean. That is, in state A, two thirds of districts spend between $6,500 and $7,500 and in state B, two thirds of districts spend between $3,250 and $3,750 per pupil. As with the range statistics, it initially appears as if state B provides greater equity. But again, as with the range statistics, when the standard deviation is divided by the mean to construct a coefficient of variation, we see that the equity across the two states is the same. That is, in each case two thirds of districts (or two thirds of pupils) fall within 7.1% of mean spending levels.

Two additional and somewhat more complex indices of horizontal equity are the McLoone index and the Gini coefficient. The McLoone index is unique to school finance and differs from other school finance equity indices in that it focuses on the distribution of resources only in the lower half of districts. Some consider the McLoone index to be an index of adequacy rather than equity. The McLoone index is calculated by first determining the position of the median pupil with respect to the object in question, usually fiscal resources. Next, the mean level of the object is calculated for all pupils below the median. Finally, the mean of the lower 50% of pupils is divided by the median for all pupils.

$$\text{McLoone Index} = \text{Mean of Lower 50\% / Median of All}$$

The closer the value is to 1.0, or the closer the lower 50% pupils are to the median pupil, the more equitable the school-funding system. Table 5.9 displays the spreadsheet calculation of the McLoone index for a 20-district sample. First, the districts are sorted from lowest to highest total revenue per pupil (or whatever the object of interest may be). Next, a cumulative pupil count is constructed to identify the district containing the median pupil. Because the 20 districts together have about 180,000 total pupils, the median pupil is the 90,000th (89,999.5th) pupil, who attends the Ferguson-Florissant school district (see Table 5.9). The revenue per pupil of Ferguson-Florissant is $7,139. Next we determine the pupil-weighted mean revenue for all districts with less than $7,139, including the portion of Ferguson-Florissant included in the lower half of the distribution (2,264.5 students). The pupil-weighted mean for the lower half comes out to $5,311. The McLoone index is $5,311/$7,139, or 0.74.

The Gini coefficient is a measure that analysts most often use for the study of income inequality. The Gini coefficient presumes a condition of perfect equity where each 1% of the individuals receive 1% of the objects. That is, graphically, with individuals along the x axis and objects along the y, the first 1% of individuals have 1% of the objects available to them, the first 2% of individuals have 2% of the objects available to them, and so on, creating a 45-degree line. If objects are unevenly distributed, however, the line will not be straight. If we sort the individuals by the number of objects they have, from low to high, we might find that the first 1% of individuals have only .5% of the total objects and that the first 2% of individuals have

Table 5.9 Spreadsheet Determination of McLoone Index (Unit = Pupil)

District	Pupils	Total Revenue per Pupil	Cumulative Pupil Count	McLoone Pupils	Median District Test	Median District Revenue	McLoone Revenue
Festus R-VI	2,672	$4,118	2,672	2,672	0	0	$11,002,081
Hillsboro R-III	3,592	$4,196	6,264	3,592	0	0	$15,072,397
Ozark R-VI	3,925	$4,263	10,189	3,925	0	0	$16,732,090
Sedalia 200	4,191	$4,301	14,380	4,191	0	0	$18,026,633
Branson R-IV	3,143	$4,312	17,523	3,143	0	0	$13,551,826
Bolivar R-I	2,350	$4,397	19,873	2,350	0	0	$10,332,154
Waynesville R-VI	5,147	$4,411	25,020	5,147	0	0	$22,703,032
Hannibal 60	3,645	$4,485	28,665	3,645	0	0	$16,347,533
Jefferson City	8,263	$5,082	36,928	8,263	0	0	$41,990,389
Raymore-Peculiar R-II	4,627	$5,113	41,555	4,627	0	0	$23,657,342
Warrensburg R-VI	3,167	$5,304	44,722	3,167	0	0	$16,798,888
Mehlville R-IX	11,799	$5,337	56,521	11,799	0	0	$62,976,106
Cooter R-IV	277	$5,408	56,798	277	0	0	$1,498,150.4
Lee's Summit R-VII	14,861	$5,952	71,659	14,861	0	0	$88,445,525
Columbia 93	16,076	$6,390	87,735	16,076	0	0	$102,731,609
Ferguson-Florissant R-II	11,949	$7,139	99,684	2,264.5	1	$7,139.0944	$16,166,479
St. Louis City	42,654	$7,649	142,338	0	0	0	0
Kansas City 33	33,642	$8,082	175,980	0	0	0	0
Wellston	747	$8,353	176,727	0	0	0	0
Ladue	3,272	$10,826	179,999	0	0	0	0
Median pupil	89,999.5						
Mean McLoone revenue	$5,311						
Median district revenue	$7,139						

Source: Calculations based on data in Table 5.6.

only the first 1% of objects. This line sags below the desired 45-degree line. Ultimately, 100% of the object must be consumed by 100% of the individuals, so the actual distribution must curve back to meet with the 45-degree line. The extent of "sag" (area between the curve and the 45-degree line), as seen in Figure 5.1, indicates the extent of inequity. The coefficient itself is the ratio of the area between the curve and the line to the total area under the 45-degree line. As such, a Gini coefficient where the area between the curve and the line approaches "0," thus the coefficient approaches "0," indicates perfect equity.

Figure 5.1 Lorenz Curve and Calculation of Gini Coefficient

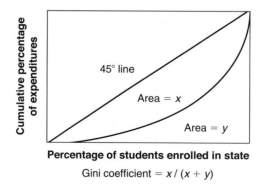

Gini coefficient = $x / (x + y)$

Table 5.10 Gini Coefficient Weighted by Property Wealth

District	Enrollment	Property Value per Pupil	Total Revenue per Pupil	E × TRPP	Cumulative % of Enrollment
Cooter R-IV	277	$19,918	$5,408	1,498,150	0.15%
Waynesville R-VI	5,147	$21,799	$4,411	22,703,032	3.01%
Wellston	747	$24,686	$8,353	6,239,839	3.43%
Hillsboro R-III	3,592	$44,725	$4,196	15,072,397	5.42%
Bolivar R-I	2,350	$45,392	$4,397	10,332,154	6.73%
Ozark R-VI	3,925	$50,363	$4,263	16,732,090	8.91%
Hannibal 60	3,645	$53,855	$4,485	16,347,533	10.94%
Festus R-VI	2,672	$56,179	$4,118	11,002,081	12.42%
Raymore-Peculiar R-II	4,627	$57,663	$5,113	23,657,342	14.99%
Warrensburg R-VI	3,167	$58,619	$5,304	16,798,888	16.75%
Sedalia 200	4,191	$60,485	$4,301	18,026,633	19.08%
Lee's Summit R-VII	14,861	$70,601	$5,952	88,445,525	27.33%
St. Louis City	42,654	$73,398	$7,649	3.26E + 08	51.03%
Kansas City 33	33,642	$75,186	$8,082	2.72E + 08	69.72%
Ferguson-Florissant R-II	11,949	$75,200	$7,139	85,305,039	76.36%
Columbia 93	16,076	$83,170	$6,390	1.03E + 08	85.29%
Jefferson City	8,263	$105,067	$5,082	41,990,389	89.88%
Mehlville R-IX	11,799	$108,448	$5,337	62,976,106	96.44%
Branson R-IV	3,143	$145,745	$4,312	13,551,826	98.18%
Ladue	3,272	$336,855	$10,826	35,421,478	100.00%

E × TRPP, enrollment times total revenue per pupil.
Source: Calculations based on data in Table 5.6.

An alternate approach is to sort the individuals not by how much of the object they have but by some other measure of their wealth, creating a hybrid measure of fiscal neutrality as well as equity. Table 5.10 displays the calculation of a Gini coefficient (as performed in the template accompanying this chapter on the Companion Website, www.prenhall.com/baker) where pupils are sorted by property wealth. The Gini coefficient is calculated for local revenue per pupil. Notice that the first 9% of the pupils receive just over 5% of the object, and the first 51% of the pupils receive only the first 37% of the object. The Gini coefficient for this distribution is .203, indicating that property-wealth related disparity in local revenues per pupil exists.

Equal Opportunity and Fiscal Neutrality Tools

Recall from Table 5.4 that measures of fiscal neutrality and equal opportunity are measures of relationship, such as correlations. Also, fiscal neutrality measures combine measures both internal and external to the school-funding system. That is, neutrality and equal opportunity measures seek to evaluate the statistical relationship

between features internal to the school-funding system, such as the distribution of per pupil revenues, and features external to the school-funding system, such as the wealth, geographic location, or demographic composition of the school district. Under ideal conditions, these internal and external features should not be associated with the distribution of the object.

Three methods that we use to assess fiscal neutrality throughout this text are simple correlations, linear trend-line (regression) analysis, and elasticities. Figure 5.2 displays an example of linear trend-line analysis of the relationship between assessed valuation per pupil and local revenues per pupil for 20 Missouri districts. Placing assessed valuation on the x axis and local revenues per pupil on the y axis, it becomes readily apparent that districts with higher assessed valuation have higher local revenue per pupil. By applying a linear trend line to the data, we can determine both the strength of the relationship between the variables and the magnitude of that relationship. The R^2 value of 0.8992 tells us the strength of the relationship, like a correlation coefficient. While correlation coefficients, r, range from -1 to $+1$, R^2 values range from only 0 to 1 (because they are the equivalent of the correlation

Figure 5.2   Fiscal Neutrality

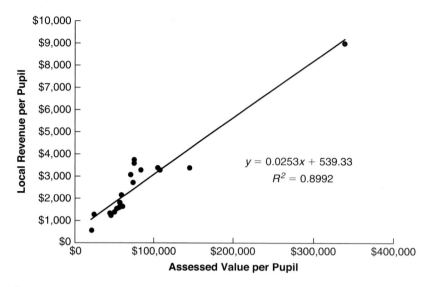

Source: Data from Table 5.6.

coefficient squared). An R^2 of 0.8992 is quite strong, equivalent to an *r* of 0.9482.

The equation $y = 0.0253x + 593.33$ is also revealing. This equation indicates the slope (0.0253) and intercept (593.33) of the trend line, but only the slope is meaningful. The intercept of 593.33 is the local revenue per pupil expected to be available to the district with $0 in assessed value per pupil (which might exist if there is a district covering only federally owned, property tax exempt land). The slope of 0.0253 indicates that each additional $1 in assessed valuation per pupil is associated with an additional $.0253 (2.5 cents) in local revenue per pupil, or that an additional $10,000 in assessed valuation is associated with an additional $253 in local revenue per pupil.

Slopes may also be expressed as elasticities to account for widely varied scales of units as with property wealth and revenues per pupil. Elasticities are slopes expressed in percent change or percent difference terms. For example, the pupil-weighted elasticity for the relationship depicted in Figure 5.2 is .642, indicating that 1% higher assessed valuation per pupil is associated with .642% higher local revenues per pupil. An elasticity of 1.0, indicating that a 1% change in *x* is associated with a 1% change in *y* indicates a perfectly elastic relationship. An elasticity of 0 indicates that values of *y* are nonresponsive, or inelastic to changes in *x*.

Benchmarking With Horizontal Equity Tools

Few if any absolutes exist in evaluating the status of school-funding systems. Authors of some previous textbooks have attempted to apply benchmarks for some equity statistics. Table 5.11 provides benchmarks by Odden and Picus (2000). Odden and Picus, and others, for example, present a widely accepted standard of 10% for the coefficient of variation. That is, a school finance system is considered equitable if two thirds of districts fall within 10% of mean revenues or expenditures per pupil.

We concur with the Odden and Picus (2000) evaluation that the stated benchmarks represent strict standards and note also that these standards are devoid of contextual considerations. Setting standards for variance statistics, or measures of horizontal equity, is particularly difficult in part because of the interconnectedness of horizontal and vertical equity concepts. For example, vertical equity adjustments in a funding formula alone can easily create gaps in the coefficient of variation in spending across districts larger than 10%. In some states, as we will discuss much more extensively in later chapters, state-aid formulas provide more than twice the aid per pupil to some districts than to others on the basis that those districts face conditions under which their operating costs are twice as high. Treating such differ-

Table 5.11   Benchmarks for Equity and Neutrality Statistics

Statistic	Range	Ideal	Stated Benchmark	Source	National Mean (1994)[a]
Horizontal equity measures					
Coefficient of variation	0 to	0	.10 or 10%	Odden & Picus, 2000, p. 62	30.06
McLoone index	0 to 1	1	.90 or .95	Odden & Picus, 2000, p. 64	.866
Gini coefficient	0 to 1	0	.05	Odden & Picus, 2000, p. 63	.152
Fiscal neutrality measures					
Correlation elasticity (with respect to property wealth)	−1 to 1	0	.5 or less with .1 or less elasticity		NA[b]
	Continuous	0			

[a] Mean for instructional expenditures per pupil for unified K–12 districts only. Hussar & Sonnenberg, 2000.
[b] Consistent property wealth measures not available across states.

ences as simple inequities, is illogical, but conventional equity-analysis tools fail to provide sufficient methods for differentiating this type of variance. In fact, a small coefficient of variation in a state with a wide variation in costs across districts could be less equitable than a higher coefficient of variation in another state.

Variance resulting from vertical equity adjustments differs substantively from variance resulting from local fiscal-capacity differences and therefore must be treated differently. In the next section, we discuss briefly how to construct horizontal equity analyses that account for vertical equity variance. We contend, however, that the creation of spending variations in the name of vertical equity does not exclude those variations from scrutiny. In Chapter 10 we provide much more sensitive tools for dissecting the rationality of differences in spending created by state-aid formulas.

Relative comparisons of equity and neutrality can be useful, and sources for comparison are increasingly available. For example, the National Center for Education Statistics (NCES) annually compiles a dataset called the *Common Core of Data*, which includes revenue and expenditure data along with student population data for all districts in all states. The common core of data includes financial data from the U.S. Census Bureau's annual financial survey of local governments. Analysts can use these data to calculate equity and neutrality indices and make annual comparisons of current expenditures per pupil, core instructional expenditures per pupil, or even cost-adjusted expenditures per pupil. Table 5.12 shows coefficients of variation for 1999–2000, including comparisons between all K–12 districts and large K–12 districts. In addition, Hussar

and Sonnenberg (2000) of the NCES have compiled a 15-year (1980–1994) history of equity statistics, including coefficients of variation, McLoone indices, and Gini coefficients on instructional expenditures per pupil across the states.

Vertical Equity Tools

In this section, we briefly present three tools that Berne and Stiefel (1984) discuss for measuring vertical equity: (a) weighted analysis of horizontal equity, (b) regression-based methods, and (c) ratio analysis. The first of these methods resolves the problem with horizontal equity analysis raised in the previous section. That is, one must treat variations in funding caused by vertical equity adjustments, or differences in spending that are intended to compensate for legitimate need differences, differently from variations in funding caused by local fiscal capacity differences. The second of these methods uses statistical modeling—regression equations—to estimate the relationship between spending differences across districts and population characteristics in those districts. For example, one might estimate the spending differences across districts associated with serving different numbers of special education or at-risk students. This approach is now more commonly addressed as the *education cost function*, and we discuss it in greater detail in Chapter 7. The final approach, ratio analysis, involves simply estimating the average resources allocated to the special population and dividing that number by the average resources allocated to the general population to generate a value that represents the *marginal cost* of services for the special population. For example, we might find

Table 5.12   Coefficients of Variation Across States (1999–2000)

All	K–12 Unified Districts				Large K–12 Unified Districts			
	Mean	CV	Percentage Children	Rank	Mean	CV	Percentage Children	Rank
Alabama	$5,698	9%	100%	7	$5,697	9%	94%	16
Alaska	$8,971	35%	100%	51	$8,282	32%	83%	50
Arizona	$5,189	14%	64%	29	$5,119	12%	59%	30
Arkansas	$5,409	11%	100%	19	$5,478	11%	58%	24
California	$6,080	17%	72%	41	$6,066	16%	71%	44
Colorado	$6,112	11%	100%	16	$6,079	9%	88%	18
Connecticut	$9,426	15%	94%	34	$9,462	15%	87%	38
Delaware	$7,996	7%	100%	5	$8,007	7%	98%	7
Florida	$5,701	6%	100%	4	$5,699	6%	100%	5
Georgia	$6,391	11%	100%	17	$6,396	11%	95%	26
Idaho	$5,239	15%	100%	33	$5,086	13%	75%	35
Illinois	$6,674	13%	65%	27	$6,861	11%	51%	25
Indiana	$6,841	14%	100%	31	$6,970	14%	81%	37
Iowa	$6,146	9%	100%	8	$6,233	8%	52%	12
Kansas	$6,271	14%	100%	30	$6,196	12%	65%	32
Kentucky	$5,962	11%	100%	18	$5,949	10%	88%	23
Louisiana	$5,700	8%	100%	6	$5,692	8%	98%	13
Maine	$7,749	17%	87%	47	$7,330	12%	51%	33
Maryland	$7,498	10%	100%	13	$7,498	10%	100%	22
Massachusetts	$8,731	18%	93%	48	$8,779	18%	85%	49
Michigan	$7,377	16%	100%	40	$7,568	16%	81%	43
Minnesota	$6,920	17%	100%	45	$7,043	18%	79%	47
Mississippi	$5,053	12%	100%	21	$4,993	11%	83%	27
Missouri	$5,992	17%	99%	46	$6,140	18%	72%	48
Nebraska	$6,176	12%	95%	23	$5,986	7%	60%	8
Nevada	$5,768	11%	100%	15	$5,694	6%	97%	3
New Hampshire	$6,706	15%	78%	32	$6,686	15%	54%	39
New Jersey	$10,627	16%	75%	39	$10,695	16%	67%	45
New Mexico	$5,784	16%	100%	36	$5,579	10%	89%	21
New York	$10,096	17%	98%	42	$10,118	16%	85%	41
North Carolina	$6,064	9%	100%	9	$6,043	9%	99%	15
North Dakota	$5,588	20%	97%	49	$5,386	10%	52%	20
Ohio	$6,520	17%	100%	44	$6,683	16%	78%	40
Oklahoma	$5,239	13%	97%	25	$5,138	8%	60%	14
Oregon	$6,661	11%	100%	14	$6,625	9%	85%	17
Pennsylvania	$7,100	16%	100%	35	$7,127	16%	85%	42
Rhode Island	$8,458	10%	98%	10	$8,446	8%	94%	11
South Carolina	$6,091	11%	100%	20	$6,080	11%	97%	29
South Dakota	$5,534	16%	99%	37	$5,331	13%	51%	36
Tennessee	$5,405	13%	98%	24	$5,426	13%	93%	34
Texas	$6,135	12%	100%	22	$6,029	8%	87%	10
Utah	$4,362	13%	100%	26	$4,335	12%	98%	31
Vermont	$7,799	16%	36%	38	$8,421	11%	14%	28
Virginia	$6,840	17%	100%	43	$6,831	17%	96%	46
Washington	$6,274	10%	99%	12	$6,226	7%	88%	9
West Virginia	$7,133	6%	100%	3	$7,123	6%	93%	4
Wisconsin	$7,700	10%	96%	11	$7,820	10%	68%	19
Wyoming	$7,412	14%	99%	28	$7,112	7%	71%	6

Source: Data from U.S. Census Bureau. *Fiscal survey of local governments, elementary and secondary school finance 1999–2000.* Retrieved from http://www.census.gov/govs/www/school.html

Table 5.13 Weighted Analysis of Vertical Equity (Equal Revenues per Pupil)

District	Enrollment	Limited-English-Proficient Pupils	Limited-English-Proficient Pupils Weight	Pupil Cost Units (Weighted Pupils)	Revenues per Pupil	Adjusted Revenues per Pupil
A	10,000	500	20%	10,100	$5,000	$4,950
B	5,000	20	20%	5,004	$5,000	$4,996
C	2,500	1,000	20%	2,700	$5,000	$4,630
D	500	10	20%	502	$5,000	$4,980
E	100	5	20%	101	$5,000	$4,950

that the *marginal cost* of services for at-risk children is 20% higher than the cost of regular education services, for a ratio of 1.2.

Tables 5.13 and 5.14 are examples of weighted horizontal equity analysis. Assume we have five districts, each of varied total enrollment and serving varied numbers of LEP students. Assume those districts receive the *same* revenues per pupil but that the cost of serving each LEP student (improving their language proficiency such that they can take advantage of other educational opportunities) is, on average, 20% higher than the cost of serving the average student. If districts receive the same revenues per pupil, then those serving more LEP pupils are at a disadvantage. To calculate that disadvantage, we construct a "pupil cost unit" measure, where we count each LEP pupil as 1.2, rather than 1.0, pupils. As a result, the district with 10,000 actual pupils, 500 of whom are LEP, has 10,100 pupil cost units (or weighted pupils). Under the current undifferentiated funding model, that district receives a total budget of $50 million ($5,000 revenues per pupil

x 10,000 pupils). When that budget is divided by pupil cost units, the adjusted revenues per pupil are only $4,950, rather than $5,000. In Chapter 8 we provide a much more thorough discussion of the measurement of marginal costs and provide a simulation of alternative ways to adjust equity analyses to accommodate different district costs.

Table 5.14 presents a case where the same districts have 20% more funding available per LEP pupil. The revenues per actual pupil differ (arguably appropriately different), but the revenues per pupil cost unit, or per weighted pupil, or adjusted revenues are the same.

Table 5.15 presents a ratio analysis that assumes that we can identify the average expenditures per regular education pupil and average expenditures per LEP pupil. If so, we can construct ratios as seen in the last column of the table. These ratios can be referred to as *implicit weights,* or weights that reflect current spending practices. As we will show in Chapter 10, many states include *explicit weights* in their school-funding formulas. Analysis of explicit weights and implicit weights involves

Table 5.14 Weighted Analysis of Vertical Equity (Vertically Equitable Unequal Revenues)

District	Enrollment	Limited-English-Proficient Pupils	Limited-English-Proficient Pupils Weight	Pupil Cost Units	Revenues per Pupil	Adjusted Revenues per Pupil
A	10,000	500	20%	10,100	$5,050	$5,000
B	5,000	20	20%	5,004	$5,004	$5,000
C	2,500	1,000	20%	2,700	$5,400	$5,000
D	500	10	20%	502	$5,020	$5,000
E	100	5	20%	101	$5,050	$5,000

Table 5.15   Ratio Analysis of Vertical Equity

District	Regular Education per Pupil Costs	Limited-English-Proficient Student per Pupil Costs	Ratio (Implicit Weight)
A	$5,247	$6,519	1.24
B	$4,832	$5,113	1.06
C	$6,320	$6,540	1.03

a combination of ex ante (for explicit weights) and ex poste (to derive implicit weights) methods.

The missing link in each of these vertical equity measurement methods is that none of these methods addresses the question of the true marginal costs of providing adequate services to the special population in question. Where, for example, does the 1.2, or 20%, marginal cost figure come from in Tables 5.13 and 5.14? Is 1.24 or 1.03 adequate? Because the concept of vertical equity is inextricably linked with educational adequacy, we address cost issues associated with vertical equity in greater detail in Chapters 8 through 10 and include a special section on "adequacy based-equity analysis" in our Chapter 10 simulations. Berne and Stiefel's (1984) methods simply produce measures of what states and/or districts are presently doing. We therefore are skeptical of the usefulness of any of these approaches—as applied in this chapter—for measuring the legitimacy of vertical equity adjustments in school funding. The weighted horizontal equity-analysis method, however, is useful for separating spending variations that result from vertical equity adjustments (whether adequate or not) from spending variations that result from local fiscal capacity differences.

Dynamic and Ecological Perspectives

The intent of the school finance equity framework is to guide the reform of public education finance systems, either through legal intervention or legislative process by informing the courts or the legislature of the status of the system. Yet, while equity measures are status measures, the reform process is a dynamic process. Further, although one may assess the status of a system in isolation, one must carry out the reform of that system in context. As noted in our previous discussion, horizontal and vertical equity generally consider ob-

jects distributed to students in isolation from any context such as community fiscal capacity, local political culture, and taste for education. Measures of equal opportunity attempt to relate the distribution of objects to limited sets of contextual information. In addition, each conceptual approach we have discussed thus far leads to measures that are snapshots of the condition of a school-funding system at a given point in time. Although many of the measures and concepts we discuss as ecological and/or dynamic do relate directly to equity per se (e.g., they are not explicitly equity measures), equity, as measured by explicit equity measures, is often unattainable unless one considers context and dynamics. In fact, snap-shots are a bit of a misnomer as well: Most of the snapping takes place long after the shot! Policy makers usually use the previous year's data to determine how to adjust the formula for the next year. This 2-year gap results in a vicious cycle of a poor district chasing the ghost of a rich district. Furthermore, because the state legislature sets rules of the chase, it's the poor tortoise that is forced to take a nap while the rich rabbit keeps on running.

Evaluating the fortitude of existing policies or potential of policy reforms or policy options requires an expanded framework that accounts for the entire political, economic, and cultural ecology involved in implementing school finance reforms and the system dynamics of the reform process. Figure 5.3 presents our expanded framework for understanding both Berne and Stiefel's (1984) elements and additional elements necessary to inform effective reform strategies. The framework includes both space (breadth of context) and time (static vs. dynamic) dimensions.

Regarding space, *internal* factors are those that are direct components of the school-funding system, under control of policy makers governing the school-funding system. *External* factors include the economy from which fiscal resources are derived, the political climate that influences the behavior of policy makers,

Figure 5.3   Expanded Dimensions of School Finance Formula Evaluation

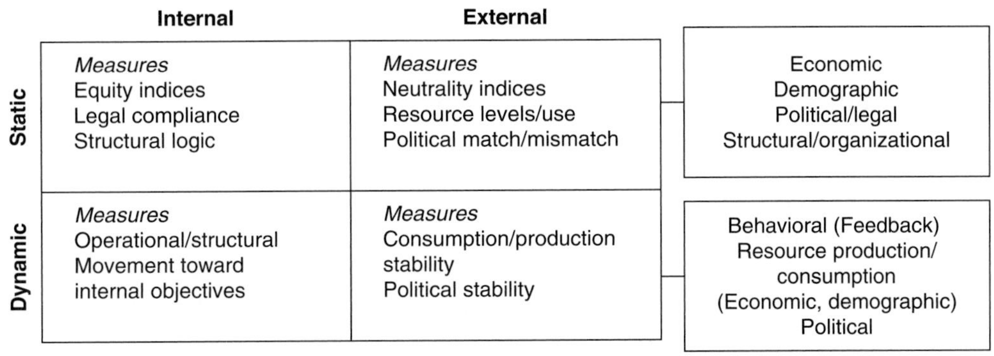

	Internal	External	
Static	*Measures* Equity indices Legal compliance Structural logic	*Measures* Neutrality indices Resource levels/use Political match/mismatch	Economic Demographic Political/legal Structural/organizational
Dynamic	*Measures* Operational/structural Movement toward internal objectives	*Measures* Consumption/production stability Political stability	Behavioral (Feedback) Resource production/ consumption (Economic, demographic) Political

and the demographics of student populations served by the public education system, which may have a variety of economic and/or political implications.

Regarding time, *static* factors are those that involve measures of the condition of the school-funding system and/or its environment at a given point in time. Such measures are typically *level* measures, such as measures of levels of performance or levels of available resources across schools or districts. *Dynamic* factors are those that involve measures of changes in the school-funding system and/or its environment over time. Such measures are typically *rate* measures, such as the rate at which per-pupil spending in low-wealth districts is converging on per-pupil spending in high-wealth districts, or the average rates of achievement gain of students. Dynamic measures are also measures of processes, such as the operational fluidity of a tax-collection, revenue-distribution system for public education.

Next, we provide two examples of dynamic concepts. The first is a dynamic internal model explicitly focused on equity. The second is a dynamic external model focused on the long-term stability of school funding, which has consequences for government efforts to attain equity. In Figure 5.4, we draw on the work of Baker and Richards (2002), on the difficulties of achieving school-funding parity in New Jersey through the various rounds of *Abbott v. Burke* discussed in Chapter 4. We provide a complete simulation in Chapter 6. Recall from Chapter 4 that the New Jersey Supreme Court mandated the legislature to achieve 100% per-pupil spending parity between the state's poorest districts, called special needs districts (SNDs), and the state's wealthiest districts, district factor groups I & J. Baker and Richards used dynamic models to run several simulations of the rates at which the state might attempt to converge SND spending on I & J spending, noting that the target, I & J spending,

Figure 5.4   Convergence

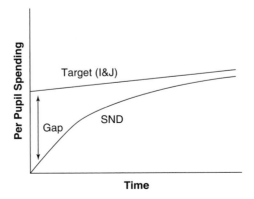

SND, special needs districts.

was a moving target. Given data on I & J spending and SND spending related to Figure 5.4, one could calculate a variety of measures that represent the rate at which the spending gap is declining over time. We call this a *dynamic parity index*. The importance of such an index is that it exceeds specifying the current status of the school-funding system and provides an insight into the direction the system is headed.

The simplified model in Figure 5.5, while not explicitly related to equity, has important equity consequences. Figure 5.5 concerns the use of resources available for achieving equity or adequacy across districts in a state. Achieving the convergence pattern presented in Figure 5.4 will require a large infusion of tax dollars to SNDs. The demand for that required tax effort is influenced by the demographic conditions of SNDs (growing or declining enrollments) and their local fiscal capacity (how poor they are), while the supply for the state's effort is contingent on statewide economic conditions and political constraints. One might presume that the state's total resource pool has a reasonable range that public education may consume, although specification of that range is a policy decision. Whatever the range, achieving a stable, equitable school-funding system requires a commitment to stabilizing state resource use within that range, realizing that maintaining that range requires a delicate balance of the rate at which state revenues are raised and the rate at which equity objectives are attempted and attained.

Aggressive pursuit of equity objectives may appear desirable to state courts. Overly aggressive mandates, however, may result in the dysfunctional and unintended policy consequence of either political backlash or economic instability, leading to less-equitable and even less-adequate statewide conditions than the pursuit of incremental improvements over a longer time frame.

Dynamic Analysis Tools

In this section, we present a limited toolkit for making dynamic evaluations of school-funding systems. The tools focus on the dynamic/internal quadrant of our framework, or more specifically—*movement toward internal objectives*. We give greater attention to contextual issues in Chapter 6, on funding formula design.

Two measures are important to understanding the rate of progress toward policy objectives: (a) the gap reduction rate (GRR) and (b) the gap reduction horizon (GRH). Intuitively, the GRR measures the rate of progress toward a particular policy objective, such as reducing spending variance across districts or converging the spending of low-wealth districts on a measure of adequacy. Choosing this target is not a trivial exercise. It defines the state's explicit equity goals. One then derives the horizon measure from the GRR. The GRH is an estimate of how many additional years the system will need to achieve the policy objective, given the current GRR.

Our first example involves a policy objective of reducing spending variance in New York State, as measured by the coefficient of variation, to the strict standard of 10%. Table 5.16 presents the coefficients of variation for New York State from 1986 to 1994. We begin by identifying the annual gap between the actual conditions and desired conditions. Regardless of whether this policy objective existed previously, our goal is to estimate the school-funding system's current rate of progress toward or away from this goal.

Figure 5.5   Dynamic Equilibrium

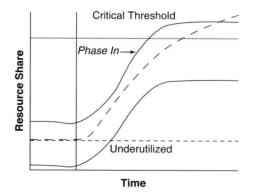

Table 5.16   Closing the CV Gap in New York

Year	New York CV	Desired	Gap	Gap Change
1986	21%	10%	11%	
1987	20%	10%	10%	−1.0%
1988	21%	10%	11%	0.7%
1989	20%	10%	10%	−0.6%
1990	21%	10%	11%	0.2%
1991	19%	10%	9%	−1.2%
1992	21%	10%	11%	1.5%
1993	19%	10%	9%	−2.0%
1994	18%	10%	8%	−1.1%
Gap reduction rate				**−0.44%**
Gap reduction horizon				**17.60**

CV, coefficient of variation.

Our next step involves estimating the average rate of change in the gap over time. Change rates can be estimated either as the change in the level of the value ($X_t - X_{t-1}$) or the percentage change in the value ($X_t - X_{t-1})/X_{t-1}$. Consider this important difference between these two approaches: When we express the average change rate as a change in the level of the value and use it to calculate a horizon, we will be predicting a horizon based on incremental movement toward the objective. If we use a percentage change rate as the GRR (where the gap itself is expressed as a percentage difference), we will approach the horizon asymptotically but never reach it. We therefore take the incremental approach. Note, however, that the gap itself remains expressed as a percentage difference between higher- and lower-resourced districts. That is, we focus on the percentage difference between districts, though not the percentage change in the percentage difference.

Table 5.16 calculates the change in the value, where the value itself, the difference in actual and desired coefficient of variation (CV), is a percentage value. An important consideration is that of how many years to include in the calculation of the change rate. We recommend at least three change periods, which requires 4 years of data. If more data are available, dates of major policy changes might serve as logical cutoff points. In Table 5.16, we used data from 1986 through 1994 to determine that the average GRR for New York was a reduction of the CV by 0.44% each year. Given a 1994 gap of 8%, an additional 17.6 years are needed to achieve a CV of 10%. We suggest that a horizon of greater than 5 years on high-priority policy objectives indicates the need to find some method for increasing the GRR, unless politicians, in fact, do not actually consider this kind of equity gap an urgent policy issue.

Table 5.17 presents a similar analysis of GRRs and GRHs, using a case analogous to that of New Jersey,

Table 5.17   Resolving Spending Disparities Between High- and Low-Capacity Districts

Year	Poor District Revenues	Wealthy District Revenues	Desired Parity	Parity Objective	Gap	Gap Ratio
1995	$6,322	$9,544	90%	$8,590	$2,268	0.36
1996	$6,575	$9,783	90%	$8,804	$2,229	0.34
1997	$6,838	$10,027	90%	$9,024	$2,187	0.32
1998	$7,111	$10,278	90%	$9,250	$2,139	0.3
1999	$7,396	$10,535	90%	$9,481	$2,085	0.28
2000	$7,692	$10,798	90%	$9,718	$2,027	0.26
2001	$7,999	$11,068	90%	$9,961	$1,962	0.25
Gap reduction rate					50.844	0.0189
Gap reduction horizon					38.59	12.98

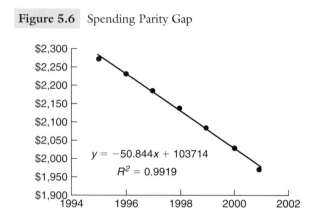

Figure 5.6   Spending Parity Gap

$y = -50.844x + 103714$

$R^2 = 0.9919$

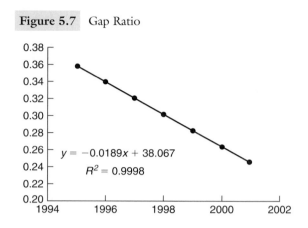

Figure 5.7   Gap Ratio

$y = -0.0189x + 38.067$

$R^2 = 0.9998$

but with fabricated data. In this case, the policy objective is to achieve parity between poor and wealthy districts, perhaps as a result of court mandate. The most significant difference between this case and the New York case is that the equity target itself, the desired revenue level for poor districts, is a moving target (unlike the 10% CV goal in Table 5.16). In our example, unlike the New Jersey Supreme Court's demand, we set a desired parity level of bringing poor-district revenues to 90% of wealthy-district revenues. We create a parity objective by multiplying 90% times the wealthy-district revenues. We estimate the gap as the parity objective minus the present status of poor-district revenues. We can also in this case estimate a gap ratio (equivalent of a range ratio). Again, alternate measures may be useful.

In this example, we take a different approach to estimating the average gap change rates and gap ratio change rates. We use $x-y$ scatter plots, where the x variable is time, in years. We can fit a linear trend line to the scatter plot in MS Excel or statistical software, and we can estimate a linear equation and goodness of fit (R^2)

measure for the trend line. (We provide Excel instructions in the simulation at the end of this chapter.)

Interpretation of the equation is similar to our discussion of fiscal neutrality tools. In this case, the slope of the equation (-50.8 or $-.0189$) represents the average annual change, or the rate at which we are closing the gap. One advantage of this approach is that we can see the shape of the trajectory. That is, we can see if we are beginning to accelerate toward our objective or decelerate. If we are accelerating or decelerating, making a curved pattern, then our straight line may be inappropriate.

Table 5.17 shows alternative measures of the gap, which, when plotted, result in one pattern of gap reduction that is more linear than the other. The R^2 value allows us to discern which pattern is best fit by a straight line. Though the differences in Figures 5.6 and 5.7 are subtle, the straight line better fits the changes in gap ratios over time than it does the changes in the gap. We therefore can be more confident in the GRR of the gap ratio and more confident in the horizon produced for gap ratio reduction to "0."

SUMMARY

We began Chapter 5 with the objective of demonstrating traditional ways of understanding and measuring equity. First we summarized an ecological perspective on policy making that takes multiple variables in a dynamic political, economic, and demographic context and seeks to assess the feasible pathways to policy success. This policy model distinguishes itself from policy analytic frameworks that measure policy outcomes or

goals in only a static fashion. Conversely, we see change, relentless, never-ending change as the single feature of the policy process that analysis must include if policy makers actually wish to attain their goals.

The lack of continuity of political leadership and the corresponding unwillingness to pursue long-term social objectives—especially ones that require higher taxes—is the single-most adverse factor mitigating against the ecological approach to policy making. Only if such long-term goals are transferred to state agencies that have the mandate to pursue such goals intelligently will static policy making be supplanted by the dynamic approach we recommend.

We next turned to the seminal work of Robert Berne and Leanna Stiefel (1984), which developed the traditional measures of school finance equity, namely vertical equity, horizontal equity, and fiscal neutrality. We explained why these concepts are important to school finance equity and how they are measured.

Finally, we explained how the study of equity gaps over time (the dynamic approach) would provide policy makers with valuable information and perspective on the status of their pursuit of equity. We provided two additional measures to demonstrate our approach, the gap reduction rate (GRR) and the gap reduction horizon (GRH). The first depicts the trajectory to closing the gap, and the second, how far out in the future the gap will be closed at the current rate of improvement.

KEY TERMS

ex ante analysis   Analysis of policy inputs or processes, such as policies themselves or resource distribution mechanisms as described in policy.

ex poste analysis   Analysis of policy outcomes, such as measures of the equity with which resources are distributed.

fiscal neutrality   A lack of relationship between the quality and quantity of schooling available, and the wealth and/or income levels and distributions of government subdivisions providing financial support for public schools. Usually measured as the relationship between taxable property wealth and per-pupil spending across public school districts within a

state, where a fiscally neutral system shows no statistical relationship between the two measures.

horizontal equity   Equal treatment of individuals, in terms of educational inputs provided. Under a horizontally equitable system, the general population of students in a state would have access to a similar quantity of similar quality schooling.

vertical equity   The differential treatment of individuals or groups of students with identifiably and measurably different educational needs. We define vertical equity in terms of differences in abilities of students to achieve specific educational outcome objectives.

REFERENCES

Baker, B. D. (2001). Living on the edges of school funding policies: The plight of at-risk, limited-English-proficient and gifted children. *Educational Policy, 15*(5), 698–722.

Baker, B. D. (2005). The emerging shape of educational adequacy: from theoretical assumptions to empirical evidence. *Journal of Education Finance, 30*(3), 259–287.

Baker, B. D., & Richards, C. E. (2002). Exploratory application of system dynamics modeling to school finance policy analysis. *Journal of Education Finance, 27*(3,) 857–884.

Berne, R., & Stiefel, L. (1984). *The measurement of equity in school finance.* Baltimore, MD: Johns Hopkins Press.

Coleman, J., et al. (1966). *Equality of educational opportunity.* Washington, DC: U.S. Government Printing Office.

Coons, J. E., Clune, W. H., & Sugarman, S. D. (1969). Educational opportunity: A workable constitutional test for state financial structures. *California Law Review, 57*(2), 305–421.

Horowitz, H. (1966). Unseparate but unequal: The emerging Fourteenth Amendment issue in public school education. *UCLA Law Review, 13*, 1147–1172.

Hussar, W., & Sonnenberg, W. (2000). *Trends in disparities in school district level expenditures per pupil. Statistical analysis report.* (NCES 2000–020.) Washington, DC: National Center for Education Statistics.

Imber, M. (1990). A typology of discrimination in education. *Readings on Equal Education, 10*, 387–397.

Odden, A. R., & Picus, L. O. (2000). *School finance: A policy perspective.* New York: McGraw-Hill.

Speakman, S. T., Cooper, B. S., Sampieri, R., May, J., Holmsback, H., & Glass, B. (1996). Bringing money to the classroom: A systemic resource allocations model applied to the New York City public schools. In L. Picus & J. Wattenbarger (Eds.), *Where does the money go? Resource allocation in elementary and secondary schools* (pp. 106–131). Thousand Oaks, CA: Corwin Press.

Underwood, J. K. (1995). School finance adequacy as vertical equity. *University of Michigan Journal of Law Reform, 28*(3), 493–519.

CHAPTER 5 SIMULATIONS

MEASURING EQUITY

Conventional Equity Measures

This simulation involves evaluating school-funding equity among 20 school districts from the state of Missouri in 2003, prior to recent reforms implemented by the Missouri legislature. While these 20 Missouri districts are provided within the Microsoft Excel equity-analysis template, any 20 districts from any state may be entered into the template as long as comparable data (assessed valuation, income, etc.) are available. The objectives of this simulation follow:

1. Learn more about the meaning of equity statistics by conducting equity analyses and communicating the findings of those analyses, using real data, but without being overburdened by calculations.
2. Learn more about how to calculate equity statistics by exploring calculations in the spreadsheet (Table 5s.1).

We encourage students with either more advanced spreadsheet skills or an interest in further pursuing the study of school finance to try to work with the statewide dataset, constructing their own formulas for equity calculations, using the template as a guide.

As an end product of this assignment, you should prepare a two- to three-page executive summary of their findings. You should also prepare summary tables of equity statistics, which you can print out from the last page (worksheet) of the Excel workbook on the Companion Website (www.prenhall.com/baker).

Working With the Equity-Analysis Template

Note: You must be working on a computer with Microsoft Excel for Windows or Macintosh, version 5.0 or later.

1. On the Companion Website (www.prenhall.com/baker), open the Microsoft Excel workbook titled: Chapter 5.xls.
2. If you are not familiar with Microsoft Excel, notice the tabs along the bottom of the workbook:

   a. Sheet 1: 20-District Dataset
   b. Sheet 2: Basic Equity Statistics

   c. Sheet 3: McLoone Index for Local Revenue per Pupil
   d. Sheet 4: McLoone Index for Total Revenue per Pupil
   e. Sheet 5: Income-Sorted Gini Coefficient for Total Revenue per Pupil
   f. Sheet 6: Elasticity for Local Revenue per Pupil
   g. Sheet 7: Elasticity for Total Revenue per Pupil
   h. Sheet 8: Summary Table

3. You have two options for approaching your analyses of the 20-district dataset:

   a. Low-tech option

      i. Print the "20-District DataSet."
      ii. Starting on the "Basic Equity Statistics" worksheet, enter the data from the 20-district data set into the appropriate green cells.
      iii. Do the same on the McLoone index worksheets. *However,* on these worksheets, you must enter your districts in order, from the lowest (top) to the highest (bottom) revenue per pupil. Be sure to keep the right data with the right districts.
      iv. Enter your data into the Gini coefficient worksheet. On this worksheet, you must enter your districts in order of lowest (top) to highest (bottom) income per pupil. Be sure to keep the right data with the right districts.
      v. Enter your data into the elasticity worksheet. This time, there is no need to sort.

   b. Higher tech option

      i. Copy and paste the data from the "20-District Dataset" worksheet into the "Basic Equity Statistics" worksheet.
      ii. For the McLoone indices, copy and paste only those variables you will need onto a separate, blank Excel worksheet. Then, use the sort function, to sort the districts by (a) local revenue per pupil for the McLoone of local revenue and (b) total revenue per pupil for the

Table 5s.1 Twenty Selected Missouri Districts (2003)

Name	Number	Enrollment	Assessed Value per Pupil	Median Household Income	General Levy ($/100)	Local Revenue per Pupil	State Revenue per Pupil	State and Local Revenue per Pupil
Festus R-VI	50,006	2,672	$56,179	$40,964	2.87	$1,612	$2,505	$4,118
Hillsboro R-III	50,003	3,592	$44,725	$48,548	2.94	$1,315	$2,881	$4,196
Ozark R-VI	22,093	3,925	$50,363	$40,352	2.75	$1,385	$2,878	$4,263
Sedalia 200	80,125	4,191	$60,485	$31,267	2.75	$1,663	$2,638	$4,301
Branson R-IV	106,004	3,143	$145,745	$32,098	2.31	$3,367	$945	$4,312
Bolivar R-I	84,001	2,350	$45,392	$29,257	2.75	$1,248	$3,148	$4,397
Waynesville R-VI	85,046	5,147	$21,799	$36,724	2.7	$589	$3,822	$4,411
Hannibal 60	64,075	3,645	$53,855	$31,962	2.86	$1,540	$2,945	$4,485
Jefferson City	26,006	8,263	$105,067	$41,924	3.23	$3,394	$1,688	$5,082
Raymore-Peculiar R-II	19,142	4,627	$57,663	$56,198	3.14	$1,811	$3,302	$5,113
Warrensburg R-VI	51,159	3,167	$58,619	$32,477	3.7	$2,169	$3,135	$5,304
Mehlville R-IX	96,094	11,799	$108,448	$53,741	3.01	$3,264	$2,073	$5,337
Cooter R-IV	78,004	277	$19,918	$31,094	2.75	$548	$4,861	$5,408
Lee's Summit R-VII	48,071	14,861	$70,601	$59,944	4.37	$3,085	$2,866	$5,952
Columbia 93	10,093	16,076	$83,170	$36,516	3.93	$3,269	$3,122	$6,390
Ferguson-Florissant R-II	96,089	11,949	$75,200	$40,500	4.74	$3,564	$3,575	$7,139
St. Louis City	115,115	42,654	$73,398	$27,156	3.73	$2,738	$4,911	$7,649
Kansas City 33	48,078	33,642	$75,186	$29,634	4.95	$3,722	$4,360	$8,082
Wellston	96,115	747	$24,686	$21,458	5.1	$1,259	$7,094	$8,353
Ladue	96,106	3,272	$336,855	$82,889	2.63	$8,859	$1,966	$10,826

Source: Data from Missouri Department of Elementary and Secondary Education. Retrieved from http://www.dese.mo.gov/schooldata/ftpdata.html

McLoone of total revenue. You can do this as follows:

1. Highlight all variables you copied and their labels.
2. Select the "sort" option from the "data" menu.
3. Select the appropriate variable as the "by" option in the dialog box.

iii. Do the same for the Gini coefficient.

Note: You must sort data in a separate Excel worksheet, because the sort function will not work in a protected worksheet. We have protected the calculations in the template so that they cannot be inadvertently and unknowingly altered.

Problem Set Questions

Write brief responses to the following questions before preparing your policy brief executive summary.

1. Compare the mean values and coefficients of variation using district versus pupil unit of analysis for the following variables:

    a. Income per pupil
    b. Property value per pupil
    c. Local revenues per pupil
    d. Total revenues per pupil

    Why do you obtain differences between values calculated by these alternate methods? What do some of the differences imply? Give examples.

2. Discuss the information provided by (a) ranges and (b) range ratios with respect to means and coefficients of variation. What do these measures add to your understanding of disparity in

    a. Income per pupil?
    b. Property value per pupil?
    c. Local revenues per pupil?
    d. Total revenues per pupil?

3. Compare the disparity of local revenues per pupil and total revenues per pupil using examples from the preceding indices. Which revenues are more disparate? What does this tell you about the role of state aid?

4. Compare the McLoone indices for local and total revenues per pupil. What does this tell you about the role of state aid? What information does this add to your findings in the previous question?

5. What does the wealth-weighted Gini coefficient tell you about the distribution of school revenues across students by income class? Do your findings support or refute your previous findings?

6. Compare the slopes and elasticities (as well as the scatter plots) of the relationship between property wealth and local revenue per pupil and property wealth and total revenue per pupil. Which is more neutral, and what factors do you believe contribute to the neutrality?

CHAPTER 6

FINANCING EQUITY

Introduction

State aid programs for local public schools date back to the late 1700s in New York State (formalized into law in 1812), beginning with flat allocations of aid intended to stimulate local communities to raise additional funds and provide publicly available schooling (Mort & Reusser, 1951, p. 371). The question of equalization, or how to allocate state aid with consideration for differences in local fiscal capacity, first emerged around 1850 as it became increasingly apparent that local support varied from town to town (Mort & Reusser, 1951, p. 373). The notion of helping one's neighbors pay for their children's education was contentious. Whatever problems we face today in funding public education, we have moved a considerable distance from the 19th-century perspective—although the distance traveled has not been accomplished without the dedicated struggle of citizens to improve education for the children of the poor and working class.

Formal methods of equalizing state aid were not elaborated in state policies until the early 1900s. Over the past several decades, policy analysts and consultants have created a variety of state school-funding formulas for resolving horizontal and vertical equity and for fiscal neutrality problems we discussed in Chapter 5. In large part, policy makers have designed and implemented these formulas in response to court demands or in an effort to fend off pending and future legal challenges. In this chapter, we present and discuss two conceptual approaches for allocating equalized state aid to local districts: (a) policies designed to directly promote equity of revenues and/or expenditures per pupil and (b) policies designed to create equal capacity among districts to raise revenues.

We present these formulas not just in terms of their mathematical derivation but also in terms of their application within their respective political, economic, and demographic environments. The Companion Website (www.prenhall.com/baker) provides a static simulation of each type of allocation formula in MS Excel (Chapter6.xls).

Goals of Funding Formulas

In general, state school finance formulas have four goals:

1. Redistribute resources from wealthier to poorer districts.
2. Improve educational efficiency.
3. Obtain or sustain political support.
4. Be affordable.

As you can see, these four goals are often mutually counter-balancing.

Redistribution Goals

Redistribution goals are the primary concern of this chapter, because they speak directly to the creation of school-funding equity across districts. That is, redistribution goals involve the collection of tax revenues to the state, and distribution of those revenues to local school districts with the specific intent of providing more resources to poorer districts and less to the wealthier ones. Just how redistributive such formulas become is also a function of the origin of the tax revenues. Setting redistribution goals involves determining how equitable a school-funding system should be, or what resource allocation objectives take priority over others. For example, is it more important to ensure that at-risk programs are adequately funded or more important to achieve a general level of spending equity in the school-funding system?

Efficiency Goals

In general, *efficiency* is defined as the use of a given level of resources to produce the maximum quantity and/or quality of output or, conversely, as minimizing the resources consumed in producing a given level of output. Critics of public education have argued that education resources have increased rapidly for the past several decades, but that productivity of schools has remained static, or even declined (Hanushek, 1986). More extensive discussion of efficiency concepts and measures appears in Chapter 11.

Political Goals

A recurring theme in this chapter is the role of politics in influencing the design and/or application of state school-funding policies. While much of the discussion that follows centers on the mathematical structure of formulas that allocate state aid to local districts, it is important to recognize that formulae must ultimately be implemented within a political, economic, and demographic environment where primarily state political leaders will then manage the formula. No matter how empirically driven or rational the formula, its application is necessarily political.

The politics of state funds for public education differ substantially from the politics of local funding, where the politics of local taxation are based primarily on garnering support of a majority of local voters for district initiatives and where local voters express their individual tastes for initiatives through their individual vote. State legislative decisions regarding education funding similarly arise from individual legislators' first looking out for their own interests as well as the interests of their constituents. At the state level, however, legislators tend to participate in more complex, game-like decision-making behaviors, such as vote trading, or "I'll vote for that package on education, if you support my environmental regulation plan." Such negotiations often lead to unexpected alliances and the adoption of policies that on the surface can be difficult to understand, absent more in-depth knowledge of the underlying politics. Our politics of school-funding class activity described at the end of this chapter exemplifies the political behavior of state legislators and the important role of negotiation.

Affordability Goals

Determining how much a state can afford to spend on education is complex. It is a function of the level of commitment of the state to high-quality education, the wealth of the state, the relative number of children to educate, and the urgency of competing social needs such as welfare, crime prevention, and health. We do have ways to measure the relative effort of states. For example, one might compare the 50 states on per-pupil public education spending against shares of the total government budget or as the ratio of per-capita income. Such measures provide comparative benchmarks for the relative effort of states and over time they provide us with path marks of progress or the lack thereof. First, in any measure of state effort, we must acknowledge that states have budgetary constraints independent of their political constraints. Not all states are equally wealthy, and this is a major source of variation in per-pupil spending nationwide. Second, for deeply complex regional and historical reasons, not all states utilize multiple sources of revenue to address their educational needs. It may be legally feasible to introduce state income taxes in states such as Florida, Texas, and New Hampshire, but it is not currently politically feasible to do so. These constraints hamper equity efforts and their sustainability over the economic long run.

Policy Design Framework

We describe state school-funding formulas as having three basic components: (a) internal policy levers, (b) critical outputs, and (c) exogenous conditions.

Policy Levers

Each type of school-funding formula has its own set of internal *policy levers*. Internal policy levers are those features of a funding formula that the policy makers who designed them can manipulate toward achieving any number of objectives, including improving equity statistics, meeting budget constraints, acquiring new resources, or securing tax cuts for constituents. We label policy levers as such on each of our school finance simulations that accompany this chapter. Some policy levers may be external to a given level of government. For example, at least in the short run, local school districts have little leeway in manipulating state-funding formulas, and the state government has little influence over the funding of federal categorical programs. When we use the term *internal policy levers,* we mean those that can be manipulated to pursue policy goals, understanding that some levers may become available in the future and some withdrawn, depending on political and economic circumstances.

Critical Output

The *critical output* of a funding formula depends largely on who is observing the output. To the legislator manipulating a policy lever with the intent of achieving tax relief for his or her constituents, the critical output is the extent of tax relief achieved. The same legislator might be even more interested in polling data on the likelihood of reelection than in the efficacy of the finance formula. To the state judicial system, the critical output might be the equity statistics presented in Chapter 5. To the state economic analyst, the critical output might be the equilibrium of the consumption of state revenue resources by the education-funding formula.

Exogenous Conditions

Exogenous conditions are those conditions that are beyond the control of policy makers but have both indirect and direct influence on the school-funding formula. Our definition of *exogenous condition* encompasses all that is not under *direct* control of policy makers or anything not explicitly a policy lever. Certainly, state economic conditions exert influence on the adequacy, equity, and stability of education resources. Additionally, demographic changes exert a variety of influences, from the effects of increased immigration on bilingual education costs, to the relationship between aging populations and their declining preferences for taxes for public education. Although we do not address the issue extensively in this chapter, the feedback effects of decisions of policy makers about education systems on issues considered exogenous in our framework, such as the economy or community demographics, are important considerations. Research indicates, for example, that schooling quality (as measured by student outcomes) affects property values positively (Haurin & Brasington, 1996), which in turn, may affect tax revenues positively, which in turn may affect positively schooling quality. This example of a virtuous reinforcing feedback loop demonstrates that few, if any, truly exogenous conditions exist in education systems.

Spending Equity Formulas

In this section, we discuss two approaches to allocating state aid to local school districts: (a) flat grants and (b) foundation programs. The goal of both funding programs is to promote a specific minimum level of spending for an identified program across the school districts within a given state. To illustrate, a flat grant of $100 for each gifted child in a district might have the goals of encouraging the identification and supplementation of instruction for gifted children, while a foundation program might ensure a minimum expenditure per pupil in K–12 education of $5,000. Thus, the goal can be narrowly or broadly defined.

Flat Grants

Flat grants, as their name implies, are simply flat amounts of aid that are allocated per actual or per weighted pupil (as in our vertical equity analysis in Chapters 5 and 10) to districts throughout a state by the state government. Flat grants were the first mechanisms used for providing state aid to local districts. The original intent of state aid was to provide tax relief to local citizens by sharing the cost of public schooling. Remember, however, that educational systems are complex: The state got the funding it is redistributing by taxing its citizens in the previous year. Whether any given child received more or less than his or her family was taxed is the central question when addressing the net redistribution of government assistance.

Policy Levers and Critical Output

Table 6.1 displays the allocation of flat-grant aid to 20 Missouri school districts. In Table 6.1, each district receives $500 in aid per pupil, regardless of property wealth, income, or any other district characteristic. Also, Table 6.1 applies a simplified assumption that districts will not alter their local spending behavior in the presence of the flat grant. It is well known that state aid distributions to local districts result in a trade-off of increased total spending and local tax relief. Local governments usually reduce their own local effort in the presence of a state subsidy. On average, one might expect each additional $1 of state aid to result in 50 cents spent on education and the other 50 cents spent to reduce the local tax burden. Each community's response to a state subsidy depends on the initial level of tax burden faced by each district and on its commitment to quality educational services relative to other services and needs.

Table 6.1 Application of Flat-Grant Program to Missouri Districts

District	Enrollment	Assessed Valuation per Pupil	Income per Pupil	Property Tax Rate	Local Revenue per Pupil	Flat Grant per Pupil	New Local Tax Rate	New Local Revenue	Total Revenue per Pupil
Festus R-VI	2,672	$56,179	$40,964	0.03	$1,612	$500	2.87%	$1,612	$2,112
Hillsboro R-III	3,592	$44,725	$48,548	0.03	$1,315	$500	2.94%	$1,315	$1,815
Ozark R-VI	3,925	$50,363	$40,352	0.03	$1,385	$500	2.75%	$1,385	$1,885
Sedalia 200	4,191	$60,485	$31,267	0.03	$1,663	$500	2.75%	$1,663	$2,163
Branson R-IV	3,143	$145,745	$32,098	0.02	$3,367	$500	2.31%	$3,367	$3,867
Bolivar R-I	2,350	$45,392	$29,257	0.03	$1,248	$500	2.75%	$1,248	$1,748
Waynesville R-VI	5,147	$21,799	$36,724	0.03	$589	$500	2.70%	$589	$1,089
Hannibal 60	3,645	$53,855	$31,962	0.03	$1,540	$500	2.86%	$1,540	$2,040
Jefferson City	8,263	$105,067	$41,924	0.03	$3,394	$500	3.23%	$3,394	$3,894
Raymore-Peculiar R-II	4,627	$57,663	$56,198	0.03	$1,811	$500	3.14%	$1,811	$2,311
Warrensburg R-VI	3,167	$58,619	$32,477	0.04	$2,169	$500	3.70%	$2,169	$2,669
Mehlville R-IX	11,799	$108,448	$53,741	0.03	$3,264	$500	3.01%	$3,264	$3,764
Cooter R-IV	277	$19,918	$31,094	0.03	$548	$500	2.75%	$548	$1,048
Lee's Summit R-VII	14,861	$70,601	$59,944	0.04	$3,085	$500	4.37%	$3,085	$3,585
Columbia 93	16,076	$83,170	$36,516	0.04	$3,269	$500	3.93%	$3,269	$3,769
Ferguson-Florissant R-II	11,949	$75,200	$40,500	0.05	$3,564	$500	4.74%	$3,564	$4,064
St. Louis City	42,654	$73,398	$27,156	0.04	$2,738	$500	3.73%	$2,738	$3,238
Kansas City 33	33,642	$75,186	$29,634	0.05	$3,722	$500	4.95%	$3,722	$4,222
Wellston	747	$24,686	$21,458	0.05	$1,259	$500	5.10%	$1,259	$1,759
Ladue	3,272	$336,855	$82,889	0.03	$8,859	$500	2.63%	$8,859	$9,359

Source: Data from Missouri Department of Elementary and Secondary Education. Retrieved June 2005 from http://www.dese.mo.gov/schooldata/ftpdata.html.

Table 6.2   Responsiveness of Critical Output to Policy Leverage: Selected Equity Measures

Option	Flat Grant per Pupil	CV	Elasticity	Total State Cost
No Aid	$0	38%	.64	$0
A	$500	32%	.55	$90 million
B	$2,000	23%	.38	$360 million

CV, coefficient of variation.

The only policy lever on a flat-grant formula is the level of the flat grant to be allocated.[1] Flat grants are not generally perceived as equalizing formulas, because they allocate the same amounts of funding to both wealthy and poor districts. Changes in the level of a flat grant, however, may have equalizing effects on at least some equity indices.

Table 6.2 demonstrates the results of the application of a flat grant at two levels (3 if you include $0), compared to a case of no state aid. For the no-state-aid case, the coefficient of variation is 38% across the 20-district sample in Table 6.1. When a $500 flat grant is added, presuming no change in local taxing behavior, the coefficient of variation is reduced to 32%. This is primarily because the mean revenue per pupil is increased from $2,991 to $3,491 per pupil, an increase in the denominator of the coefficient of variation. Note also that the elasticity is slightly reduced with each increase in state aid per pupil. What happens to the coefficient of variation when the flat grant is increased to $2,000? What happens to the elasticity coefficient? Do you think the flat grant is an efficient means of reducing inequality of per pupil spending? Why or why not?

While improvements to equity and neutrality are important, the effects of these changes on the state budget are not trivial. Note that providing only a $500 flat grant per pupil to these 20 school districts costs the state $90 million and increasing that grant to $2,000 costs the state nearly $360 million.

Examples in Practice

Flat grants most often exist in current state policies for providing categorical programs. Most states have used one of the equalization schemes that follow in this chapter for their general fund. Categorical aid flat grants across the states include New York's allocation in the 1990s of $196 per gifted child, or New Jersey's flat grant of $1,102 per limited-English-proficient child. More discussion of categorical aid flat grants appears in Chapter 8.

Some states, including Wyoming, Vermont, and Kansas, have funding systems that are *full state control* or state-dominated funding models. In these cases, the base state aid per pupil is the equivalent of a flat, or block, grant. The intent of such models is that the flat grant alone should suffice to provide an adequate education. Thus, the flat grant is both adequate and equitable. Wyoming's block grant is allocated based on an analysis of the cost of an adequate education that we discuss in greater detail in Chapter 9. Vermont implemented a flat-grant program in 1998 (referring to it as a guaranteed yield program), allocating a base state aid per-pupil flat grant of approximately $5,100 in 1999–2000, and Kansas implemented a flat-grant program in 1992 (referring to it as a foundation program) with a flat grant of $3,870 per weighted pupil in 2001–2002 (down to $3,863 per pupil from 2002 through 2005). In both Kansas and Vermont, regardless of what they have chosen to call their funding formulas, the states implemented uniform statewide property taxes to partially support a uniform statewide base aid, or flat grant. Arguably, as preferences for adequacy-based funding schemes increase, and power increasingly shifts from local districts to states, flat grants are likely to increase in popularity. Depending on what kind of tax systems are used to collect the state funding, an adequate statewide flat grant may be more equitable than a foundation program funded by sales taxes. Only by examining both sides of the equation can we determine the net redistributional consequences of the funding system.

---

[1]This is true in a qualified sense. Recently, some states offer flat grants to charter schools and even to private schools on a per-pupil basis that is unrelated to the actual cost of the schooling or to the identified needs of the children in them. For an interesting case study, see Richards, Sawicky, and Shore (1996).

Foundation Aid Formulas

The concept of foundation aid formulas dates back to 1924, when described by George D. Strayer and Robert M. Haig as follows:

> To carry into effect the principle of "equalization of educational opportunity" and "equalization of school support" as commonly understood it would be necessary (1) to establish schools or make other arrangements sufficient to furnish the children in every locality within the state with equal educational opportunities up to some prescribed minimum; (2) to raise the funds necessary for this purpose by local or state taxation adjusted in such manner as to bear upon the people in all localities at the same rate in relation to their tax-paying ability; and (3) to provide adequately either for the supervision and control of all the schools, or for their direct administration, by a state department of education. (Strayer & Haig, 1924)

As described by Strayer and Haig (1924), foundation-aid formulas account for differences in local capacity to fund public schools and have the objective of bringing each school district up to a *foundation level* of funding. The **foundation level** is the target level of minimum funding per pupil to be available to school districts and/or charter schools.

Foundation aid (state aid) is the share of the foundation level of funding to be allocated from a state's general fund budget (or specific school fund). Usually, "state aid" per se is funding allocated out of state general funds (from sales and/or income tax) from the state to local school districts on an equalized basis, according to the amount of property tax revenue that districts raise when implementing the required tax rate.

The **required tax rate (RTR)** is typically the school district property tax rate or levy required by the state in order to receive state aid sufficient to raise district revenues per pupil to the foundation level. (The RTR is also sometimes referred to as the required local effort, RLE.)

It is very important to notice that, for Strayer and Haig (1924), the notions of "equity" and "equal educational opportunity" were qualified by the phrase, "up to some prescribed minimum." Although states have used foundation formulas to pursue absolute horizontal equity (equal dollars per pupil in rich and poor districts), the original design was not intended to accomplish this but rather to provide an equal minimum foundation.

Local capacity usually is defined as the local assessed property value per pupil of the district, because property taxes have dominated local finance of public education. Local assessed property value per pupil is usually used as the basis for measuring fiscal capacity in school finance because property taxes have dominated the local finance of public education. In a foundation program, a district's state aid per pupil (SAPP) is the difference between the foundation level set by the state legislature and what the district can raise locally, given the state RTR times its local assessed valuation per pupil (AVPP):

$$SAPP_d = FAPP_d - (RTR_d \times AVPP_d)$$

Table 6.3 provides a sample application of a foundation aid program to two districts. The foundation level is $5,000 per pupil, and the RTR is 1%, or 10 mills. District A has assessed valuation per pupil of $100,000. If District A applies the RTR of 1% to its assessed valuation per pupil, the yield is $1,000 per pupil. The difference between that yield and the foundation aid per pupil, or the state aid per pupil, is $4,000 for District A. In this example, however, District A may raise additional revenues by levying in excess of the 1% required rate. If District A levies a 2% tax rate, it gains another $1,000 per pupil of local revenues. Note that District B's local revenues per pupil from applying the RTR of 1% equal the foundation level, leaving District B with no state aid.

Table 6.4 displays the application of foundation funding to our 20-district sample with a foundation

Table 6.3   Application of Foundation Aid to Two Sample Districts

District	Foundation Aid per Pupil	Required Tax Rate	Assessed Valuation per Pupil	Local Yield	State Aid per Pupil	Actual Local Tax Rate	Local Revenue per Pupil	TRPP
A	$5,000	1%	$100,000	$1,000	$4,000	2%	$2,000	$6,000
B	$5,000	1%	$500,000	$5,000	$0	.8%	$4,000	$4,000

TRPP, total revenue per pupil.

Table 6.4 Application of a Foundation Program to Missouri Districts

District	Enrollment	Assessed Valuation per Pupil	Income per Pupil	Original Tax Rate	Required Tax Rate	New Tax Rate	New Local Revenue per Pupil	Foundation Level	State Aid per Pupil	Total Revenue per Pupil
Cooter R-IV	277	$19,918	$31,094	2.75%	2.75%	2.75%	$548	$5,000	$4,452	$5,000
Waynesville R-VI	5,147	$21,799	$36,724	2.70%	2.75%	2.75%	$599	$5,000	$4,401	$5,000
Wellston	747	$24,686	$21,458	5.10%	2.75%	5.10%	$1,259	$5,000	$4,321	$5,580
Hillsboro R-III	3,592	$44,725	$48,548	2.94%	2.75%	2.94%	$1,315	$5,000	$3,770	$5,085
Bolivar R-I	2,350	$45,392	$29,257	2.75%	2.75%	2.75%	$1,248	$5,000	$3,752	$5,000
Ozark R-VI	3,925	$50,363	$40,352	2.75%	2.75%	2.75%	$1,385	$5,000	$3,615	$5,000
Hannibal 60	3,645	$53,855	$31,962	2.86%	2.75%	2.86%	$1,540	$5,000	$3,519	$5,059
Festus R-VI	2,672	$56,179	$40,964	2.87%	2.75%	2.87%	$1,612	$5,000	$3,455	$5,067
Raymore-Peculiar R-II	4,627	$57,663	$56,198	3.14%	2.75%	3.14%	$1,811	$5,000	$3,414	$5,225
Warrensburg R-VI	3,167	$58,619	$32,477	3.70%	2.75%	3.70%	$2,169	$5,000	$3,388	$5,557
Sedalia 200	4,191	$60,485	$31,267	2.75%	2.75%	2.75%	$1,663	$5,000	$3,337	$5,000
Lee's Summit R-VII	14,861	$70,601	$59,944	4.37%	2.75%	4.37%	$3,085	$5,000	$3,058	$6,144
St. Louis City	42,654	$73,398	$27,156	3.73%	2.75%	3.73%	$2,738	$5,000	$2,982	$5,719
Kansas City 33	33,642	$75,186	$29,634	4.95%	2.75%	4.95%	$3,722	$5,000	$2,932	$6,654
Ferguson-Florissant R-II	11,949	$75,200	$40,500	4.74%	2.75%	4.74%	$3,564	$5,000	$2,932	$6,496
Columbia 93	16,076	$83,170	$36,516	3.93%	2.75%	3.93%	$3,269	$5,000	$2,713	$5,981
Jefferson City	8,263	$105,067	$41,924	3.23%	2.75%	3.23%	$3,394	$5,000	$2,111	$5,504
Mehlville R-IX	11,799	$108,448	$53,741	3.01%	2.75%	3.01%	$3,264	$5,000	$2,018	$5,282
Branson R-IV	3,143	$145,745	$32,098	2.31%	2.75%	2.75%	$4,008	$5,000	$992	$5,000
Ladue	3,272	$336,855	$82,889	2.63%	2.75%	2.63%	$8,859	$5,000	$0	$8,859

Source: Data from Missouri Department of Elementary and Secondary Education. Retrieved June 2005 from http://www.dese.mo.gov/schooldata/ftpdata.html.

level of $5,000 per pupil and RTR of 2.75% (27.5 mills). Note that in this simulation, we allow districts for which property taxes originally exceeded the RTR to decrease their local taxes toward the RTR. Resulting local revenues range from $548 to $8,859 per pupil. When state aid is added, total revenues range from the foundation level of $5,000 to $8,859, with one district remaining independent from the formula.

Two alternatives exist for the case where District B has even higher assessed valuation per pupil. The first alternative is simply to leave District B alone, allowing it to apply whatever tax rate it wishes and spend what it wishes on its schools. The second alternative is to impose a *recapture* provision, whereby any dollars raised above the foundation level with the RTR would be submitted to the state for redistribution. This approach both improves equity statistics, by lowering the top as well as raising the bottom, and infuses additional funds into the available state revenue pool. However, complete or even partial *recapture* provisions are rarely politically palatable.

Equal per-pupil spending was never intended to be the primary goal of foundation aid formulas. As such, they do not typically achieve this goal. However, if the funding levels are sufficiently high, one can view the foundation approach as an attempt to create educational adequacy. Foundation formulas gained popularity from the 1970s to 1990s primarily as a means of responding to and fending off equity litigation. Whether a foundation formula is built on adequacy principles depends largely on the derivation of the foundation level of funding. In most cases, foundation levels are derived relative to existing spending levels for some or all districts and not relative to any particular cost or adequacy target. For example, one might use the mean or median spending of all districts in a state or, as mandated by the New Jersey court, the mean spending of the highest spending districts in the state. This particular approach in New Jersey only ensured a half-century of court litigation. Although the New Jersey foundation-funding model often resulted in the temporary improvement of equity statistics, it did not necessarily ensure educational adequacy. More often, legislators simply remove the foundation level of funding from the legislature's budget constraint, given the number of pupils to be served:

$$\text{Total Budget Constraint} = \text{Available Revenues}_s + (\text{RTR}_s \times \text{Total Assessed Valuation}_s)$$

Then:

$$\text{Foundation} = \text{Total Budget Constraint/Pupils}$$

That is, the foundation is derived by summing total available state revenues and total revenues generated by required local tax rates, then dividing that "total budget constraint" by all of the state's pupils. Even where foundation aid programs are initially implemented with adequacy ideals in mind, state budget constraints tend to dictate changes (or lack thereof) to foundation aid over time.

Policy Levers and Critical Output

The two policy levers of a foundation program are the foundation level and the RTR. We can manipulate each toward different outcome objectives. We encourage you to run sensitivity analyses of each lever on different outcomes using the simulation at the end of this chapter. One approach to sensitivity analysis is to hold one lever constant (foundation = $5,000) while incrementally adjusting the other (RTR from 0% to 5%). When making these adjustments, record and compare outcome measures. Increasing the required local tax rate, for example, increases the burden placed on local voters to fund public education. If we keep the foundation level constant, local voters are responsible for greater and greater shares of the total cost with each incremental increase to RTR. As a result, the total state cost (one critical output) is decreased. Of course, if we can use increased RTR to decrease state cost, then we can combine increased RTR with increased foundation levels at the same state cost, toward greater equity or adequacy.

Table 6.5 displays the application of four alternative combinations of policy leverage to the 20-district sample. The objective was to create policy options that each met the budget constraint of no greater than $1 billion in state revenue. Note that increased required tax rates allow substantial increases to the foundation level. Of course, this approach is only realistic if political and economic conditions permit. Note that increasing foundation aid results in incremental improvement to both the dispersion measure (coefficient of variation) and the neutrality measure (elasticity).

Examples in Practice

Foundation aid formulas dominate current school finance policies across states, whether as a portion, or basic framework of entire state-funding systems. We note, however, that several states refer to their aid

Table 6.5   Sensitivity Analysis of Four Alternative Foundation Programs

| Option | Foundation | Required Tax Rate | Selected Equity Measures | | Total State Cost |
			Coefficient of Variation	Elasticity	
A	$4,500	1.0%	12%	.17	$667 million
B	$4,750	1.1%	11%	.15	$698 million
C	$5,000	1.2%	11%	.14	$728 million
D	$6,000	1.6%	9%	.12	$908 million

programs as foundation programs while it is questionable whether that characterization is appropriate. Conventional examples include Massachusetts' foundation aid program with a foundation of $6,442 in 1998–1999. Slight variants include the first tier of Connecticut's *Education Cost Sharing Program*, which uses a foundation level of spending ($5,775 in 1998–1999) to establish what it refers to as a minimum expenditure requirement (MER), which must be met by all districts and determines state share of the foundation according to local property wealth. New Jersey's school finance program establishes a T&E Budget (Thorough and Efficient Budget) for each school district, where the foundation level across districts, or T&E budgets, ranged from $6,554 to $7,244 in 1998–1999.

In some cases it can be difficult, for example, to discern between a flat-grant program partially funded by a statewide property tax and a simple foundation program. Kansas and Vermont are examples where the state imposes a local property tax rate, then guarantees a set foundation level for that tax rate. Arguably, because both states recapture excess property tax revenues— essentially adding all property tax revenues to a pool with other state revenues for funding the foundation level across districts—the systems function more like a statewide flat grant.

Revenue-Raising Equity Formulas

Alternatives to formulas designed to generate specific levels of spending across districts are formulas designed to provide districts with comparable revenue-raising capacity, regardless of local fiscal capacity. In this section, we discuss the guaranteed tax base formula as the basic prototype.

Guaranteed Wealth/Tax-Base Formulas

Guaranteed tax base formulas are based on the ideal that any district in a state should have comparable "opportunity" to raise revenues for education. The **guaranteed tax base (GTB)** is the taxable property wealth per pupil guaranteed by the state. Because property values are most often the tax base for raising local education revenue, the most common strategy employed in GTB programs is to provide all districts the opportunity to raise revenue as if they have a guaranteed level of assessed property value per pupil. That guaranteed level of property wealth is the guaranteed tax base.

Table 6.6 provides a two-district example of a GTB formula. In the example, District A has assessed valuation per pupil of $100,000, and District B has assessed valuation per pupil of $500,000. In this example, we do not impose an RTR. Rather, the formula

Table 6.6   Two-District Example of a Guaranteed Tax Base

District	Guaranteed Tax Base	Local Tax Rate	Guaranteed Revenue per Pupil	Assessed Value per Pupil	Actual Local Revenue per Pupil	State Aid per Pupil	Total Revenue per Pupil
A	$500,000	1%	$5,000	$100,000	$1,000	$4,000	$5,000
B	$500,000	.8%	$4,000	$500,000	$4,000	$0	$4,000

works such that districts select a tax rate based on local voter preferences, and the state guarantees the revenue that would be generated by applying that tax rate to the GTB of $500,000. For district A, a tax rate of 1% would generate $5,000 per pupil given the GTB. However, applying the 1% rate to district A's assessed value per pupil generates only $1,000 per pupil. As a result, the state provides the difference between the local revenue raised and the revenue that would have been raised at the guaranteed wealth level, or $5,000 − $1,000 = $4,000 in SAPP.

$$SAPP = LTR \times (GTB - AVPP)$$

Where LTR is the adopted local tax rate

District B's assessed valuation per pupil (AVPP) is equal to the GTB. As such, District B receives no state aid. If District B's assessed value exceeded the guaranteed wealth, we would again have the option of either allowing District B to exercise its right to raise whatever revenues it chooses or to impose recapture on revenues raised above what the district would have raised with the same tax rate at the guaranteed wealth level.

Policy Levers and Critical Output for the GTB Formula

In its purest form, the GTB formula has only one policy lever: the guaranteed wealth level. In most cases, the guaranteed wealth level is expressed in relative terms, as a percentile wealth among districts in a state using either pupil or district unit of analysis. That is, the GTB level might be the assessed valuation of the 75th percentile district or of the district with the 75th percentile pupil when we rank districts by assessed valuation. As a matter of practicality, most GTB formulas also include a minimum RTR, and many also include a maximum tax rate up to which the state will share in revenue raising.

Implementing a minimum tax rate establishes a "foundation" level of spending, in that it guarantees that all districts will have revenue at least equal to the minimum tax rate times the guaranteed wealth. Such formulas are also sometimes referred to as **guaranteed yield** formulas. Despite this guarantee, **matching aid** (state aid allocated to school districts on the basis of a defined matching rate) does not yield uniformly high spending in low-capacity districts. In Missouri, for example, several districts receiving around 70% matching rates still levy only the minimum formula tax rate of

$2.75 per $100 in assessed valuation, while others receiving much lower matching rates levy much higher taxes (Table 6.7). Revenues per pupil in Missouri remain highly associated with assessed value per pupil.

The **matching rate** is the rate at which matching aid is provided, usually depending primarily on the ratio of a district's taxable property wealth per pupil to a guaranteed level of taxable property wealth per pupil. Matching rates may be modified with income or other factors.

Table 6.8 applies sensitivity analysis to the GTB formula, adjusting both RTRs and guaranteed wealth levels (expressed as district-unit percentiles). The critical output shows that increasing the guaranteed wealth level comes at substantial cost to the state but generally results in improved equity, as measured by the coefficient of variation. Note also that increases to the GTB should yield improved elasticity. Required tax rates have a slightly different effect under the GTB than under the foundation formula. While increases to the RTR shifted the burden for funding the foundation to local districts, increases to RTR under the GTB increase both local burden and state burden to provide matching funds.

Examples in Practice

Missouri's school-funding formula (until recently) was one example of a relatively straightforward GTB formula. The objective of the Missouri formula is to provide districts with a GTB at the level of the 90th percentile pupil, with a minimum RTR of $2.75 per $100 assessed valuation (residential property assessed at 19%). Many states use GTB formulas in conjunction with other methods in what we discuss later in this chapter as combination formulas.

One common criticism of GTB formulas that research has validated extensively is that simply providing the districts equal opportunity to spend based on assessed valuation rarely yields comparable spending levels across communities and rarely results in substantial improvements to fiscal neutrality (Monk, 1984). In practice, wealthy communities remain more likely to use state aid under GTB programs for tax relief than for increased spending (Richardson & Lamitie, 1989). Also, property wealth equalization may not adequately address income disparities across districts. For example, two separate studies on the GTB program in Kansas, which allows districts to raise funds above the foundation, confirm significant differences in median family income between districts opting to raise additional

Table 6.7 Application of a Guaranteed Tax Base Formula to Missouri Districts

District	Enrollment	Assessed Valuation per Pupil	Income per Pupil	Original Tax Rate	Original Total Revenue	New Tax Rate	Guaranteed Wealth	Local Revenue per Pupil	State Revenue per Pupil	Total Revenue per Pupil
Cooter R-IV	277	$19,918	$31,094	2.75%	$548	1.12%	$155,301	$223	$1,518	$1,742
Waynesville R-VI	5,147	$21,799	$36,724	2.70%	$589	1.19%	$155,301	$260	$1,593	$1,853
Wellston	747	$24,686	$21,458	5.10%	$1,259	2.52%	$155,301	$621	$3,285	$3,906
Hillsboro R-III	3,592	$44,725	$48,548	2.94%	$1,315	2.35%	$155,301	$1,053	$2,603	$3,655
Bolivar R-I	2,350	$45,392	$29,257	2.75%	$1,248	2.23%	$155,301	$1,010	$2,446	$3,457
Ozark R-VI	3,925	$50,363	$40,352	2.75%	$1,385	2.40%	$155,301	$1,208	$2,517	$3,725
Hannibal 60	3,645	$53,855	$31,962	2.86%	$1,540	2.61%	$155,301	$1,406	$2,649	$4,056
Festus R-VI	2,672	$56,179	$40,964	2.87%	$1,612	2.69%	$155,301	$1,514	$2,671	$4,185
Raymore-Peculiar R-II	4,627	$57,663	$56,198	3.14%	$1,811	3.00%	$155,301	$1,729	$2,928	$4,656
Warrensburg R-VI	3,167	$58,619	$32,477	3.70%	$2,169	3.57%	$155,301	$2,093	$3,452	$5,544
Sedalia 200	4,191	$60,485	$31,267	2.75%	$1,663	2.71%	$155,301	$1,637	$2,566	$4,202
Lee's Summit R-VII	14,861	$70,601	$59,944	4.37%	$3,085	4.70%	$155,301	$3,315	$3,977	$7,292
St. Louis City	42,654	$73,398	$27,156	3.73%	$2,738	4.09%	$155,301	$3,000	$3,347	$6,347
Kansas City 33	33,642	$75,186	$29,634	4.95%	$3,722	5.49%	$155,301	$4,126	$4,396	$8,522
Ferguson-Florissant R-II	11,949	$75,200	$40,500	4.74%	$3,564	5.25%	$155,301	$3,952	$4,209	$8,161
Columbia 93	16,076	$83,170	$36,516	3.93%	$3,269	4.55%	$155,301	$3,783	$3,281	$7,064
Jefferson City	8,263	$105,067	$41,924	3.23%	$3,394	3.95%	$155,301	$4,153	$1,985	$6,138
Mehlville R-IX	11,799	$108,448	$53,741	3.01%	$3,264	3.69%	$155,301	$3,999	$1,728	$5,726
Branson R-IV	3,143	$145,745	$32,098	2.31%	$3,367	2.50%	$155,301	$3,646	$239	$3,885
Ladue	3,272	$336,855	$82,889	2.63%	$8,859	2.63%	$155,301	$8,859	$0	$8,859

Source: Data from Missouri Department of Elementary and Secondary Education. Retrieved June 2005 from http://www.dese.mo.gov/schooldata/ftpdata.html.

Table 6.8   Sensitivity Analysis of GTB Level and Required Tax Rate on Equity, Neutrality, and Cost

	Selected Equity Measures			
Option	GTB	CV	Elasticity	Total State Cost (in millions)
A	50th percentile	33%	.56	$12.11
B	75th percentile	26%	.44	$47.40
C	80th percentile	26%	.32	$116.90
D	90th percentile	27%	.20	$297.90

CV, coefficient of variation; GTB, guaranteed tax base.

funds and districts opting out (Baker, 2001b; Duncombe & Johnston, 2004). We discuss this issue in greater detail later in this chapter in our section on the economics of intergovernmental aid.

Previously in the chapter, we have referred repeatedly to combination formulas—that is, the use of flat grants, GTBs, or foundation formulas as only part of a general state aid program—but we have not explained these combination formulas. Two-tier formulas can take many forms. We present one approach in Table 6.9. This formula involves a foundation program as its first-tier program. Two unique features of the first tier are that it includes a uniform statewide property tax rate and recaptures excess revenues generated by that tax rate from high property wealth districts. States can use those recaptured revenues to lessen the burden on other state revenue sources for funding foundation aid to poorer districts.

The second tier of the formula is a GTB formula, using a 75th percentile tax base equalization. In Table 6.9, for simplicity, all districts are imposing a uniform second-tier tax rate. Typically, this tax rate would vary across districts, because implementing this tax is entirely at local discretion. Note that with the GTB formula, the uniform tax rate of 0.2% guarantees second-tier revenue of $154 per pupil.

Policy Levers and Critical Output for the Two-Tier Formula

The policy levers in the two-tier model shown in Table 6.9 are more complicated, in terms of both their effects on equity and their various political implications. The policy levers include the foundation level, the Tier-I RTR and the Tier-II guaranteed wealth level. One might also include a policy lever setting a cap on Tier-II tax revenues at some defined level.

As in the previous foundation program, increases to Tier-I aid result in increased equity across districts but also increase the budget cost to the state quite dramatically. Increases to Tier-I foundation aid may also decrease districts' need or desire to use Tier-II taxes. State legislators, however, may use the second tier as a way to save funds on the first tier (Table 6.10). For example, if the legislature removes $1 per pupil from the first tier, it initially saves $1 times all pupils in the state. Many, but not all, districts might choose to make up the $1 revenue loss with local option taxes. If so, for those who do, the state will need to pick up only a portion of the $1 across only those pupils in districts below the 75th percentile of wealth. Such strategies may also have adverse equity consequences, if rich districts elect to pick up the extra dollar in local tax effort, while poor do not.

Our inclusion of a recapture provision on the first tier creates another potential political game. Recapture provisions, or "Robin Hood" provisions, have historically been among the least politically palatable policies in school finance, especially among those districts required to send revenues generated by local property taxes "back to the state" or to other districts. **Recapture** is simply redistribution of revenue generated by a specific tax revenue source. Two policy levers, the foundation level or the RTR, can be used to reduce numbers of districts included in the recapture group and to garner political support. Raising the foundation level decreases the likelihood that the RTR times the local property wealth of any district exceeds the foundation. Lowering the RTR has the same effect. Both options, however, are expensive, in that they require making up the difference (tax rate option) or increasing aid (foundation option) with "other" state revenues.

Table 6.9 Two-Tier Foundation and GTB Formula (Tier-I Foundation = $5,000)

District	Enrollment	Assessed Valuation per Pupil	Tier-I Required Levy	Tier-I Local Share	Tier-I State Aid	Tier-II GTB	Tier-II Optional Levy	Tier-II Local Share	Tier-II State Aid	Tier-I Revenue per Pupil	Tier-II Revenue per Pupil	Total Revenue per Pupil
Cooter R-IV	277	$19,918	2.75%	$548	$4,452	$77,193	0.20%	$40	$115	$5,000	$154	$5,154
Waynesville R-VI	5,147	$21,799	2.75%	$599	$4,401	$77,193	0.20%	$44	$111	$5,000	$154	$5,154
Wellston	747	$24,686	2.75%	$679	$4,321	$77,193	0.20%	$49	$105	$5,000	$154	$5,154
Hillsboro R-III	3,592	$44,725	2.75%	$1,230	$3,770	$77,193	0.20%	$89	$65	$5,000	$154	$5,154
Bolivar R-I	2,350	$45,392	2.75%	$1,248	$3,752	$77,193	0.20%	$91	$64	$5,000	$154	$5,154
Ozark R-VI	3,925	$50,363	2.75%	$1,385	$3,615	$77,193	0.20%	$101	$54	$5,000	$154	$5,154
Hannibal 60	3,645	$53,855	2.75%	$1,481	$3,519	$77,193	0.20%	$108	$47	$5,000	$154	$5,154
Festus R-VI	2,672	$56,179	2.75%	$1,545	$3,455	$77,193	0.20%	$112	$42	$5,000	$154	$5,154
Raymore-Peculiar R-II	4,627	$57,663	2.75%	$1,586	$3,414	$77,193	0.20%	$115	$39	$5,000	$154	$5,154
Warrensburg R-VI	3,167	$58,619	2.75%	$1,612	$3,388	$77,193	0.20%	$117	$37	$5,000	$154	$5,154
Sedalia 200	4,191	$60,485	2.75%	$1,663	$3,337	$77,193	0.20%	$121	$33	$5,000	$154	$5,154
Lee's Summit R-VII	14,861	$70,601	2.75%	$1,942	$3,058	$77,193	0.20%	$141	$13	$5,000	$154	$5,154
St. Louis City	42,654	$73,398	2.75%	$2,018	$2,982	$77,193	0.20%	$147	$8	$5,000	$154	$5,154
Kansas City 33	33,642	$75,186	2.75%	$2,068	$2,932	$77,193	0.20%	$150	$4	$5,000	$154	$5,154
Ferguson-Florissant R-II	11,949	$75,200	2.75%	$2,068	$2,932	$77,193	0.20%	$150	$4	$5,000	$154	$5,154
Columbia 93	16,076	$83,170	2.75%	$2,287	$2,713	$77,193	0.20%	$166	$0	$5,000	$166	$5,166
Jefferson City	8,263	$105,067	2.75%	$2,889	$2,111	$77,193	0.20%	$210	$0	$5,000	$210	$5,210
Mehlville R-IX	11,799	$108,448	2.75%	$2,982	$2,018	$77,193	0.20%	$217	$0	$5,000	$217	$5,217
Branson R-IV	3,143	$145,745	2.75%	$4,008	$992	$77,193	0.20%	$291	$0	$5,000	$291	$5,291
Ladue	3,272	$336,855	2.75%	$9,264	−$4,264	$77,193	0.20%	$674	$0	$5,000	$674	$5,674

GTB, guaranteed tax base.

Source: Data from Missouri Department of Elementary and Secondary Education. Retrieved December 2004 from http://www.dese.mo.gov/schooldata/ftpdata.html.

Table 6.10   Using the Second Tier to Save State Funds on the First Tier

Option	Foundation	Required Tier-I Tax Rate	Tier-II GTB	Hypothetical Tier-II Tax Rate	Minimum Revenue per Pupil	State Cost (millions)
A	$5,000	1.1%	75th percentile	.2%	$5,720	$21.02
B	$4,000	1.1%	75th percentile	.5%	$5,801	$13.37

GTB, guaranteed tax base.

Some, including Hoxby (2001) argue that income taxes are generally more appropriate taxes for meeting redistribution goals such as uniform first-tier revenues. Hoxby recommends phasing out the state required property tax rate on the first tier of this formula, using only other state revenues for redistribution. Hoxby recommends, however, using property taxes for the second tier of this type of formula, because property taxes allow local voters to raise additional funds for their schools, improving school quality in their district, and ultimately improving the values of the properties being taxed at the second tier.

Other Two-Tier Approaches

Texas uses a cost-adjusted foundation program as the first tier of funding, supported by a uniform tax rate. The second tier of the formula allows districts to raise additional revenues at a guaranteed yield of $27.14 per pupil per each penny of property tax rate. The second tier of the Texas formula includes a somewhat creative and politically contentious recapture provision on districts with assessed valuation per pupil in excess of $305,000 per pupil as of 2003–2004. The recapture provision requires districts with high-assessed valuation to choose among options for "donating" excess revenues, wealth credits so-to-speak, or pupil-funding credits either to a state pool, or other specific districts. Some have suggested that district revenues raised by wealthy districts beyond this recapture provision constitute a third tier of the Texas formula.

Vermont, like Kansas, allows districts to raise supplemental revenues on top of the basic education grant. Vermont took a particularly creative and very aggressive approach to recapturing second-tier funds. Vermont's "sharing pool" allows districts to opt into a pool of districts wishing to supplement the first tier. Once in the pool, districts choose their desired spending levels. Then, based on assessed valuation of partic-ipating districts, the state applies a uniform tax rate to districts in the pool to generate the necessary revenues to cover budget requests. This means, for example, that if 10 districts enter the pool, and one is wealthy and nine are poor, then the one wealthy district may pay the majority of second-tier funding for all districts in the pool. Further, if wealthy districts opt out, choosing private fund-raising instead, one middle-wealth district might end up paying the bill for the rest of the districts in the pool. Needless to say, this Vermont provision was not politically palatable to many districts, and from the provision's outset, the state supplemented the "shark pool," as it became known, with other state revenues (see Baker, 2001a). Vermont has since changed the policy to a guaranteed yield, matching aid formula, where an additional 1% of tax yields an additional 1% revenue, regardless of taxable property wealth.

Beyond Property Wealth Equalization

As noted previously, one failure of tax base equalization programs is that they rarely achieve sufficient fiscal neutrality and, in particular, property wealth equalization formulas rarely achieve neutrality with respect to income across districts. Recall from Chapter 1 that voter choices to spend on public education at given levels depend primarily on (a) their tastes for public education goods and services, (b) the price of an additional unit of education in taxes, and (c) the ability of the voter to pay for education, usually in terms of their income. Within this framework, property value equalization can play either of two roles. First, we might consider property values of residents, if they can be easily liquidated, to partially represent a voter's ability to pay.

Alternatively, we can view property value measures as primarily an index of the local "tax price" of public services. For example, the local property wealth of any given community may consist of a mix of industrial, agricultural, and residential properties. Those who vote for taxes for schools in communities are primarily (or at least disproportionately with respect to the value of property) the local residential property owners. Consider a case where the average housing unit value in a community is $100,000. If each household has one child in the local schools, and no other properties exist in the district, then the average property wealth per pupil is $100,000. As a result, to raise $1,000 per pupil in local revenue, each residential taxpayer must pay a 1% (or $1,000 each) tax.

Now, consider the case where the same town includes a large corporate complex, or even more dramatically, oil or natural gas deposits the value of which equals the total value of all housing units in the district. When we include these properties in the calculation of district assessed valuation per pupil, the value increases to as much as $500,000 or even $1,000,000. Yet the residential property owner still pays taxes on his or her $100,000 home. If assessed value per pupil is $500,000, each homeowner would be required to pay only $200 (instead of $1,000), or .2%, in taxes for an additional $1,000 in revenue for the schools. That is, the "tax price" in this district is much lower than the tax price in the first.

Bringing income into the picture allows us to measure the relative burden of these different tax prices on residents. Assume that each family in both districts has an income of $50,000 per year. In the first district, each family pays $1,000 in taxes to raise $1,000 in revenue for the schools, meaning that each pays the equivalent of a 2% income tax rate. Resident taxpayers in the second district who pay only $200 each pay the equivalent of a .4% tax rate for the same revenue. Studies have validated residents' propensity to use valuable nonresidential properties for both tax relief and increased spending on their schools (Baker, 2001a).

Further, districts of comparable assessed valuation per pupil and housing unit values may have very different average income per pupil, affecting the rate at which they choose to take advantage of similar tax prices. That is, even if the tax price is similar, if residents have very different ability to pay, they will choose different tax rates for education. State school-funding formulas attempt to account for income differences, or fiscal capacity differences, in a variety of ways, still primarily relying on property taxes as the central measure of wealth. Three such approaches are (a) using income weights to adjust property wealth equalized aid, (b) including income sensitivity measures to limit individual tax burdens faced by residents, or (c) calculation of complex fiscal capacity indices for districts including measures of family incomes to adjust aid allocations.

Income Weighting

Application of income weights to property wealth equalized aid is perhaps the most common method of accommodating district income differences. Note that it is particularly pertinent to account for local income differences in funding systems (e.g., GTBs) that rely on local voters to set spending levels to ensure that districts have comparable ability to spend. Table 6.11 presents an example of income weighting. In the example, each district's aggregate taxable income per pupil is indexed relative to the median district's income per pupil. This can be done in a variety of ways, but the objective is to obtain a relative income weight whereby a district with income above the median receives a weight of less than 1.0, and a district with income below the median receives a weight of greater than 1.0. One approach is to calculate the ratio of each district's income to the median income, then divide that ratio into 1.0 (invert the ratio):

$$\text{District Income Weight (DIW)} = 1/(\text{District Income}/\text{Median Income})$$

Consider the following sample calculation:

Step 1: DIW = $1/(50,000$ district income$/40,000$ median income)

Step 2: $50,000/40,000 = 1.25$ (district has 25% higher income than median)

Step 3: $1/1.25 = 0.8$ (median need is 25% higher than district need, or $.2/.8 = .25$)

The weight must be inverted if it is to be used as multiplier for appropriately adjusting state aid. In the case of our sample district, because it has higher than median income, we wish to adjust its aid downward. We do so by multiplying the district income weight times the funding that would have been received through a pure GTB model, or by allocating only 80% of the GTB aid. If the district had lower than median income, the ratio would be greater than 1.0, and the

Table 6.11 Income Weighting

District	Enroll-ment	Assessed Valuation per Pupil	Income per Pupil	Original Tax Rate	Req-uired Tax Rate	New Tax Rate	Guara-nteed Wealth	Local Revenue per Pupil	GTB State Revenue per Pupil	Income Weight (Rela-tive to Median)	Income-Weighted Aid per Pupil	Total Revenue per Pupil
Cooter R-IV	277	$19,918	$31,094	2.75%	2.75%	2.75%	$155,301	$548	$3,723	1.18	$4,385	$4,932
Waynesville R-VI	5,147	$21,799	$36,724	2.70%	2.75%	2.75%	$155,301	$599	$3,671	1.00	$3,661	$4,260
Wellston	747	$24,686	$21,458	5.10%	2.75%	4.49%	$155,301	$1,108	$5,864	1.71	$10,007	$11,115
Hillsboro R-III	3,592	$44,725	$48,548	2.94%	2.75%	2.80%	$155,301	$1,251	$3,092	0.75	$2,332	$3,583
Bolivar R-I	2,350	$45,392	$29,257	2.75%	2.75%	2.75%	$155,301	$1,248	$3,022	1.25	$3,783	$5,031
Ozark R-VI	3,925	$50,363	$40,352	2.75%	2.75%	2.75%	$155,301	$1,385	$2,886	0.91	$2,619	$4,004
Hannibal 60	3,645	$53,855	$31,962	2.86%	2.75%	2.75%	$155,301	$1,481	$2,790	1.15	$3,196	$4,677
Festus R-VI	2,672	$56,179	$40,964	2.87%	2.75%	2.75%	$155,301	$1,545	$2,726	0.89	$2,437	$3,982
Raymore-Peculiar R-II	4,627	$57,663	$56,198	3.14%	2.75%	3.04%	$155,301	$1,756	$2,973	0.65	$1,937	$3,693
Warrensburg R-VI	3,167	$58,619	$32,477	3.70%	2.75%	3.56%	$155,301	$2,090	$3,446	1.13	$3,886	$5,975
Sedalia 200	4,191	$60,485	$31,267	2.75%	2.75%	2.75%	$155,301	$1,663	$2,607	1.17	$3,054	$4,717
Lee's Summit R-VII	14,861	$70,601	$59,944	4.37%	2.75%	4.30%	$155,301	$3,035	$3,641	0.61	$2,224	$5,259
St. Louis City	42,654	$73,398	$27,156	3.73%	2.75%	3.62%	$155,301	$2,658	$2,966	1.35	$4,000	$6,658
Kansas City 33	33,642	$75,186	$29,634	4.95%	2.75%	4.85%	$155,301	$3,649	$3,888	1.24	$4,804	$8,453
Ferguson-Florissant R-II	11,949	$75,200	$40,500	4.74%	2.75%	4.66%	$155,301	$3,506	$3,734	0.90	$3,376	$6,882
Columbia 93	16,076	$83,170	$36,516	3.93%	2.75%	3.86%	$155,301	$3,210	$2,784	1.00	$2,792	$6,003
Jefferson City	8,263	$105,067	$41,924	3.23%	2.75%	3.19%	$155,301	$3,351	$1,602	0.87	$1,399	$4,750
Mehlville R-IX	11,799	$108,448	$53,741	3.01%	2.75%	2.97%	$155,301	$3,223	$1,393	0.68	$949	$4,172
Branson R-IV	3,143	$145,745	$32,098	2.31%	2.75%	2.75%	$155,301	$4,008	$263	1.14	$300	$4,308
Ladue	3,272	$336,855	$82,889	2.63%	2.75%	2.63%	$155,301	$8,859	$0	0.44	$0	$8,859

GTB, guaranteed tax base.

Source: Data from Missouri Department of Elementary and Secondary Education. Retrieved December 2004 from http://www.dese.mo.gov/schooldata/ftpdata.html.

district would receive greater than the original GTB aid. Several mathematical alternatives exist for constructing income weights.

Fiscal Capacity Indices

The state of Tennessee takes a more complex approach to estimating the local (county) capacity of districts to raise funds for education. The Tennessee Advisory Commission on Intergovernmental Relations (TACIR) provides fiscal capacity indices used to determine the required local share in the basic education program formula (a type of foundation formula). Fiscal capacity is calculated for each of the 95 county areas based on the factors that best predict the amount of revenue local governments in Tennessee can be expected to raise for education. The factors that TACIR found best predict actual local revenue for education include:

- Tax base: total taxable sales and equalized assessed property values
- Per capita income
- Ratio of residential and farm property assessment to total property assessment
- Ratio of average daily membership of students in public schools to total population

Tennessee uses the percentages calculated with the TACIR formula to divide responsibility for the local share of the basic education program (BEP) formula among the counties. The state pays 75% of the cost of the BEP classroom components and 50% of the nonclassroom components. Tennessee multiplies the TACIR fiscal capacity percentages by statewide local share of BEP funding (after deducting the state-paid amount) to determine the amount for which each county area is responsible. This calculation produces the state and local percentage shares that the state uses to determine each school district's funding.

Income Sensitivity

A recent approach accounting for individuals' income differences rather than district average income differences is Vermont's use of income-sensitive property taxes. Vermont limits the property taxes on an individual with income (modified adjusted gross income) of less than $75,000 to 2% of that income. (This applies to property tax liability on primary residence and up to 2 acres or to the tax due on the property after taking a $15,000 exemption from the fair market value of the house. See Picus, 1998.)

Summary Across the States

In 1998–1999, 24 states relied on local assessed property value per pupil alone as the basis for equalizing state aid. Ten states (Connecticut, Iowa, Maine, Maryland, Massachusetts, New Hampshire, New Jersey, New York, Ohio, and Pennsylvania) included personal income along with assessed valuation per pupil; four states (Virginia, Tennessee, Kentucky, and Nebraska) used assessed valuation, personal income, and other revenue sources; and eight states used assessed valuation and other revenue sources as of 1998–1999 (see www.nces.ed.gov/edfin).

Equity Beyond Annual Operating Expenses: Facilities Equity in the 21st Century

An issue of increasing importance concerns the equity and adequacy of school facilities. Note that we have devoted the majority of attention in this chapter to the equalization of annual operating funds—funds that districts use to pay teachers, administrators, and other school staff; purchase educational materials, supplies, and equipment; and keep the lights and heating or cooling systems running throughout the year. Local school districts must also be able to construct and renovate facilities that are adequate to meet the needs of their student populations, whether those populations are growing, declining, or changing in their basic educational needs. Crampton, Thompson, and Hagey (2001) estimated that unmet funding needs for school infrastructure across the states exceeded $266 billion, resulting in 5-year costs per pupil ranging from $271 per pupil in Florida to $3,385 per pupil in Utah. Infrastructure needs include deferred maintenance (bringing facilities up to good condition), new construction, renovation, retrofitting, additions, and other major improvements.

The quality of schooling facilities can have indirect effects on equity of annual operating funds. For example, architects and engineers generally assume that schools constructed in the year 2000 were approximately 10% to 15% more cost efficient to operate than schools built just 10 years earlier. Districts with the luxury of operating new facilities with up-to-date mechanical systems are likely to spend less of their operating funds on utilities, leaving more for instruction.

State-aid formulas for supporting infrastructure are less evolved than aid formulas for equalizing annual operating budgets. In fact, Seilke (2001) indicates that 12 states (Idaho, Iowa, Louisiana, Michigan, Missouri, Nebraska, Nevada, North Carolina, North Dakota, Oklahoma, Oregon, and South Dakota) provided no state aid for infrastructure in 1998–1999. This was, however, a slight improvement from 1993–1994, when 16 states provided no state aid for infrastructure. Of the states with aid programs, 21 used some form of equalization in the allocation of aid for facilities, most often with respect to local assessed valuation per pupil. Only 1 state, Hawaii, provided full state funding for facilities.

The lack of state legislative attention to infrastructure needs is, in part, a function of state courts' ignoring facilities' disparities in school finance equity litigation. As we discuss in Chapter 7, the New Jersey court paid substantial attention to facilities adequacy in that state's most recent round of litigation. The Texas court in the *Edgewood* (1989) decision discussed in Chapter 4 also addressed facilities equity as a critical component of an overall equitable school-funding system (Clark, 2001).

Tax and Revenue Limits in School Finance Policies

Ever since state legislatures and supreme courts have retained new responsibilities for funding public education, legislatures have also become increasingly involved in regulating local tax policies. Two basic motives exist for legislation or constitutional provisions limiting taxation or revenue collection. The first motive may be expressed either in terms of fiscal austerity, or protections against "overtaxation." That is, state legislators pass policies that curb local spending behavior, and perhaps their own state spending behavior, in an effort to control the growth of bureaucracy and/or protect the voting public from being forced to pay excessive taxes or excessive tax increases without adequate participation. In many cases, when a state legislature imposes limits on local taxation with this motivation, local voters have the opportunity to override the limits. Policies intended to curb spending or limit tax burden typically take the form of (a) limitations on rates of increases allowed in local property taxation, (b) limitations on rates of increases allowed in the reassessment of property values, or (c) limitations on allowable local tax rates, with options for local voter override, perhaps with a two-thirds' majority.

The second motive is maintenance of equity in education revenues per pupil. State legislatures may impose limitations on the authority of local school districts to raise revenues above that which is declared adequate by the state. Essentially, the goal of such tax limits is to produce good equity statistics, including limited ranges, range ratios, and coefficients of variation in revenues per pupil. Such limits have become increasingly popular in two-tiered funding formulas in recent years, where it is assumed that the state takes care of adequate funding in the first tier and that local districts have the opportunity to provide limited supplements as a second tier. Some states, such as Kansas, limit second-tier revenues to a 31% supplement of the base state aid per pupil. One problem with such limits is that they provide legislatures with an "equity shield" when they choose not to provide sufficient aid to education. Equity statistics can remain acceptable, while adequacy erodes substantially. As you will be see in Chapter 7, the pursuit of adequacy litigation is more complicated than equity litigation.

With California's Proposition 13 as the most frequently cited example, strong criticisms have been levied against the state limitation of local spending on public schools for purposes of achieving greater equity and fiscal neutrality. Most such criticisms cite the tendency of tax limits to level down spending, or produce equitable inadequacy (Fiscel, 1989). Some recent evidence suggests that over time, tax limits level down not only spending but also student achievement (Downes & Figlio, 1998). Given the mixed evidence on production functions, it may be an interesting approach to test the negative production of educational achievement during suppressed spending.

Notes on the Economics of Intergovernmental Aid and School-Funding Formulas

Recall the demand function for local public goods and services:

Local Demand = f(Income, Tax Price, Tastes)

Where local demand is most often measured by the amount of local tax revenues generated for the public service, on the assumption that demand for expenditures translates to demand for outcomes. The introduction of state aid, or transfer payments from the state to local districts, may influence this model in a variety of ways. We first introduced this idea in Chapter 3. As described, one general response of voters is to partially reduce local effort when state aid is provided, using only a portion of the aid to increase total spending on the public service. The tax-relief response may occur under either a foundation or GTB program. Guaranteed tax base aid serves to decrease the tax price for each additional $1 of education revenues for all districts below the GTB level. The decreased tax price allows the median voter to increase consumption or maintain consumption and take tax relief. Foundation aid, or other lump-sum-type grants, such as targeted flat grants, may be seen as an income supplement. The increased income allows the median voter to spend more on education and take some tax relief. Studies of the relationship between income changes and education spending changes over time suggest that each 1% change in income is accompanied by an approximately .5% increase in education spending (Baker & Richards, 1999).

Economic theory suggests that price decreases should stimulate more consumption than income increases, but empirical analyses of the effects of different types of grants on local spending behavior produce similar results for both lump-sum (foundation or block-type) grants and matching (GTB-type) grants (Gramlich, 1977). This discrepancy (or lack of) is referred to as the "flypaper effect." While one would expect block grants from state to local governments to be passed on to voters as tax relief, they tend instead to "stick where they hit." That is, the block grants lead to increased local government spending. Duncombe and Yinger (2000) map how property tax relief and school aid are essentially "flip sides of the same coin" depending on the method by which aid is allocated. In particular, Duncombe and Yinger draw parallels between aid programs and various tax rebate strategies, noting the following two examples:

1. A homestead exemption is equivalent to a state matching grant, where the matching rate is equal to the ratio of the exemption to the median house value. This form of matching aid would provide more aid to districts with low property wealth but would not be as redistributive as a school matching grant of the power-equalizing type.

2. A property tax rebate, which is not tied to actual property taxes, is equivalent to a lump-sum school aid program. If the rebate is based on household income, then this would be similar in form to a lump-sum grant where income is the fiscal capac-

ity measure. The rebate equivalent to a foundation aid program would be very redistributive, but the rebate would vary across school districts depending on property values and costs. (Duncombe & Yinger, 2000, p. 13)

As discussed previously, Richardson and Lamitie's (1989) study of Connecticut aid found that, when voters and local administrators can anticipate future levels of unrestricted state aid (in this case, GTB aid), they adjust local spending behavior accordingly. As a result, Richardson and Lamitie endorse a state strategy of targeted unanticipated grants (TUGs) and short-lived unanticipated grants (SLUGs) to increase total education support in Connecticut by retaining local effort and to ensure that supplemental aid is spent on legislative priorities. This approach, however, is only as valid as the legislatively targeted programs are important.

The simulations exercises at the end of this chapter and computer simulation available on the Companion Website (www.prenhall.com/baker) allow the user to manipulate local tax responses to different types of state aid. The response to flat grant or foundation aid is treated as a response to lump sum aid or supplement to local income. The simulation uses grant elasticities. A grant elasticity is a measure of the extent to which total expenditures per pupil rise as a function of lump sum aid. If, for example, the elasticity is 1.0, for each dollar in aid received, total expenditures on education go up $1. That is, local voters take no tax relief and choose instead to spend all new aid on education.

Price elasticities are used for GTB simulations. That is, how much does total revenue change when the tax price of an additional dollar of revenue is decreased? A negative price elasticity suggests that as price is decreased, demand (as measured by total expenditure) increases.

Dynamic and Contextual Perspective

In this section, we discuss the dynamics of achieving equity objectives and the importance of understanding the context in which those objectives are to be achieved. This section is based, in part, on an article by Baker and Richards (2002) and serves as a prelude to the dynamic simulation that accompanies this chapter. We begin this section with a review of the basic premises of systems theory as first presented by Jay W. Forrester (1968) in his seminal work, *Principles of Systems*.

Figure 6.1 Reinforcing Feedback

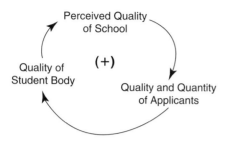

Figure 6.2 Balancing Feedback

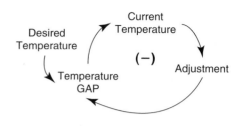

Forrester (1968) and others, including Senge (1990) in *The Fifth Discipline,* discuss feedback loops as central features of dynamic systems. Two basic forms of feedback occur in dynamic systems, (a) reinforcing, or positive, feedback and (b) balancing, or negative, feedback. In reinforcing feedback, actions within the cycle continually reinforce one another, producing an overall pattern of acceleration either in a positive or negative direction. One relatively simple example of positive feedback is that of the relationship between perceived quality, application rates, and actual quality of private schools or colleges (see Figure 6.1). As perceived quality increases, applications increase, allowing greater selectivity of students, leading to higher actual and perceived quality, and so on.

Connecticut's program of providing an additional 25% aid per pupil to districts based on a 3-year average of the percentage of pupils failing the state mastery test yielded a disturbing example of positive feedback. Arguably, the increased funding received by districts as a function of increased failures promoted inefficiency and increased resource dependence over time. This led to more rapid increases in failure rates, resulting in further increases in funding, and so on. Between 1993–1994 and 1997–1998, 5 of the 10 lowest performing districts in the state were also among the 10 districts that declined at the fastest rate (including the four fastest rates of decline). Similar arguments might be made regarding positive feedback in the long-term relationship between identification rates of special education pupils and funding received for serving those pupils, especially where state special education finance formulas are sensitive to identification rates.

Balancing feedback typically involves convergence on some externally established objective, depicted in Figure 6.2. The classic example discussed by Senge (1990) is one of achieving the right shower temperature. The person taking the shower has an ideal temper-

ature in mind. When she first turns on the water, there is likely to be a discrepancy, or gap between the actual and desired temperature. So she adjusts the temperature and evaluates the effects of the corrective action. If a gap remains, the temperature is adjusted again.

Most school finance reforms, especially those intended to achieve equity in a presently inequitable system, involve balancing feedback, resulting in the convergence pattern discussed in Chapter 5 (Figure 5.4). In particular, the problem of achieving equity involves balancing feedback where monitoring and management of the gap are a constant, cyclical process, just as in the case of the shower example.

Also like the shower example, the reinforcing feedback of achieving equity objectives does not exist in a vacuum. The cycle is subject to any number of exogenous events, like the flush of a toilet or use of a hot-water-consuming appliance by a family member while you're taking a shower. Examples of exogenous influences on achieving parity include events that affect the economy that provides revenues necessary for achieving the objective. Unlike the shower example, where the desired temperate is constant, equity or adequacy objectives may change over time, though often, one can still express them in constant terms. This is the case, for example, with the New Jersey finance parity problem posed in Chapter 5, where the goal was to achieve parity between the state's poorest districts and the state's wealthiest districts, but where revenues of the wealthiest districts continue to grow.

Policy Leverage in Dynamic Systems

We have mentioned policy levers on numerous occasions in this chapter. Thus far, we have considered only direct policy leverage, or features of funding formulas that may be directly manipulated by policy makers that in turn directly influence the equity outcomes of the

Figure 6.3   Direct Policy Leverage

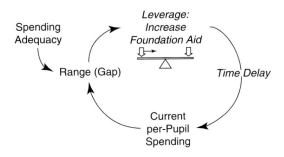

Figure 6.4   Indirect, Systemic Policy Leverage

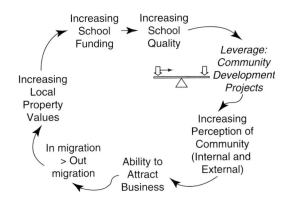

formula. Indeed, many such decisions have a variety of effects on broader economic and demographic conditions, which in turn have effects on available revenues for public education and the demand for educational services. Figure 6.3 presents adjustments to foundation aid as a corrective action toward achieving adequate spending across school districts.

Figure 6.4 displays what we refer to as indirect, or systemic, policy leverage. Systemic policy leverage involves applying the minimum necessary force to some point on the system to achieve the maximum desirable effect, generating sustainable outcomes. For example, one might pursue a number of community-based development projects in hopes of improving overall quality of life or at least the perception of quality, attracting businesses and increasing immigration of more families preferring high-quality public services, leading to increased property values and increased revenues for schooling, reinforcing improvement of quality of living in the community. Of course, additions to foundation aid as direct policy leverage might yield some similar systemic effects, stimulating productive positive feedback.

Policy leverage may be static or adaptive. To this point, in our examples of school-funding formulas, we have discussed only static leverage. That is, we assume a system to be flawed because of poor equity indicators or some other issue. We then focus on either one or several equity measures as critical output and "tweak" our policy levers, attempting to positively influence our equity measures, closing the gap between actual and desired conditions. Figure 6.5 depicts static leverage, such as a one-time increase in foundation aid intended to close a gap between wealthy and poor districts. Note that where the policy leverage is this static, the gap

shortly returns. One might argue that many state school finance reforms have been nearly this static, achieving equity or adequacy for fleeting moments before eroding over time as a function of failure to provide necessary revenues to maintain the formula.

The misunderstanding revealed by such common practices is that a broken system can instantaneously be fixed by either simply putting enough money into that system or changing the structure of the system at a given point in time and that once the system is fixed, it will remain fixed without further attention. Fixing a school-funding system, however, takes time and must be undertaken with cognizance of environmental conditions and constraints. Furthermore, maintaining the system also takes time and must also involve consideration of environmental conditions and constraints.

Figure 6.6 displays *adaptive leverage*. Three critical skills are involved in adaptive leverage:

1. *System Monitoring:* The first critical element of adaptive leverage is learning to monitor the system, or to measure the gap between actual and desired conditions not only in static terms but also in dynamic terms. An example of a static term is, How big is the gap at a given point in time? Examples of dynamic terms are, How big is the gap? Is it growing or shrinking, and by how much? What is the average gap over time? What is the convergence rate? What is the gap-reduction horizon, given maintenance of current conditions and policies?

2. *System Anticipation:* The second critical element is to apply policy leverage with an eye toward future rather than present conditions. That is, we should apply policy leverage not only to create the best

Figure 6.5   Static Leverage

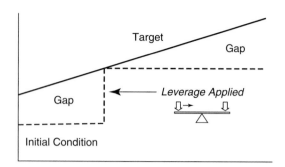

Figure 6.6   Adaptive Leverage

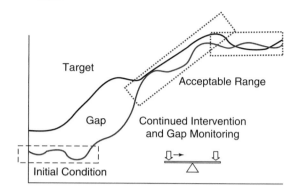

possible set of present outcomes but also to achieve a sustainable rate of gap reduction, such that systems can achieve high-priority goals within a reasonable horizon. We specifically choose the word *anticipation* over *forecasting* because we do not necessarily mean predicting a specific set of future conditions but rather anticipating how the system might behave if certain conditions were present.

3. *System Contextual Awareness:* Adaptive leverage requires cognizance of not only critical output related directly to policy objectives, such as equity statistics, but also of critical output related to production and consumption of system resources and system stability, as addressed in Chapter 5 (Figures 5.3 to 5.5).

Adaptive leverage is critical in developing beneficial tax policy. Consider, for example, the application of skills 2 and 3, sustainability and contextual awareness; it would make little sense to impose a new tax policy that would generate enough revenues for perfect equity in an economy unlikely to sustain the tax policy.

We close this section with our opinion, shared by other system dynamics advocates, regarding the best way to develop monitoring, anticipation, and contextual awareness skills. Forrester (1968), Senge (1990), and Dorner (1996) point to numerous examples of how our mental models of how things work most often fail us. All of these authors promote the virtues of using dynamic computer simulations for making the assumptions behind our mental models more specific, leading to improved understanding of system behavior. Forrester notes:

> To know the behavior that follows from assumptions about parts of a system can be achieved only through modeling and computer simulation. (Forrester, 1994, p. 4)

We encourage you to use this chapter's simulation and the support materials on the Companion Website (www.prenhall.com/baker) to enhance your own monitoring, anticipation, and contextual awareness skills.

SUMMARY

You should now have a better understanding of the four major goals of school-funding formulas: (a) Redistribute resources from wealthier to poorer districts; (b) improve educational efficiency; (c) obtain or sustain political support, and (d) be affordable. Just how redistributive formulas are requires a careful look at both the tax side and the redistribution side of the equation. We have neglected efficiency in this chapter out of ne-

cessity. We discuss productivity, standards, and efficiency in Chapter 11, because these topics are now central to the current school finance reform movement.

We sought to clarify the structure of school finance funding formulas by emphasizing their core common features: (a) internal policy levers; (b) critical outputs; and (c) exogenous conditions. All finance policies have these three characteristics, and they are fundamental to studying the anatomy of school finance. We then explored these three features of finance formulas by examining the flat grant, the foundation grant, the GTB formula, and combination formulas. We further emphasized that our notions of equity and equal opportunity have evolved historically. The original foundation formula devised by Strayer and Haig (1924), which is the parent of most school finance formulas today, was intended to equalize spending up to some prescribed minimum, not to accomplish absolute equity of spending. Since the Civil Rights Movement, and the school finance litigation attending it, states have adapted the original foundation formula to pursue horizontal equity rather than early notions of adequacy. This formula is static, however, as are all of its current variants. The foundation formula is organized to produce year-to-year distribution formulas without reference to prior year's results.

We concluded our discussion by introducing a dynamic model, one that examines the results of a particular funding model over several years, and by introducing ways to measure the impact of multi-year funding on our equity goals. We sought to demonstrate why *only a dynamic model* would meet the modern definition of horizontal equity. Further, we offered three critical skill sets required of all would-be modelers seeking to accomplish goals in a dynamic, complex, and adaptive system: (a) system path marking; (b) anticipation of possible futures; and (c) a deep understanding of the contextual model mimicking the actual system and the extent to which it helpfully models the actual system. These three skills will increase our capacity to understand why we fail to accomplish equity, efficiency, and performance goals and most importantly, they will increase our capacity to sustain our approximations of them.

KEY TERMS

foundation level Target level of minimum funding per pupil to be available to school districts and/or charter schools.

foundation aid (state aid) The share of the foundation level of funding to be allocated from a state's general fund budget (or specific school fund). Usually, "state aid" per se is funding allocated out of state general funds (from sales and/or income tax) from the state to local school districts on an equalized basis, according to the amount of property tax revenue that districts raise when implementing the required tax rate.

guaranteed tax base (GTB) The taxable property wealth per pupil guaranteed by the state. For example, if a state guarantees a tax base of $150,000 per pupil, but a district only has a tax base of $75,000 per pupil, at whatever local property tax rate the district adopts, the state will provide matching aid to reach the level of yield a district with $150,000 in per-pupil property wealth would achieve. In this case, the state would provide $1 for each $1 raised locally, because local taxable wealth is one half of guaranteed taxable wealth.

guaranteed tax base formula A state-to-school district financial aid allocation formula whereby the state provides each district the opportunity to raise school revenue *as if* the district had a specific guaranteed level of taxable property wealth. In its purest form, a GTB formula does not require any minimum level of local tax effort. Usually, a minimum requirement does exist.

guaranteed yield Some choose to characterize a guaranteed tax base formula that requires a minimum tax rate as a guaranteed yield formula. That is, every district is guaranteed a yield equal to at least the required local effort times the guaranteed tax base. In effect, this approach is also the same as a foundation formula, where the guaranteed yield equals the foundation level.

matching aid Another name for state aid allocated to school districts on the basis of matching local effort. That is, state aid received is tied to local effort adopted and allocated at a defined matching rate.

matching rate The rate at which matching aid is provided, usually depending primarily on the ratio of a district's taxable property wealth per pupil to a guaranteed level of taxable property wealth per pupil. Matching rates may be modified with income or other factors.

recapture (revenue sharing) Recapture is simply redistribution of revenue generated by a specific tax revenue source. Recapture usually refers to statewide redistribution. Income and sales taxes collected into a state's general fund and allocated to school districts through either a foundation or guaranteed tax base formula are necessarily recaptured. That is, some communities will generate more tax revenue than would be allocated back to them through the formula. *Recapture* usually refers to provisions that redistribute property tax revenues. For example, if a district implements the required local effort but raises in property tax revenues more than its assigned foundation level per pupil, the state may "recapture" the additional revenue. If, instead, it is assumed that the required local effort is actually a state revenue source to support the foundation formula, this recapture is the same as redistribution of any other state revenues.

required tax rate   A required tax rate (RTR) is typically the school district property tax rate or levy required by the state in order to receive state aid sufficient to raise district revenues per pupil to the foundation level. The RTR is also sometimes referred to as the required local effort (RLE).

REFERENCES

Baker, B. D. (2001a). Balancing equity for students and taxpayers: Evaluating school finance reform in Vermont. *Journal of Education Finance, 26*(spring), 239–248.

Baker, B. D. (2001b). *Wide of any reasonable mark: Evaluating the Kansas School District Finance Act.* Expert testimony prepared on behalf of plaintiff districts in *Montoy v. Kansas.*

Baker, B. D., & Richards, C. (1999). A comparison of conventional linear regression and neural network methods for forecasting education spending. *Economics of Education Review, 18*(4), 405–415.

Baker, B. D., & Richards, C. (2002). Exploratory application of system dynamics modeling to school finance policy. *Journal of Education Finance, 27*(3), 857–884.

Clark, C. (2001). Texas state support for school facilities 1971–2001. *Journal of Education Finance, 27*(2), 683–700.

Crampton, F. E., Thompson, D. C., & Hagey, J. M. (2001). Creating and sustaining school capacity in the twenty-first century: Funding a physical environment conducive to student learning. *Journal of Education Finance, 27*(2), 633–652.

Dorner, D. (1996). *The logic of failure: Why things go wrong and what we can do to make them right.* New York: Metropolitan Books.

Downes, T., & Figlio, D. N. (1998). *School finance reforms, tax limits, and student performance: Do reforms level-up or dumb down? Working paper.* Department of Economics, Tufts University. Medford, MA. Retrieved May 1, 2007, from http://ase.tufts.edu/econ/papers/9805.pdf

Duncombe, W., & Johnston, J. M. (2004). The impacts of school finance reform in Kansas: Equity is in the eye of the beholder. In J. M. Yinger (Ed.), *Helping children left behind: State aid and the pursuit of educational equity* (pp. 147–194). Cambridge, MA: MIT Press.

Duncombe, W., & Yinger, J. (2000). *Property tax relief and state education aid: Two sides of the same coin?* Unpublished manuscript.

Edgewood Indep. Sch. Dist. v. Kirby, 777 S.W.2d 391 (Tx. 1989).

Fiscel, W. (1989). Did *Serrano* cause Proposition 13? *National Tax Journal, 42*(4), 465–473.

Forrester, J. W. (1968). *Principles of systems.* Waltham, MA: Pegasus Communications.

Forrester, J. W. (1994). Systems dynamics, systems thinking, and soft OR. *Systems Dynamics Review, 10*(2). Retrieved from http://web.mit.edu/sdg/www/D-4405-2. SD.SysTh.SoftOR.pdf

Gold, S., Smith, D., & Lawton, S. (1995). *Public school finance programs of the United States and Canada: 1993–94.* Albany, NY: American Education Finance Association Center for the Study of the States, The Nelson A. Rockefeller Institute of Government.

Gramlich, E. (1977). Intergovernmental grants: A review of the empirical literature and compensation. In W. Oates (Ed.), *The political economy of fiscal federalism.* Lexington, MA: Lexington Books.

Hanushek, E. A. (1986). The economics of schooling: Production and efficiency in public schools. *Journal of Economic Literature, 24*(6), 1141–1177.

Haurin, D. R., & Brasington, D. (1996). *The impact of school quality on real house prices: Interjurisdictional effects. Working paper.* Dept. of Economics, Ohio State University. Retrieved May 1, 2007, from http://www.econ.ohio-state.edu/pdf/haurin/haurin.pdf

Hoxby, C. (2001). All school finance equalizations are not created equal. *Quarterly Journal of Economics, 116*(4), 1189–1231.

Monk, D. H. (1984). Stalking full fiscal neutrality: The distinction between school district wealth and tastes. *Educational Theory, 34*(I), 55–69.

Mort, P. R., & Reusser, W. C. (1951). *Public school finance: Its background, structure and operation.* New York: McGraw-Hill.

Picus, L. (1998). *Sensitive property taxes and school finance reform in Vermont.* Paper presented at the Annual Meeting of the American Education Research Association, San Diego, CA.

Richards, C. E., Sawicky, M.B., & Shore, R. (1996). *Risky business: The private management of public schools.* Washington, DC: Economic Policy Institute.

Richardson, G. P., & Lamitie, R. E. (1989). Improving Connecticut school aid: a case study with model-based policy analysis. *Journal of Education Finance, 15,* 169–188.

Seilke, C. (2001). Funding school infrastructure needs across the states. *Journal of Education Finance, 27*(2), 653–662.

Senge, P. (1990). *The fifth discipline: The art and practice of the learning organization.* New York: Doubleday.

Strayer, G. D., & Haig, R. M. (1924). *The financing of education in the State of New York* (pp. 173–175). Report of the Educational Finance Inquiry Commission, New York.

FINANCING EQUITY

Static Model of Equity Formulas

This simulation demonstrates the application of five different funding formula types to a sample of 20 school districts from the state of Missouri before implementing its new school finance formula (SB 287). As with the equity-analysis template, we can import data for 20-district samples from other states. We provide instructions for doing so in our section on technical issues, later in the simulation.

This simulation has several objectives, and several different uses. We use the simulation both for in-class lab activities, focused on the politics of consensus building in school finance, and for homework assignments focused on developing individual students' insights into the economics and politics of funding formula alternatives.

Getting Started

To begin this simulation, open the Microsoft Excel workbook on the Companion Website (www.prenhall.com/baker) to Chapter6.xls. A screen will appear that asks you whether you wish to "enable" or "disable" macros. You should choose to "enable" macros, or the simulation will not function properly. For example, the buttons on the home page of the simulation are intended to navigate you to the various formula types. Those buttons will not work if you "disable" macros. Macros are explained in greater detail in the technical issues section, later in the simulation.

Once you have opened the simulation, you should see a screen like the one depicted in Figure 6s.1. Single clicking any of the yellow buttons labeled with the various formula types (discussed earlier in this chapter) will take you to a simulation of that formula type. For example, if you click the button for the "Foundation," it will take you to an interface such as that in Figure 6s.2.

As we discussed in this chapter, each formula type has its own set of "Policy Levers." On each simulation interface, blue numbers labeled "Policy Levers" indicate the policy levers. Note that the foundation formula has two policy levers:

1. Foundation level
2. Required local tax rate

Figure 6s.1   Opening Screen of Chapter 6 Simulation

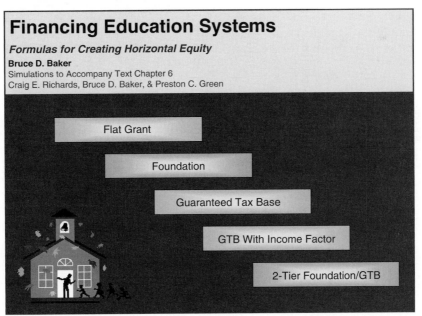

GTB, guaranteed tax base.

Figure 6s.2 Simulation Interface Example (Foundation Formula)

Policy Levers

Foundation Level	$ 6,000
Required Tax Rate	1.20%

Cost Data

Total State Cost (millions)	$ 908.32

(Return to Main Menu)

Equity Outcomes

Mean	$ 8,038
CV	9%
McLoone	94%
FRR	0.30

(Click to Recalculate Equity)

Neutrality Outcomes

Elasticity	0.12
WW Gini	0.00

(Click to Calculate Gini)

(Click to View Graph)

Foundation Formula

District	Enrollment	Assessed Valuation per Pupil	Income per Pupil	Original Tax Rate	Required Tax Rate	New Tax Rate	New Local Revenue per Pupil	Foundation Level	State Aid per Pupil	Total Revenue Per Pupil
Cooter R-IV	277	$19,918	$31,094	2.75%	1.20%	2.75%	$548	$6,000	$5,761	$6,308.73
Waynesville R-VI	5,147	$21,799	$36,724	2.70%	1.20%	2.70%	$589	$6,000	$5,738	$6,326.98
Wellston	747	$24,686	$21,458	5.10%	1.20%	5.10%	$1,259	$6,000	$5,704	$6,962.77
Hillsboro R-III	3,592	$44,725	$48,548	2.94%	1.20%	2.94%	$1,315	$6,000	$5,463	$6,778.21
Bolivar R-I	2,350	$45,392	$29,257	2.75%	1.20%	2.75%	$1,248	$6,000	$5,455	$6,703.58
Ozark R-VI	3,925	$50,363	$40,352	2.75%	1.20%	2.75%	$1,385	$6,000	$5,396	$6,780.62
Hannibal 60	3,645	$53,855	$31,962	2.86%	1.20%	2.86%	$1,540	$6,000	$5,354	$6,894.00
Festus R-VI	2672	$56,179	$40,964	2.87%	1.20%	2.87%	$1,612	$6,000	$5,326	$6,938.18
Raymore Peculiar R-II	4,627	$57,663	$56,198	3.14%	1.20%	3.14%	$1,811	$6,000	$5,308	$7,118.66
Warrensburg R-VI	3,167	$58,619	$32,477	3.70%	1.20%	3.70%	$2,169	$6,000	$5,297	$7,465.47
Sedalia 200	4,191	$60,485	$31,267	2.75%	1.20%	2.75%	$1,663	$6,000	$5,274	$6,937.51
Lee's Summit B-VII	14,861	$70,601	$59,944	4.37%	1.20%	4.37%	$3,085	$6,000	$5,153	$8,238.06
St Louis City	42,654	$73,398	$27,156	3.73%	1.20%	3.73%	$2,738	$6,000	$5,119	$7,856.97
Kansas City 33	33,642	$75,186	$29,634	4.95%	1.20%	4.95%	$3,722	$6,000	$5,098	$8,819.49
Ferguson Florissant R-II	11,949	$75,200	$40,500	4.74%	1.20%	4.74%	$3,564	$6,000	$5,098	$8,662.09
Columbia 93	16,076	$83,170	$36,516	3.93%	1.20%	3.93%	$3,269	$6,000	$5,002	$8,270.53
Jefferson City	8,263	$105,067	$41,924	3.23%	1.20%	3.23%	$3,394	$6,000	$4,739	$8,132.86
Mehlville R-IX	11,799	$108,448	$53,741	3.01%	1.20%	3.01%	$3,264	$6,000	$4,698	$7,962.91
Branson R-IV	3,143	$145,745	$32,098	2.31%	1.20%	2.31%	$3,367	$6,000	$4,251	$7,617.77
Ladue	3,272	$336,855	$82,889	2.63%	1.20%	2.63%	$8,859	$6,000	$1,958	$10,817.03

CV, coefficient of variation; FRR, federal range ratio; WW, wealth weighted.

Each interface has two types of "Critical Output." One critical output is the total cost of the policy option in question, expressed in millions of dollars. Remember, the cost represented is the cost of the given policy option across only the 20 districts in the sample. This particular critical output is of primary interest to legislators in the budget-planning process.

The second set of critical output indicators consists of the equity and neutrality indicators. Each simulation interface provides means, coefficients of variation, McLoone indices, federal range ratios, elasticities, and income-sorted Gini coefficients. All calculations involve the pupil unit of analysis. Recall from the equity-analysis exercise in Chapter 5 that McLoone indices and income-sorted Gini coefficients require resorting districts. Federal range ratios do as well. Because changes to the policy levers can change the rankings of districts by total revenue per pupil, the districts must be resorted to make appropriate McLoone, Gini, and federal range ratio (FRR) calculations. You do this automatically by clicking the YELLOW buttons.

You must click these yellow buttons after each change in policy levers, or McLoone indices, Gini coefficients, and federal range ratios are likely to be incorrectly calculated. If you scroll down the worksheet, you will notice that the various equity statistics are calculated in exactly the same way as they were in the equity-analysis template. The macro buttons for recalculation simply take the data from the main work-sheet, copy it, paste it, and sort it in the appropriate location on the worksheet.

For a visual representation of your policy options, you may click the "View Graph" button. Each graph is a bar graph of district state and local revenue, with districts sorted by property wealth per pupil from left to right as in Figure 6s.3.

When you increase state aid to the school districts in the simulation, you may notice that many if not all of the districts choose to lower their local tax rates, assuming those tax rates are above the required minimum rate for receiving aid. We have included this feature in an effort to make the simulation somewhat realistic. Districts will lower their tax rates only if they are above the minimum and only if they receive state aid. Tax rate reductions are based on an assumption that no state aid previously existed (an oversimplified, false assumption, but necessary for making the simulation reasonably straightforward). We provide more details on the assumptions and equations behind the tax relief feature in our technical details section, later in the simulation.

In-Class Group Activity: Politics of Equity (90–120 Minutes)

In this section we describe an activity that Professors Baker and Richards use regularly, with slight variations, in their courses on school finance policy. The activity is best run with a flexible time frame to allow

Figure 6s.3 Sample Graph Output

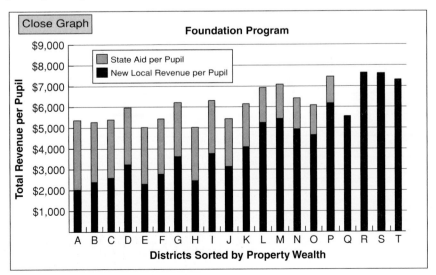

students to "get into it" at various stages rather than cutting them off too soon. Often, it will take some time for more tentative student groups to become comfortable with the simulation itself and with the political games that may be played with the simulation.

The activity can be done with any or all of the formula types. Our experience suggests that the foundation formula is easiest to work with for this particular activity. The course instructor plays the role of the judicial branch of state government. This role is generally passive, perhaps involving the setting of specific benchmarks that the legislature must meet. While we are not necessarily proponents of this particular benchmark, one we commonly use is that viable policy options must have a coefficient of variation (CV) of less than 10%. Similarly, to expedite the activity, we give students a budget constraint up front. A budget constraint that works well in this simulation is $700 million.

Requirements

- Judicial Requirement: CV = <.10
- Legislative Budget Constraint: = $700 million

Students should work in teams of two or three as representatives of one or more school districts. One approach is to assign teams to represent districts similar in wealth. For example, a class of 20 might be divided as shown in Table 6s.1.

This approach can create strange bedfellows as the political negotiations progress. Note that under this approach, group 10 is unlikely to be affected by any policy options. As such, the exercise may be uninteresting for those students. One alternative is to split districts S&T as shown in Table 6s.2.

While this may seem strange, it is perhaps more likely that two small wealthy districts in the state would be near or even adjacent to larger poorer districts than for all legislative districts in the state to be a mix of wealthy and poor. There are numerous ways to group the school districts into legislative districts. Student legislators can also each represent a single district. In our experience, the best method is for each student representative to look out for the interests of more than a single district.

Following is a description of the procedures that Professor Baker used when conducting the activity:

Overview

In teams, you will be assigned to serve as legislators representing two or three school districts. Your goal is to represent the voters in your districts to the best of your ability. That is, come up with and lobby for a school finance formula that gives your voters what they want. If you don't, you know what will happen when election time rolls around.

Table 6s.1	Recommended Grouping of School Districts into Legislative Districts
Teams (2 students each)	**Representing Districts**
1	A&B
2	C&D
3	E&F
4	G&H
5	I&J
6	K&L
7	M&N
8	O&P
9	Q&R
10	S&T

Table 6s.2	Alternative Arrangement of School Districts into Legislative Districts
Teams (2 students each)	**Representing Districts**
1	A&S
2	C&D
3	E&F
4	G&H
5	I&J
6	K&L
7	M&N
8	O&P
9	Q&R
10	B&T

Phases

1. *Tinkering:* You will need to spend some time tweaking the policy levers and tinkering with the simulation to figure out how to create desirable policies for your districts. This will probably take about 20 minutes or so. Your goal is to come up with three policy proposals to put on the table for discussion in the legislative session. Ultimately, the legislators will consider only one of those proposals in the final vote, so consider various strategies when you come up with your three options. Your options must all meet the judicial requirements and budget constraints stated previously.

2. *Proposals:* Each team will list their three proposals on the board (perhaps projected instead) when ready. Teams may then take some time to test out how other teams' proposals affect them.

3. *Elimination:* We will go through each set of three proposals, one at a time. Each team except the team proposing the options will cast one vote as to which option stays on the table. At the end of this process, each team will have one of their options remaining.

4. *Lobbying:* This process will go on as long as it must. The goal is to create a consensus vote on any one of the remaining options. When any group believes they have achieved a majority (one vote per team), they may call for a vote. Alternatively, if a group believes they have a majority that favors a new compromise proposal, they may call for a presentation of that proposal and a return to lobbying (which may be brief if consensus on the compromise already exists).

Teams should use summary tables such as Table 6s.3 to tally their policy options.

Role of the Instructor

The role of the instructor throughout the first phase is to monitor students' understanding of how the simulation works, and if necessary to ask questions that prompt the students to try new things. Students can easily get trapped in a particular type of policy option (e.g., adjusting only foundation level and not working with required local effort). The instructor should create a summary table of proposed options on a black or white board, or on a projected spreadsheet. The latter is handy, because it allows the instructor to move back and forth between testing proposed policy options with the simulation in front of the class and displaying the summary table. It is also much easier to delete a policy option during the elimination phase, or sort policy options from high to low by required local effort or foundation level. During the lobbying phase, the class should have time to relax and really talk it out with other teams and their own team members. Teams may cast individual votes in the final phase or vote as a block.

Problem Set Questions

Instructions

This assignment is a group assignment and receives a group grade. The purpose of this assignment is to explore the potential and limitations of various school finance funding formulas for accomplishing equity under the typical demographic, political, and economic constraints that states face. The simulation we have

Table 6s.3 Sample Output Summary Table

Option	Cost	Found	RTR	CV	McLoone	Gini	W/L	Your Gain

CV, coefficient of variation; RTR, required tax rate; W/L, winners/losers.

developed is quite complex. The dataset is drawn from Missouri in 2003–2004. We have protected the formulas so that you cannot accidentally alter them. However, this simulation is quite easy to use, because the data are supplied, and all we are asking you to do is alter critical parameters and test the results against the various equity and fiscal neutrality measures you have been studying. It is important to present both numerical results and your interpretation of them. Your best results should explain why you consider them to be best. (Unfortunately, policy trade-offs are inevitable, and one school district's "best formula" is another school district's "worst formula.") You need to explain what trade-offs you are making and state the explicit values you are pursuing in your recommended solution to the problem. So, to summarize, as you address each question, attempt to address the following (though it may not be possible to address all of the following in each response):

1. An explicit statement of the goal.
2. An explicit statement of the underlying values that the goal represents.
3. The exact formula you recommend, the parameter settings you used, and the equity and neutrality indicators produced by the simulation.
4. Your interpretation of the indicators.
5. Your overall assessment of the efficacy of the formula.
6. Your estimate of the political feasibility of implementing the formula.
7. Your estimate of the financial feasibility of implementing the formula.

Questions

1. Can use of a flat-grant formula improve equity? Why or why not? (What parameters must one use to accomplish equity? What do critical outputs look like? Costs? Equity?)
2. Can use of a foundation formula improve equity? Why or why not? (What parameters must one use to accomplish equity? What do critical outputs look like? Costs? Equity?)
3. Can use of a GTB improve equity? Why or why not? (What parameters must be used to accomplish equity? What do critical outputs look like? Costs? Equity?)
4. Who benefits the most under each formula, and why?

5. Who benefits the least under each formula, and why?
6. What are the advantages of a combination formula?
7. Assume you are a high-wealth district. (Pick one from the dataset, and identify it in your answer.) Which formula would you prefer most, and why? What specific allocation and parameters would you use under each formula to maximize the benefit to your own district? Why?
8. Assume you are a low-wealth district. (Pick one from the dataset, and identify it in your answer.) Which formula would you prefer most, and why? What specific allocation and parameters would you use under each formula to maximize the benefit to your own district? Why?
9. Assume you are an average-wealth district. (Pick one from the dataset, and identify it in your answer.) What formula would you prefer most, and why? What specific allocation and parameters would you use under each formula to maximize the benefit to your own district? Why?
10. Assume each district has one vote. Construct a formula (you can use any model you wish) where a majority of districts would benefit from the plan, and vote for it.
11. Assume each district has a pupil-weighted vote where every 100 students equals one vote. Now construct a plan that would get a simple majority of voters to approve it. How does it differ from the results in the previous answer? Why?

Technical Details

In this section, we address a few of the technical details underlying the simulation and other technical issues that may enhance students' learning experiences when using the simulation.

What Are Macros, and Why Are They in This Simulation?

Macros are visual basic programming code that you can use to write viruses (malicious code). So you should generally exercise caution when opening spreadsheets or other documents that contain macros. We assure you that we have not, in any way, attempted to include malicious code in this simulation. The macros in this simulation serve two functions: (1) navigation, taking you from one formula type to another, and to graphic output and back, and (2) recalculation. Regarding recalculation, you may recall that the equity-analysis template required sorting and resorting of certain data for making appropriate calculations. The macros in this simulation simply automate those functions.

Optimizing With the Solver

Technically minded students will often be predisposed to seek the mathematically optimal solution for each simulation. While testing mathematical optimality may help to understand the technical workings of the simulation, it can draw attention away from important economic and political implications of policy options. You can use a tool called SOLVER in Microsoft Excel to quickly demonstrate optimal policy leverage combinations.

For example, you might wish to "minimize local tax rate" while maintaining a CV = .10 and Budget Constraint = $20 million. To run this particular optimization problem, you must first "unprotect" the foundation aid worksheet by selecting "unprotect" from the "Tools/Protection" menu. Next, select "Solver" from the Tools menu. A dialog box will appear, with three types of information to be added.

Set target cell: For the preceding example, we set the target cell as the cell containing the required local effort (B3), and set that cell to be minimized.

By changing cells: The cells that are to be manipulated are B2 and B3, or the two policy levers.

Subject to constraints: The constraints we have imposed are that the CV cannot exceed .10 and that the budget shall equal $20 million. Because of the way we have framed the problem, the CV will be maximized within our constraint.

The solver provides the output shown in Table 6s.4.

How Do I Import My Own Data into the Simulation?

As with the solver option, entering your own data into the simulation requires unprotecting each worksheet into which you would like to enter new data. To enter your own data, you must have access to comparable data to that used in the simulation, for a sample of 20 school districts, or aggregations of statewide data into 20 groups. Data must be available on (a) assessed valuation per pupil, (b) income per pupil (median family income measures will do) and (c) tax rates. Replace data only in these columns on any given worksheet. Other columns include important calculations that may be accidentally overwritten when the worksheet is unprotected.

Table 6s.4   MS Excel Solver Output: Interface of Simulation

Microsoft Excel 9.0 Answer Report
Worksheet: [Chapter6.xls]Foundation
Report Created: 3/13/2007 10:54:35 AM
Target Cell (Min)

Cell Name	Original Value	Final Value		
B3 Required Tax Rate	1.00%	1.40%		
Adjustable Cells				

Cell Name	Original Value	Final Value		
B2 Foundation Level	$5,000	$5,507		
B3 Required Tax Rate	1.00%	1.40%		
Constraints				

Cell Name	Cell Value	Formula	Status	Slack
E3 CV	10%	E3<=0.1	Binding	0
B6 Total State Cost (millions)	$20.00	B6 = 20	Binding	0

The solver indicates that the minimum required tax rate that can be imposed, while meeting our equity and budget constraints, is 1.4% and will achieve a foundation level of $5,507. This output does not apply to data currently in the simulation.

Advanced "Tax Response" Simulations

You've probably noticed by now that the simulation also includes two simulations labeled as advanced simulations. These versions of the GTB and foundation formulas allow you to test assumptions regarding how local districts may respond to changes in state aid. That is, to what extent are local districts expected to take some of the additional aid provided through the formula and apply that aid toward tax relief? Earlier in Chapter 6, we discussed grant and price elasticities:

- The response to flat grant or foundation aid is treated as a response to lump-sum aid, or supplement to local income. The simulation therefore uses grant elasticities. A grant elasticity is a measure of the extent to which total expenditures per pupil rise as a function of lump-sum aid. If, for example, the elasticity is 1.0, that would mean that for each dollar in aid received, total expenditures on education go up $1. Local voters take no tax relief and choose instead to spend all new aid.

- For GTB simulations, the simulation uses price elasticities. That is, how much does total revenue change when the tax price of an additional dollar

of revenue is decreased? A negative price elasticity suggests that, as price decreases, demand (as measured by total expenditure) increases.

The advanced simulations include relatively simple, adjustable elasticity parameters. We use adjustable parameters because the elasticities are not well-known for the sample of districts in question (see Figure 6s.4).

Foundation Formula and Grant Substitution Parameter

For the foundation formula, we use a grant substitution parameter, which when set to 1.0, results in no change in local tax effort regardless of the level of foundation aid provided (see Figure 6s.5).

When you change the grant substitution parameter, new local tax rates and new local revenue are calculated as follows:

- Total Revenue per Pupil = (GSP × SAPP) + (OTR × AVPP)
- New Local Revenue per Pupil = TRPP − SAPP
- New Tax Rate = LRPP/AVPP

(AVPP, assessed valuation per pupil; GSP, grant substitution parameter; LRPP, local revenue per pupil; OTR, other tax revenue; SAPP, state aid per pupil; TRPP, tax rate per pupil.)

Figure 6s.4   Opening Screen of Chapter 6 Simulation

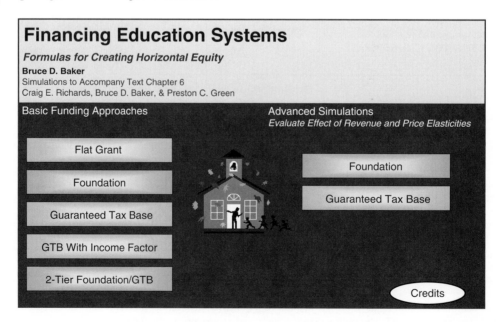

Figure 6s.5 Policy Levers

Foundation level	$5,000
Required tax rate	1.00%
Grant substitution parameter	1.00

Figure 6s.6 Policy Levers

Wealth guarantee (%ile)	75%
Price elasticity	-2.50

Example

District A
Grant Substitution Parameter at 1.0

- Total Revenue per Pupil = $(1.0 \times \$3,351) + (1.34\% \times \$164,869) = \$5,556.59$
- Local Revenue per Pupil = $\$5,556.59 - \$3,351 = \$2,205$
- Tax Rate = $\$2,205/\$164,869 = 1.34\%$

Grant Substitution Parameter at .90

- New Total Revenue per Pupil = $(.90 \times \$3,351) + (1.34\% \times \$164,869) = \$5,221.45$
- Local Revenue per Pupil = $\$5,221 - \$3,351 = \$1,870$
- Tax Rate = $\$1,870/\$164,869 = 1.13\%$

When the grant substitution parameter is set at .90, the district applies 90% of the state aid toward additional expenditures (90% sticks) and uses 10% of the grant toward tax relief. Grant substitution parameters between 0 and 1 therefore are the most useful.

Guaranteed Tax Base

As described in this simulation and earlier in Chapter 6, for the GTB formula, we use a price elasticity parameter, because the assumption is that matching aid functions as an adjustment to the price of an additional dollar of school revenue (see Figure 6s.6).

When you adjust price elasticity, new local revenues and new tax rates are calculated as follows:

- New Local Revenue per Pupil = (OTR × AVPP) × ((Expenditure Elasticity × Tax Price Change) + 1)
  - Wealth Ratio = AVPP/GTB (for AVPP < GTB, else 1.0)
  - Expenditure Elasticity = Wealth Ratio × Price Elasticity + 1
  - Tax Price Change = Wealth Ratio − 1
- New Tax Rate = LRPP/AVPP

Example

District J: Price Elasticity −1.0

- Wealth Ratio = $\$269,827/\$360,111 = .75$
- Expenditure Elasticity = $.75 \times -1 + 1 = .251$
- Tax Price Change = $.75 - 1 = -.25$
- New LRPP = $(1.214\% \times \$269,827) \times ((.251 \times -.25) + 1) = \$3,275 \times .93725 = \$3,070$
- New Tax Rate = $\$3,070 / \$269,827 = 1.14\%$

The price elasticity tells us how much of the *change in tax price* will be used to take savings and how much will be used to purchase more good/service. Note that the *tax price* is expressed in terms of the *wealth ratio*, or ratio of actual assessed value per pupil to guaranteed assessed value per pupil. The *tax price change* is the difference between the wealth ratio when the GTB aid is applied, and the wealth ratio of the town where local wealth and the GTB are the same. In this example, it is calculated that District J will apply approximately 94% of its previous local revenue/taxes toward total revenue, taking just over 6% as savings/tax relief.

Additional Problem Set Questions

Grant Elasticity

1. Assume a grant substitution parameter of .85. How easy/difficult is it to achieve equity and adequacy with a foundation aid formula? How might this change your approach to the allocation of foundation aid?

2. Pick 2 districts, and compare their response at 2 or 3 different foundation levels, holding required tax rate constant.

3. Pick 2 districts, and compare their response at 2 or 3 different required tax rates, holding foundation constant.

Price Elasticity

1. Assume a price elasticity parameter of −1.0. How easy/difficult is it to achieve equity and adequacy with a foundation aid formula? How might this

change your approach to setting the GTB? How does local tax response influence state budget planning?

2. Pick 2 districts, and compare their response at 2 or 3 GTB levels, holding the price elasticity at −1.0.

3. Pick 2 districts, and compare their response at 2 or 3 GTB levels, holding price elasticity at −2.5.

4. What are the implications for using a GTB approach to achieving equity? Fiscal neutrality?

5. What are the implications for introducing new money into the aid formula? That is, how is the price elasticity related to total state cost? And how is the price elasticity related to which districts benefit most as total cost to the state increases?

EDUCATIONAL ADEQUACY

CHAPTER 7

UNDERSTANDING AND MEASURING EDUCATIONAL COSTS AND ADEQUACY

Introduction

From 1986 to 1999, total current expenditures on K–12 public education increased nearly 50%, from $213.4 billion to $311.6 billion in constant dollars (inflation adjusted), according to estimates from the National Center for Education Statistics (Hussar & Gerald, 2001). Over the same time period, current expenditures per pupil increased 24%, to $6,696. From these two sets of figures, we can estimate that about half the increase was due to enrollment growth, but the other half was due to real-dollar increases. In comparison, real-dollar growth in per capita income in the United States grew by about 20% to 25%. In other words, real growth in income nearly matched the growth in enrollment but not the growth in real spending. In this chapter, we seek to establish criteria for answering following questions:

1. How much educational spending is adequate?
2. What do we mean by *adequate*?
3. Is adequacy determined solely by the needs of the child?
4. If spending is inadequate, how do we determine what is adequate?

We begin with a discussion of school finance litigation brought on the basis of state education clauses, with the intent of advancing educational adequacy. Next, we present a theoretical discussion of the concept of educational adequacy, delineating between input-based and outcome-based perspectives, marginal versus absolute outcome perspectives, and expenditure versus resource-based methods for measuring educational adequacy. We then discuss the growing movement among state legislatures to use empirical analyses to define adequate spending in order to inform the design of cost-based school finance formulas. We then summarize recent attempts across states to measure the costs of providing a constitutionally adequate education. We critique various available input-based and outcome-based methods for measuring education costs when applied for purposes of measuring educational edequacy. We conclude this chapter by discussing state attempts in New Jersey and Wyoming to implement school finance formulas around input adequacy goals and measurement and provide a hypothetical example of formula implementation based on outcome adequacy goals and measurement.

State Constitutions and Educational Adequacy

Adequacy challenges to school finance formulas have been brought primarily under the education clauses of state constitutions. Every state has an education clause, which defines the state's duty to provide an education to its citizens (McUsic, 1991). (Thro, 1989, argues that Mississippi does not have an education clause.) Scholars have placed education clauses into four categories based on the strength of this guarantee (Cover, 2002; Dayton, 2001; Fogle, 2000; Mills & McLendon, 2000; Thro, 1989). Table 7.1 includes these four categories. Category I provisions, which are the weakest education clauses, merely require the state to provide a system of public education. For instance, New York's education clause requires the legislature to provide "for the maintenance

Table 7.1   Categories of Education Clauses

Category I: Weak Clauses (Merely Require Provision)	Category II: System Meets a Standard of Quality	Category III: Specific Educational Mandates	Category IV: Provide That Education Is Fundamental
Alabama	Arkansas	California	Georgia
Alaska	Colorado	Indiana	Illinois
Arizona	Delaware	Iowa	Maine
Connecticut	Florida	Massachusetts	Michigan
Hawaii	Idaho	Nevada	Missouri
Kansas	Kentucky	Rhode Island	New Hampshire
Louisiana	Maryland	South Dakota	Washington
Mississippi	Minnesota	Wyoming	
Nebraska	Montana		
New Mexico	New Jersey		
New York	North Dakota		
North Carolina	Ohio		
Oklahoma	Oregon		
South Carolina	Pennsylvania		
Utah	Tennessee		
Vermont	Texas		
	Virginia		
	West Virginia		
	Wisconsin		

Adapted from Dayton (2001).

and support of a system of free common schools, wherein all the children of this state may be educated" (New York Constitution Article 11, § 1).

Category II provisions "mandate that the system of public schools meet a certain minimum standard of quality, such as 'thorough and efficient'" (Thro, 1989, p. 1662). For example, Colorado's constitution provides, "The general assembly shall, as soon as practicable, provide for the establishment and maintenance of a thorough and uniform system of free public schools throughout the state" (Colorado Constitution Article 9, § 2).

Category III clauses contain specific educational mandates and preambles that state their purpose. Rhode Island's education clause is typical of this category. It provides the following:

> The diffusion of knowledge, as well as of virtue among the people, being essential to the preservation of their rights and liberties, it shall be the duty of the general assembly to promote public schools and public

libraries, and to adopt all means which it may deem necessary and proper to secure to the people the advantages and opportunities of education and public library services. (Rhode Island Constitution Article 12, § 1)

Finally, Category IV provisions "impose the greatest obligation on the state legislature" because "they provide that education is 'fundamental,' 'primary,' or 'paramount'" (Thro, 1989, p. 1667). Washington's education clause, for example, declares that it "is the paramount duty of the state to make ample provision for the education of all children residing within its borders, without distinction or preference on account of race, color, caste, or sex" (Washington Constitution Article 9, § 1).

In theory, the strength of the education clause should correlate with plaintiffs' success (Dayton, 2001; Thro, 1994). Examination of successful school finance litigation, however, reveals that the language of education clauses does not serve as an accurate predictor of success or failure (Dayton, 2001).[1]

---

[1]Dayton (2001) observes that although "[t]here is no strong correlation between the strength of constitutional language and the outcome of school funding cases . . . it should be noted that factors unrelated to constitutional language (differences in factual findings, constitutional histories, decisions based on equal protection rather than education article language, etc.) may have skewed the results in reported cases" (Dayton, 2001, p. 457 footnote 2).

Characteristics of Successful Third-Wave Adequacy Litigation

Scholars have recognized *Rose v. Council for Better Education, Inc.* (1989) as the seminal third-wave case. In *Rose,* the Kentucky Supreme Court held that the state's entire educational system violated its education clause by failing to provide its students with an adequate education. The remainder of this section identifies characteristics of successful third-wave adequacy litigation.

Courts Have Assumed the Task of Defining an Adequate Education

In most successful third-wave adequacy litigation, courts have identified the components of an adequate education and then ordered the legislature to develop a remedy that accomplishes the constitutional mandate. In *Rose,* the Kentucky Supreme Court adopted an outcomes-based definition of adequacy:

> [A]n efficient system of education must have as its goal to provide each and every child with at least seven of the following capacities: (i) sufficient oral and written communication skills to enable students to function in a complex and rapidly changing civilization; (ii) sufficient knowledge of economic, social and political systems to enable the student to make informed choices; (iii) sufficient understanding of governmental processes to enable the student to understand the issues that affect his or her community, state and nation; (iv) sufficient self knowledge and knowledge of his or her physical wellness; (v) sufficient grounding in the arts to enable each student to appreciate his or her cultural and historical heritage; (vi) sufficient training or preparation for advanced training in either academic or vocational fields so as to enable each child to choose and pursue life work intelligently; and (vii) sufficient levels of academic or vocational skills to enable public school students to compete favorably with counterparts in surrounding states, in academics or in the job market (*Rose v. Council for Better Education, Inc.,* 1989, p. 212).

The supreme courts of Arkansas (*Lake View School District No. 25 of Phillips County v. Huckabee,* 2002, *Lake View I*), Massachusetts (*McDuffy v. Secretary of the Executive Office of Education,* 1993), and New Hampshire (*Claremont v. Governor,* 1997) have adopted *Rose*'s definition of outcomes-based adequacy.

In *Campbell County School District v. State* (1995), the Wyoming Supreme Court not only defined adequacy in terms of outcomes but also identified a number of educational inputs necessary to achieve those outcomes. The court ruled that an adequate education

"must be defined as graduating from high school equipped for a role as a citizen, participant in the political system and competitor both intellectually and economically" (*Campbell,* 1995, p. 1278). The court also identified sets of educational inputs needed to achieve this outcome goal:

> To fulfill the constitutional command of "equality of financing will achieve equality of quality," the legislature must state and describe what a "proper education" is for a Wyoming child. The constitution requires it be the best that we can do. The legislature, in fulfilling its constitutional duty, must define and specify what that is. Trial testimony indicated aspects of a quality education will include:
>
> 1. Small schools, small class size, low teacher/student ratios, textbooks, low personal computer/student ratios.
> 2. Integrated, substantially uniform substantive curriculum decided by the legislature through the State Superintendent of Public Instruction and the State Board of Education with input from local school boards.
> 3. Ample, appropriate provision for at-risk students, special problem students, talented students.
> 4. Setting of meaningful standards for course content and knowledge attainment intended to achieve the legislative goal of equipping all students for entry to the University of Wyoming and Wyoming Community Colleges or which will achieve the other purposes of education.
> 5. Timely and meaningful assessment of all students' progress in core curriculum and core skills regardless of whether those students intend to pursue college or vocational training. (*Campbell,* 1995, p. 1279)

An Adequate Education Must Prepare Students for Contemporary Society

Several state high courts have found that an adequate education must adapt to the needs of contemporary society (Rebell, 2001; Verstegen, 2003). For instance, in *DeRolph v. State* (2000), the Ohio Supreme Court explained: "What was deemed thorough and efficient when the state's Constitution was adopted certainly would not be considered thorough and efficient today. Likewise, an educational system that was considered thorough and efficient twenty-five years ago may not be so today" (p. 1001). Similarly, the New Hampshire Supreme Court declared in *Claremont v. Governor* (1997) that "[m]ere competence in the basics—reading, writing, and arithmetic—is insufficient in the waning days of the twentieth century to insure that this State's public school students are fully integrated into the world around them" (p. 1359).

In *Campaign for Fiscal Equity v. State* (2003), the New York high court rejected the state's argument that it had satisfied its duty to provide a "sound basic" education by providing New York City students with an 8th- or 9th-grade education:

> A high school education is today as indispensable as a primary education was in 1894. Children in the 21st century need the opportunity for more than a ninth grade education to be productive citizens. Back in the 19th century, a high school education was not needed to obtain a good job. Now, a high school education is a prerequisite to most good jobs. Those who lack a high school education and have obtained good jobs have done so in spite of, not because of, the lack of a high school education. While it may be true that there will always be menial low-skills jobs, and thus a need for people to fill them, it should not be the purpose of the public schools to prepare students for those jobs, which are limited in number and dwindling (p. 331).

A Correlation Exists Between Educational Funding and Outcomes

Another characteristic of successful third-wave adequacy litigation is that courts have found a correlation between poor academic performance and educational spending. In *Rose* (1989), for example, the Kentucky Supreme Court cited a "substantial difference" in the curricula offered by rich and poor school districts, "particularly in the areas of foreign language, science, mathematics, music and art" (p. 197). Poor school districts also had less school funding and higher teacher/student ratios than their more affluent counterparts. The court also observed that "achievement test scores in the poorer districts are lower than those of rich districts and expert testimony clearly established that there is a correlation between those scores and the wealth of the district" (p. 197), and "Kentucky's overall effort and *resulting* achievement in the area of primary and secondary education are comparatively low, nationally" (p. 197, emphasis added).

Similarly, in *Lake View School District No. 25 of Phillips County v. Huckabee* (2002) (*Lake View I*), the state of Arkansas disputed a claim that it was not providing students with an adequate education by asserting that "there is no correlation between enhanced school funding and better school performance" (p. 488). The state pointed out that it had increased spending on education in response to the Arkansas

Supreme Court's declaration in *DuPree v. Alma School District No. 30 of Crawford County* (1983) that the school finance system was unconstitutional and that student performance had not significantly improved. The court rejected this claim, in part, because the state's efforts to "correct the course of educational deficiencies in Arkansas are dependent on quality teachers" (p. 489). The state had failed to ensure that its poor school districts would have quality teachers. The state's entry level for teacher salaries was the lowest of the nine states comprising its region and was ranked 48th nationally. Moreover, the court noted that serious disparities in teacher salaries existed in Arkansas, and poor school districts were losing teachers because of low pay. Moreover, in *Campaign for Fiscal Equity v. State* (2003), the New York Court of Appeals held that the plaintiffs established a correlation between the school finance system and the poor performance of New York City students. The court found that increased funding could enable New York City schools to provide better teachers, facilities, and instrumentalities of learning; and that such spending would in turn improve student outcomes.

Courts Have Rejected Local Control and Separation and Powers Defenses

A fourth hallmark of successful school finance litigation is that courts have rejected legal defenses that have defeated second-wave equity litigation, such as the doctrines of local control and separation of powers. *Claremont School District v. Governor* (1997) (*Claremont II*), a New Hampshire case, is illustrative. In *Claremont II*, the New Hampshire Supreme Court struck down the school finance system because the state's disproportionate tax burdens prevented the state from providing an adequate education. The court rejected the argument that local control justified local property taxation. As the court explained:

> We recognize that local control plays a valuable role in public education; however, the State cannot use local control as a justification for allowing the existence of educational services below the level of constitutional adequacy. The responsibility for ensuring the provision of an adequate public education and an adequate level of resources for all students in New Hampshire lies with the State. [W]hile local governments may be required, in part, to support public schools, it is the responsibility of the [State] to take such steps as may be required in each instance effectively to devise a plan and sources of funds sufficient to meet the constitutional mandate. (pp. 475–476, internal quotations omitted)

In *Rose v. Council for Better Education, Inc.* (1989), defendants argued on appeal that the trial court violated the separation of powers by directing the legislature to raise taxes. The Kentucky Supreme Court disagreed with this assertion. The trial court defined the definition of an "efficient" education, identified the characteristics of such an education, and discussed possible methods for increasing the funding necessary to satisfy the constitutional mandate. These activities met the judiciary's role of interpreting the constitution. The trial court, however, did not engage in legislative activities, such as directing the legislature "to enact any *specific legislation*, including raising taxes" (*Rose*, 1989, p. 214). Furthermore, the Kentucky Supreme Court observed that the legislature would develop the specifics of the remedy.

Emerging Trends in Adequacy Litigation

The Role of Vertical Equity

An emerging trend in adequacy litigation is that courts have begun to recognize the concept of vertical equity: Certain types of students may need increased resources in order to achieve adequate outcomes (Ryan & Saunders, 2004). The New Jersey Supreme Court has been particularly active in this regard. In *Abbott v. Burke* (1990) (*Abbott II*), the court held that the state had failed to provide students from poor, urban school districts (special needs districts, or SNDs) with an adequate education. The court then ordered the legislature to provide SNDs with the inputs necessary to achieve this outcome: (a) funding substantially equal to that of affluent districts, and (b) educational programming that would address the educational concerns of SNDs.

In *Abbott v. Burke* (1997) (*Abbott IV*), the New Jersey Supreme Court addressed the constitutionality of the state's Comprehensive Educational Improvement and Financing Act (CEIFA). The CEIFA defined an adequate education in terms of academic standards and provided funding on the basis of what a hypothetical school district would need to achieve these standards. The CEIFA also provided aid for two supplemental programs designed to address the disadvantages of SNDs: demonstrably effective program aid (DEPA), and early childhood program aid (ECPA). DEPA provided aid for instructional, school governance, health, and service programs, while ECPA provided aid for early childhood programming, such as full-day kindergarten and preschool classes.

The New Jersey Court found that the CEIFA's adoption of outcomes-based standards to define a thorough and efficient education was facially constitutional. However, the court found that the hypothetical district model, which did not incorporate the characteristics of SNDs, was unconstitutional because it failed to ensure that SNDs would receive funding sufficient to attain the statute's academic standards. Also, the DEPA and ECPA were not based on studies of the students' actual needs or the costs of meeting those needs. Furthermore, the statute failed to remedy the facilities problems of the SNDs. The court ordered the legislature to guarantee substantial parity between the SNDs and affluent districts by the beginning of the 1997–1998 school year. The court then remanded the case to the state superior court to oversee the assessment of the educational and facilities needs of the SNDs and to implement a plan to address these problems. On remand, the superior court adopted an educational package that included whole-school reform, full-day kindergarten, full-day prekindergarten, school-based health and social services, an accountability system, and increased funding for facilities.

In *Hoke County Board of Education v. State* (2004), the North Carolina Supreme Court upheld a trial court finding that the state had failed to provide at-risk students in the plaintiff school district with an adequate education. The state high court held that ample support existed for the trial court's conclusion that the state had failed "to identify 'at-risk' students and to address their needs with educational resources that would provide tutoring, extra class sessions, counseling, and other programs that target 'at-risk' students in an effort to enable them to compete among their non 'at-risk' counterparts and thus avail themselves of their right to the opportunity to obtain a sound basic education" (p. 390). The state high court also affirmed the trial court's order that the state assess its allocation of resources such that at-risk students in the plaintiff districts could receive an adequate education. The North Carolina Supreme Court, however, reversed the lower court's remedial order that the state provide prekindergarten classes to at-risk students attending low-needs districts. The North Carolina Supreme Court ruled in this fashion because there was no proof that the provision of pre-kindergarten classes was the sole means to address the needs of at-risk students. The trial court's remedial order also violated the doctrine of separation of powers because such a remedy "would effectively undermine the authority and autonomy of the government's other branches" (p. 393).

The Role of Adequacy Studies

Another emerging trend in third-wave adequacy litigation is that courts are commissioning studies to determine the cost of an adequate education in developing constitutional remedies to inadequately funded systems (Ryan & Saunders, 2004). Five state high courts have commissioned cost of adequacy studies. In *Campbell County School District v. State* (1995), the Wyoming Supreme Court ordered that "[a] cost of education study and analysis must be conducted and the results must inform the creation of a new funding system" (p. 1279). In *Abbott v. Burke* (1997) (*Abbott IV*), the New Jersey Supreme Court remanded the case to the state superior court to assess educational and facilities needs of SNDs and to implement a plan that would enable the state to provide SNDs with an adequate education. In *Campaign for Fiscal Equity v. State* (2003), the New York Court of Appeals commissioned a study to determine the cost of providing an adequate education for New York City.

In *Lake View School District No. 25 of Phillips County v. Huckabee* (2004) (*Lake View II*), the Arkansas Supreme Court recalled its mandate-releasing jurisdiction of a school finance case and appointed two Masters to evaluate the measures taken by the legislature to enact a school-funding formula that would provide students with an adequate education. In *Montoy v. State* (2005) (*Montoy V*), the Kansas Supreme Court ruled that the state legislature must carry out a "cost analysis" study that was included in legislation designed to address the court's ruling in *Montoy IV* (2005), which stated that the school-funding system was constitutionally inadequate. Both the Wyoming and Kansas supreme courts have addressed the question of whether the adequacy study can be based on past expenditures. In *State v. Campbell County School District* (2001), the Wyoming Supreme Court ruled on an adequacy study partially based on statewide averages of past district expenditures. The court ruled that professionally developed estimates would not necessarily result in an unconstitutional system, although the actual measurement of educational costs was superior. Also, the court rejected the argument that a system based on past expenditures was fatally flawed because it was based on a system that had been declared unconstitutional. Although the state's supreme court had ruled in 1995 that the "old system had

resulted in unconstitutional disparities between districts, absent was a holding that the system, as a whole, was underfunding education" (*State v. Campbell County School District*, 2001, p. 538). While some districts were indeed inadequately funded, other districts were not. Thus, the record did not conclude that a system based on statewide averages would result in an inadequate education. In *Montoy V*, the Kansas Supreme Court ruled that an adequacy study that was based on prior spending was constitutionally permissible, as long as the study "corrects for the recognized inadequacy of those expenditures and ensures that a reliable method of extrapolation was adopted" (*Montoy V*, p. 939). However, the court found that the legislature's alternative proposed cost study was flawed because it examined only educational inputs. The court also required the cost study to compute the cost of educational outputs. The Arkansas, New Jersey, and New York courts have employed special masters to aid in the costing out and implementation of adequate remedies. The Arkansas and New Jersey courts have adopted the findings of their experts. In *Lake View School District No. 25 v. Huckabee* (2005) (*Lake View III*), the Arkansas Supreme Court adopted the findings of its two special masters that the state had failed to provide a constitutionally adequate system.

On remand from *Abbott IV*, a New Jersey superior court adopted an educational package recommended by the special master that included whole-school reform, full-day kindergarten, full-day pre-kindergarten, school-based health and social services, an accountability system, and increased funding for facilities. In *Abbott v. Burke* (1998) (*Abbott V*), the New Jersey Supreme Court held that these various proposals comported with the state's statutory and regulatory definitions of an adequate education. Therefore, the court held that the proposals should be immediately implemented.

In contrast to *Abbott V*, the New York high court held in *Campaign for Fiscal Equity v. State* (2006) that a trial court may not adopt a referee's report recommending that the state provide New York City's public schools with $5.63 billion in additional annual operating funds, phased in over 4 years, and to expend a minimum of $9.179 billion on capital improvements over the next 5 years. The Court of Appeals of New York found sufficient support in the record for the plan submitted by the New York State Commission on Education Reform plan (Zarb Commission) (see Governor's Commission on Education Reform, 2004), which had contracted Standard and Poor's School Evaluation

Services to conduct a cost study. Thus, adopting the referee's report violated the doctrine of separation of powers.

Reliance on State-Accountability Systems

A third emerging trend in adequacy litigation is that courts may rely more on accountability systems developed by state legislatures to determine whether states are providing an adequate education (Dayton, Dupre, & Kiracofe, 2004; Liebman & Sabel, 2003; Ryan & Saunders, 2004). The National Commission of Excellence's report, *A Nation at Risk: The Imperative for Educational Reform* (1983), which warned that the public school system was creating a "rising tide of mediocrity that threatens our very future as a Nation and a people" (p. 5), is widely seen as the catalyst for the accountability movement (Dyson, 2002; Heise, 1998). The No Child Left Behind Act (NCLB) of 2001 has also encouraged the development of accountability systems. NCLB requires states to develop accountability systems that apply to all public schools. States must bring all students to the level of "proficient" by 2013–2014. NCLB requires each state, school district, and school to make adequate yearly progress (AYP) toward meeting state standards.

State accountability systems identify educational outcomes and use assessment mechanisms to determine whether students are meeting these standards (Ryan & Saunders, 2004). Accountability systems make it easier for courts to measure adequacy because they do not have to develop their own standards. Rather, courts merely have to determine whether students are failing to meet the standards of the accountability system and whether increased funding would enable students in low-performing districts to meet these standards.

Montoy v. State (2005), a Kansas school finance case, is illustrative. In *Montoy*, the Kansas Supreme Court held that the state had failed to provide schools with high proportions of minority and disadvantaged students with an adequate education, in violation of the state constitution. The court found that the current school finance system failed to satisfy the legislature's own definition of a suitable provision for the finance of education, which was based on student academic performance and school accreditation standards. The court cited a study commissioned by the legislature that concluded that the school finance system needed an additional $850 million to satisfy the legislature's standard (Augenblick, Meyers, Silverstein, & Barkis, 2002).

In this regard, *Montoy* departed from most successful adequacy litigation, in which courts have identified the components of an adequate education and then ordered the legislature to develop a remedy that achieves this mandate (Roelke, Green, & Zielewski, 2004). For example, in *Campaign for Fiscal Equity v. State* (2003), the New York Court of Appeals adopted its own definition of an adequate education, a meaningful high school education, and then ordered the implementation of a cost study to determine the cost of an adequate education. By contrast, the Kansas Supreme Court did not have to develop its own standard of adequacy but instead could rely on the legislature's own definition of a suitable education. Rather, the court merely had to compare the legislature's funding effort with its own commissioned study.

The major limitation of state accountability systems as a litigation tool is that state legislatures may lower standards to avoid constitutional liability. This phenomenon has already occurred with respect to NCLB. Several states have responded to NCLB by lowering testing standards, redefining schools in need of improvement, and redefining proficiency standards (Almeida, 2004; Losen, 2004). This scenario may cause plaintiffs to challenge the constitutionality of the state accountability standards. Several courts have held that the standard for adequacy must reflect the needs of contemporary society (*Campaign for Fiscal Equity v. State*, 2003; *DeRolph v. State*, 2000). If state accountability standards fall below this high level, plaintiffs may assert that the standards are unconstitutional because they do not measure the skills that students need to be contributing members of contemporary society (Almeida, 2004).

Substantive Due Process Challenges

In the future, plaintiffs may employ the due process clause of the Fourteenth Amendment to challenge the adequacy of school-funding systems. The due process clause forbids the state to "deprive any person of life, liberty, or property, without due process of law" (U.S. Constitution, Amendment XIV, § 1). Due process has two components: procedural and substantive. Procedural due process requires the state to provide notice and an opportunity for a person to be heard before depriving a person of a protected interest. Substantive due process prohibits states from depriving a person of a protected interest in an arbitrary or capricious manner.

States that require students to pass high-stakes graduation tests in order to receive a diploma might be especially susceptible to a substantive due process challenge to the adequacy of their school-funding systems (Dyson, 2002). In *Debra P. v. Turlington* (1981), the Fifth Circuit held that a high school graduation test violates a person's substantive due process right to a high school diploma if the test is arbitrary and capricious, frustrates a legitimate state interest, or is fundamentally unfair in that "it encroaches upon concepts of justice lying at the basis of our civil and political institutions" (p. 404). In *Debra P.*, the court held that the state's use of a high school graduation test was fundamentally unfair because the test covered material that was not taught in the schools. Similarly, students in districts with poor passage rates might argue that inadequate funding is frustrating the state's ability to provide students with the opportunity to master the competencies required by the state accountability system.

Limitations of Adequacy Litigation

Adequacy litigation has several limitations that may reduce the impact of this approach. The first limitation is that the concept of adequacy is extremely complicated. Adequacy claims not only demand "a prescription of some minimum inputs into schools, but also of outputs from schools" (Cover, 2002, p. 425). A further complication is that adequacy measures invite "measurements of many education sectors, including but not limited to teacher experience, class size, reading levels, and enrichment programs, in addition to state funding" (p. 425). Because of this complexity, a number of courts have refused to assume the task of determining the components of an adequate education. These courts held that the issue was not "justiciable," or appropriate for judicial review, because of the unavailability of judicially manageable standards. These courts also ruled that defining the elements of an adequate education would place them in the role of the legislative and executive branches, in violation of the doctrine of separation of powers.

In *Committee for Educational Rights v. Edgar* (1996), for example, the Illinois Supreme Court dismissed a claim that the state had failed to satisfy the education clause's mandate of providing "high quality public educational institutions and services" (Illinois Constitution Article 10, § 1) because of justiciability and separation of powers concerns. The components of a high-quality education could not be ascertained, because the constitution provided no guidance, and education was not within the judiciary's field of expertise.

"Rather," the court explained, "the question of educational quality is inherently one of policy involving philosophical and practical considerations that call for the exercise of legislative and administrative discretion" (*Committee for Educational Rights v. Edgar*, 1996, p. 1191). Furthermore, if the court assumed the role of determining whether the educational system was of sufficient quality, it "would largely deprive members of the general public of a voice in a matter which is close to the hearts of all individuals in Illinois" (*Committee for Educational Rights v. Edgar*, 1996, p. 1191). Such a result would be unfortunate because "[s]olutions to problems of educational quality should emerge from a spirited dialogue between the people of the State and their elected representatives" (p. 1191).

In *Pawtucket v. Sundlun* (1995), the Rhode Island Supreme Court also dismissed an adequacy challenge because no judicially enforceable standards existed for measuring whether the state was providing an "efficient" education. The court refused to create such standards because it found that the proper forum for this request was the state legislature, not the judiciary. Moreover, the court cited the New Jersey Supreme Court's struggle to define the components of an adequate education as a reason not to assume this task:

> [T]he absence of justiciable standards could engage the court in a morass comparable to the decades-long struggle of the Supreme Court of New Jersey that has attempted to define what constitutes the "thorough and efficient" education specified in that state's constitution. . . . Beginning with *Robinson v. Cahill*, . . . the New Jersey Supreme Court has struggled in its self-appointed role as overseer for more than twenty-one years, consuming significant funds, fees, time, effort, and court attention. The volume of litigation and the extent of judicial oversight provides a chilling example of the thickets that can entrap a court that takes on the duties of a Legislature. (*Pawtucket v. Sundlun*, 1995, p. 59)

The Rhode Island Supreme Court's discussion in *Pawtucket* (1995) raises another weakness of adequacy litigation: Even if plaintiffs win, legislatures may refuse to cooperate. This legislative recalcitrance might have caused the Alabama and Ohio Supreme Courts to retreat from previous decisions holding that their school finance formulas were inadequate (Thomas, 2004). In *Opinion of the Justices* (1993), the Alabama Supreme Court held that a trial court decision that invalidated the school finance system was binding unless appealed. In 1993, the trial court issued a remedial order requiring the state to develop a performance-based public educational system. In *Ex Parte James* (1997), the Alabama Supreme Court held that the trial court had the power to implement a remedy plan but that the trial court had acted prematurely by not giving the legislature sufficient time to develop a remedy. Five years later, the Alabama Supreme Court dismissed the case on separation of powers grounds (*Ex Parte James*, 2002). The court noted that the state constitution contained a provision that explicitly prohibited the judiciary from exercising legislative and executive powers. Accordingly, "any specific remedy that the judiciary could impose would, in order to be effective, necessarily involve a usurpation of that power entrusted exclusively to the Legislature" (*Ex Parte James*, 2002, p. 819). In *State ex rel. State v. Lewis* (2003), the Ohio Supreme Court ended a 12-year lawsuit challenging the adequacy of the state's school finance system. The court issued four decisions declaring the school finance system inadequate. In *Lewis*, the Ohio Supreme Court found that the school finance formula was still unconstitutional, but it issued a writ of prohibition barring the trial court from overseeing legislative efforts to remedy the deficiencies. The writ of prohibition was necessary to prevent the judiciary from "encroach[ing] upon the clearly legislative function of deciding what the new legislation will be" (*State ex rel. State v. Lewis*, 2003, p. 202).

Equal Educational Opportunities Act of 1974

Limited-English-proficiency and English-language-learner (LEP/ELL) students may be able to mount an adequacy challenge under the Equal Educational Opportunities Act (EEOA) of 1974. Section 1703 of the EEOA provides:

> [N]o state shall deny equal educational opportunity to an individual on account of his or her race, color, sex, or national origin, by . . . the failure by an educational agency to take appropriate action to overcome language barriers that impede equal participation by its students in its instructional programs. (EEOA, 2006)

Unlike Title VI, the EEOA specifically creates a private right of action. Section 1706 states that "[a]n individual denied an equal educational opportunity, as defined by this subchapter may institute a civil action in an appropriate district court of the United States against such parties, and for such relief as may be appropriate" (EEOA, 2006). Section 1720 of the act defines an "educational agency" as a "local education agency" or "state educational agency" (EEOA, 2006).

In *Castaneda v. Pickard* (1981), the Fifth Circuit Court of Appeals established a three-pronged analysis for analyzing the appropriateness of a school district's language remediation program under the EEOA. First, the court must "examine carefully the evidence the record contains concerning the soundness of the educational theory or principles upon which the challenged program is based" (p. 1009). Second, the court must determine "whether the programs and practices actually used by a school system are reasonably calculated to implement effectively the educational theory adopted by the school" (p. 1010). Third, the court must determine whether the district's program was overcoming language barriers: "[i]f a school's program, although premised on a legitimate educational theory and implemented through the use of adequate techniques, fails, after being employed for a period of time sufficient to give the plan a legitimate trial, to produce results indicating that the language barriers are actually being overcome, that program may . . . no longer constitute appropriate action" (p. 1010).

Applying the *Castaneda* test, a federal district court in *Flores v. Arizona* (2000) held that Arizona's provision of $150 per LEP student violated the EEOA by failing to provide these students with an adequate education. The state's educational programs passed the first prong of the *Castaneda* test because experts generally regarded those programs as sound designs for the effective instruction of LEP students. The educational programs failed the second prong, however, because the state-provided funding was inadequate to implement the state's programs. The court identified the following deficiencies: "1) too many students in a classroom, 2) not enough classrooms, 3) not enough qualified teachers, including teachers to teach ESL [English as a second language] and bilingual teachers to teach content area studies, 4) not enough teacher aids, 5) an inadequate tutoring program, and 6) insufficient teaching materials for both ESL classes and content area courses" (p. 1239). The court further held that the state's funding of LEP/ELL students "is arbitrary and capricious and bears no relation to the actual funding needed to ensure that ELCB students . . . are achieving mastery of its specified 'essential skills'" (p. 1239).

Summary of Legal Issues

During the third wave of school finance litigation, plaintiffs have primarily argued that educational funding systems are inadequate in violation of education clauses. In most successful adequacy litigation, courts have assumed the role of defining an adequate education, while leaving it to legislatures to develop specific strategies to achieve these goals. In successful litigation, courts have also made it clear that these adequacy standards must adapt to the needs of contemporary society. Also, courts have rejected claims that no correlation exists between funding and educational outcomes. Furthermore, courts have rejected legal defenses that have defeated numerous second-wave equity lawsuits, such as the doctrines of local control and separation of powers. In future school finance litigation, courts may define adequacy in terms of vertical equity, may call for adequacy studies, and may use state accountability systems to determine whether states are satisfying their constitutional duty.

Adequacy litigation has many limitations that may reduce its effectiveness. A major limitation of adequacy litigation is that this concept is exceedingly difficult to define. This complexity might be the reason that several courts have adequacy challenges on justiciability and separation of powers grounds. Another limitation of adequacy litigation is that, even if plaintiffs win, the legislature may balk at developing a remedy, causing the court to eventually wear down and dismiss the case.

In addition to traditional adequacy litigation—in which plaintiffs assert that states have failed to provide poor school districts with a sufficient funding in violation of state education clause—alternative strategies exist. Segregated urban school districts have attained adequacy aid through *Milliken v. Bradley* (1977) (*Milliken II*). A major limitation of *Milliken II* aid is that such funding is designed merely to address the effects of intentional discrimination. In the future, plaintiffs may mount substantive due process challenges to inadequately funded school systems. Finally, LEP/ELL students may challenge inadequate educational funding through the EEOA.

Key Concepts in the Measurement of Costs

In this section, we present key concepts for understanding the meaning and measurement of educational adequacy. We discuss adequacy in terms of inputs to or outcomes of schooling, with outcomes measured as either absolute or marginal benefits of schooling. We also discuss the measurement of adequacy via accounting (expenditure-based) or resource-cost analyses.

Input-Based Versus Outcome-Based Definitions of Adequacy

Analysts can conceptualize adequacy in terms of inputs to schooling or outcomes from schooling. Input-based approaches to adequacy consider the fiscal resources required for purchasing a set of human and material inputs that constitute a suitable or thorough and efficient education: for example, the adequate number of teachers and administrators and the necessary materials, supplies, and equipment. Policy makers who opt for input-based models often assume that the quality of resources obtained are reasonably equal from school to school and that schools can use the resources with reasonably equal effectiveness. Because neither assumption holds in the real world and large, observable inequities in outcomes persist, even after delivery of dollar-equal inputs, a burgeoning research literature on outcome-based approaches has sought to usurp the position of the input-based models.

Outcome-based approaches focus on student, school, or district-level performance indices. Increasingly, analyses determine outcomes with respect to state standards for district or school accreditation. Policy makers who opt for the outcome approach assume that a school that yields adequate outcomes, or achieves accreditation, must have access to adequate resources. Further, the school that yields adequate outcomes with the fewest resources must also be the most efficient. Unfortunately, outcome-based models face problems even more complex than those of the input variety.

Continued refinement of both input- and outcome-based models is necessary, as we will discuss in detail throughout this chapter. In particular, neither adequately addresses the ecological features of schooling. Input models are presently based on assumptions that we (or someone much wiser than us) can know and can prescribe that set of educational inputs that will lead to desired educational outcomes. Although evidence regarding outcome effects of specific interventions such as comprehensive school reforms or class-size reduction (CSR) in specific contexts is increasing, we still know very little about how to best combine and integrate interventions to produce desired outcomes optimally. For example, some recent research has validated that CSR policies produce small, positive achievement gains, indicating that funding an adequate education might involve funding at a level that would support small class sizes (Finn & Achilles, 1999). However, other analyses show that CSR is among the more expensive reforms to implement, and when compared with other options, such as improving the education level of teachers, CSR policies are relatively cost-ineffective (Brewer, Krop, Gill, & Reichart, 1999).

Outcome models suffer the limitations of available data on the full array of inputs to schooling that influence outcomes as well as precision, depth, and breadth of outcome measures. For example, student outcomes are a function of both schooling resources and family and community resources, or nonschooling resources. Recent research, for example, documents significant differences in the rate of achievement gain of high and low socioeconomic status students solely as a function of summer learning (Alexander, Entwistle, & Olsen, 2001). As such, would it be reasonable to reduce the public subsidy to traditional public schools where higher percentages of children engage in summer learning at parent expense? Can (or should) state-supported *educational adequacy* be means tested for assumed private contributions?

Where outcome measures are too narrow, for example, including only reading and math tests of minimum proficiency, one might be able to estimate the minimum costs of achieving just those outcomes, but one would have no idea whether those districts spending the least to achieve those outcomes have done so at the expense of other important academic, cognitive, and affective outcomes. A major recent criticism of state-accountability systems adopted under NCLB of 2001 is that those systems have led to even greater disparity across student populations in the availability and quality of programming related to nontested areas (e.g., arts, physical education, advanced courses).

Other difficulties emerge where outside factors influence resources available to schools. Numerous cases in school finance exist where schooling resources vary widely and student population characteristics vary commensurately. For example, low-performing children who happen to be poor attend districts with fewer resources that are also segregated by race and class, and these systems are compared against higher-performing children who happen to be individually wealthier and attend districts with more resources. In such cases, outcomes may appear to increase with respect to changes in resources (achievement is correlated with spending). Analysts have difficulty, however, decomposing the effects of the additional schooling resources and non-schooling resources associated with the higher performance of wealthier students attending schools with more resources and the lower performance of lower-income students attending schools with fewer resources.

In other cases, schooling resources across a state are relatively uniform but schooling performance varies, with some schools performing quite well and others quite poorly. While the uniform level of funding is apparently adequate for some students, it is not for others. Yet there is no effective way to extrapolate what funding would be adequate for all students by observing the relationship of inputs to outcomes because of the limited variance of inputs. Such conditions tend to exist in states with greater control over funding, including tax limits or revenue caps that limit local citizens from expressing their demand for higher-quality schooling (e.g., Kansas or California) (Theobald & Picus, 1991). Where adequate outcomes do exist in such a system, a major influence on those outcomes may be nonschooling resources. Where the state exerts greatest control over public equity of resources, parents with a high demand for quality education likely will substitute their private dollars to raise the level of inputs so that their child enjoys a competitive advantage.

Adequacy litigation discussed previously in this chapter can be classified as input- or outcome-based. For example, the series of *Abbott v. Burke* cases in New Jersey were input-based adequacy cases, with evolving definitions of input adequacy. Initially, input adequacy for litigant districts was defined by the New Jersey courts as exact parity between poor and wealthy districts' fiscal inputs. More recently, the New Jersey court has defined adequate inputs as the inputs required for implementing whole-school reform models presumed to yield positive outcomes for low-income students.

As we discussed earlier in this chapter, *Rose v. Council for Better Education* (1989) in Kentucky is the first major outcome-based adequacy decision, with the court requiring school districts across the state to produce students proficient across seven major outcome areas. A recent policy issue has arisen that casts doubt on the commitment of legislators to thoughtful funding of education. Some critics question whether state legislatures may simply define a set of inputs or outcomes as suitable or thorough and efficient as a Machiavellian strategy to fend off adequacy litigation. For example, New Jersey now refers to the basic level of aid required for implementing appropriate whole-school reforms as "T&E," or "thorough and efficient" funding. Is it so, simply if the legislature declares it so?

Other states such as Texas have recently defended their state funding systems on the basis that all districts achieved accreditation under the state's outcome evaluation system. That is, the state board of education set criteria for suitable outcomes, and all districts met those outcomes. The inputs to schooling therefore must be suitable or thorough and efficient. Of course, state boards of education are themselves a part of the political process. Their standards may be high or low depending on their perception of what the current political climate will accept. Because the vast majority of school systems in the 50 states are functioning as accredited schools, and the performance of these schools varies quite widely, standards must also vary quite widely. For evidence, see *Primary Progress, Secondary Challenge: A State-by-State Look at Student Achievement Patterns* (Hall & Kennedy, 2006).

Absolute Versus Marginal Outcomes

An important consideration in measuring outcomes is whether the outcomes of interest are *absolute* or *marginal* benefits. Absolute benefits are *levels* of student performance attained by participating in public education. The recent standards movement across states suggests that the purpose of public schooling is to produce a set of absolute benefits or raise all students' performance to a defined minimum level. In most, if not all cases, state standards and the tests used to assess them involve a minimum set of knowledge and skills attainable by a majority of students.

Economist Paul Samuelson has defined a "collective consumption good" (1954, p. 387) as one that yields comparable marginal benefits to all who choose to participate.

Marginal benefits of schooling are performance *gains* or *value-added gains* that analysts may attribute to the schooling resources allocated to the child. From our perspective, it seems reasonable to conclude that state policy makers should be concerned that every school provides both basic levels of mastery of necessary educational skills and value-added learning for each student at a rate appropriate to each grade level. The educational and cost implications of marginal versus absolute outcome measurement vary significantly by student abilities and/or prior achievement levels.

For lower-ability or lower-achieving students, a more reasonable approach may be to emphasize absolute benefits that these students should attain by the time they exit the public schooling system. The greater

their difficulties and/or the lower their initial achievement, the greater the effort, and likely the greater the cost of achieving those absolute outcomes. Many higher-ability children will surpass minimum standards well in advance of their expected time of completion, leaving two options. First, we may adhere to measuring absolute benefits and simply allow them to exit the system early and purchase, on their own, whatever additional education they desire. This solution creates obvious equity concerns for bright children once they have exited the public education system. Second, we may choose to provide additional opportunities at public expense, either within or outside of the public K–12 school system, to provide marginal benefits beyond the absolute expectation. This latter option, however, requires supplemental resources. (We addressed this notion previously under the concept of *vertical equity* in Chapter 5.) Another option might be to allow students to graduate when they have demonstrated mastery of the content and then provide them with the equivalent value of their remaining education as a voucher to any state-funded college or technical school program. The net cost to the system will be zero, and the value added to the student will be very high.

Some suggest that use of marginal benefit analysis negates the effects of nonschool resources (Walberg, 2001). That is, family resources affect the level at which a child enters the public schooling system but do not affect the rate at which the child continues to learn while attending the school system. Existing research suggests the contrary, including the aforementioned study finding that summer learning alone has significant effects on students' annual achievement gains (Alexander et al., 2001).

Measuring Input- Versus Outcome-Based Adequacy

Now that we have discussed some of the thorny theoretical issues attending the conceptualization of adequacy in school finance, we examine various methods of measuring adequacy. Transforming the concept of adequacy into a measure first requires us to define four terms we find are frequently imprecisely used:

Expenditure: Funds spent by an organization, or allocated to organizational subunits (and subsequently spent by those units), for purposes of maintaining the operations of those units. For example, funds expended by a high school science department for purchasing materials, supplies, and equipment or funds expended by district-level administration for the annual operations of the district central office.

Resource: People, time, space, and materials required to provide a specific set of educational services that requires a budget allocation. For example, the numbers of teachers, levels of experience, and teacher time allocated toward providing a particular academic program. Levin and McEwan (2001) refer to resources as "ingredients."

Price: Dollar value of a given resource. For example, the price, in salary and benefits, of hiring a teacher with A, B, and C qualifications to carry out X, Y, and Z duties. Ideally, the competitive market for the resources in question determines the prices for the resources in question. This, of course, means that the price of a given resource may vary across different schools or districts if they are subject to different market conditions.

Cost: The aggregation or summation of the prices of resources required for providing a specific set of educational services. The cost of providing a particular set of educational services equals what must be spent in order to achieve a defined set of outcomes, if the system in question—the school—can produce those outcomes efficiently.

In our view, analyses must relate *cost* to the cost of producing some level of educational output, whether arrived at via input or outcome orientation. Because cost is necessarily tied to producing some level of outcomes, cost necessarily varies across students and contexts. The concept of vertical equity returns!

To use a Kansas analogy, the cost of producing a corn crop that meets accepted standards for yield and quality might average $1,000 per acre. This cost includes the price of seed, chemicals, labor, water, machinery, etc. Our ability to produce high-quality corn at this cost depends on a number of conditions beyond our control. We're not corn farmers or commodities traders, but we're guessing that it would cost quite a bit more, in terms of irrigation alone, to grow a comparable quantity of corn of similar quality in the deserts of New Mexico or Arizona as compared to the wetter, more fertile areas of Northeastern Kansas. That is, the production costs are less where conditions are more favorable.

If government has an interest in the production of corn or the sustenance of corn farming (two different policy goals), then government can implement policies or use financial subsidies to support corn farming or corn farmers. In an effort to make comparable the quality of living for Arizona and Kansas corn farmers, government might need to provide significant additional resources to those Arizona corn farmers. In the case of corn, however, a more logical policy would be to encourage the growing of corn only where it's cheaper to grow corn or to let natural conditions determine which farmers succeed and which fail. That's where corn and kids are different.

Adequacy Analysis Applied

Determining the adequacy of public elementary and secondary education is, at best, a difficult task. In attempting to determine adequacy, several models currently are in practice. Important considerations for undertaking studies of educational adequacy include (a) conceptual, (b) contextual, and (c) technical considerations.

Conceptual: Is a state legislature guided by *input* or *outcome* standards of adequacy? That is, does a legislature perceive an adequate education to consist of a prescribed set of educational inputs, such as numbers of teachers per pupil, materials, and supplies and facilities? Or does the legislature perceive an adequate education to be reflected in certain student outcome measures? Certain methods for measuring the cost of educational adequacy focus on schooling inputs, while others focus on schooling outcomes. Where a state legislature's emphasis is on achieving adequate outcomes, the state should use outcome-based, or performance-oriented, analyses.

Contextual: The political, economic, and demographic context of each state differs. Some states are more economically and demographically complex than others. Some states are more politically diverse than others. Different methods may work better in different contexts. Key contextual questions include the following: Does political consensus exist around desired inputs or outcomes? Is the state relatively homogenous in geography, demographics, and economics?

Technical: Related to the political, demographic, and economic complexity of a state are a variety of technical concerns. Different methods have different technical strengths and weaknesses. Key questions include the following: If the state were highly heterogeneous, is the method in question sufficiently rigorous for estimating cost variations across districts of different characteristics serving varied student populations? Does the state collect sufficient data for estimating costs and cost variations?

In recent years, a handful of consulting teams including Management Analysis and Planning & Associates (MAP) (www.edconsultants.com) and Augenblick, Palaich, and Myers (www.apaconsulting.net) have worked with states to generate estimates of the cost of an adequate education. In doing so, they each have created approaches to adequacy analysis such as the *basket of educational goods and services,* used by MAP in Wyoming, or *successful schools method,* used by Augenblick and colleagues in Ohio and more recently in Maryland. Some recent literature classifies adequacy analysis into three categories: (1) cost function or inference from outcomes by statistical analysis; (2) empirical observation, or *successful schools*; and (3) professional judgment (see, e.g., Picus, 2001).

We choose to reclassify adequacy studies according to their principal methods (drawing on the work of Taylor, Baker, & Vedlitz, 2005), as we describe in the following sections.

Average Expenditure Studies

Before the 1990s, concepts regarding educational adequacy were often guided by the average or median expenditures of school districts in the prior year. A common presumption was that median spending was adequate, and that states should strive to bring the lower half of districts up to the median. As early as 1951 (in referring to a study conducted in 1930–1931), Mort and Reusser describe setting foundation funding according to the average expenditures of the well-organized districts of average wealth (Mort & Reusser, 1951).

With increased prevalence of state standards and assessments, consultants and policy makers in the early 1990s turned their attention to the average expenditures of school districts meeting a prescribed set of outcome standards, rather than the simple average or median of all districts. This approach is called the *successful schools model.*

Successful schools studies use outcome data on measures such as attendance and dropout rates and student test scores to identify that set of schools or school districts in a state that meets a chosen standard of success. Then, the average of the expenditures of those schools or school districts is considered adequate (on the assumption that some schools in the state can succeed with that level of funding). Modified successful schools analyses include some consideration of how schools used the resources. This is done in either of two ways. In most cases, analysts may analyze data on how schools use the resources to identify and exclude peculiar, or outlier, schools or districts from the successful schools sample. Alternatively, analysts might seek patterns in resource allocation to identify those schools that allocate resources in such a way as to produce particularly high outcomes, with particularly low expenditures. Early successful schools analyses in Ohio used data on district resource allocation as a partial basis for modifying the sample of districts to be used for calculating average costs of achieving standards (Augenblick, 1997).

Resource Cost Studies

The **resource-cost model (RCM)** is a method that analysts have used extensively to measure the costs of educational services (Chambers, 1999; Hartman, Bolton, & Monk, 2001). In general, RCM is a method for measuring costs of services, existing or hypothetical, adequate or not. The RCM methodology typically involves three steps:

1. Identify and/or measure the resources (people, space, and time) used in providing a particular set of services.
2. Estimate resource prices and price variations from school to school or school district to school district.
3. Tabulate total costs of service delivery by totaling the resource quantities (resource intensity) and the prices.

Analysts have used RCMs for calculating the cost of providing adequate educational services since the early 1980s.

Two relatively new variants of RCMs have been specifically tailored to measure the costs of an adequate education: (a) *professional judgment*-driven RCM and (b) *evidence-based* RCM. They differ in the strategy for identifying the resources required to provide an adequate education. In **professional judgment** studies, focus groups of educators and policy makers prescribe the basket of educational goods and services required to provide an adequate education. In evidence-based studies, analysts derive resource needs for staffing and staff development from proven-effective comprehensive school reform models such as Robert Slavin's Roots and Wings/Success for All that focus on improving educational outcomes in high-poverty schools (cited in Odden, 2000). More recent evidence-based analyses attempt to integrate a variety of proven-effective input strategies such as CSR, specific interventions for special student populations, and comprehensive school reform models, rather than relying on a single reform model.

Because analysts recently have broadened **evidence-based** strategies to include and blend a variety of reform strategies, in this book, we use the phrase *evidence based* rather than *cost of comprehensive school reforms* to describe the approach. Our terminology, however, may lead to a blurred distinction between evidence-based and professional judgment models. One might assume, for example, that a panel of well-informed professionals would prescribe inputs for schools based at least partly on the professionals' knowledge of research literature on effective reform strategies. The subtle distinction between this and *evidence-based* analysis is that evidence-based analysis requires an empirical research basis for recommended resource configurations. Further, in evidence-based analysis, the consultants conducting the cost study provide the recommendations, and evidence-based analysis typically does not include panels of experts from schools and districts in the state.

Statistical Modeling Studies

Less common among recent analyses of educational adequacy are statistical methods that may be used to estimate either (a) the quantities and qualities of educational resources associated with higher or improved educational outcomes or (b) the costs associated with achieving a specific set of outcomes, in different school districts, serving different student populations. The first of these methods is known as the *education production function* and the second is known as the *education cost function*. The two are highly interconnected and—like successful schools analysis—require policy makers to establish explicit, measurable outcome goals.

Analysts can use education production-function analysis to determine which quantities and qualities of educational resources are most strongly, positively associated with a designated set of student outcomes. For example, is it better for a school to have more teachers or fewer teachers with stronger academic preparation at the same total cost to maximize some desired outcome? Further, analysts can use education production-function analysis to determine whether different resource quantities and qualities are more or less effective in districts serving different types of students (economically disadvantaged, ELLs), or in different types of districts (large urban or small, remote rural).

Cost-function analyses, like production-function analyses, use certain statistical equations. **Education cost-function analysis** is a statistical model in which educational expenditures are the dependent variable and where (a) student outcomes, (b) student characteristics, (c) schooling characteristics, and (d) relative efficiency are expected to influence current/historical spending. In cost-function analysis, the goal is to estimate the cost of achieving a desired set of educational outcomes and further to estimate how those costs differ in districts with certain characteristics, serving students with certain characteristics. For example, the costs of achieving state average outcomes in a high-poverty urban district may differ greatly from the costs of achieving the same outcomes in an affluent suburb. A cost function that analysts have estimated with existing data on district spending levels and outcomes, and including data on district and student characteristics, can be useful for predicting the average cost of achieving a desired level of outcomes in a district of average characteristics serving a student population of average characteristics. Further, the cost function is useful to generate a cost index for each school district that indicates the relative cost of producing the desired outcomes in each school district. For example, per-pupil costs of achieving target outcomes likely would be higher than average in small, rural school districts, in school districts with high percentages of economically disadvantaged and LEP children, and in districts that have higher competitive wages for teachers.

The cost function is an extension of the production function. In cost-function studies, the goal is to estimate directly, in a single model, the costs of achieving desired outcomes, while with a production-function model, the goal is to identify those inputs that produce desirable outcomes and subsequently estimate the cost of those inputs. To date, cost-function studies have narrowly specified outcome measures, including primarily measures of student achievement in core subject areas.

Reconciling the Various Approaches

In a perfect world, with perfect information regarding the relationship between resource mix and student outcomes (for guiding bottom-up analysis), perfect data on student outcomes and perfect measures of district inefficiency (for guiding top-down analysis), resource cost, and statistical cost-function analysis would produce the same results. Each type of analysis would eliminate all distortions in cost estimates. Resulting distortions of resource-oriented versus performance-oriented analyses may be quite similar or quite different.

Ideally, investigators using resource-cost approaches for calculating the cost of adequacy would have perfect information regarding the lowest cost mix of resources that would lead to the desired educational outcomes for a given set of students under a given set of conditions. As noted, analysts most often achieve resource mix either by following the recommendations of expert panels (professional judgment) or by identifying specific educational reform models that researchers believe to be effective–and not by estimating the relationship between resource mix and existing student outcomes. To date, evidence on the effectiveness or the cost-effectiveness of comprehensive school reforms that commonly guide such analyses remains questionable at best (Bifulco, Bordeaux, Duncombe, & Yinger, 2002; Borman & Hewes, 2002; Borman, Hewes, Overman, & Brown, 2003; Levin, 2002). When the prescribed resource mix is not the most efficient mix that a district could purchase at a given total cost, resource-cost analyses will lead to distortions in cost indices, and these distortions may have differential effects across districts of varied size or of varied student populations. For example, the resource intensity required to achieve a passing score on the New York State Regents Exam in a certain type of district may be over- or under-stated by expert panels or prescribed models. Most cost indices produced by resource-cost analyses include at least some such distortion.

Similar problems exist in the estimation of statistical models of costs. Statistical models of costs rely on existing school district expenditure data and on relationships between expenditure data and current levels of student outcomes. Analysts attempt to subtract inefficiencies from expenditure data. That is, it is possible that a district with a specific set of characteristics currently spends more than necessary to achieve its current level of outcomes. Further, common patterns of inefficiency may exist across all, or similar, sets of districts in a state. Where some or all of these inefficiencies go unmeasured, actual costs (assuming either average, or maximum efficiency) of outcomes may be overstated for some or all districts.

Findings of Recent Cost Studies

The growing track record regarding adequacy analysis, replication of analyses in the same states under different sponsorship, and application of alternative methods under the same sponsorship in some states provide increased opportunities to compare the results of adequacy studies and ascertain whether certain patterns exist. In this section, we review the findings of selected studies of the cost of an adequate education, focusing first on basic costs, then on additional costs associated with district characteristics and student-population characteristics.

Table 7.2 summarizes the findings of average expenditure studies since 1996. Note that, in general, average expenditure estimates vary within a state as a function of choosing different desired outcome standards. That is, when consultants select that set of districts that achieve very high outcome standards, expenditures are often higher than when consultants select a set of districts meeting more modest outcome standards. This finding may occur for a variety of reasons. First, the logical assumption that it costs more to achieve higher outcomes may hold. However, because average expenditure studies fail to control for a variety of other district factors, the higher spending rates of highly successful schools are often a function of high-wealth communities that choose to spend more on their schools and at the same time, due to socioeconomic conditions, have high-performing children. A recent study in Illinois made some attempt to accommodate this shortcoming by grouping schools by poverty rates. In Illinois, among low-poverty schools, schools achieving the 80% standard spent, on average, $4,470 per pupil, while schools achieving the 100% standard spent $5,270 (Augenblick & Myers, 2001).

It can be extremely difficult to make apples-to-apples comparisons of cost figures generated by adequacy studies, especially where methods vary. The cost figures presented in Table 7.2 include estimates from successful schools. Successful schools analyses typically involve taking simple averages of expenditures of districts

Table 7.2   Findings From Successful Districts—Average Expenditure Studies

State	Author	Estimate Type[a]	Includes Special Education	Year	Base Cost	Regionally and Inflation Adjusted
New York	Standard and Poor's, 2004	Mean	Yes	2004	$12,679	$11,300
New Jersey	Augenblick et al., 2006	Low	No	2005	$ 8,493	$ 7,108
Ohio	Legislature	Low	No	1999	$ 5,560	$ 7,080
Maryland	Augenblick & Myers, 2001	Low	No	2000	$ 5,969	$ 6,789
Illinois	Augenblick & Myers, 2001	Low	No	2000	$ 5,965	$ 6,722
Missouri	Augenblick & Myers, 2003	Low	No	2002	$ 5,664	$ 6,717
Connecticut	Augenblick & Palaich, et al., 2005	Low	No	2004	$ 6,846	$ 6,338
Illinois	Augenblick & Myers, 2001	Low	No	2000	$ 5,594	$ 6,304
Kansas	Augenblick & Myers, 2001	Low	No	2001	$ 4,547	$ 5,928
Ohio	Legislature	Low	No	1996	$ 3,930	$ 5,432
Minnesota	Augenblick & Palaich, et al., 2006	Low	No	2004	$ 5,198	$ 5,378
Colorado	Augenblick & Myers, 2003	Low	No	2002	$ 4,654	$ 5,294
Alternative Estimates						
Rhode Island (Low)[a]	Wood, 2007	Low	No	2005	$ 8,780	$ 8,498
New York (High)	Standard and Poor's 2004	Mean	Yes	2004	$13,420	$11,961
Ohio	Legislature	Low	No	1999	$ 4,446	$ 5,662

Note that where multiple estimates are provided, either the "low" estimate or "recommended" base cost (by report authors) is included in Table 7.2.

[a]Rhode Island estimates are alternative estimates to cost-function estimates provided in Table 7.4 and represent average school-level estimates.

Sources:

Augenblick and Myers, Inc. (2001). *A procedure for calculating a base cost figure and an adjustment for at risk pupils that could be used in the Illinois school finance system.* The Education Funding Advisory Board.

Augenblick and Myers, Inc. (2001). *Calculation of the cost of a suitable education in Kansas in 2000–2001 using two different analytic approaches.* Kansas Legislative Coordinating Council.

Augenblick and Myers, Inc. (2001). *Calculation of the cost of an adequate education in Maryland in 1999–2000 using two different analytic approaches.* Maryland Commission on Education Finance, Equity and Excellence. Annapolis, MD.

Augenblick and Myers, Inc. (2003). *Calculating the cost of an adequate education in Colorado using the professional judgment and the successful school districts approaches.* Colorado School Finance Project.

Augenblick and Myers, Inc. (2003). *Calculation of the cost of an adequate education in Missouri using the professional judgment and the successful school district approaches.* Missouri Education Coalition for Adequacy.

Augenblick, Palaich and Associates, Inc. (2005). *Estimating the cost of an adequate education in Connecticut.* The Connecticut Coalition for Justice in Education Funding.

Augenblick, Palaich and Associates. (2006). Estimating the cost of an adequate education in Minnesota.

Augenblick, Palaich, et al. (2006). *Report on the cost of education. New Jersey Department of Education.* Date not provided on document (study conducted in 2002, summary of findings released in 2006).

Standard and Poor's School Evaluation Services. (2004). *Resource adequacy study for the New York State Commission on Education Reform.* New York.

Wood, R. C., and Associates. (2007). *State of Rhode Island education adequacy study.* Joint Committee to Establish a Permanent Foundation Aid Formula for Rhode Island.

meeting specific standards. The *base cost* generated from these studies is typically the cost of meeting standards in a district with favorable demographics. Modified successful schools analyses may involve a variety of filters to select specific districts based on how they spend their money, or based on how much they spend to achieve a given outcome. *Base* costs generated from modified successful schools analyses are typically the average expenditures of lower-spending, or efficient-spending, districts with favorable demographics.

Table 7.3 summarizes findings of resource-cost studies, most of which have employed professional judgment panels to discern the appropriate mix of resources for schools. Table 7.3 includes estimates of resource costs for Kentucky, where analysts used an evidence-based approach. Regional and inflation-adjusted estimates vary widely. Again, one might suspect that some of this variation is due to differences in desired outcomes among states. That is, if professional judgment panels in Oregon were specifying a resource mix toward achieving a lower outcome standard than professional judgment panels in Missouri, then it would be reasonable that the cost of achieving those standards would be lower. Yet the link between inputs and outcomes in resource-based analyses remains relatively loose, and analysts have not yet attempted to use resource-cost analysis to estimate the costs of achieving alternative outcomes in the same state context, in the same year.

Table 7.3 is dominated by professional judgment studies for which base costs are produced for districts of varied size. Base costs reported in the table are the base costs for a large, or scale-efficient (lowest cost-size group) district. Most professional judgment studies report base costs as costs of providing regular education programs before add-ons for economically disadvantaged, at-risk, or disabled students. Some professional judgment studies report average, or mean costs, which are typically the costs of providing adequate educational services in a district of average characteristics. As one might expect, average costs are likely to be higher than base costs.

Table 7.4 summarizes the findings from selected recent statistical models of education costs. These statistical models in particular present major advancements over average expenditure studies, in that they not only include a direct link between expenditures and outcomes but also use rich data on district characteristics and student population demographics. The models therefore are useful to simulate the costs of achieving state average outcomes in a district of aver-

age characteristics. Further, one can estimate how the costs of achieving average outcomes vary in districts with high-need student populations and how costs vary when one changes the outcome target to higher- or lower-than average outcomes. As with successful schools analysis, findings from New York State indicate that striving for higher outcome standards necessarily costs more, even in generally lower-cost districts.

Authors of cost-function studies typically report the cost of achieving desired outcomes in a district of average characteristics. Studies vary as to whether they include children with disabilities (e.g., Duncombe, Lukemeyer, & Yinger, 2004; Duncombe & Yinger, 2005, 2006; Gronberg, Jansen, Taylor, & Booker, 2004; Imazeki & Reschovsky, 2004b).

Looking across Tables 7.2 to 7.4, one might notice that, in general, successful schools studies have historically produced lower cost estimates than professional judgment studies. This does not make sense if base costs from professional judgment are intended to represent the costs per pupil of achieving (not exceeding) desired outcomes in a school or district that theoretically has no additional higher-need students. By contrast, successful schools estimates compute average actual spending (including inefficiency) of schools with at least some higher-need students and schools that either meet or exceed standards. As such, successful schools estimates should invariably come out higher than professional judgment base costs. Such significant gaps in logic and inconsistencies in findings make these studies highly vulnerable to criticism. Table 7.5 compares cost estimates across methods, on the same state in the same year. The table shows that when consultants applied both successful schools and professional judgment analyses, they consistently found higher costs via professional judgment analysis. On the one hand, these differences occur because successful schools cost estimates are typically based on districts with low student needs—favorable demographics. However, professional judgment base costs assume no additional student needs.

In Kansas, professional judgment cost estimates indicated that the state needed $5,811 (2001 dollars) in operating expenditures per pupil to achieve desired state outcomes in a large district with no special needs students. In the actual lowest-need large Kansas district, that figure is $5,839. However, that district already meets the same state standards with the equivalent funding of $5,131 per pupil (2003–2004), raising

Table 7.3   Findings From Input-Based, Resource Cost Studies

State	Study Method	Author	Estimate Type[a]	Includes Special Education	Year	Base Cost	Regionally and Inflation Adjusted
New York	PJ	American Inst. for Research, 2004	Mean	Yes	2002	$12,975	$12,257
Washington	EB	Conley & Rooney, 2007	Mean	Yes	2005	$11,326	$10,627
Wisconsin	PJ	Inst. for Wisconsin's Future, 2002	Base	No	2002	$ 8,730	$ 9,872
Kentucky	PJ	Verstegen, 2003	Mean	Yes	2003	$ 8,438	$ 9,673
Missouri	PJ	Augenblick & Myers, 2003	Base	No	2002	$ 7,832	$ 9,288
Maryland	PJ	Management, Analysis & Planning, 2001	Mean	Yes	1999	$ 7,461	$ 9,003
Washington	PJ	Ranier Institute, 2003	Mean	Yes	2001	$ 7,753	$ 8,541
Connecticut	PJ	Augenblick, Palaich, et al., 2005	Base	No	2004	$ 9,207	$ 8,524
Montana	PJ	Augenblick & Myers, 2002	Base	No	2002	$ 6,004	$ 8,523
Arkansas	EB	Picus et al., 2003	Mean	Yes	2002	$ 6,741	$ 8,477
Indiana	PJ	Augenblick & Myers, 2002	Base	No	2002	$ 7,094	$ 8,389
North Dakota	PJ	Augenblick, Palaich, et al., 2004	Base	No	2002	$ 6,005	$ 8,219
Nebraska	PJ	Augenblick & Myers, 2003	Base	No	2001	$ 5,845	$ 7,931
Kentucky	EB	Picus et al., 2003	Mean	No	2003	$ 6,893	$ 7,902
Colorado	PJ	Augenblick & Myers, 2003	Base	No	2002	$ 6,815	$ 7,752
Kansas	PJ	Augenblick & Myers, 2001	Base	No	2001	$ 5,811	$ 7,577
Maryland	PJ	Augenblick & Myers, 2001	Base	No	2000	$ 6,612	$ 7,520
Nevada	PJ	Augenblick, Palaich, et al., 2006	Base	No	2004	$ 7,229	$ 7,263
Oregon	PJ	Oregon Qual. Educ. Comm., 2000	Base	No	1999	$ 5,448	$ 6,868
Tennessee	PJ	Augenblick, Palaich, et al., 2006	Base	No	2003	$ 6,200	$ 6,816
New Jersey	PJ	Augenblick, Palaich, et al., 2006	Base	No	2005	$ 8,016	$ 6,709
Minnesota	PJ	Augenblick, Palaich, et al., 2006	Base	No	2005	$ 5,938	$ 5,865
Alternative Estimates							
Maryland (High)	PJ	Management, Analysis & Planning, 2001	Mean	Yes	1999	$ 9,313	$11,237

[a] In PJ studies, a "base" cost is typically the cost of the regular education program at the district level per pupil for the district size, where per-pupil base costs were lowest (usually, though not always, the largest district prototype). Mean costs are the statewide average costs of model estimates, which include average district size, average labor costs, and average student population characteristics, generally leading to higher values.

EB, evidence based; PJ, professional judgment.

Sources:

American Institutes for Research and Management Analysis and Planning, Inc. (2004, March). *The New York adequacy study: Determining the cost of providing all children in New York an adequate education. Volume 1—Final Report.* New York: Campaign for Fiscal Equity.

Augenblick and Myers, Inc. (2001). *Calculation of the cost of a suitable education in Kansas in 2000–2001 using two different analytic approaches.* Kansas Legislative Coordinating Council.

Augenblick and Myers, Inc. (2001). *Calculation of the cost of an adequate education in Maryland in 1999–2000 using two different analytic approaches.* Maryland Commission on Education Finance, Equity and Excellence. Annapolis, MD.

Augenblick and Myers, Inc. (2002). *Calculation of the cost of an adequate education in Indiana in 2001–2002 using the professional judgment approach.* Indiana State Teachers Association.

Augenblick and Myers, Inc. (2002). *Calculation of the cost of a suitable education in Montana in 2001–2002 using the professional judgment approach.* Montana School Boards Association.

Augenblick and Myers, Inc. (2003). *Calculating of the cost of an adequate education in Colorado using the professional judgment and the successful school district approaches.* Colorado School Finance Project.

Augenblick and Myers, Inc. (2003). *Calculation of the cost of an adequate education in Missouri using the professional judgment and the successful school district approaches.* Missouri Education Coalition for Adequacy.

Augenblick and Meyers, Inc. (2003). *Calculation of the cost of an adequate education in Nebraska in 2002–03 using the professional judgment approach*. Nebraska State Education Association.

Augenblick, Palaich and Associates, Inc. (2004). *Calculation of the cost of an adequate education in North Dakota in 2002–03 using the professional judgment approach*. North Dakota Department of Public Instruction.

Augenblick, Palaich and Associates, Inc. (2004). *An estimation of the total cost in 2002–03 of implementing the results of the school finance adequacy study undertaken by Augenblick, Palaich and Associates, Inc.*

Augenblick, Palaich and Associates, Inc. (2005). *Estimating the cost of an adequate education in Connecticut*. The Connecticut Coalition for Justice in Education Funding.

Augenblick, Palaich and Associates. (2006). *Estimating the cost of an adequate education in Minnesota*.

Augenblick, Palaich and Associates. (2006). *Estimating the cost of an adequate education in Nevada*. Legislative Commission's Committee to Study School Financing Adequacy.

Augenblick, Palaich, et al. (2006). *Report on the cost of education*. New Jersey Department of Education. Date not provided on document (study conducted in 2002, summary of findings released in 2006).

Conley, D., & Rooney, K. (2007). *Washington adequacy funding study*. Eugene, OR: Education Policy Improvement Center.

Institute for Wisconsin's Future. (2002). *Funding our future: An adequacy model for Wisconsin school finance*.

Management, Analysis and Planning, Inc. (2001). *A professional judgment approach to determining adequate education funding in Maryland*. The New Maryland Education Coalition.

Picus, L. O., and Associates. (2003). *A state of the art approach to school finance adequacy in Kentucky*. Kentucky Department of Education.

Picus, L. O., and Associates. (2003). *An evidence based approach to school finance adequacy in Arkansas*. Arkansas Joint Committee on Educational Adequacy.

Ranier Institute. (2003). *What will it take? Defining a quality education in Washington and a new vision of adequacy for school funding*.

Verstegen, D. A. (2003). *Calculation of the cost of an adequate education in Kentucky*. Council for Better Education.

serious questions regarding the validity of the relationship between professional judgment cost estimates and outcomes.

Despite the growing sophistication of researchers' efforts to estimate the cost of an adequate education, it remains an inexact science. Further, estimation of the cost of an adequate education necessarily occurs in a highly political and litigious context. Because estimation of costs under each method involves numerous judgments, and because those judgments may be influenced by political motives, findings do vary. Table 7.6 lists findings from selected studies, which used similar methods on the same states. The most intriguing findings in Table 7.6 are for Ohio, where various constituents continue to duel over which group of schools will be identified as successful and used as the basis for calculating costs.[2]

In Illinois, consultants provided 40 separate successful schools cost estimates for unified districts, varying widely on the basis of outcome standards and other inclusion criteria, resulting in a range of costs of approximately 14%. Findings varied by outcome goal, poverty rates, and an efficiency filter, which was used

to select out districts engaging in inefficient spending practices. Analysts from Standard and Poor's used a similar approach in a recent study of costs in New York (*Resource Adequacy Study for the New York State Commission on Education Reform*, 2004).

The summer of 2004 saw a flurry of adequacy analyses in the state of Texas, including two separate cost–function studies and one professional judgment study of selected districts. The studies emerged as support documents for a legislative committee considering ways to redesign their state aid formula and as part of litigation to be heard in district court in August 2004. Analysts performed the cost functions in Table 7.6 with different years of data. As such, they are all adjusted to school year 2004 dollars.

Note the apparently large discrepancies in cost–function estimates for the state of Texas, at similar outcome levels. Imazeki and Reschovsky (2004a), on behalf of plaintiffs, estimate the average cost of a 55% pass rate on the state assessment to be $7,352 in regionally adjusted 2004 dollars. By contrast, Taylor (2004), on behalf of the legislature, estimates the average cost to be $6,295 to $6,495.

---

[2]The findings for Ohio represent analyses that the Governor's Office prepared using 43 districts meeting 20 of 27 1999 standards; the Senate, using 122 districts meeting 17 of 18 1996 standards; the House, using 45 districts meeting all 18 original standards in 1999; and the House again, in an amended bill using 127 districts meeting 17 of 18 standards in 1996 and 20 of 27 standards in 1999.

Table 7.4   Findings From Statistical Models of Education Costs

State	Author	Estimate Type[a]	Includes Special Education	Year	Base Cost	Regionally and Inflation Adjusted
New York	Duncombe, Lukemeyer, & Yinger, 2003, 2004	Mean	No	2004	$14,107	$12,573
Texas (55%)	Imazeki & Reschovsky, 2004	Mean	Yes	2002	$ 6,950	$ 7,227
Illinois (55%)	Baker, 2006	Mean	No	2005	$ 7,506	$ 7,010
Minnesota	Haveman, 2004	Mean	No	2002	$ 6,236	$ 6,864
Missouri (17.5/26.6%)	Baker, 2006	Mean	Yes	2005	$ 6,163	$ 6,599
Kansas	Duncombe & Yinger, 2006	Mean	No	2007	$ 6,120	$ 6,346
Texas (55%)	Gronberg, Jansen, Taylor, & Booker, 2004	Mean	Yes	2002	$ 5,950	$ 6,187
Rhode Island (Mean)	RC Wood, 2007	Mean	No	2005	$ 9,362	$ 9,062
Alternative Estimates						
New York (140)	Duncombe, Lukemeyer, & Yinger 2003, 2004	Mean	No	2000	$14,083	$14,508
New York (160)	Duncombe, Lukemeyer, & Yinger 2003, 2004	Mean	No	2000	$15,139	$15,596
New York (150)	Duncombe, Lukemeyer, & Yinger 2003, 2004	Mean	No	2000	$14,716	$15,160
Texas (70%)	Imazeki & Reschovsky, 2004	Mean	Yes	2002	$ 9,787	$10,177
Texas (70%)	Gronberg, Jansen, Taylor, & Booker, 2004	Mean	Yes	2004	$ 6,523	$ 6,423
Texas (55%)	Gronberg, Jansen, Taylor, & Booker, 2004	Mean	Yes	2004	$ 6,483	$ 6,383

[a]All cost–function estimates are mean cost estimates. NY estimate is the mean weighted for enrollment. As such, NYC significantly raises this estimate. We include the pupil-weighted version for NY for comparison with successful schools and professional judgment results from NY. The Texas Imazeki and Reschovsky estimates are also pupil weighted. Other estimates are not pupil weighted.

Note: Outcome standards are listed in parentheses next to state name. For Texas and Illinois, models were estimated to the cost of achieving a 55% proficiency rate. For Missouri, models were estimated to the cost of achieving a 17.5% proficiency rate in Math and 26.6 in Language Arts (Missouri's standards for 2005). In New York, a 200-point index developed by the authors was used and set to a value of 140. Alternative estimates, applying higher outcome standards, are shown in the lower half of the table.

Sources:

Baker, B. D. (2006). *Estimating the cost of alternative outcome standards in Illinois.* Prepared for the Chicago Reporter.

Baker, B. D. (2006). *Missouri's school finance formula fails to guarantee equal or minimally adequate educational opportunity to Missouri schoolchildren.* Committee for Educational Equality.

Duncombe, W. D., Lukemeyer, A., & Yinger, J. (2003). Financing an adequate education: A case study of New York. In W. F. Fowler, Jr. (Ed.), *Developments in school finance: 2001–02, fiscal proceedings from the annual state data conferences of July 2001 and July 2002* (pp. 127–154). Washington, DC: U.S. Department of Education, National Center for Education Statistics.

Duncombe, W., Lukemeyer, A., & Yinger, J. (2004). *Education finance reform in New York: Calculating the cost of a "sound, basic education" in New York City. Working Paper #28.* Syracuse, NY: Education Finance and Accountability Program. Center for Policy Research. Maxwell School of Syracuse University. Retrieved March 1, 2006, from http://www-cpr.maxwell.syr.edu/pbriefs/pb28.pdfp.3.

Duncombe, W., & Yinger, J. (2006). *Estimating the costs of meeting student performance outcomes mandated by the Kansas State Board of Education.* Topeka, KS: Kansas Legislative Division of Post Audit. Retrieved March 1, 2006, from http://www.kslegislature.org/postaudit/audits_perform/05pa19a.pdf

Gronberg, T., Jansen, D., Taylor, L., & Booker, K. (2004). *School outcomes and schools costs: The cost function approach.* College Station, TX: Busch School of Government and Public Service, Texas A&M University. Retrieved March 1, 2006, from http://bush.tamu.edu/research/faculty_projects/txschoolfinance/papers/SchoolOutcomesAndSchoolCosts.pdf

Haveman, M. (2004). *Determining the cost of an adequate education in Minnesota.* Minneapolis: Minnesota Center for Public Finance Research.

Imazeki, J., & Reschovsky, A. (2004). *Estimating the costs of meeting the Texas educational accountability standards.*

Wood, R. C., and Associates. (2007). *State of Rhode Island education adequacy study.* Joint Committee to Establish a Permanent Foundation Aid Formula for Rhode Island.

Table 7.5   Differences in Estimates by Method in Same State

State	Cost–Function	Successful Districts	Professional Judgment	% Difference
New York	$12,573	$11,300	$12,257	−8%
Colorado		$ 5,294	$ 7,752	−46%
Connecticut		$ 6,338	$ 8,524	−34%
Kansas	$ 6,346	$ 5,928	$ 7,577	−28%
Maryland		$ 6,789	$ 7,520	−11%
Minnesota	$ 6,864	$ 5,378	$ 5,865	−9%
Missouri	$ 6,599	$ 6,717	$ 9,288	−38%
New Jersey		$ 7,108	$ 6,709	6%

Estimates drawn from Tables 7.2 to 7.4.

Taylor, Baker, and Vedlitz (2005) explain:

The two cost-function analyses for Texas cover essentially the same school districts in a similar time frame. However, the studies differ in a number of key respects (see Taylor 2004) not the least of which is that the plaintiff's estimate (Imazeki & Reschovsky [2004b]) is the unweighted average of district cost projections while the Legislature's estimates (Gronberg et al.) are pupil-weighted averages. Because Texas has so many small districts with correspondingly high cost projections, this difference in weighting alone can explain all of the difference in estimated average cost at the 55% passing performance standard.[3] (Taylor et al., 2005, p. 15)

Findings of reported professional judgment and evidence-based analyses are also problematic to compare and often provide no opportunity to reconcile differences, as with the Texas cost functions. In Maryland, for example, the state's consultants and special interest consultants dealt differently with costs associated with special education. Table 7.6 compares minimum adequacy costs for Maryland in each study, excluding children with disabilities. In Maryland, the finding of $6,612 was from the state-sponsored study, but the legislature eventually chose to adopt (for 5-year phase-in) the even lower finding from the successful schools analysis.

Cost-Based General Education Aid Formulas

In this section, we present examples of adequacy-based general education aid formulas. Because adequacy analyses can use either an input- or outcome-based perspective, the resultant funding formulas also can use either an input- or outcome-based perspective. Ongoing major adequacy-based reforms in Wyoming and New Jersey have emphasized input-based funding. While outcome-based adequacy formulas have yet to be implemented, we discuss the possibilities in this section, with reference to analyses performed in New York and recent analyses and policy discussions in Texas.

Input-Based Adequacy Formulas

Wyoming and New Jersey have both sought to ensure educational adequacy using input-based adequacy finance formulas. In Wyoming, the first objective was to determine the cost of providing an adequate basic education to all Wyoming students, and the second objective was to design a school-funding policy consistent with the findings of the cost analysis. This section describes, in detail, the influence of the empirical data, along with economic, political, and judicial forces impinging on that implementation process. In New Jersey, a state with nearly a half-century of school finance litigation, a long effort to achieve adequate fiscal inputs to schooling for children in its poor urban districts has been underway. Despite significant increases in spending since the 1970s, the litigant districts have continued to produce substandard outcomes. We examine how New Jersey has attempted to ensure adequate uses of existing resources by mandating that SNDs (urban and poor) implement specific whole-school reform models.

---

[3] Unweighted, Gronberg et al. (2004) estimate at the 55% pass rate is $7,375 using 2004 data, and $7,304 using 2002 data (both in adjusted 2004 dollars) (Taylor, 2004).

Table 7.6 Comparison of Findings From Different Sources, Same Method on the Same State

Authors	Estimate Type	Includes Disabilities	Estimate Year	Estimate	Regionally and Inflation Adjusted
Successful Schools					
Illinois					
Augenblick et al. (2001)	Low		2000	$ 5,594	$ 5,182
Augenblick et al. (2001)	Low		2000	$ 5,965	$ 5,525
New York					
Standard & Poor's (2004)	State Mean	Yes	2004	$13,420	$ 9,782
Standard & Poor's (2004)	State Mean	Yes	2004	$12,679	$ 9,242
Ohio					
Legislature (2001)	Low		1999	$ 5,560	$ 5,778
Legislature (2001)	Low		1999	$ 4,446	$ 4,620
Augenblick et al. (2001)	Low		1996	$ 3,930	$ 4,581
Professional Judgment					
Maryland					
Augenblick et al. (2001)	Base	Yes	2000	$ 6,612	$ 5,967
Management, Planning & Analysis (2001)	State Mean	Yes	1999	$ 9,313	$ 8,917
Management, Planning & Analysis (2001)	State Mean		1999	$ 7,461	$ 7,143
Cost Function					
New York					
Duncombe et al. (2004) (Syracuse U.)	State Mean		2004	$14,107	$10,282
Duncombe et al. (2003) (Syracuse U.) [140]	State Mean		2000	$14,083	$11,864
Duncombe et al. (2003) (Syracuse U.) [150]	State Mean		2000	$14,716	$12,397
Duncombe et al. (2003) (Syracuse U.) [160]	State Mean		2000	$15,139	$12,753
Texas					
Imazeki & Reschovsky (2004) [55%]	State Mean	Yes	2002	$ 7,476	$ 6,444
Gronberg, Jansen, Taylor, & Booker (2004) [55%]	State Mean	Yes	2004	$ 6,483	$ 5,291
Imazeki & Reschovsky (2004) [70%]	State Mean	Yes	2002	$ 9,135	$ 7,874
Gronberg, Jansen, Taylor, & Booker (2004) [70%]	State Mean	Yes	2004	$ 6,523	$ 5,323

Note: Expressed in 2004 constant dollars.
Adapted from Taylor, Baker, & Vedlitz (2005).

Sources:

American Institutes for Research and Management Analysis and Planning, Inc. (2004, March). *The New York adequacy study: Determining the cost of providing all children in New York an adequate education. Volume 1—Final Report.* New York: Campaign for Fiscal Equity.

Augenblick and Myers, Inc. (2001). *A procedure for calculating a base cost figure and an adjustment for at risk pupils that could be used in the Illinois school finance system.* The Education Funding Advisory Board.

Augenblick and Myers, Inc. (2001). *Calculation of the cost of an adequate education in Maryland in 1999–2000 using two different analytic approaches.* Maryland Commission on Education Finance, Equity and Excellence. Annapolis, MD.

Augenblick, Palaich and Associates, Inc. (2004). *An estimation of the total cost in 2002–03 of implementing the results of the school finance adequacy study undertaken by Augenblick, Palaich and Associates, Inc.*

Baker, B. D. (2006). *Estimating the cost of alternative outcome standards in Illinois.* Prepared for the *Chicago Reporter.*

Duncombe, W. D., Lukemeyer, A., & Yinger, J. (2003). Financing an adequate education: A case study of New York. In W. F. Fowler, Jr. (Ed.), *Developments in school finance: 2001–02, fiscal proceedings from the annual state data conferences of July 2001 and July 2002* (pp. 127–154). Washington, DC: US Department of Education, National Center for Education Statistics.

Duncombe, W., Lukemeyer, A., & Yinger, J. (2004). *Education finance reform in New York: Calculating the cost of a "sound, basic education" in New York City. Working Paper* #28. Syracuse, NY: Education Finance and Accountability Program. Center for Policy Research. Maxwell School of Syracuse University. Retrieved March 1, 2006, from http://www-cpr.maxwell.syr.edu/pbriefs/pb28.pdfp.3.

Gronberg, T., Jansen, D., Taylor, L., & Booker, K. (2004). *School outcomes and schools costs: The cost function approach.* College Station, TX: Busch School of Government and Public Service, Texas A&M University. Retrieved March 1, 2006, from http://bush.tamu.edu/research/faculty_projects/txschoolfinance/papers/SchoolOutcomesAndSchoolCosts.pdf

Imazeki, J., & Reschovsky, A. (2004). *Estimating the costs of meeting the Texas educational accountability standards.*

Management, Analysis and Planning, Inc. (2001). *A professional judgment approach to determining adequate education funding in Maryland.* The New Maryland Education Coalition.

Standard and Poor's School Evaluation Services. 2004. *Resource adequacy study for the New York State Commission on Education Reform.* New York.

Wyoming's Cost-Based Block Grant

Earlier in this chapter, we discussed an adequacy analysis for the state of Wyoming by MAP in 1997 (Guthrie et al., 1997) and described in the literature by James Guthrie and Richard Rothstein of MAP (Guthrie & Rothstein, 1999). This study and the finance reforms that followed represent one of the first major attempts to link a more precise empirical analysis of education costs to the redesign and implementation of a state school finance policy. As with any school-funding formula, the Wyoming Resource Block Grant Model remains a work in progress; the Wyoming State Supreme Court, which expressed opinions on various features of the formula in February of 2001, reviewed it.

Wyoming's cost-based block grant formula provides a classic example in school finance of blending political considerations and economic constraints with consultant recommendations and court opinions. Some of the components of the new funding formula were based significantly on the MAP recommendations. Some modifications to the formula were implemented with economic constraints in mind, and still other components of the formula were added purely as political concessions.

While MAP based many of its recommendations on empirical analysis, many other recommendations in the MAP report ranged from speculative cost-based suggestions according to practices in other states,[4] to completely arbitrary recommendations.[5] Yet these recommendations were all contained in a series of reports purported to provide the Wyoming legislature with cost-based estimates. Following are descriptions of the recommendations that Wyoming adopted, the economically motivated modifications, and the politically motivated modifications.

Policy Implementation

First and foremost, MAP recommended that its cost-based estimates for providing an adequate education to Wyoming children be implemented as a resource-based block grant, and that the grant be provided in full, by the state to each local school district. MAP based the cost analysis that yielded the adequacy figure on specific prototypical school designs, which had been constructed by a panel of state experts and outside consultants. MAP determined, however, that local school districts should have the freedom to use their block grant to provide whatever mix of resources they choose. For example, a district could opt to hire more teachers at lower salaries, or pay higher salaries and increase class sizes. In many ways, this was the original political concession of the resource-based block grant model, but one that consultants for MAP as well as legislators assumed politically necessary. In Wyoming, consultants and legislators perceived it as politically unpalatable for the legislature to dictate how education should be structured within schools, even if the legislature was to be allocating the full cost of operating schools from the state coffers, based on specific resource configurations.

Having accepted the block grant approach, the next question for the Wyoming legislature was whether it could, or even wanted to, fully fund the block grant to levels that MAP identified in its various simulations of prototypical school costs. The various MAP simulations involved alternative pupil/teacher ratios; the simulation called MAP 3 was based on the state's expert education panel recommendations. Judge Nicholas Kalokathis, in his February 23, 2001, decision, noted:

> The MAP study was presented to the legislature in 1997 with four computer simulations of various funding scenarios including Example 3 (MAP 3) which was the result of consultation with the Wyoming experts concerning class size and the required number of teachers. MAP 3 was not funded by the legislature, and to do so would have cost an additional $75,000,000. The budget actually adopted by the legislature resulted in fewer teachers and larger classrooms for middle and high schools than provided for in the MAP 3 model. (*State of Wyoming et al. v. Campbell*, 2001, ¶14)

---

[4] This was the case, for example, for the recommendation regarding the costs of bilingual education programs. Recommendations were based on current spending behavior in Connecticut school districts. For example, original recommendations for costs of bilingual education were based on current spending behavior in Connecticut school districts.

[5] This was the case, for example, for many components of the small school weight, where only the very smallest school costs were actually analyzed. For example, to determine small-district weighting, consultants conducted the equivalent of a back-of-the-napkin estimation of the additional per-pupil costs of the very smallest schools, and then drew a linear slope between that higher cost level and the prototype cost. Also, for gifted education, consultants recommended a weight based on the weight already in place in Wyoming and not on actual cost analysis. This was also the case for adjustments to be made for gifted education, which were based only on prior Wyoming state aid policies.

Recognizing potential economic constraints, Judge Kalokathis noted:

> Considering the revenue deficits the state believed it was facing in the years 1997–99, the legislature's motivation to shave the recommended class size and avoid the corresponding costs is understandable. However, if its approach fails to provide a proper education as commanded by the constitution, this court cannot condone the result. (*State of Wyoming et al. v. Campbell,* 2001, ¶63)

As per the MAP recommendations, the legislature made several adjustments to the block grant level to accommodate both the different costs of meeting the needs of individual students and the different costs of providing adequate education under different circumstances. We discuss the details of such policies across states later in this chapter, but provide an overview of their application in the Wyoming context here. Wyoming implemented the following MAP recommendations in the new finance policy:

1. An adjustment to help districts serve economically disadvantaged youth (EDY), with additional aid for districts with large EDY populations, including $500 per EDY and supplemental aid for districts enrolling more than 150% above state average EDY levels.

2. An adjustment of $900 per limited-English-speaking (LES) pupil.

3. Nine dollars per pupil in average daily attendance to support gifted programs.

4. Adjustments to accommodate both geographic differences in costs (Wyoming Cost of Living Index, WCLI) and inflation of costs over time.

5. An adjustment for small schools, which provided supplemental grants for elementary schools enrolling fewer than 30 students and high schools enrolling fewer than 200 students, and included sliding scales of supplemental aid for elementary schools enrolling 30 to 200 students and high schools enrolling 200 to 400 students.

Regarding individual student needs, the court and MAP consultants each emphasized that the prototypical models, which included small class sizes, provided additional support for students with special needs, regardless of supplemental funding. For the specific needs of EDY students and the cost-basis of recommendations for meeting those needs, the court expressed concern that the $500 per low-income student

recommendation was arbitrary and not cost-based, and further that the cutoff of 150% above state-average EDY percentages used for receiving additional aid was also arbitrary and had no empirical basis. Further, the court expressed concern that the $900 per LES pupil was based merely on experiences in another state, Connecticut. The court accepted the arbitrary treatment of gifted education due to lack of contradictory evidence and on the basis that small class sizes should support appropriate opportunities (*State of Wyoming et al. v. Campbell,* 2001, ¶77–82). Similarly, Judge Kalokathis expressed concern regarding arbitrary cutoff selections for receipt of small school aid.

In addition to the preceding elements of Wyoming's school finance reform, an intriguing further adjustment provided additional aid for small school districts, many of which already benefited from aid for small schools. The original MAP report did not include the small-district adjustment, but an addendum by MAP included the recommendation that qualifying small districts receive $50,000 for each attendance center in addition to the one in which the district office is located, that districts with less than 900 students receive an additional amount for administration, and districts with fewer than 1,100 students receive additional funds for maintenance and operations costs (*State of Wyoming,* 2001, ¶25). Small districts originally proposed this politically motivated amendment, which became known as the "small-school settlement," in 1999 in exchange for their withdrawal from litigation. Regarding this adjustment, Judge Kalokathis noted, "Disparate treatment of schools based on arbitrary standards cannot be justified. We affirm the trial court's decision and hold the small school district adjustment unconstitutional" (*State of Wyoming,* 2001, ¶100).

As of February of 2001, the judicial summary of the MAP proposal and resource-based block grant model adopted by the Wyoming legislature was as follows:

1. The cost-based model approach chosen by the legislature which relies upon past statewide average expenditures is capable of supporting a constitutional school finance system.

2. The funding legislation must be modified as follows, on or before July 1, 2002, in order to provide a constitutionally adequate education appropriate for our times:
   - The model and statute must be adjusted for inflation each biennium, with 1996–97 as the base year, utilizing the Wyoming cost of living

index (WCLI), beginning in 2002–03, so long as a cost of education model using historic costs is relied upon for the basis of education funding. The legislature shall conduct a review of all components of the model in 2001 and every five years thereafter to assure it remains an accurate reflection of the cost of education.

- Administrative and classified salaries must be adjusted to account for differences in experience, responsibility, and seniority.
- Cost of maintenance and operation, including utility costs, must be determined by either development of a formula which uses enrollment measured by ADM, building square footage, and number of buildings in the district or actual costs fully reimbursed, subject to state oversight.
- Pending future development of an accurate formula with which to distribute adequate funds, actual and necessary costs of educating economically disadvantaged youth and limited English speaking students shall be funded, subject to state oversight.
- The costs of providing teachers and equipment for vocational and technical training must be included as line items in the MAP model and funded accordingly.
- Any small school adjustment must be based on actual differences in costs which are not experienced by larger schools.
- Any small school district adjustment must be based on documented shortfalls under the MAP model that are not equally suffered by larger districts.
- Statewide average costs must be adjusted for cost-of-living differences using either the entire WCLI or another reasonable formula which includes a full housing component to cover costs not included in the benefits portion of the salary component. (*State of Wyoming*, 2001, ¶2)

The court concluded with two notes regarding the adequacy of educational facilities:

1. The legislature must fund the facilities deemed required by the state for the delivery of the "full basket" to Wyoming students in all locations throughout the state through either a statewide tax or other revenue raising mechanisms equally imposed on all taxpayers.
2. All facilities must be safe and efficient. Safe and efficient facilities are those that attain a score of 90 or above for building condition, an educational

suitability score and technological readiness score of 80 or above, and a score of 4 for building accessibility. (*State of Wyoming*, 2001, ¶2)

The Wyoming case raises important political, economic, and technical questions regarding the future of similar endeavors. We do not propose answers to these questions, because the specific contexts in states are so varied. However, we do believe that policy makers should strive for a culture of open decision making, with policy transparency that allows both participants and observers to understand the policy tensions and their resolution. A culture of transparency supports open government and, ultimately, the possibility of policy reform if the decisions made are not sustainable over the long run.

1. What are the best policy processes to use so that an appropriate balance between political negotiation, economic constraints, and use of empirical findings supports positive education policy decisions?
2. What can policy analysts who specialize in education finance do to shift the debate from point in time, or static, assessments of adequacy to longer-term assessments that better focus on sustainable progress toward adequacy in light of the very real political, economic, and empirical constraints we now confront?
3. How do we sort out the competing metrics, indicators, and technical considerations in empirical studies that researchers and consultants conduct so that politicians and courts can better sift through the evidence and separate the wheat from the chaff?

The first question is perhaps the most difficult to answer, although extreme examples appear relatively straightforward. Most state constitutions place responsibility for defining "suitable" or "thorough and efficient" on legislatures. In the case of legislature-consultant relationships, the legislature may choose to agree or not with consultant recommendations. In studies using professional judgment models, and for which the legislature concurs with the validity of the service-delivery model (or basket of goods and services), ignoring the cost of providing that basket becomes more difficult for the legislature. In the extreme case, with or without agreement on the service-delivery model, it is unlikely that any state court would allow a legislature to choose $0 as the basic funding level per pupil. Legislatures, however, have not done a particularly good job of meeting children's adequacy needs, and the expensive and extensive amount of litigation in the United States (a phenomenon unique to the United States among highly developed societies) suggests rather strongly that other models might be better.

The second question is particularly complex. State judges, as in Wyoming, have frequently written off the validity of legislative claims that the state simply cannot afford the level of funding that consultants recommend or that the court requests. While claims currently on the record may or may not be valid, we must accept the possibility that economic conditions can exist under which a judicially mandated or consultant-recommended spending target is unattainable or unsustainable. In such cases, we must establish more flexible frameworks for evaluating both the status and dynamics of adequacy. Our dynamic equity indicators, including gap-reduction rates and horizons, are among possible solutions for measuring progress toward objectives.

Regarding the third question, some issues are clearer than others. On the one hand, politicians, judges, and consultants can quibble incessantly over subtle differences in alternative inflation indices or geographic cost indices and whether each index appropriately represents cost differences in the state context in question. Such debates will most likely hinge on who stands to gain the most from each alternative. These debates are unlikely to be resolved by courts, consultants, or politicians. On the other hand, despite the relative precision of the MAP study, the consultants made several recommendations with little or no more legitimate cost justification than most purely politically derived policies. MAP's recommendations for cutoff points for small-school adjustments, discussed previously, are one example. Also, MAP recommended a slight increase to existing aid for gifted education but provided no evidence regarding costs. Due to lack of contradictory evidence, the court accepted this recommendation.

Finally, the Wyoming experiment has a few potentially adverse outcomes. First, the Wyoming reform—while taking positive and progressive steps toward a more thoughtful financing policy than previous reforms regarding the notion of adequacy—may have inadvertently opened a Pandora's box regarding judicial

analysis of the cost-basis of state-aid programs. Second, the approach to measuring education costs and implementing the cost-based, fully funded formula may have adverse economic effects on the education sector within a state, in that it establishes a fixed price for educational public goods and services and eradicates any influence of local demand for levels of the goods or services above state-defined adequate levels. If underfunded over time, this model runs the risk of making the state's entire public education sector noncompetitive with other industries, reducing the desirability of professions in the education sector and reducing the quality of the public education workforce.

The California experience in this regard following Proposition 13 is a noteworthy case study in the undesirable policy consequences of statewide control of equity when coupled with systematic underfunding. We have very few full-state-funding models to study over time, but the California case suggests the likelihood that local demand will be suppressed in pursuit of affordable statewide equity if local supplementary contributions are suppressed, as was the case in California through property tax limitations.

Reallocating Resources in New Jersey

New Jersey's approach to funding adequacy differs from that of Wyoming in several respects. New Jersey did not directly tie its recent move toward an adequacy model for funding education to any empirical analysis of the cost of an adequate education for all New Jersey students. Rather, New Jersey's reform hinged on the assumption that years of litigation on behalf of the state's poor, urban districts, SNDs, had led to adequate funding levels but largely inefficient use of funding in the SNDs. The goal of the new funding program, as mandated by the court in *Abbott V* (1998), was to ensure that districts serving large percentages of low-income students have adequate resources available to provide a "proven effective" whole school reform model.[6]

New Jersey schools wishing not to research and select their own model would use the default model selected by the state, Slavin's Roots and Wings/Success for All (Slavin, Karweit, & Madden, 1989). Implementation of this program did not necessarily mean further increases in funding for SNDs (Odden & Picus, 2000), but rather enforced changes in the use of

---

[6] This phrase is in quotes because substantial debate remains over the extent to which the success of Slavin's model (Slavin, Karweit, & Madden, 1989), as measured by any number of student outcomes, is supported by nonbiased empirical research.

existing funds. The adequate funding level was set at $8,664, a level comparable to resources already available in SNDs. The legislature called this new adequate level of funding the "Thorough and Efficient," or "T&E" funding level. Each district in the state is assigned a T&E funding level.

The state based the $8,864 amount for implementing whole-school reforms on expert testimony of Allan Odden, who presented his own findings and findings of others regarding whole-school reforms implementation costs. A consultant to the legislature (Allan Odden) identified Roots and Wings/Success for All as the Cadillac (most expensive) option (Odden & Picus, 2000, p. 74). Therefore, if funds were sufficient to support Success for All, they must be sufficient to support other options, including Levin's Accelerated Schools, Comer School Development Project, and Little Red Schoolhouse.

Consultant analysis of current revenues of schools in New Jersey's SNDs revealed that most schools in those districts had funds that were more than sufficient for operating Success for All and that most schools could actually expand the model and still have additional resources available.

Finally, like the court in Wyoming, the *Abbott V* (1998) decision in New Jersey also emphasized the legislature's responsibility for ensuring adequate facilities. The court ordered the commissioner of education to establish facility efficiency standards, including the following example for elementary schools:

1. Adequate classroom space for class sizes of 15 in pre-kindergarten, 21 in kindergarten through grade 3, and 23 in grades 4 and 5;

2. Space or scheduling accommodations for 90 minutes of reading daily for students in grades 1 through 3 in class sizes of no more than 15;

3. Toilet rooms in all pre-kindergarten and kindergarten classrooms;

4. Cafeteria and/or gymnasium with stage for breakfast, lunch, large group presentations, instrumental music and student performances;

5. Computer room for keyboard and computer instruction; and

6. Media center. (Erlichson, 2001, p. 676)

The court did not intend the facility design standards merely to comply with basic health and safety guidelines but to "represent the instructional spaces, specialized instructional areas, and administrative spaces that are determined by the commissioner to be educa-

tionally adequate to support the achievement of the core curriculum content standards including the provision of required programs in Abbott districts and early childhood education programs in the districts in which these programs are required by the state" (Erlichson, 2001, p. 672). What is unique about the New Jersey situation is that the *Abbott V* (1998) decision did not focus on what new level of funding might be considered adequate but instead focused on how certain districts should be required to use those funds in order to provide adequate services for their particular student populations. *Abbott V* (1998) and the legislation that followed represent a new degree of judicial and legislative involvement in curriculum and educational processes, under the umbrella of educational adequacy, raising new questions of just how far courts and legislatures should go in dictating what goes on in the classroom. New Jersey, in contrast to other states, focused on inputs with established per-pupil expenditures and defined facilities requirements, on school processes with whole-school reform models, and on student outcomes with statewide standardized testing in elementary, middle, and high school, and school report cards spelling out the current year results and the 3-year trend.

Outcome-Based Adequacy Approaches: A Hypothetical Application to New York

Because outcome-based adequacy simultaneously addresses required basic levels of aid and required differences in aid to accommodate costs associated with achieving specific outcomes with different populations, in different settings, we present only an introduction to the basic concept of outcome-based funding in this brief section. We discuss outcome-based adequacy funding in greater detail at the conclusion of our presentations of adequacy for special populations and adequacy under varied conditions. In theory, an outcome-based adequacy formula is designed to provide aid at levels sufficient to achieve a specific level of outcome. Setting aside questions of vertical equity for later discussion, the goal would be to use a cost function to estimate the cost of achieving a specific level of outcomes in the district of average characteristics (scale, sparsity, etc.) and serving a student population of average characteristics. Assuming some positive estimated relationship between available revenues and student outcomes, if legislators desire higher outcomes, costs will increase. The interesting

Figure 7.1   Sensitivity of Costs to Different Outcome Targets in New York State

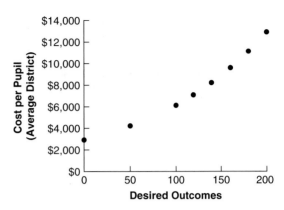

Desired Outcome Level (0–200)	Cost per Pupil in Average District
0	$2,861
50	$4,161
100	$6,070
120	$7,055
140	**$8,201**
160	$9,532
180	$11,079
200	$12,878

Source: Data from William Duncombe, Maxwell School, Syracuse University.

twist introduced into the political environment is that legislators are forced to consider the outcomes they desire, when setting the price they are willing to pay.

An extensive body of literature by William Duncombe and colleagues at the Maxwell School of Public Affairs at Syracuse University has applied cost–function analysis to New York's public schools (e.g., Duncombe, Lukemeyer, & Yinger, 2003, 2004).

These analyses take on new meaning in the wake of the New York State High Court of Appeals ruling in favor of plaintiffs in *Campaign for Fiscal Equity* (CFE). Sadly, the outcome-based analysis of Duncombe and colleagues has played little role in the deliberation over remedies to the CFE litigation.

Figure 7.1 shows the effect of changing desired outcomes on the required based funding level for the district of average characteristics. That is, what would it cost (based on cost-function analysis) to achieve the desired outcomes in that district?

Figure 7.1 shows that controlling for a number of district, school, and pupil characteristics, raising the median student's score from 120 to 140 would require an additional $946 in per-pupil spending, but raising the score from 140 to 160 would cost $1,331 per student. In short, the cost is more per point, the

higher the definition of outcome adequacy. High standards of adequacy are quite expensive! We suspect that the data underestimate the true cost of reaching very high levels of adequacy because of the very high costs associated with elevating the quality of the teacher labor force sufficiently and of making other structural adjustments such as smaller class sizes and lengthening of the school day and school year to attain such high definitions of adequacy.

While cost-function analysis can be helpful for setting basic, or average, levels of aid required to achieve certain outcomes, the greatest value of cost-function analysis for guiding the design of aid formulas is that cost functions can simultaneously accommodate each of the various factors that may influence costs across districts and can fold all of those cost differences into a single cost index for adjusting the average aid. As you will see in the next few chapters, cost adjustments and vertical equity accommodations in aid formulas have become quite complex (if not entirely convoluted) since the 1970s. After we discuss the various approaches for applying cost and vertical equity adjustments in state aid formulas in Chapters 8 and 9, we will return to a more thorough discussion and application of aid formulas using cost functions and outcomes in Chapter 10.

SUMMARY

As we have discussed in this chapter, education finance consultants promote a handful of methods for studying education costs, identifying adequate spending levels,

and differentiating costs by district and/or student characteristics. Consultancies of this type often arise in response to school finance litigation, which has increasingly focused on achieving outcome adequacy in education. A policy based on empirical analysis can only be as good as the analysis on which the policy was based! Where analytical methods are intended to directly inform policy, resultant policies can be only as robust as the analyses from which they were derived. We therefore must pass judgment on these methods with respect to court requirements.

Various methods for estimating the cost of an adequate education and cost variations by district and student characteristics each have their strengths and weaknesses. Some methods are stronger and more empirically valid, at least for some purposes. For example, where state legislatures have an interest in understanding costs as they relate specifically and explicitly to student outcome standards, analysts should use statistical methods that estimate directly the relationship between costs and outcome measures. The connection between resources and outcomes proposed in professional judgment analyses is at best, speculative. Resource cost analyses, however, may be most useful where states define adequate education partly or entirely on the basis of curricular opportunities that should be made available to students. Perhaps most problematic in the context of state policy design are evidence-based approaches to resource identification, such as those used in Arkansas and Kentucky (Odden, Picus, & Fermanich, 2003a, 2003b).

The exercise of adequacy analysis is ultimately intended to measure the cost of implementing educational standards promulgated by state legislatures and potentially reviewed by state courts. Professional judgment approaches purport to use state standards to guide resource specification, which may be reasonable where state standards mention specific resources such as curricular offerings. Evidence-based models do not measure the cost of implementing specific state standards but, rather, the cost of implementing specific educational models, in some cases commercial products, promoted by individuals or teams of model developers. That is, a cost analysis guided by Robert Slavin's comprehensive school reform model Roots and Wings/Success for All, done for the state of Kentucky, measures Slavin's definition of an adequate education and Slavin's preferred set of educational and social outcomes, not the Kentucky legislature's preferred set of outcomes, unless the legislature is willing to explicitly defer to the model on this issue (Odden et al., 2003b).

A final important issue regarding adequacy analyses in the context of school finance litigation is the source of those analyses. Until recently, state legislatures were the sponsors of most adequacy analyses, in an effort to inform policy redesign. In some cases, state courts had ordered those analyses. The recent successful use of legislative-sponsored analyses by plaintiffs challenging present funding has spawned a flurry of analyses across states, sponsored primarily by special interest and activist groups apparently hoping to use those studies as evidence of flaws or shortcomings in existing funding. These studies may produce findings useful to plaintiffs in articulating the shortcomings of existing funding. However, we argue that the burden on plaintiffs to validate that the study of education costs they sponsored represents an accurate measurement of the costs of achieving the legislature's standards, is much greater than when the study is sponsored, overseen, and accepted (or at least not refuted) by the legislature.

Theoretically, results of input (resource cost) versus outcome (cost-function)-based analysis should be reconcilable. Both rely on assumptions of estimating the appropriate *intensity* of resources of specific *quality* for a given student population under a given set of circumstances. Ideally, the identification of resource intensity and quality in input-based analysis is contingent on achieving some set of desired outcomes. Assuming good information on the relationship between certain resource configurations and student outcomes, results of a resource-cost analysis could be quite similar to results of a cost function. This assumes a lot, however. First, significant debate remains over the *best* ways to configure educational resources (primarily teaching staff) and the best indicators of quality resources. A potential approach to filling this void involves the detailed analysis of resource allocation by schools producing desired outcomes. Yet this approach assumes that what succeeds in one school or set of schools will also succeed in other, similar schools. Second, estimating prices for teachers with specific qualities can be difficult, because present teacher pay is not highly related to quality attributes.

Despite their virtues, other issues plague cost functions and may reduce their reliability for determining the appropriate resource intensity and quality needed to achieve certain outcomes. On the resource-quality side, cost functions suffer from the same difficulty in estimating prices of quality resources. (In Chapter 13 in a section on teacher labor markets, we develop a more extensive discussion of teacher wages and prices.) In addition, by basing cost estimates on present spending behavior across districts and the outcomes achieved across districts, cost functions are built on the assumption that resource intensity and quality that produce certain outcomes in one context should lead to similar outcomes in a different context. While cost-function studies include "controls" for student population and district structural differences, not all contextual differences can be adequately measured. Ideally, one would be able to measure how costs and outcomes change over time and within districts or how changing total spending and internal resource allocations lead to changes in student outcomes, within districts in order to discern more precisely, the costs of improving outcomes.

Lest we leave you with the impression that the primary path to school success is optimizing resource mixes, let us assure you we have a healthy respect for the local ecology of the school and the many intangibles that compose it, including leadership, community involvement, culture, and *esprit de corps*. Nonetheless, because this is a textbook on education finance, we hope we have made the case that, for all of their shortcomings, rigorous empirical analyses of education costs may significantly, positively influence the design of state aid formulas, which presently are based primarily on political preferences and state budget constraints.

KEY TERMS

cost   The aggregation or summation of the prices of resources required for providing a specific set of educational services. The "cost" of providing a particular set of educational services equals what must be spent in order to achieve a defined set of outcomes, if the system in question – the school – is able to produce those outcomes efficiently.

education cost-function analysis   A statistical model in which educational expenditures are the dependent variable and where (a) student outcomes, (b) student characteristics, (c) schooling characteristics, and (d) relative efficiency, are expected to influence current/historical spending.

evidence-based analysis   A variant of resource cost modeling where consultants or outside experts prescribe, based on their own interpretation of research evidence on educational reforms, a model of input quantities and qualities for providing a specific service or set of services.

expenditure   Funds spent by an organization, or allocated to organizational subunits (and subsequently spent by those units), for purposes of maintaining the operations of those units. For example, funds expended by a high school science department for purchasing materials, supplies, and equipment or funds expended by district level administration for the annual operations of the district central office.

price   Dollar value of a given resource. For example, the price, in salary and benefits, of hiring a teacher with A, B, and C qualifications to carry out X, Y, and Z duties. Ideally, the competitive market for the resources in question determines prices. This, of course, means that the price of a given resource may vary across different schools or districts if they are subject to different market conditions.

professional judgment analysis   A variant of resource cost modeling where panels of professional educators are selected to prescribe based on their knowledge and experience, the quantities and qualities of resources to be included in a resource cost model of a specific service or set of services.

resource   People, time, space, and materials required for providing a specific set of educational services that requires a budget allocation. For example, the numbers of teachers, levels of experience, and teacher time allocated toward providing a particular academic program. Levin and McEwan (2001) refer to resources as "ingredients."

resource-cost model (RCM)   The general approach to identifying resource quantities, qualities, and related prices for providing specific educational (or any) services.

REFERENCES

Abbott v. Burke, 575 A.2d 359 (N.J.1990) (*Abbott II*).

Abbott v. Burke, 693 A.2d 417 (N.J. 1997) (*Abbott IV*).

Abbott v. Burke, 710 A.2d 450 (N.J. 1998) (*Abbott V*).

Alexander, K. L., Entwisle, D. R., & Olsen, L. S. (2001). Schools, achievement, and inequality: A seasonal perspective. *Educational Evaluation and Policy Analysis, 23*, 171–191.

Almeida, T. A. (2004). Refocusing school finance litigation on at-risk children: *Leandro v. State of North Carolina. Yale Law and Policy Review, 22*, 525–569.

Augenblick, J. (1997). *Recommendations for a base figure and pupil-weighted adjustments to the base figure for use in a new school finance system in Ohio.* Report presented to the School Funding Task Force, Ohio Department of Education.

Augenblick, J., & Myers, J. (2001). *A procedure for calculating a base cost figure and an adjustment for at risk pupils that could be used in the Illinois school finance system.* Submitted to the Education Funding Advisory Board.

Augenblick, J., Myers, J., Silverstein, J., & Barkis, A. (2002). *Calculation of the cost of an adequate education in Kansas in 2000–2001 using two different analytic approaches.* Submitted to the Legislative Coordinating Council, State of Kansas.

Baker, B .D. (2005). The emerging shape of educational adequacy: From theoretical assumptions to empirical evidence. *Journal of Education Finance, 30* (3), 277–305.

Bifulco, R., Bordeaux, C., Duncombe, W., & Yinger, J. (2002). *Do Whole School Reform Programs Boost Student Performance? The Case of New York City.* New York: Smith-Richardson Foundation.

Borman, G., Hewes, G., Overman, L., & Brown, S. (2003). Comprehensive school reform and achievement: A meta-analysis. *Review of Educational Research, 73* (2), 125–230.

Borman, G. D., & Hewes, G. (2002). The long-term effects and cost effectiveness of success for all. *Educational Evaluation and Policy Analysis, 24* (4), 243–266.

Brewer, D., Krop, C., Gill, B. P. & Reichardt, R. (1999). Estimating the cost of national class size reductions under different policy alternatives. *Educational Evaluation and Policy Analysis, 21,* 179–192.

Campbell County Sch. Dist. v. State, 907 P.2d 1238 (Wyo. 1995).

Campaign for Fiscal Equity v. State, 801 N.E.2d 326 (N.Y. 2003).

Campaign for Fiscal Equity v. State, 861 N.E.2d 50 (N.Y. 2006).

Castaneda v. Pickard, 648 P.2d 989 (5th Cir. 1981).

Chambers, J. (1999). *Measuring Resources in Education: From Accounting to the Resource Cost Model Approach.* Working Paper Series, Working Paper No. 1999–16. National Center for Education Statistics, Office of Education Research and Improvement. Washington, DC: U.S. Dept. of Education.

Claremont v. Governor, 703 A.2d 1353 (N.H. 1997) (*Claremont II*).

Committee for Educ. Rights v. Edgar, 672 N.E.2d 1178 (Ill. 1996).

Cover, A. (2002). Is "adequacy" a more "political question" than "equality"?: the effect of standards-based education on judicial standards for education finance. *Cornell Journal of Law and Public Policy, 11,* 403–439.

Dayton, J. (2001). *Serrano* and its progeny: an analysis of 30 years of school funding litigation. *West's Education Law Reporter, 157,* 447–464.

Dayton, J., Dupre, A., & Kiracofe, C. (2004). Education finance litigation: A review of recent state high court decisions and their likely impact on future litigation. *West's Education Law Reporter, 186,* 1–14.

Debra P. v. Turlington, 644 F.2d 397 (5th Cir. 1981).

DeRolph v. State, 728 N.E.2d 993 (Ohio 2000)

Duncombe, W., & Yinger, J. (2006). *Estimating the costs of meeting student performance outcomes mandated by the Kansas State Board of Education.* Topeka, KS: Kansas Legislative Division of Post Audit. Retrieved March 1, 2006, from http://www.kslegislature.org/postaudit/audits_perform/05pa19a.pdf

Duncombe, W. D., Lukemeyer, A., & Yinger, J. (2003). Financing an adequate education: A case study of New York. In W. F. Fowler, Jr. (Ed.), *Developments in school finance: 2001–02, fiscal proceedings from the Annual State Data Conferences of July 2001 and July 2002* (pp. 127–154). U.S. Department of Education, National Center for Education Statistics. Washington, DC: U.S. Department of Education.

Duncombe, W., Lukemeyer, A., & Yinger, J. (2004). *Education finance reform in New York: Calculating the cost of a "sound, basic education" in New York City. Working Paper #28.* Syracuse, NY: Education Finance and Accountability Program. Center for Policy Research. Maxwell School of Syracuse University. Retrieved March 1, 2006, from http://www-cpr.maxwell.syr.edu/pbriefs/pb28.pdfp.3

Duncombe, W., & Yinger, J. (2005). *How much more does a disadvantaged student cost? Center for Policy Research, Working Paper #60.* Syracuse, NY: Maxwell School of Citizenship and Public Affairs, Syracuse University. Retrieved March 1, 2006, from http://www-cpr.maxwell.syr.edu/cprwps/pdf/wp60.pdf

DuPree v. Alma School District No. 30 of Crawford County, 651 S.W.2d (Ark. 1983).

Dyson, M. R. (2002). Leave no child behind: Normative proposals to link educational adequacy claims and high stakes assessment due process challenges. *Texas Forum on Civil Liberties and Civil Rights, 7,* 1–70.

Equal Educational Opportunities Act of 1974, 20 U.S.C. § 1701 *et seq* (2007).

Erlichson, B. A. (2001). New schools for a new millenium: Court-mandated school facilities construction in New Jersey. *Journal of Education Finance, 27*(2), 663–682.

Ex parte James, 713 So.2d 869 (Ala. 1997).

Ex parte James, 836 So.2d 813 (Ala. 2002).

Finn, J., & Achilles, C. (1999). Tennessee's class size study: Findings, implications, misconceptions. *Educational Evaluation and Policy Analysis, 21,* 97–110.

Flores v. Arizona, 172 F.Supp. 1225 (D. Ariz. 2000).

Fogle, J. (2000). *Abbeville County School District v. State*: The right to a minimally adequate education in South Carolina. *South Carolina Law Review, 51,* 781–805.

Gronberg, T., Jansen, D., Taylor, L. L., & Booker, K. (2004). *School outcomes and schools costs: The cost function approach.* College Station, TX: Busch School of Government and Public Service, Texas A&M University. Retrieved March 1, 2006, from http://bush.tamu.edu/research/faculty_projects/txschoolfinance/papers/SchoolOutcomesAndSchoolCosts.pdf

Guthrie, J. W., & Rothstein, R. (1999). Enabling Adequacy to Achieve Reality: Translating Adequacy Into State

School Finance Distribution Arrangements. In H. F. Ladd, R. Chalk, & J. S. Hansen (Eds.), *Equity and Adequacy in Education Finance: Issues and Perspectives* (pp. 209–259). Washington, DC: National Academy Press.

Hall, D., & Kennedy, S. (2006). *Primary progress, secondary challenge: A state-by-state look at student achievement patterns.* Washington, DC: The Education Trust. Retrieved March 1, 2006, from http://www2.edtrust.org/NR/rdonlyres/15B22876–20C8–47B8–9AF4–FAB148A225AC/0/PPSCreport.pdf

Hartman, W., Bolton, D., & Monk, D. (2001). A synthesis of two approaches to school-level financial data: The accounting and resource cost model approaches. In W. Fowler (Ed.), *Selected Papers in School Finance, 2000–01.* National Center for Education Statistics, Office of Educational Research and Improvement. Washington, DC: U.S. Dept. of Education.

Hoke County Bd. of Educ. v. State, 599 S.E.2d 365 (N.C. 2004).

Hussar, W., & Gerald, D. (2001). *Projections of education statistics to 2011.* Office of Educational Research and Improvement, National Center for Education Statistics Washington, DC: U.S. Department of Education.

Imazeki, J., & Reschovsky, A. (2004a). Estimating the costs of meeting the Texas educational accountability standards. Testimony presented on behalf of plaintiff districts in *West Orange Cove v. Neeley.* Austin, TX.

Imazeki, J., & Reschovsky, A. (2004b). Is No Child Left Behind and un (or under) funded federal mandate? Evidence from Texas. *National Tax Journal, 57*(5), 571–588.

Lake View Sch. Dist. No. 25 v. Huckabee, 91 S.W.3d 472 (Ark. 2002) (*Lake View I*).

Lake View Sch. Dist. No. 25 v. Huckabee, 144 S.W.3d 741 (Ark. 2004) (*Lake View II*).

Lake View Sch. Dist. No. 25 v. Huckabee, 220 S.W.3d 645 (Ark. 2005) (*Lake View III*).

Levin, H. M. (2002). *The cost effectiveness of whole school reforms. Urban Diversity Series No. 114.* ERIC Clearinghouse on Urban Education. Institute for Urban and Minority Education.

Levin, H. M., & McEwan, P. J. (2001). *Cost-Effectiveness Analysis* (2nd ed.). Thousand Oaks, CA: Sage Publications.

Liebman, J. S., & Sabel, C. F. (2003). A public laboratory Dewey barely imagined: The emerging model of school governance and legal reform. *New York University Review of Law and Social Change, 28,* 183–304.

Losen, D. (2004). Challenging racial disparities: The promise and pitfalls of the No Child Left Behind Act's race-conscious accountability. *Howard Law Journal, 47,* 243–298.

McDuffy v. Secretary of the Exec. Office of Educ., 615 N.E.2d 516 (Mass. 1993).

McUsic, M. (1991). The use of education clauses in school finance reform litigation. *Harvard Journal on Legislation, 28,* 307–340.

Milliken v. Bradley, 433 U.S. 267 (1977) (*Milliken II*).

Mills, J., & McLendon, T. (2000). Setting a new standard for public education revision 6 increases: The duty of the state to make "adequate provision" for Florida schools. *Florida Law Review, 52,* 329–409.

Montoy v. State, 102 P.3d 1160 (Kan. 2005).

Mort, P., & Reusser, W. (1951). *Public school finance.* New York: McGraw-Hill, p. 388.

National Commission of Excellence. (1983). *A nation at risk: The imperative for educational reform.* Washington, DC: U.S. Government Printing Office.

No Child Left Behind Act of 2001, 20 U.S.C.A. §§ 6301–7916 (2004).

Odden, A. R. (2000). Costs of sustaining educational change via comprehensive school reform. *Phi Delta Kappan, 81*(6), 433–438.

Odden, A., & Picus, L. (2000). *School finance: A policy perspective.* New York: McGraw-Hill.

Odden, A. R., Picus, L. O., & Fermanich, M. (2003a). *An evidence based approach to school finance adequacy in Arkansas.* Little Rock AR: Arkansas Joint Committee on Educational Adequacy.

Odden, A. R., Picus, L. O., & Fermanich, M. (2003b). *A state of the art approach to school finance adequacy in Kentucky.* Kentucky Department of Education.

Opinion of the Justices, 624 So.2d 107 (Ala. 1993).

Pawtucket v. Sundlun, 662 A.2d 40 (R.I. 1995).

Picus, L. O. (2001). How much is enough? Adequacy has replaced equity as the top school finance issue. *American School Board Journal, 188*(12), 28–30.

Rebell, M. (2001). Educational adequacy, democracy, and the courts. In T. Ready, C. Edley, & C. Snow (Eds.), *Achieving high educational standards for all* (pp. 218–267). Washington, DC: National Academy Press.

Resource Adequacy Study for the New York State Commission on Education Reform. (2004). New York: Standard and Poors, School Evaluation Services.

Roelke, C., Green, P., & Zielewski, E. (2004). School finance litigation and legislation: The unfulfilled promise of the third wave. *Peabody Journal of Education, 79,* 104–133.

Samuelson, P. (1954). The pure theory of public expenditure. *Review of Economics and Statistics, 36*(4), 387–389.

Slavin, R., Karweit, N., & Madden, N. (1989). *Effective Programs for Students at Risk.* Boston: Allyn & Bacon.

State ex rel. State v. Lewis, 789 N.E.2d 195 (Ohio 2003).

State [of Wyoming] v. Campbell County School District, 19 P.3d 518 (Wyo. 2001).

Taylor, L. L. (2004). *Estimating the cost of education in Texas.* Prepared for the Texas Office of the Attorney General. Testimony prepared on behalf of the Texas legislature in the case of *West Orange Cove v. Neeley.* Austin, TX.

Taylor, L. L., Baker, B. D., & Vedlitz, A. (2005). *Measuring educational adequacy in public schools*. College Station, TX: Busch School of Government and Public Service, Texas A&M University.

Theobald, N. D., & Picus, L. O. (1991). Living with equal amounts of less: Experiences of states with primarily state funded school systems. *Journal of Education Finance, 17*(1), 1–6.

Thomas, T. A. (2004). Ubi jus, ibi remedium: The fundamental right to a remedy under due process. *San Diego Law Review, 41*, 1633–1645.

Thro, W. (1989). To render them safe: The analysis of state constitutional provisions in public school finance reform. *Virginia Law Review, 75*, 1639–1679.

Thro, W. (1994). Judicial analysis during the third wave of school finance litigation: The Massachusetts decision as a model. *Boston College Law Review, 35*, 597–617.

Verstegen, D. (2003). *Calculating the cost of an adequate education in Kentucky*. Prepared for the Council for Better Education.

United States Constitution Amendment XIV, § 1.

Walberg, H. (2001). Improving learning in Kansas public schools: The reasonable basis and constructive effects of quality performance accreditation. Expert Testimony in the case of *Montoy v. Kansas*.

ADDITIONAL READINGS

Consultancies for States or Special Interests

Augenblick, J. (1997). *Recommendations for a base figure and pupil weighted adjustments to the base figure for use in a new school finance system in Ohio*. Prepared for The School Funding Task Force, under contract with the Ohio Department of Education. Davis, CA: Management Analysis and Planning.

Augenblick, J., Alexander, K., & Guthrie, J. (1995). *Report of the panel of experts: Proposals for the elimination of the wealth based disparities in education*. Report Submitted by Ohio Chief State School Officer Theodore Sanders to the Ohio State Legislature.

Augenblick, J., & J. Myers (2001). *Calculation of the cost of an adequate education in Maryland in 2000–2001 using two different analytic approaches*. Submitted to the Maryland Commission on Education Finance, Equity and Excellence (Thornton Commission).

Augenblick, J., & Myers, J. (2001). *A procedure for calculating a base cost figure and an adjustment for at risk pupils that could be used in the Illinois school finance system*. Submitted to the Education Funding Advisory Board.

Augenblick, J., & Myers, J. (2002). *Calculation of the cost of an adequate education in Indiana in 2001–2002 using the professional judgment approach*. Submitted to the Indiana State Teachers Association.

Augenblick, J., & Myers, J. (2003). *Calculating the cost of an adequate education in Colorado using the professional judgment and successful school districts approaches*. Submitted to Colorado School Finance Project.

Augenblick, J., & Myers, J. (2003). *Calculation of the cost of an adequate education in Missouri using the professional judgment and the successful school districts approaches*. Submitted to the Missouri Education Coalition for Adequacy.

Augenblick, J., & Myers, J. (2003). *Calculation of the cost of an adequate education in Nebraska in 2002–2003 using the professional judgment approach*. Submitted to Nebraska State Education Association, Greater Nebraska Schools Association, Lincoln Public Schools, Nebraska Association of School Boards, Nebraska Coalition for Educational Equity and Adequacy, Nebraska Council of School Administrators, Nebraska Rural Communities Association, Omaha Public Schools, Westside Community Schools.

Augenblick, J., Myers, J., Silverstein, J., & Barkis, A. (2001). *Calculation of the cost of an adequate education in Kansas in 2000–2001 using two different analytic approaches*. Submitted to the Legislative Coordinating Council, State of Kansas.

Augenblick, J., Palaich, & Associates. (2003). *Calculation of the cost of an adequate education in North Dakota in 2002–03 using the professional judgment approach*. Submitted to the North Dakota Department of Public Instruction.

Calvo, N. A., Picus, L. O., Smith, J. R., & Guthrie, J. (2000). *A review of the Oregon Quality Education model*. Submitted to the Oregon Department of Education.

Chambers, J. G. (1984). *The development of a program cost model and cost-of-education model for the state of Alaska. Volume II: Technical report*. Stanford, CA: Associates for Education Finance and Planning.

Chambers, J. G., & Parrish, T. B. (1982). *The development of a resource cost model funding base for education finance in Illinois*. Report prepared for the Illinois State Board of Education. Stanford, CA: Associates for Education Finance and Planning.

Conley, D., & Freund, W. (2003). *"What will it Take" Project. Washington Quality Education Model*. ED477192 *Final Report*. Seattle, WA: Rainier Institute.

Duncombe, W. D. (2002). *Estimating the cost of an adequate education in New York*. Working Paper No. 44. Center for Policy Research. Maxwell School of Citizenship and Public Affairs. Syracuse, NY: Syracuse University.

Ehlers, J., Hayward, G. C., & Picus, L. O. (2002). *Wyoming education finance: Small district report.* Submitted to Wyoming State Legislature. Davis, CA: Management Analysis and Planning.

Guthrie, J., et al. (2001). *A professional judgment approach to determining adequate education funding in Maryland.* Submitted to The *New* Maryland Education Coalition. Davis, CA: Management Analysis and Planning.

Guthrie, J., Hayward, G. C., Smith, J. R., Rothstein, R., Bennett, R. W., Koppich, J. E., Bowman, E., DeLapp, L., Brandes, B., & Clark, S. (1997). *A proposed education resource block grant model for Wyoming school finance.* Submitted to Wyoming State Legislature. Davis, CA: Management Analysis and Planning.

Guthrie, J., & Smith, J. R. (1998). *Wyoming education finance issues: Programs for students with special needs (disadvantaged, limited English proficient, gifted).* Submitted to Wyoming State Legislature. Davis, CA: Management Analysis and Planning.

Guthrie, J., & Smith, J. R. (1998). *Wyoming education finance issues: Reconsideration of Wage Rate Cost Adjustments.* Submitted to Wyoming State Legislature. Davis, CA: Management Analysis and Planning.

Hayward, G. C. (2002). *Wyoming education finance: Modifying the maintenance and operations adjustment to comply with the ruling of the Wyoming Supreme Court.* Submitted to Wyoming State Legislature. Davis, CA: Management Analysis and Planning.

Hayward, G. C., Guthrie, J. Smith, J. R., & Bowman, E. (1998). *Wyoming education finance issues: Small schools Report.* Submitted to Wyoming State Legislature. Davis, CA: Management Analysis and Planning.

Myers, J., & Silverstein, J. (2003). *Calculation of the cost of an adequate education in Montana in 2001–2002 using the professional judgment approach.* Submitted to Montana School Boards Association, Montana Quality Education Coalition, Montana Rural Education Association, Montana Association of School Business Officials, Montana Association of County School Superintendents.

Norman, J. (2002). *Funding our future: An adequacy model for Wisconsin school finance.* Madison, WI: Institute for Wisconsin's Future.

Odden, A. R., Picus, L. O., & Fermanich, M. (2003). *A professional judgment approach to school finance adequacy in Kentucky.* Kentucky Department of Education. N. Hollywood, CA: Lawrence O. Picus & Assoc.

Odden, A. R., Picus, L. O., & Fermanich, M. (2003). *A state of the art approach to school finance adequacy in Kentucky.* Kentucky Department of Education.

Picus, L. O., Hayward, G. C., & Ehlers, J. (2002). *Wyoming education finance: Small schools report.* Submitted to Wyoming State Legislature. Davis, CA: Management Analysis and Planning.

Seder, R. C., Picus, L. O., & Smith, J. R. (2002). *Wyoming education finance: Estimating the costs of services for at risk students.* Submitted to Wyoming State Legislature. Davis, CA: Management Analysis and Planning.

Smith, J. R. (2002). *Wyoming education finance: Proposed revisions to the cost based block grant.* Submitted to Wyoming State Legislature. Davis, CA: Management Analysis and Planning.

Smith, J. R., et al. (1998). *Wyoming education finance issues report: Reconsideration of the housing cost adjustment.* Submitted to Wyoming State Legislature. Davis, CA: Management Analysis and Planning.

Smith, J. R., & Guthrie, J. (2000). *An exploration of educational and demographic conditions affecting New Hampshire's adequacy aid.* Submitted to the New Hampshire Legislature Adequate Education and Education Financing Commission. Davis, CA: Management Analysis and Planning.

Verstegen, D. (2003). *Calculating the cost of an adequate education in Kentucky.* Prepared for the Council for Better Education.

Wolkoff, M. J. (2002). *Wyoming education finance: Regional price adjustment.* Submitted to Wyoming State Legislature. Davis, CA: Management Analysis and Planning.

Wolkoff, M. J., & Podgursky, M. (2002). Wyoming education finance: Wyoming school district employee compensation. Submitted to Wyoming State Legislature. Davis, CA: Management Analysis and Planning.

State Agency Reports

Morgan, J. G. (2003). *Funding public schools: Is the BEP adequate?* Comptroller of the Treasury, Office of Education Accountability, State of Tennessee.

Pennsylvania House of Representatives. (2002). *Report of the Select Committee on Education Funding.* Mario Civera, Jr., Chair.

South Carolina Education Oversight Committee. (2003). *Progress report on the study of sufficient funding.*

Thornton, A. (2002). *Final report: Commission on Education Finance, Equity and Excellence.* Submitted to Governor Parris Glendening, State of Maryland.

Independent Reviews or Analyses

Ohio Coalition for Equity and Adequacy of School Funding. (2001). *Determining the Cost of an adequate education: Yet another failed attempt.* Columbus, OH: Author.

Major Books

Ladd, H. F., Chalk, R., & Hansen, J. S. (Eds.). (1999). *Equity and adequacy in education finance: Issues and perspectives*. Committee on Education Finance, Commission on Behavioral and Social Sciences and Education. Washington, DC: National Academy Press.

Ladd, H. F., & Hansen, J. S. (Eds.). (1999). *Making money matter: financing America's schools*. Committee on Education Finance, Commission on Behavioral and Social Sciences and Education. Washington, DC: National Academy Press.

Levin, H. M., & McEwan, P. J. (2001). *Cost-Effectiveness Analysis* (2nd ed.). Thousand Oaks, CA: Sage Publications.

Selected Resource Cost Literature

Chambers, J. G. (1999). *Measuring resources in education: From accounting to the resource cost model approach*. Working Paper Series, National Center for Education Statistics, Office of Educational Research and Improvement. Working Paper #1999–16. Washington, DC: U.S. Department of Education.

Chambers, J. G. (1999). Patterns of Expenditures on Students with Disabilities: A Methodological and Empirical Analysis. In T. B. Parrish, J. G. Chambers, & C. M. Guarino (Eds.), *Funding special education: Nineteenth annual yearbook of the American education finance association* (pp. 89–123). Thousand Oaks, CA: Corwin Press.

Hartman, W. T., Bolton, D., & Monk, D. H. (2001). A synthesis of two approaches to school-level financial data: The accounting and resource cost model approaches. In W. Fowler (Ed.), *Selected Papers in School Finance, 2000–01*, National Center for Education Statistics, Office of Educational Research and Improvement. Washington, DC: U.S. Department of Education.

Education Cost-Function Studies That Estimate Cost of Achieving Specific Outcomes (Basic Cost)

Duncombe, W. D., & Lukemeyer, A. (2002). *Estimating the cost of educational adequacy: A comparison of approaches*. Paper presented at the Annual Meeting of the American Education Finance Association, Albuquerque, NM.

Duncombe, W. D., Lukemeyer, A., & Yinger, J. (2003). Financing an adequate education: A case study of New York. In W. F. Fowler, Jr. (Ed.), *Developments in school finance: 2001–02, fiscal proceedings from the Annual State Data Conferences of July 2001 and July 2002* (pp. 127–154). U.S. Department of Education, National Center for Education Statistics. Washington, DC: US Department of Education.

Reschovsky, A., & Imazeki, J. (1998). *The development of school finance formulas to guarantee the provision of adequate education to low-income students*. In W. J. Fowler,

Jr., (Ed.), *Developments in school finance*, 1997 (NCES 98–212). Washington, DC: U.S. Department of Education, National Center for Education Statistics.

Reschovsky, A., & Imazeki, J. (1999). *Does the school finance system in Texas provide students with an adequate education?* Paper presented at the Annual Meeting of the American Education Finance Association. Seattle, WA.

Reschovsky, A., & Imazeki, J. (2001). Achieving educational adequacy through school finance reform. *Journal of Education Finance, 26*(4), 373–396.

Selected Recent Studies on and Reviews of Comprehensive School Reforms

Bifulco, R. C., Bordeaux, C., Duncombe, W., & Yinger, J. (2002). *Do whole school reform programs boost student performance? The Case of New York City*. New York: Smith-Richardson Foundation.

Borman, G. D., & Hewes, G. (2002). The long-term effects and cost effectiveness of success for all. *Educational Evaluation and Policy Analysis, 24*(4), 243–266.

Borman, G. D., Hewes, G., Overman, L., & Brown, S. (2003). Comprehensive School Reform and Achievement: A Meta-Analysis. *Review of Educational Research 73*(2), 125–230.

Levin, H. M. (2002). *The cost effectiveness of whole school reforms*. Urban Diversity Series. (No. 114) ERIC Clearinghouse on Urban Education. New York: Institute for Urban and Minority Education.

Evaluations of the Effectiveness of Efficiency Analysis

Bifulco, R., & Bretschneider, S. (2001). Estimating school efficiency: A comparison of methods using simulate data. *Economics of Education Review, 20*, 417–429.

Bifulco, R., & Duncombe, W. (2002). Evaluating school performance: Are we ready for prime time? *Developments in school finance 1999–2000*. Office of Educational Research and Improvement, National Center for Education Statistics. Washington, DC: U.S. Department of Education.

Other Related Literature

Abbott v. Burke, 693 A.2d 417 (N.J. 1997) (*Abbott IV*).

Almeida, T. A. (2004). Refocusing school finance litigation on at-risk children: *Leandro v. State of North Carolina*. *Yale Law and Policy Review, 22*, 525–569.

Andrews, M., Duncombe, W., & Yinger, J. (2002). Revisiting economies of size in American education: Are we any closer to consensus? *Economics of Education Review, 21*, 245.

Augenblick, J., Meyers, J., Silverstein, J., & Barkis, A. (2002). *Calculation of the cost of a suitable education in*

Kansas 2000–2001 using two different analytic approaches. Prepared for the Legislative Coordinating Council.

Baker, B. D., & Duncombe, W. (2003). *Balancing district needs and student needs: The role of economies of scale adjustments and student need weights in school finance formulas.* Manuscript.

Ealy, C. (2003). Achieving equity and adequacy in Texas school funding: a Delphi approach. Unpublished doctoral dissertation, Texas A&M University.

Education Commission of the States. (2001, September). *A survey of finance adequacy studies.* Denver, CO: Author.

Roelke, C., Green, P., & Zielewski, E. (2004). School finance litigation and legislation: The unfulfilled promise of the third wave. *Peabody Journal of Education, 79,* 104–133.

Legal Citations and Cases

Campbell County Sch. Dist. v. State, 907 P.2d 1238 (Wyo. 1995).

Campaign for Fiscal Equity v. State, 801 N.E.2d 326 (N.Y. 2003).

Castaneda v. Pickard, 648 F.2d 989 (5th Cir. 1981).

Claremont v. Governor, 703 A.2d 1353 (N.H. 1997) (*Claremont II*).

Colorado Const. Art. 9, § 2.

Committee for Educ. Rights v. Edgar, 672 N.E.2d 1178 (Ill. 1996).

Cover, A. (2002). Is "adequacy" a more "political question" than "equality"?: the effect of standards-based education on judicial standards for education finance. *Cornell Journal of Law and Public Policy, 11,* 403–439.

Dayton, J. (2001). *Serrano* and its progeny: an analysis of 30 years of school funding litigation. *West's Education Law Reporter, 157,* 447–464.

Dayton, J., Dupre, A., & Kiracofe, C. (2004). Education finance litigation: A review of recent state high court decisions and their likely impact on future litigation. *West's Education Law Reporter, 186,* 1–14.

Debra P. v. Turlington, 644 F.2d 397 (5th Cir. 1981).

Due Process Clause, U.S. Const. Amend. XIV, § 1.

DuPree v. Alma Sch. Dist. No. 30 of Crawford County, 651 S.W.2d 90 (Ark. 1983).

Dyson, M. R. (2002). Leave no child behind: Normative proposals to link educational adequacy claims and high stakes assessment due process challenges. *Texas Forum on Civil Liberties and Civil Rights, 7,* 1–70.

Enrich, P. (2003). Race and money, courts and schools: tentative lessons from Connecticut. *Indiana Law Review, 36,* 523–559.

Ex parte James, 713 So.2d 869 (Ala. 1997).

Ex parte James, 836 So.2d 813 (Ala. 2002).

Fogle, J. L. (2000). *Abbeville County School District v. State*: The Right to a Minimally Adequate Education in South Carolina. *South Carolina Law Review, 51,* 781–805.

Hoke County Bd. of Educ. v. State, 599 S.E.2d 365 (N.C. 2004).

Ill. Const. Art. 10, § 1.

Lake View Sch. Dist. No. 25 v. Huckabee, 91 S.W.3d 472 (Ark. 2002).

Lake View Sch. Dist. No. 25 v. Huckabee, 144 S.W.3d 741 (Ark. 2004).

Liebman, J. S., & Sabel, C. F. (2003). A public laboratory Dewey barely imagined: The emerging model of school governance and legal reform. *New York University Review of Law and Social Change, 28,* 183–304.

Losen, D. (2004). Challenging racial disparities: The promise and pitfalls of the No Child Left Behind Act's race-conscious accountability. *Howard Law Journal, 47,* 243–298.

McDuffy v. Secretary of the Exec. Office of Educ., 615 N.E.2d 516 (Mass. 1993).

McUsic, M. (1991). The use of education clauses in school finance reform litigation. *Harvard Journal on Legislation, 28,* 307–340.

Milliken v. Bradley, 418 U.S. 717 (1974) (*Milliken I*).

Milliken v. Bradley, 433 U.S. 267 (1977) (*Milliken II*).

Mills, J., & McLendon, T. (2000). Setting a New Standard for Public Education Revision 6 Increases: The Duty of the State to Make "Adequate Provision" for Florida Schools. *Florida Law Review, 52,* 329–409.

Missouri v. Jenkins, 515 U.S. 70 (1995).

Montoy v. State, 102 P.3d 1160 (Kan. 2005).

N.Y. Const. Art. 11, § 1.

No Child Left Behind Act of 2001, 20 U.S.C.A. §§ 6301–7916 (2004).

Opinion of the Justices, 624 So.2d 107 (Ala. 1993).

Pawtucket v. Sundlun, 662 A.2d 40 (R.I. 1995).

Rebell, M. (2001). Educational Adequacy, Democracy, and the Courts. In T. Ready, C. Edley, & C. Snow (Eds.), *Achieving High Educational Standards for All* (pp. 218–267). Washington, DC: National Academy Press.

R.I. Const. Art. 12, § 1.

Rose v. Council for Better Educ., 790 S.W.2d 186 (Ky. 1989).

Ryan, J. E., & Saunders, T. (2004). Foreword to symposium on school finance litigation: Emerging trends or new dead ends? *Yale Law and Policy Review, 22,* 463–480.

State ex rel. State v. Lewis, 789 N.E.2d 195 (Ohio 2003).

Thomas, T. A. (2004). Ubi Jus, Ibi Remedium: The Fundamental Right to a Remedy under Due Process. *San Diego Law Review, 41,* 1633–1645.

Thro, W. (1989). To render them safe: The analysis of state constitutional provisions in public school finance reform. *Virginia Law Review, 75,* 1639–1679.

Thro, W. (1994). Judicial Analysis during the Third Wave of School Finance Litigation: The Massachusetts Decision as a Model. *Boston College Law Review, 35,* 597–617.

Wash. Const. Art. 9, § 1.

CHAPTER 8

CHILD-BASED COSTS AND VERTICAL EQUITY

Introduction

Vertical equity is the appropriately differentiated treatment of those with different educational needs (see Chapter 5). Vertical equity concerns are arguably the centerpiece of educational adequacy litigation. Many educational adequacy cases have sought to establish a minimum baseline of funding across all schools and districts in a state; however, as many if not more have focused their efforts on achieving adequate additional support for special needs populations including children at-risk and limited-English-proficient (LEP) children.

Successful challenges to state education clauses are vital for otherwise unprotected and under-protected special student populations. What do we mean by otherwise unprotected, or under-protected? All children are protected by state and federal equal protection clauses against arbitrary and capricious differential treatment or deprivation of their fundamental interests without due process. However, equal protection challenges most successfully advocate for equal treatment, or *horizontal equity* of inputs, and not *appropriately differentiated treatment*—vertical equity. Hence the emergence in the 1970s of a rigid federal statutory framework, followed by similar state statutory frameworks protecting the rights of children with specific disabilities. Children *at-risk* lack similar statutory protection, and federal statutory protection for LEP children remains largely untested.

More complicated alternatives for promoting vertical equity through legal action involve *outcome equity* and *substantive due process* challenges. Equal protection challenges can succeed for at-risk and LEP children as long as state or federal courts are willing to recognize a right to differentiated funding in order to

have equal opportunity to achieve desired outcome. That right is strengthened when the outcome of interest is a fundamental interest guaranteed in state constitutional language. In such cases, plaintiffs may argue that states have violated their substantive due process rights by not providing sufficient additional resources for them to achieve the outcome—a constitutionally defined property interest—in question.

Reconceptualizing Vertical Equity as Adequacy

In an alternative view of vertical equity (see Chapter 5), it is a form of adequacy, where the cost of an adequate instructional program is differentiable by student need (Underwood, 1995). The cost of instructional programs varies both by the programmatic needs of the child (child-based differences) and by the organizational setting (school- and district-based differences) in which those needs are to be met. We begin this section with a discussion of *child-based differences* in costs and conclude it with a discussion of *school- and district-based differences*.

We can also reconceptualize vertical equity as outcome equality, or equal opportunity to achieve a given set of outcomes. The distinctions between outcome equal opportunity and individualized adequacy, while seemingly subtle, are important. Equal opportunity to achieve a desired outcome standard requires limitation of opportunity surpluses. Opportunity surpluses exist where some students or groups of students have a higher probability of achieving desired outcomes as a result of both uncontrollable and controllable factors.

In a common opportunity surplus, children with the greatest socioeconomic advantages attend those schools with the highest levels of educational resources, while economically disadvantaged children with much greater educational need (often in nearby schools or districts) have access to significantly lower resources. The result is a significant disparity in educational outcomes.

A pure conception of educational adequacy accepts that if resource levels in the less well-funded school or district can be deemed *adequate,* then the extent that resources in the better-funded school or district exceed *adequacy* (the opportunity surplus margin) is irrelevant. The problem with opportunity surpluses, under an equal opportunity or *vertical equity* framework, is that when one child or group of children has an opportunity surplus, that surplus diminishes the value of the opportunities of other children, even if those opportunities are perceived to be adequate. Employers or selective colleges and universities will continue to prefer graduates of higher-quality secondary schools.

Ideally, the goal in policy development is to ensure that all districts in a state, regardless of size, location, or fiscal capacity, can provide both an adequate basic education to all students and can adequately accommodate the special needs of their varied student populations. That task is easier said than done!

Child-Based Differences: A Conceptual View

We begin with a conceptual discussion of the costs associated with accommodating child-based differences. Three questions guide our discussion:

1. Who are the students who have special needs that may have associated different costs?

2. What outcomes do we expect these students to attain from supplemental services?

3. What are the supplemental (or marginal) costs of attaining those outcomes?

Regarding the first question, researchers and policy makers have identified two aggregate groups of students who require supplemental resources to attain adequate benefits from participating in public schooling: (a) students with disabilities as classified under the Individuals with Disabilities Education Act (IDEA) and (b) fringe populations, or populations statistically in the minority who are marginalized by the core curriculum but who are not consistently statutorily protected across states (Baker, 2001c). These populations

include at-risk, LEP, and gifted and talented students. We discussed earlier (see Chapter 7), an extensive statutory framework (including IDEA, the Americans with Disabilities Act, and Section 504) protects opportunities for students with disabilities, and some legal protections also exist for LEP students in Section 1703 of the Equal Educational Opportunities Act (EEOA) of 1974. Currently no Supreme Court precedents exist regarding the application of the EEOA to define adequate services for LEP students. State-level emphasis on at-risk populations, defined primarily as low-income students, are largely a response to federal programs initially designed to provide support to schools serving high percentages of low-income children. State support, including state statutory protection for gifted children, is arguably a function of political activism. By addressing these specific populations, we by no means intend to suggest that these are the only students with special needs. Rather, these are the populations most frequently recognized in school finance policy today. In this section, we present a broadened conception of vertical equity that is responsive but not restricted to the needs of these populations.

We show our conception of the costs associated with special education needs in Figures 8.1 through 8.4 (originally presented by Baker and Friedman-Nimz, 2003). We express special needs in these figures as variations in ability levels (in relation to any particular outcome), recognizing that some students are highly able, some are disabled, and most students have both abilities and disabilities in varying degrees. We also consider the case of students who enter a system with learning deficits, some as specific as LEP and others deficits associated with or diagnosed with physical deficits such as visual or auditory impairments. Central to our conception is the question of expected outcomes and outcome measurement, addressing the second question noted earlier: What outcomes do we expect these students to attain from supplemental services?

Historical emphasis on the needs of students with disabilities or learning deficits, combined with the more recent standards movement, leads us to Figure 8.1, or the cost of achieving absolute benefits—standards—across students of differing abilities or performance levels.

The horizontal line in Figure 8.1 labeled "basic cost" represents the average cost of bringing the average child to the desired (usually the average, or slightly below average) outcome level. We can assume that students of above-average abilities will require fewer

Figure 8.1   Marginal Costs of Outcomes

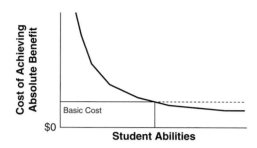

resources to achieve the same outcome standard, and children who are already there or can achieve the standard independently will require no resources. Students with disabilities or other deficits, will require more costly than average resources to achieve the standard, and some students' disabilities may be so extreme that they simply cannot achieve the academic outcome standard with any calculable set of resources. Turnbull and colleagues propose an alternative framework for evaluating *quality of life* outcomes for children with disabilities (Turnbull, Turnbull, Wehmeyer, & Park, 2003).

If we expect children of varied abilities to achieve comparable marginal benefits from education, then Figure 8.2 is a more appropriate representation of cost differences. Figure 8.2 suggests that each school picks a target range of student abilities to which it tailors its core curriculum, yielding an average rate of progress through curricular materials for the average, or targeted child. Some students, however, regularly deviate in either one direction or the other in their abilities to accomplish curricular tasks. Those with disabilities, with learning difficulties, or who are entering the system with deficits will require additional support, at additional costs to achieve comparable rates of gain. In reality, however, for these children to achieve compa-

rable absolute benefit as well, we should attempt to achieve accelerated rates of gain. This is especially true for children who have average or higher ability but simply enter the system with learning deficits.

The major difference between Figure 8.2 and Figure 8.1 is in the implications for higher-ability and more advanced children. Figure 8.2 suggests that additional resources are required for the high-ability child to continue to achieve gains or marginal benefits. Assume, for example that a bright child has already finished his or her math homework, or even mastered the entire year's worth of math curriculum by the midpoint of the year. Additional resources as simple as providing the student a more advanced book so that he or she may learn independently or providing access to individualized computer curricula might be sufficient for the student to achieve appropriate marginal benefits.

We have already alluded to the importance of considering both marginal and absolute benefits for children lagging behind on outcome standards. That is, it is not enough to get children falling behind to learn at the same rate as the average child if we expect them to achieve standards in a reasonable amount of time. This perspective, however, applies only to those capable of learning at an accelerated rate but whose performance has lagged for one reason or another, perhaps a child with a learning difference such as dyslexia, or a child from an economically disadvantaged background. We also recognize the relevance of context in Figure 8.2 by recognizing that individual schools or districts likely tailor their curricula to their average students.

Figure 8.3 addresses how costs of achieving marginal benefits might differ across different educational

Figure 8.3   Marginal Costs of Differentiated Service Delivery (for Marginal Benefit Across Settings)

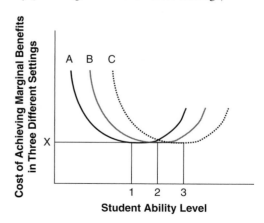

Figure 8.2   Marginal Costs of Differentiated Service Delivery (for Marginal Benefit)

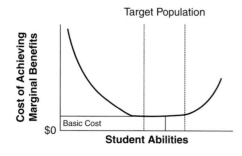

Figure 8.4   Costs of Achieving Marginal and Absolute Benefits Across Different Settings

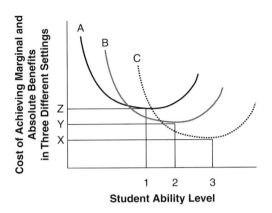

settings where the high-ability child requiring supplemental resources in School A may be the average-ability child in School C, learning at the appropriate rate with that school's average set of resources. Figure 8.4 reintroduces absolute benefits, indicating that schools serving higher proportions of children with disabilities and learning deficits require higher levels of resources than schools with fewer such children. That is, the average cost of achieving absolute benefits for the average student in School A will be more than that of School C. This premise is validated by the cost–function research introduced in Chapter 7.

The practical implications of Figures 8.1 through 8.4 are that state school finance policies must be sensitive both to differences in the needs of individual students and to overall differences in student populations across schools. That is, ideally, state school finance formulas should include aid adjustments or categorical allocations that support curricular differentiation and related services for students with special needs across all schools, such that comparable *marginal* benefits can be achieved. Also, school finance formulas should provide supplemental aid to raise the average level of educational resources available in schools serving large numbers of students with learning disabilities and deficits so as to increase their chances of achieving desired *absolute* benefits.

One unfortunate implication of Figures 8.3 and 8.4 is that education might be most efficiently provided when students are segregated into different schools or tracks by ability levels. Transportation costs alone reduce the likelihood of such policies being truly cost-effective. Furthermore, schools face the logistical

problem of where to place students with high abilities in some academic subjects who are low in others. Finally, we must consider the social costs and social benefits of having students across strata interact with one another. In less pragmatic language, we must also consider the ethical implications of segregating students by ability, particularly when such abilities are themselves produced by privilege. Nevertheless, children with extreme disabilities or extremely high abilities may reap the greatest benefits from participating in opportunities that a district can efficiently provide only in a segregated setting.

Baker and Richards (1998), for example, promote the virtues of providing wealth-equalized scholarships for low-income gifted and talented students to attend private summer and weekend programs. This approach places the student who year-round is most likely from a School C environment with too few resources to appropriately modify curriculum temporarily into a School A environment, where the child may benefit both from more appropriate curricula and from more stimulating peer interactions.

Individual Educational Needs Versus Sociological Proxies

In education policy research in general, and in cost analysis in particular, two types of measures capture differences in student-population characteristics and related needs: sociological proxies and individual educational needs. The contrast between **marginal costs** based on district poverty rates and marginal costs based on counts of LEP students is relatively straightforward.

Education cost studies, in particular cost–function models, include measures of the share of children in poverty in a school district not as a measure of the individual educational programming needs of any one or a group of students in the district, but as a broad proxy measure of the socio-economic conditions in the district, which most often relate quite strongly with educational outcome differences. Clearly, not each child identified as living in poverty or qualifying for subsidized lunch will require specific, measurable supplemental educational programs or services. Rather, additional financial leverage, perhaps played out in reduced class sizes or improved teacher quality, can have positive marginal effects on the outcomes of populations disproportionately from impoverished family backgrounds. By contrast, counts of children with limited English language skills relate more directly to the need for additional tutoring and language instruction involving specialized teachers in contact with specific students.

While poverty measures are the most common sociological proxy in education cost analysis, race and ethnicity variables can also be useful for characterizing social/cultural and socio-economic differences between school districts that may be strongly associated with student outcomes. A substantial body of research indicates the presence of racial achievement gaps above and beyond comprehensive sets of socio-economic measures (Baker, Keller-Wolff, & Wolf-Wendel, 2000; Garms & Smith, 1970; Hanushek, Kain, Markman, & Rivken, 2003; Rothstein, 2004). With only a few exceptions, however, researchers and policy analysts have avoided this issue in the estimation of marginal costs, in part because of confusion over sociological proxies versus educational need indicators (Downes & Pogue, 1994; Imazeki & Reschovsky, 2004). Few researchers or policy analysts seem comfortable with the notion that race, for example, might be an indicator of educational need at the level of the individual student, and professional judgment panels are unlikely to propose race-differentiated curriculum. At the sociological level, however, comprehensive school reforms, class size reduction, and even educational vouchers have had differential affects on student outcomes (achievement, attainment, etc.) by race, often showing more significant improvements for African-American poor children than for their white peers (Finn, Gerber, Achilles, & Boyd-Zaharias, 2001; Grismer, Flanagan, & Williamson, 1998).

Measures of Child Poverty

Critics, including ourselves throughout this text, often raise concern about providing financing based on counts of students that may be influenced by district officials, such as rates of children qualifying for subsidized lunch. Because policy makers do not intend poverty measures in school finance policies to identify individual students' needs, but rather to predict the likelihood that children requiring additional learning support exist in certain schools, greater flexibility exists in measuring poverty at the school or district level. Nonetheless, no method is best for all circumstances. Free lunch counts are based on children living in families at 130% the U.S. Census Bureau poverty rate and are annually adjusted but not regionally sensitive. At this higher threshold, one would certainly expect subsidized lunch counts to be much higher than counts of

children in families qualifying at the poverty level. In Kansas, for example, among the state's large districts, census poverty rates range from near 0% to just under 30%. Free lunch count rates range from 0% to 65%.

Critics of subsidized lunch counts often complain that they bear little relationship to census poverty rates. The range differences for districts in Kansas appear, superficially, to validate this concern. However, we find that, statistically, census poverty rates explain about 92% of the variation in free lunch counts across these districts. Further, on average, a 1% difference in census poverty rate is associated with a 3.35% difference in free lunch rate. This difference does not imply necessarily that free lunch rates are exaggerated or over-reported but, rather, that a large share of Kansas families live at income levels between 100% and 130% of the census poverty level. In fact, the number of families in that band is greater than the number of families below 100%. Nationally, using subsidized lunch rates from school year 1999–2000 and U.S Census poverty rates, poverty rates explain about 85% of variance in subsidized lunch rates. On average, a 1% difference in census poverty rate is associated with a 2% difference in subsidized lunch rate. Variance in this relationship among states depends on the numbers of families in each state that lie in the income range between the poverty level itself, and 130% of that poverty level, among other possible explanations.

Ultimately, when selecting a sociological proxy for vertical equity adjustment, one would like to find the proxy that effectively predicts educational outcome deficiencies that school or district officials cannot manipulate and that does not create perverse incentives. Clearly, funding on the basis of poor performance directly would create such incentives. The alternative is to discern which poverty or other socio-economic proxy best predicts outcome deficiencies across districts.

Costs and Child-Based Differences

Research Evidence on Costs

Previously in this chapter, we have begun to address our first question, Who are the students who have special needs that may have associated different costs? We have identified special education students, LEP, at-risk, and gifted and talented students, and we have differentiated between expected cost differences when applying alternative outcome expectations. The more arduous task, however, is identifying the *specific* populations in need, identifying their specific educational needs, and measuring the marginal costs associated with meeting those specific needs.

We define marginal costs as the additional costs, above and beyond the costs of educating the regular education or average child. In policy conversation, these costs are sometimes referred to as "excess costs," or the cost exceeding the basic education funding level (often the level of foundation aid).

Students With Disabilities

Although exact current expenditures are unknown, the Center for Special Education Finance (CSEF) estimates that expenditures on special education services in the United States exceeded $50 billion in 1999 or $8,080 per special education student (Chambers, Parrish, & Harr, 2004).

Tom Parrish (1997), in *Special Education in an Era of School Reform,* notes that accurate current expenditure data are unavailable because states were last required to report such data for the 1987–1988 school year.

The recent Special Education Expenditures Project (SEEP) (http://www.csef-air.org/pub_seep.php) has attempted to produce new estimates of total special education spending, on special education students relative to general education students, and spending on special education students in different contexts. Major findings of SEEP include:

- The total spending to provide a combination of regular and special education services to students with disabilities amounted to $77.3 billion, or an average of $12,474 per student. Students with disabilities for other special needs programs (e.g., Title I, ELL, or gifted and talented students) received an additional $1 billion, bringing the per-student amount to $12,639.

- The **additional expenditure** to educate the average student with a disability is estimated to be $5,918 per student. This is the difference between the total expenditure per student eligible for special education services ($12,474) and the total expenditure per regular education student ($6,556).

- Based on 1999–2000 school year data, the total expenditure to educate the average student with disabilities is an estimated *1.90 times* that expended to educate the typical regular education student with no special needs. This ratio has actually declined since 1985, when Moore et al. estimated it (1988) to be 2.28.

- Excluding expenditures on school facilities, the ratio of current operating expenditures on the typical special education student is *2.08 times* that expended on the typical regular education student with no special needs.

The authors of SEEP explain that they have evaluated the "additional expenditures" associated with special education rather than "excess costs," the language of earlier special education spending studies (Chambers et al., 2004). Additional expenditures are merely the amount that public schools have spent, historically, on special education students. Additional expenditures are not costs, because no specific quality of service exists, and because no outcome standard is associated with the spending patterns (other than the average of current practice).

Local education agencies received $3.7 billion in federal IDEA funding in 1999–2000, accounting for 10.2% of the additional total expenditure on special education students (or $605 per special education student), and about 7.5% of total special education spending. If Medicaid funds are included, federal funding covers 12% of the total additional expenditure on special education students (i.e., 10.2% from IDEA and 1.8% from Medicaid) (Chambers et al., 2004).

Hamilton Lankford and Jim Wyckoff (1999) found that special education spending in New York State grew at a rate 50% faster than general education spending from 1980 to 1993. Despite the apparent high spending and rate of growth of spending since the 1970s, a 1996 Phi Delta Kappa/Gallup Poll found that 47% of adults said that America is spending *too little* of its total education budget on students with special needs, *41%* said that spending is *about the right amount,* and only *5%* said that spending is too high (Elam, Rose, & Gallup, 1996, cited in Parrish, 2001). Although the federal government had promised to achieve 40% funding of special education by 1982 when the federal allocation was initially set at 5% in 1978, the rate never exceeded 12.5%. Parrish (2001) estimates that 1996 federal allocations cover about 8% of the nation's special education costs.

Table 8.1 summarizes additional costs by disability level and disaggregation of costs by specialized and generalized services received. As mentioned, the average special education student had total expenditures of $12,525 compared to the average regular education student at $6,556. As one might expect, expenditures rise for higher severity categories of children with disabilities and children with multiple disabilities. Again,

Table 8.1 Average Expenditures per Pupil by Disability in 1999–2000 Special Education Expenditure Project

Student Population	Total	Ratio to Average	Special Education Services	% Special Education
Average non special education student	$ 6,556			
Average special education student	$12,525	1.90	$ 8,126	65%
Specific learning disability	$10,558	1.60	$ 5,507	52%
Speech/language impairment	$10,958	1.70	$ 6,334	58%
Other health impairment	$13,229	2.00	$ 8,754	66%
Emotional disturbance	$14,147	2.20	$ 9,885	70%
Orthopedic impairment	$14,993	2.30	$10,888	73%
Mental retardation	$15,040	2.30	$11,393	76%
Hearing impairment/deafness	$15,992	2.40	$11,006	69%
Traumatic brain injury	$16,542	2.50	$12,459	75%
Autism	$18,790	2.90	$15,219	81%
Visual impairment/blindness	$18,811	2.90	$13,796	73%
Multiple disabilities	$20,095	3.10	$16,098	80%
Pre-school	$13,426	2.00	$10,013	75%
Students placed in non-public schools	$25,580	3.90	$25,580	100%

Source: Adapted from Exhibit B1, Chambers, J. G., Shkolnik, J., & Perez, M. (2005). Total expenditures for students with disabilities: Spending variation by disability. Retrieved October 2006, from http://www.csef-air.org/publications/seep/national/Final_SEEP_Report_5.PDF

these average expenditure patterns might serve as guidelines for a weighting system on special education funding, but these patterns merely reflect average expenditures of current services, with no measure of the adequacy of student outcomes.

More dated research by Chambers (1999) applies a resource-cost model approach to estimating more precise cost differences across educational settings and student needs. Chambers provides a conceptual framework for the empirical measurement of the marginal costs of serving students with disabilities. Chambers notes that while "ideally, student needs would be based on an objective set of personal attributes or competencies, . . . most of the literature relies on the use of student disabilities as a way of categorizing students for the purpose of cost or expenditure analysis" (1999, p. 95).

Chambers's (1999) approach to resource-cost analysis in special education involves five dimensions: (a) type of environment, (b) grade levels, (c) service prototype, (d) primary disability, and (e) student need.

Type of Environment: Chambers's definition of type of environment refers to whether a school is organized departmentally or non-departmentally, where middle and secondary schools are more likely to be departmentally organized.

Grade Levels: Chambers points out that within departmentalized and non-departmentalized environments, students are grouped by grade levels, which he organizes as (a) preschool, (b) kindergarten, (c) primary grades 1–3, (d) intermediate grades 4–8, and (e) traditional high school grades 9–12.

Service Prototype: *Service prototype* refers to a combination of the type of placement (regular classroom, outside the regular classroom, or separate facility) and the percentage of time spent in that placement. Chambers suggests that the service prototype is a way of describing the intensity of service needs for a special education student.

Primary Disability: As noted previously, while Chambers prefers to identify student needs based on detailed individual characteristics, the practical reality is that student disabilities are most often and most easily classified according to federally defined categories of disabilities (as used in Tables 8.2 and 8.3.)

Student Need: Because federally defined disability categories are still quite broadly defined, Chambers relies on subjective responses of special educators to classify the level of student

Table 8.2   Marginal Cost Weightings by Grade, Placement, Disability, and Curricular Adaptation for Hypothetical Student

Dimension	Designation	Weight
Environment	Nondepartmentalized	1.24
Grade level	5th Grade	1.03
Disability	Learning disability	1.00
Student need	Minor adaptation	1.17
	Total Cost (weight)	**1.49**

needs for individual students, where the level of need refers to the extent of curricular, behavioral, or medical–physical adaptations necessary to provide instructional services.

Using data on special education services in Massachusetts in the 1990s, Chambers conducted an analysis of marginal costs of special education services at the intersections of the various dimensions listed previously. Chambers found that on average, the cost of educating a special education student in a non-departmentalized setting was 2.17 times the cost of educating the regular education student; in a departmentalized setting, the cost was 1.21 times regular education costs; and in an external assignment, the cost was 8.38 times regular education costs.

Following are two examples that draw on the marginal cost findings of Chambers (1999). In the first (Table 8.2), we have a 5th-grade student in a non-departmentalized setting who is learning disabled and requires minor curricular adaptation.

Chambers (1999) found that marginal costs for students in grades 4–8 in non-departmentalized settings were 3% above (1.03 times) costs for grades 1–3 in non-departmentalized settings. In addition, the ratio of base expenditures for a student with disabilities compared to a regular education student was 1.24 for non-departmentalized settings. Finally, students requiring minor curricular adaptation had marginal costs 17% above (1.17 times) those requiring no curricular adaptation. Multiplying the weights across the dimensions, we find that this student has a marginal cost to his or her education, or cost factor, of 1.49 (1.03 × 1.24 × 1.17 = 1.49).

Our second student (Table 8.3) faces more significant barriers, including orthopedic impairments as well as two additional disabilities. This student is also in a nondepartmentalized setting and requires the 1.24 base weight. Chambers found that a child with orthopedic impairment on average has marginal costs 2.68 times the costs for a learning disabled child. Chambers found that the child with two additional disabilities has yet another 18% higher costs (1.18). The student requires major physical–medical support (1.44) and minor curricular adaptation (1.17).

As a result, the cost factor for this student is 6.61 (1.24 × 1.17 × 1.44 × 2.68 × 1.18 = 6.61). That is, the costs of providing reasonable specialized services for this child are nearly seven times the costs for the average child.

Table 8.3   Marginal Cost Weightings by Grade, Placement, Disability, and Curricular Adaptation for Another Hypothetical Student

Dimension	Designation	Weight
Environment	Nondepartmentalized	1.24
Grade level	Primary	1.00
Disability	Orthopedically impaired	2.68
Disability	Two additional disabilities	1.18
Student need	Minor curricular adaptation	1.17
Student need	Major physical/medical support	1.44
	Total Cost (weight)	**6.61**

To obtain a more comprehensive understanding of the derivation of these indices and specifics of how they work, we strongly recommend reading Chambers's (1999) original work, *The Patterns of Expenditures on Students with Disabilities*. Our goal here is merely to introduce the framework for analyzing cost differences by need and placement and to provide a limited set of examples for uses of findings from such analyses.

Analysts and policy makers must use information on special education costs by need and placement with caution. While resource-cost analysis and special education cost indexing may be useful for measuring adequacy or vertical equity for students with special needs, such cost indices may yield unintended consequences if directly applied in school finance policies as adjustments to state aid. As we will discuss in greater detail later in this chapter, allocating higher levels of aid based on student classifications or placements may stimulate over-identification or excessive use of restrictive placements by local district leaders attempting to maximize revenue.

Finally, an increasing concern is whether the rapid growth rate in special education costs has adversely affected, or *encroached* upon, available resources for the general population (Lankford & Wyckoff, 1999). That is, if total education revenues grow more slowly than special education costs, regular education resources will decline. Lankford and Wyckoff in particular find that when total revenues are constrained, perhaps by overall economic conditions or by local fiscal capacity, encroachment of regular education funds increases or is higher. A recent National Research Council (NRC) report, *Making Money Matter: Financing America's Schools* (Ladd & Hansen, 1999), suggests that while the problem of encroachment may exist, it may be more productive to address whether the current "entitlement and categorical approach to educating children with disabilities best serves their learning needs," rather than to continue pitting one student population against another for access to finite resources (Ladd & Hansen, 1999, p. 222). The NRC recommends more integrated approaches to placement, improving the capacity of schools to accommodate students in integrated environments, improving accountability for special education students' outcomes, and providing schools and parents greater control over the use of public funds to accomplish these tasks (Ladd & Hansen, 1999).

Children At-Risk

Cost estimates and/or guidelines for achieving vertical equity for at-risk and LEP pupils have been presented in literature and applied in state policies for several years, despite limited empirical bases. The most common estimates indicate a cost of serving both at-risk and LEP pupils at 1.2, or 120% of the cost of educating the "typical" student (Parrish & Hikido, 1998; Parrish, Matsumoto, & Fowler, 1995). A recent NRC report noted the following with respect to the 1.2 weighting for at-risk pupils:

> While this indicator may be the best currently available for determining a weighting for students in poverty and is easily understood, it results from federal budget decisions about what to spend on Title I, not on a calculation of the costs of education of poor children and of compensating for prior deprivation that may affect their education performance. (Ladd & Hansen, 1999, p. 127)

Results from early, published analyses of the costs of serving at-risk pupils vary widely. Goertz (1988; cited in Odden & Picus, 2000, p. 212), for example, found that in a study of schools in 17 districts, Chapter I expenditures ranged from $175 per pupil in a district with an expenditure range of $175 to $1,070, to $2,500 per pupil. Several authors address costs of serving at-risk children in terms of the costs of operating comprehensive school-reform models tailored to the needs of at-risk populations. Odden and Picus cost out the ingredients of offering the Roots and Wings/Success for All, whole-school reform program focused on improving achievement of at-risk pupils in a school of 500 pupils, arriving at approximately $1,000 per pupil, or $500,000 (Odden & Picus, 2000, p. 213).

Most recently, Duncombe and Yinger (2005) used cost–function analysis to isolate the additional costs of bringing at-risk children to desired outcome levels in New York State, applying alternative measures of poverty concentration. The authors find a weight of 149% above (249% of) average costs when measuring poverty by U.S. Census Bureau rates and about 110% when measuring poverty by rates of children qualifying for subsidized lunch.

Limited-English-Proficient Children

Studies of the costs of providing bilingual education or transitional programming have also produced widely varying results, ranging from less than an extra 5% (Carpenter-Huffman & Samulon, 1981, and Gonzalez, 1996, cited in Odden & Picus, 2000, p. 214) to an extra 100% (Chambers & Parrish, 1983, cited in Odden &

Picus, 2000, p. 214). Parrish (1994) estimated the costs of serving LEP students under alternative instructional models in California (Parrish, 1994). Parrish (1994) found the average total marginal cost of serving LEP students to be $361 (marginal instructional cost = $186, administration and support cost = $175). Across four approaches to service delivery, marginal costs were approximately 18% above classroom costs; classroom costs ranged from $1,409 to $1,978 per pupil, and total costs, including support for LEP students, ranged from $1,756 to $3,505 per pupil. Parrish and Hikido (1998) note that the $361 marginal cost is only 8% above average expenditures per pupil in California, which at the time were $4,598 (Parrish & Hikido, 1998).

Most recently, Duncombe and Yinger (2005) used cost–function analysis to isolate the additional costs of bringing ELL/LEP children to desired outcome levels in New York State. The authors note, "In a typical aid formula, the extra weight for a pupil from a poor family or with LEP is about 25%. We estimate that these extra weights should be between 111 and 215 percent" (Duncombe & Yinger, 2005).

Gifted Children

Presently, little evidence exists regarding the resource costs of adequate services for gifted children. Baker and Friedman-Nimz (2003) apply a cursory analysis of adding qualified gifted education specialists to elementary schools of approximately 400 students, yielding marginal costs of .3 to .6 per gifted pupil (assuming 5% of the student population as *primary beneficiaries* of services).

Chambers' (1999) National Center for Education Statistics (NCES) working paper, *Measuring Resources in Education*, provides a few additional insights into resource costs for gifted children as experienced in Ohio, but that work is limited to personnel costs and is estimated with data on current practices rather than ideal conditions. Using average caseloads and contact hours, and average expenditures per pupil hour, the average cost per participating pupil for K–12 gifted and talented instruction was approximately $2,061 (regular teaching assignment) or $1,655 (special education teaching assignment) (Chambers, 1999, p. 108). These costs were comparable in Chambers' analyses to costs per pupil hour of providing self-contained bilingual/multicultural programs (regular teaching assignment) or costs per pupil hour of providing programs for the develop-

mentally handicapped (special education teaching assignment). Case loads, or class sizes, for gifted education in Ohio ranged between 15 and 20. The report did not provide marginal cost estimates. Expenditures per pupil in Ohio were approximately $5,550 in 1996, leading to a marginal cost of about 30% to 37%, similar to that found by Baker and Friedman-Nimz (2003).[1]

Findings From Educational Adequacy Studies

Table 8.4 summarizes the marginal cost findings of 10 separate state-level, input-based analyses of the cost of providing an adequate education. Base costs are reported as regionally and inflation adjusted, but marginal costs are not similarly adjusted; therefore, marginal need weights are calculated against non-adjusted base costs. Across these studies, marginal costs for children in poverty range from 25% (Tennessee) to over 100%, with one very low outlier from a study in Kentucky by Verstegen (2003). Weights for LEP/ELL range from about .50 to over 1.0.

It is important to understand that these studies are not necessarily weighting the same pupils, because the studies may measure poverty in different ways. We therefore attempt to make more direct comparisons in Table 8.5. For Table 8.5, we estimate the regression slopes between "adequacy cost per pupil" for each district in each state and subsidized lunch rates reported in the NCES *Common Core of Data*, Public School Universe File in school year 1999–2000. Table 8.5 is based on an analysis originally presented by Bruce Baker in the *Journal of Education Finance* (2006). Table 8.5 includes only those districts with 2,000 or more students in each state, so as to avoid higher costs associated with small districts.

Table 8.5 shows that in Minnesota, based on a cost–function model using data-envelopment analysis, a district with 100% children qualifying for subsidized lunch would have costs per pupil about 86% above the district with 0% children qualifying for subsidized lunch. Most slope values fall between .60 and .80, indicating that on average a district with 100% children in poverty would have costs per pupil ranging from 60% to 80% more than the district with 0% children in poverty. Only the Arkansas evidence-based study falls well out of line with these estimates. Verstegen's (2003) Kentucky study did not supply district-by-district

---

[1] Based on pupil-weighted average of current expenditures less state aid allocation for special education using U.S. Census fiscal survey of local governments 1996.

Table 8.4   Marginal Costs of Student Needs From Recent Input-Based Adequacy Studies

State	Authors	Regionally and Inflation Adjusted	Poverty Margin (Scale Effic.)	LEP/ELL Margin (Scale Effic.)	Poverty Weight	LEP Weight
Colorado	Augenblick and Myers (2003a)	$7,504	$2,501	$3,874	0.37	0.57
Kansas	Augenblick et al. (2001)	$7,577	$2,578	$5,993	0.44	1.03
Kentucky	Verstegen (2003)	$7,601	$ 817	$ 817	0.12	0.12
Maryland	Augenblick and Myers (2001)	$7,325	$9,165	$6,612	1.39	1.00
Maryland	Guthrie et al. (2001)	$7,941	$7,038		1.04	—
Missouri	Augenblick and Myers (2003b)	$9,259	$2,744	$4,446	0.35	0.57
Montana	Augenblick and Myers (2003c)	$8,592	$1,810		0.30	—
Nebraska	Augenblick and Myers (2003d)	$7,827	$2,436	$5,682	0.42	0.97
North Dakota	Augenblick et al. (2003)	$8,065	$2,192	$4,651	0.37	0.77
Tennessee	Augenblick et al. (2003)	$5,636	$1,262	$4,544	0.25	0.90

ELL, English language learner; LEP, limited English proficiency.

data, but those numbers likely would fall out of line as well. Further, evidence-based analysis on Wyoming, also by Lawrence O. Picus and Associates (Odden et al., 2005), shows little need-related variation. With the exception of one district in the state of Wyoming (Riverton), however, relatively little variation occurs in student-population characteristics.

In Chapter 5, we discussed Berne and Stiefel's (1984) approaches to performing vertical equity–adjusted horizontal equity analysis. We presented simple analyses including pupil weights of 1.2 for both at-risk and LEP students. We included no other cost adjust-ments. In Chapter 5 we also summarized variation in funding across states, comparing variation across all districts and variation across large (scale-efficient) districts. Removing economies of scale-related costs (discussed further in Chapter 9) changed the analysis substantially. What if we examine only large districts and then use 100% need weights for children in poverty? This approach is similar to that proposed and applied by Robert Bifulco in a *Journal of Education Finance* article in the fall of 2005, evaluating racial disparities in school funding.

Table 8.6 applies this approach to state and local revenue data from 2002–2003. Taking this approach

Table 8.5   Relationship Between Median-Centered Indexed Costs and Subsidized Lunch Rates (K–12 Districts Enrolling >2,000 Students, Not Weighted)

State	Method (Author)	Relationship Between Indexed Costs and Subsidized Lunch Rates[a]	
		Estimate	R-squared
Minnesota	Cost–function/data envelopment analysis	0.855[b]	0.468
Kansas	Cost–function (D&Y, 2006)	0.799	0.769
Texas	Cost–function (R&I, 2004)	0.739	0.610
New York	Cost–function (D, L & Y, 2004)	0.687	0.385
Texas	Professional judgment (MAP, 2004)[c]	0.624	0.707
Nebraska	Professional judgment (A&M, 2002)	0.611	0.694
Kansas	Professional judgment (A&M, 2002)	0.598	0.697
New York	Professional judgment (AIR/MAP, 2004)	0.381	0.283
Texas	Cost function (TAMU, 2004)	0.354	0.741
Arkansas	Evidence based (Odden et al., 2005)	0.176	0.780

[a] School year 2000 subsidized lunch rate (NCES *Common Core of Data*, 2000, Fiscal/Non-Fiscal Longitudinal File).
[b] Slope reduces to .4137, but r-squared increases to .7265 if Minneapolis and St. Paul are dropped.
[c] Analysis conducted for only a small subset of districts.
Source: Data from Baker, 2006.

Table 8.6 Comparison of Horizontal Equity Across States Adjusted and Not Adjusted at 100% Difference for Poverty (Large Districts Only)

State	Not Adjusted for Student Need			Adjusted for 100% Difference in Poverty Cost		
	State and Local Rev. PP	Coefficient of Variation	Rank	State and Local Rev. PP	Coefficient of Variation	Rank
Hawaii	$10,382	0.0%	1	$ 7,762	0.0%	1
District of Columbia	$14,239	0.0%	2	$ 8,710	0.0%	2
Nevada	$ 6,947	4.8%	3	$ 5,770	4.3%	3
West Virginia	$ 7,926	7.1%	6	$ 5,501	10.7%	4
Florida	$ 6,923	9.1%	11	$ 5,070	12.2%	5
Minnesota	$ 9,634	13.8%	30	$ 8,037	12.3%	6
Iowa	$ 8,456	8.3%	9	$ 6,882	13.0%	7
South Dakota	$ 6,177	7.7%	7	$ 5,267	13.2%	8
Oregon	$ 7,101	10.4%	13	$ 5,619	13.3%	9
Kentucky	$ 6,644	9.3%	12	$ 4,784	13.4%	10
Indiana	$ 7,690	12.5%	27	$ 6,213	13.7%	11
Utah	$ 5,367	13.9%	31	$ 4,474	13.8%	12
Nebraska	$ 7,827	6.6%	5	$ 6,386	14.0%	13
Delaware	$10,061	11.5%	21	$ 7,730	14.2%	14
Arkansas	$ 6,427	11.9%	24	$ 4,690	14.4%	15
Wyoming	$ 9,458	12.0%	25	$ 7,747	15.2%	16
Tennessee	$ 5,937	12.2%	26	$ 4,274	15.6%	17
Washington	$ 7,728	11.1%	17	$ 6,137	16.2%	18
New Mexico	$ 6,714	11.2%	19	$ 4,404	16.4%	19
Wisconsin	$ 9,536	8.6%	10	$ 7,887	16.6%	20
Montana	$ 7,382	5.7%	4	$ 4,389	16.9%	21
South Carolina	$ 7,441	11.9%	23	$ 5,356	17.0%	22
New Hampshire	$ 8,966	15.8%	35	$ 7,703	17.9%	23
Louisiana	$ 6,541	10.9%	16	$ 4,203	18.0%	24
Massachusetts	$11,203	18.9%	46	$ 9,196	18.5%	25
Colorado	$ 7,682	10.8%	15	$ 6,476	18.7%	26
Maine	$ 8,967	11.8%	22	$ 6,984	19.4%	27
Oklahoma	$ 5,652	7.9%	8	$ 3,886	19.7%	28
North Carolina	$ 6,827	15.5%	34	$ 5,178	19.7%	29
North Dakota	$ 6,952	16.9%	38	$ 5,903	20.1%	30
Rhode Island	$10,243	10.5%	14	$ 8,092	20.3%	31
Mississippi	$ 5,623	11.2%	18	$ 3,628	20.3%	32
Maryland	$ 9,357	13.4%	28	$ 7,593	20.8%	33
Alaska	$ 8,003	23.3%	50	$ 6,333	20.9%	34
Georgia	$ 8,295	15.0%	33	$ 6,179	21.4%	35
Kansas	$ 7,731	11.4%	20	$ 6,256	21.6%	36
Idaho	$ 6,007	18.8%	45	$ 4,933	22.3%	37
Connecticut	$11,735	15.9%	36	$ 9,953	22.4%	38
New Jersey	$13,856	20.0%	49	$10,975	23.5%	39
Missouri	$ 7,620	18.3%	44	$ 5,997	23.9%	40
Alabama	$ 6,370	13.6%	29	$ 4,642	24.9%	41
Virginia	$ 8,263	20.0%	48	$ 6,752	24.9%	42
Ohio	$ 8,868	19.8%	47	$ 7,117	25.3%	43
Vermont	$10,644	17.8%	42	$ 8,015	25.5%	44
Michigan	$ 9,068	14.9%	32	$ 7,439	26.5%	45
Pennsylvania	$ 9,604	17.5%	40	$ 7,860	27.2%	46
Texas	$ 7,369	16.3%	37	$ 5,466	28.1%	47
Arizona	$ 6,932	17.6%	41	$ 4,190	30.4%	48
California	$ 8,364	17.5%	39	$ 5,415	31.9%	49
New York	$12,137	17.9%	43	$ 8,974	35.6%	50
Illinois	$ 9,815	32.7%	51	$ 6,673	39.9%	51

Rev. PP, revenue per pupil.

Source: Data from National Center for Education Statistics/U.S. Census Bureau (2002–2003). *Fiscal Survey of Local Governments (F-33) 2002–2003.*

substantially changes state equity rankings. For example, Minnesota moves from 30th to 6th in ranking for need-adjusted equity when student needs are taken into account; this result suggests that a great deal of the variance that leads to the ranking of 30 is actually "good" variance, or higher levels of funding in districts with greater poverty. In contrast, Kansas drops from 20th to 36th because the state's aid formula fails to accommodate student needs among large districts.

Current Policy Toolkit for Promoting Vertical Equity

In this section, we begin with a discussion of the typical toolkit of policy options used in the pursuit of vertical equity, or individualized adequacy: (a) pupil weights, (b) flat grants, (c) resource-based funding, (d) percentage reimbursement, and (e) discretionary grants (Parrish & Wolman, 1999). These five major categories belie the vast number of permutations that the 50 states actually practice. Accordingly, direct comparisons of states' accommodations for students' special needs can be very difficult. Sometimes, it can be difficult to tell whether supplemental aid is being received for and used toward a specific purpose.

Two basic delineations are helpful: (a) aid supplements for special populations can either be applied as separate categorical aid programs, or as adjustments to general aid, and (b) cost adjustments for student needs may be additive, or multiplicative with other cost adjustments. We will provide more specific discussion of the second point later in this chapter. On the first point, categorical aid programs typically place special revenues into separate funds for restricted use. From an analyst's perspective, this approach can make it easier to determine whether districts are receiving aid for specific purposes. Later in this section, we present several tables of state revenues received by local districts for at-risk and LEP pupils. We do not report data for many states where aid is available, because the aid is included as an adjustment to general aid and is not readily measurable.

Tools in the Toolkit

Now we discuss the pros and cons of each of the five typical policy options that states use to achieve vertical equity:

1. Weighted-pupil formulas
2. Flat-grant and census-based formulas
3. Resource-based formulas
4. Percentage-reimbursement formulas
5. Discretionary grants

Weighted-Pupil Formulas

Under a weighted funding system, state supplemental aid is allocated on a per-student basis where the amount of aid is based on the funding weight associated with each student. For example, a gifted child might be weighted 1.12 (Texas), such that a district receives 12% additional aid (12% × base aid allocation per pupil) per each gifted child identified, or an LEP child might be weighted at 20% (1.20). In general, states tend to either use weighted-pupil formulas as the basis for adjustments for several student populations or not at all. The exception is that a state may choose to use a weighted-pupil system for programs for at-risk, bilingual, and/or gifted students, but the state may have a separate formula of a different type for children with disabilities. This is largely a result of recent court litigation on the use of weighted-pupil formulas for programs for children with disabilities.

Table 8.7 presents a weighted-pupil system that includes weights for at-risk and for LEP pupils. The weighted-pupil model is applied to large school districts in Cook County, IL. Currently, Illinois does not use such a system, instead relying heavily on local property tax decisions. The weight for at-risk pupils—measured by qualifying for subsidized lunch—is 1.09 above basic cost. This weight is based on the recent work of William Duncombe and John Yinger (2005). This weight implies that the cost of educating at-risk pupils is 2.09 times the foundation level, which in this case is $6,106 (the minimum estimated cost for Cook County school districts based on a 2004–2005 analysis). The weight for LEP pupils is 103%, implying that the costs for an LEP child are 2.03 times average costs. To calculate aid associated with weighted pupils, states often use formulas that begin by calculating total weighted-pupil counts. For example, in Table 8.7, the City of Chicago has over 400,000 actual pupils, 85% of whom qualify for free or reduced-price lunch. However, only 14% are LEP. To estimate the weighted-pupil count for Chicago, we multiply 1.09 times the 85% of 415,000 and 1.03 times the 14% of 415,000, and add that to the 415,000, generating a weighted-pupil count approximately double the actual pupil count. Funding is allocated per weighted pupil, leading

Table 8.7 Weighted-Pupil Formulas

District Name	Enrollment	% LEP/ELL	% Poverty	Current Expenditures per Pupil 2005	Base Aid per Pupil	Poverty Weight	LEP Weight	Weighted Pupils	Budget	Budget per Pupil
Maywood-Melrose Park-Broadview 89	5,840	11.8	74.8	$ 7,451	$6,106	1.09	1.03	11,310	$69,060,655	$11,826.47
City of Chicago School Dist. 299	415,598	14.0	85.4	$ 9,758	$6,106	1.09	1.03	862,391	$5,265,758,139	$12,670.32
Thornton Twp H S Dist. 205	6,554	1.0	40.7	$11,277	$6,106	1.09	1.03	9,529	58,184,423	$ 8,877.70
Cicero School District 99	13,552	44.2	78.7	$ 7,420	$6,106	1.09	1.03	31,346	191,397,694	$14,123.73
J S Morton H S District 201	7,566	7.7	47.9	$ 9,912	$6,106	1.09	1.03	12,116	73,982,395	$ 9,778.27
Community High School Dist. 218	5,134	8.7	35.0	$12,247	$6,106	1.09	1.03	7,553	46,116,656	$ 8,982.60
Cons. High School District 230	8,348	1.5	5.5	$11,047	$6,106	1.09	1.03	8,977	54,816,244	$ 6,566.39
Palatine C C School Dist. 15	12,740	13.7	23.5	$ 9,662	$6,106	1.09	1.03	17,800	108,689,204	$ 8,531.67
Evanston C C School Dist. 65	6,504	7.5	39.3	$12,983	$6,106	1.09	1.03	9,793	59,793,325	$ 9,193.32
Wheeling C C School Dist. 21	7,070	30.2	28.9	$11,026	$6,106	1.09	1.03	11,496	70,196,499	$ 9,928.78
Orland School District 135	5,912	2.1	8.2	$ 9,766	$6,106	1.09	1.03	6,568	40,102,594	$ 6,783.83
Township H S Dist. 211	12,956	3.7	12.5	$12,809	$6,106	1.09	1.03	15,215	92,902,840	$ 7,170.64
Comm. Cons. Sch. Dist. 59	6,312	18.1	28.9	$10,993	$6,106	1.09	1.03	9,477	57,867,107	$ 9,167.79
Schaumburg C C School Dist. 54	14,914	8.4	8.7	$10,729	$6,106	1.09	1.03	17,618	107,575,894	$ 7,213.32
Maine Township H S Dist. 207	6,920	5.2	15.2	$14,270	$6,106	1.09	1.03	8,437	51,513,459	$ 7,444.68
Township High School Dist. 214	11,923	6.6	11.3	$14,167	$6,106	1.09	1.03	14,202	86,717,909	$ 7,273.16

Note: Hypothetical formulation based on data on Illinois school districts.
ELL, English language learner; LEP, limited English proficient.
Source: Data from Illinois Department of Education. Data provided to author by staff from the *Chicago Reporter.*

to a per-pupil allocation for Chicago of $12,670. This implies that costs per pupil in the City of Chicago are approximately double the minimum costs per pupil.

We might expect some overlap between children in poverty and children with LEP. In this approach, however, we have no well-defined way to estimate how one might alter the weights when a combination of needs occurs. As it turns out, this weighted-pupil cost estimate for the City of Chicago is slightly lower than the cost estimate produced by cost–function analysis ($13,417) using the same year of data, set to an outcome composite score of 55% proficiency.

Advantages of Weighted-Pupil Formulas

One perceived advantage of weighted aid is that pupil weights may accommodate cost differences across districts by the student needs of those districts. For example, in Table 8.7, Cicero, a district where nearly 80% of students qualify for free or reduced lunch and 44% are LEP, ends up with a foundation level per pupil of $14,123, more than double the base of $6,106. Meanwhile, Orland, a district with less than 10% students in poverty and 2% LEP students, ends up with a foundation level per pupil of only $6,783.

Another perceived advantage of pupil weights is that analysts may allocate them as enhancements to district general funds rather than as categorical funds. As in the example in Table 8.7, analysts may integrate pupil weights with the calculation of "adjusted foundation" levels or customized foundation levels for each district in a state based on the individual needs of students in that district. The legislature may choose to restrict the use of weighted funds that enhance a district's foundation level, requiring those funds to be transferred to special accounts and expended on only the intended services, or the legislature may choose to allow local districts flexibility in providing special services to all children with their enhanced general funds. Where funds remain flexible and integrated with general funds, the compliance burden associated with fund accountability is reduced. Often, weighted aid for special education remains treated as categorical, while other weights are treated as general fund enhancements intended to accommodate district-level special needs.

Using weights in the calculation of adjusted foundation levels has the added benefit of equalizing, or cost sharing the supplemental funds within the equalization or cost-sharing formula for general funds. For example, in the case of a low-wealth district with high numbers of weighted pupils, the resulting higher-adjusted foundation level requires the state to share a larger percentage of a larger value. In the case of a wealthy district with a high weighted-pupil count, the wealthy district would pay a larger share of the higher-adjusted foundation level. Thus, pupil-weighted aid results in a higher rate of equalization than strict categorical grants to students independent of district wealth. In sum, pupil-weighted aid is more equalizing when it is included into the foundation formula than when it is not included.

As we will discuss later, in two-tiered formulas (where weights are applied on the first tier, and local districts raise additional revenue in the second tier), weights are only partially equalized. That is, districts have varied ability to supplement their weighted aid (and the programs for which that aid is intended).

Finally, a political advantage of pupil weights for school district officials and special population advocates, but not necessarily for legislators, is that when base aid allocations increase, weighted aid necessarily increases, unless the legislature consciously chooses to decrease the weight.

Disadvantages of Weighted-Pupil Formulas

Recent literature in special education finance finds potential problems with pupil-weighting systems that differentiate funding on the basis of specific disabilities or placement (Parrish, 2000, 2001). In particular, some states provide higher weights for students identified with more severe disabilities and for students receiving services in more restrictive placements. These higher weights have a rational connection to the cost differences associated with meeting the needs of students with more severe and multiple disabilities, and with the higher costs of providing services in some settings. However, allocating weights in this manner in policy provides district officials with a number of perverse incentives. One perverse incentive is that district administrators may increase their revenue by identifying more students with disabilities in general, and by identifying more students with more severe disabilities in particular (Cullen, 2003). Second, contrary to current trends toward inclusion of students with disabilities in regular education programs, and contrary to the mandate of IDEA that districts provide students with special accommodations in the least restrictive environment (LRE), differential weights based on placements may actually encourage districts to place students with disabilities in more restrictive placements since these placements receive a higher subsidy.

Niskanen (1968) describes the tendency of public officials to exhibit "budget-maximizing" behaviors. Niskanen argues that public officials cannot be driven by the same motives that guide the behavior of business leaders in market-based systems, such as profit seeking through competitive price setting and cost minimization, leading to greater productive efficiency. Rather, public officials can seek only to maximize their domain and to increase their own power base by increasing total revenue flow of their organization and hiring more personnel.

Other critics of pupil-weighting systems argue that pupil-weighting systems are poor at containing costs over time. These critics point to the concurrent dominance of pupil-weighting systems and rapid growth in numbers of pupils identified with disabilities during the decade following implementation of P.L. 94–142, now IDEA. This argument is also consistent with Niskanen's (1968) theories of budget maximization. A different limitation of pupil weights is that smaller districts may have too few students to generate useful levels of aid for providing services in-house, and cooperative options may not be available (Baker, 2001b, 2001d). For example, Texas uses a pupil weight of 12% per pupil for gifted education. A district with 500 pupils reporting the maximum allowable 5%, or 25 pupils, as gifted would have received a grand total of $7,161 (12% × $2,387 × 25) to provide gifted education services at the 1998 Texas foundation level. While a district four times that size might be able to purchase a single, entry-level gifted education specialist, the district of 500 pupils faces the prospect of either supplementing the $7,161 with general funds to purchase a specialist; purchasing a portion of an existing teacher's time, who may not have special qualifications for serving gifted children; or purchasing materials, supplies, or equipment without the guidance of a specialist or an organized program or model in which to use those resources. Furthermore, these 25 students may be widely dispersed throughout the district and come from any of 13 grade levels, making the prospects of using such limited funding unlikely.

Finally, when policy makers add supplemental funds to general funds for "flexible" use, those supplemental funds may or may not end up benefiting the intended recipients (e.g., no guarantee exists that funds brought in through pupil weights will actually be spent on gifted programs, unless specified in state accounting requirements). This is one area where states might be more advantaged by developing Web-based curricula for small numbers of students in dispersed settings with widely diverse "gifts" or "needs" and/or encouraging the use of vouchers for the purchase of such services privately, as Baker and Richards have suggested (1998).

Policy Levers and Critical Output of Weighted-Pupil Formulas

Once a legislature has opted for a pupil-weighting system, the primary policy lever is the level of weight to be applied to each special population. Such weights should be driven by empirical research on the marginal costs of providing special services; actual weights, however, are far more often driven by a combination of political preferences and budget constraints. The weight can be only as high as the state budget will bear, and it is in the interest of legislators to lobby for increases to the weight that brings the most revenue back to the school districts of their constituents.

Where a school-funding formula includes many weights, the political gaming around weights can become overwhelming, detracting entirely from discussions of what to do about general funding levels. Legislators often avoid legislation that increases base-funding levels because it benefits all districts similarly (though unevenly as a result of weighted-pupil distributions). Policies that benefit all students can achieve majority support only in the presence of a benevolent majority. More often, legislators seek opportunities for consensus building around adjustments to funding formulas that have the greatest positive influence on the constituents of the sponsoring coalition. Pupil-weighting systems provide ideal opportunities for such gaming behaviors.

Furthermore, interchanging weighted pupils for actual pupils in both conversation and analyses may conceal political motives and the adverse effects of politically derived decisions. Politically motivated weights or adjustments to weights may erode horizontal equity but not promote any legitimate vertical equity objective. In some states, as many as 25% to 30% of the base enrollment is added to district enrollments through pupil weights for funding purposes, large portions of which may be politically motivated. When equity analyses are performed on a per-weighted-pupil basis, as recommended by Berne and Stiefel (1984) (see Chapter 5), such disparities remain concealed.

Other levers on pupil-weighting systems include the basis on which the weights are allocated and whether limits are to be applied to the number of students to which the weight can be applied, or number of years that a weight can be applied to a particular student. Regarding the allocation basis, some states apply weights to full-time equivalent (FTE) students, perhaps based on contact hours in the relevant program. For example, if five LEP students each spend 20% of their day in bilingual education programs, they are counted as 1.0 FTE for bilingual education. The resultant funding using this allocation basis differs substantially from funding results obtained if we count the LEP students as 5.0 FTE. Nonetheless, their limited-English capacity is an obstacle to learning for the entire day.

For bilingual programs for LEP pupils, states sometimes limit the number of years for which student qualifies to 2 years, on the assumption that language deficiencies for any individual child should be remediated within that time. Pupil weights for gifted education programs are often limited to either 3% or 5% of a district's population. The goal of such limits is both (a) to constrain state spending on bilingual or gifted programs by limiting revenue-maximizing behaviors of local district officials and (b) to make state revenues for bilingual or gifted education more predictable. Such limits are less politically palatable for students with disabilities, because disabilities typically cannot be eliminated in a specific time frame, and parents of students with disabilities can successfully challenge district officials' failure to identify and respond to their children's special educational needs. Some states, however, have accomplished the mathematical equivalent of identification limits for students with disabilities by alternative, more politically palatable means.

The primary critical output that analysts must measure is the extent to which districts across a state receive adequate supplemental revenue to provide the special services needed by students in each district. Assuming that pupil weights applied in policy represent marginal costs, and that those costs are consistent across districts (a wishful assumption), pupil-weighting programs should fare well on this output measure. Other influences on this critical output include the disparity of general education resources that districts can use to supplement special education resources toward meeting district-level costs. Other important critical output includes (a) cost containment, or a budget constraint, and (b) the effectiveness of local district behavioral responses to the children in need. Pupil-weighting programs fare poorly on these output measures.

Flat-Grant and Census-Based Formulas

Flat-grant funding is based on a fixed funding amount per student and may be allocated either per identified special need student, or per total student population, assuming fixed portions of special needs students across districts. In the latter case, flat-grant funding is referred to as census-based funding. In the former case, allocation per special need student, flat grants are mathematically similar to pupil weights. For example, referring to the weighted-pupil formula in Table 8.7, we could say that at-risk pupils are allocated a weight of .25, or a flat grant per at-risk pupil of $1,000 (.25 × $4,000).

In a census-based funding system, we might assume that 15% of students in all districts are expected to have disabilities. We might further assume that the average cost of meeting the needs of those students is $4,000 over the foundation level (excess costs), or the equivalent of 2.0 × $4,000 = $8,000 per special education pupil. We could say that the flat grant, or census-based formula, allocates $4,000 supplemental dollars per special education student, assuming a fixed special education proportion of 15%, or we could say that the census-based formula provides a block grant equal to $600 per pupil, total enrollment ($4,000 × .15 = $600). Note that a pupil-weight with a cap, or fixed portion of students that qualify for the weight, is mathematically equivalent to the census-based block grant.

Advantages of Flat-Grant and Census-Based Formulas

Because need-based flat grants are the mathematical equivalent of pupil weights, we direct our attention here to census-based block grants, which have gained popularity in recent years as a politically palatable method for containing costs of programs for students with disabilities. The primary advantage of allocating flat-grant funds on the basis of district total enrollment and assumed fixed proportions of pupils in need is the removal of the connection between identification rates, service levels, and funding received. These flat-grant funds do not provide an incentive to provide more costly services for more students, because more funding cannot be obtained by doing so. Any local choice to provide more costly services or to identify more students as having disabilities can result only in encroachment on district general funds.

Another advantage occurs by allocating census-based grants with fewer accounting requirements regarding segregation of funds and respective services. As with pupil weights, policy makers may integrate block-grant funds with district general funds in order to allow local district officials the opportunity to determine how to combine and use all funds for optimal service provision for regular and special education students. One might argue that this approach not only reduces incentives to "over-identify" but also promotes inclusion of special education students in regular classrooms and allows districts to use special education personnel in ways that benefit all children. As we will discuss later in this chapter, the balance between cost-containment objectives and promoting preferred practices at the local level is a delicate one that has been achieved with varied degrees of success in states attempting census-based funding reforms.

Disadvantages of Flat-Grant and Census-Based Formulas

Perhaps the most significant disadvantage of census-based funding approaches is that they fail to accommodate the costs associated with differences in student needs across districts. For example, the $600 per-pupil allocation discussed previously is based first on an assumption that all districts have approximately 15% students with disabilities. Further, the $600 is based on the assumption that the average cost of meeting the needs of that 15% is comparable across districts, or that the number of students with both severe, low-frequency, high-cost disabilities and the number of students with non-severe, high-frequency, low-cost disabilities is similar across districts. In reality, such uniformity of need is unlikely. As a result, policy makers in states using census-based funding formulas have included safety valves, or severity adjustments, as well as separate funding programs to accommodate catastrophic costs. Later in this chapter, we discuss recent research on such severity adjustments and the case of Vermont's three-tiered policy. Other disadvantages of flat grants are relatively minor by comparison. First, unlike pupil weights, a legislature can neglect to increase the level of a flat grant on an annual basis, even in years when other aid is increased. This, of course, is to the disadvantage of advocates but to the potential advantage of legislators. Also, when flat grants are allocated per special need pupil, like pupil weights, they are subject to the same critical-mass shortcomings as pupil weights.

Policy Levers and Critical Output in Flat-Grant and Census-Based Formulas

Like pupil weights, the primary policy lever in flat-grant formulas is the level of the grant itself. Secondary is whether that grant is to be allocated on a census basis or on a need basis. Limits may also be applied where politically palatable, as in the case of years of participation for LEP pupils, or identification caps for gifted pupils. Where limits are applied to a need-based flat grant, the grant becomes the equivalent of a census-based grant.

Again the critical output is whether the funding system provides each district with an equitable and adequate opportunity to meet its cost needs, specifically the costs of serving the special population that are over and above the district's general education resource levels per pupil. As previously mentioned, these costs are sometimes referred to as "excess costs." Implemented without adjustments, census-based flat grants can fare quite poorly on this measure. When it comes to (a) cost containment and (b) local behavioral responses, census-based grants fare much better, though some argue that inadequate census-based grants encourage local administrators to "under serve" children with special needs in an effort to avoid increased encroachment on general education funds.

Resource-Based Formulas

Resource-based funding relies on an allocation of specific education resources, usually teaching staff, but sometimes classroom units. For example, in both Kansas and Missouri (under the current formula being phased out), the states pay a fixed portion of each FTE special education teacher's salary, with local districts making up the difference. In several other states, the state pays a fixed portion of operating each classroom that is used for special education students, including both personnel and non-personnel costs. Again, local districts are left to pay the remaining share.

Some states share the cost of resources with local districts based on measures of local district fiscal capacity. For example, Virginia shares the cost of purchasing one gifted education specialist per 1,000 pupils, where the cost-sharing ratio is based on the state's fiscal capacity index for allocating general fund equalization aid.

Advantages of Resource-Based Formulas

Like pupil-weighting systems, resource-based systems generally accommodate differences in programming needs across districts. Policy makers may allocate more resources where needed to serve more special needs students, or where students require more significant curricular intervention. Depending on resource allocation, resource-based funding may allow sufficient flexibility in the use of personnel for providing services to students with special needs in the regular classroom, providing opportunity for incidental benefit to other students who are not classified. Under these circumstances, resource-based funding should neither stimulate over-identification nor cause excessively restrictive placements. For example, in gifted education, personnel partially purchased with state funds might either coordinate school-wide enrichment activities or operate a self-contained classroom.

Disadvantages of Resource-Based Formulas

One disadvantage of the resource-based approach is that aid allocated only for personnel reimbursement ignores additional resource costs—especially facilities costs in districts where space is both scarce and costly. Allocating aid per classroom unit partially resolves this issue but may limit the flexibility of resource use by promoting programs that operate in self-contained classrooms and segregation of funds for accounting purposes. A related issue is that resource-based programs may be tied to more cumbersome compliance burdens regarding the management of and accounting for resources intended for special populations. Baker (2003) finds some evidence that districts in states using resource-based funding for special education tend to spend slightly more on administration than districts in states using other approaches, though the significance of this effect remains questionable.

Finally, resource-based funding systems that tie funding levels to the levels of resources provided may also promote revenue-maximizing behavior among district officials. That is, district officials may identify more students in need of services, or students in need of more intensive services, in order to receive more teaching-unit allocation and thus the funding to partially pay for those teaching units.

Policy Levers and Critical Output in Resource-Based Formulas

The policy levers on a resource-based funding system differ from either a pupil weight or flat-grant system, but the critical output remains the same. The primary policy levers follow:

1. The level at which the state will share in the cost of the resource

2. The numbers and types of resources that districts can purchase with state funds for serving a given number of students with a defined set of special needs

3. The strictness of the accountability system over spending

Secondary in importance is how the state and local districts will share in the cost of the resources. Will the state pay a flat portion across all districts, or will the state cost share on a wealth-equalized, sliding scale basis?

Depending on the breadth of resources that the formula covers, resource-based formulas may fare quite well on measures of whether local districts have adequate resources to meet their students' needs. As previously mentioned, resource-based models raise some concerns regarding cost containment because they can, under some circumstances, promote budget-maximizing behavior.

Percentage-Reimbursement Formulas

Under a percentage-reimbursement system, the amount of state supplemental aid a district receives is based on its prior-year expenditures for the program. States generally reimburse only the percentage of expenses the state can afford in a given year, and states generally set guidelines as to which expenses are reimbursable or which are considered allowable costs. As with resource-based formulas, the state may choose to reimburse a fixed percentage across all districts or may use a sliding scale based on district fiscal capacity. For example, in the 1990s, Connecticut reimbursed districts' actual expenditures on special education programs based on a sliding scale, from 30% to 70%, based on a combination of local property wealth and income (Baker, 1995).

Advantages of Percentage-Reimbursement Formulas

The greatest advantage of percentage-reimbursement programs is that they precisely accommodate significant cost differences across districts resulting from either the varied levels of services that districts provide, to differences in the prices of resources required for providing those services. Where supplemental funding successfully meets district-level needs, one result should be decreased encroachment on general funds. Recent research by Baker (2003) indicates that districts in states using percentage reimbursement programs for special education generally have more funding available to use on their core instructional programs. That is, special education is less of a drain on general education funds in states that use percentage reimbursement (Baker, 2003).

Disadvantages of Percentage-Reimbursement Formulas

Depending on the scope of "allowable costs" and the relationship between levels of service provided and levels of reimbursement received, percentage reimbursement programs may fare quite poorly on cost containment. One of the most significant disadvantages associated with percentage reimbursement programs is the compliance burden that typically accompanies the management and accounting of funds spent on special services, for allowable costs. The necessity for segregation of funds for accounting purposes can also have the unintended consequence of promoting segregation of services, reducing incidental benefit, and promoting restrictive placements.

Policy Levers and Critical Output in Percentage-Reimbursement Formulas

Like resource-based models, the primary policy levers on percentage reimbursement models are the average rate the state will pay toward reimbursement and the scope of reimbursable expenses. Again, secondary, but not less important, is whether the state will pay a fixed portion, or use a wealth-equalized sliding scale.

Percentage reimbursement programs may best meet actual district needs, presuming local district administrators are allocating resources with the primary intent of meeting their students' special needs. Like resource-based programs, however, percentage reimbursement programs that allow districts to increase identification rates and service levels in order to maximize revenues may fare poorly on cost-containment measures.

Discretionary Grants

Discretionary grants from states to local districts are a fifth source of funding for categorical programs. Some states use discretionary grants to fund programs such as gifted education. Discretionary grants are grants rewarded on an application basis and are sometimes competitively accepted. Discretionary grants are usually available above and beyond a basic set of resources, for purposes of creating and evaluating innovative programs. Discretionary grants are rarely used and generally are considered unacceptable as the principal means of funding programs for students with special needs.

Integration of Supplemental Aid with General Funds

For decades, little attention has been paid to the integration of general education funding formulas and supplemental aid formulas. Often, state-level reform of general and special education funding occurs at different times, under different circumstances, and with little consideration for integration of the two. For example, Vermont has been applauded for its special education finance reform (called Act 230), implemented in 1990. Act 230 created a state/local cost-shared census-based funding system for special education and was implemented simultaneously to service-delivery reforms intended to promote greater inclusion of students with disabilities. From 1990 through 1998, however, Vermont had dramatic wealth-related disparities in general education funds, which resulted in the Vermont Supreme Court overturning the state's foundation formula as unconstitutional in 1997. In 1996, general fund revenues per pupil ranged from $3,417 in Victory to $11,298 in Winhall. It is difficult to conceive how a census-based block grant could afford districts with such disparate general revenues, comparable ability to provide special education services. In 1998, Vermont began to phase in its general education finance reform known as Act 60 (Baker, 2001a). In 1997, the Ohio Supreme Court recognized the equity implications of providing un-equalized supplemental funds for special populations in conjunction with under-equalized and/or questionably adequate general funds, noting, "Funds for handicapped students, for instance, whose education costs are substantially higher are disbursed in a flat amount per unit. If the actual cost exceeds the funds received, wealthier districts are in a better position to make up the difference (Parrish & Wolman, 1999, p. 248). The Ohio court's finding points out that supplemental state aid allocations determined absent consideration for the general aid formula can result in illogical or undesirable outcomes. In an analysis of ever-expanding categorical funding programs in California, Murphy and Picus (1996) note:

> . . . encroachment in California varies in terms of both expenditures per pupil and in terms of the percentage of the general fund that the encroachment represents. As a result, this system could result in a loss of equity, potentially damaging the state's claim that it has achieved the level of equity demanded in the *Serrano* lawsuit. (p. 386)

Figure 8.5 Differential Effects of Flat Aid on Poor and Wealthy Districts

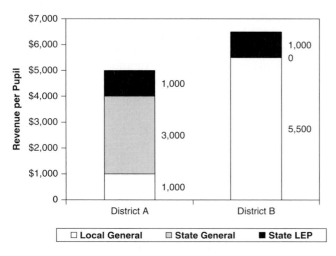

LEP, Limited English Proficient.

Figure 8.5 presents a simplified illustration of this problem, where district A is a poor local district, relying heavily on state general fund aid, and district B is a much wealthier local district receiving no state aid for its general fund. District A can raise only $1,000 per pupil from local property taxes and receives $3,000 per pupil in general fund aid from the state, for a general fund of $4,000 per pupil. District B, on the other hand, raises $5,500 per pupil from local sources alone. Assume each district has an LEP student and that the state allocates $1,000 in supplemental aid per LEP student to supplement its general program. District A now has $5,000 to provide both general and supplemental services for its LEP student, while district B has $6,500. If the $5,500 in district A is insufficient, the district likely will choose to either not serve or under serve the child in question or will be forced to draw on general funds, which in theory, are allocated to other pupils in that district. Now consider which district, A or B, is more likely to be impacted by LEP pupils. Assuming socioeconomic correlates hold, and district B serves many more needy pupils, for each LEP pupil where the combination of local resources and supplemental aid is insufficient, an additional burden is placed on the district's already lagging general fund.

Finally, if supplemental funds provided via pupil weights are to be adequate, we must give simultaneous consideration to the adequacy of both the base figure by which the weight will be multiplied and the weight itself. For example, the empirical literature, or even standard practices, may dictate that the average marginal cost of

educating a child with a learning disability is 1.90, or 90% above the average cost of educating the average child. We cannot simply take the 90% weight and apply it to a state's foundation level, for example, Texas 2004 Tier-I foundation level of $2,537, because $2,537 is not representative of the average cost of educating the regular education student in Texas but, rather, is an arbitrary base funding figure derived from legislative budget constraints. The average instructional expenditures per pupil alone for that year were closer to $5,000 per pupil. We therefore assume the instructional costs for the child with learning disabilities to be approximately $1.9 \times 5,000$, or $9,500 per pupil, an equivalent weight of 3.75 with respect to the $2,537 base figure.

Survey of Existing Policies

Finance Policies for Students With Disabilities

The appendix to this chapter presents a detailed summary of state special education finance policies from 1994–1995 as reported in Parrish and Wolman (1999), *Trends and Developments in Special Education Funding: What the States Report.* At the time, 18 states used pupil-weighting systems for funding special education programs. Of those 18 states, 7 states used pupil weights tied to a student's disabling condition, 6 states used weights tied to placements, 1 state used weights tied to services received, 3 states used weights tied to total special education enrollment, and 1 state used weights tied to both placement and condition.

Among the remaining states, 10 used flat-grant funding. This excludes California, which more recently made the change to a census-based funding formula. Of those 10 states, 5 (Massachusetts, Montana, North Dakota, Pennsylvania, and Vermont) allocated special education funds on a census basis (total district enrollment). One state allocated flat grants based on services received, 3 states allocated flat grants based on special education enrollments, and 1 state allocated flat grants based on type of placement.

Another 10 states used resource-based funding programs in 1994–1995. Three of those states allocated funds specifically for the purchase of special education personnel. Six states allocated funds on the basis of classroom units (this includes California, which has since changed its formula), and 1 state allocated resources on the basis of "allowable costs," a method more common under percentage-reimbursement programs.

Table 8.8 Summary Analysis of Special Education Formulas

	Number of States	Expenditure 1993–1994	State Share 1993–1994	Percent Expenditure 1987–1988	Percent Enrollment 1987–1988
Flat grant	10	$5,176	1.86	10.64	11.18
Pupil weight	18	$4,838	8.20	11.28	10.56
Percentage reimbursement	12	$5,903	4.14	11.69	10.67
Resource based	10	$5,792	3.60	12.64	10.68

Adapted from Parrish and Wolman (1999).

Finally, 12 states used percentage-reimbursement programs in 1994–1995. Only 1 of those states (Hawaii) based reimbursement rates on placements and conditions. Of the remaining 11 states, 6 based reimbursements on actual prior-year expenditures and 5 based reimbursements on a set of allowable costs.

Parrish and Wolman (1999) also report special education expenditure data across the states, which are included in Table 8.8. Those authors reported average expenditures per special education student and revenue shares for 1993–1994 for select states (Parrish & Wolman, 1999, p. 216) and percentages of K–12 expenditures allocated to special education and percentages of students served in special education programs for all states for 1987–1988 (Parrish & Wolman, 1999, p. 218).

Table 8.8 provides a summary analysis of expenditures by formula type. While not definitive by any means, this analysis appears to show that states using percentage-reimbursement and resource-based programs spend somewhat more per special education pupil than states using pupil weights. Interestingly, states using flat grants in 1993–1994 had slightly elevated student identification rates in 1987–1988, perhaps serving as the impetus for census–based reforms in the early 1990s. Note, however, that this is a cursory and exploratory use of these data. Further analysis using appropriately collected data is required before conclusions are appropriate.

Finance Policies for At-Risk, Limited-English-Proficient, and Gifted Children

In this section we discuss funding programs for at-risk, LEP, and gifted children, which use the same basic mechanisms as funding programs for children with disabilities. The appendices of this chapter include tables that summarize state aid programs for at-risk, LEP,

and gifted and talented students for school year 1998–1999. Each table contains the type of formula used and the allocation basis for funding as reported in Seilke et al. (2001) *Public School Finance Programs of the United States and Canada.*

In addition to policy descriptors from Seilke et al., the tables include estimates of state revenues per total student enrollment, per expected need student, and per expected need student as a percentage of core instructional expenditures per pupil. This last estimate is intended to measure state aid in terms of its implicit marginal cost of educating the special need student. Based on actual state aid allocations, this figure estimates the average percentage above core instructional expenditures that the state allocates for serving children in the special population. These figures are from Baker's (2001c) research entitled *Living on the Edges of School Finance Policies: The Plight of At-Risk, Limited English Proficient and Gifted Children* and are based on local district revenues received from their respective states in school year 1995–1996, as reported in the NCES *Common Core of Data* (Baker, 2001b). Reports by Baker and McIntire (2003) and Baker and Friedman-Nimz (2003) provide more recent data for gifted education programs.

For at-risk and LEP students, Baker (2001c) estimated expected need using U.S. Census Bureau data aligned with district boundaries provided by NCES in the *Common Core of Data.* Census measures included numbers of children enrolled in districts that are considered at-risk, on the basis of poverty measures and on the numbers of children who speak English "Not Well," used for estimated LEP student populations (Parrish & Hikido, 1998, used similar methods). Similar options were not available for estimating numbers of gifted and talented children, unless one chooses to assume that if low income must predict remedial need, then high income predicts giftedness. As a result,

Baker assumed a uniform distribution of 5% gifted regardless of socioeconomic strata for estimating gifted education aid per need pupil.

At-Risk Pupils

In 1998–1999, 38 states provided funding specifically designated for compensatory programs for at-risk children and/or to accommodate district-level needs in districts serving large proportions of low-income students. Of those states, the largest share used some form of pupil-weighting system for allocating aid, typically based on numbers of children qualifying for free or reduced price lunch through the National School Lunch Program. A relatively large number of states used flat grants, and in some cases, as discussed previously, it is impossible to discern differences between the two.

In the majority of cases, states intended funding to support remediation through tutors, mentoring, extended-day programs, and summer programs. Out of legitimate concern that funds allocated purely on an income basis might be inefficiently distributed with respect to remedial needs, states are increasingly using performance criteria for identifying students (Baker, Keller-Wolff, & Wolf-Wendel, 2000). For low-performing poor schools that make determined efforts to improve, one of the ironies of using performance criteria becomes the loss of the funding that enabled improvement.

Title I, or Chapter I, of the Elementary and Secondary Education Act of 1965, the nation's largest federal public education program by far, continues to provide some federal funding to supplement state and local efforts to meet the needs of economically disadvantaged children, amounting to approximately $8 billion per year in recent years. In an analysis of school district revenues, Parrish and Hikido (1998) found that 99.2% of districts enrolling expected poverty populations in excess of 25%, or their enrollments received federal Chapter I funding in 1991–1992 at an average rate of $257 ($207 cost and need adjusted) per pupil or $793 ($781 cost and need adjusted) per target pupil. Districts with fewer students in poverty received less funding per enrolled pupil and similar if not slightly higher amounts per target pupil. (Baker, 2001c, replicated Parrish and Hikido's, 1998, p. 31, methods for his research.) Baker and Duncombe (2004) identify a total of 38 states providing some form of financial support to meet the needs of at-risk children. The authors report that 21 states included provisions in general aid programs, and 25 states allocated categorical aid separate from general aid programs. Baker and Duncombe (2004) and Carey (2002) estimate *implicit weights* of the amount of aid that local districts receive from states to accommodate children in poverty (Carey, 2002). *Implicit weights* are measures of aid actually allocated to local districts, whereas *explicit weights* are those specified in state school finance policies. Implicit-weight analysis involves estimating the population in need, most commonly with census data, estimating the aid allocated to that population, and determining the ratio of need-targeted aid to average, or general, education revenues (Baker & Duncombe, 2004, pp. 203–204). Using Carey's weights, 11 states (out of 39) had a poverty weight above 25%. Only two states had weights this high using Baker and Duncombe's estimates. Three of the New England states (Connecticut, New Hampshire, and Massachusetts) had particularly high poverty weights, and all of these states had statutory poverty weights of 25% or higher. We discuss implicit weight analysis further in Chapter 10.

Limited-English-Proficient Pupils

Funding for bilingual education programs and other services for LEP students existed in 29 states in 1998–1999. Baker and Markham (2002) found that many states not providing supplemental funding for LEP children had significant estimated LEP populations and included districts exceeding 25% LEP.

A handful of states reported in Seilke et al. (2001) suggest that programs for LEP children are primarily a federal responsibility, through ESEA Title VII funding. Baker and Markham (2002) indicate that federal aid, for the most part, has provided negligible support to local districts (see Chapter 3).

Parrish and Hikido (1998) find similarly that even among districts with the highest percentages of LEP students in 1991–1992, only 19.8% received federal Title VII funding. They further note that "Because this [Title VII] is a discretionary rather than a formula grant program, these funds do not flow heavily to districts with high concentrations of LEP students" (p. 75).

Of the 29 states providing supplemental funding for LEP students, half used pupil weights. Most remaining states used flat grants, and a handful used other methods. Pupil weights for LEP children vary widely in their magnitude and allocation basis. For example, a pupil weight can be allocated per actual enrolled pupil with language remediation needs or on the basis of remedial contact hours. In that latter case, if six children receive an hour a day each of second-language support, and a full day of services consists of 6 hours, then the 6 hours of service provided may sum to 1.0 FTE children. We then multiply 1.0 FTE by the pupil weight to yield the weighted-pupil funding. This is likely why Kansas, for example, which weights LEP pupils at 20%, allocates less than 1% of core expenditures per estimated LEP pupil. Other states such as Florida and Texas appear to be allocating more funds than their weights would suggest. This is likely because the estimated LEP aid per LEP pupil is based on census bureau data, which may under-represent actual numbers of pupils identified and served in Florida and Texas school districts.

Gifted and Talented Pupils

State definitions of gifted and talented children vary widely (Stephens & Karnes, 2000). As a result, actual prevalence is difficult if not impossible to estimate. While some states specify particular percentiles on standardized achievement tests or cut-off scores on intelligence tests, most allow considerable flexibility to local districts. In 1995, 31 states mandated identification of gifted children, but only 24 (only those states with legislative mandates and not administrative rules or department of education guidelines) mandated services for those children (Baker, 1995).

A relatively large number of states, 42, allocate funding for programs for gifted and talented children, a possible testament to the strength of parent lobbying groups. While funding is allocated, however, much of the funding appears to be negligible, and 8 states provide only discretionary and/or competitive grants to select districts applying for a finite pot of funds. Fourteen states used flat-grant programs, and 8 states used pupil-weighted programs for financing gifted education in 1998–99. Flat grants ranged widely, from $55 per 3% pupils (Arizona), to $320 per 2% pupils (Washington), and pupil weights range widely, from .12 in Texas to .6 in Louisiana. Among these states, several placed identification limits on the funds, ranging from 2%–3% (Arizona, New York, Washington) to 7% (Colorado), making them the equivalent of census-based funding. Actual funding ranged widely as well, from less than 1% above core expenditures to over 20% in South Carolina.

States used resource-based and percentage-reimbursement programs more often for gifted children than for at-risk and LEP children. This is likely because gifted children are included under the umbrella of special education in many states, and resource-based and percentage-reimbursement programs are more commonly used for special education programs.

Baker and Friedman-Nimz (2003) and Baker and McIntire (2003) estimate the aid that local districts receive from states for providing gifted education services, finding aid per target populations (estimated at flat 5%), ranging from only a few dollars to over $600 per pupil (South Carolina) and nearly $2,000 per pupil (Florida). Implicit weights of state aid ranged from less than 1% to over 30% (Baker & Friedman-Nimz, 2003; Baker & McIntire, 2003).

Summary of Funding and Revenues for At-Risk, Limited-English-Proficient, and Gifted Children

Table 8.9 provides a summary of 1998–1999 funding programs local district revenues from state sources for serving at-risk, LEP, and gifted children. On average, states allocated about $670 per at-risk pupil and $212 per enrolled pupil. Of the 29 states that allocated funding for LEP students, the 12 that reported categorical allocations provided somewhat higher levels of funding per expected need pupil, but less funding per total enrolled pupils. This latter finding occurs because the numbers of LEP pupils are relatively few in comparison to low-income pupils. While many more states (42) provided funding for gifted education, most provided less funding per expected need pupil or per enrolled pupil.

Changing the Behavioral Dynamics of Supplemental Aid Programs

Throughout this chapter, we have raised the issue of the revenue-maximizing response of local district officials when state supplemental aid is tied to numbers of children identified and served, resources consumed locally, or differential costs of services and alternative placements. Figure 8.6 depicts a systems diagram of the problem. One might assume that the magnitude of state aid available for gifted or LEP children significantly influences local program participation rates, even where actual prevalence of LEP children is also considered. Increases in local identification rates result in increases both in local program costs (because more children need to be served) and in state aid received.

Table 8.9   Summary of Funding for At-Risk, Limited-English-Proficient, and Gifted Children

	At-Risk	Limited English Proficient	Gifted and Talented
States with funding[a]	38	29	42
In general aid formula	21	12	
Categorical	25	19	
Allocation method in 1998–1999[b]			
Flat grant	8	7	14
Pupil weight	15	12	8
Percentage reimbursement	0	1	5
Resource based	1	3	4
Discretionary or competitive	3	1	9
Other	2		
Average categorical aid per pupil[c]	$212 (23)[d]	$66 (12)	$30 (18)
Average categorical aid per need pupil	$673	$1025	$594

[a] Baker and Duncombe (2004).

[b] U.S. Department of Education, National Center for Education Statistics. *Public School Finance Programs of the United States and Canada: 1998–99*. NCES 2001–309; Compilers Catherine C. Sielke, John Dayton, C. Thomas Holmes, of the University of Georgia and Anne L. Jefferson of the University of Ottawa. William J. Fowler, Jr., Project Officer. Washington, DC.

[c] Calculations by author using data from *U.S. Census Fiscal Survey of Local Governments* (Public Elementary and Secondary School Finance) 2002–03 & *NCES CCD Local Education Agency Universe Survey 2002–03*.

[d] Number of states reporting.

As Figure 8.6 shows, at this point, either of two circumstances may exist, but we suggest that either leads to the same behaviors of local officials. On the one hand, costs can increase at a greater rate than state revenues, leading to declining local general revenues per pupil. Rather than responding to the stress on the general fund budget, evidence suggests that many

local administrators respond somewhat illogically by attempting to generate even more state revenues via increased local identification, despite the increased costs associated with this option. Perhaps they assume that if economies of scale can be achieved, supplemental aid will eventually balance local costs. If on the other hand, state revenues increase at a faster rate than local costs, local officials may also respond by identifying more students to obtain more revenue, and thus increase the volume and flexibility of general funds. In either case, the result is a distribution of services that may only partially reflect the actual needs of students.

The systems diagram in Figure 8.6 can be read as follows. Beginning in the upper left, we present state policy as "available aid per need pupil" with a plus sign, indicating that it adds resources to the system, but depends on "local identification rates," which the state may or may not constrain. From the right upper side of the flow cycle, we also see that "actual local need" is an influencing factor, but that it may constrain the numbers if few actual-need-pupils are in the district or conversely may increase identification rates if the district is higher than average in need-pupils. After determining state aid, the district undertakes a given level of education that results in "local program costs," which in turn tend to have a negative impact on general

Figure 8.6   System Dynamics of Identification and Service-Based Funding

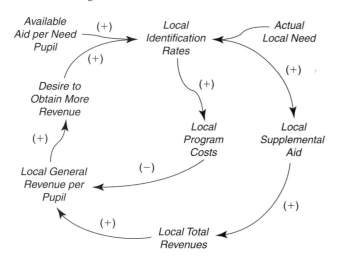

revenues, because states under-fund the programs. On the right side of the system-dynamic model, the district supplements the state aid with local resources, which is partially covered by increases in "local total revenues," generated via tax levy, and partially covered, as we just noted, by general revenues.

These additional local pressures increase the "desire to obtain more revenue" and put pressure on the state to increase its funding for service. The multi-year result of this dynamic usually creates a growing burden on the local district, insufficient funds for general education, and internal political pressures on the system that pit children with special needs against the general needs population. At the state level, it generates growing pressure to cap the system, shift more of the burden to local districts, find other policy approaches that cost less money (e.g., mainstreaming), and it generates internal political pressures on the system that pits special education funding against general education funding.

Now we can better understand that the intent of census-based reforms has been to limit local revenue-maximizing behavior by breaking the linkage between students identified and services provided and revenue received. A major shortcoming of census-based funding that both Vermont and Pennsylvania administrators have identified has been the inability of census-based funding to accommodate differences in student needs across districts. One possible solution is to develop safety valves, or severity adjustments, that help districts with disproportionate populations of special needs students. In doing so, however, policy makers run the risk of re-initiating the feedback cycle in Figure 8.6, as local district officials strive to document their exceptional needs.

Under ideal circumstances, policy makers would know the actual incidence (occurrence) or prevalence (existence) of need for each school or district in the state and would not have to rely on identification rates determined by local officials and influenced by existing policies. While local district identification rates are "endogenous" to the system, actual incidence or prevalence is "exogenous."

Parrish, Kaleba, Gerber, and McLaughlin (1998) present one alternative for estimating differences in the incidence of disabilities across districts (see also, Parrish, Gerber, Kaleba, & Brock, 2000). The alternative approach comes from a study in which the authors analyze the incidence of disabilities across California school districts in an effort to derive an "incentive-less" severity adjustment for the state's relatively new census-based funding formula. The authors use a variety of indirect, exogenous measures in a regression model to predict incidence of severe, high-cost disabilities across districts. They select six indirect measures including poverty, social class, language proficiency, agency size, agency resource capacity, and urbanicity and use those measures to predict local identification rates. Parrish et al. found that the models explained 42% of the variability in severe, high-cost disabilities across districts. One implication of this finding is that it may be reasonable to use models constructed with "exogenous" variables, such as census data on poverty, to predict need across districts and identify cases where exceptional needs and additional funding are needed. The authors note, however, that while their findings suggest that "some set of factors beyond district control (e.g., poverty and/or urbanicity) could serve as the basis for valid and reliable adjustments to state special education funding," their own analysis "does not support the use of such measures as reliable proxies for variation in the incidence of severe and/or high cost students in California" (Parrish et al., 2000, p. 34).

A significant drawback of the statistical proxy approach is that it relies on indirect measures of incidence that may have objectionable implications or may appear related to incidence as a result of objectionable local behaviors. For example, 42 states exhibit a positive relationship between numbers of students identified as having disabilities and numbers of children in poverty.[2] This may occur because more children born into poverty and attending high-poverty districts are indeed more likely to have legitimate disabilities. It may also occur because district officials in more poverty-stricken districts are more likely to identify students as having disabilities for a variety of reasons, including the desire to generate more revenue or the desire to remove "difficult" children from the regular classroom. Despite the potential objectionable policy implications of the poverty measure—that poor children are more likely disabled—a possible equity benefit of the exogenous poverty measure for predicting exceptional needs is that it would more often result in increased special education funding in districts serving higher percentages of children in poverty.

---

[2] Based on analysis performed by Baker (2002–Spring) using 1997 school district poverty data from a special tabulation of the *Common Core of Data* and 1999 special education prevalence rates from the Public Education Agency Universe Survey of the *Common Core*. Complete tabulations of these data are reported in Baker, Skrtic, and Wortman (2002).

Figure 8.7 Actual and Predicted Values

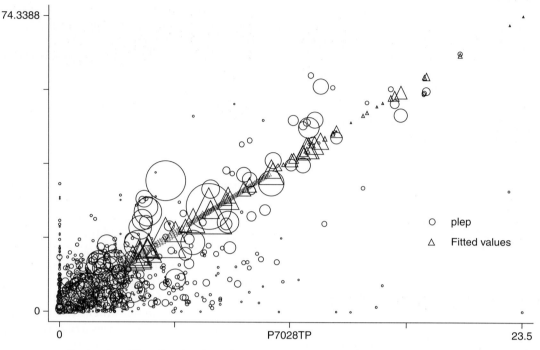

Bubble size represents district size. The triangles show the prevalence rates for each district. plep, percent limited English proficient; P7028TP, percent of children between 5 and 17 who speak English "not well" or "not at all."

Source: Figure created by authors using data on the percentage of population speaking English "not well" or "not at all" from the U.S. Census Bureau and the National Center for Education Statistics (2000) and data on school district rates of Limited-English-Proficiency students from the Texas Education Agency (2000).

Fortunately, we can estimate the prevalence of need for LEP students with more direct measures. Parrish and Hikido (1998), for example, used U.S. Census data on numbers of children residing in school districts who speak English "Not Well" or "Not at All." We can also use exogenous census measures to estimate the extent to which districts are over- or understating need, or to raise questions as to whether certain districts face extenuating circumstances. Figure

8.7 presents a graph of the relationship between the census variable (p7028TP) and district-identified prevalence on the *y* axis, where the circles represent the districts, of varied size (different-size circles). Figure 8.7 also includes the predicted prevalence rates for each district (triangles). One interpretation is that circles that fall above the line of triangles may be over-identifying need, while circles falling below the line of triangles may be under-identifying need.

SUMMARY

Vertical equity is the emerging centerpiece of state school finance formulas and potentially an emerging centerpiece of district-to-school allocation formulas, as we will discuss in greater detail in Chapter 15. Until recently, consensus was relatively strong regarding the "who" questions of vertical equity, but very little consensus or political will existed regarding the amount of

support needed. To some extent, the "how-much" question hinges on whether policy makers should allocate funding toward what might be considered "reasonable interventions" or service-delivery models, or whether a higher standard of moving toward "outcome equity" is required. Arguably, in the modern policy context, where the No Child Left Behind Act of 2001 provides an outcome-orientation framework and where closing gaps is a central concern, improved outcome equity must be the goal for all children. This is indeed a costly proposal, where current state aid formulas typically allocate on the order of 20% to 25% times basic aid for children in poverty, where input-based studies suggest the need for 35% to 50% additional funding (over minimum, basic funding), and where outcome-based studies indicate the need for as much as double the average expenditure per pupil for children from impoverished backgrounds and children with English language deficiencies to achieve desired outcomes.

We also believe that many conceptual difficulties are yet to be resolved regarding vertical equity, some of which intersect in awkward ways with current legal frameworks. In short, equal protection clauses make no guarantee of appropriately unequal treatment. As discussed in Chapter 7, some state courts have interpreted state education clauses as requiring vertical equity, in relation to educational adequacy. While Underwood's conception of vertical equity as educational adequacy is useful, it is overly narrow, assuming that vertical equity can exist only where individual students' needs may be identified and accommodated toward a specific level of outcome. By contrast, we believe that both sociological/collective and individual needs are present, and education finance policy can be leveraged to address both. For example, policy makers can design state school finance packages to address aggressively the erosion of social capital that at times occurs in poor urban centers suffering inter-generational poverty. Further, we believe that vertical equity can exist in a more purely relative sense.

We suggest replacing current notions of vertical equity with the following framework:

1. **(Pure) Equity of inputs (or educational processes):** Consistent with current views on horizontal equity, which may define inputs in dollars per pupil or educational programs and resources of "comparable quality" (which may come at varied input prices). Analysts may evaluate equity of inputs under standard "equal-treatment" frameworks, which consider differential treatment of individuals or groups on bases not related to educational need to be active discrimination.

2. **(Pure) Equity of outcomes:** This is perhaps the most difficult of policy objectives to achieve, either for individual children or groups, in part because pure equity of outcomes requires compressing all educational need-related variance in student outcomes—both the top and bottom. Federal courts have already denied this framing in the context of desegregation litigation (*Missouri v. Jenkins*, 1995). Nonetheless, education is a positional good (as framed by Koski & Reich, 2006): That is, the value of one child's minimally adequate education is necessarily diminished by the value of other children's super-adequate education.

3. **Equity of opportunity to achieve specific level of outcomes:** This is perhaps the most practical of vertical equity objectives and the most consistent with current standards-based accountability systems under the No Child Left Behind Act. Nonetheless, this is a costly proposition in terms of the magnitude of vertical equity adjustments that are necessary to increase the opportunities for children in poor, urban areas to achieve desired educational outcomes at a sufficient rate. This approach differs subtly from pure equity of outcomes in that leveling down is not a requirement. The positional nature of education, however, is neglected. In some state constitutional contexts, courts may consider sufficient educational outcomes to be a property interest of children of the state. In that case, litigants may challenge failure to provide sufficient vertical equity adjustment (e.g., passive discrimination) leading to deprivation of the property interest as a violation of children's due process rights.

Whatever the framework or perspective, in the present policy context, pure equity of educational inputs clearly is no longer a sufficient policy objective, especially because America's children are so disparately sorted across our nation's schools and communities and because such large disparities in educational outcomes and economic opportunities persist.

The appendix to this chapter includes a series of tables that summarize state-aid formula attempts since the mid-1990s to accommodate vertical equity concerns both for children with disabilities and for children we identify as on the *fringes* of state school finance policy. Many of these policies likely have already changed substantially. We expect even more to change, perhaps before this text is published. Vertical equity and need-adjusted school financing are perhaps the most rapidly evolving area in applied school finance policy research and practice. We expect continued emphasis, coupled with significant unrest, on questions of vertical equity for the foreseeable future.

KEY TERMS

additional expenditure Margin of difference in actual spending on a specific student or student population relative to the average student or average population, regardless of outcome attained.

marginal cost Additional costs of achieving constant outcomes with a specific student or student population, relative to the "average" student or average student population.

REFERENCES

Augenblick, J., & Myers, J. (2001). *Calculation of the cost of an adequate education in Maryland 2000–2001 using two different analytic approaches.* Submitted to the Maryland Commission on Education Finance, Equity and Excellence (Thornton Commission).

Augenblick, J., & Myers, J. (2003a). *Calculating the cost of an adequate education in Colorado using the professional judgment and successful school districts approaches.* Submitted to Colorado School Finance Project.

Augenblick, J., & Myers, J. (2003b). *Calculation of the cost of an adequate education in Missouri using the professional judgment and successful school districts approaches.* Submitted to the Missouri Education Coalition for Adequacy.

Augenblick, J., & Myers, J. (2003c). *Calculation of the cost of an adequate education in Montana 2002–2003 using the professional judgment approach.*

Augenblick, J., & Myers, J. (2003d). *Calculation of the cost of an adequate education in Nebraska in 2002-2003 using the professional judgment approach.* Submitted to Nebraska State Education Association, Greater Nebraska Schools Association, Lincoln Public Schools, Nebraska Association of School Boards, Nebraska Coalition for Educational Equity and Adequacy, Nebraska Council of School Administrators, Nebraska Rural Communities Association, Omaha Public Schools, Westside Community Schools.

Augenblick, J., & Myers, J., Silverstein, J., & Barkis, A. (2001). *Calculation of the cost of an adequate education in Kansas in 2000–2001 using two different analytic approaches.* Submitted to the legislative coordinating Council, State of Kansas.

Augenblick, J., Palaich, R., et al. (2003). *Calculation of the cost of an adequate education in North Dakota in 2002–2003 using the professional judgment approach.* Submitted to the North Dakota Department of Public Instruction.

Baker, B. D. (1995). *The economic health of gifted education in three northeastern states. An analysis of public school programs and private opportunities in New York, New Jersey and Connecticut.* ERIC Clearinghouse on Gifted Education. Retrieved from http://eric.ed.gov/ ERIC Docs/data/ericdocs2/content_storage_01/0000000b/ 80/25/71/1a.pdf

Baker, B. D. (2001a). Balancing equity for students and tax-payers: Evaluating school finance reform in Vermont. *Journal of Education Finance, 26*(4), 437–462.

Baker, B. D. (2001b). Gifted children in the current policy and fiscal context of public education: A national snapshot and state level equity analysis of Texas. *Educational Evaluation and Policy Analysis, 23*(3), 229–250.

Baker, B. D. (2001c). Living on the edges of school finance policy: The plight of at risk, limited English proficient and gifted children. *Educational Policy, 15,* 699–723.

Baker, B. D. (2001d). Measuring the outcomes of state policies for gifted education: An equity analysis of Texas school districts. *Gifted Child Quarterly, 45*(1), 4–15.

Baker, B. D. (2003). State policy influences on the internal allocation of school district resources: Evidence from the Common Core of Data. *Journal of Education Finance, 29*(1), 1–24.

Baker, B. D. (2006). Evaluating the reliability, validity and usefulness of education cost studies. *Journal of Education Finance, 32*(2), 170–201.

Baker, B. D., & Duncombe, W. (2004). Balancing district needs and student needs: The role of economies of scale adjustments and pupil need weights in school finance formulas. *Journal of Education Finance, 29,* 195–222.

Baker, B. D., & Friedman-Nimz, R. C. (2003). Gifted children, vertical equity and state school finance policies and practices. *Journal of Education Finance, 28,* 523–556.

Baker, B. D., Keller-Wolff, C., & Wolf-Wendel, L. E. (2000). Two steps forward, one step back: Race/ethnicity and student achievement in education policy research. *Educational Policy, 14,* 511–529.

Baker, B. D., & McIntire, J. (2003). Evaluating state school funding for gifted education programs. *Roeper Review, 26,* 173–179.

Baker, B. D., & Markham, P. (2001). *State school funding policies and limited English proficient students.* Unpublished Manuscript. University of Kansas, Department of Teaching and Leadership.

Baker, B. D., & Markham, P. (2002). State school funding policies and limited English proficient children. *Bilingual Research Journal, 26*(3), 659–680.

Baker, B. D., & Richards, C. E. (1998). Equity through vouchers: The special case of gifted children. *Educational Policy, 12*(4), 363–379.

Baker, B. D., Skrtic, T., & Wortman, J. (2002). *Report to the Kansas Special Education Advisory Council, April 9, 2002.* Retrieved from http://www.kansped.org/ksde/advisory/seac/min02-04.pdf

Berne, R., & Stiefel, L. (1984). *The measurement of equity in school finance: Conceptual, methodological and empirical dimensions.* Baltimore: Johns Hopkins Press.

Bifulco, R. (2005). District-level Black–White funding disparities in the United States 1987 to 2002. *Journal of Education Finance, 31*(2), 172–194.

Carey, K. (2002). *State poverty–based education funding: A survey of current programs and options for improvement.* Washington, DC: Center on Budget and Policy Priorities.

Chambers, J. G. (1999). Patterns of expenditures on students with disabilities: A methodological and empirical analysis. In T. B. Parrish, J. G. Chambers & C. M. Guarino (Eds.), *Funding special education: Nineteenth annual yearbook of the American Education Finance Association* (pp. 89–123). Thousand Oaks, CA: Corwin Press.

Chambers, J., Parrish, T., & Harr, J. (2004). *What are we spending on special education services in the United States?* Center for Special Education Finance. American Institutes for Research. Retrieved from http://www.csef-air.org/publications/seep/national/ AdvRpt1.PDF

Council of State Directors of Programs for the Gifted and Talented. (1996). *1996 State of the States Gifted and Talented Education Report.*

Cullen, J. B. (2003). The impact of fiscal incentives on student disability rates. *Journal of Public Economics, 87*(7–8), 1557.

Downes, T. & Pogue, T. (1994). Adjusting school aid formulas for the higher cost of educating disadvantaged students. *National Tax Journal, XLVII,* 89–110.

Duncombe, W., & Yinger, J. (2005). How much more does a disadvantaged student cost? *Economics of Education Review, 24*(5), 513–532.

Equal Educational Opportunities Act. (Section 1703 of the EEOA of 1974).

Finn, J. D., Gerber, S. B., Achilles, C. M., & Boyd-Zaharias, J. (2001). The enduring effects of small classes. *Teachers College Record, 103,* 145–183.

Garms, W. J., & Smith, M. C. (1970). Educational need and its application to state school finance. *The Journal of Human Resources, 5,* 304–317.

Grismer, D., Flanagan, A., & Williamson, S. (1998). Does money matter for minority and disadvantaged students? Assessing the empirical evidence. In W. Fowler (Ed.),

Developments in school finance, 1997 (pp. 13–30). Washington, DC: U.S. Department of Education.

Guthrie, J., et al. (2001). *A professional judgment approach to determining adequate education funding in Maryland.* Submitted to the New Maryland Education Coalition. Davis, CA: Management Analysis and Planning.

Hanushek, E. A., Kain, J. F., Markman, J. M., & Rivken, S. G. (2003). Does the ability of peers affect student achievement? *Journal of Applied Econometrics* 18, 527–544.

Imazeki, J., & Reschovsky, A. (2004). Is No Child Left Behind an un (or under) funded federal mandate? Evidence from Texas. *National Tax Journal, 57,* 571–588.

Koski, W. S., & Reich, R. (2006). Why "Adequate" isn't: The retreat from equity in educational law and policy and why it matters. *Emory Law Review, 56*(3).

Ladd, H., & Hansen, J. (1999). *Making money matter: Financing America's schools.* Committee on Education Finance, Commission on Behavioral and Social Sciences and Education, National Research Council. Washington, DC: National Academy Press.

Lankford, H., & Wyckoff, J. (1999). The allocation of resources to special education and regular instruction in New York State. In Parrish et al. (Eds.), *Funding Special Education* (pp. 147–175). Thousand Oaks, CA: Corwin.

Moore, M. T., Strang, E. W., Schwartz, M., & Braddock, M. (1988). *Patterns in special education service delivery and cost.* ERIC Document Reproduction Service No. ED 303 027. Washington, DC: Decision Resources.

Murphy, J., & Picus, L. O. (1996). Special program encroachment on school district general funds in California: Implications for Serrano equalization. *Journal of Education Finance, 21*(3) 366–386.

Niskanen, W. A. (1968). Nonmarket decision making: The peculiar economics of bureaucracy. *The American Economic Review, 58*(2), 293–305.

Odden, A. R., & Picus, L. O. (2000). *School finance: A policy perspective.* New York: McGraw-Hill.

Odden, A. R, Picus, L. O., Goetz, M., Fermanich, M., Seder, R., Glenn, W., & Nelli, R. (2005). *An evidence based approach to recalibrating Wyoming's block grant school funding formula.* Wyoming Legislative Select Committee on Recalibration.

Parrish, T. B. (1994). A cost analysis of alternative instructional models for limited English proficient students in California. *Journal of Education Finance, 19,* 256–278.

Parrish, T. B. (1997). *Special education in an era of school reform.* Center for Special Education Finance. American Institutes for Research. Retrieved from http://eric.ed.gov/ERICDocs/data/ericdocs2/content_storage_01/0000000b/80/22/c7/bd.pdf

Parrish, T. (2000). *Disparities in the identification, funding and provision of special education.* Submitted to the Civil

Rights Project for the Conference on Minority Issues in Special Education in Public Schools.

Parrish, T. (2001). Special education finance. In McLaughlin, M. (Ed.), *Special education finance in an era of school reform.* Washington, DC: Federal Resource Center of the Regional Resource and Federal Centers Network.

Parrish, T., Gerber, M., Kaleba, D., & Brock, L. (2000). *Adjusting special education aid for severity: The case of census-based funding in California.* Palo Alto, CA: Center for Special Education Finance, American Institutes for Research.

Parrish, T. B., & Hikido, C. S. (1998). *Inequalities in public school district revenues.* NCES 98–210. Washington, DC: National Center for Education Statistics.

Parrish, T. B., Kaleba, D., Gerber, M., & McLaughlin, M. (1998). *Special education: Study of incidence of disabilities: Final report.* Sacramento: California Department of Education.

Parrish, T. B., Matsumoto, C. S., & Fowler, W. J., Jr. (1995). *Disparities in public school district spending 1989–90: A multivariate, student-weighted analysis, adjusted for differences in geographic cost of living and student need.* NCES 95–300R. Washington, DC: National Center for Education Statistics.

Parrish, T. B., & Wolman, J. (1999). Trends and new developments in special education funding: What the states report. In Parrish, T. B., Chambers, J. G. & Guarino, C. M. (Eds.), *Funding special education: Nineteenth annual yearbook of the American Education Finance Association* (pp. 203–229). Thousand Oaks, CA: Corwin Press.

Reschovsky, A., & Imazeki, J. (1998). The development of school finance formulas to guarantee the provision of adequate education to low-income students. In W. J. Fowler, Jr., (Ed.), *Developments in school finance* (NCES 98–212). Washington, DC: U.S. Department of Education, National Center for Education Statistics.

Reschovsky, A., & Imazeki, J. (2001). Achieving educational adequacy through school finance reform. *Journal of Education Finance, 264,* 373–396.

Rivken, S. G. (2003). Does the ability of peers affect student achievement? *Journal of Applied Econometrics, 18,* 527–544.

Rothstein, R. (2004). *Class and schools: Using social, economic, and educational reform to close the black–white achievement gap.* New York: Teachers College Press.

Seilke, C. C., Dayton, J., Holmes, C. T., Jefferson, A. L., & Fowler, W. J., Jr., et al. (2001). *Public school finance programs of the United States and Canada 1998–99.* NCES 2001–309. Washington, DC: U.S. Department of Education, National Center for Education Statistics.

Stephens, K. R., & Karnes, F. A. (2000). State definitions for the gifted and talented revisited. *Exceptional Children, 66,* 219–238.

Turnbull, H. R., III, Turnbull, A. P., Wehmeyer, M., & Park, J. (2003). A quality of life framework for special education outcomes. *Remedial and Special Education, 24*(2), 67–74.

Underwood, J. K. (1995). School Finance Adequacy as Vertical Equity. *University of Michigan Journal of Law Reform, 28,* 493–519.

U.S. Census Bureau & National Center for Education Statistics. (2000). *School district demographics system, Census 2000 special tabulation.* Retrieved from http://nces.ed.gov/surveys/sdds/

U.S. Census Bureau. (2002–2003). *Fiscal survey of local governments (F–33). 2002–2003.*

Verstegen, D. (2003). *Calculating the cost of an adequate education in Kentucky.* Prepared for the Council for Better Education.

Appendix to Chapter 8: Finance Policy Tables

Table 8a.1 State Special Education Finance Policies 1994–1995

State	Formula Type[a]	Allocation Basis[a]	Special Education Funds for Target Population Only[a]	Mean Aid per Pupil	Percent Support by Source[b]			Percent K–12 Expenditures	Percent K–12 Enrollment
					Fed	State	Local		
Alabama	Pupil weights	Special education enrollment	X					13.1%	13.0%
Alaska	Flat grant	Type of placement						12.5%	9.1%
Arizona	Pupil weights	Disabling condition						9.5%	9.2%
Arkansas	Pupil weights	Type of placement	X					6.6%	10.0%
California	Resource based	Classroom unit	X	$5,580	5%	71%	24%	10.1%	9.0%
Colorado	Flat grant	Special education enrollment	X	$3,409	9%	31%	60%	10.5%	8.5%
Connecticut	Percentage reimbursement	Actual expenditures		$8,501	4%	37%	59%	15.1%	14.8%
Delaware	Resource based	Classroom unit	X					11.7%	11.4%
District of Columbia								8.0%	3.2%
Florida	Pupil weights	Disabling condition		$5,059	6%	56%	38%	12.8%	11.2%
Georgia	Pupil weights	Disabling condition	90%					12.0%	8.1%
Hawaii	Percentage reimbursement	Placement and condition						13.0%	6.6%
Idaho	Percentage reimbursement	Actual expenditures	X					11.0%	8.9%
Illinois	Resource based	Allowable costs		$2,758	17%	63%	20%	21.2%	11.6%
Indiana	Pupil weights	Disabling condition		$4,270	11%	70%	19%	7.6%	10.3%
Iowa	Pupil weights	Type of placement		$6,867	7%	54%	39%	10.5%	11.6%
Kansas	Resource based	Number of special education staff	X					11.2%	9.7%
Kentucky	Pupil weights	Disabling condition		$3,951	6%	94%	0%	12.8%	11.4%
Louisiana	Percentage reimbursement	Actual expenditures	X					11.3%	8.1%
Maine	Percentage reimbursement	Allowable costs	X	$4,744	8%	59%	33%	9.4%	12.8%
Maryland	Flat grant	Special education enrollment		$7,909	5%	26%	69%	11.1%	12.9%
Massachusetts	Flat grant	Total district enrollment		$7,131	6%	30%	64%	16.4%	15.7%
Michigan	Percentage reimbursement	Allowable costs	X	$7,069	6%	34%	60%	9.2%	9.4%
Minnesota	Percentage reimbursement	Actual expenditures	X	$7,144	6%	70%	24%	13.4%	11.4%

(continued)

Table 8a.1 State Special Education Finance Policies 1994–1995 *(continued)*

State	Formula Type[a]	Allocation Basis[a]	Special Education Funds for Target Population Only[a]	Mean Aid per Pupil	Percent Support by Source[b]			Percent K–12 Expenditures	Percent K–12 Enrollment
					Fed	State	Local		
Mississippi	Resource based	Number of special education staff	X					9.7%	11.4%
Missouri	Resource based	Number of special education staff	X	$3,597	10%	30%	60%	10.5%	12.1%
Montana	Flat grant	Total district enrollment		$3,068	14%	60%	26%	6.6%	11.7%
Nebraska	Percentage reimbursement	Allowable costs	X					7.4%	11.3%
Nevada	Resource based	Classroom unit	X	$8,218	4%	40%	56%	16.5%	8.6%
New Hampshire	Pupil weights	Type of placement						13.7%	9.4%
New Jersey	Pupil weights	Placement and condition						7.6%	15.3%
New Mexico	Pupil weights	Services received		$5,511	9%	90%	1%	13.1%	10.8%
New York	Pupil weights	Type of placement	X					20.8%	9.4%
North Carolina	Flat grant	Services received	X	$2,422	15%	76%	9%	8.1%	9.8%
North Dakota	Flat grant	Total district enrollment		$4,479	10%	31%	59%	11.1%	9.9%
Ohio	Resource based	Classroom unit						18.4%	10.6%
Oklahoma	Pupil weights	Disabling condition						17.0%	10.7%
Oregon	Pupil weights	Special education enrollment						10.3%	9.2%
Pennsylvania	Flat grant	Total district enrollment						9.3%	11.2%
Rhode Island	Percentage reimbursement	Actual expenditures		$5,858	5%	36%	59%	15.8%	14.1%
South Carolina	Pupil weights	Disabling condition	85%					8.7%	12.1%
South Dakota	Percentage reimbursement	Allowable costs	X	$4,052	13%	49%	38%	9.5%	11.0%
Tennessee	Resource based	Classroom unit						7.3%	11.8%
Texas	Pupil weights	Type of placement	X					7.7%	9.3%
Utah	Pupil weights	Type of placement	X					9.0%	10.1%
Vermont	Flat grant	Total district enrollment		$7,813	5%	39%	56%	10.9%	10.0%
Virginia	Resource based	Classroom unit		$4,700	9%	23%	68%	9.8%	10.6%
Washington	Pupil weights	Special education enrollment		$6,593	6%	62%	32%	10.2%	9.0%
West Virginia	Flat grant	Special education enrollment						9.9%	13.0%
Wisconsin	Percentage reimbursement	Allowable costs						14.1%	9.7%
Wyoming	Percentage reimbursement	Actual expenditures						11.1%	9.9%
U.S. Average				$5,395	7%	44%	49%	12.2%	10.7%

[a]*Source:* Data from Parrish, T. B., & Wolman, J. (1999). Trends and new developments in special education funding: What the states report. In T. B. Parrish, J. G. Chambers, & C. M. Guarino (Eds.), Funding special education: Nineteenth annual yearbook of the American Education Finance Association (pp. 206–208). Thousand Oaks, CA: Corwin Press.

[b]*Source:* Data from Parrish and Wolman (1999, pp. 216–218).

Table 8a.2 Policies for Compensatory Education and Programs for At-Risk Students 1998–1999

State	Formula Type[a]	Allocation Basis[a]	Use of Funds[a]	Aid per ADA[b]	Aid per Need Pupil[b]	Percent of Core Expenditures per Pupil[b]
Alabama	Flat grant	$100 per at-risk pupil based on academic performance and income.	After school, summer, tutoring, weekend, and parents as teachers.			
Arizona	Discretionary grants (available)			$49.92	$770	27.3%
Arkansas			K–3 school year, K–3 summer school, and college prep.	$16.41	$323	12.3%
California	District need	Prior resources, district revenue, and low-income and LEP pupils. Tied to federal allocations.	Economic Impact Aid, Reading programs, and Native American Indian Education Program.			
Colorado	Pupil weights	25% families on temporary family assistance + 25% projected underperforming.		$6.65	$315	9.8%
Connecticut				$32.66	$2,493	48.1%
District of Columbia		Resources included in general formula.				
Florida	Pupil weights	Drop-out prevention and teenage parent (39.9%), 9–12 Educational Alternatives (13.8%).		$110.46	$2,330	82.8%
Georgia	Pupil weights	Developmentally delayed K–3, reading, math, and writing deficiencies 5–9.				
Illinois	Pupil weights	.44% × adults without diploma; .40 × single parent households; .16 × poverty count.	Adult education programs.	$36.22	$1,460	49.4%
Indiana				$0.03	$2	0.1%
Iowa	Pupil weights	.10 × free lunch count + additional funding for early childhood at risk. Based on ADA, achievement levels, and at-risk count.	Summer programs (salaries and instructional assistants).	$17.05	$1,672	53.5%
Kansas				$2.62	$230	6.8%
Kentucky	Pupil weights	.17 × free and reduced lunch count.	Flexible.			
Louisiana						
Maryland	Pupil weights	.25 × Title I-eligible pupils. $2,228 elementary; $1,794 high school; based on income.	Tutoring, mentoring, extended day.	$121.33	$4,399	117.3%
Massachusetts	Flat grant					

(continued)

225

Table 8a.2 Policies for Compensatory Education and Programs for At-Risk Students 1998–1999 *(continued)*

State	Formula Type[a]	Allocation Basis[a]	Use of Funds[a]	Aid per ADA[b]	Aid per Need Pupil[b]	Percent of Core Expenditures per Pupil[b]
Michigan	Pupil weights	.115 × federal Title I eligible.	Instructional, and noninstructional services for "at-risk" pupils.	$108.69	$5,225	161.7%
Minnesota	Flat grant	$3,530 eligible pupil units based on free and reduced (prorated at 60%) lunch count.		$5.36	$525	15.9%
Mississippi	Flat grant (general fund add-on)	20% weight or approximately $650 per low-income pupil.		$303.09	$2,943	118.4%
Missouri	Flat grant/pupil weight	20% per free and reduced lunch eligible.				
Nebraska	Pupil weights (sliding scale)	5%–30% per free and reduced lunch eligible.				
New Jersey	Flat grant (variable)	20%–40% free lunch receive $316 per pupil; >40% receive $448 per pupil. "Demonstrably Effective Program Aid" also available.		$155.10	$5,744	104.8%
New Mexico	District weight (based on need cluster)	Based on rank order of districts involving Title I eligibility, LEP, mobility, and dropout rates. "Set aside" funds.	1–8 remediation.	$0.10	$2	0.1%
New York						
North Carolina	Flat grant	50% of funds allocated at $45.53 per ADM; 50% allocated on $265 per low-income pupil basis.	Remediaton, drop-out prevention, safe schools, etc.	$90.62	$1,932	63.5%
Ohio	Pupil weight	.25 × eligible pupils.		$56.55	$2,786	110.5%
Oklahoma	Pupil weight	.25 for students in poverty, students in foster homes, or neglected and delinquent students.				
Oregon	Pupil weight					
Pennsylvania	Pupil weight	.26 times free and reduced lunch count (K–3) or times number not meeting state standards (4–12).	Academic assistance	$15.54	$859	25.9%
South Carolina				$165.77	$2,088	73.0%
Texas	Pupil weight	.2 × free and reduced lunch count.	Flexible	$269.71	$6,760	191.4%
Utah	Discretionary grants	Low-income pupils.		$19.33	$1,421	53.2%
Vermont	Pupil weight	.25 × low-income pupils.				
Virginia	Resource based	9 instructional positions per 1,000 eligible students (cost share).		$92.65	$2,249	82.6%
Washington	Flat grant	Based on 4th- and 8th-grade performance and poverty percent. $390 per Learning Assistance Program (LAP) student. Additional funds to high-impact districts.		$154.98	$5,344	143.8%
Wisconsin	Competitive grants	Pre-school to grade-5 programs.				
Wyoming				$9.61	$590	13.5%

[a]*Source:* Data from Seilke, C. C., Dayton, J., Holmes, C. T., Jefferson, A. L., & Fowler, W. J., Jr., et al. (2001). *Public school finance programs of the United States and Canada 1998–99.* NCES 2001–309. Washington, DC: U.S. Department of Education, National Center for Education Statistics.
[b]*Source:* Data from Baker, B. D. (2001c). Living on the edges of school finance policy: The plight of at risk, limited English proficient and gifted children. *Educational Policy, 15,* 699–723.
ADA, average daily attendance; LEP, limited English proficient.

Table 8a.3 Policies for Limited-English-Proficient Students 1998–1999

State	Formula Type[a]	Allocation Basis[a]	LEP Aid per Pupil[b]	LEP Aid per Expected LEP Pupil[b]	Percent of Core Expenditures per Pupil[b]
Arizona	Pupil weight	6% per eligible pupil.			
Colorado	Flat grant	$400 per eligible LEP pupil, $200 per bilingual.	$0.94	$120	2.3%
Connecticut	Flat grant/pupil weight	10% per eligible pupil.	$38.66	$3,647	129.6%
Florida	Pupil weight	20.1% per eligible pupil.	$60.31	$1,058	29.5%
Hawaii			$8.03	$1,199	40.5%
Illinois					
Iowa	Pupil weight	19% per eligible pupil.	$0.00	$1	0.0%
Kansas	Pupil weight	20% per FTE eligible pupil (contact hours).			
Maryland	Flat grant	$1,350 per eligible pupil.	$4.63	$607	16.2%
Michigan	Flat grant	Eligible pupil.			
Minnesota	Resource based	68% LEP teacher per 40 LEP pupils + 47% supplies and equipment.	$6.98	$1,745	52.9%
Nebraska	Pupil weight	25 × eligible pupil.			
New Jersey	Flat grant	$1,102 per eligible pupil.	$24.83	$1,435	26.2%
New Mexico	Pupil weight	50% per eligible pupil.	$0.03	$1	0.0%
New York	Pupil weight	16% per eligible pupil.			
North Carolina	Resource based	Eligible schools receive base of $9,400 for 1/2 teacher assistant + funds per LEP pupil + funds for LEP concentration.	$5.20	$634	20.8%
North Dakota	Flat grant	$300 per eligible student.			
Oklahoma	Pupil weight	25% per eligible pupil.			
Oregon	Pupil weight	.5 per eligible student.			
Rhode Island	Flat grant	Defined allocation per eligible pupil.			
Texas	Pupil weight	10% per eligible pupil.	$14.63	$644	18.2%
Utah	Discretionary grants				
Vermont	Pupil weight	20% per eligible pupil.			
Virginia	Resource based	Nine instructional positions per 1,000 eligible students (cost share).			
Washington	Flat grant	$664 per eligible pupil.	$27.65	$1,553	41.8%
West Virginia					
Wisconsin	Percentage reimbursement	Prior-year costs.			

[a]*Source:* Data from Seilke, C. C., Dayton, J., Holmes, C. T., Jefferson, A. L., & Fowler, W. J., Jr., et al. (2001). *Public school finance programs of the United States and Canada 1998–99.* NCES 2001–309. Washington, DC: U.S. Department of Education, National Center for Education Statistics.

[b]*Source:* Data from Baker, B. D. (2001). Living on the edges of school finance policy: The plight of at risk, limited English proficient and gifted children. *Educational Policy, 15,* 699–723.

Table 8a.4 Policies for Gifted and Talented Students 1998–1999

State	Program Mandate 1993–1994[a]	Aid Formula 1993–1994[b]	Aid Formula 1998–1999[c]	Allocation Basis 1998–1999[c]	Aid per 5% FTE[e]	Aid Percent of Current Expenditures[e]
Alabama	Yes	Resource based	Pupil weight	Eligible pupil.		
Alaska	Yes	Pupil weight	Flat grant	$55 per 3% pupils or $1,000 (greater of two).		
Arizona	Yes	Flat grant			$58	.71%
Arkansas	Yes	Pupil weight	Pupil weight	Varied by count & fiscal capacity.	$9	.16%
California	No	Flat grant	Flat grant		$250	3.84%
Colorado	Yes	Discretionary grant	Flat grant	$6,500 per district + flat grant per 7% enrolled pupils + other special-purpose grants.	$368	4.75%
Delaware	Yes	Discretionary grant	Pupil weight			
Florida	Yes	Pupil weight	Pupil weight	Eligible pupil.	$1,832	32.8%
Georgia	Yes	Discretionary grant	Pupil weight	1.64 or 64% per eligible pupil.		
Hawaii	Yes	Percentage reimbursement			$450	6.89%
Idaho	Yes	Flat grant	Flat grant	Enrollment.		
Illinois	Yes	Flat grant	Flat grant/resource	Either grant per 5% FTE pupils or $5,000 per teacher.	$191	3.01%
Indiana	No	Discretionary grant	Discretionary grant	Support for program planning, implementation, or continuation.	$219	3.41%
Kansas	Yes	Resource based	Resource based	Number of staff.		
Kentucky	Yes	Percentage reimbursement	Resource based	Teachers and coordinators.		
Louisiana	Yes	Pupil weight	Pupil weight	.6 × eligible pupils.		
Maine	Yes	Percentage reimbursement	Percentage reimbursement	Approved costs.		
Maryland	No	Discretionary grant	Discretionary grant	Program improvement plans.	$116	1.57%
Massachusetts	No	Flat grant	Discretionary grant			
Michigan	No	Resource based	Resource based	Teachers in districts; Summer institutes; comprehensive service centers.	$24	.36%
Minnesota	No	Discretionary grant	Discretionary grant			
Mississippi	Yes	Flat grant	Flat grant (general fund add-on)		$.04	0%

(continued)

228

State	Program Mandate 1993–1994[a]	Aid Formula 1993–1994[b]	Aid Formula 1998–1999[c]	Allocation Basis 1998–1999[c]	Aid per 5% FTE[e]	Aid Percent of Current Expenditures[e]
Missouri	Yes	Discretionary grant	Discretionary grant	Reimbursement of approved program costs.		
Montana	Yes	Discretionary grant	Discretionary grant	Support for teacher training, innovation, and program continuation.	$22	.38%
Nebraska	No	None	Discretionary grants	Approved programs.		
Nevada	No	None	Discretionary grant			
New Mexico	No	None	Flat grant		$147	2.02%
New York	No	Flat grant	Flat grant	$196 per 3% ADA.		
North Carolina	Yes	Flat grant	Flat grant	For 4% ADM.	$649	10.4%
North Dakota	No	None	Discretionary grant			
Ohio	Yes	Resource based	Resource based	Salary allowance and per-pupil cost allowance (classroom unit).	$1.68	.03%
Oklahoma	Yes	Pupil weight	Pupil weight	.34 per eligible pupil.	$84[d]	1.11%
Oregon	Yes	Percentage reimbursement	Discretionary grant			
Pennsylvania	Yes	Percentage reimbursement				
South Carolina	Yes	Flat grant	Flat grant	Per eligible pupil for (a) academic, (b) artistic, and (c) advanced placement programs.	$738	11.99%
South Dakota	Yes	Percentage reimbursement	Repealed			
Tennessee	Yes	Resource based	Resource based	Allowable costs of service option selected.		
Texas	Yes	Pupil weight	Pupil weight	.12 per 5% ADA.	$321[d]	5.86%
Utah	Yes	Flat grant	Flat grant	Eligible pupil.	$416	8.01%
Virginia	Yes	Resource based	Resource based	One instructional position per 1,000 eligible students (cost share).	$538	8.24%
Washington	No	Flat grant	Flat grant	$320 per 2% FTE.	$99	
West Virginia	Yes	Discretionary grant	Discretionary grant			1.52%
Wyoming	No	Flat grant	Flat grant		$63	.94%

[a]2001.

[b]Prior-year data used. Fiscal year 2000 data not available.

[c]Council for State Directors of Programs for the Gifted (1994, 1995). State of the States Gifted and Talented Education Report.

Golds, S.D., Smith, D.M., & Lawton, S.B. (1995). Public school finance programs of the United States and Canada: 1993–94. Albany, NY: American Education Finance Association Center for the Study of the States, The Nelson A. Rockefeller Institute of Government.

[e]U.S. Department of Education, National Center for Education Statistics. (2001). Public School Finance Programs of the United States and Canada: 1998–99. NCES 2001–309; Compilers, C. Sielke, J. Dayton, C. T. Holmes, University of Georgia; & A. L. Jefferson, University of Ottawa. W. J. Fowler, Jr., Project Officer. Washington, DC.

ADA, average daily attendance; ADM, average daily membership; FTE, full-time equivalent.

CHAPTER 9

EDUCATION COSTS AND DISTRICT EXOGENOUS CONDITIONS

Introduction

Beyond individual student needs, a variety of organizational, structural, and geographic factors influence the cost of providing comparable services across schools and districts. Such factors include but are not limited to the following:

Geographic Variations in the Prices of Educational Inputs: As we noted previously in our definition of price (see Chapter 7), markets influence prices. The market price for comparable teachers, for example, differs among districts and states. Presumably, district hiring and the uniform salary schedule they offer would tend to equalize teacher quality within the district. However, high-ability teachers can be quite sensitive to local variations in working conditions, and this inevitably adversely affects challenging schools in their efforts to recruit talented teachers.

Scale of School or District: Analyses most often define scale (size) in terms of numbers of pupils and most often address scale at the district level. Analyses may address scale in terms of either the scale at which productivity is maximized, at which cost is minimized, or where greatest efficiency is achieved.

Sparsity of Student Population: Sparsity is typically defined in terms of the number of pupils in residence per square mile. Because sparsity primarily affects transportation costs more than annual operating costs, we do not address the specifics of sparsity here.

Grade Level: Some state's funding formulas account for differences in costs associated with providing educational services at different grade levels. We do not address the technical issues associated with grade-level differences in cost here, but we note that *many* studies, input and outcome based, do find higher costs per pupil for providing secondary education (see, e.g., Gronberg, Jansen, Taylor, & Booker, 2004).

Geographic Variations in Prices and Wages

Geographic variations in the prices paid by school districts for educational resources are a function of both discretionary (demand side) and cost (supply side) factors. Discretionary factors are those factors within the control of local administrators, such as the choice to hire more experienced or more highly educated teachers at a higher price, or the choice to heat school buildings to 73 degrees instead of 68 degrees during winter. Cost factors are those factors that are beyond the control of local administrators, such as the availability of qualified science teachers and local market prices for utilities or for materials, supplies, and equipment. The goal in establishing a geographic cost of education index is to identify specifically those cost differences outside of the control of local administrators, or, for example, the different costs of a teacher given the same levels of education and experience.

To date, most analyses and applications of geographic cost differences specifically involve differences in the price of teachers, because personnel represent approximately 80% of local school budgets (Peternick et al., 1998, cited in Ladd, Chalk and Hansen, 1999, p. 125). The National Academy of Sciences (NAS) report *Making Money Matter* (Ladd & Hansen, 1999) identifies three personnel-based price indices: (a) Barro's average teacher salary index (Barro, 1992, cited in Ladd & Hansen, 1999); (b) McMahon and Chang's cost-of-living index (McMahon & Chang, 1991, cited in Ladd & Hansen, 1999); and (c) Chambers's teacher-cost index (Chambers, 1995, cited in Ladd & Hansen, 1999), which the NAS report refers to as the "most sophisticated" of existing approaches for "examining national differences in teacher salaries and distinguishing the cost of education from actual education expenditures" (Ladd & Hansen, 1999, p. 125).

Alternate Approaches

Historically, analysts have used three basic approaches to address differences in competitive wages for teachers across school districts or broader regions within states. The three basic approaches to adjustments include (a) cost-of-living adjustments, (b) competitive (comparable) wage adjustments, and (c) hedonic wage-model adjustments. (For a more complete review with analysis of pros and cons of each method, see Duncombe & Goldhaber, 2004.)

Cost of Living

Cost-of-living adjustments are intended to compensate teachers and other school employees across school districts or regions within a state for differences in costs of maintaining *comparable* quality of living. Cost-of-living adjustments typically assume some basket of basic goods and services required for attaining a specific quality of living. Analysts identify goods and services of a specific quality level and estimate the price differences for purchasing those goods or services across regions in a state. The basket of goods typically includes things such as housing, food, clothing, child care, and health care.

At least two major problems exist in using cost-of-living adjustments for adjusting school aid. First, wealthy, generally more advantaged school districts in and around more desirable locations often show higher costs of the basket of goods and services. Using an index based on such findings results in supporting very different rather than similar quality of life across teachers within a state. One might imagine an extreme case where a cost-of-living adjustment considers only

housing prices across two school districts: one with palatial estates and another, a neighboring slum of decaying multifamily housing units. Funding schools or paying teachers on the basis of the differences in housing unit values—such that the teachers in the affluent district can afford palatial estates and the teachers in the slum can afford to live in the slum—clearly supports a different, not similar, quality of life. States including Colorado, Florida, and Wyoming use cost-of-living type indices in their school-aid formulas.

Competitive Wage

Analysts estimate **competitive- (comparable) wage** adjustments for teachers by evaluating the competitive wages of workers in other industries requiring similar education levels and professional skills as teachers. To the extent that competitive wages for similar work (at similar levels of experience, education, age, etc.) vary across regions or school districts within a state, so, too, must competitive wages for teachers. The underlying assumption is that teacher's wages must be competitive with other local industries requiring comparable skills, or teachers might choose to work in those industries instead of education. Because local labor markets vary, competitive teacher wages must vary. (For a more thorough discussion of comparable wage indices, see Taylor, 2005.)

Unfortunately, little is known about the mobility of teachers into other supposedly comparable or competitive professions and vice versa, and less is known about the potential role of wages in influencing mobility into and out of the teaching profession from other professions. Podgursky, Monroe, and Watson (2004) note, "Examination of non-teaching earnings for exiting teachers finds little evidence that high-ability teachers are leaving for higher pay" (Podgursky, Monroe, & Watson, 2004, p. 507).

According to Duncombe and Goldhaber (2004), states including Massachusetts, Ohio, and Tennessee have used measures of average private wages to construct cost adjustments to school aid.

Hedonic Wage

Hedonic-wage adjustments focus specifically on teachers' employment choices within the field of education and attempt most directly to provide each school district with comparable opportunity to recruit and retain teachers of similar quality. A vast body of educational research indicates that teachers' job choices are driven primarily by location and work conditions including but not limited to student-population characteristics. Neither cost-of-living indices nor competitive-wage indices address work conditions of teachers. Among those work conditions that are typically considered outside of the control of local school administrators are student-population characteristics, crime and safety issues, and to some extent facilities' quality and age. A well-estimated hedonic-wage index should capture the negative effects of difficult work conditions on teacher choices, resulting in higher index values for the cost of recruiting a teacher of comparable quality into more difficult working conditions, assuming all else equal. This is easier said than done (Duncombe & Goldhaber, 2004). Other factors beyond the control of local school administrators may include the remoteness of a school district and access to local amenities. Hedonic-wage indices also include consideration of cost-of-living factors. Where cost-of-living adjustments alone may support a better quality of life (rather than similar quality of life) for teachers in more affluent school districts, a hedonic approach can counter some of this effect with work condition and location factors that often contrast with cost-of-living measures.

Shortcomings of the hedonic approach most often relate to the availability of sufficient, detailed data to capture expected patterns of competitive-wage variation in relation to teacher quality. Presently, teacher wages vary both within and across school districts primarily as a function of years of service and degree level, due to the deeply embedded single-salary schedule. Sadly, little evidence shows that either years of service or degree level (as typically compensated in the single-salary schedule) is a good measure of teacher quality. In most cases, the best one can do in estimating a hedonic-wage model is to control for these two major factors and then discern the extent that work-condition factors and costs of living influence the differences in wages across districts for teachers at similar experience and degree levels. Ideally, available data would include measures of teachers' own test scores and/or the selectivity of the undergraduate institutions attended by teachers: two teacher-quality factors more frequently associated with improved student outcomes. Even when better teacher-quality measures are available, if few or no teachers with strong academic backgrounds work in schools with adverse working conditions, analysts can have difficulty estimating what incentives are needed to attract those teachers. The State of Texas presently uses a teacher-wage adjustment based on a hedonic-wage model.

Applications to School Finance Policy

Among the three approaches (cost of living, competitive wage, and hedonic wage), hedonic-wage indices are most appropriate for use at the district level. For example, districts that have the most difficult working conditions locally need to provide the necessary competitive wage to attract teachers of at least minimum desired quality. That is, policy makers can and should use indices based on hedonic-wage models to influence within-labor-market, cross-district sorting of teachers, where labor markets might be defined as metropolitan areas or other within-state regions more highly aggregated than individual districts, cities, or towns.

Other wage indices, such as competitive wage and cost-of-living indices, are problematic when applied to individual districts, because they are more likely to provide recruitment and retention advantages to those districts already advantaged within labor markets (wealthier suburbs over neighboring poor urban districts in the same metropolitan area). That is, at the microlevel, between two neighboring districts in the same region of a state, housing and other costs likely would be higher or competitive wages higher in the more affluent of the neighboring districts. Providing additional incentives to attract teachers to the more advantaged district in the same labor market as other disadvantaged districts would be inappropriate. Indeed, poorly estimated hedonic indices that fail to capture additional costs of difficult working conditions suffer the same problem, though usually to a lesser extent.

Instead of applying district-level indices, policy makers might apply comparable wage or cost-of-living indices to the consolidated metropolitan statistical area or core-based statistical area, covering a wide array of districts of varied need, but neither compensating for nor against those needs. The downside of even this approach is that districts in economically depressed regions of a state will likely be assigned lower competitive wage or cost-of-living indices, making it difficult to recruit in new, higher-quality teachers from other regions of the state. In effect, the index will reinforce the depressed state of the local economy.

Integration With Student-Need Weights

Ideally, a well-estimated hedonic-wage index would capture at least some of the additional costs associated with bringing similar-quality teachers into more difficult settings. Unfortunately, data issues pertaining to the measurement of teacher quality typically mute (or perhaps negate entirely) this desired *combat pay* effect. Whether a wage index fully accounts for teacher quality influences how that wage index should be integrated with other cost adjustments, such as additional funding for at-risk children.

The underlying premise of providing additional funding to schools or districts serving greater proportions of at-risk children is that these children will need more contact with teachers of comparable quality if we expect them to achieve the same outcomes as other children. That is, they need a higher quantity of teachers of similar quality. If the wage index compensates the cost of recruiting teachers of similar quality into schools with more at-risk children, then the at-risk adjustment need only compensate for the costs associated with the higher quantity of teachers needed. However, where the wage index does not fully capture additional costs associated with comparable quality, the at-risk adjustment must compensate for both quality and quantity.

Where a metropolitan area uses a comparable-wage or cost-of-living index, with no differential for difficult work conditions across districts within the area, the general aid formula will need larger weightings for at-risk children. Student-need weights must compensate for required differences in both teacher quantity and competitive wages. If a well-estimated hedonic-wage index can capture the competitive-wage difference associated with disadvantaged student populations, separate weights for at-risk children might be smaller, because they need to compensate only for teacher quantity differences.

Summary of Pros and Cons for Cost-of-Living, Competitive-Wage, and Hedonic-Wage Adjustments

Table 9.1 summarizes the cost-of-living, competitive-wage, and hedonic-wage approaches, their application, strengths, and shortcomings. First and foremost, it is important to differentiate between the goals of the methods. The only one of the three methods that attempts to capture the complete context of nonpecuniary factors that may influence a teacher's choice to work in one district versus another is the hedonic-wage approach. Among the three, cost-of-living

Table 9.1   Approaches to Measuring Wage Variation Across Settings

Approach	Goal	Data	Geographic Unit	Strengths	Shortcomings
Cost of living	Address uncontrollable costs to employees of living in commutable distance to work (comparable quality of life for teachers).	Basket of local goods/services in area of commutable distance.	Labor market (CBSA/CMSA).	Less influenced by current teacher compensation.	Most often supports higher quality of living for teachers in "advantaged" districts.
Competitive wage	Provide wage required to keep a person with specific education/ knowledge/skills in teaching within a specific labor market.	Wages of comparable professions (based on place of work).	Labor market (CBSA/CMSA).	Less influenced by current teacher compensation.	Teachers don't typically move to "comparable" professions.
				Based on competitive labor market assumptions.	Influenced by inequities across local/ regional economies.
Hedonic wage	Provide wage required for recruiting and retaining teacher of specific quality attributes.	Wages of teachers by background attributes, location, and working conditions.	School district.	Only approach to consider localized work conditions.	Strongly influenced by the current single-salary schedule.

CBSA, core-based statistical area; CMSA, consolidated metropolitan statistical area.

approaches are most problematic, primarily because they most often lead to supporting higher quality of living for teachers in advantaged school districts, which serve more-advantaged student populations. Cost-of-living approaches are even more problematic when applied to districts rather than broader labor markets as a unit of analysis, because they provide incentives for teachers in disadvantaged districts to take better jobs at a higher wage in neighboring more-advantaged districts.

Competitive-wage indices are a significant improvement over cost-of-living indices, but the relationship between private-sector wages and teacher wages remains tenuous and poorly understood. Further, financing schools on the basis of private-sector wages may, in part, lead to reinforcing economic disparities across a state. Indeed, the same is partly true of hedonic-wage models, which, lacking sufficient teacher-quality measures, may indicate the necessity for lower wages in school districts with lower housing costs and generally lower private and public sector wages.

National Center for Education Statistics Indices

In the 1990s, the National Center for Education Statistics (NCES) commissioned Jay Chambers of the American Institutes for Research (AIR) to develop a national teacher-cost index, based on data from the NCES *Schools and Staffing Surveys of 1987–88 and 1993–94* (http://nces.ed.gov/surveys/sass/).

Chambers's (1999) teacher-cost index uses a multiple-regression approach called the hedonic-wage model to estimate differences in the price of teachers across and within states. The wage model estimates cost-related differences while holding constant discretionary differences. As discretionary factors, Chambers includes teacher characteristics such as educational preparation; experience levels; composition of teachers with respect to race, gender, age, and maturity; and job characteristics including class size, subject matter, and type of classes. Most of these factors—which involve "who is hired" and "how they are assigned"—are within the discretion of local administrators; however, as we mentioned earlier, segmented labor markets often limit the willingness of highly qualified applicants to work in urban districts. Administrators may hire more- or less-experienced individuals, and assign them heavier or

lighter workloads, contingent, of course, on the role of local labor unions and quality of labor supply.

Chambers's cost factors include those that affect the desirability of a particular geographic location such as climate, composition of student enrollment, crime rates, and proximity to an urban area. These factors are clearly outside of the control of local administrators, who may, for example, have to pay a premium to attract comparable teachers to either a remote rural setting or blighted urban school with high percentages of difficult students and high rates of crime. Chambers's goal is to use the equations to conduct a simulation to address the following question:

> How much more or less does it cost to recruit and employ similar school personnel (i.e. exhibiting similar discretionary factors) in different school districts (characterized by different sets of cost factors) at different points in time (i.e. in different school years)? (1999, p. 258)

Chambers also estimates cost indices for administrators, other noncertificated staff, and nonpersonnel (utilities, materials, supplies, etc.) costs. Each of these indices attempts to separate cost-related differences from discretionary differences. Chambers then constructs a weighted average of these indices, according to their share of typical school budgets, in order to construct an overall geographic cost of education index (CEI). A particularly difficult issue in the development or application of wage indices is the identification of all of the relevant factors that might influence whether districts truly have comparable ability to purchase teachers of comparable quality and qualifications. For example, if one district simply has nicer facilities than another, will it have a competitive advantage on teacher recruitment, allowing it to pay the same, yet attract more desirable candidates? Is the same true of student population differences? Chambers calls these "hedonic wages," or things that add pleasure to your work that you are willing to trade off against higher wages.

As an alternative, the NCES contracted Lori Taylor of Texas A&M to produce a comparable-wage index for teacher labor markets across the country in 2005 (Taylor, 2005). Taylor's comparable-wage index uses data from the Individual Public Use Microdata Sample (IPUMS 5%). The integrated public use microdata system draws 5% and 1% samples from the decennial census. Taylor uses the 5% sample for estimating the NCES CWI.

IPUMS contains information on earnings, place of work, occupation, and demographics. The unit of analysis is the labor market, with urban district wage indices calculated for corresponding metropolitan areas and rural district wage indices based on corresponding rural areas, which usually include multiple counties. To construct the comparable-wage index, Taylor uses earnings data on college graduates to construct a regression model in which the dependent variable is the log of the annual wage. Independent variables include race, educational attainment, amount of time worked, occupation and industry of each individual in the national sample, and an indicator variable for each labor market area.

Unfortunately, IPUMS data are decennial, and significant regional convergence or divergence of comparable wages over a 10-year period is likely. Taylor addresses this problem by generated annual updates of the comparable-wage index (CWI) using data from the

Occupational Employment Statistics (OES) data set from the Bureau of Labor Statistics. The OES data contain average annual earnings by occupation but provide no information about individual worker characteristics and thus cannot be used for developing the baseline index. Analysts use the OES data to determine the rate of wage increase, by occupation and labor market, and then apply them to baseline CWI values to generate updates.

Figure 9.1 displays the county-level map of the new CWI, with shading representing CWI values where 1.0 is the national average. The key to Figure 9.1 shows the ranges of the CWI associated with each shading, where the darkest regions are those with 36% to 63% above average competitive wages. In at least a few areas around the country, relatively high-wage labor markets are immediately adjacent to well-below-average-wage labor markets. For example, on the southeastern boundary of the Kansas City metropolitan area, competitive wages

Figure 9.1   County-Level NCES Comparable Wage Index 2004

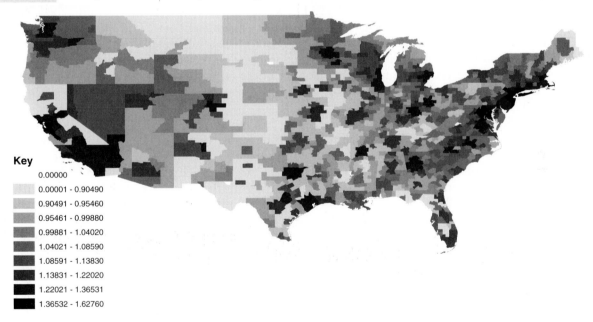

Key

	0.00000
	0.00001 - 0.90490
	0.90491 - 0.95460
	0.95461 - 0.99880
	0.99881 - 1.04020
	1.04021 - 1.08590
	1.08591 - 1.13830
	1.13831 - 1.22020
	1.22021 - 1.36531
	1.36532 - 1.62760

Source: Data from Taylor, L. L., & Glander, M. (2006). *Documentation for the NCES Comparable Wage Index Data File* (EFSC 2006-865). U.S. Department of Education. Washington, DC: National Center for Education Statistics. Retrieved April, 2007, from http://www.nces.ed.gov/edfin/pdf/2006865.pdf

drop abruptly from 19% above national average to 14% below. Such abrupt changes raise some concern for direct application of the index in state school finance policy. A difference of greater than 30% in wage adjustment along a county border could create significant labor market distortion, drawing teachers into jobs in school districts on the outer fringe of those areas defined as labor markets (usually metropolitan area labor markets). Recall that a CWI is not intended to capture district-to-district working condition differences. Abrupt changes in competitive wages between labor markets may disadvantage higher poverty rural and small-town districts that lie on the edge, but just outside of higher-wage metropolitan areas. Those caveats aside, the new NCES CWI presents an intriguing alternative perspective on wage variation across and within states.

Comparisons of Wage/Cost Indices: The Case of Wyoming

As part of ongoing litigation and court oversight, the Wyoming legislature is required to revisit the cost basis of its cost-based block-grant funding formula every 5 years. In 2005, one of the components revisited was the underlying wage adjustment, which until then had been based on the Wyoming cost-of-living index (WCLI). The top panel of Figure 9.2 shows the distribution of the Wyoming cost-of-living index across Wyoming school districts. The WCLI is a typical cost-of-living index based on the average costs of a basket of goods and services including housing values, among other things. The primary beneficiary of the WCLI is Teton School District #1, or Jackson Hole, which receives a WCLI value of 140, or 40% above state average. This value is driven largely by the cost of housing in this elite tourism area of the state, immediately south of Yellowstone National Park.

Critics have raised two concerns regarding the WCLI. First, the WCLI provides too much additional support to Teton #1. While adjustment is intended to aid districts in compensating teachers, the most recent recalibration report and other previous studies show that full amount of additional support is not actually reflected in teacher wages in the district (Odden et al., 2005).

That is, Teton #1 clearly can recruit comparable teachers as other districts using only about 50% of their WCLI adjustment. Second, the WCLI overlooks the potential difficulty in remote rural districts and higher-poverty districts of recruiting and retaining teachers.

The bottom panel of Figure 9.2 shows an alternative hedonic-wage index. Unfortunately, the hedonic index was built on a model that included insufficient data on teacher quality, a common problem in hedonic modeling. Evidence of the need for higher wages in higher-poverty districts for recruiting quality teachers therefore is limited. In addition, Wyoming does not have the types of large, poor urban districts that exist in other states.

The most obvious difference between the hedonic index and the WCLI is the reduction in index value of Teton #1. More remote districts also receive slightly higher indices than previously, and the overall range of indices is reduced.

Inflation

Analysts can measure inflation in terms of changes in either the total cost of providing comparable educational services over time or the prices of educational resources, or inputs, over time. The approach to measuring differences in prices over time is similar to measuring differences in prices across geographic regions. The goal is to measure the differences in price that are a function of changes that are beyond the control of local school administrators and boards of education. For example, when measuring changes in the prices of teachers over time simply by calculating average salaries, one might overstate inflation by either (a) the aging and concurrent increased experience levels of the overall teacher population or (b) the tendency of districts to hire more highly qualified teachers over time. Maintenance of an experienced teacher pool and the choice to hire teachers with more credentials are within the discretion of local administrators. However, changes in local cost-of-living or in the availability of teachers within the broader labor market are not. An appropriate education-inflation index must measure those changes in resource prices and costs that are beyond the control of local administrators.

Chambers (1997) compares several alternative inflation indices with an inflationary cost of education index (ICEI) as a companion to his geographic cost of education index, derived by the same methods (hedonic wage model) using the same data as part of the same analyses. Table 9.2, originally reported in Chambers (1997), compares several inflation indices.

Figure 9.2 Geographic Distribution of the Wyoming Cost of Living Index Versus the Hedonic Model

Wyoming Cost of Living Index

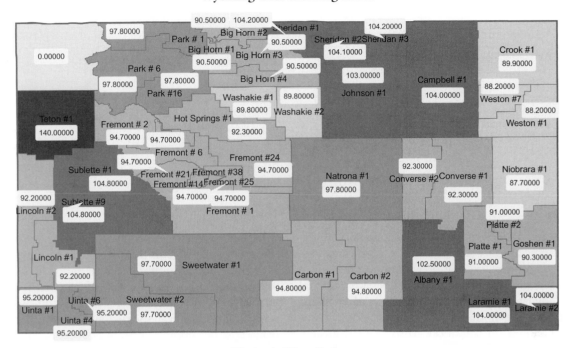

Hedonic Wage Index

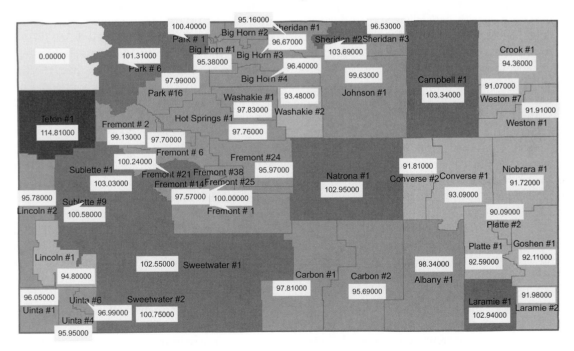

1. Darker shades associated with higher wage index values.
2. Index values reported in call-out bubbles.

Source: Adapted from Baker, B. D. (2005). Estimating an hedonic wage model for the State of Wyoming. In L. O. Picus et al., *Recalibration of the Wyoming Cost-Based Block Grant, Wyoming Legislature.* Retrieved January 2006, from http://legisweb.state.wy.us/2006/interim/schoolfinance/Recalibration/WY%20RecaFinal.pdf

Table 9.2   Comparison of Inflation Indices 1987 Through 1994

Description of Index	Inflation Index by Sample Year			Percentage Change by Time Interval	
	1987–1988	1990–1991	1993–1994	FY1988 to FY1991	FY1991 to FY1994
Standard price deflator					
Consumer price index	100.0	115.6	126.3	15.6	9.3
Gross domestic product deflator	100.0	115.5	124.8	15.5	8.1
School price index	100.0	117.6	130.0	17.6	10.5
Net services index	100.0	115.5	130.5	15.5	13.0
Modified employment cost index	100.0	117.2	128.3	17.2	9.5
Cost of education index	100.0	115.0	126.4	15.0	9.9

FY, fiscal year.
Source: Adapted from Chambers, 1997, p. 16 (Table III–1A).

Hanushek and Rivkin (1996) recommend using the gross domestic product (GDP) deflator, which measures public expenditures on education with respect to domestic consumer and investment goods and services. That is, the GDP deflator measures what the consumer might have spent on other things, if the consumer had not spent that money on education. Mishel and Rothstein (1996) recommend the net services index of the Bureau of Labor Statistics, which focuses on growth in personnel costs in industries with generally static productivity. The elementary and secondary school price index (SPI) purports to measure changes in the prices of education inputs over time. (See Chambers, 1997, pp. 2–3, for a more through discussion; http://nces.ed. gov/pubsearch/pubsinfo.asp?pubid=9743.)

Some suggest that education prices typically increase at a faster pace than consumer prices because consumer prices are heavily influenced by improvements in manufacturing productivity (see Ladd et al., 1999, p. 131). Chambers (1997) found consumer price index and inflationary cost of education index inflation rates from 1987 through 1994 to be quite comparable. Chambers notes, however, that while annual differences among the indices appear small, the cumulative effects of choosing alternative indices may be quite significant in the long run. For example, Chambers notes that "A difference of 2.5 percent like the one observed between the SPI and the ICEI in the first time interval amounts to about a 64 percent difference compounded over 20 years, and a 110 percent difference compounded over 30 years" (1997, p. xiii).

The application of inflation indices in policy involves several important considerations that influence whether adequacy is truly maintained. For example, differences emerge in total cost over time when inflation is applied to the prices of individual resources rather than the aggregate cost of education. Table 9.3 displays an example using Guthrie and Rothstein's (1999) prototypical elementary school. The initial total cost per pupil in 1997 was $6,165. The first two columns of data show expenses across functions and budget shares, followed by the various inflation rates applied to resource inputs. The budget-share-weighted average inflation rate is 3.3621%.

On the one hand, we can apply the 3.3621% change rate, compounded over time to the $6,165. On the other, we can apply the individual price inflation indices to each category of resource, assuming constant enrollment (because our resources are expressed in totals rather than per pupil). The last two rows of the Table 9.3 display the results of these alternative approaches. Note that by 1998 a $10 per-pupil difference has emerged, and by 2002 a $67 per-pupil difference has emerged. Why is this so, if the weighted average of the individual indices is 3.36%? The $67 difference occurs because each time individual prices, rather than total cost, are inflated, the budget shares change. As a result, if one category of resources is growing at a rate much faster than the initial weighted average rate, each year that category of resources will consume a larger portion of the budget, despite resource levels remaining constant.

The shortcomings of aggregate cost-inflation indices over time can be quite significant, yielding a seemingly unexplainable budget squeeze on districts. One solution is to annually update the inflation index

Table 9.3 Comparison of Aggregate Cost Versus Input Price Inflation

	1997	Weight	Inflation	1998	1999	2000	2001	2002	Weight
Personnel costs									
Teachers	$828,660	46.67%	3.37%	$858,901	$890,295	$922,888	$956,731	$991,872	46.82%
Substitutes	$10,173	0.57%	3.67%	$10,551	$10,944	$11,351	$11,774	$12,212	0.58%
Aids/paraprofessionals	$35,986	2.03%	3.67%	$37,325	$38,713	$40,154	$41,648	$43,197	2.04%
Support staff	$62,150	3.50%	3.37%	$64,418	$66,772	$69,217	$71,755	$74,390	3.51%
Media staff	$41,433	2.33%	3.37%	$42,945	$44,515	$46,144	$47,837	$49,594	2.34%
Media assistant									
Administrative	$64,185	3.62%	4.40%	$67,116	$70,183	$73,390	$76,746	$80,255	3.79%
Clerical staff	$45,362	2.55%	3.70%	$47,237	$49,194	$51,235	$53,365	$55,587	2.62%
Operations staff	$68,603	3.86%	2.13%	$70,440	$72,340	$74,304	$76,336	$78,437	3.70%
Other costs									
Materials and supplies	$61,950	3.49%	2.33%	$63,408	$64,901	$66,428	$67,992	$69,592	3.29%
Equipment	$37,837	2.13%	2.33%	$38,728	$39,639	$40,572	$41,527	$42,505	2.01%
Categorical programs	$153,810	8.66%	6.00%	$163,248	$173,266	$183,898	$195,183	$207,160	9.78%
Activities	$2,167	0.12%	2.33%	$2,218	$2,270	$2,323	$2,378	$2,434	0.11%
Professional development	$26,352	1.48%	2.33%	$26,971	$27,605	$28,254	$28,918	$29,598	1.40%
Assessment	$7,200	0.41%	2.33%	$7,369	$7,542	$7,720	$7,901	$8,087	0.38%
Maintenance and operations	$93,064	5.24%	2.67%	$95,574	$98,151	$100,798	$103,517	$106,308	5.02%
Administration and miscellaneous	$159,323	8.97%	2.33%	$163,068	$166,901	$170,823	$174,839	$178,948	8.45%
Transportation	$77,180	4.35%	2.67%	$79,261	$81,399	$83,594	$85,849	$88,164	4.16%
Aggregate inflation		100.00%	3.36%						
Index calculation									
Annual resource-based grant	$1,775,434			$1,838,780	$1,904,630	$1,973,096	$2,044,293	$2,118,341	
Input price inflated grant per pupil	$6,165			$6,385	$6,613	$6,851	$7,098	$7,355	
Annual grantif constant inflated foundation	$6,165			$6,375	$6,592	$6,816	$7,048	$7,288	

Source: Hypothetical comparison based on initial cost estimates from Wyoming. Data from Guthrie and Rothstein (1999).

by reevaluating individual resource-price inflation and weights derived from budget shares, acknowledging the subtle changes in those shares over time. A second, mathematically similar solution is to annually apply input price rather than aggregate cost inflation.

One caveat regarding inflation indices is that they are difficult to implement as policy in the public sector, where legislative budget allocations occur annually. It is often both economically and politically infeasible for a legislature in 1 year to bind future legislatures to a specific rate of growth for their expenditures on public education. This is not to suggest, however, that use of inflation indices in state education finance policy is entirely futile. One might argue that including such indices at least requires future legislatures to consciously and publicly choose to ignore inflation if they wish not to maintain adequate funding increases. We conclude that states should fund independent or quasi-independent agencies to report important indicators and their trends so that the political process can proceed with accurate information.

Economies of Scale, Sparsity, and Remoteness

The notion that costs per pupil vary by district size, sparsity, and location is relatively well accepted in school finance. But why do cost differences exist by school district size, or more precisely, what role does size or enrollment alone play in dictating district costs per pupil? It is important to distinguish, for example, between costs related to the scale of operation, and costs related to the location and geography of operation. For the annual operation of schools, factors that affect personnel costs tend to be the most significant factors influencing total costs. Less significant to annual operating budgets (though certainly not unimportant) are costs associated with food, transportation, and other facilities operations. The majority of annual operating expenditures of public school districts are allocated to salaries and wages of school and district personnel. K–12 education is a personnel-intensive service industry. The personnel cost equation is essentially:

$$\text{Price} \times \text{Quantity} = \text{Cost}$$

where *price* refers to the competitive wage that a school district must offer to attract teachers and/or administrators and other staff with specific qualities. Equality of educational opportunity requires that price or wage reflects the price of recruiting teachers of specific qualities and that sufficient resources exist such that each district can attract sufficient quantities of teachers with those qualities. *Quantity* simply indicates the quantity of teachers and other staff required to provide the appropriate educational programs/services.

District Structure and Location-Related Cost Variation

District geographic factors may affect either the price or the quantity or both of school personnel.

- **Costs Related to District or School Size (Enrollment):** School size primarily affects teacher-quantity requirements. Small districts unable to consolidate due to geographic isolation must operate inefficiently small classes simply to provide sufficient curricular opportunities, in terms of both depth and breadth.[1]

- **Costs Related to Sparsity:** District sparsity, which states often measure by numbers of pupils per square mile, most directly affects transportation costs. The further apart and further the linear distances from schools that students live, the greater the costs of transporting those students to schools, where those costs are driven by driver hours, fuel costs, vehicle numbers, and vehicle maintenance. However, once those students have arrived at school, cost effects of sparsity are limited. Sparsity *may* affect annual operating costs of schools in two other ways. A district may be so sparse, or spread out that additional schools are required for very small numbers of students. In this case, the costs of sparsity are related to the costs of operating low-enrollment schools, where necessary. Finally, sparsity of a district may affect teacher travel, either for specialized teachers splitting time between distant facilities, or simply for recruitment of high-quality teachers to distant locations. These costs associated

---

[1] Note that while *small class size* is a preferred educational reform for many, and one we promote throughout this text, the issue with very small remote schools and districts is that to simply offer a diverse high school curriculum, including advanced course options across math, English, science, and so on, requires class sizes of three to five students or even fewer.

with sparsity may be more directly associated with remoteness.

- **Costs Related to Remoteness:** Costs associated with remoteness overlap significantly with costs associated with sparsity. The primary cost effects of remoteness likely result from prices of recruiting quality teachers and other school staff. Remoteness also likely affects the prices of other goods and services (food delivery, materials and supplies, equipment, maintenance and repair contracts etc.). Often, remoteness significantly limits (if not eliminates entirely) competitive bidding. However, these costs are a much smaller share of total annual operating costs than are core personnel costs.

One can view the concept and/or measurement of **economies of scale** in education from either of two perspectives:

1. What is the school or district size at which students can achieve maximum output for a given level of input?
2. What is the school or district size at which students can achieve a given level of output at minimum cost?

Analysts can examine economies of scale via the education-production function or via the education-cost function. Analysis of production typically occurs at the school or classroom level, where it is assumed that most teaching and learning occur. Cost measurement, on the other hand, typically occurs at the district level, because districts are the organizational units that raise revenues, receive intergovernmental transfers, and internally allocate resources. While findings remain mixed on both production and cost fronts, Andrews, Duncombe, and Yinger note:

> Cost function results indicate potentially sizeable cost savings up to district enrollment levels between 2,000 and 4,000 students, and that sizeable diseconomies of size may begin to emerge for districts above 15,000 students. At the school level, production function studies provide some evidence that moderately sized elementary schools (300 to 500 students) and high schools (600 to 900 students) may optimally balance economies of size with the negative effects of large schools. (2002, p. 2)

While the production perspective is important, the cost perspective on economies of scale is of primary interest in school finance policy. This is because the measurement of cost differences across districts of varied size has direct implications for the design of state school-funding formulas. For example, providing comparable education services in a district with only 300 pupils costs 25% more than average, then the state may choose to allocate an additional 25% aid per pupil. Legislators should be cognizant, however, of the anticonsolidation incentive created by such policies.

Is it possible to reconcile the results from the school-level production–function studies, and district-level cost–function studies? Cost–function research suggests consolidation of very small rural districts may save money, as long as districts are kept at a moderate size, and transportation times remain reasonable. Increasing district size beyond 2,000 students in a sparsely populated area will probably not save significant money. A district of 2,000 is consistent with schools in the size range suggested in the production–function research (Baker & Duncombe, 2004).

Figure 9.3 presents the scale effect found in a cost–function analysis of Texas school districts performed in 2000. In general, econometric analyses of the influence of scale on costs per pupil result in sharply dropping curved functions, with, as noted previously, cost minimization achieved somewhere above 2,000 pupils. The highest costs, exceeding twice the minimum costs, tend to occur in districts much smaller than 100 pupils.

Table 9.4 summarizes the additional costs associated with small district size from six separate resource-cost studies, using professional judgment panels. In each case, the district of minimum costs is represented with a cost index of 1.0. The minimum cost district is typically a larger, scale-efficient district. In Kansas analysts estimated that a district with 200 students had costs 48% above those of a district with 11,200 students. In North Dakota, in contrast, analysts estimated that a district with 208 students had costs only 9% above a large district, and in Nebraska a district with 182 students had costs 93% above the minimum. When aggregated, all of the findings in Table 9.4 together suggest that costs generally level off in districts with approximately 5,000 students and increase most sharply in districts with fewer than 300 students. This finding is consistent with recent comprehensive reviews of economic literature (Andrews, Duncombe, & Yinger, 2002).

Later in this chapter, we discuss how some states choose to accommodate economies of scale in their aid formulas. Many, however, do not, despite the presence

Figure 9.3   Economies of Scale and District Costs as Estimated via Cost–Function Analysis for the State of Texas

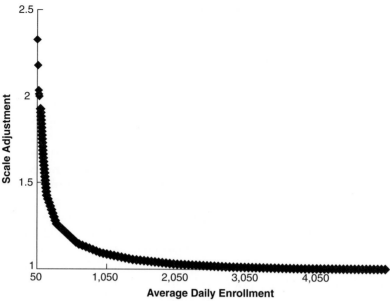

Source: Data from Alexander, Gronberg, Jansen, Keller, Taylor, and Triesman (2000).

of numerous small, remote, and sparse school districts. Further, among those who do, insignificant variation occurs in existing policies, few to none of which are based on empirically rigorous analyses.

Evidence of School-Level Economies of Scale: The Case of Wyoming

To date, most research on education costs has focused on cost differences associated with district size, not school size. Underlying district cost differences are differences in the size of schools and required staffing configurations for those schools. One reason for the lack of analyses on school-level costs is the lack of precise data on school-level expenditures. In recent years, such data have become available in Wyoming.

Baker (2007) constructs a series of school-level education cost–function models to estimate the relative cost of achieving a common outcome goal (50% proficiency rate on Wyoming state assessments, WyCAS) across districts of varied size, controlling for differences in regional competitive wages (using the hedonic index previously discussed) and differences in student populations. Baker used two approaches for

the school-size measure. First, Baker placed schools in enrollment categories to capture economies of scale differences as a step function by school size. Second, he used a third-order polynomial equation to generate a cost curve.

Elementary Schools

Figure 9.4 addresses scale-related costs for elementary schools in Wyoming. On average, elementary schools enrolling less than 50 students cost about 59% more to operate than elementary schools enrolling more than 250 students. On average, elementary schools enrolling 50 to 150 students cost about 20% more to operate than elementary schools enrolling more than 250 students. That margin is reduced to 10% for schools enrolling 150 to 250 students. All coefficients are highly statistically significant, estimated with robust standard errors clustering schools within districts.

Secondary Schools

Figure 9.5 addresses scale-related costs for high schools. High school costs appear more significantly affected by economies of scale. Very small high schools cost 75% more than scale-efficient high schools to operate. High

Table 9.4   Estimated Cost Adjustments for Economies of Scale (Resource Cost)

Enrollment	Kansas	Montana	Colorado	Missouri	North Dakota	Nebraska
96					1.7	
125			2.4			
130				1.53		
182						1.93
200	1.48					
208		1.33			1.09	
364				1.09		
400						1.4
430	1.27		1.52			
598					1	
748		1.11				
1,196				1.08		
1,300	1.15					1.31
1,500			1.18			
1,740		1				
4,380				1		
5,200			1			
7,499					1.11	
8,450		1.04				
11,200	1					
12,500						1
18,370				1.04		
29,970			1.02			

Source: Data from Baker (2005).

Figure 9.4   Elementary Economies of Scale

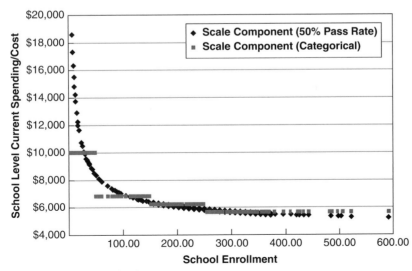

Source: Data from Wyoming Public Schools.

Figure 9.5   High School Economies of Scale

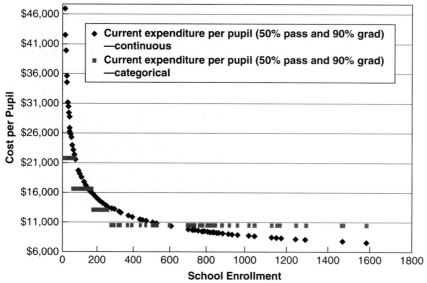

Source: Data from Wyoming Public Schools.

schools enrolling 50 to 150 students cost 46% more to operate. Even for high schools with 150 to 250 students, costs are greater than 20% higher than for high schools with greater than 250 students. Numbers of schools in each category prohibited larger size classifications. Note that in the high school model, outcome measures are positive and statistically significant, indicating the expected effect that higher outcomes come with higher average costs.

Current Policies Across States

In this section of the chapter, we address the practical side of implementing district and school-level cost adjustments. Specifically, we address the application of geographic input price adjustments and economies of scale adjustments, the theoretical basis and derivations of which we discussed in Chapter 8.

Geographic Input Price Differences

An NAS report noted, "the handful of states which currently take account of differences in the cost of education from place to place do so by using state wage indices (Ohio), consumer price indices (Colorado, Florida, Wyoming), or regression analysis using state rather than national data (Texas)" (Ladd & Hansen, 1999, p. 126).

Example Application: The Texas Wage Index
Figure 9.6 shows the 1990 Texas hedonic-wage index.

Cost indices used in state-aid formulas often are set to a minimum of 1.0 rather than a median of 1.0. How the index is set should depend on the underlying base cost by which the index is multiplied. If the base cost is intended to represent average or median costs, then a median-centered index should be used. If the base is intended to represent minimum costs, then the index may be set to 1.0. In Texas, the base-aid figure was not tied to cost at all, and by 2002–2003 had reached a level of $2,537 per weighted pupil.

Other considerations when applying a wage/input price index in school finance policy are (a) the share of the basic funding to receive the adjustment and (b) whether the index should be used to adjust state aid used for matching additional district effort above and beyond the first tier.

In Texas, under the foundation school program (FSP), 71% of first-tier aid was adjusted with the 1990 cost index. As a political compromise, 50% of second-tier funding was adjusted. Addressing the first tier only, the index was applied as follows:

1. 71% of Basic Allotment (2,537) times CEI = ABA
One determines the adjusted basic allotment (ABA)

Figure 9.6 1990 Texas Cost of Education Index (Hedonic Wage Index)

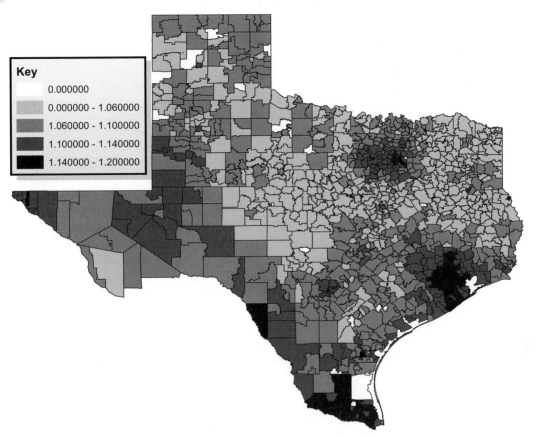

Key
	0.000000
	0.000000 - 1.060000
	1.060000 - 1.100000
	1.100000 - 1.140000
	1.140000 - 1.200000

Source: Data from Texas Education Agency.

first by multiplying the cost index (CEI) times the basic allotment for each district.

2. Scale adjustments to ABA made next = AA

Then, one determines the adjusted allotment (AA) by applying the economies of scale and sparsity adjustments to the ABA. That is, the underlying assumption is that scale affects personnel demands (as discussed herein), and therefore has multiplicative, not additive, effects with wage.

Then, one multiplies the scale- and wage-adjusted ABA times the weighted-pupil count (weighted average daily attendance [WADA]), which includes the various student-need adjustments. The assumption here is that pupil needs are then multiplicative with both scale- and wage-related costs. Regarding wage variation, this may be true where student-need weights address only the need for additional quantities of personnel and not the additional costs of recruiting staff of similar quality. Regarding scale, we know less about how marginal costs

associated with student needs interact with district size. The multiplicative application suggests that if general education costs 20% more in a smaller district, then the marginal costs (student-need weight) for at-risk or bilingual education will increase another 20% over those basic costs and the need weight. Future analyses must pay more attention to this particular issue. In the Texas case, however, like the base aid, existing pupil need weights are not derived from cost analysis.

Example Application: Missouri's New "Dollar-Value Modifier"

Increasingly, as states modify or completely overhaul their aid formulas, states are paying more attention to a multitude of cost factors, including competitive wages. However, despite significant advancement in our understanding of teacher wages and a track record of relatively rigorous statistical methods applied in states such as Texas, other states continue to adopt policies based on far less rigorous analyses or none at all. The apparent goal of wage adjustment in the political context has been to capitulate to the interest of major metropolitan areas in states.

A recent dramatic overhaul of Missouri school finance (Senate Bill 287) provides a stereotypical example. For the past 10 to 15 years in Missouri, under the state's guaranteed tax base formula, suburban districts in the state have quickly ratcheted upward their spending levels, in part, in competition with the state's two largest cities, whose funding levels and teacher salaries were increased dramatically in the early 1990s as a function of desegregation litigation. Rural districts fell well behind in per-pupil revenues, with many hovering below $4,000 per pupil as recently as 2003.

Missouri's recent reforms focused most directly on leveling up funding in rural and small-town districts from the implicit base funding of approximately $4,100 per pupil to a new base of $6,117 derived from successful schools analysis. In addition, the state added a new-student need weight for limited-English-proficient (LEP) students (.60) and the weight for at-risk students (counting free and reduced lunch) was increased from .20 to .25. Missouri then distributed a pot of leftover funds (about $15 million) across small districts (<350 students). The state plans to implement the structure over a 3-year period, starting in 2006–2007.

The new need-based formula left suburban districts wanting their piece of the cost-adjustment pie. And they got it, with a dollar-value modifier (DVM). Missouri's new DVM is based roughly on cost-of-living factors and calculated (a) on a regional basis if the district is in a *micro*politan or metropolitan area or (b) on a county basis for districts outside of core-based statistical areas. In general, the DVM increases the foundation level for the state's metropolitan areas and increases that aid similarly for urban core and suburban districts. As a political compromise, Missouri truncated the range of the index at both its lower and upper end, limiting the range to about 10% (1.0 to 1.1034). The DVM is multiplied times the student need adjusted basic funding per pupil.

More Problematic Approaches: Kansas Cost-of-Living Adjustment

Among the most problematic approaches recently adopted in state school finance policy is the Kansas cost-of-living adjustment. In fact, although the adjustment is relatively small, the Kansas Supreme Court

considered it so problematic that the court has continued to prohibit its implementation.

In the spring and summer of 2005, during a regular and a special legislative session on school finance in response to a high court order to improve the adequacy of school funding and reduce the political distortions in cost adjustments, the Kansas legislature passed a series of modifications to the state's weighted-pupil formula, including modest increases to base aid, at-risk funding, and bilingual education.

In addition to these, and other changes, the legislature passed a special adjustment to local taxing authority so that 17 districts across the state could raise additional Tier-I funds to compensate for high cost of living. The 17 districts would be those with average single-family housing prices greater than 25% above the state average. In effect, the adjustment would be a high-priced house-need weight.

By the end of the special summer 2005 session on school finance, the Cost of Living adjustment (based solely on housing values) remained the only provision that the Kansas Supreme Court continued to stay. In a special hearing on the adjustment in August 2005, plaintiffs provided a geographic portrayal of the application of the adjustment with respect to the locations of poor and minority students in the state. A modified version of that evidence appears in Figure 9.7.

As one might expect, when one goes to the extreme of providing a special cost adjustment solely on the basis of housing price, that adjustment exclusively favors wealthy suburban districts, in this case, the state's two major university towns (Manhattan and Lawrence). In the Kansas City metropolitan area in particular, the adjustment would provide additional funding in nearly all but the area's highest-need district, Kansas City.

Economies of Scale, Sparsity, and Remoteness

According to the NAS report *Making Money Matter*, 15 states use some form of cost adjustment for either small schools or small school districts. The report notes that "Some states adjust for large size. They accord large districts added per pupil revenue, presumably justified because there are diseconomies in operating unusually large organizations. Other states adjust for unusual small size districts, schools, or both" (Ladd & Hansen, 1999, p. 129).

Figure 9.7   Kansas Cost-of-Living Adjustment

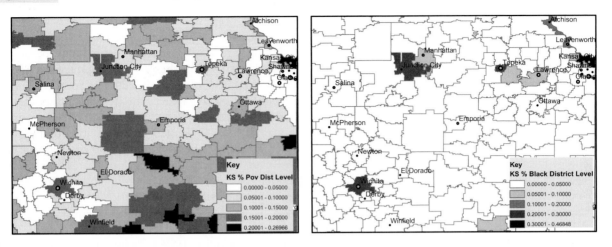

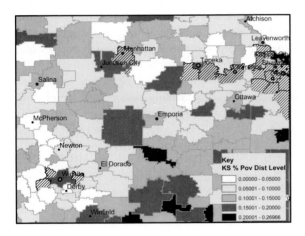

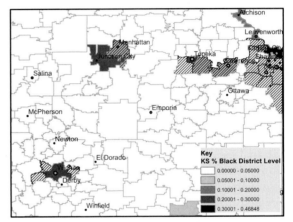

The report also notes, "No two states have adopted a distribution scheme that contains a similar formula component or approach specifying additional revenues a school or district should receive because of enrollment size" (Ladd & Hansen, 1999, p. 129).

State aid adjustments for scale can occur in several aid programs: basic operating aid, transportation aid, and facilities aid, and through a special categorical aid program for isolated rural districts. (Scale adjustments can be made in other categorical programs. We did not consider these in classifying aid systems.)

Basic Operating Aid
Scale adjustment to the basic operating aid program can occur by additions to the foundation level, changes in pupil weights, or additions to the calculated aid level. Research suggests that district enrollment levels above 2,000 probably do not result in significant cost savings and that costs per student can go up significantly as enrollment falls below 500 students (Andrews, Duncombe, & Yinger, 2002). In general, aid adjustments should reflect factors outside of district control. In addition, states may not want to subsidize geographically small districts that can feasibly merge with a neighboring district. Thus, scale adjustments should reflect both district enrollment size and sparsity. States should measure sparsity by a factor outside of district control, such as pupil density (pupils per square mile), rather than distance between schools, which can be affected by district decisions about the size and location of its schools.

Approximately half of the states make some scale adjustment to their basic operating aid system. While many of the states making adjustments are rural states where economy of scale is likely to be a major concern, several other states with significant rural areas make no scale adjustment at all (Idaho, Iowa, Kentucky, Mississippi, Missouri, New Hampshire, Tennessee, Virginia, Wisconsin). Of the 24 states with adjustments, all but one consider district enrollment (16 states), school enrollment (10 states), or both (3 states) in setting the adjustments. In addition, 13 states include some type of adjustment for sparsity or isolation. Of the states with district enrollment thresholds (to receive the adjustment), most are below 2,000 students. Of the states with an isolation factor, only two use pupil density as the principal criteria. Distance between schools is the more common method for determining isolation. Most states allow for a larger adjustment as the enrollment becomes smaller.

Transportation Aid

Transportation costs per student can vary depending on the number of students transported, length of bus trip, bus utilization rates, condition of roads, and regional costs associated with bus driver salaries and fuel costs. Ideally, a transportation aid formula would account for factors directly affecting transportation costs that are outside of a district's control (Alexander, 1990). External factors that reflect the effects of isolation on transportation costs include pupil density, bus miles on state-approved routes (or pupil bus miles for students eligible for transportation), or linear density (approved students divided by bus miles traveled). Forty-five states have some sort of aid program for transportation that is either part of the foundation program (12 states) or a separate categorical aid program (33 states). One advantage of including transportation aid in the foundation program is that it will be wealth equalized. Thirteen states use either pupil density or linear density in calculating aid levels. Another 11 states use bus miles, pupil miles, or some combination of bus miles and number of students in calculating transportation aid (2 states used both a density measure and miles measure). A large share of states use either the number of students transported to calculate aid, or some share of actual costs, which could be under district control.

Building Aid

Building expenditures per pupil are likely to be higher in sparsely populated school districts, both because of some relatively fixed costs for certain types of facilities and additional classroom space per student, because of lower class sizes. On the other hand, in places such as New York City, square-foot building costs can exceed the national average by 3 or 4 times. Some states should consider sparsity adjustments for building aid programs similar to those in basic operating aid programs, and other states should consider urbanicity adjustments. However, with very rare exceptions, states do not adjust building-aid levels for district size and sparsity. Several states actually set minimum school-size levels for districts to receive state funding (Georgia and West Virginia) (U.S. Department of Education, 2001; Walker & Sjoquist, 1996). At least in the case of West Virginia, the school-size restrictions have forced districts to consolidate to get state funding (Purdy, 1996).[2]

Two approaches for adjusting for economies of scale in school-funding formulas include the school-based block grant approach used in Wyoming for compensating the high cost of operating exceptionally small schools, or a sliding-scale pupil-weighting approach based on cost-function analyses as presented in Chapter 8. For example, cost-function coefficients may suggest that instructional costs in the district serving 100 pupils are 50% higher than in the district serving 2,500 pupils and that instructional costs in the district serving 300 pupils are 20% higher than in the district serving 2,500 pupils. Assuming that the district serving 2,500 pupils represents the minimum on the "J" curve, that district would receive a 1.0 weight times the basic cost. The district serving 100 pupils would receive a 1.5 weight, and the district serving 300 pupils would receive a 1.2 weight.

Adjustments for economies of scale may present additional complexities regarding the integration of other adjustments. For example, scale economies for general education programs and supplemental education programs are likely quite different across the same set of districts. That is because the scale of general education programs and special education programs is quite different. For example, total district enrollments for a group of districts may range from 100 to 2,000 and have measurable cost differences per unit of production with

---

[2] Arizona provides a 5% increase in new facilities funding for rural districts. In California, the Office of Public School Construction provides an increase in new construction funding of 12% for projects that house less than 101 students or by 4% if it houses between 101 and 200 students (Opresko, 2000).

a minimum of 1.0 at 2,000 students and as much as 1.8 at 100 students. The same set of districts may have from 5 to 15 students with special needs in districts enrolling about 100 students to 100 to 300 students with special needs in districts enrolling about 2,000 students. It is unlikely that the same 1.8/1.0 ratio used for general education funding is appropriate to apply to funding for students with special needs. In fact, scale economies may be inconsequential for these students, many of whom require intensive individualized services in any setting, and many of whom are served in regional centers and cooperative agencies in the smallest districts.

A final concern regarding economies of scale weightings relates to the incentive provided to local school officials to continue operating schools or districts at inefficient production levels because doing so allows them to maximize revenue. Ladd and Hansen raise the question:

> Presumably, population sparsity and rural remoteness can trigger the need for a "necessary" small school. Here, it is generally acknowledged, the state has an obligation to allocate added revenues to ensure that students are fairly treated. However, if a community merely chooses to have a small school in order to take advantage of the sense of engagement that such an institution may offer, is the state still obligated to pay the added costs? (1999, p. 130)

It is conceivable, for example, that two very small districts, experiencing declining enrollments may be within reasonable geographic distance from one another to consolidate, but may choose not to because of the expected, often substantial, loss in annual revenues per pupil.

Example Application: Texas Scale and Sparsity Adjustments

The Texas foundation school program (FSP) includes a series of cost adjustments intended to simultaneously accommodate costs associated with differences in district size and sparsity. The FSP also includes a separate block-grant program for allocating transportation aid. The FSP assumes the sparsity adjustment to Tier-1 aid to be related to nontransportation operating costs. Very small districts (130 average daily attendance [ADA] or less) in Texas are effectively provided a min-

imum base budget by setting the funded pupils for those districts above the actual ADA using a set of decision rules based on grade levels offered and distance to the nearest high school district.[3]

Small districts with 130 to 1,600 students receive either of two weights, a higher weight of .0004 if the district is greater than 300 square miles (thereby sparse) and a lower weight of .00025 if the district is less than 300 square miles. Districts with 1,600 to 5,000 pupils may receive midsized district-weighted funding, with a weight of .000025. However, high-property wealth districts are excluded from the midsized district weight. (The FSP defines high-property wealth districts as those with property values exceeding $305,000 per pupil in WADA in 2002–2003.) In Texas, small and midsized district weights are applied to each district's ABA. In 2002–2003, the basic allotment per pupil was $2,537. That basic allotment is multiplied times a cost of education index, which adjusts for differences in teacher wages in different parts of the state, to yield the ABA. As such, the wage index and scale and sparsity adjustments have multiplicative effects.

The end result of the Texas scale and sparsity index appears as Figure 9.8. The y axis represents the magnitude of the adjustment, relative to the ABA. Districts may receive as much as 63% above (1.63) their ABA through small-district weighting. For districts with fewer than 1,600 pupils, the figure shows two separately sloping lines. The steeper of the two lines represents the cost index for small, sparse districts larger than 300 square miles, and the more gradual slope represents the index for small, less-sparse districts. Districts with 1,600 to 5,000 pupils fall on the gradual sloping line that descends to a value of 1.0.

Example Application: Kansas Scale Adjustments

The Kansas economy of scale weight, or "low enrollment weight," is less complex than the Texas weight. In 1992, under court pressure (though no formal decree), the Kansas legislature adopted a new, cost-adjusted two-tiered formula called the School District Finance Act. As part of that formula, the legislature followed a governors' task force recommendation to make adjustments for economies of scale. Kansas calculated the weight as

---

[3]The decision rules for setting the fundable ADA of very small districts are as follows: (1) If the district has less than 130 students in ADA, offers a K–12 program and either enrolls at least 90 students or is greater than 30 miles by bus from the nearest high school, the district receives aid for 130 students. (2) If the district offers a K–8 program and has at least 50 students, or is 30 miles from the nearest high school district, the district receives aid for 75 students. (3) If the district offers a K–6 program and has at least 40 students or is 30 miles by bus route from the nearest high school district, the district receives funding for 60 students.

Figure 9.8 Texas Scale and Sparsity Adjustment

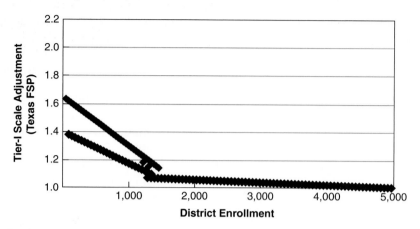

FSP, foundation school program.

Source: Authors constructed simulations based on data from Texas Foundation School Program and Kansas School District Finance Act.

follows: The median general fund budget per pupil of districts with 75 to 125 pupils represented the relative cost in districts with 100 pupils, the median budget per pupil of districts with 200 to 400 pupils represented the cost in districts with 300 pupils, and the median general fund budget per pupil in districts with over 1,900 pupils represented the cost per pupil in districts with over 1,900 pupils. (Note that Kansas did not include separate adjustments or provisions for sparsity in the scale adjustment. Rather, it uses a separate, density-based formula for providing transportation aid.) Kansas derived a weighting scheme by "connecting the dots" between the districts with 100 pupils, 300 pupils, and 1,900 pupils to yield the pattern shown in Figure 9.9. Unlike the Texas formula, Kansas does not make adjustments to the base before adjusting for scale.

These calculations resulted in ratios for Kansas of 214% for 100 or fewer pupils, 158% for 300 pupils, and no weight for districts with 1,900 or more students. (Kansas modified the School District Finance Act so that districts in 1999 with 1,725 students would received a weight of 1.0632.)

Figure 9.9 Kansas Scale Adjustment

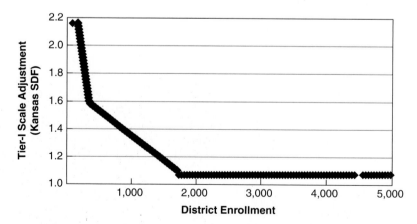

SDF, School District Finance Act.

Source: Authors constructed simulations based on data from Texas Foundation School Program and Kansas School District Finance Act.

Comparing Texas and Kansas, the smallest districts in Kansas receive a much higher weight, especially compared to Texas small districts under 300 square miles. For districts with 300 to 1,000 pupils, the Kansas weight runs relatively parallel to the Texas weight for districts over 300 square miles, but the Kansas weight is significantly higher than Texas districts with small land area.

Finding the Right Drivers of Need-Based Funding: Avoiding Endogeneity

When setting pupil need or district characteristic cost adjustments in state school finance policy, a primary goal is to avoid measures that are *endogenous* to the system. What do we mean by endogeneity? **Endogeneity** as we use it is a statistical modeling term, but one that relates nicely to policy design concerns. In short, measures that are **endogenous** to the system are those that can be influenced within the system itself. Exogenous

measures are those that are completely outside of the system. Of course, no measure is completely outside the system. For example, varied quality of schools (measured by outcomes) from one side of an island to another can, of course, influence where individuals choose to live, influencing the demographic makeup of each community. The goal in designing a weighted student-funding formula is to identify those factors outside of control of school officials that best predict the needs of the school and its student population, where *needs* specifically refer to the various factors that affect the ability of teachers and administrators to influence student outcomes and the resulting different costs of achieving desired student outcomes.

Figure 9.10 provides a schematic guide to identifying exogenous cost factors. Ideally, one would identify that set of purely exogenous measures that identify precisely and accurately which schools are likely to have lower student outcomes and where higher costs are associated with improving those outcomes. This logic applies to both student need and school location

Figure 9.10   Finding Exogenous Need/Cost Indicators

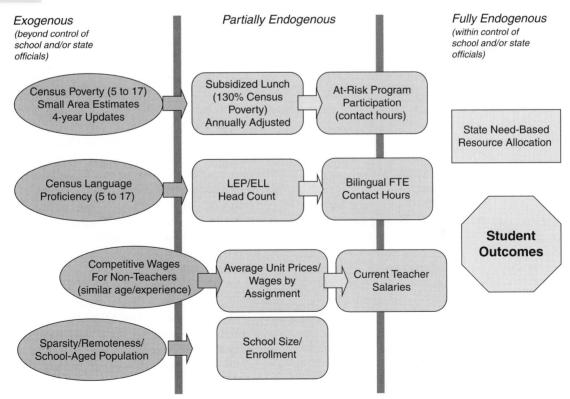

ELL, English language learner; FTE, full-time equivalent; LEP, limited English proficient.

factors. In most states, the best possible exogenous factors would include U.S. Census Bureau small-area estimates of children between age 5 and 17 enrolled in public schools and (a) living in poverty and (b) speaking English "not well" or "not at all." These two factors serve as good sociological predictors of at-risk and LEP shares of students.

These measures, however, have a handful of problems. First, language-proficiency data are gathered only decennially. Poverty measures for small areas, including school districts, are measured decennially and updated annually (U.S. Census Bureau, no date, http://www.census.gov/www/saipe/district.html). However, these data are also measured by residential location, creating inaccuracies where interdistrict choice models are involved, both on the sending and receiving end, including charter school enrollments (for which no specific data would be available) or interdistrict desegregation plans (which higher-poverty residents of one district might be enrolled in another). Alternatively, one might turn to the next best options, which include school-counted subsidized lunch rates and LEP student counts. Subsidized lunch rates are defined in federal policy and can be audited for over-count with reasonable precision. Further, subsidized lunch rates tend to be highly correlated with census poverty rates (e.g., correlation = .92 across large Kansas districts), though at a different average level due to different income thresholds. The second need indicator, LEP/ English language learner (ELL) counts, should be based on precise, state-mandated definitions for identifying LEP, such that these counts may also be audited for precision and accuracy. Nonetheless, audits typically catch only overreporting, not underreporting, and under-reporting may be problematic where incentive to identify and serve is insufficient.

We argue that states should avoid taking the next step to the right in Figure 9.10, basing funding on special program participation rates or contact hours. Doing so can encourage school officials to inflate contact hours or participation in specialized, segregated services even if not educationally appropriate. Or, if weighted funding is too low to cover costs of special programs and services (leading to a net loss per hour provided), local administrators may simply forgo the weighted funding and provide no services to the population in question (usually LEP/ELL).

A secondary issue with subsidized lunch counts is the tendency for secondary-grade subsidized lunch counts to be underreported. One might assume that the lower rates of qualifying for subsidized lunch among secondary students is a function of parents of older students being more established in their careers and no longer in poverty. We side with the alternative, well-documented view that, due to a variety of reasons including but not limited to stigma, reporting rates are simply lower at the secondary level. One approach for correcting this underreporting is to use K–8 reporting rates to predict 9–12 rates based on feeder school relationships.

One would not want to fund on the basis of low performance itself. Indeed, it may be reasonable to want to drive more funding into a school that is low performing. However, financing directly on the basis of low performance also means reducing that funding as performance improves, even if the external conditions that initially led to lower performance have not changed. This simply does not make sense. Further, and more pessimistically, where no consequences exist for individual students if they fail state tests (relieving school personnel of more serious ethical concerns), school administrators and teachers may actually deemphasize state tests and reap financial benefits for doing so if that de-emphasis leads to increased failure rate. In short, funding on the basis of low performance itself is a bad idea.

Identifying the correct approach for adjusting for teacher wages is also wrapped up in questions of endogeneity. As discussed previously, if one wishes to identify differences in wages required to recruit teachers of similar qualifications to higher- versus lower-need schools in the same labor market, one must have access to data showing substantive differences either in pay currently received by teachers in those schools or in teacher quality across those schools at the same pay. Current teacher salaries across schools in several states are fully endogenous to the system, governed by a single salary schedule attached to experience and degree levels. As such, current salary data are of limited use in identifying necessary wage differentials across schools or islands.

Alternatively, one might look to wages of similarly educated, similarly experienced professionals in comparable occupations to determine an appropriate competitive wage by Public Use MicroData Area (PUMA). Even then, in more remote areas where school personnel make up a larger share of the local economy, schooling wages (endogenous) may strongly influence local competitive wages.

School-size factors are also not immune to endogeneity concerns. One would not, for example, want to establish a system that provides a disincentive for charter schools to grow their enrollments (because they would lose small-school adjustment). Further, one would not necessarily want to establish a system that supports a greater than necessary number of small, higher-cost schools where geography and demography would allow for more efficient delivery of educational services.

SUMMARY

As with pupil weights for student needs, cost adjustments to accommodate scale and sparsity—in combination with cost adjustments to accommodate geographic differences in input prices—are largely idiosyncratic across states. Scale adjustments in their present form are based on empirical analyses of costs associated with scale that range dramatically in technical depth and most often involve arbitrarily and/or politically defined cut-points as to who will receive additional aid and who will not. Finally, the way in which cost adjustments, like scale and geographic price adjustments, are combined varies widely, with some states choosing to add one adjustment to another, and other states choosing to multiply one times another. Rarely, if ever, are these decisions based on thoughtful and thorough empirical analyses of how different types of costs vary in combination with one another. This is particularly true of the relationship between district need adjustments and student-need adjustments.

KEY TERMS

competitive (comparable) wage   Wages and wage variations for workers in professions other than the reference group (teachers) that might compete directly for workers in the reference group. If other professions, requiring similar education and experience to the reference group, earn more in one area of a state than in another, it can be inferred that wages for the reference group should vary similarly.

cost of living   Differences in "cost" from one location to another, in providing *comparable quality of living*.

economies of scale   Refers generally to the concept that costs of output typically decline with the volume of output, or size of the institution. In education, scale is most often measured as numbers of enrolled students.

endogeneity (endogenous)   Endogeneity is formally a statistical modeling term meaning that the relationship between outcome and input measures is circular. In this chapter, endogeneity refers to those situations where the cost factor in question may be influenced by available revenue. For example, students counted as requiring funding for special needs may be identified in increasing numbers where funding is available.

hedonic wage (model)   Wages and wage variations that are sensitive to desirability of localized working conditions and preferences for local amenities.

sparsity   By dictionary definition, *sparse* is the antonym of *dense*. Most often, sparsity measures in school finance are operationalized as density measures, such as numbers of residents or pupils per square miles.

REFERENCES

Alexander, M. D. (1990). Public school pupil transportation: Rural schools. *Journal of Education Finance, 16,* 226–246.

Alexander, C., Gronberg, T., Jansen, D., Keller, H., Taylor, L., & Triesman, P. (2000). *A study of uncontrollable variations in the costs of Texas public education: A summary report prepared for the 77th Texas legislature.* Austin, TX: Charles A. Dana Center, University of Texas at Austin.

Andrews, M., Duncombe, W., & Yinger, J. (2002). Revisiting economies of size in American education: Are we any closer to a consensus? *Economies of Education Review, 21,* 245–262.

Baker, B. D. (2005). The emerging shape of educational adequacy: From theoretical assumptions to empirical evidence. *Journal of Education Finance, 30*(3), 259–287.

Baker, B. D. (2007). *Evaluating marginal costs with school level data: Implications for weighted student formulas.* Working Paper, Lawrence, KS: University of Kansas.

Baker, B. D., & Duncombe, W. D. (2004). Balancing district needs and student needs: The role of economies of scale adjustments and pupil need weights in school finance formulas. *Journal of Education Finance, 29*(2), 97–124.

Chambers, J. (1997). *Measuring inflation in public school costs.* Working paper No. 97–43. Project Officer, W. J. Fowler, Jr. Washington, DC: U.S. Department of Education. National Center for Education Statistics. Retrieved from http://nces.ed.gov/pubs97/9743.pdf

Chambers, J. (1998). *Geographic variations in public schools' costs.* Working Paper No. 98–04. Project Officer, W. J. Fowler, Jr. Washington, DC: U.S. Department of Education. National Center for Education Statistics.

Chambers, J. G. (1999). Patterns of variation in the salaries of school personnel: What goes on behind the cost index numbers? *Journal of Education Finance, 25,* 255.

Duncombe, W. D., & Goldhaber, D. (2004). *Estimating geographic cost of education differences: A case study of Maryland.* Paper presented at the annual meeting of the Association for Budget and Financial Management. Chicago.

Gronberg, T., Jansen, D., Taylor, L., & Booker, K. (2004). *School outcomes and schools costs: The cost function approach.* College Station, TX: Bush School of Government and Public Service, Texas A&M University. Retrieved March 1, 2006 from http://bush.tamu.edu/research/faculty_projects/txschoolfinance/papers/SchoolOutcomesAndSchoolCosts.pdf

Guthrie, J. W., & Rothstein, R. (1999). Enabling adequacy to achieve reality: Translating adequacy into state school finance distribution arrangements. In H. F. Ladd, R. Chalk, & J. S. Hansen (Eds.), *Equity and adequacy in education finance: Issues and perspectives* (pp. 209–259). Washington, DC: National Academy Press.

Hanushek, E. A., & Rivkin, S. G. (1996). Understanding the 20th century growth in U.S. school spending. *Journal of Human Resources, 32*(1), 35–67.

Ladd, H. F., Chalk, R., & Hansen, J. S. (1999). *Equity and adequacy in education finance: Issues and perspectives.* Washington, DC: National Academy Press.

Ladd, H., & Hansen, J. (1999). *Making money matter: Financing America's schools.* Committee on Education Finance, Commission on Behavioral and Social Sciences and Education, National Research Council. Washington, DC: National Academy Press.

Mishel, L., & Rothstein, R. (1996, July 25). *Alternative options for deflating education expenditures over time.* Paper presented at the National Center for Education Statistics (NCES) Summer Data Conference, Washington, DC.

National Center for Education Statistics and U.S. Department of Education. (2001). *Public school finance programs of the United States and Canada: 1998–99.* NCES 2001-309. Washington, DC. Author.

Odden, A. R., Picus, L. O., Goetz, M., Fermanich, M., Seder, R., Glenn, W., & Nelli, R. (2005). *An evidence based approach to recalibrating Wyoming's block grant school funding formula.* Prepared for the Wyoming Legislative Select Committee on Recalibration.

Opresko, A. (2000). *School construction: The nation and selected states.* Albany: New York Bureau of Budget.

Podgursky, M., Monroe, R., & Watson, D. (2004). The academic quality of public school teachers: An analysis of entry and exit behavior. *Economics of Education Review, 23*(4), 507–518.

Purdy, H. (1996). An economical, thorough and efficient school system and the West Virginia School Building Authority. Economy of Scale Numbers, EDRS. *Public school finance programs of the United States and Canada: 1998–99.* NCES 2001-309. Washington, D.C.: National Center for Education Statistics and U.S. Department of Education.

Taylor, L. (2005). *Comparable wages, inflation and school finance equity.* Working Paper #540. College Station, TX: Bush School of Government and Public Service. Texas A&M University.

U.S. Census Bureau. (no date). *Small area income and poverty estimates, school district special tabulation.* Retrieved from http://www.census.gov/hhes/www/saipe/

U.S. Department of Education, National Center for Education Statistics. (2001). *Public School Finance Programs of the United States and Canada: 1998–99.* NCES 2001–309. Washington, DC: Author.

Walker, M. B., & Sjoquist, D. L. (1996). Allocation of state funds for construction and renovation of schools in Georgia. *Journal of Education Finance, 22,* 161–179.

Additional Reading

Taylor, L. L., & Fowler, W. J., Jr. (2006). *A comparable wage approach to geographic cost adjustment* (NCES 2006-321). U.S. Department of Education. Washington, DC: National Center for Education Statistics.

ADVANCED ADEQUACY TOPICS AND SIMULATIONS

Introduction

This chapter provides more advanced insights and analyses related to the study of educational adequacy and vertical equity. Our study of advanced topics in school finance adequacy in this chapter builds directly on the work in Chapters 8 and 9. Without a thorough understanding of these two previous chapters, Chapter 10 will be very difficult to comprehend, unless you come to it with a fairly high level of expertise from other sources. In the first section, we propose a new series of tools for evaluating increasingly complex state-aid formulas. The primary objective of our new toolkit is to provide straightforward and transparent measures and indices of the extent that current aid formulas achieve adequacy goals. We conclude this section with a synthesis of our new indices tied specifically to emerging causes of action in school finance litigation. In the final section, we provide frameworks for developing cost-based aid formulas using hypothetical examples of policy proposals in the states of Texas and Kansas on the Companion Website (www.prenhall.com/baker).

New Tools for Evaluating Aid Formulas

To reiterate a major theme discussed in Chapters 7 to 9, in the modern era of school finance, it is no longer sufficient to argue that all children should have the same dollars allocated to their education. Rather, each child has a particular educational program that is adequate for him or her, and each child's program incurs different sets of educational costs (Underwood, 1995). As we discussed in Chapter 7, the requirement of differential, need-based financing of public education can be tied to substantive due process claims in school finance litigation. Plaintiffs have made their cases based on a determination that the state's school finance policy does not make sufficient adjustments such that children of varied needs have comparable opportunities to succeed on state-outcome standards (see Chapter 7). In this section, we summarize the current state of knowledge regarding additional costs associated with student needs and district characteristics. We also discuss methods for evaluating current state school finance policies and designing new policies against this backdrop.

Because many, though not all, states have built their current school finance policies on the assumption that some children need more resources than others, current revenues and expenditures across local school districts typically include two types of variations: (a) variations due to the local wealth or fiscal capacity of school districts and (b) variations due to differences in need and related costs. The conventional equity analysis tools that we presented in Chapter 5 are ineffective at sorting out these two sources of variance. The typical school finance equity statistics including coefficients of variation, ranges, range ratios, and McLoone indices, as calculated in Chapter 5, assume that all variance in per-pupil spending promotes inequality and assume that the ideal condition is one where all districts have the *same* educational resources. In fact, that version of the ideal condition may be anything but ideal for the district that has high concentrations of very high-need students or is in a region with excessively high labor costs.

A coefficient of variation for educational revenues that exceeds 20% or 30% and range ratios that exceed 2.0 may be entirely appropriate. Such seemingly large amounts of variation in resources across districts within a state may actually be required:

1. If some districts in the state have significantly higher costs associated with providing comparable opportunities

2. Or if some districts incur higher-than-average costs as a result of external environmental conditions over which school districts have little or no control that limit the districts' ability to produce outcomes comparable to those with students from more nurturing environments

To complicate matters further, one cannot simply assume that cost adjustments adopted by legislatures and included in state-aid formulas are empirically determined indicators of real cost. Rather, as discussed by Baker and Duncombe (2004), cost adjustments in state-aid formulas are derived in a political context and most likely represent a state's balance of political power as much if not more so than the real differences in costs faced by local public schools. Further, Baker and Green (2005) demonstrate how legislators can actually use the tools intended to differentiate per-pupil expenditures based on legitimate differences in resources required to accomplish state-mandated outcomes.

An illustrative example of the use of political power to differentiate per-pupil expenditures occurred in the 2005 legislative session in Kansas. Legislators representing wealthy, suburban districts proposed a new cost adjustment for districts in high-cost regions of the state. High cost was to be determined by identifying those districts with median housing unit values more than 25% above state average housing unit values. Obviously, such a cost adjustment would lead directly to wealth-related variance and would also pour additional funds into districts serving student populations with lower rather than higher needs.

Less obviously self-interested cost adjustments abound in state policies throughout the country. In some cases, the rationale alone raises significant questions, as in the preceding example. In other cases, the effect of cost adjustments is questionable, and policy makers may need to run simulations in order to determine the impact in advance of adoption. For example, again in Kansas, the legislature has adopted a cost adjustment for children attending school in new facilities that channels more in *cost-adjusted* aid to wealthy, growing suburbs than to poor urban districts in metropolitan areas. This effect occurs because the new-facilities

adjustment is significantly larger than adjustments for at-risk or limited-English-proficient (LEP) children. In Alabama, the state determines foundation aid by a count of teacher units, applying 15% more aid per teacher unit for teachers holding a master's degree. Like the Kansas new facilities cost adjustment, this cost adjustment has the effect of providing less funding for districts with higher concentrations of poor and minority students, because minority teachers, who invariably teach minority students in Alabama, are significantly less likely to hold a master's degree than are their white peers (Baker & Green, 2005).

Most researchers and the education media continue to rely on arbitrary cost adjustments for measuring the relative adequacy of financial resources across districts and across states (Carey, 2003; Rubenstein, 2003). Others continue to assume that cost adjustments adopted by state legislatures are the best empirical estimates of cost, using aid-formula cost adjustments to account for vertical equity/adequacy in their analyses. Thankfully, state court judges have recognized the shortcomings of such analyses. In *Montoy v. State* (2001), Kansas presented equity analyses based on aid-formula pupil weightings in order to assert that the current Kansas aid formula is equitable. Regarding the analyses, Judge Terrence Bullock noted that the defense expert, "testified he believes Kansas has a 'substantial amount' of school equity, but in so opining he also testified that he *assumed* the Kansas system of weighting was based on actual costs to educate, which it is not" (*Montoy v. State*, 2001). In fact, through more thorough analyses of costs and needs of local districts in Kansas, other researchers have found significant flaws and questionable political origins of the state's current pupil-weighting system (Baker & Duncombe, 2004; Baker & Green, 2003; Baker & Green, 2005; Baker & Imber, 1999; Duncombe & Johnston, 2004; Green & Baker, 2002).

How does one critique the cost-basis or rationality of aid-formula adjustments, commonly implemented as pupil weights or flat grants? A simple resolution to these problems is to continue to use conventional equity statistics but limit analyses to districts of with similar costs. That is, measure the variance in resources among districts with similar student populations (to account for student-need–related costs) in similar regions (to account for regional price variations) of a state and of similar size (to account for economies of scale). Unfortunately, for differences in student needs, this approach reduces our ability to compare the resources available in high- and low-need districts. High-poverty districts could have similar resources to one another, and low-poverty districts could also have resources similar to one another. The average level of resources in high-poverty districts might be lower or even the same as that of low-poverty districts. Conventional equity statistics would mask this problem. However, between-group comparisons could be made. Subgroup analysis can be a useful way to remove districts facing high costs as a result of lacking economies of scale. You will see throughout this section that we frequently focus on districts enrolling greater than 2,000 or 5,000 pupils in order to isolate those districts perceived to be scale efficient.

Next, we propose a series of possible analyses, beginning with methods that decompose individual cost adjustments in order to make *best comparisons* with cost benchmarks. We also discuss the evaluation of systems of cost adjustments as a whole. We argue that more important than the rationality of any single cost adjustment in a state-aid formula is the collective net of effects of the complete package of cost adjustments on high- and low-need districts. Finally, we discuss the evaluation of systems that include both variance in revenues per pupil due to cost adjustments and variance in revenue per pupil due to allowance of local discretion in taxation.

Evaluation of Individual Cost Adjustments

Our first and least comprehensive approach for tackling cost adjustments in state-aid formulas is to address them one at a time, both in terms of the basic rationality of the cost adjustment and in terms of the magnitude of the effect of the cost adjustment. We ask the following policy questions:

1. Does it make sense to begin with the assertion that the cost adjustment should be included in the aid formula?
2. Is the cost adjustment, as written in policy and as applied in the allocation of dollars to local districts, sufficiently related to the actual costs incurred?

One might certainly question the surface validity of the Kansas legislature's attempt to adopt a cost adjustment based on district housing unit values on the basis that local housing costs influence necessary teacher wages, especially because the preponderance of

empirical evidence suggests quite the opposite (see Chapter 13). As we discuss in Chapter 13, a number of factors related more commonly with high poverty and low housing unit values more likely lead to higher costs of recruiting and retaining teachers of quality similar to those who work in districts with high-priced houses and more advantaged students. As such, this type of adjustment may be overturned at even the most deferential level of rational basis analysis. Answering the second question requires some evidence on education costs associated with the adjustment and the effectiveness of the adjustment at helping districts meet those costs.

We begin with a discussion of dollar comparisons of cost adjustments for children with LEP and recent evidence on the costs of providing adequate educational services for those children in five states (Kansas, Missouri, Nebraska, Colorado, and North Dakota). Next, we address the calculation of *implicit weights* because, quite simply, a pupil weight as written in state policy is not always what it appears to be. Finally, we briefly address a simple rationality test: Do districts with more students in need actually receive more need-based funding? While the answer to this question should be obvious, Baker (2001) found that in many cases, districts predicted by census bureau data to have greater poverty or LEP rates did not actually receive a greater share of poverty or LEP-based aid.

Dollar Comparison Against Cost Benchmarks

As we discussed in Chapter 8, in recent years, consultants have conducted resource-cost analyses to estimate the cost of an adequate education in Kansas, Missouri, Nebraska, Colorado, and North Dakota (Augenblick and Myers, Inc., 2002, 2003a, 2003b, 2003c; Augenblick, Palaich and Associates, Inc., 2004). Each of those states, except Missouri, has a cost adjustment for LEP children within its aid formula. In some cases, that cost adjustment is tied to the delivery of bilingual education programming rather than to the count of LEP children. The top section of Table 10.1 includes consultants' estimates of the adequate basic aid requirement for scale-efficient (larger) districts in each state. Immediately below the basic aid figure is consultants' estimated additional cost per LEP child. Note that the state achieves adequacy for LEP children by the combination of basic and supplemental funding. For example, in Kansas, consultants estimated that a district serving 11,200 pupils had basic costs per pupil of $5,811 in 2001. The estimated adequate LEP

Table 10.1   Relative Adequacy Comparisons for Limited-English-Proficiency Children

	Kansas[a]	Colorado	Missouri[b]	North Dakota	Nebraska
Basic adequacy estimates					
"Adequate" basic aid	$5,811	$6,815	$7,832	$6,005	$5,845
"Adequate" LEP adjustment	$5,993	$4,837	$4,746	$6,046	$5,682
Adequacy for LEP child	$11,804	$11,652	$12,578	$12,051	$11,527
Revenue guaranteed by aid formula					
Minimum guaranteed foundation	$4,107	$4,202	$4,043	$2,287	$4,814
LEP adjustment in aid formula	$744	$400	$—	$300	$1,204
Base revenue per LEP child	$4,851	$4,602	$4,043	$2,587	$6,018
Percent adequate	41%	39%	32%	21%	52%
Current expenditures (average district)[c]					
Mean current expenditures per pupil	$6,501	$6,435	$6,570	$5,839	$6,371
Mean % LEP	4.9%	10.1%	1.2%	0.0%	5.9%
Mean % Poverty	11.1%	10.2%	13.8%	10.3%	11.4%
Current expenditures (high % LEP/ELL district)[c]					
Mean current expenditures in top 10% LEP	$6,390	$6,733	$8,286	$4,929	$5,614
Minimum current expenditures in top 10% LEP	$5,112	$5,912	$4,571	$4,929	$5,314
Mean % LEP in top 10% LEP districts	13.3%	25.8%	4.7%	1.6%[d]	25.3%
Mean % poverty in top 10% LEP districts[e]	15.7%	18.4%	30.3%	11.2%	16.7%
Adequacy comparisons					
Computed "adequate" revenue per pupil	$7,010	$8,507	$8,783	$6,365	$7,688
Mean as % of adequate	91%	79%	94%	77%	73%
Minimum as % of adequate	73%	69%	52%	77%	69%

[a]Kansas: Minimum Foundation = 1.0632 × $3,720 = $3,955 (2001).
[b]Missouri: Minimum Foundation = .0275 × 147,022 = 4,043 (2003). Actual amount was reduced due to budget shortfall.
[c]Districts enrolling greater than 2,000 pupils.
[d]North Dakota districts did not report LEP/ELL counts in the NCES/LEAU. Census data used as proxy.
[e]U.S. Census Percent 5 to 17 in Poverty.
LEP, limited English proficiency; ELL, English language learner.
Source: Baker, Green, & Markham, unpublished manuscript, 2004.

adjustment for a district of that size was $5,993, for a total allocation per LEP child of $11,804 (assuming that child is not also from an economically disadvantaged background).

The next section of Table 10.1 includes the minimum guaranteed state and local revenue available to an LEP child. For example, in 2001 the basic allotment in large districts in Kansas was $4,107, and the LEP/bilingual education adjustment was $744, for a cumulative basic allocation of $4,851 or less than half that deemed adequate by the legislature's own consultants. The case is similar for the other states in Table 10.1, with only Nebraska exceeding 50% of adequacy for LEP children in its basic formula allotment, due to both Nebraska's higher general aid and slightly larger LEP supplement.

The basic formula allotment comparisons to adequacy estimates in the upper portion of Table 10.1 likely underestimate the actual resources available in local school districts for LEP children. However, basic formula allotments do represent that amount of funding *guaranteed* by the state to be available.

The lower sections of Table 10.1 compare actual current expenditures per pupil to adequacy targets rather than comparing the minimum amount guaranteed by aid formulas. Note that current expenditure data include expenditure of federal funds as well as expenditures on children with disabilities. A debatable point is whether state legislatures alone are responsible for ensuring adequate funding regardless of federal effort or whether states may combine federal funds with state and local funds to achieve state-defined adequacy targets. Because Table 10.1 uses adequacy estimates for large, scale-efficient districts, we calculate average current expenditures per pupil for only large districts (enrolling > 2,000 pupils (which is the lower threshold identified by Andrews, Duncombe, & Yinger, 2002, as the point at which district level costs begin to level off.) Current expenditures are reported for the average large district and for the average of large districts in the top 10% of districts by LEP student concentration.

In Kansas, Nebraska, and North Dakota (1 district), large districts with high-LEP populations spend less per pupil than large districts on average. Large districts with high-LEP concentrations also tended to have higher poverty rates than low-LEP-concentration districts. Adequacy estimates at the bottom of Table 10.1 are based on calculated adequate base aid, estimated adequate poverty weights, LEP weights, and poverty and LEP shares. For example, $7,010 per pupil for a high-concentration-LEP Kansas district includes a base aid of $5,811, a poverty supplement of 15.7% times the estimated poverty weight of .44 times the base ($5,811), and an LEP supplement of 13.3% times the LEP weight of 1.03 times the base. Note that in this analysis, we use U.S. Census Bureau data instead of free or reduced price lunch rates for poverty estimates, resulting in a significantly lower poverty estimate than used in state policy and in analyses by Augenblick and Myers, Inc., 2002, 2003a, 2003b, 2003c, and Augenblick, Palaich and Associates, Inc., 2004. Hence, Table 10.1 includes conservative estimates of the cost of adequacy in high-LEP districts. Even with conservative estimates, high-LEP-concentration districts fall consistently short of adequate funds across the states under investigation, and the minimum-spending, high-concentration-LEP district in each state falls substantially below adequate levels.

Implicit-Weight Calculation

One oversimplification in the previous example is that we assumed that the Kansas pupil weight of .20 (under policies in 2004, the weight has since been increased), which is based on contact hours in bilingual education programs, actually translates to 20% additional aid per LEP child in a Kansas school district. In this section, we discuss the many ways in which a pupil weight might not be exactly what it appears to be and why it can be particularly difficult to compare pupil weights from one state-aid formula to another.

Can we simply compare pupil weights in aid formulas with these benchmarks? For example, is a .20 weight always more adequate than a .10 weight? Many reasons explain why this does not work very well. Most are related to the fact that cost adjustments are applied in so many different ways, making it particularly difficult to compare cost adjustments in one state school finance formula to cost adjustments in another. A further complication is that base-aid formulas define

adequacy at substantially different levels, even in similar regions of the United States. Because most vertical equity adjustments are relative to base aid, the same 20% adjustment can have significantly different net effects.

Table 10.2 compares cost adjustments for at-risk and LEP students in Kansas and Texas, two states that use extensively cost-adjusted two-tiered aid formulas. For at-risk pupils, Kansas uses a pupil weight of .10 times students who qualify for free lunch. Texas uses a weight of .20 times students who qualify for free or reduced-price lunch. Kansas bases total pupil counts on September 20th enrollments, while Texas bases enrollments on average daily attendance, which may actually disadvantage districts with economically deprived students who miss school more frequently. The Kansas .10 weight is multiplied by the base aid per pupil of $3,863, to yield $386 per at-risk pupil. The Texas .20 weight is multiplied by the scale and wage-adjusted allotment, yielding an average of $569 per pupil (and minimum possible of .20 × $2,537 = $507). One can readily see how the various steps in the calculation process and multitude of factors in addition to the single-pupil weight can lead to very different results, even if the weights were initially the same. Although the Texas weight is twice the size of the Kansas weight, its net difference is only $183 (569 − 386 = 183). Another way to compare is to set the Kansas percentage at 20, and that would produce a supplement of twice $386, or $772, which is considerably more than the $569 that the same 20% secures in Texas. We are belaboring this point because we want to emphasize that simple tables of comparison on the percentage of supplement are not valid comparisons.

To further complicate matters, as discussed in Chapter 9, the availability of state aid can influence local behavior regarding identification of student needs. Therefore, seeking *exogenous* measures of need can be useful. We frequently turn to U.S. Census Bureau school district special tabulation data for these measures. For example, we use U.S. Census Bureau poverty rates for children between the ages of 5 and 17 and for children between the ages of 5 and 17 who speak English not well or not at all to predict school district need. Because a stricter standard is applied, census bureau poverty rates tend to underestimate free and reduced-price lunch rates. Similarly, census statistics on language proficiency appear to underestimate need. Census bureau measures, while imperfect, do provide us with more comparable measures across states. As mentioned, Kansas counts only children qualifying for free lunch, whereas Texas includes children

Table 10.2   Calculation of Implicit Weights for Kansas and Texas At-Risk and Bilingual Program Weights

Need Category	Supplemental Aid	Mean Tier-I Aid	Implicit Weight	Current Instructional Spending	Implicit Weight
LEP children					
Kansas					
Bilingual aid per FTE pupil[a]	$773	$4,939	0.16	$3,540	0.22
Bilingual aid per LEP child[b]	$374	$4,939	0.08	$3,540	0.11
Bilingual aid per child who speaks English "not well" or "not at all"[c]	$1,139	$4,939	0.23	$3,540	0.32
Texas					
Bilingual aid per ADA pupil[d]	$284	$3,574	0.08	$3,780	0.08
Bilingual aid per LEP pupil[e]	$245	$3,574	0.07	$3,780	0.06
Bilingual aid per child who speaks English "not well" or "not at all"[f]	$846	$3,574	0.24	$3,780	0.22
Economically disadvantaged					
Kansas					
Compensatory aid per free lunch pupil[g]	$386	$4,939	0.08	$3,540	0.11
Compensatory aid per child in poverty[h]	$778	$4,939	0.16	$3,540	0.22
Texas					
Compensatory aid per ADA pupil[i]	$569	$3,574	0.16	$3,780	0.15
Compensatory aid per child in poverty[j]	$1,329	$3,574	0.37	$3,780	0.35

[a]Computed as 6 contact hours of bilingual education. Based on FTE Bilingual Education counts in Kansas Department of Education FY03 General Fund and Legal Max file.
[b]NCES Local Education Agency Universe Survey number of Limited English Proficient Pupils (school year 2000–2001).
[c]U.S. Census Bureau, number of children between ages of 5 and 17 who speak English "Not Well" or "Not at All."
[d]Bilingual education pupils in Average Daily Attendance from Texas Education Agency's FM02 file.
[e]NCES Local Education Agency Universe Survey number of Limited English Proficient Pupils (school year 2000–2001).
[f]U.S. Census Bureau, number of children between ages of 5 and 17 who speak English "Not Well" or "Not at All."
[g]Children qualifying for National School Lunch Program, "Free Lunch" category. Based on FTE reports in Kansas Department of Education FY03 General Fund and Legal Max file.
[h]Based on rates of poverty reported in U.S. Census 2000, for children aged 5 to 17.
[i]ADA compensatory education students, excluding "pregnant" classification, and related aid.
[j]Based on rates of poverty reported in U.S. Census 2000, for children aged 5 to 17.
ADA, average daily attendance; FTE, full-time equivalent; LEP, limited English proficiency.
Source: Adapted from Baker and Duncombe (2004).

qualifying for reduced-price lunch, and Kansas uses a program contact-hour method for determining full-time equivalent (FTE) participants in bilingual education programming.

Using census bureau estimates of need, the Kansas weight translates to $778 per child in poverty and the Texas weight to an average of $1,329 per child in poverty. Thus, although the Texas weight is twice the size of the Kansas weight, against the expected number of Texas children qualifying, Texas children receive $227 (16%) less than they might if both formulas were equivalent.

One can calculate **implicit weights** by comparing the supplemental allotment to the average available resources per pupil, assumed to crudely represent the expenditure per pupil for regular education. While Kansas uses a higher base aid per pupil in the first tier of its aid formula (Kansas, $3,863, compared to Texas, $2,537), current instructional spending per pupil is slightly higher in Texas than in Kansas. Average current expenditures per pupil or current instructional expenditures per pupil measures more accurately represent district resources than artificial funding formula values such as base-aid figures. With respect to average current instructional expenditures and U.S. census poverty rates, the Kansas implicit poverty weight is .22 and the Texas implicit poverty weight is .35.

Even more variation exists between the two states in the treatment of bilingual education programs. Texas bases its student counts on average daily attendance of LEP students. Kansas counts FTE pupils in bilingual education programs as the sum of 6 contact hours; a student receiving bilingual services all day, every day would count as 1 FTE. Kansas uses an explicit weight of .20, and Texas uses a weight of .10. The implicit weights, with respect to census data on children who speak English not well or not at all, and with respect to average current instructional spending per pupil, are .32 for Kansas and .22 for Texas. That is, though the Kansas categorical weight is twice as large, the total cost yield of that weight is only about 1.5 times as large as the Texas weight. Implicit weights can be a valuable tool for understanding the local impact of different approaches to providing cost adjustments.

Need-Effect Rationality Tests

Finally, we address a simple test of the rationality of a formula cost adjustment. Is the targeted aid reaching the target population? In the case of aid for bilingual education programs or language remediation, we would expect districts with larger shares of children who speak English not well or not at all to be receiving more of that targeted aid. Strangely, Baker (2001) did not always find this to be the case. In fact, Baker found that "only 63% of reporting states allocated compensatory aid in significant positive relation to expected need and only 46% of reporting states allocated LEP aid in accordance with expected need across districts" (2001, p. 717). We recommend the use of simple correlation tests and/or scatter plot analysis between categorical or supplemental aid per pupil received and expected need, predicted with exogenous measures.

Figure 10.1 displays a scatter plot (bubble plot, with bubble size representing district enrollment) of the relationship between bilingual program aid received per pupil (all enrolled pupils) and the census demographic measure of the percentage of children between the ages of 5 and 17 who speak English not well or not at all. Clearly, some positive relation exists between the two measures, and a reasonably strong relationship exists among communities with a higher percentage of non-English-speaking students. Note, however, that one should gauge correlations in policy analysis against expected policy outcomes rather than against a single statistical expectation. In this case, one would expect a nearly perfectly linear relationship

Figure 10.1   Relating Kansas Bilingual Program Aid per Pupil With Census 2000 Demographics

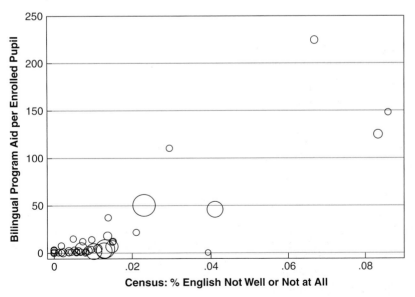

Bubble size represents district size.

Source: Data from U.S. Census Bureau (2000) percentage of children between age 5 and 17 speaking English "not well" or "not at all" and from bilingual funding allocations from the Kansas Department of Education.

between a state's allocation of aid for bilingual education programs and the residential location of non-English-speaking children. Figure 10.1 reveals that many communities with lower shares of non-English-speaking children appear to choose not to provide bilingual education services or not to receive state aid for doing so. The aid mechanism appears to result in a barrier to local behavior or initiating programming when certain minimum thresholds are not met.

Analysis of the Collective Need Effects of Cost-Adjustment Systems

Because state-aid formulas may include a multitude of weights and those weights can counter-balance one another, it is also necessary to evaluate pupil-weighting systems as a whole, in addition to dissecting the rationality of individual weights. Analyzing each weight can tell us about financial support for a specific group of children with special educational needs relative to a variety of adequacy and equity standards. Analyzing the system as a whole tells us whether district-wide aggregates of children are receiving comparable resources. Returning to our Texas and Kansas comparisons, we might, for example, evaluate and compare the cumulative effects of cost adjustments on the first tier of each state's general operating aid formula. As discussed previously, both states adjust for economies of scale, but Texas differentiates its scale weights by sparsity as well. Kansas uses a sparsity adjustment for transportation aid, which Texas provides as a separate allotment. Texas provides a relatively small, flat-grant, new instructional facilities allotment, while Kansas includes a weight of .25 times all students attending a new facility in the first 2 years of operation. Also as discussed previously, Kansas and Texas use a variety of student-need weights, including weights for at-risk children and bilingual education programs. Texas also includes a weight for gifted children (which Kansas includes within a separate special education aid program), and Texas includes special education weights as part of the general aid formula.

What then, is the balance of all of these effects, and how might we evaluate that balance? From a rationality perspective, based on existing empirical research, one might argue that one appropriate analysis would be to test whether districts with more students in poverty receive, on average, more cost-adjusted first-tier aid. That is, because it generally costs more to achieve desired outcomes in districts serving more

children from economically deprived backgrounds, poverty is treated as an overriding cost factor. As such, if we can construct an index of the cumulative effects of first-tier cost adjustments for each district in a state, we should find that, on average, districts with more children in poverty receive higher cost adjustments—that is, if we believe poverty to be an overriding cost factor. Because other cost factors, such as costs associated with scale, can be large and can result in shifting aid from poor urban to rural areas, one may choose to make comparisons among districts of similar size.

One can calculate an aggregate implied cost index for each school district by either of two methods, depending on the type of cost adjustments used in the state's aid formula:

1. If a state uses weighted pupil counts to provide aid, one can calculate a weighted-pupil/actual pupil ratio for each district, or weighting ratio.
2. Where the state uses a formula that results in a cost-adjusted first-tier aid value, but not necessarily a weighted-pupil count, one can divide each district's cost-adjusted first-tier aid by the base aid per pupil.

Either approach results in cost indices for each district that represent the cumulative effects of first-tier cost adjustments on the aid received by those districts:

$$\text{Implied Cost Index} = \text{Cost-Adjusted Aid per Pupil/Unadjusted Base Aid per Pupil}$$

or

$$\text{Implied Cost Index} = \text{Weighted-Pupil Count/Actual Enrolled Pupils}$$

For example, in Texas, the implied index for a small remote district might be calculated via the first method, as follows:

Basic Allotment	= $2,537
Adjusted Basic Allotment (ABA)	= $2,537 × (1.06) Geographic Wage
Index	= $2,645
Adjusted Allotment	= $2,645 (ABA) × Small District Adjustment
	= $4,195
Foundation School Program (FSP) Aid per Pupil	= $4,195 (Adjusted Allotment) × Various Pupil Need Weights = $5,786

Implied Cost Index = \$5,786 (cost-adjusted aid per pupil)/\$2,537 (unadjusted aid per pupil)
= 2.28

Whereas in Kansas, the implied cost index for a small remote district might be calculated via the second method, as follows:

Total Enrollment $\quad\quad$ = 150
At-Risk Weighted FTE $\quad$ = 25 × .10 = 2.5
Bilingual Program FTE $\quad$ = 125 contact hours/
$\quad\quad\quad\quad\quad\quad\quad\quad\quad$ 6 × .20 = 4.17
Vocational Program FTE = 50 contact hours/
$\quad\quad\quad\quad\quad\quad\quad\quad\quad$ 6 × .50 = 4.17
Transportation-
$\quad$ Weighted FTE $\quad\quad$ = 100 × .25 = 25
Low-Enrollment-
$\quad$ Weighted FTE $\quad\quad$ = 129
Total Weighted FTE $\quad$ = 315

Implied Cost Index = 315.01 Weighted FTE/
$\quad\quad\quad\quad\quad\quad\quad\quad\quad$ 150 FTE = 2.10

Once we have calculated implied cost indices, we can evaluate the need effects of these indices. We typically focus on need effects related to economic disadvantage and to LEP status. Need effects can be evaluated visually or statistically. Visual analysis allows one to discern (a) whether districts with greater student needs, such as increased poverty concentrations, are receiving greater total cost adjustment; (b) how much additional support is being provided via cost adjustments; (c) whether increases in implied cost index are strongly or only weakly associated with increases in need; and (d) whether increases in implied cost index are linearly or nonlinearly associated with differences in need.

Figure 10.2 compares the poverty effects of first-tier cost adjustments in Kansas and Texas. The aggregate first-tier cost adjustments are on the y axis, and the census measure of the percentage of children in poverty is on the x axis.[1] Because both states have numerous small, sparse, and remote districts, Figure 10.2 includes only those districts enrolling greater than 2,000 pupils. As such, Figure 10.2 asks the question,

Do larger districts in Kansas and Texas that have more children in poverty receive more in cost adjustment? In Texas, the answer is quite solidly, yes, while in Kansas little discernable relationship exists between poverty and first-tier cost adjustments. This occurs largely because other weights in the Kansas formula, such as new facilities weighting, are larger than poverty and bilingual education weights and are disproportionately received by very low-poverty districts (note the very low-poverty large district that receives nearly the highest cost adjustment among Kansas large districts). Figure 10.2 reveals a potentially significant illogical imbalance in the cost adjustments in the Kansas aid formula.[2]

One can perform more rigorous tests of the balance of cost adjustments via correlation and/or regression analysis. Table 10.3 provides slope coefficients and R^2 values for the relationships between first-tier cost adjustments and poverty and LEP status of Kansas and Texas districts. Table 10.3 confirms that among larger districts, no discernable positive poverty effect exists in Kansas' aid formula, whereas in Texas, a sizable poverty effect occurs. Interestingly, while Texas' implicit weights for LEP children were smaller than those for Kansas, Texas possesses a much stronger and more consistent LEP effect. This occurs because the geographic wage index in Texas provides additional support to many districts with very high-LEP populations. Across small and large districts, Kansas possesses a positive poverty effect, mainly because several very small, rural districts in Kansas have among the state's highest poverty percentages. These districts benefit slightly from the poverty weight but substantially from the scale weight. The positive poverty effect of the Kansas low-enrollment weight provides no consolation for large, high-poverty districts in Kansas.

Analysis of Systems Including Cost-Adjustment Variance and Variance Due to Local Control

One can evaluate school finance systems as a whole by methods similar to those used for the first tier of a school finance system. One can choose to evaluate

---

[1] For comparison purposes, we have removed special education weighting and gifted and talented weighting from the Texas first tier (because they are a separate aid program in Kansas) and added the new facilities allotment (which is included as a general fund weight in Kansas). We have also removed transportation weighting from the Kansas formula (which is included as a separate allotment in Texas).
[2] This is based on analysis of Kansas policies in 2004, prior to recent changes resulting from judicial action.

Figure 10.2   Comparison of Poverty Effects for Kansas and Texas First-Tier Aid

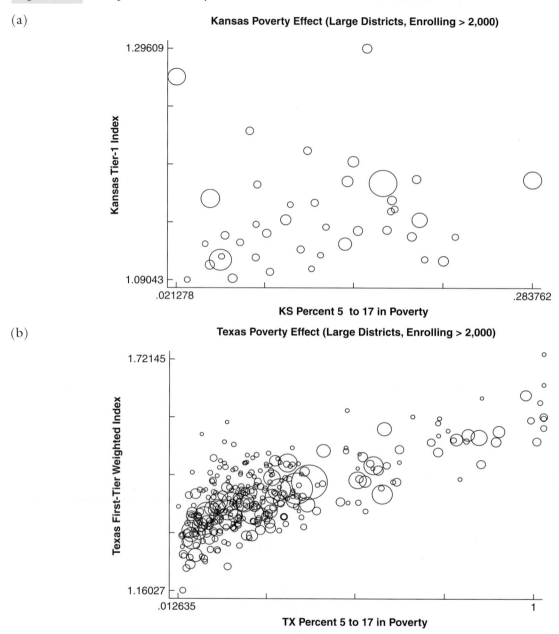

(a)

Kansas Poverty Effect (Large Districts, Enrolling > 2,000)

(b)

Texas Poverty Effect (Large Districts, Enrolling > 2,000)

Bubble size represents district size.
Source: Adapted from Baker and Duncombe (2004)

per-pupil revenues directly or to construct an implied cost index for per-pupil revenues. Direct comparisons of per-pupil dollar values are useful where dollar-value benchmarks are available, or where specific interest exists in determining how many more dollars are received per pupil in need. Ratios, or implied indices, are useful for determining whether districts that need more resources, have more resources. That is, ratios apply a relative rather than absolute standard. As will be discussed at the end of this section, these alternative views relate to different types of challenges in school finance litigation.

Table 10.3   Estimates of Poverty and Language Proficiency Status Effects for Kansas and Texas Tier-I Aid

Cost Factor	Kansas		Texas	
	Estimate	Sig. R^{2a}	Estimate	Sig. R^{2a}
Effects of scale index alone on student need				
Scale index and poverty	0.40*	0.02	−0.01	0.00
Scale index and LEP	−2.69*	0.04	−0.52**	0.05
Effects of Texas geographic wage index				
Wage index and poverty			0.07**	0.13
Wage index and LEP			0.61**	0.34
Effects of Tier-I index (comparable components) on student need				
Tier I index and poverty				
All districts	0.47**	0.01	0.26**	0.19
Large (>2,000) districts	0.03	0.00	0.28**	0.65
Texas large districts limited to Kansas range (<28.4%)			0.36**	0.25
Tier I index and LEP				
All districts	−1.63*	0.02	0.79**	0.05
Large (>2,000) districts	1.01*	0.12	1.39**	0.48
Texas large districts limited to Kansas range (<7.8%)			1.56**	0.28

*Statistically significant from zero at 5% level. **Statistically significant at the 1% level.
[a]Adjusted R^2 of regression of Tier-I index on enrollment, enrollment squared, poverty, and LEP shares.
LEP, limited English proficiency.
Source: Adapted from Baker and Duncombe (2004).

Individual Need-Effects Analysis

As with Tier-I cost-adjustment systems, we can apply need-effects analysis to state and local school district revenues as a whole. Again, standard comparisons include testing the relationship between state and local revenues and measures of the population of students in poverty or measures of the population of limited English proficient students. Good exogenous measures are ideal but not always available. Even if the first tier of a state's aid formula is sufficiently sensitive to local district needs, it is conceivable that the system as a whole is not. This is especially the case where second-tier local discretionary revenues become a dominant feature of the school finance system. In Texas, for example, in 2003–2004, second-tier revenues had reached approximately 40% of operating revenues. If second-tier revenues are highly associated with wealth and income, it is conceivable that greater amounts of second-tier revenue are raised by districts with lower needs, especially as relates to children from economically deprived backgrounds. Some states, however, make efforts to carry over adjustments to first-tier aid into matching aid received on the second tier.

Figure 10.3 displays the LEP effect of state and local revenue per pupil for Texas districts enrolling more than 2,000 pupils. Note that Figure 10.3 includes only those districts with 0% to 30% LEP students. This limitation is applied for comparison purposes with Figure 10.4, which displays the LEP effect for large Nebraska districts. Many Texas districts have much larger LEP populations. Our desire was to compare the LEP effects across the same range of need. The Texas LEP effect in Figure 10.3 is smaller than the LEP effect for the first tier alone, which is primarily due to the additional second-tier revenues raised by districts with relatively small LEP populations. In spite of the significant role of second-tier revenues in the Texas funding system, the LEP effect remains positive.

In contrast, Figure 10.4 displays a negative (though not statistically significant) LEP for the state and local revenues per pupil in Nebraska districts. Nebraska has far fewer large districts, making it more difficult to identify a pattern. However, the districts with the highest LEP populations clearly have the fewest resources per pupil.

The slope of the trend line for Nebraska districts is approximately –$380. This slope indicates that moving from a district with 0% LEP to a district with 100% LEP is associated with a drop in state and local revenues of $380 per pupil.

Figure 10.3   Limited-English-Proficiency Effect of State and Local Revenue per Pupil for Texas K–12 Districts (ADA > 2,000)

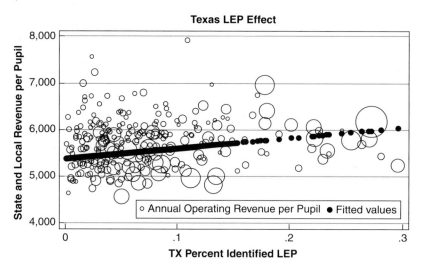

ADA, average daily attendance; LEP, limited English proficiency.
Bubble size represents district size.

Source: Data from Texas Education Agency (no date).

Figure 10.4   Limited-English-Proficiency Effect of State and Local Revenue per Pupil for Nebraska K–12 Districts (Enrollment > 2,000)

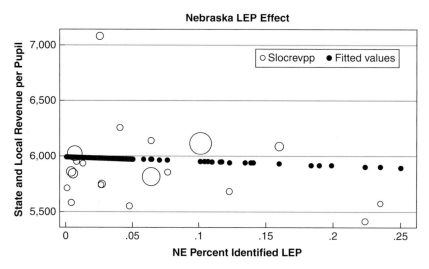

LEP, limited English proficiency; slocrevpp, state and local revenue per pupil.
Bubble size represents district size.

Source: Data from Nebraska Department of Education (2002–2003a, 2002–2003b).

Note that because these analyses address only one need factor at a time, other analyses may explain why Nebraska school districts with more LEP children have fewer resources per pupil. It is plausible, though unlikely, that districts with more LEP children have fewer children from economically disadvantaged backgrounds. In addition, other cost factors may simply be higher in districts with few LEP children. We must explore these possibilities with additional visual and statistical analyses. Assessing relationships among districts of similar size is also generally important, especially in geographically diverse states (Texas) and/or states with vast, sparse, rural areas.

Combining Need-Effect Analysis With Need-Effect Benchmarks

Although analysts can easily judge a decline in revenues associated with an increase in need as problematic, analysts can have difficulty determining whether a positive slope is *positive enough*. Knowing when a need effect is positive enough requires a benchmark, preferably generated by empirically rigorous cost analysis. In recent years, Texas has experienced a flurry of such analyses, which proliferated even more rapidly with litigation in 2004. (It is a pity that litigation is still the most predominant method of generating cost research and that states are seldom inclined to conduct it on their own until threatened with even higher expenses if they do not.) The analyses have applied both resource-cost and cost-function methods. Note, however, that the analyses applied resource-cost methods on only a limited subset of districts (plaintiff districts in *West Orange Cove Consolidated Independent School District et al. v. Alanis*, 2003).

Table 10.4 presents the poverty effects and LEP effects of current state and local as well as state, local, and federal revenues of Texas districts, and it presents the *would-be* poverty effects of revenues generated for Texas districts under resource-cost estimates provided by Smith and Seder (2004) of Management Analysis and Planning Associates (MAP) and by economists from Texas A&M University provided for the Texas Joint Select Committee on Public School Finance.

Table 10.4 shows that, across all districts, a 1-unit difference (0% poverty to 100% poverty) is associated with $1,131 more, on average, in state and local revenues per pupil (current operating expenditures). The addition of federal aid doubles that number. Consultants for MAP provided different estimates in which they included and excluded limits on LEP and poverty-population estimates, referring to the different estimates as *bounded* and *unbounded*, respectively. In either case, the MAP need effects (across only plaintiff districts) were much larger than the need effects of current revenues. Need effects for unbounded estimates were much higher. However, cost–function analysis prepared for the Texas legislature produced much more modest need effects. In fact, the poverty effect of the cost function was somewhere between the poverty effect of state and local revenue alone and the poverty effect of revenue including federal aid (which is poverty targeted). When translated to a pupil weight, the poverty effect of the Texas cost function was approximately .30 to .35. Recall that when translated

Table 10.4 Comparing Limited-English-Proficiency and Poverty Effects of Current Revenue and Cost Estimates in Texas

	Poverty Effect		LEP Effect	
	All Districts	**>2,000**	**All Districts**	**>2,000**
District revenues				
M&O Only	$1,131	$1,091	$628	$1,006
r-squared	0.13	0.29	0.02	0.09
M&O with Federal	$2,224	$2,165	$1,723	$2,175
r-squared	0.31	0.53	0.07	0.18
MAP analysis				
Unbounded	$4,336	$4,334	$8,244	$8,281
r-squared	0.87	0.89	0.67	0.68
Bounded	$2,678	$2,679	$5,428	$5,461
r-squared	0.78	0.80	0.59	0.62
Cost function analysis	$1,404	$1,362	$1,430	$1,731
r-squared	0.40	0.63	0.15	0.35

LEP, limited English proficiency; MAP, Management Analysis and Planning Associates.
Source: Data from Texas Education Agency (no date); Gronberg, Jansen, Taylor, & Booker (2004); and cost-study findings from Smith and Seder (2004) prepared on behalf of plaintiff districts in *West Orange Cove v. State* (2003) (see Chapter 7).

into the Tier-I formula, a .35 vertical-equity adjustment may have quite a different dollar impact.

Cost-Alignment Analysis

Cost-alignment analysis makes more direct and more comprehensive comparisons between estimated costs and/or indices of costs and actual revenues available to school districts. Further, because cost-alignment tests consider all cost factors simultaneously, they reduce the possibility that overlooking potential counterbalancing cost factors will misguide us. Two basic questions are associated with cost-alignment analysis:

1. Relative to specific cost/dollar values, do school districts presently have what they need, and if not, how much do current dollar values deviate from need?

2. Relative to one another and by reference to empirically estimated cost indexes, do the districts that need more resources (e.g., have higher costs) have more resources?

We propose the following three categories of measures for addressing these questions: (a) cost-deficit measures, (b) cost-deviation measures, and (c) relative cost and need measures.

Cost-Deficit Measures

The first measure deals with comparisons of actual-to-adequate dollar values. One approach is to simply concern oneself with those districts and those children whose current educational resources are lower than their estimated needs. One might calculate percentages of districts and/or percentages of students in districts with subadequate funding. One might also calculate the average deficit across these students and the total funding required to eliminate the deficit. We propose the following, relatively simple, calculations for evaluating cost deficits and their effect on pupils:

> *Share of students below* x% *adequacy*
> *Average deficit per pupil*

Share of Students Below X% Adequacy: One might begin by calculating the percentage of all students in a state who attend districts with revenues below adequacy targets. Next, one might expand the analysis by calculating the percentage of students attending districts less than 95% of their adequacy target, 90% of their adequacy target, and so on. It may be useful to

combine these calculations with measures of the average characteristics of districts that are below adequacy targets. Such a calculation and distribution could provide important exploratory data on where the critical areas of underfunding among districts might lie. One important element in such an analysis is to keep track of how many students are potentially affected and how much. If 50% of all students are in the 5% below-adequate category, it is less significant than 25% of all students 50% below adequate. These two concepts are often referred to in the strategic planning literature as scope (how wide) an impact, and intensity (how deep) an impact. District aggregation often obfuscates scope and impact. One method of controlling for this is to calculate the average deficit per pupil.

Average Deficit per Pupil: For those districts with revenues below their adequacy target, one might calculate the deficits in per-pupil revenues from the adequacy target. One can then calculate a weighted average, based on student enrollments, across all districts that fall below their adequacy targets.

Cost-Deviation Measures

States may also find utility in addressing not only districts that currently receive less funding than necessary but also districts that may currently be overcompensated by state policy. Where resources are scarce, the state may need to reallocate aid, perhaps by shifting cost adjustments from one set of districts to another. It may be useful to evaluate the average of deviations both above and below the estimated costs of achieving desired outcomes. For example, Figure 10.5 presents a comparison of actual (diamonds) and adequate (Gronberg, Jansen, Taylor, & Booker, 2004) (solid line) revenues for Texas school districts. Several districts currently fall below the line (negative deviations), and several are above the line. Some districts likely are above the line due to additional (Tier II) local effort applied to a strong property tax base. Note, however, that Texas is among the few states that apply recapture to Tier-II revenues. Districts also may be above the line as a result of cost adjustments in the current Tier I that are not well aligned with actual costs. It may be technically, though perhaps not politically, feasible to reallocate these misaligned cost adjustments to districts currently below their target.

To determine the overall extent to which district resources deviate from adequate targets, we propose

Figure 10.5 Comparison of Actual and Target Revenues for Texas Districts

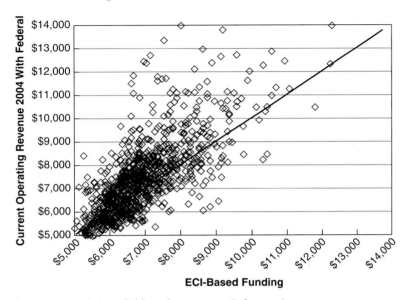

Note: Diamonds show actual revenues, and the solid line shows target (adequate) revenues. ECI, education cost–function index.

Source: Data from Texas Education Agency (2004, special request of author). Underlying "adequacy" target data based on Gronberg et al. (2004).

the use of *mean absolute percent error analysis* (MAPE).

Mean Absolute Percent Error Analysis: The mean absolute percent error is the average of the absolute deviations between one measure and another. When using MAPE to evaluate absolute costs, one measures absolute error by comparing actual revenues per pupil to predicted adequate revenues per pupil. One takes the absolute value for each district's difference, over or under, from predicted cost. The average of those deviations is the MAPE. Errors *over cost* are treated the same as errors *under cost*. The point is to measure overall alignment rather than deficits alone. MAPE is a measure of the goodness of the fit of actual distributions to predicted adequacy targets. MAPE assumes a reasonably linear trend between the *x* and *y* coordinates.

Relative Cost and Need Measures

Each of the previous indicators focused on whether each district had too little or too much revenue per pupil relative to empirical estimates of adequate resources. A critical question in alignment analysis is whether the districts that need more resources actually get more resources relative to their need. One can use

correlation and slope analysis used to address this question:

> *Correlation Analysis:* One can estimate correlations either between actual resources and predicted costs or between implicit indices of costs generated from actual resources and empirically estimated cost indices. Again, such correlations assume a relatively linear relationship.

> *Slope Analysis:* One can also perform slope analysis either between actual resources and predicted costs or between implicit indices of costs generated from actual resources and empirically estimated cost indices.

Visual inspection is also a useful tool for discerning the relative alignment of actual revenues and costs. Figure 10.6 displays the relationship between costs per pupil (on the *x* axis) and state and local operating revenues per pupil on the *y* axis for Texas school districts enrolling over 2,000 students. As is our usual protocol, we show district size by the size of the bubbles in the graph. While we do not see a strikingly strong correlation ($r = .4196$, weighted for enrollment), we do at least see a general pattern of districts with higher costs having more resources. We can

Figure 10.6   Alignment of Texas Revenues and Costs

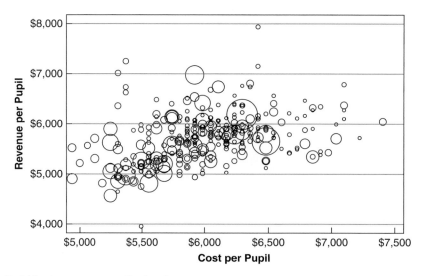

Correlation = .4196. Bubble size represents district size.

Source: Data from Texas Education Agency (2004, special request of author). Underlying "adequacy" target data based on Gronberg et al. (2004).

Figure 10.7   Alignment of Kansas Revenues and Costs

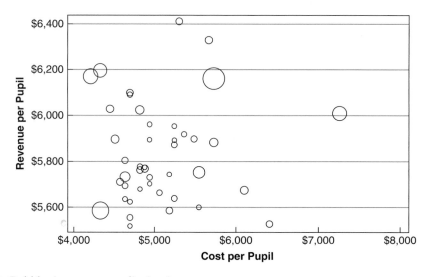

Correlation = .1551. Bubble size represents district size.

Source: Data from Kansas Department of Education (2004). Cost estimates prepared by authors.

calculate a line of best fit to determine the magnitude of this relationship.

Figure 10.7 displays a comparable analysis for school districts in Kansas with 2,000 or more pupils. Among the larger districts in Kansas, no discernable relationship whatsoever exists between revenues per

pupil and predicted costs. Thus, while current revenues do not appear well aligned with costs in Texas among the larger districts, they are certainly far better aligned with costs than are revenues among large districts in Kansas. It is difficult to determine how disequalizing the alignment is for each state in a national

Table 10.5   Cost-Alignment Indices in School Finance

Alignment Measure	Variable 1	Variable 2	Interpretation
Correlation (or R-squared)	Implicit cost index	Empirically based cost index	If districts that have higher costs have more revenue per pupil, R^2 approaches 1.0.
	Actual revenues per pupil	Empirically based cost per pupil	If districts that have higher costs have the revenue per pupil to match, R^2 approaches 1.0.
Trendline slope	Implicit cost index	Empirically based cost index	The ideal condition of slope = 1.0 indicates that each unit difference in estimated cost index is associated with a unit difference in implicit index. Assuming the implicit index to be on the y axis, a slope from 0 to 1.0 indicates that the implicit index is less sensitive to costs than necessary. A slope of >1.0 indicates that the implicit index is more sensitive to costs than needed. And a negative slope indicates that districts that need more resources, actually receive less.
	Actual revenues per pupil	Empirically based cost per pupil	Again, the ideal condition is a slope of 1.0 but with slightly different meaning. A slope of $1 indicates that, on average, a district needing $1 more in resources has $1 in resources. A slope >$1 indicates that a district that needs an additional $1, on average, has additional resources exceeding $1 and so on.
MAPE	Implicit cost index	Empirically based cost index	Indicates whether districts have the appropriate amount (relative to cost) of revenue above or below the median (as a percentage). For example, districts might on average, deviate 10% from what they should have (costs), relative to one another. Measure relates to relative adequacy or equal protection concerns.
	Actual revenues per pupil	Empirically based cost per pupil	Indicates whether districts have the appropriate amount (relative to cost) of revenue above or below target revenue, or costs per pupil (as a percentage). For example, districts might on average, deviate 10% from what they should have (costs). Measure relates to absolute adequacy concerns.

MAPE, mean absolute percentage error.

context without having comparably estimated cost indices for all states.

Summary of Alignment Indices

Table 10.5 summarizes applications of alignment indices. In particular, one can apply either correlation or MAPE analysis to either dollar values or implicit and estimated cost indices. Different applications yield different meanings. For example, if one applies MAPE analysis to actual revenues and empirically estimated costs, one can discern, on average, whether districts have approximately the correct amount of financial resources relative to their specific target. When one applies MAPE analysis to implicit and estimated cost indices, one can discern whether districts have the correct amount of resources relative to their peers. Inter-

pretations of correlation analysis are roughly the same whether applied to dollar costs or cost indices because correlation analyses tell us whether the rank order of districts' actual and needed resources is comparable. Slope analysis can tell us more precisely whether the differences in actual revenues or implicit indices are sufficiently sensitive to costs and needs.

Simulation 10.1: Cost-Adjusted Equity Analysis

Perhaps the best and most comprehensive approach to evaluating the effectiveness of state-aid policies with regard to adequacy and vertical equity is to re-estimate conventional equity and fiscal neutrality statistics (see Chapter 5) using empirically justifiable cost adjustments.

Analysts can calculate cost-adjusted revenues or expenditures simply as follows:

Actual Revenues per Pupil/Cost Index = Cost-Adjusted Revenues per Pupil

As we've noted previously in this text, analysts use this approach quite frequently, but most often apply it poorly with arbitrary and/or incomplete adjustments for factors influencing costs; some researchers choose simply to accept legislatively adopted cost adjustments as if they were empirical estimates of costs. Analysts must conduce cost-adjusted equity analysis with comprehensive cost indices, accounting for a full array of district-associated costs and student-need associated costs that affect the opportunities and outcomes for children with special educational needs. We prefer that comprehensive indices of costs be estimated via cost-function analysis, but resource-cost analysis may also be a useful tool for generated comprehensive indices. A second-order problem, one almost completely ignored in policy, is the measuring of hedonic benefits to wealthy communities in homogeneous neighborhoods that make it easier to teach, provide positive home-school contributions to student learning, and other benefits seldom measured. A complete accounting of costs would include such positive externalities as a deduction from the amount of state aid that would otherwise be provided. Because we have no hope of seeing this put into practice, we argue instead that cost adjustments should be strongly biased in favor of otherwise educationally and economically disadvantaged students.

Simulation 10.1 (see the Companion Website, www.prenhall.com/baker) displays the importance of using comprehensive cost indices in place of (a) conventional adjustments for student needs and geographic price variation, (b) legislatively adopted weights, or (c) no cost adjustment. The following specific simulation options are available:

1. *No cost adjustment:* Evaluates the dispersion of current expenditures per pupil across districts.
2. *Weighted-pupil index (formula adjustment) (WPI):* One constructs the WPI by dividing the weighted FTE count for each district by the actual FTE count for each district.
3. *Input price adjustment: National Center for Education Statistics (NCES) Geographic Cost of Education Index (GCEI) 1993–1994:* Analysts use the NCES GCEI to adjust for input prices. To make the adjustment, one divides the current expenditures per pupil for each district by the GCEI for that district. The input-price-adjusted expenditures represent the purchasing power of the per-pupil expenditures.
4. *Need adjustment (Parrish, Matsumoto, & Fowler, 1995):* The need-adjustment method is comparable to the method presented in Chapter 5. As a default, we apply the weights that Parrish, Matsumoto, and Fowler (1995) use, but one can change those weights in the simulation.
5. *Combined input price and need:* This method combines the need adjustments for at-risk and bilingual education with the GCEI.
6. *Cost-function adjusted:* Cost-function analysis was applied to Kansas school district data to produce the index. The index was created by predicting the resources required for each district to achieve average outcomes, and then by representing those resources with respect to state average required resources (scale centered at 1.0, or 100).

Except for need and input price, indices may not be combined. The simulation will apply the first index, from top to bottom, selected with a "1." Figure 10.8 displays the interface for the simulation.

When performing cost-adjusted equity analyses, discerning the different meanings of equity statistics can be difficult. For example, what does it mean if there is more variance (a larger coefficient of variance or Gini coefficient) in unadjusted resources than cost-function-adjusted resources? What does it mean if application of a weighted pupil index removes nearly all variance in spending? Table 10.6 provides some guidelines for interpreting your findings.

Following are a few examples of the types of differences you might find in the simulation when you use different cost. Figures 10.9 and 10.10 compare the distribution of resources by district size (a) using no cost adjustment (Figure 10.9) and (b) using the weighted-pupil index (Figure 10.10). Note that Figure 10.9 presents a pronounced curved pattern whereby progressively smaller districts have progressively more resources per pupil. This pattern is a function of the state's economies of scale, or small-district weight. In Figure 10.9, little variation occurs in spending above and beyond that policy.

Figure 10.10 removes the effects of state policies, such as the small-district weighting, to reveal all districts within a relatively narrow band of per-pupil resources. As noted in Table 10.6, the variations observed in Figure 10.10 are those variations in resources across districts that exceed state-imposed differences. Note

Figure 10.8   Simulation Control Panel

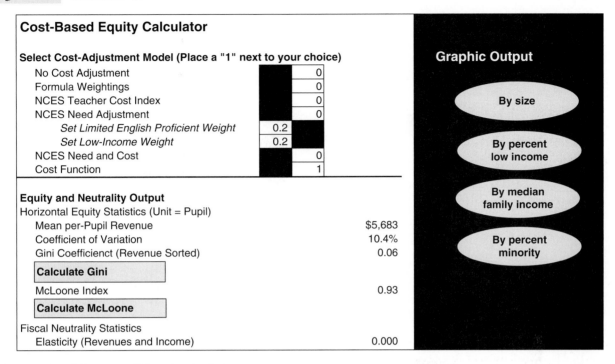

NCES, National Center for Education Statistics.

Source: From the Companion Website (www.prenhall.com/baker).

Table 10.6 Guidelines for Interpreting Dispersion Measures

Type of Adjustment	What Do the Dispersion Measures Mean?
None	Measures the sum of the variations in spending both associated with cost differences and not associated with cost differences. Also measures the sum of variations associated with local discretion and state policy, where state policy is intended to accommodate cost differences.
Weighted Pupil Index	Measures only that variance associated with local discretionary spending differences. Assumes all state policies to be rationally related to cost differences.
Input Price	Measures variations in the ability of districts to purchase specific resources, e.g., teachers. Accommodates only input price differences, not differences in required quantities (e.g. scale differences).
Student Need Index	Measures variations in resources above and beyond crude estimates of differences in costs of meeting student needs. Does not accommodate input price differences or cost differences associated with district structural characteristics (scale, etc.).
Cost–Function Index	Measures variations in resources above and beyond statistically estimated cost differences. Accommodates cost differences associated with (a) price difference, (b) student population differences, and (c) district structural differences.

Figure 10.9   Distribution of Resources by Enrollment, No Adjustment

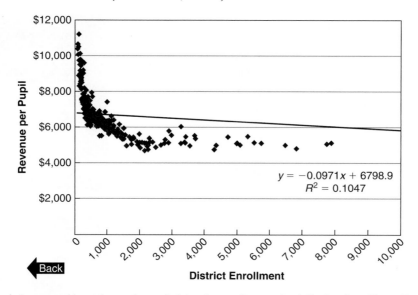

$$y = -0.0971x + 6798.9$$
$$R^2 = 0.1047$$

Source: Hypothetical simulation created by authors using underlying data on Kansas school districts from Kansas Department of Education (2004). From the Companion Website (www.prenhall.com/baker).

Figure 10.10   Distribution of Resources by Enrollment, Weighted Pupil Adjustment

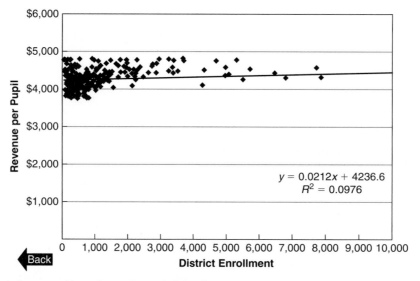

$$y = 0.0212x + 4236.6$$
$$R^2 = 0.0976$$

Source: Hypothetical simulation created by authors using underlying data on Kansas school districts from Kansas Department of Education (2004). From the Companion Website (www.prenhall.com/baker).

that because the state imposes strict local revenue limits, districts that have reached their limit fall in a horizontal line at the top of the distribution, and districts choosing to raise no additional revenues locally fall in a horizontal line along the bottom.

Note that the only other resource-adjustment option in the simulation that accounts for costs associated with economies of scale is the cost-function adjustment (Table 10.6). The cost-function adjustment for economies of scale is based on empirical analyses,

Figure 10.11 Distribution of Resources by Enrollment, Cost–Function Adjustment

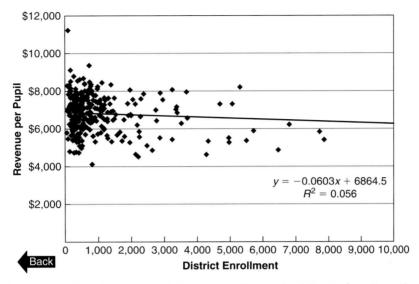

$$y = -0.0603x + 6864.5$$
$$R^2 = 0.056$$

Source: Hypothetical simulation created by authors using underlying data on Kansas school districts from Kansas Department of Education (2004). From the Companion Website (www.prenhall.com/baker).

while the pupil-weight adjustment for scale is based on political preference and power.

Using the cost–function adjustment produces the pattern in Figure 10.11. Under the weighted-pupil adjustment (Figure 10.10), larger districts appeared to have slightly more in cost-adjusted revenue per pupil. Under the cost–function adjustment, larger districts appear to have less. Note that the range of cost-adjusted revenues under the weighted-pupil adjustment is from approximately $3,800 per pupil to approximately 25% above that, while the range in cost-function-adjusted revenues per pupil is from approximately $4,000 per pupil to more than twice that value. When one uses formula weightings, the coefficient of variation on the interface is 5.8%. But, when one uses cost–function estimates, coefficient of variation increases to 21%. That is, in terms of the value of districts' education dollars toward achieving student outcomes, a substantial amount of variation in resources across Kansas districts develops.

Using a mix of arbitrary student need (.2 for at-risk and LEP) and input-price adjustments (NCES GCEI) but no adjustments for economies of scale can be particularly misleading where numerous small districts exist. In fact, this approach can be worse than making no adjustments at all. Figure 10.12 displays the effects of applying input price and arbitrary

student-need weights by district size. Because the NCES geographic price index in particular indicates much higher competitive wages in major metropolitan areas, the price index serves to deflate the value of education dollars in large, scale-efficient districts and inflate the value of education dollars in small, rural districts. As a result, the slope of the trend line is more strongly negative than would be the case if one were to apply no adjustment (Figure 10.9). And when one applies no adjustment, the negative slope of the trend line is still larger than when one applies correct adjustments. We encourage you to explore the simulation further.

Where Comprehensive Cost Indices Are Unavailable
Estimating comprehensive cost indices for performing cost-adjusted equity analysis may not always be technically feasible. Precise estimation of education cost indices from cost–function analyses requires advanced statistical knowledge, specialized statistical software, and a ton of good data on schooling inputs and outcomes across all school districts. Estimation of comprehensive cost indices by resource-cost analysis is a cumbersome task requiring the determination of appropriate resource mix across numerous prototypical schools and districts of differing size and student needs. Where comprehensive cost indices are unavailable

Figure 10.12   Distribution of Resources by Enrollment, Input Price, and Student Need

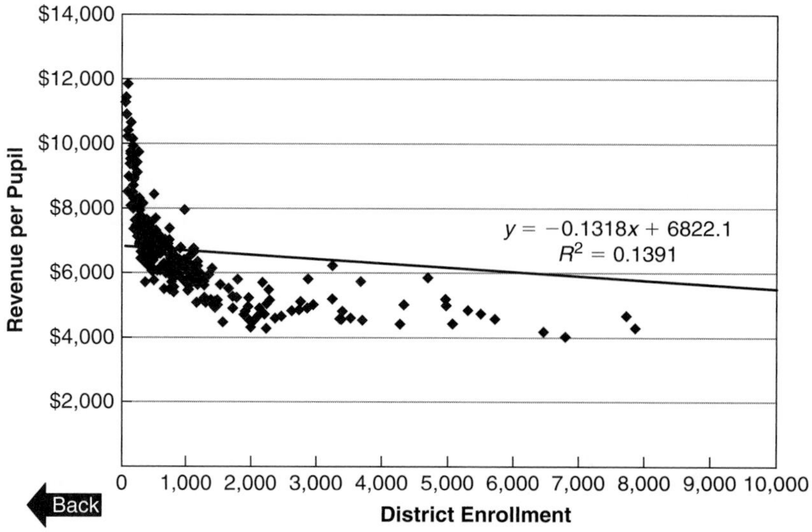

Source: Hypothetical simulation created by authors using underlying data on Kansas school districts from Kansas Department of Education (2004). From the Companion Website (www.prenhall.com/baker).

or incalculable, one can take some steps to improve on traditional equity analyses:

1. Remove small, scale-inefficient districts with fewer than 2,000 (or 5,000 pupils depending on available sample size).
2. Separate K–12 from K–8 or other grade-level organized districts.
3. Use an appropriate index for input-price variation, where the primary input of interest is the classroom teacher.
4. Use student-need adjustments that fall within the range of adjustments generated by recent cost analyses (.35 to 1.0 for economically disadvantaged and .2 to 1.2 for LEP).

   a. Preferred weights for poverty:
      i. 1.10 × subsidized lunch rate
      ii. 1.49 × census poverty rate

   b. Preferred weights for LEP/English language learner (ELL) students
      i. 1.03 × LEP/ELL-student head count

Obviously, due to the wide range of available cost indices for student needs, this approach will lack precision. Further, the removal of small districts from analyses in states where small districts are the norm sig-

nificantly limits analyses. Limited analyses, however, are more useful than faulty ones. In Chapter 13, we discuss issues related to teacher labor markets and the estimation of competitive wages, raising some questions about frequently used indices of input-price variation.

Next we present an example of a cost-based aid formula applied to school districts in Texas. This simulation appears on the book's Companion Website (www.prenhall.com/baker/chpt10b.xls) and is titled Cost-Based Aid Simulation: Texas 27 District Model). The cost-based aid simulation of school districts in Texas is followed by a cost-guided aid simulation of school districts in Kansas. In this simulation, we show how existing policy levers might be used to *morph* a state-aid formula to more closely match, or align with, district-level cost estimates. Check the Companion Website (www.prenhall.com/baker) for a simulation of this aid formula.

Simulation 10.2: Proposal for Cost-Based Aid Formulas: Application to Texas

As illustrated throughout the first half of this chapter, numerous new methods are available for deconstructing and critiquing today's increasingly complex state-aid formulas. We prefer, however, to apply these same concepts and many of the same measures to reconstruct, redesign, and reinvent a new breed of school finance formulas. In this section, we present two approaches to the development of new state aid formulas: cost-based and cost-guided aid formulas.

Cost-Based Formulas: Policy makers may use cost-based aid formulas to set the overall level of foundation aid. In cost-based formulas, the adjustments applied to that foundation aid are directly informed by empirical analysis of costs. In particular, cost-based formulas replace politically derived cost adjustments with cost adjustments derived from empirical analysis, such as a single comprehensive cost index derived from cost–function analysis.

Cost-Guided Formulas: Cost-guided aid formulas are not necessarily directly based on cost estimates and may or may not require complete overhaul of current aid formulas. A cost-guided aid formula may include conventional aid formula features such as pupil weights or need-based flat grants. A cost-guided formula differs from the current approach in that the indices we presented earlier in this chapter guide the adjustment of individual formula levers in order to improve the overall alignment of the formula with empirically estimated costs. Analysts can successfully *cost-morph* formulas with sufficient existing policy levers.

Table 10.7 summarizes the characteristics of the 27 hypothetical Texas school districts in the simulation. The districts are statistical aggregates of real Texas school districts by geographic type/locale and by poverty. We assigned each hypothetical district a cost-index value based on the cost function estimated by Alexander et al. (2000) for the 77th Texas Legislature. We averaged cost indices for each of the 27 groups in Table 10.7. Notice, for example, that very small districts have higher cost–function indices to

Table 10.7 Sample District Characteristics and Cost Indices Based on Texas Data

Group	Locale	Poverty	Refined Average Daily Attendance	Percent Disabled	Percent Poverty	Percent LEP	Cost Index (CFI)
1	Large central city	High	60, 324	7.31%	25.34%	6.74%	1.00
2	Large central city	Low	51,625	7.31%	16.15%	3.17%	0.95
3	Large central city	Very high	121,686	7.43%	40.91%	8.73%	1.07
4	Large central city	Very low	12,001	6.06%	5.86%	1.36%	0.89
5	Large town	High	7,284	10.18%	25.91%	1.88%	0.95
6	Large town	Low	5,384	7.10%	17.63%	2.14%	0.93
7	Large town	Very high	6,624	8.70%	50.65%	5.74%	1.01
8	Mid-size central city	High	17,069	8.36%	25.39%	2.61%	1.00
9	Mid-size central city	Low	17,693	7.46%	16.87%	3.28%	0.95
10	Mid-size central city	Very high	20,171	7.36%	57.86%	7.87%	1.04
11	Mid-size central city	Very low	1,782	6.17%	5.63%	0.63%	0.91
12	Rural	High	933	7.81%	24.81%	1.46%	1.11
13	Rural	Low	864	7.26%	17.12%	1.15%	1.09
14	Rural	Very high	1,522	7.39%	49.47%	4.99%	1.20
15	Rural	Very low	650	6.19%	9.11%	0.91%	1.12
16	Small town	High	2,549	7.18%	26.00%	2.28%	1.01
17	Small town	Low	2,462	6.52%	16.89%	1.20%	0.94
18	Small town	Very high	3,484	6.10%	47.60%	4.36%	1.05
19	Small town	Very low	2,378	6.62%	11.25%	1.87%	0.96
20	Urban fringe of mid-size city	High	1,438	8.31%	26.29%	0.84%	1.11
21	Urban fringe of mid-size city	Low	3,063	8.28%	17.13%	1.07%	1.00
22	Urban fringe of mid-size city	Very high	12,311	6.41%	82.13%	10.04%	1.06
23	Urban fringe of mid-size city	Very low	4,224	7.29%	8.16%	0.67%	0.91
24	Urban fringe of large city	High	25,692	7.23%	26.03%	5.24%	1.02
25	Urban fringe of large city	Low	8,323	8.14%	17.20%	2.54%	0.96
26	Urban fringe of large city	Very high	3,456	6.81%	61.83%	8.57%	1.12
27	Urban fringe of large city	Very low	29,237	5.73%	7.83%	1.92%	0.88

CFI, cost–function index; LEP, limited English proficient.
Source: Based on data on Texas School Districts (Texas Education Agency, 1999–2000) and cost index values from Alexander, Gronberg, Jansen, Keller, Taylor, and Triesman (2000).

Figure 10.13   Policy Levers on First Tier of Cost-Adjusted Adequate-Funding Formula

Defined Inputs	
Required funding for median outcomes at maximum efficiency	**4,800**
Policy Levers	
Desired % increase in outcomes	**0%**
Efficiency target	**80%**
Expenditure/outcome elasticity	**1.00**
Percent of base to fund with statewide nonresidential rate	**20%**
Required local residential effort toward base (unadjusted)	**0.75%**
Include income adjustment to local residential effort (1 = Yes)	**1**
Statewide Nonresidential Property Tax Output	
Total nonresidential value (millions)	**$36,968**
Revenue to be raised with nonresidential tax (millions)	**$510**
Required nonresidential tax rate	**1.38%**
State Cost and Local Share Output	
Total state cost (millions)	**$1,793**
Cost to state general funds (millions)	**$1,282**
Local residential tax share (millions)	**$759**
Local residential tax share (% of total state and local)	**30%**
Property tax share	**50%**
Mean Per-Pupil Revenue	**$6,014**

Source: Based on simulation of underlying data in Table 10.7 (Alexander et al., 2000; Texas School Districts, 2003–2004).

compensate for their relative inefficient economies of scale. Also, notice that among similar geographic districts, districts with higher poverty levels and larger LEP populations also have higher cost indices.

In a cost-based aid formula, these cost indices can replace all individual pupil weights or cost adjustments. One subtle difference in the application of the cost–function index, as presented here, relative to a conventional pupil-weighting scheme applied to foundation aid, is that the cost–function indices center around 1.0. Values greater than 1.0 and less than 1.0 are present. The value of 1.0 represents the costs of achieving target outcomes in a district of average characteristics. If the cost–function index is to be used *as-is,* the analyst must set foundation aid at an average-cost level rather than base-cost level, such that each district's cost adjusted Tier-I aid per pupil is described as follows:

$$\text{Cost Adjusted Tier-I per Pupil} = \text{Cost Index} \times \text{Cost of Outcomes in Average District}$$

Figure 10.13 presents the policy levers that might be available to policy makers for managing the cost-adjusted first tier. Whereas the first tier of the FSP has a multitude of policy levers for managing both revenues and expenditures, the cost-adjusted first-tier formula has only two expenditure-related levers. A handful of tax policy and revenue-related levers are also included. (See Chapter 3 for issues related to tax policy and differential taxation of residential and nonresidential properties.) The expenditure-related levers differ somewhat from conventional funding-formula expenditure levers. The formula has entirely removed the ability to manipulate cost adjustments, because the formula aggregates all cost adjustments into the single cost–function estimated index.

Determining the foundation spending level differs from determining the spending level for conventional foundation aid programs. One determines the foundation spending level as a function of two factors: (a) the desired increase in student outcomes and (b) the expected level of efficiency at which districts should strive to produce those outcomes. Note that in this particular version of the simulation, we apply oversimplified assumptions to these levers. This simulation is for conceptual/illustrative purposes only.

For the first factor (increased outcome), assume, for example, that the median district and student characteristics could produce median outcomes with $4,800 per pupil *if* that district functioned at maximum efficiency. Now, assume that the district functions at 80% efficiency instead of 100% efficiency. It might cost $6,000 ($4,800/.80) per pupil to achieve median outcomes in that district. It is likely unreasonable to assume that all districts can function at 100% efficiency. One may perform econometric analyses of efficiency to discern the ranges of efficiency at which districts currently operate with respect to one another. Within those ranges, one may specify reasonable targets. Raising the efficiency target lowers the required base aid or foundation allotment. (See Chapter 11 for more extensive discussion of the concept and measurement of efficiency.) In the simulation, one can set not only the desired level of outcomes and efficiency but also the desired growth in outcomes over time. Assume again that the district of median characteristics can achieve median outcomes, at 80% efficiency, with $6,000 per pupil. Now, accept the oversimplified assumption that a 1% increase in inputs, on average, yields a 1% increase in outcomes. Assume that the present median performance level is deemed unacceptable, and that the goal is to increase the performance level by 5%. With an input–outcome elasticity of 1.0, this will require a 5% increase in foundation allotment, or a foundation of $6,300. That is, desiring higher outcomes requires more money. Rather than making decisions solely on the basis of dollar values, legislators are forced to make decisions about dollar values, in terms of their preferences for outcome levels. Assume perhaps more realistically, that the input–outcome elasticity is .20. In this case, a 5% increase in outcomes will require a 25% increase in foundation allotment.

As the efficiency and desired outcome levers interact, they can produce rather dramatic effects. In short, at lower efficiency levels and smaller input–outcome elasticities, it will take much larger increases to foundation allotments to yield a unit of performance improvement. While very high efficiency rates may reduce required spending increases, setting efficiency targets too high may produce unreasonable expectations regarding the output that districts should be able to produce given the aid they receive.

Table 10.8 presents a hypothetical simulation output of cost-adjusted base aid per pupil, based on the district characteristics and cost indices in Table 10.7. A variety of additional hypothetical conditions is also included for estimating each district's base aid, such as the assumed cost of achieving average outcomes in the average district and assumed average efficiency of school districts. As such, the *levels* of aid in Table 10.8 are not necessarily meaningful but the relative amounts of aid are. Note, for example, that an economies of scale component exists, whereby small rural districts receive higher aid per pupil. Poverty effects, however, are also quite strong, such that a very high-poverty urban or urban fringe district receives nearly as much as a lower-poverty rural district. Poverty effects are also quite strong, and in this example, nearly as strong as geographic/locale effects, on average.

Table 10.8 Sample Base Aid per Pupil, Adjusted for Costs by Locale and Poverty, Based on Texas Data

Locale	Poverty				Average
	Very High	High	Low	Very Low	
Large central city	$6,711	$6,300	$5,981	$5,603	**$6,149**
Large town	$6,377	$5,960	$5,847		**$6,061**
Mid-size central city	$6,580	$6,271	$5,981	$5,704	**$6,134**
Rural	$7,556	$6,994	$6,877	$7,072	**$7,125**
Small town	$6,645	$6,336	$5,952	$6,025	**$6,240**
Urban fringe of mid-size city	$6,690	$6,992	$6,283	$5,729	**$6,424**
Urban fringe of large city	$7,062	$6,418	$6,020	$5,515	**$6,253**
Average	**$6,803**	**$6,467**	**$6,134**	**$5,941**	**$6,351**

Source: Based on simulation of underlying data in Table 10.7 (Alexander et al., 2000; Texas School Districts, 2003–2004).

Table 10.9 First-Tier Tax Rates, Adjusted for Median Family Income

Locale	Poverty (%)				Average (%)
	Very High	High	Low	Very Low	
Large central city	0.74	0.86	1.03	1.37	**1.00**
Large town	0.62	0.72	0.71		**0.68**
Mid-size central city	0.62	0.75	0.79	1.25	**0.85**
Rural	0.59	0.69	0.74	0.82	**0.71**
Small town	0.59	0.68	0.77	0.90	**0.73**
Urban fringe of mid-size city	0.50	0.67	0.80	0.99	**0.74**
Urban fringe of large city	0.57	0.81	0.97	1.36	**0.93**
Average	**0.60**	**0.74**	**0.83**	**1.11**	**0.81**

Table 10.9 examines the tax policy side of the formula. As we discussed in Chapter 5, appropriate adjustments for local fiscal capacity can be particularly important for adjusting local tax burdens and making the tax policy side of a school finance formula more progressive. The present simulation includes a relatively simple option for using the median household income of districts as a basis for adjusting the required local tax rate on residential properties that provides partial support for the first tier. Applying the income adjustment produces the required local tax rates on residential property in Table 10.9, assuming a 75-cent base rate. Note that on average, required tax rates increase as poverty rates decrease.

Table 10.10 shows the revenue influence of this policy option. Applying the income adjustment to a 75-cent base residential tax rate, and using a $1.38 flat rate for statewide nonresidential property taxation (to fund 20% of the first tier) leads to a first tier funded at

50% by property tax. The total state share is $1.8 billion, and local residential property tax share is $759 million (or 30% of the total of about $2.6 billion). The statewide nonresidential tax covers about $516 million (20%) of the total state costs.

Figure 10.14 addresses the progressiveness of the tax burden using the income adjustment. Figure 10.14 relates median household income, on the horizontal axis, to median property taxes paid by residential property owners, expressed as a percentage of median household income. That is, property taxes are essentially expressed as an income tax equivalent. Figure 10.14 shows that applying the income adjustment to base tax rates produces a relatively progressive tax system or one where families with higher median income tend to pay a higher percentage of income to support the first tier.

Table 10.11 and Figure 10.15 present the results of removing the income adjustment but maintaining

Table 10.10 Cost of Implementing Formula With Income Progressive Residential Property Tax

State Cost and Local Share Output

Total state cost (millions)	**$1,793**
Cost to state general funds (millions)	**$1,282**
Local residential tax share (millions)	**$759**
Local residential tax share (% of total state and local)	**30%**
Property tax share	**50%**

Source: Based on simulation of underlying data in Table 10.7 (Alexander et al., 2000; Texas School Districts, 1999–2000).

Table 10.11 Cost of Implementing Formula With Unadjusted Tax Rates (75-Cent)

State Cost and Local Share Output

Total state cost (millions)	**$1,911**
Cost to state general funds (millions)	**$1,401**
Local residential tax share (millions)	**$640**
Local residential tax share (% of Total State and Local)	**25%**
Property tax share	**45%**

Source: Based on simulation of underlying data in Table 10.7 (Alexander et al., 2000; Texas School Districts, 1999–2000).

Figure 10.14 Property Tax Progressiveness with Respect to Income (First-Tier Residential Property Tax)

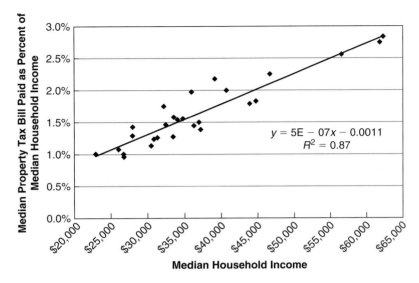

Source: Based on simulation of underlying data in Table 10.7. Data from NCES (2001–2002) and Texas School Districts (2003–2004), with cost index data from Alexander et al. (2000). From the Companion Website (www.prenhall.com/baker).

all other levers at the same levels. That is, residents in all districts pay a 75-cent property tax rate for the first tier, regardless of district median household income. Removing the income adjustment reduces revenues generated by residential property taxes in this simulation because the income adjustment tends to increase tax rates on larger urban and suburban areas, resulting in increased total state cost, unless the base rate for residential or for nonresidential properties increases.

Figure 10.15 Alternative Property Tax Progressiveness With Respect to Income (First-Tier Residential Property Tax)

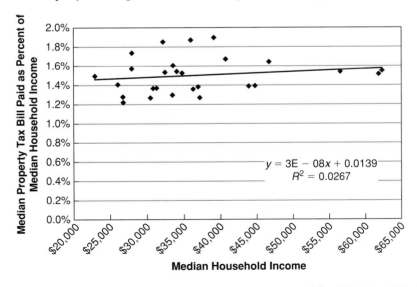

Source: Based on simulation of underlying data in Table 10.7 (Alexander et al., 2000; Texas School Districts, 2003–2004). From the Companion Website (www.prenhall.com/baker).

Figure 10.15 shows that the result of imposing a flat-base residential property tax is a relatively flat tax burden. That is, expressed as an income tax equivalent, the residential property tax rate is generally flat. However, the uniform tax rate does differentially affect district residents by household income, with a range of tax burden from about 1.2% of income to over 1.8% of income.

We encourage you to explore the Texas cost-based aid formula simulation (Simulation 10.2) on the Companion Website (www.prenhall.com/baker).

Cost-Guided Aid Formulas: Morphing Kansas Aid With Existing Levers

An important question for policy makers is whether the current aid formula, with its available policy levers, is manipulable such that revenues become significantly more aligned with costs. We have referred repeatedly to the poor alignment of the current Kansas aid formula with respect to cost estimates, especially among the state's larger districts. In short, wealthy suburban districts receive greater cost adjustment than poor urban districts with high-need populations. The aid formula includes cost adjustments for scale, economically disadvantaged students, and LEP students in bilingual education programs. The problem is not necessarily with the availability of levers but with the imbalance in the settings of those levers.

Figure 10.16 summarizes the current status of Kansas Tier-I policy levers. In 2004–2005, at-risk children, classified as those qualifying for free lunch, receive a weight of 10%, and each FTE in bilingual education programs receives a weight of 20%. The state has a very large-scale adjustment, which places the district with 300 pupils at 58% above base aid, and the district with 100 pupils at 114% above base aid. However, the current formula also includes a correlation weight, which raises the basic allotment for large districts, narrowing the effective range of the scale weight. Kansas set the current correlation weight for large districts at 6.32%, such that no district will receive less than 6.32% above the base state aid per pupil. This quirk of the Kansas aid formula allows one to significantly raise the correlation weight but lower the base aid per pupil, effectively raising the base aid for large districts but not small ones. Finally, the state uses a weight of 25% for each child who attends a new school facility for the first 2 years of operation, and the state provides additional, negotiated new-facilities support (ancillary new-facilities aid) for districts claiming even higher costs of opening new facilities than can be covered with the 25% weight. The effect of both of these provisions is to pump significant additional Tier-I

Figure 10.16   Current Status of Kansas Tier-I Policy Levers

Morphing the Current Tier I	
Pupil weights	
At-risk	0.10
Bilingual	0.20
Vocational	0.50
New facilities	0.25
Ancillary new facilities (% previous)	100%
Correlation	6.32%
Base state aid per pupil	$3,863
Total cost of morphed Tier I	$2,171
Transportation	$77
Hold harmless	0
Total with hold harmless and transportation	$2,248
Increase (decrease) in Tier-I cost	**($2)**

Source: Based on simulation created by authors using data on Kansas School Districts (no date).

Figure 10.17   Difference Between Actual 2003–2004 Aid and Cost of Achieving Average Outcomes

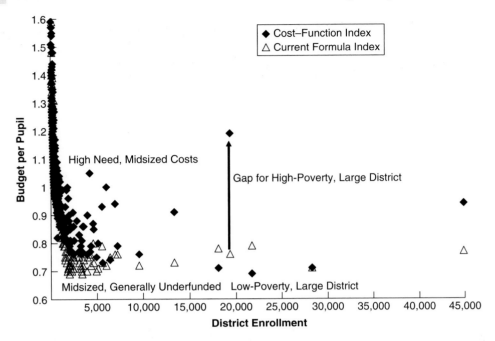

Source: Based on simulation created by authors using data on Kansas School Districts (no date).

support into wealthy suburban, sprawling districts. As of 2003–2004, Kansas set base aid per pupil at $3,863, producing a simulated cost for 2004–2005 approximating that which the state spent in 2003–2004 ($2 million difference).

Figure 10.17 graphs districts' 2003–2004 Tier-I revenues and estimated costs per pupil by district size. A particularly revealing cluster of districts occurs around the 20,000-student range. Among the three hollow triangles (current lever settings) are two fast-growing, affluent suburbs and the state's poorest urban community between them. Note that under current lever settings, the poor urban community receives less Tier-I aid than its affluent neighbors in the same metropolitan area. Note that the state's largest urban district, with an enrollment of 45,000, also receives less in cost-adjusted Tier-I aid than these two affluent suburban districts.

Figure 10.18 displays the alignment of the current Tier-I allocations and cost–function indices the authors of this text (Baker index) as well as Duncombe and Johnston (2004) estimated. Figure 10.18 also displays a cost index generated by resource-cost analysis from an adequacy study by Augenblick and Myers

Figure 10.18   Alignment With Current Law and Various Cost Indices

Alignment Tests (equal protection)	
Mean Absolute Percent Error	
Baker & Green, 2004	6.8372%
Duncombe & Johnston, 2004	6.4751%
Augenblick & Meyers, 2002	9.4884%
AVERAGE	**7.6%**
Correlation	
Baker & Green (2004) Cost Index	0.882
Duncombe & Johnston (2004) Cost Index	0.894
Augenblick & Myers (2002) Cost Index	0.819
AVERAGE	**0.865**

Source: Based on simulation created by authors using data on Kansas School Districts (no date).

(2002). (Later, in Figure 10.21, we base the alignments tests on indexed costs rather than dollar values.)

Figure 10.19 displays the outcomes of one option that districts can accomplish with approximately $155 million additional funding. We chose this particular budget constraint because the Kansas House of Repre-

Figure 10.19   Morphed Option at $155 Million Budget Constraint

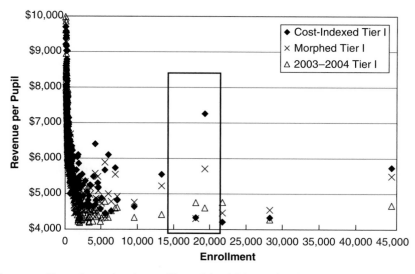

Source: Based on simulation created by authors using data on Kansas School Districts (no date).

sentatives passed a plan of this magnitude in the spring of 2004. The plan ultimately failed in the Senate because it required some new taxes. In Figure 10.19, the Xs mark the new position of districts after *morphing* the aid formula by adjusting the formula policy levers as shown in Figure 10.20. Significant increases resulted to both at-risk and bilingual education program weights. We eliminated new facilities weight, and in-

creased large-district funding dramatically by increasing the correlation weight. Base aid decreased from $3,863 to $3,525, but the new effective base increased, because the new effective base is 1.2 × $3,525, or $4,230 (compared with 1.0632 × $3,863 = $4,107).

Important changes in alignment are achieved by this allocation of funding, even though the allocation

Figure 10.20   Policy Levers and Alignment Output

Morphing the Current Tier I		**Alignment Tests (equal protection)**	
Pupil weights		*Mean Absolute Percent Error*	
At-risk	0.50	BAKER	5.0864%
Bilingual	0.50	Duncombe & Johnston	6.1163%
Vocational	0.50	Augenblick & Myers	6.9468%
New facilities	0.00		
Ancillary new facilities (% previous)	0%	**AVERAGE**	**6.0%**
Correlation	20.00%		
		Correlation	
Base state aid per pupil	3,525	Baker Cost Index	0.909
		Duncombe & Johnston Cost Index	0.896
Total cost of morphed Tier I	$2,292	Augenblick & Myers Cost Index	0.899
Transportation	$77		
Hold harmless	38	**AVERAGE**	**0.901**
Total with hold harmless and transportation	$2,407		
Increase (decrease) in Tier-I Cost	**$157**		

Augenblick & Myers, 2002; Baker, B.D. (2005). The emerging shape of educational adequacy: From theoretical assumptions to empirical evidence. *Journal of Education Finance, 30*(3), 277–305; Duncombe & Johnston, 2004.

Source: Based on simulation created by authors using data on Kansas School Districts (2004).

Figure 10.21 Comparison of Current and Morphed Tier I

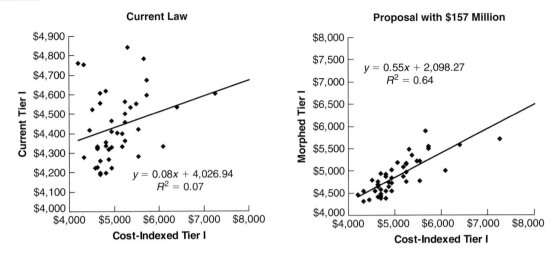

falls well short of targets identified in the legislature's own adequacy study. Notice in particular that the very high-need urban district that had previously received less in cost-adjusted aid than its wealthy suburban peers now receives significantly more. This district (Kansas City, KS) still falls well short of target revenues (for average outcomes). The state's largest district does much better, and overall, the morphed formula places far more districts near their target funding (black diamonds).

Figure 10.20 shows improvements to alignment statistics. Previously, the mean absolute percentage errors between actual and estimated cost indices ranged from just under 7% to over 9%. Under the new plan, MAPEs range from just over 5% (compared to our index) to just under 7% (compared to an index constructed from Augenblick and Myers' 2002 analysis).

More striking are the differences in alignment among the state's larger districts. Figure 10.21 displays the relationship between cost-indexed Tier-I funding and current settings for policy levers in the left panel and cost-indexed Tier-I funding and proposed settings for policy levers in the right panel. Under current lever settings, a negligible relationship exists between cost-indexed funding and actual aid. That is, no relationship exists between need and existing pupil weightings. Under the proposed adjustments, the relationship increases dramatically. Note that the R^2 goes from .07 to .64. However, the slope of the trend line of .55 sug-

gests that, while this proposal represents a dramatic improvement, the new proposal is still not sufficiently sensitive to need (slope is between 0 and 1). That is, a district needing $1 more is receiving, on average, only 55 cents more in aid per pupil.

Comparison of Cost-Based and Cost-Guided Aid Formulas

Both cost-based and cost-guided aid formulas have, of course, pros and cons. Certainly, taking the plethora of existing politically derived pupil weights in a state's school finance formula and replacing them with a single, empirically derived weight sounds appealing from the perspective of a researcher or policy analyst. It's simple, and it depoliticizes vertical-equity adjustments in school finance. These benefits alone should be sufficient reason to adopt cost-based formulas. Many state legislators, however, are still uncomfortable with the thought of relinquishing control over aid allocation to an econometric equation. First, the problem of relinquishing political control over the adjustment of individual weights takes certain bargaining chips off the legislative table. Second, concern remains over the "black box" of calculations underlying the education cost function.

Legislators should be comforted by the fact that increasingly, cost-function analysis and resource-cost analysis are producing more similar findings regarding cost variations across schools and districts. Indeed, numerous assumptions that researchers adopt when modeling costs may influence estimates of who needs more and who needs less. Developing cost-based aid formulas requires a closer relationship between researchers and legislators such that legislators may better understand underlying assumptions and how they may ultimately influence policy. Funding models driven by empirical cost–function analysis place legislators in the particularly uncomfortable, but appropriate, position of setting financing targets by explicitly declaring the schooling outcomes they desire. Upon setting a desired 55% pass rate as the basis for funding estimates in Texas, the Texas legislature was greeted by a headline in the *Houston Chronicle* reading "Study: Education Plan Lacking: Findings Show 45% of State's Students Would Be Left Behind" (2004). This is the kind of reverse political pressure that leads politicians with real resource and taxation constraints wanting to dodge empirical studies that simply confirm what they already know: they should be spending a lot more than current political constraints allow. Litigation, however, remains a potent force insofar as it makes the cost of hiding true costs worse than the cost of facing the problem.

Cost-guided aid formulas may provide a useful middle ground for state legislators to move politically derived aid formulas toward empirically estimated benchmarks. In cost-guided formulas, legislators retain the power to adjust individual components of aid formulas, allowing the creation of specific incentives to identify and serve special student populations or promote increased efficiency in the delivery of specific educational services. Unlike purely politically derived systems, legislatures have a greater obligation to insure the relative balance of cost adjustments and retain alignment with overall indices of cost. In addition, policy makers can use a range of cost indices derived from alternative methods under varied assumptions upon which to base alignment. For example, while the cost indices that the authors Duncombe and Johnston (2004) and Augenblick and Myers (2002) produced vary in apparently significant ways, the indices also share important commonalities with one another and highlight sharp differences with current policy. All three empirically estimated indices have smaller overall economies of scale effects than current policy, and all three have much larger student-need effects than current policy. Through morphing or even a cost-guided

overhaul, policy makers can choose to align aid with one or more of the indices to achieve a significantly more rational policy than current policies.

Discussion

In this chapter, we have covered substantial ground regarding current and future issues in educational adequacy and the evaluation and redesign of state-aid formulas. In this era of outcome-based standards and accountability, increasingly diverse student populations, and increasingly complex aid formulas, states continue to need to develop more precise tools and methodological standards for evaluating the fairness, logic, and empirical basis of existing state school finance policies. We have attempted to provide some of those tools and a framework for their application. We cannot emphasize, enough, however, the uniqueness of each state's circumstances and the resulting need to individually tailor any and all analyses to those circumstances. More conventional equity and fiscal neutrality analyses (see Chapter 5) may be useful for initial dissection of Missouri or Wisconsin school finance policies, which continue to be plagued by strong property wealth-related disparities resulting from those states' locally controlled matching aid programs. Still, appropriately cost-adjusted analyses will produce more precise findings. States such as Kansas and Texas with complexly layered cost-adjusted financing schemes require more detailed analysis of need effects and appropriate cost adjustment for more conventional equity statistics. Conventional analysis of either Kansas or Texas school finance policies (see Chapter 5) will likely result in meaningless or even erroneous findings.

We are realistic in our expectation that state school finance policies will never be perfectly empirically based. The empirics themselves are far from perfect. The art of estimating the cost of achieving specific educational outcomes continues to improve, as do the data for estimating costs. Yet we continue to measure only narrow sets of available educational outcomes, specifically, students' academic achievement in reading, writing, and mathematics. In contrast, state courts have defined adequate schooling much more broadly as preparing children for productive participation in future economies and preparing children to be active, engaged civic participants. Rarely are civic engagement or even civic knowledge and comprehension among the measured outputs of schooling. In addition, we continue to use only crude proxies to estimate the social context in which children grow to be productive, engaged citizens, focusing specifically on measures of poverty and language proficiency status, and sidestepping more difficult questions of race and culture.

Even if we were able to adopt new school finance policies based on the empirics of today, we must recognize that our policies are based on the knowledge base and technologies of teaching and learning today, and we must exercise extreme caution so as not to fix those technologies firmly into place for the foreseeable future. State school finance policies should include incentives to stimulate the emergence of new, more effective and more efficient technologies, which, over time, may reshape our understanding of education costs. For example, the role of computer technology and high-bandwidth transmission in broadening curricular offerings in remote, sparse rural communities may alter, though not necessarily reduce, the costs of educational service delivery. Analysts, policy makers, and educators know little about either the resource costs of service delivery or the outcome-based costs of distance learning with current technologies—or of course, with future technologies. Finally, the rationality and empirical basis of state school finance formulas will likely continue to be a function of state political processes, at least for the foreseeable future. Increasingly, that political process is negotiated not only by branches of a state's legislature but also by the state courts, arguably as an equal though not necessarily superior branch of state government. Increasingly, courts are demanding empirical support for funding levels established by legislatures:

> Let the Court be crystal clear. If school funding is not based on actual costs incurred by our schools in providing a suitable education for our children, no one, not this Court, not the Supreme Court, not the schools, not the public, and not even the Legislature itself will ever be able to objectively determine whether that funding meets the dual requirements of our Constitution, those being 1) adequacy and 2) equity. This is why the Courts of our sister States have moved unanimously and in a rising tide to this position and that is the absolute essence of this Court's ruling in the case at bar.
>
> Judge Terrence Bullock
> May 11, 2004
> *Montoy v. Kansas* 99 C 1738

Judicial mandate, even including appointment of special masters' of the court to oversee reform as in Arkansas in 2003–2004, is unlikely to be a panacea for ensuring empirically based aid formulas. However, judicial pressures are also unlikely to have little or no effect on even the most intractable legislatures. The political tug-of-war between legislative branches, governors, and state courts in the presence of increased empirical evidence regarding costs will likely result in some positive morphing of state school finance policies.

SUMMARY

In this chapter, we focused first on the idea that traditional equity measures are not particularly helpful for assessing adequacy aid formulas. Traditional equity measures cannot distinguish variations in per-pupil expenditure that are intended to compensate for the special educational needs of children in the district from those that are politically derived, because legislators from powerful rural or wealthier districts can manipulate the formulas to advantage their own constituents. In short, it is necessary to rethink the problem in order to disentangle vertical equity from horizontal equity.

We examined several approaches to assessing the vertical equity of specific cost adjustments for specific educational needs, for example, those of LEP students. We compared empirically determined costs and other approaches to estimating the size of the vertical adjustment required for specific extraordinary educational needs, arguing that empirically determined cost analysis is superior to all others but faces political resistance because it removes degrees of freedom for legislative horse-trading. We acknowledged that expert opinion and other efforts to assess real needs without conducting empirically sophisticated cost analyses might be an important intermediary step in those states where the political climate simply will not support empirically determined cost analysis.

Finally, we provided new measures for estimating the ratios of predicted to actual costs using correlation coefficients, slopes, and MAPE as statistical methods that would provide more useful information to policy makers. We gave you simulations to play with, but have admittedly provided limited guidance. The simulations are available so that you may develop a better intuitive understanding of the complex counter-balancing relationships among various kinds of vertical equity cost adjustments. We also supplied data samples from three states so that you might gain more insight via cross-state comparisons. We hope these simulations have been helpful, and we appreciate your feedback on their utility.

KEY TERMS

cost-alignment analyses Make more direct and more comprehensive comparisons between estimated costs and/or indices of costs and actual revenues available to school districts. Because cost-alignment tests consider all cost factors simultaneously, they reduce the possibility that overlooking potential counterbalancing cost factors will misguide us.

cost-based formulas Policy makers may use cost-based aid formulas to set the overall level of foundation aid. In cost-based formulas, the adjustments applied to that foundation aid are directly informed by empirical analysis of costs. In particular, cost-based formulas replace politically derived cost adjustments with cost adjustments derived from empirical analysis, such as a single comprehensive cost index derived from cost-function analysis.

cost-guided formulas Cost-guided aid formulas are not necessarily directly based on cost estimates and may or may not require complete overhaul of current aid formulas. A cost-guided aid formula may include conventional aid formula features such as pupil weights or need-based flat grants. In a cost-guided formula, the indices guide the adjustment of individual formula levers in order to improve the overall alignment of the formula with empirically estimated costs. Analysts can successfully *cost-morph* formulas with sufficient existing policy levers.

implicit weights (implicit costs) One can calculate implicit weights by comparing the supplemental allotment to the average available resources per pupil, assumed to crudely represent the expenditure per pupil for regular education.

REFERENCES

Alexander, C., Gronberg, T., Jansen, D., Keller, H., Taylor, L., & Triesman, P. (2000). *A study of uncontrollable variations in the costs of Texas public education: A summary report prepared to the 77th Texas Legislature.* Charles A. Dana Center. University of Texas at Austin.

Andrews, M., Duncombe, W., & Yinger, J. (2002). Revisiting economies of size in American education: Are we any closer to consensus? *Economics of Education Review, 21,* 245–262.

Augenblick and Myers, Inc. (2002). *Calculation of the cost of a suitable education in Kansas in 2000–2001 using two different analytic approaches.* Kansas Legislative Coordinating Council.

Augenblick and Myers, Inc. (2003a). *Calculating the cost of an adequate education in Colorado using the professional judgment and the successful school district approaches.* Colorado School Finance Project.

Augenblick and Myers, Inc. (2003b). *Calculation of the cost of an adequate education in Missouri using the professional judgment and the successful school district approaches.* Missouri Education Coalition for Adequacy.

Augenblick and Myers, Inc. (2003c). *Calculation of the cost of an adequate education in Nebraska in 2002–03 using the professional judgment and the successful school district approaches.* Nebraska State Education Association.

Augenblick, Palaich and Associates, Inc. (2004). *Calculation of the cost of an adequate education in North Dakota in 2002-03 using the professional judgment approach.* North Dakota Department of Public Instruction.

Baker, B. D. (2001). Living on the edges of school funding policy: The plight of at-risk, limited English proficient and gifted children. *Educational Policy, 15*(5), 699–723.

Baker, B. D., & Duncombe, W. D. (2004). Balancing district needs and student needs: The role of economies of scale adjustments and pupil need weights in school finance formulas. *Journal of Education Finance, 29*(2), 97–124.

Baker, B. D., & Green, P. C. (2003). Commentary: The Application of Section 1983 to School Finance Litigation. *West's Education Law Reporter, 173*(3), 679–696.

Baker, B. D., & Green, P. C. (2005). Tricks of the trade: Legislative actions in school finance that disadvantage minorities in the post-Brown era. *American Journal of Education, 111*(May) 372–413.

Baker, B. D., & Imber, M. (1999). "Rational educational explanation" or politics as usual? Evaluating the outcome of educational finance litigation in Kansas. *Journal of Education Finance, 25*(1), 121–139.

Carey, K. (2003). *The funding gap report 2003.* The Education Trust. Retrieved June 2006 from www.edtrust.org

Duncombe, W., & Johnston, J. (2004). The impacts of school finance reform in Kansas: Equity is in the eye of the beholder. In Yinger, J. (Ed.), *Helping children left behind: State aid and the pursuit of educational equity* (pp. 147–194). Cambridge, MA: MIT Press.

Green, P. C., & Baker, B. D. (2002). Circumventing Rodriguez: Can plaintiffs use the Equal Protection Clause to challenge school finance disparities caused by inequitable state distribution policies? *Texas Forum on Civil Liberties and Civil Rights, 7*(2), 141–165.

Gronberg, T., Jansen, D., Taylor, L., & Booker, K. (2004). *School outcomes and school costs: The cost function approach.* Austin, TX: Texas Joint Select Committee on Public School Finance. Retrieved April 26, 2004, from http://www.capitol.state.tx.us/psf/Reports/school%20outcomes%20and%20school%20costs.doc2.pdf

Kansas Department of Education. Division of School Finance. (no date). *General fund and legal max FY03.* Retrieved from www.ksde.org

Kansas Department of Education. Division of School Finance. (no date). *General fund and legal max FY04.* Retrieved from www.ksde.org

Montoy v. State. No. 99-C-1738 (Shawnee County, Nov. 21, 2001).

National Center for Education Statistics. (2000–2001). *Common core of data, local education agency universe survey.* Retrieved from www.nces.ed.gov/ccd

National Center for Education Statistics and U.S. Census Bureau. (no date). *School district demographics system.* Retrieved from http://nces.ed.gov/surveys/sdds/

Nebraska Department of Education. (2002–2003a). *Nebraska annual financial report.* Retrieved from http://ess.nde.state.ne.us/ASPX/DownloadHome.aspx

Nebraska Department of Education. (2002–2003b). *Nebraska state of the schools report.* Retrieved from http://reportcard.nde.state.ne.us/Main/DataDownload.aspx

Parrish, T. B., Matsumoto, C. S., & Fowler, W. J. (1995). *Disparities in public school district spending 1989–90: A multi-variate, student-weighted analysis, adjusted for differences in geographic cost of living and student need.* NCES 95-300R. Washington, DC: National Center for Education Statistics.

Rubenstein, R. (2003). National evidence on racial disparities in school finance adequacy. In W. J. Fowler (Ed.), *Developments in school finance, 2001–02,* pp. 91–110. Washington, DC: U.S. Department of Education, National Center for Education Statistics.

Smith, J., & Seder, R. (2004). *Estimating the costs of meeting state educational standards.* Davis, CA: Management Analysis and Planning, Inc.

Study: Education plan lacking: Findings show 45% of state's students would be left behind. (2004, April 25). *Houston Chronicle.*

Texas Education Agency. (no date). *Public Education Information Management System (PEIMS), Snapshot file.* Retrieved from http://www.tea.state.tx.us/perfreport/snapshot/

Underwood, J. K. (1995). School finance adequacy as vertical equity. *University of Michigan Journal of Law Reform, 28*(3), 493–519.

U.S. Census Bureau. (2000). *School district demographics system. Census 2000.* Washington, DC: Author. Retrieved from http://nces.ed.gov/surveys/sdds/

West Orange Cove Consolidated Independent School District et al. v. Alanis, 107 S.W.3d (Tex. 2003).

PRODUCTIVITY AND EFFICIENCY

CHAPTER 11

PRODUCTION, COST, AND EFFICIENCY

Introduction

In this chapter, we provide an overview of economic theories and methods related to the productivity and efficiency of public schools. We have touched upon many of these issues in previous chapters, but here we synthesize a comprehensive model of the economics of public schooling to reveal the interrelated nature of education production, costs, spending, and efficiency. Understanding efficiency is especially important, as it provides a springboard for understanding how we may design future policies to improve performance while controlling costs.

In Chapter 10 we addressed two approaches to adequacy: inputs and outcomes. Understanding the production and efficiency of schooling requires understanding the relationship between inputs and outcomes, and the extent to which education systems use the right mix and amount of inputs to produce desired levels of outcomes. The contribution of resource mix is a second-order contribution. If we assume that inputs such as given levels of teacher quality, class size, and instructional materials each have their independent effects on student achievement, is it possible that they also have synergistic effects—especially over the long run—that are above and beyond their independent effects? This second-order effect is a resources mix effect. The sum can be greater than the parts.

In this chapter, we ask, What is the appropriate way to measure the outcomes of schooling? How should we measure the inputs of schooling? What do we know from the research literature regarding the appropriate mix, level, and types of resources required for productive schools?

We begin with a review of the concepts of education production, education costs, and the demand for public education. In the first section, we develop a systems model of the relationship between education production, cost, and demand. Next, we provide a brief overview of research on educational productivity, with references to numerous other studies on the topic. We then discuss the concept and measurement of efficiency both in formal economic terms and in practical, applied terms in public education research and policy analysis. We conclude with a discussion of cost-effectiveness analysis as an alternative, more straightforward approach to generating similar insights to those produced by economic efficiency analyses.

Conceptual View of Production, Costs, and Spending

In Chapter 3 we first introduced the concept of the median voter model of the demand for public education. Note that while we emphasize this model throughout this text, the median voter model is only one approach to characterizing demand for local public goods and services. We indicated previously that analysts typically measure the demand for public education in terms of the price that voters are willing to pay for the level or type of education they desire. That is, analysts may use spending on education as a measure of demand for educational services, presuming spending may be influenced directly by voters. In the case of state-controlled school finance systems, state average or total spending on education is a measure of state average demand for public education, but by way of representative government, not direct referenda.[1] Recall that we express the demand for public education as follows:

$$\text{Spending} = f(\text{Voter Tastes, Fiscal Capacity, Tax Price})$$

That is, spending on public education is a function of voter tastes, capacity to spend, and the price in taxes of an additional unit of public education. As discussed previously, a major assumption of the model requires that voters set spending, or schooling input levels, with full information that the input level chosen will yield a desired level of outcomes. Voters do not simply choose to spend at a given level regardless of the quality of product they receive. An interesting policy question becomes, What is the effect of poor information (or a poor technology of educational production) on the levels that voters are willing to spend? Presumably, the weaker the causality between marginal increases in spending and marginal increases in student achievement, the lower overall levels of spending will be. If this is true, then it behooves the policy community to spend on research that will tighten the causal linkages.

In Chapter 8 we discussed the education cost function as a tool for estimating adequate funding levels across schools of different types and sizes and across students with varied educational needs. Recall that we defined the education cost function as follows:

$$\text{Cost} = f(\text{Desired Outcomes, Student Inputs, Schooling Input Prices, Schooling Structural Characteristics})$$

That is, the cost of education is a function of the desired level of output, a variety of student inputs (including their family background characteristics and prior academic preparation), and the prices of the inputs required for providing education, most importantly the prices of teachers. In addition, as we discussed in Chapter 8, many schooling structural characteristics beyond control of local administrators also may influence costs.

Perhaps the best-known and most frequently cited economics equation in educational policy research is the education production function, which became popularized in the battle over whether schooling resources matter, which to date, has yet to be resolved (see, e.g., Hanushek, 1996; Hedges & Greenwald,

1996). We may define a simple education production function as follows:

$$\text{Student Outcomes} = f(\text{Schooling Inputs, Student Inputs, Environmental Inputs})$$

That is, student outcomes are a function of schooling inputs, student inputs, and environmental inputs. Schooling inputs may include financial inputs to schooling and/or the resources purchased with those financial inputs such as teachers with specific educational or experiential qualifications. Student-level inputs are as described in the cost function (i.e., including student socioeconomic background as well as prior academic preparedness). Environmental inputs are those factors that influence students and their families positively or negatively, including the quality of the air, water, and food supply; the state of the economy; and war and natural disasters. An extensive body of research since the report by Coleman et al. in 1966 has focused on the relationship between schooling inputs, student inputs, and student outcomes using education production functions, the primary focus of which has been to identify those schooling inputs that may influence student outcomes. Most of these models presume stability of the environmental factors.

As we mentioned earlier, voters or state legislators set spending levels, or schooling input levels, on the assumption that given levels of spending shall yield given levels of student outcomes. In theory, increases in schooling inputs should yield increases in production, or schooling outcomes. The existence of these relationships, however, is contingent on educational leaders' efforts and/or capacity to maximize outcomes for any given set of inputs and to marginally increase outcomes as additional inputs become available. In other words, the school leaders who are consumers of resources on behalf of children need knowledge of best practice and need implementation expertise to apply resources effectively.

Linking the Functions

We have found it useful in our teaching experiences to consider each of the three major equations of the economics of public education systems just discussed (i.e., spending, cost, and student outcomes) as components of an integrated systems model. Viewing each as a separate, independent equation, where a set of independent

---

[1]Blomberg and Hess (2000) discuss extensively the differences in the behaviors of local voters voting directly on spending referenda and state legislators making budget allocation decisions.

variables influences a given dependent variable, promotes what Richmond and Peterson (1997) describe as "Laundry List Thinking" (Richmond & Peterson, 1997, pp. 1–7). In the absence of an integrated systems model, each individual input has its own independent influence on the outcome of interest; outcomes do not influence inputs, and inputs are unassociated with one another.

Production function research in particular has attempted for years to test whether each or any of a plethora of teacher characteristics, classroom practices, class sizes, and/or teaching support staff configurations possess individual linear relationships with student outcomes. Hanushek (1996), for example, summarizes a list of 90 studies, including 377 attempts to identify causal relationships between individual schooling inputs and student outcomes. The recent development in the cost–function literature (discussed in Chapter 7), including the complex problem of dealing with student outcomes as an independent variable, piqued our interest in providing a systems perspective on the economics of education.

Figure 11.1 displays the relationship between the demand function and the production function. In the demand function (from right to left), community tastes for education and community wealth and income influence the community's choice of spending level. Community wealth, most notably property wealth (which may or may not be associated with income), influences the tax price of education and also influences the spending level. Somewhat unconventionally, we choose to include wealth, in addition to income, as a partial measure of ability to pay in addition to recognizing that property wealth influences spending via its influence on tax price.

We assume that school systems set spending levels according to desired student outcomes, with actual levels of student outcomes to be determined via the production function. Typically, educational researchers and economists have been concerned with either labor market outcomes, such as job placement and wages or standardized test scores, presumed to influence educational attainment and ultimately wages. The dotted link between spending and student outcomes in Figure 11.1 represents that assumed relationship. For the production function (from left to right), we decompose our community into parents and nonparents. We make the simplified assumption that nonparents may influence the demand function but are less likely to influence production (except through demand). We assume that a variety of student background characteristics, including their parents' tastes for public education (perhaps indicated by their own education levels) and their parents' wealth and income, are strong influences on student outcomes. Parent income, for example, may influence prenatal, neonatal, and early childhood health and well-being in addition to the ability to purchase supplemental educational opportunities as the child becomes of school age.

Figure 11.2 presents the relationship between the education cost function and the education production function. Student outcomes influence education costs (right to left), a relationship that can be stated in either of two ways. First, we can suggest that one may base a hypothetical cost on a desired level of outcomes. Alternatively, we can suggest that the actual cost

Figure 11.1   Linking Spending (Demand) and Production

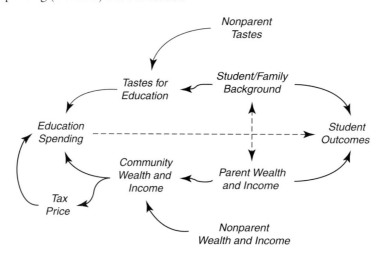

Figure 11.2 Linking Cost and Production

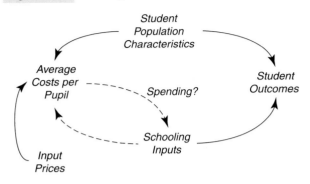

Education production (left to right), as in the previous diagram, is a function of student–population characteristics and of schooling inputs. That is, education systems expend fiscal inputs to purchase schooling inputs (at given prices), and those schooling inputs (including quantities and qualities of teachers, facilities, materials, supplies, and equipment) influence student outcomes. The question that emerges in this diagram is whether actual spending behavior of districts toward achieving their present level of outcomes is truly representative of the minimum cost of schooling inputs required to achieve that same level of outcomes with that same group of students. This question of "efficiency" is the centerpiece of a later section of this chapter and is a critical element in cost–function analysis that we chose to overlook while we encouraged you to build your analytic skills and knowledge base in previous chapters.

(based on current spending) is related to current outcomes. That is, we may have a desired set of outcomes that would cost x to achieve, but we may presently spend only $x - y$, achieving somewhat lower outcomes. In addition to being influenced by student-population characteristics, education costs are a function of both the quantity and prices of schooling inputs.

Figure 11.3 integrates all three functions into one systems model. We describe the aggregate adult community as the group of parents and nonparents who influence local and state policy, including education spending,

Figure 11.3 Systems Model of Production, Cost, and Demand in Public Education

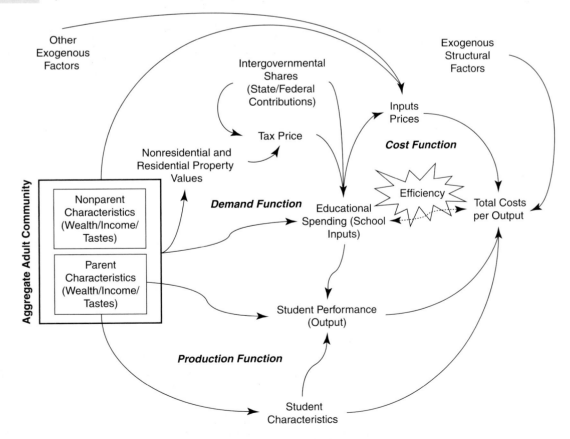

and the group of parents that influence the education, health, and well-being of students in the system. Note that if we focus solely on the public education system, we might consider parents of home-schooled or privately schooled students to be the equivalent of nonparents. As in our previous diagrams, parent characteristics and student characteristics along with schooling inputs influence student outcomes through the production function. However, parent characteristics (as one component of the community) also influence schooling inputs, with an expectation of outcomes.

In the demand model, characteristics of the aggregate voting adult community, along with tax prices or the price to the median voter of an additional unit of education, influence schooling fiscal inputs. Note that we include the role of intergovernmental aid in this diagram, a role we discussed in Chapter 6. That is, aid from federal or state governments to local districts may influence the tax price to local voters. Alternatively, aid could increase their fiscal capacity. In this diagram, we also assume that a variety of other exogenous factors influence the prices of educational inputs. These factors might include labor market variables that affect teacher prices as in Chambers' wage indices discussed in Chapter 8.

We might add other intriguing connections to the diagram, but we have omitted them in order to maximize simplicity in this already-complex diagram. For example, we might include a feedback connection between student outcomes and residential property values, indicating that, as student outcomes improve, and public perception of the community improves, housing values increase. These effects might also increase desirability for business relocation to the community, resulting in a positive effect on nonresidential property values as well.

A potential problem area, or point of interest, in the model is the reconciliation of total costs per output, from the education cost function, and education spending levels that the demand model generates. On the one hand, measuring the amount spent that produced a given level of outcomes may be the most straightforward measure of the costs to produce that level of outcomes. In this case, we do not need to represent spending and cost separately in the diagram. However, schools and districts may generally be unable, or perhaps even unwilling, to achieve the maximum possible outcomes for a given set of inputs. In this case, spending and costs are two different things. Costs are the theoretical costs associated with achieving the most cost-effective possible outcomes, which dif-

fers from the amount spent that produced a given level of outcomes. That difference, or the dotted line between costs and spending in Figure 11.3, is efficiency.

Understanding Efficiency

Economists generally discuss two types of efficiency with respect to public education finance: (a) allocative efficiency and (b) pure technical efficiency. (For a more thorough discussion, consult Pindyck & Rubinfeld, 1995.)

> **Allocative Efficiency:** An allocation is efficient if goods cannot be reallocated to make someone better off without making someone else worse off.
>
> **Technical Efficiency (Input Efficiency):** A particular allocation of inputs into the production process is technically efficient if the output of one good cannot be increased without decreasing the output of another good.

In public education finance, analysts most often associate *allocative efficiency* with the distribution of resources across schools and districts and discuss this efficiency in the context of state school finance equalization (Hoxby, 1996; Lankford, 1985). In this context, *allocative efficiency* refers to the fact that parents can choose the level of public good (education) they wish their child to receive by a combination of voting at the ballot box for higher or lower taxes or voting with their feet by moving to a district with programs more suited to their preferences (if their preferences are inconsistent with their present community). That is, *allocative efficiency* means that individuals receive only that level of public good they demand (based on their demand determinants)—no more, no less. Hoxby (1996) and others suggest that the optimal means toward attaining allocative efficiency is local school finance, driven by the previously discussed model of demand for local public goods and services and Charles Tiebout's (1956) *A Pure Theory of Local Expenditures.*

Tiebout characterized the mechanism by which individuals sort themselves among communities based on their preferences for local public goods and the prices of those goods. Under this process, for example, the individual with low fiscal capacity to pay for education but high preferences for quality education might choose to purchase a low-value property in a high-wealth, high—education-preference community, allowing that individual

Figure 11.4   Technical Efficiency

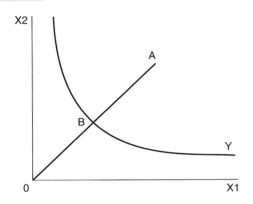

to pay a reasonable tax price (due to the relatively high wealth of the community as a whole) and still receive the desired quality of education. (Chapter 2 provides additional discussion of the concept of *allocative efficiency* and its relationship to Tiebout processes).

Figure 11.4 represents technical efficiency. Schools choose among combinations of inputs X1 and X2 to produce Y units of output. Y represents the outcomes attainable with combinations of X1 and X2, if those resources are used efficiently. A reduction in X1 must be accompanied by an increase in X2, and vice versa, to maintain Y outcomes. Let's assume that a school uses quantities of X1 and X2 that place the school in the location of A. We may measure the efficiency of the school by taking the ratio of the length of OA to the length of OB. We find that the school that uses this combination of resources to produce Y outcomes is inefficient. That is, in this case, the school is using excess of both X1 and X2 to produce the given set of outcomes (Y), and this is empirically shown by the resulting ratio of less than 1 (OB/OA < 1).

Duncombe and Miner (1996) note that one shortcoming of technical efficiency is that it ignores the relative resource prices and cost of production:

> It is possible for a technically inefficient district to have lower spending than a technically efficient district providing the same level of service because the mix of production factors it uses are less costly. For example, assume the wage of teacher's aides in a district is much lower than that of teachers. A technically efficient district that uses all teachers could have higher expenditures than an inefficient district producing the same level of

education outcome with a mix of aides and teachers. A local government is said to be *cost efficient* if there is no other way to combine inputs to produce the same level of output at a lower cost, given relative resource levels. *Cost efficiency provides the most comprehensive measure of productive efficiency.* (p. 144, emphasis added)

Measuring Efficiency: Methodological Issues

Analysts can measure efficiency with respect to either production or costs. As noted previously, school districts can combine resources and use them to maximize outcomes, or productivity. All schools or districts, however, deviate at least slightly from their theoretical maximum production. This deviation is *production inefficiency*. Alternatively, schools can produce a given level of output with a theoretical minimum cost. Again, schools or districts producing given levels of outcomes do so at levels higher than the theoretical minimum. That deviation is *cost inefficiency*. Assuming that measures of production inefficiency fully account for differences in costs of production due in part to differences in input prices across schools, the two measures of inefficiency are equivalent.

Since the 1980s, analysts have employed various methods to estimate the efficiency of schools. Those methods fall broadly into two categories: (a) methods based on equations fit by regression analysis to data on school spending and performance and (b) methods that use numerical optimization algorithms to identify maximum efficiency for each school or district. Recent research indicates advantages to each method under different conditions.

Regression-Based Methods
Regression-based methods, or econometric approaches for studying efficiency involve estimating equations or mathematical models to represent the production or cost frontier. Regression-based methods can be either deterministic or stochastic. Further, regression-based methods may measure efficiency relative to an average response function or relative to a production frontier.

Deterministic Approach: Average Response Function
One "efficiency analysis"[2] approach used commonly in consultation with state legislators involves comparing

---

[2]Efficiency analysis is in quotes here because we later establish standards for analyses that we believe qualify to be legitimate efficiency analyses, given today's technologies.

schools or districts with "average production efficiency" levels by fitting a multiple linear regression production function to student performance data.

Typically, this would involve fitting a curve similar to that in Figure 11.4 through the middle of a scatter plot of districts (rather than across the tops of the most efficient districts). One would assume that districts above the curve are above average efficiency and that districts below the curve are below average efficiency. Such methods, however, are very sensitive to even subtle changes in the way in which the regression line is fit to the data. Schools identified as "inefficient" may vary widely simply as a result of adding or removing one or a handful of independent variables from the regression, or fitting a curve in place of a straight line.

Figure 11.5 presents a simplified example of the bivariate relationship between expenditures per pupil and the percentage of students passing the Texas statewide assessments. Three lines are fit to the data to represent "average efficiency," or the expected percentage of students passing state tests at each level of expenditures per pupil. The gray dashed curve (a second-order polynomial) produces the best fit ($R^2 = 0.24$) but actually

indicates a decline in productivity for the highest spending levels, a theoretically questionable finding. More important, however, are districts in the sample that are above one line but below others. Further, distances from the curves for the same districts vary widely, such that some districts are extreme outliers from one curve but not the others. An important question discussed in greater detail as we present existing research on educational efficiency is whether or not efficiency measurement methods are "ready for prime time." (We borrow this phrase from the title of a useful article on this topic by Duncombe & Bifulco, 2000.) That is, are efficiency analyses methods sufficiently refined and stable to inform policy and to use to scrutinize the effectiveness of school leaders?

Deterministic Approach: Production Frontier

One relatively straightforward variant of the average response function is a method known as corrected ordinary least squares (COLS). *Ordinary least squares* (OLS) refers to the standard method for estimating a regression equation, or line or curve of best fit. Analysts use COLS to estimate a frontier rather than average

Figure 11.5   Identifying Average Efficiency Across Texas Districts

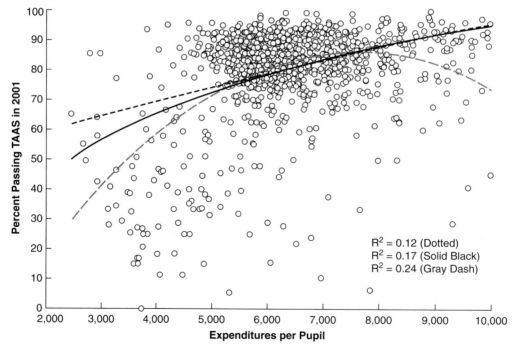

TAAS, Texas Assessment of Academic Skills.

Source: Data from http://www.tea.state.tx.us, Snapshot 2000 dataset

Figure 11.6 Estimation of a Production Frontier

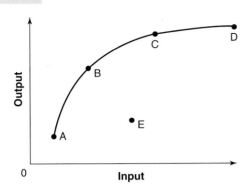

Figure 11.7 Deterministic and Stochastic Cost Frontiers

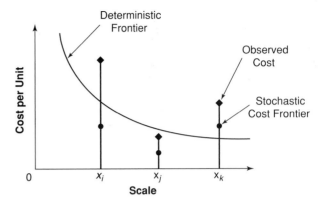

Source: Adapted from Anderson and Kabir (2000).

response. Figure 11.5 shows that several points fall above the curve and several below the curve. The distance from each point below the curve to the curve is negative, and the distance from each point above the curve to the curve is positive. If we slide the curve upward, such that no distance from a point to the curve is greater than 0, we have a production frontier as in Figure 11.6. The adjustment to make the largest *residual* 0 is the correction in COLS.

Stochastic Approach

Stochastic frontier analysis is a regression-based alternative to deterministic OLS methods. Anderson and Kabir (2000) provide Figure 11.7 as a comparison of deterministic versus stochastic frontier analysis.

Figure 11.7 displays the cost per unit of outcome (*y* axis) with respect to school district scale (*x* axis). As discussed in Chapter 9, costs per unit of outcome decline with respect to district scale. Our curve in Figure 9.3 and the curve in Figure 11.7 are deterministic cost functions. Anderson and Kabir (2000) note, however, that district-level productivity varies from the deterministic function partly due to inefficiency but also partly due to factors beyond district control (considered a *noise* term). Stochastic frontier analysis separates inefficiency from noise for each district, identifying a separate expected cost per unit of production for each district, given the exogenous characteristics and resource levels of that district. In theory, the distance of each district's actual cost to its stochastic estimated cost frontier should measure the district's inefficiency without including random variations beyond district control.

Random variations of conditions may be either favorable or unfavorable to districts. In Figure 11.7, note that the inefficiency of district X_i with respect to its sto-

chastic cost frontier is greater than it is with respect to the deterministic frontier. This suggests that district X_i experiences random, favorable conditions, and as a result, district X_i should actually face lower costs per unit of production than estimated by the deterministic frontier. District X_j also experiences random, favorable conditions such that even though district X_j is relatively efficient with respect to the deterministic function, it is relatively inefficient with respect to its stochastic cost frontier. District X_k, on the other hand, faces unfavorable, random conditions, such that its measured inefficiency is reduced with respect to those conditions. Bifulco and Duncombe (2000) indicate that, while unmeasured exogenous conditions might have favorable or unfavorable random effects on districts, so might measurement errors on student outcomes.

Numerical Maximization Methods

Since the early 1980s, analysts have used more flexible methods for efficiency analysis than those just described. In 1978, Charnes, Cooper, and Rhodes introduced **data envelopment analysis (DEA)** as a numerical maximization method for measuring the efficiency of not-for-profit and governmental agencies. Data envelopment analysis "weights inputs and outputs in a way that maximizes the efficiency index for each district" (Duncombe & Miner, 1996, p. 144).

As depicted in Figure 11.4, DEA identifies those districts in a sample of districts that produce the maximum outcomes at given levels of inputs. DEA methods assign those districts an efficiency index of 1.0 and create a frontier by connecting the dots, so-to-speak, between districts maximizing production at each level of input (as in Figure 11.6). Using DEA, analysts express efficiency of districts below the frontier as a ratio of the output of those districts compared to the frontier.

Researchers have used several versions of DEA to study school district efficiency. Bessent and Bessent (1980), for example, used the basic formulation of Charnes et al. (1978) to study the efficiency of schools in Houston, Texas.

A shortcoming of early DEA efficiency analyses is that they assumed constant returns to scale (e.g., that expected production would be similar regardless of scale) and that they failed to accommodate the various environmental factors that may influence district costs and productivity, including student population characteristics and population sparsity. Subsequent analyses by McCarty and Yaisawarng (1993), Deller and Rudnicki (1993), and others have applied DEA methods that account for differences in returns to scale and differences in environmental influences.

Improvements in efficiency analysis that help to account for factors beyond school district control, including economies of scale and student population characteristics, are critically important. Note that our example in Figure 11.5 assumes that all districts in Texas should be able to get the same proportion of students to pass the statewide test if they are simply given the same amount of money. Given our discussions of vertical equity in Chapter 8, this assumption is obviously flawed.

Somewhat like OLS regression analysis, DEA is a deterministic approach to understanding schooling efficiency. That is, both regression equations and DEA produce defined production or cost frontiers and subsequently measure efficiency for all districts relative to those frontiers. One particular problem with deterministic methods is that they assume that we have measured all possible variables that are beyond district control that may affect their productivity and further that "noise," or random variation in our measures of productivity, is not present. DEA, like other deterministic methods, attributes all deviations from the frontier to inefficiency.

Efficiency and Education Costs

At this point, it is particularly relevant to address the role of efficiency in understanding education costs, especially when estimating cost functions as discussed in Chapters 8 and 10. District-level education costs estimated via education cost functions may vary widely simply as a function of inefficiency. If, for example, certain types of districts, perhaps large urban districts, are prone to significant inefficiencies but we do not have accurate measures of those inefficiencies, the relatively high spending behavior of those districts and relatively low productivity of those districts will inflate their costs of achieving a given set of outcomes.

Figure 11.8 depicts the spending per pupil for three districts and costs per pupil of achieving a given set of

Figure 11.8   Cost of Achieving Average Outcomes by District Size

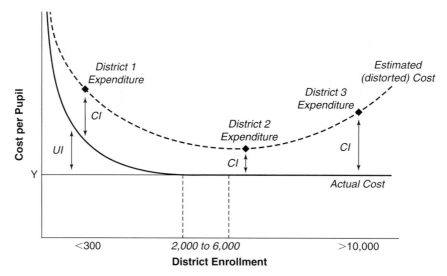

CI, controllable efficiency; UI, uncontrollable inefficiency.

outcomes, by scale, assuming average student population characteristics. Depicted spending levels are purely hypothetical. Inefficiencies most likely vary irregularly across districts of different size and/or irregularly across districts by any number of characteristics. Inefficiencies vary as a function of factors both within and outside of local district administrators' control. Increased costs of outcomes that result from operating at too small a scale are one form of inefficiency but a form of inefficiency that *may be* beyond the control of local boards of education or administrators, assuming geographic isolation (uncontrollable inefficiency, UI, in Figure 11.8).

Inefficiencies that should be within the control of local administrators are (a) increased costs of outcomes resulting from poor recruitment and hiring practices, (b) noncompetitive bidding where competitors exist, or (c) simply ineffective delivery of curriculum and instruction. Administrators engaging in these inefficient practices should be able to reduce their inefficiencies, moving toward expenditure levels closer to costs (reducing controllable inefficiency, CI), where the cost curve may represent the costs of achieving desired outcomes at either *average* or *perfect* efficiency.

Districts 1 to 3 in Figure 11.8 vary in their relative *CI*. District 1 is a small district producing outcomes at spending levels slightly above actual costs. District 2 is a larger district producing desired outcomes at very near actual costs, but District 3 is a larger district apparently spending far more than necessary to achieve desired outcomes. The differences in apparent inefficiency likely result from factors within the control of administrators and from unmeasured (or poorly measured) factors with random, positive and negative effects on district efficiency.

Duncombe and Yinger (1999) tested the effects of controlling for efficiency on education cost in New York State. Duncombe and Yinger performed cost–function analyses with the following two assumptions: First, they assumed that the given spending levels of school districts represented the spending required for those districts to achieve given outcomes, given their student populations and other conditions. Second, Duncombe and Yinger assumed that districts might be functioning with varied degrees of inefficiency. They found, for example, that controlling for inefficiency, Yonkers, an urban district just north of New York City, received a cost index of 191.91, compared to a cost index of 276.81 when not controlling for inefficiency. The implication of this finding is that much of Yonkers's relatively high spending and low

production can be attributed to inefficiency rather than conditions beyond district control.

Again, critical questions that we will address later in this chapter are, Do the various methods for cost-efficiency analyses effectively and consistently identify more- and less-efficient school districts? And do the analytical methods reveal reasons for the observed inefficiencies?

A Brief Review of Research

In this section we briefly summarize factors related to productivity and efficiency. Ultimately, the goal of policy makers is to identify those factors that may be manipulated toward improving productivity and efficiency. Unfortunately, one shortcoming of the studies discussed in this section is that they apply what we have previously identified as "laundry list thinking." Chapters 12 and 13 focus on two general approaches to policy: market-based and government-regulated approaches. In this section, we address micro-level findings regarding district-level variables that policy makers might used as policy levers.

Factors Influencing Productivity

Since the 1960s, researchers have sought to identify schooling inputs that influence educational productivity using education production functions. Early analyses of education production, or student outcomes, by Coleman et al. (1966) suggested that student background characteristics were the dominant influences on student academic achievement, and that schooling resources, or at least differences in schooling resources observed at the time, seemed to make little difference. Coleman's findings suggested to many that there was little hope of narrowing gaps in student outcomes between high- and low-socioeconomic status (SES) students, or even of raising the minimum performance bar for low-SES students. (For a recent synopsis of the Coleman report see Haller and Kleine, 2001.)

Referring to our approach for modeling school-funding policies in Chapter 6, one might classify as *exogenous conditions* the student SES characteristics that Coleman identified as most significantly related to student achievement. Bear in mind that, while student SES characteristics were more significant determinants of student achievement than other variables that Coleman explored, these characteristics still explained very little of the differences in student achievement. (See Haller &

Kleine, 2001, p. 33.) More recent production function studies have focused primarily on *policy levers* for improving educational productivity, including class sizes and teacher qualifications, while controlling for *exogenous conditions* (Finn & Achilles, 1999; Wenglinsky, 1997). Ideally, just as we constructed policy simulations that allowed us to test the effects of changing finance policy levers on equity and adequacy measures, we should be able to construct simulations based on empirical research on education production that allow us to tweak policy levers such as education spending and/or pupil to teacher ratios and assess effects on student performance. Unfortunately, modeling productivity is a far more complex task than modeling equity.

One central issue raised initially by the Coleman (1966) report was whether adding more money to the system is likely to improve performance. Can money alone be an effective policy lever? Many school finance equity reforms have been predicated on the assumption that it can. Coleman's findings were pessimistic in this regard, but several studies with findings both favoring and opposing the influence of fiscal inputs have followed (Hanushek, 1996; Hedges & Greenwald, 1996). If increases in total resources produce either small or nonsignificant results, attention should shift to how schools may use existing resources or to determining what types of purchased schooling inputs are more likely to lead to improved student outcomes. One school finance policy implication of shifting the emphasis from total fiscal resources to efficient resource allocation is that states should consider targeting aid in order to promote more productive resource allocation. New Jersey's attempt to require certain districts to implement specific whole-school reforms is one example of state intervention in district resource allocation. Yet, existing empirical evidence (or lack thereof) on the effectiveness of these reforms makes it difficult to simulate or even speculate the efficiency advantages of this strategy. We address other state approaches to improving efficiency through targeted resource allocation in Chapter 12.

Existing production function research provides little firm empirical evidence on the expected effects of policy levers (Hanushek, 1996; Hedges & Greenwald, 1996). Since the 1990s, policy makers and analysts have generally accepted the premise that money certainly can matter in public education but that the money must be used wisely. Acceptance that money matters has emerged slowly and tentatively out of the cloud of dust raised in heated debate over the topic that seemed to dominate the entire decade of the 1990s (dating back to the 1960s).

Specifically, the education production–function genre is often characterized by the battle of the meta-analyses over whether money matters (Hanushek, 1996; Hedges & Greenwald, 1996). Tables 11.1 and 11.2 summarize first Hanushek's, then Hedges and Greenwald's scorecards of production–function studies conducted through the early 1990s.

Hanushek's (1996) scorecard points out that the majority of studies find nonsignificant relationships between the various potential policy levers and student achievement outcomes. Further, while positive significant relationships tend to outnumber negative significant relationships, the presence of negative significant relationships in many studies casts reasonable doubt on positive significant findings. Hanushek's general conclusion regarding education production–function

Table 11.1   Hanushek's Scorecard

	Resources	Teacher/Pupil Ratios	Teacher Education	Teacher Experience	Teacher Salary	Expend. Per Pupil	Admin. Inputs	Facilities
Number of Estimates		277	171	207	119	163	75	91
Statistically significant	Positive	15	9	29	20	27	12	9
	Negative	13	5	5	7	7	5	5
Statistically insignificant	Positive	27	33	30	25	34	23	23
	Negative	25	27	24	20	19	28	19
	Unknown	20	26	12	28	13	32	44

Source: Adapted from Hanushek, E. (1996). School resources and student performance. In G. Burtless (Ed.), *Does money matter?* (pp. 43–73). Washington, DC: The Brookings Institution.

Table 11.2 Hedges and Greenwald's Scorecard Summary of Results of Combined Significance Tests of Longitudinal Studies[a]

		Teacher/Pupil Ratio[c]		Teacher Education			Teacher Experience	
		Hanushek	New Universe	Hanushek	New Universe	New Universe[d]	Hanushek	New Universe
Positive	Full-Analysis Sample	Yes	Yes	Yes	No	Yes	Yes	Yes
	Robustness Sample[b]	No	**Yes**	No	No	**Yes**	Yes	**Yes**
Negative	Full-Analysis Sample	Yes	Yes	Yes	Yes	No	No	No
	Robustness Sample	No	**No**	Yes	Yes	**No**	No	**No**

[a]Evidence of positive effects indicates that the null hypothesis was rejected at $\alpha = 0.05$ level; evidence of negative effects indicates that the null hypothesis was rejected at $\alpha = 0.05$ level.

[b]The robustness samples are the middle 90%, with 5% trimmed from each side of the distribution.

[c]The signs have been reversed in those studies that use the variable pupil–teacher ratio or class size, to be consistent with the teacher–pupil ratio, so that $\beta > 0$ means that smaller classses have greater outcomes.

[d]Represents a "dichotomous" sample created using only those equations that indicated the possession of a master's degree. Those equations with continuous variables (for example B.A. to Ph. D.) were excluded from this subsample (*paraphrased from Hedges & Greenwald*, 1996).

Source: Adapted from Hedges, L., & Greenwald, R. (1996). Have times changed? The relation between school resources and student performance. In G. Burtless (Ed.), *Does Money Matter?* (pp. 74–92). Washington, DC: The Brookings Institution.

research is that research has found no reliable production function between schooling resources and student achievement, where schooling resources range from per-pupil expenditures to teacher salaries, experience, and education levels.

Hedges and Greenwald (1996) reanalyzed the findings of the production function studies that Hanushek (1996) reviewed and also gathered their own *universe* (in theory, all existing) of studies. In their scorecard, Hedges and Greenwald conclude that evidence of positive effects of reduced pupil-to-teacher ratios, teacher education levels, and teacher experience levels is reliable. Given the resource implications of each of these variables, Hedges and Greenwald conclude that financial resources do matter.

Far more studies have been conducted identifying possible inputs to schooling with consequences for student achievement than we can possibly discuss in this brief section. We can point out, however, the apparent contradictions of existing findings and the related difficulties of using those findings to inform school finance policies.

Methodological Considerations

We conclude this brief section on education production–function research with a few notes on the statisti-cal methodologies than analysts use for evaluating education production. The methodological rigor of the analyses of schooling productivity has evolved over the years, but the quality of such studies and the resultant validity of their findings remain inconsistent. Following are four standards and two ideals that we encourage you to consider when you evaluate production–function research, perform your own analyses, or review research and evaluation proposals that address questions of educational productivity:

1. **Whenever Possible, Analyses Should Use Student-Level Data** (Hanushek, Rivken, & Taylor, 1996). Hanushek et al. (1996) show quite decisively that when analyses use school-average, district-average, or even state-average performance indicators (resulting in loss of much of the variation in student-level performance), the effects of resources on student achievement are inflated. Student-level data have become increasingly available over the past decade, including comprehensive state-level data systems of annual student value-added achievement and national data sets available from the National Center for Education Statistics (www.nces.ed.gov) including the *National Educational Longitudinal Study of 1988* (NELS, 1988, http://www.nces.ed.gov/surveys/ nels88/) and

the more recent Early Childhood Longitudinal Study (ECLS; http://www.nces. ed.gov/ecls/).

2. **Analyses Should Measure Outcomes in Value-Added Terms** (Wright, Horn, & Sanders, 1997). As we discussed in Chapters 7 and 10, on educational adequacy, marginal achievement gains are a far more useful indicator of the influence of schools on students than are simple measures of performance levels. Hanushek (1986, p. 1157) provides an extension of this rationale. However, we must still recognize that school remains only a part of each child's learning day and year.

3. **Analyses Must Consider the Hierarchical Structure of Schooling Data** (Wenglinsky, 1997). In recent years, greater attention has been given to the hierarchical structure of schools and the difficult-to-measure interdependencies of students learning within the same classroom or school and/or differential influence of school-, district-, or even state-level policy variables on students in different schools and/or classrooms. Wenglinsky (1997), for example, uses hierarchical and structural models to show that expenditures at some levels of the schooling system did influence student achievement (notably, instructional expenditures and central administrative expenditures), while expenditures at other levels did not (notably school-level administration and capital outlay). Further, Wenglinsky showed that student SES influenced both individual student achievement and also influenced school climate, which in turn influenced student achievement.

4. **Straight Lines and Laundry Lists Don't Always Suffice.** We cannot assume that the relationship between financial resources and/or other schooling inputs and student outcomes is linear, or even that it conforms to a simple economic expectation of diminishing returns. Figlio (1999) for example, finds that a flexible *translog* functional form[3] is a more effective means for measuring complex relationships between schooling inputs and outcomes.

Figlio's (1999) *translog* production function reveals small, statistically significant effects of financial resources on student outcomes. It is also likely that schooling production involves numerous complex interactions among supposed independent variables at various levels of the hierarchy of schooling.

A fifth standard we had considered was the importance of adjusting schooling inputs to reflect regional purchasing power differences across districts. Most education production–function studies that attempt to evaluate whether fiscal inputs matter assume that $1 of fiscal input carries similar purchasing power across districts. The importance of such adjustments, while theoretically reasonable, remains empirically questionable. Taylor (1997), for example, found production functions on student level, national data to be relatively insensitive to regional cost adjustments.

Finally, we hold two ideals regarding the analysis of education production that may, for the time being, be less reasonable requirements for *gold standard* empirical research: First and foremost, analyses must give more attention to the measurement of schooling outcomes. At the very least, we must focus on schooling achievement measures empirically validated to be associated with more long-term measures of success such as educational attainment and earnings.

Second we must begin to explore in greater detail and with greater methodological rigor, the dynamics of change over time. That is, we must study how changes in resource allocation patterns and teaching practices in districts over time influence changes in student value added over time, rather than constantly studying differences in productivity across districts, hoping that one day we might make the less-productive districts like the more-productive districts by adjusting levers such as class sizes and/or teacher salaries to be more similar. Recall that we have alluded in this section to the possibility of constructing dynamic simulations of schooling production, where one might adjust specific policy levers including class sizes or teacher qualifications and observe the likely influence of these levers on a variety of social and academic outcomes. We hold the firm belief that understanding cross-sectional differences in production, or differences in inputs and outcomes across schools, can only minimally inform our understanding of how schooling production changes within schools over time.

---

[3]Note that this flexible form is the same as that used by Texas researchers in constructing their education cost function discussed in our chapter on educational adequacy (Chapter 7). Although infrequently used, this *translog* approach appears to consistently produce superior fit to complex education production and cost data (Figlio, 1999).

Factors Influencing Educational Efficiency

Since the 1990s, a handful of researchers have attempted to study the relative efficiency of public schools and factors that affect that efficiency. Some of the research discussed in this section is the same as that discussed previously under methods for studying efficiency. Currently, findings and methods for studying efficiency are evolving simultaneously and are arguably still at very early stages of development.

In 1996, David M. Anderson presented a *quadriform* approach to studying efficiency. Anderson's quadriform approach was based on linear regression equations of both student outcomes and of current operating expenditures per pupil. We preface Anderson's findings with the concern that quadriform analysis has never been shown to be a reliable method for schooling efficiency analysis, and we will discuss that further later in this chapter. Nonetheless, Anderson constructed the following rubric for classifying the efficiency of Michigan school districts:

1. *Efficient schools* have higher than expected outcomes with lower than expected expenditures (i.e., positive residuals with respect to outcomes and negative residuals with respect to expenditures).
2. *Inefficient schools* have lower than expected outcomes and higher than expected expenditures.
3. *Lighthouse schools* have higher than expected outcomes and higher than expected expenditures.
4. *Frugal schools* have lower than expected scores and lower than expected outcomes.

Anderson's (1996) goal was to identify both the alterable and unalterable factors associated with the efficiency of school districts in Michigan. Anderson's outcome measures included scores on Michigan State Assessments and percentages of students taking the ACT. Unalterable school characteristics included school size, demographics, and region; and alterable school characteristics included teacher salaries, class sizes, and the allocation of resources within schools.

Anderson found the following:

1. Salary is negatively related to efficiency.
2. Class size is positively related to efficiency (larger is more efficient). With larger class size, little loss of teaching effectiveness occurs, but the reduction in instructional costs is considerable.

3. For rural schools, higher spending shares on instruction were positively associated with efficiency. Resource allocation was not associated with efficiency for urban schools.
4. For urban schools, teacher experience was negatively associated with efficiency, and teacher level of education was positively associated with efficiency.
5. In rural schools, library quality mattered, and guidance counselors had positive effects, but in urban schools, guidance counselors had negative effects.

Duncombe and Miner (1996), in the early stages of a series of analyses of the costs and efficiency of New York schools, used a version of DEA to identify factors associated with district efficiency. Regarding factors beyond district control, they found that measures of districts' combined wealth (a composite of income and property wealth) and the proportion of commercial and industrial property in a district were associated with greater cost efficiency. Regarding factors within district control, they found that cost efficiency was negatively associated with the percentage of tenured teachers and with the percentage of the budget allocated to salaries and benefits.

Anderson and Kabir (2000), using the stochastic frontier approach discussed earlier, found that the cost frontier declines with school membership, or that smaller school districts tend to be less efficient. They also found that teachers' educational experience exerted a positive influence on efficiency (p. 22). While this might appear to contradict Anderson's (1996) and Duncombe and Miner's (1996) findings regarding teacher experience and efficiency, a notable difference in the studies is that Anderson and Kabir estimated their stochastic cost frontier to school districts in Nebraska, a much more rural state than either Michigan or New York. As we will discuss in greater detail in Chapter 12, Gronberg and Jansen (2001), like Anderson and Kabir, used stochastic frontier analysis to find that charter schools in Texas were relatively efficient compared to public schools serving similar student populations.

Precision and Accuracy of Efficiency Analysis

Finally, we address the current usefulness of efficiency analyses for directly informing education finance policies. Since the 1990s, consultants to state legislators have used efficiency and related analyses to identify relatively high-performing schools and relatively low-performing schools. One example is a recent evaluation by Augenblick and Myers of the organization of Kansas' public schools using a linear regression model[4] of student achievement outcomes to identify "unusually low performers" with respect to their predicted performance levels. Augenblick and Meyers targeted districts identified as unusually low performers for observation and discussed those districts as potential candidates for consolidation or reorganization. The implications for local district administrators of being identified as leaders of low-performing schools or districts are quite serious.

We have discussed here how each of the following might significantly change the list of identified districts: (a) the mere shape of the line fit to the data, (b) the inclusion or exclusion of one or more measures, or (c) the separation of random variation from true inefficiency. The political implications of these apparently subtle technical issues should not be taken lightly.

Academic researchers evaluating state-of-the-art methods for estimating efficiency and using simulated data in which actual efficiency can be known have found that currently available methods cannot place more than 31% of schools in their true performance quintiles (Bifulco & Bretschneider, 2001). Bifulco and Duncombe (2000), in subsequent analyses with simulated data, compared the accuracy of COLS, stochastic frontier estimation (SFE), and several variants of DEA for identifying district inefficiency in a data set with varying degrees of (a) measurement error and (b) endogeneity (cyclical relationships between outputs and inputs). In short, they found that some methods worked well with some kinds of data and others with other kinds of data. Unfortunately it is difficult, if not impossible, to assess the extent to which actual data suffer from measurement error or endogeneity (though reasonable statistical tests for endogeneity do exist). Therefore, it is difficult to select the best method for any given circumstance. As such, Bifulco and Duncombe conclude:

It would be difficult to defend implementing performance-based financing or management programs with estimates of school performance whose correlation with true performance is not higher than 0.30. (2000, p. 24)

Typically, consultancies with state legislators that claim to identify underperforming or inefficient districts use methods far inferior to those tested by Bifulco and Bretschneider (2001) or Bifulco and Duncombe (2000). It is critically important that research in this area continue to progress to a point where we can more confidently assign efficiency indices to schools and districts. Researchers should evaluate existing models for identifying inefficient districts for stability over time. That is, district leaders should not be condemned for their ineffectiveness simply as a result of one estimated regression equation, given a single year, or averaged handful of years of data. Researchers must use alternative data and model specifications to ensure that classifications are appropriate. Bad efficiency analyses will never be ready for prime time, but we are hopeful that more refined methods will be in the near future.

Have School Finance Reforms Improved or Reduced Productivity?

A growing body of research attempts to test specifically whether state school finance reforms lead to changes in student outcomes, including overall increases or declines in outcomes, or improvement in the equity of student outcomes (e.g., raising the bottom end, though not necessarily closing the gap) (Downes, 2003; Downes & Figlio, 1998). These studies attempt to test whether new money introduced into low-wealth schools via school finance reform leads to improved outcome levels and improved outcome equity. Like the Tennessee class size studies (Finn & Achilles, 1999), these studies measure changes over time in student outcomes, and their relationship to changes in

---

[4]The linear regression model that Augenblick and Meyers used did not conform to even the most basic production–function standards, no less our *gold standard* set forth in this chapter. Augenblick and Myers specified the model that they used to predict district aggregated performance as follows: Combined standardized state assessment scores = *f*(percent free/reduced lunch, tax rate (mills), population density, assessed valuation, natural log of enrollment, per pupil spending for instruction). They specified all relationships as linear. The authors did not use value-added outcomes, and they excluded substantial influences on student performance, including numbers of students with disabilities (SPED) and numbers of students with limited English proficiency (LEP). The authors identified 36 districts as "unusually low performing." Replication analyses using student-level performance data and including LEP and SPED counts alone produce an overlap of no more than 3 to 5 districts with the Augenblick and Myers (2001) "low performers."

state policies. (For an exceptional overview of this topic, see Downes, 2002.)

Whether school finance reform as a general concept leads to improved student outcomes, depends largely on the type of reform implemented. The following are questions you might be led to ask in seeking to determine the effectiveness of school finance reforms in your state:

1. Did the reform include significant new money, and did that that money lead to more adequate schooling inputs for previously low-funded, low-performing schools?
2. Did the reform include tax or spending limits, in an effort to enforce equitable inputs (often in conjunction with less emphasis on relative adequacy)?
3. Was the reform proactive or court ordered?

The first two questions are largely empirical and relatively straightforward to answer. Significant debate remains on the third question. The difficulty with answering the third question is that the effectiveness of reforms appears to be more dependent on the type of reform implemented than on the reason for the reform. Certain types of reforms tend to produce more consistently positive or more consistently negative results regarding long-term spending and outcomes. The literature on reforms including tax limits typically finds that tax limits level down spending and tax limits may level down student performance (Downes & Figlio, 1998). In general, Downes and Shah (1995) show that the stringency of constraints on local discretion determines the effects of reforms on the level and growth of spending.

Downes (2002) makes a strong case for more detailed study of specific reforms, noting the difficulty of comparing or classifying reforms across states. More recent, empirically rigorous literature on significant state-specific school finance reforms indicates positive results with respect to achievement outcomes. Two of these studies focus on school finance reform in Vermont (Downes, 2003) and in Kentucky (Flanagan & Murray, 2003). In each state, funding to low-wealth districts was increased dramatically. In Vermont, Tom Downes (the same economist who co-authored an empirically rigorous analysis of the leveling-down effect), found that Vermont's school finance reform (Act 60), which significantly increased funding in low-property-wealth districts, has also led to increased performance outcomes for children from low-wealth districts and that performance outcomes have improved more rap-

idly in low-wealth districts than in high-wealth districts. Note that since Downes's (2003) analyses, Vermont has modified Act 60 to increase the foundation level of funding to $6,800 per pupil over the next few years. Downes studied only the effects of the increase to $5,100 per pupil. Flanagan and Murray (2003) found similarly positive achievement effects from Kentucky's education reform act.

Finally, Deke (2003) in a study of the infusion of new revenues into Kansas districts in the early 1990s, found, "Using panel models that, if biased, are likely biased downward, I have a conservative estimate of the impact of a 20% increase in spending on the probability of going on to postsecondary education. The regression results show that such a spending increase raises that probability by approximately 5%" (p. 275).

A Cost-Effectiveness Perspective

Cost-effectiveness analysis provides an appealing alternative to econometric analyses for evaluating and improving schooling efficiency. A **cost-effectiveness** analysis shows the relationship between the cost of implementing a particular program or strategy and the expected or actual effects of that strategy on student outcomes, for example, the expected achievement points gained per dollar spent on a new reading strategy. Cost-effectiveness analysis is a management decision tool, and one that management can use at various levels of education policy in order to evaluate and improve educational efficiency. Policy makers can use cost-effectiveness analysis to compare the relative effectiveness (productivity) of various programs or strategies. Those programs or strategies involve different uses of educational resources. By continually evaluating and selecting the most productive strategies, shifting resources toward productive strategies and away from nonproductive strategies, policy makers may incrementally improve the technical efficiency of schooling. The organizational level at which this occurs will be defined primarily by policy preferences regarding local control and state interventions.

Economist Henry M. Levin presented a technical guide to conducting cost-effectiveness analysis in education in 1983, updated with coauthor Patrick McEwan in 2001. In this section, we present an overview of Levin's cost-analysis methods. We then review existing policy research on the cost-effectiveness of CSR policies, an issue that has received significant attention in recent years.

Table 11.3   Cost-Effectiveness Analysis of Two Dropout-Reduction Programs

Option	Input Measure (Costs of Ingredients per Pupil)	Outcome Measure(s) (Improvement/Dropout Reduction)	Input per Unit of Outcome (C/E Ratio)
Dropout-Reduction Program B	$147	10%	$14.7
Dropout-Reduction Program A	$353	25%	$14.1

Types of Cost Analyses

Levin identifies four major types of cost analysis in education: (a) cost-effectiveness; (b) cost–benefit; (c) cost–utility; and (d) cost-feasibility. Cost-feasibility analysis addresses only the cost side of the equation, asking simply whether the program or policy option in question is affordable. Descriptions and examples of the other three methods of cost analysis follow.

Each type of cost analysis involves estimating the costs of policy options. Levin discusses extensively the ingredients methods for estimating costs. See our discussion of input-based cost-analysis methods, and specifically, the *resource-cost model*, in Chapter 8, which is analogous to Levin's ingredients method.

Cost-Effectiveness

Cost-effectiveness analysis involves relating the costs of policy options to the outcomes or expected outcomes of those policy options. That is, cost-effectiveness analysis involves direct comparisons of schooling inputs and outcomes. Where educational programs are

concerned, outcome measurements typically take the form of assessments of student achievement related to the goals of the program or policy option in question.

Table 11.3 presents an example of a cost-effectiveness comparison of two programs for dropout reduction. The first has a cost of $147 per pupil and the second a cost of $353 per pupil. On a feasibility basis alone, policy makers might choose Program B. Program B has a proven track record of 10% reduction in dropout rates, while Program A has a track record of 25% reduction. Dividing the cost estimates by the outcome measures yields the cost per unit of outcome, or cost-effectiveness (C/E) ratio. Both programs are comparable in terms of their C/E ratios, with the more expensive program possessing a slight advantage.

Cost–Benefit

Cost–benefit analysis puts both inputs and outcomes into monetary terms. A **cost–benefit** analysis shows the relationship between the cost of implementing a specific program or strategy, and the short- or long-term financial benefits of doing so. Tables 11.4 and 11.5 present

Table 11.4   Cost–Benefit Analysis of Attending College

Option	Input Measure (Cost of Ingredients)	Outcome Measure (Savings or Monetary Gain)	Input per Unit of Outcome (Cost/Benefit Ratio) or Net Benefit (Cost–Benefit)
Attend college	Cost of tuition, room and board, and lost wages	Wage of college graduate	Cost/benefit ratio
Enter workforce	Cost of room and board	Earnings (and returns on savings) during expected college attendance period and subsequent wages	Cost/benefit ratio

Table 11.5   Cost–Benefit Analysis of Lease Versus Purchase of Computers

Option	Input Measure (Cost of Ingredients)	Outcome Measure (Savings or Monetary Gain)	Input per Unit of Outcome (Cost/Benefit Ratio)
Lease computers	Lease contract cost (cumulative over period, adjusted to future value)	Future value of savings from lease payment	Cost/benefit ratio
Purchase computers	Up-front purchase cost (adjusted to future value)	Future value of asset (computers after depreciation)	Cost/benefit ratio

conceptual examples. A typical cost–benefit example related to education for an individual is the comparison of the costs and benefits of attending college or graduate school. Both costs and benefits may be measured in monetary terms with relative ease, and net benefits may be calculated by subtracting costs from monetary benefits. Table 11.4 is a simplified version of cost–benefit analysis. A more elaborate version would include present-value comparisons of the two options and lost wages while attending college.

More practical uses of cost–benefit analysis for school administrators involve costs and benefits of lease versus purchasing options and a variety of other facilities operations upgrades, including replacement of heating and cooling systems. Use of cost–benefit analysis to select the best options for equipment acquisition or facilities management may allow district administrators to reallocate resources from plant and auxiliary services to cost-effective instructional programs.

Levin and McEwan (2001, p. 18) provide the example of cost–benefit analysis applied to dropout reduction, referring to estimates of the costs of alternative dropout-reduction programs and the likely long-term savings to taxpayers of implementing alternative programs.

Cost–Utility

Cost–utility analysis is similar to cost-effectiveness analysis but includes an additional dimension: the usefulness of (or constituents' preferences for) a particular set of outcomes. A **cost–utility** analysis shows the relationship between the cost of implementing a specific program or strategy, the outcomes of that strategy, and

the values of key stakeholders for those particular outcomes. For example, two programs, such as those we presented in our cost-effectiveness example, might have similar C/E ratios. However, those programs might address completely or partially different objectives, and relevant constituents may have different preferences for those objectives.

Table 11.6 provides an example of a cost–utility analysis using two reading and two math programs designed to supplement the core curriculum. Let us assume that district officials can choose to implement either a math or a reading supplemental program. That is, math or reading programs in this case are substitutes, not complements. The district arrives at the costs for each supplemental program via ingredients analysis. Then the district obtains outcomes either via research reports on the programs or internal evaluation of the programs if they have already been in use. The district might arrive at utility measures via surveys of relevant constituents including parents, board members, teachers, and/or even community business leaders. The cost–utility analysis in Table 11.6 rated increasing math performance with a utility of 8 on a 10-point scale and rated increasing reading performance with a utility of 4.

The first step in the analysis involves multiplying the expected (or measured) effectiveness of the programs times their utility, yielding the *expected utility* of each option. The second step in the analysis involves dividing the costs by the expected utility to create a cost–utility ratio. Conceptually, the cost–utility ratio is similar to a cost-effectiveness ratio where program outcomes are weighted by constituent preferences.

Table 11.6 Cost–Utility Analysis

Option	Input Measure (Costs of Ingredients)	Outcome Measure(s) (Student Performance Gains/Probability of Success)[a]	Utility Measure (Priority or Preference for Alternative Outcomes)[b]	Expected Utility (Outcome × Utility)	Cost/Utility Ratio
Math Program A	$530	.5	8	4.0	$132.50
Math Program B	$230	.4	8	3.2	$ 71.88
Reading Program A	$375	.7	4	2.8	$133.93
Reading Program B	$295	.6	4	2.4	$122.92

[a]Percent of children improving by 1 grade level.
[b]Preference rating of constituents.

Application to Policy Analysis: Alternative Perspectives on the Cost-Effectiveness of Class-Size Reduction Policies

Cost-effectiveness analysis has arguably not received the attention that it should either as a local district management tool or as a tool for education policy analysis. One topic that researchers have addressed on multiple occasions since the 1990s using cost-effectiveness analysis is class-size reduction (CSR). Public interest in CSR grew upon release of the Tennessee STAR studies, based on a large-scale, longitudinal, experimental study conducted in the late 1980s (Finn & Achilles, 1990, 1999). Finn and Achilles concluded that "The results are definitive: (a) a significant benefit accrues to students in reduced-size classes in both (math and reading) subject areas and (b) there is evidence that minority students in particular benefit from the smaller class environment, especially when curriculum-based tests are used as the learning criteria" (1990, p. 557). The STAR studies and related studies led to significant policy directives including a statewide effort to reduce class size in California and extensive discussion of potential federal interventions to help states reduce class sizes.

Not long after CSR had picked up momentum on the basis that it was one of few policy options with well-documented effects, researchers and policy makers began to question whether CSR might be too costly. In this section, we present a brief summary of Finn and Achilles' (1990, 1999) findings regarding the effects of CSR, we address concerns raised by Brewer, Krop, Gill, and Reichardt (1999) regarding

the potential costs of federal interventions, and we conclude with a review of two different analyses of the cost-effectiveness of CSR. We do not intend our review to provide definitive answers regarding the cost-effectiveness of CSR but rather to illuminate the usefulness of cost-effectiveness analysis as a tool for policy evaluation. In fact, the issues surrounding the viability of CSR as a policy option extend well beyond simply understanding relative cost-effectiveness, requiring more systemic thinking, as we will discuss in Chapter 13, on teacher labor markets.

Table 11.7 presents Finn and Achilles' (1990, 1999) findings regarding the effectiveness of CSR and differential effectiveness of CSR for minority students. Note that these findings are specific to K–3 CSR policies. Finn and Achilles found, as previously noted, that CSR benefited all students but had greater benefits for minority students than for white students. Some of the ongoing debate over the Tennessee STAR study (Finn & Achilles, 1990, 1999) is over the magnitude of the effects of CSR. Just how much does CSR improve student performance relative to other options? Even if CSR were to produce dramatic improvements, if the costs of CSR were substantially higher, CSR might not be cost-effective.

Brewer et al. (1999) raised questions regarding the costs of implementing nationwide CSR. At that time, the Clinton administration was discussing the possibility of a federal plan to purchase 100,000 teachers in order to help school districts reduce class sizes. Brewer et al. used existing data on students and staffing from the *Common Core of Data* and *Schools and Staffing Survey* as well as projections of enrollment growth to estimate the additional classes

Table 11.7 Difference Between Small Class Means and Larger Class Means

Scale (Test)	Group	Grade Level			
		K (n = 5, 738)	1 (n = 6, 572)	2 (n = 5, 148)[a]	3 (n = 4,744)[a]
Word study skills	White	0.15	0.16	0.11	
	Minority	0.17	0.32	0.34	
	All	0.15	0.22	0.20	
Reading	White	0.15	0.16	0.11	0.16
	Minority	0.15	0.35	0.26	0.35
	All	0.18	0.22	0.19	0.25
Math	White	0.17	0.22	0.12	0.16
	Minority	0.08	0.31	0.35	0.30
	All	0.15	0.27	0.20	0.23

Note: Table abbreviated (Basic Skills First test percent passing data not included).
[a] Excluding pupils whose teachers received STAR training.
[b] Total language scale in grade 3 (not reading).
Source: Abbreviated and adapted from Finn and Achilles (1999).

required for reducing all class sizes to 20, 18, and 15 students. They found that national CSR would range in cost from $2 billion to $11 billion per year, not accounting for the likely increases in teacher salaries as demand for teachers increased and not accounting for the construction costs of new classrooms.

Table 11.8 displays the Brewer et al. (1999) scenario for reducing class sizes to 20 nationwide. In the first year of the program, an additional 103 thousand classes would be needed and an annual operating cost of over $5 billion, or an additional $448 per pupil. While not conducting cost-effectiveness analyses,

Brewer et al. raise the question as to whether similar resources might be put to better use.

Two recent studies apply cost-effectiveness analysis directly to CSR. Addonizio and Phelps (2000) synthesize effectiveness estimates for CSR from several studies and construct cost estimates for implementing CSR. Addonizio and Phelps (2000) focus, in particular, on the idea that CSR policies are subject to diminishing returns, citing Akerhielm (1995). Rather than comparing CSR to other policy options, Addonizio and Phelps compare the marginal cost of each .01 standard deviation gain in student achievement yielded by incremental

Table 11.8 Brewer et al. (1999) Estimates of the Cost of National Class Size Reduction

Year	New Classes (Class Size = 18)	Operational Costs in Billions (Current Dollars)	Per-Pupil Operational Costs
1998–1999	102,687	$5.049	$448
1999–2000	101,337	$5.083	$454
2000–2001	99,928	$5.148	$465
2001–2002	99,345	$5.263	$481
2002–2003	97,468	$5.306	$489
2003–2004	98,450	$5.517	$511
2004–2005	98,466	$5.674	$527
2005–2006	96,088	$5.688	$530
2006–2007	95,854	$5.832	$544
2007–2008	96,370	$6.028	$562

Source: Data from Brewer et al. (1999).

Figure 11.9   Diminishing Marginal Returns of Class-Size Reduction

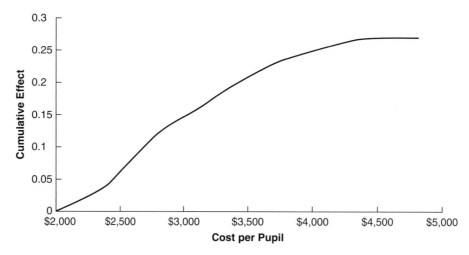

Source: Data from Addonizio & Phelps (2000).

reductions in class size. That is, they compare the cost-effectiveness of reducing class size from 30 to 25, from 25 to 21.4, and so on. Figure 11.9 displays the cumulative achievement effects of incremental reductions in class size as presented by Addonizio and Phelps (2000).

Addonizio and Phelps' (2000) cost-effectiveness estimates are displayed in Table 11.9. They find, for example, that the marginal cost of each additional .01 standard deviation in student achievement improvement is lowest ($7,500) when moving from class sizes of 25 to 21.4. Costs of marginal gains increase dramatically below class sizes of 16.67, and no marginal gains are realized below class sizes of 13.64.

Doug Harris (2002) took a somewhat different approach to studying the cost-effectiveness of CSR, evaluating the trade-offs between using additional resources for CSR versus using those resources for increased teacher salaries. Harris's goal was to identify the optimal combination of teacher salary and class size. That is, given a finite sum of resources, what combination of class size and teacher salary will be most productive? Harris defines productivity in terms of students' future wages, extrapolating from expected academic achievement gains.

Table 11.10 displays one portion of Harris's (2002) analyses. Harris finds, for example, that CSR

Table 11.9   Marginal Returns of Class-Size Reduction

Teachers	Class Size	Change in Class Size	Difference in Cumulative Effect Size	Teacher Cost per Pupil	Total Cost	Marginal Cost of .01 Gain
5	30			$2,000	$300,000	
6	25	−5	0.04	$2,400	$360,000	$15,000
7	21.4	−3.6	0.12	$2,800	$420,000	$ 7,500
8	18.75	−2.65	0.17	$3,200	$480,000	$12,000
9	16.67	−2.08	0.22	$3,600	$540,000	$12,000
10	15	−1.67	0.25	$4,000	$600,000	$20,000
11	13.64	−1.36	0.27	$4,400	$660,000	$30,000
12	12.5	−1.14	0.27	$4,800	$720,000	∞

Source: Data from Addonizio & Phelps (2000).

Table 11.10 Harris's (2002) Estimates of Costs per Pupil for Raising Student Achievement

Test Score Gain	Class Size	Cost per Pupil	Teacher Salaries	Cost per Pupil
	16.2		$40,582	
0.01	15	$ 210	$41,090	$ 31
0.05	10.7	$1,287	$43,490	$163
0.1	7	$3,251	$47,370	$402

Source: Data from Harris (2002).

costs $210 per pupil to raise student test scores by .01 standard deviation, while increasing teacher salaries costs only $31 per pupil to raise student test scores by the same amount. Harris's general conclusion is that "Reducing class sizes is neither cost-effective nor optimal. This conclusion is further reinforced by the fact that the benefits attributed to class size reduction do not include the negative effect of class size reduction on teacher quality" (Harris, 2002, p. 183).

Summary and Synthesis

It is important to note the connection between cost-effectiveness and efficiency. Cost-effectiveness analysis is about identifying those programs or policies that are highly productive at relatively low cost. The efficient education system (school or district) is the system that uses fiscal input to purchase the mix of resources (quantities and qualities) that maximizes productivity. In theory, if district officials make appropriate decisions regarding substitutions of internal resource allocation, based on cost-effectiveness analysis, their school or district should become more efficient. Further, if policy options such as CSR are effective, but not cost-effective, we should expect states and/or school districts that implement those policies to be less efficient or decline in efficiency. In fact, some of the previously discussed analyses of factors affecting efficiency support the notion that larger class sizes may be associated with greater efficiency.

SUMMARY

In this chapter, we have grappled with some of the more complex theoretical and technical issues underlying education production, costs, and efficiency. These issues are important not only to understanding the material presented in subsequent chapters on reform strategies for improving educational productivity and efficiency but also for deepening your understanding of previous chapters, particularly Chapters 7 to 10, on educational adequacy. We urge you to revisit our discussions of educational adequacy in Chapters 7 through 10 with special attention to conceptions and measurement of educational efficiency.

Perhaps the most important conclusion that can be drawn from our discussion of the measurement of educational efficiency is just how little we know about how well different types of schools, serving different types of children achieve desired outcomes. Even the most technically advanced methods for efficiency analysis remain surprisingly inaccurate. Yet, substan-

tially less well-developed, less-precise, and less-accurate methods continue to play a role in the education policy arena. In that arena, such analyses are largely pseudo-science, inherently political in their purposes, and one must view them critically. It is particularly problematic, given the state of the art, to label certain school districts as inefficient producers of outcomes, or to suggest that generally, districts of a certain type overspend and/or under-produce. Such findings, most often inaccurate, become fodder for arguments to hold constant or reduce existing—and probably already insufficient—funding of public schools.

The remaining chapters address common and emerging approaches to educational reform. We assert that policy makers propose educational reforms with the primary objectives of improving educational productivity and efficiency, the latter being the ultimate objective. Policy makers argue for market competition among schools, based on the notion that market competition improves outcomes at comparable costs (efficiency). Policy makers who argue for providing financial incentives on the basis of performance apply similar assumptions regarding the relationship between competition and efficiency. In Chapters 12 and 14, we evaluate these assumptions. In Chapter 13, we temporarily digress to discuss teacher labor markets and the relationship between teachers, teaching quality, and school productivity.

Some researchers assert that teacher quality may be improved at less cost than increasing teacher quantity, thus leading to greater efficiency than current pressures to reduce class size. Finally, in Chapter 15, we discuss the ways in which public school districts and private and charter schools presently allocate resources as well as what little researchers know about the relationship between resource use and school or district efficiency.

KEY TERMS

allocative efficiency   An allocation is efficient if goods cannot be reallocated to make someone better off without making someone else worse off.

cost–benefit   Relationship between the cost of implementing a specific program or strategy and the short- or long-term financial benefits of doing so.

cost-effectiveness   Relationship between the cost of implementing a particular program or strategy and the expected or actual effects of that strategy on student outcomes. For example, the expected achievement points gained per dollar spent on a new reading strategy.

cost–utility   Relationship between the cost of implementing a specific program or strategy, the outcomes of that strategy, and the values of key stakeholders for those particular outcomes.

data envelopment analysis (DEA)   A numerical maximization method used for conducting productive or cost-efficiency analysis.

stochastic frontier analysis   A statistical modeling, regression-based approach to efficiency analysis where the error term—the difference between the actual and predicted spending for a given level of outcome—is decomposed into a random component and a component representing inefficiency.

technical efficiency (input efficiency)   A particular allocation of inputs into the production process is technically efficient if the output of one good cannot be increased without decreasing the output of another good.

REFERENCES

Addonizio, M. F., & Phelps, J. L. (2000). Class size and student performance: A framework for policy analysis. *Journal of Education Finance, 26*(2), 135–156.

Akerhielm, K. (1995). Does class size matter? *Economics of Education Review 14*(3), 229–241.

Anderson, D. M. (1996). Stretching the tax dollar: Increasing efficiency in urban and rural schools. In L. O. Picus & J. Wattenbarger (Eds.), *Where does the money go? Resource allocation in elementary and secondary schools* (pp. 156–177). Thousand Oaks, CA: Corwin Press.

Anderson, J. E., & Kabir, M. (2000). *Public education cost frontier models: Theory and an application.* Paper presented at the Annual Meeting of the American Education Finance Association, Austin, TX.

Augenblick, J., & Myers, J. (2001). *A comprehensive study on the organization of Kansas school districts.* Prepared for the Kansas State Board of Education. Retrieved from www.ksbe.org

Bessent, A., & Bessent, E. (1980). Determining the comparative efficiency of schools through data envelopment analysis. *Educational Administration Quarterly, 16,* 57–75.

Bifulco, R., & Bretschneider, S. (2001). Estimating school efficiency: A comparison of methods using simulate data. *Economics of Education Review, 20.*

Bifulco, R., & Duncombe, W. (2000). Evaluating school performance: Are we ready for prime time? In W. Fowler (Ed.), *Developments in School Finance, 1999–2000.* Washington, DC: National Center for Education Statistics, Office of Educational Research and Improvement.

Blomberg, B. S., & Hess, G. D. (2000). *The impact of voter initiatives on economic activity.* Working paper, Department of Economics, Wellesley College, Wellesley, MA.

Brewer, D., Krop, C., Gill, B. P., & Reichardt, R. (1999). Estimating the costs of national class size reductions under different policy alternatives. *Educational Evaluation and Policy Analysis, 21*(2), 179–192.

Charnes, A., Cooper, W. W., & Rhodes, E. (1978). Measuring efficiency of decision making units. *European Journal of Operational Research, 3,* 429–444.

Coleman, J., Campbell, E. Q., Hobson, C. J., McPartland, J., Mood, A. M., Weinfield, F. D., et al. (1966). *Equality of educational opportunity.* Washington, DC: U.S. Government Printing Office.

Deke, J. (2003). A study of the impact of public school spending on postsecondary educational attainment using statewide school district financing in Kansas. *Economics of Education Review,* pp. 275–284.

Deller, S., & Rudnicki, E. (1993). Production efficiency in elementary education: The case of Maine public schools. *Economics of Education Review, 12,* 45–57.

Downes, T. (2002). *Do state governments matter? A review of the evidence on the impact on educational outcomes of the changing role of the states in the financing of public education.* Working Paper, Federal Reserve Bank of Boston.

Downes, T. (2003). *School finance reform and school quality: lessons from Vermont.* Paper presented at the annual meeting of the American Education Finance Association. Orlando, FL.

Downes T., & Figlio, D. (1998). *School finance reforms, tax limits and student performance: Do reforms level up or level down?* Working Paper 98–05. Department of Economics, Tufts University.

Downes T., & Shah, M. (1995). *The effect of school finance reform on the level and growth of per pupil expenditures.* Working Paper. Department of Economics, Tufts University.

Duncombe, W., & Bifulco, R. (2000). Evaluating school performance: Are we ready for prime time? In W. Fowler (Ed.), *Developments in school finance 1999–2000.* Washington, DC: National Center for Education Statistics, Office of Educational Research and Improvement.

Duncombe, W., & Miner, J. (1996). Productive efficiency and cost-effectiveness: Different perspectives in measuring school performance. In R. Berne (Ed.), *Study on cost effectiveness in education: Final report.* Albany, NY: The University of the State of New York. The State Education Department.

Duncombe, W., & Yinger, J. (1999). Performance standards and education cost indexes: You can't have one without the other. In H. F. Ladd, R. Chalk, & J. S. Hansen (Eds.), *Equity and adequacy in education finance: Issues and perspectives* (pp. 260–97). Washington, DC: National Academy Press.

Figlio, D. N. (1999). Functional form and the estimated effects of school resources. *Economics of Education Review, 18*(2), 242–252.

Finn, J. D., & Achilles, C. M. (1990). Answers and questions about class size: A statewide experiment. *American Educational Research Journal, 27*(3), 557–577.

Finn, J. D., & Achilles, C. (1999). Tennessee's class size study: findings, implications, misconceptions. *Educational Evaluation and Policy Analysis, 21*(2), 97–109.

Flanagan, A., & Murray, S. (2003). *A decade of reform: The impact of school reform in Kentucky.* Paper presented at the American Education Finance Association annual meeting. Orlando, FL.

Gronberg, T. J., & Jansen, D. (2001). *Navigating newly chartered waters: An analysis of Texas charter school performance.* Texas Public Policy Foundation.

Haller, E., & Kleine, P. (2001). *Using educational research: A school administrator's guide.* New York: Longman.

Hanushek, E. A. (1986). The economics of schooling: production and efficiency in public schools. *Journal of Economic Literature, 24,* 1141–1177.

Hanushek, E. (1996). School resources and student performance. In G. Burtless (Ed.), *Does Money Matter?* (pp. 43–73). Washington, DC: The Brookings Institution.

Hanushek, E. A., Rivken, S. G., & Taylor, L. (1996). Aggregation and the estimated effects of school resources. *Review of Economics and Statistics, 78*(4), 611–627.

Harris, D. (2002). Identifying optimal class sizes and teacher salaries. In Levin, H. M., & McEwan, P. (Eds.), *Cost effectiveness and educational policy.* Larchmont, NY: Eye on Education.

Hedges, L., & Greenwald, R. (1996). Have times changed? The relation between school resources and student performance. In G. Burtless (Ed.), *Does money matter?* (pp. 74–92). Washington, DC: The Brookings Institution.

Hoxby, C. M. (1996). Are efficiency and equity in school finance substitutes or compliments? *Journal of Economic Perspectives, 10*(4), 51–72.

Lankford, R. H. (1985). Efficiency and equity in the provision of public education. *The Review of Economics and Statistics, 67*(1), 70–80.

Levin, H. M. (1983). *Cost effectiveness: A primer.* Newbury Park, CA: Sage Publications.

Levin, H. M., & McEwan, P. J. (2001). *Cost-effectiveness* (2nd ed.). Thousand Oaks, CA: Sage Publications.

McCarty, T., & Yaisawarng, S. (1993). Technical efficiency in New Jersey school districts. In H. Fried, K. Lovell, & S. Schmidt (Eds.), *The measurement of productive efficiency* (pp. 271–287). Oxford, UK: Oxford University Press.

Pindyck, R. S., & Rubinfeld, D. L. (1995). *Microeconomics* (3rd ed.). Englewood Cliffs, NJ: Prentice Hall.

Richmond, B., & Peterson, S. (1997). *An introduction to systems thinking.* Hanover, NH: High Performance Systems.

Taylor, C. (1997). Does money matter? An empirical study introducing resource costs and student needs to educational production function analysis. In W. Fowler (Ed.), *Developments in school finance 1997*. Washington, DC: National Center for Education Statistics, Office of Educational Research and Improvement.

Tiebout, C. (1956). A pure theory of local expenditures. *Journal of Political Economy*, 41–424.

Wenglinsky, H. (1997). School district expenditures, school resources and student achievement: Modeling the production function. In W. Fowler (Ed.), *Developments in school finance 1997*. Washington, DC: National Center for Education Statistics, Office of Educational Research and Improvement.

Wright, S. P., Horn, S. P., & Sanders, W. L. (1997). Teacher and classroom context effects on student achievement: Implications for teacher evaluation. *Journal of Personnel Evaluation in Education, 11*(1), 57–67.

CHAPTER 12

PROMOTING PRODUCTIVITY AND EFFICIENCY
COMPETITIVE MARKETS

Introduction

In this chapter, we address the role of market-based policies as mechanisms for promoting productivity and efficiency in schooling. The topic of market-based policies in education, often centered on school-choice and voucher policies, has raised considerable debate over the years. Beginning with Milton Friedman's *Capitalism and Freedom* in 1962 to the more recent *Politics Markets and America's Schools* by Chubb and Moe (1990), economists have long argued that public education systems would benefit from the competitive aspects of market economies. Other prominent economists have responded to these claims with significant concerns, including Henry Levin's critique that privatization and competition may lead to significant erosion of the common principles of public schooling in America (Levin, 1983).

As we discuss in detail throughout this chapter, the interplay between public education and private markets has become increasingly complex over the years, including market competition between public and private schools, pseudo market competition among public schools, and the introduction of various forms of private providers of educational services from management to remediation and evaluation. Opinions on these more complex relationships are similarly politically heated. Hill, Pierce, and Guthrie (1997) discuss how contracting of management and educational services can "transform America's schools," while Bracey (2002) suggests that such ventures are merely one component of an all-out *War Against America's Public Schools.*

We begin this chapter with a discussion of how competitive markets are related to allocative and productive efficiency. We emphasize policies for improving productivity and cost-efficiency. Next we provide a framework, involving active and passive privatization, for understanding different approaches to integrating public education and private markets. Throughout this chapter, we discuss the least-biased empirical research on the extent to which market-based policies have, or have not, helped to improve productivity and efficiency of America's public schools. However, we provide few, if any, definitive answers to this question.

Markets, Privatization, and Efficiency

Notwithstanding early independent private schools, the original education marketplace consisted of local communities providing public schooling services of varied quality, and consumers selecting their place of residence at least partially on the basis of the quality of public services available. We have addressed the issue of local demand and neighborhood sorting, the Tiebout (1956) process, at several points throughout the text. Most often, Tiebout processes are associated with allocative efficiency. Hoxby describes the theoretical relationship between Tiebout processes and efficiency as follows:

> The incentives that schools have to be productive are generally increased by Tiebout choice because it gives households more information and leverage in the principal-agent problem that exists between them and the people who run their local schools. Self-sorting of students is generally increased by Tiebout choice, and people sort themselves so as to maximize private allocative efficiency (their own welfare). Self-sorting may produce poor *social* allocative efficiency, however. Each school may be more productive given its student body but students may be sorted so that good peers are not in contact with the students who would benefit from them most. (Hoxby, 2000, p. 1210)

According to Hoxby, Tiebout choice alone can help improve both private allocative efficiency and productive efficiency. Hoxby argues that the primary reason that Tiebout choice and local property taxation improve productive efficiency is that school officials are motivated to improve schooling performance because public perception of higher-quality schools leads to higher local property values, which in turn, lead to more revenues from the same tax rate for the schools (Hoxby, 1996).

Voucher advocates view as insufficient the notion that (a) Tiebout choice alone creates market-based incentives for the improvement of public education and that (b) Tiebout choice creates options for parents/taxpayers when selecting a community. The increasing role of state intervention to equalize schooling quality by shifting funding from local property taxes to state income and sales taxes interferes, to varying degrees, with the espoused advantages of Tiebout choice.

Increased state involvement in financing and controlling traditional public schools is one likely reason for the resurgence of interest and activity in alternative market-based policies throughout the 1990s, including school-choice policies such as vouchers and charter schools. Certainly, the research and public policy literature of the late 1980s through early 1990s, much of which stemmed from *A Nation at Risk* (U.S. National Commission on Excellence in Education, 1983), reflected this point of view. Concurrently, school finance equity litigation had matured, and state involvement, as measured by shares of total funding, had peaked.

We delineate public–private relationships in education systems as *passive* and *active* forms of privatization, acknowledging the murkiness of this delineation. In its simplest form, passive privatization involves creating policies that allow private providers to participate in the delivery of public education services using public financial support. Voucher programs—which provide direct tuition assistance or tax credit assistance to parents to assist parents in sending their children to either public or private schools—make up one form of passive privatization.

Active privatization involves a direct contractual relationship between local, state, or federal government and a private provider of an educational or related service. As we discuss in greater detail later in this chapter, that contractual relationship should contain a handful of key elements to truly constitute an active privatization relationship.

Passive Privatization

Passive Privatization in Theory

Policies promoting passive privatization, especially voucher programs, have received much attention in economic literature. Whether passive privatization leads to greater efficiency than public bureaucracy depends on a handful of basic assumptions about competitive markets. Some argue, for example, that public bureaucracies, functioning as monopolies and deriving their revenues from taxation, have no incentive to operate efficiently (Niskanen, 1968). Rather, the incentive of public bureaucracies is to *revenue maximize* and disregard cost-efficiency, making it difficult for taxpayers, as consumers, to understand the relationship between cost and quality. The central economic argument of choice advocates is that allowing parents to choose either public or private schools and having the public tax dollars travel with the child creates market competition for access to revenues. As institutions compete for revenue, they must learn how to maximize output, given revenue, on the assumption that consumers will make their choices based on output.

Manski was among the first to formally associate the effects of competition on efficiency in schooling through computational modeling (1992; as discussed in McEwan, 2000b). Manski, like others,[1] assumed that public schools maximize rents, or the difference between actual expenditures and the expenditures that consumers value. Arguably, consumers value expenditures that lead to improved outcomes. The margin between district actual expenditures and those expenditures that yield a given level of outcomes (or cost of a given level of output) is inefficiency. Manski assumes private schools to operate in a perfect competitive economy. As such, private schools must maximize productivity, given their level of revenue, reducing inefficiency in order to attract new customers. When school systems introduce vouchers, making it more economically feasible for public school students to exit and attend private schools, public schools must respond by increasing outputs without increases in inputs in order to operate at efficiency levels comparable to private schools.

---

[1]Most notably, Niskanen (1968) promoted the theory that public bureaucracies function as budget-maximizing bureaus.

McMillan (1999) among others, suggests that choice programs increase parental monitoring of schools, which in turn increases the effort of both public and private schools. McEwan (2000b), however, points out that a potential adverse effect of choice programs is not only that private schools might attract away the "better" students, or cream skim, but that private schools might also attract the children of parents more likely to monitor their public schools more closely. That is, voucher programs may lead to cream skimming of "involved" parents, resulting in a reduction of oversight of public schools.

Manski's (cited in McEwan, 2000b) expectation of improved efficiency will occur only if initial differences in public and private school efficiency exist. A substantial body of literature addresses the question of whether private schools, on average, are better or more efficient than public schools. Later in this chapter, we address this research and the existing but limited research on whether choice programs influence efficiency.

Finally, some voucher advocates argue that vouchers may also serve as a solution to equity and adequacy problems. Heise and Nechyba (1999) state:

> [V]ouchers are an attractive remedy in education adequacy suits because they address at least three of the factors giving rise to current inequalities in public education. By enabling parents to choose private schools for their children, vouchers provide the means for them to escape the political peculiarities of systems that allocate more per pupil resources to the well off. By removing education-related incentives for high-income

households to separate themselves from poor neighborhoods, vouchers introduce a desegregating force into society. Finally, by reducing housing prices in high quality public school districts and raising them in low quality districts, vouchers help more low-income families afford to live in areas with better public schools.

Passive Privatization in Practice

The reality of voucher policies in American public education diverges substantially from the theoretical discussions of programs where any student may choose any public or private school, carrying with him or her a tax-subsidized voucher that will meet the full costs of tuition. To date, in the United States, publicly funded voucher programs have been attempted only as small-scale, targeted programs. In addition to voucher programs funded by public tax dollars, several programs operated by private nonprofit foundations provide aid in the form of vouchers for low-income public school students to attend private independent or religious schools.

Table 12.1 presents a framework for understanding the design of voucher programs. (This framework, which we present as our own, is strongly influenced by the RAND report *Rhetoric vs. Reality* [Gill, Timpane, Ross, & Brewer, 2001], which we discuss at several points throughout this chapter.) First and foremost is the question of the policy objective of the voucher or choice program. Although economic theorists from Milton Friedman (1962) to Chubb and Moe (1990) have long promoted large-scale voucher programs as the panacea for making system-wide improvements to

Table 12.1 Regulatory and Financing Dimensions of Voucher Programs

	Policy Objective	
	Productive Efficiency	Equity and/or Adequacy
Regulatory Dimension		
Schools	a. Public/private b. Market-based accountability	a. Public/private b. Some state accountability (and information dissemination)

Students	a. All
	b. Minimal state intervention regarding
	   admissions policies
		a. Targeted by income or
		b. Students in underperforming
		   schools
		c. No barriers to participation

Financing Dimension		
Revenue collection	a. Broad-based state tax (sales, income)	a. Progressive broad-based tax (income)
Distribution	a. Flat "cost-based" tuition voucher	a. Means tested or targeted b. Transportation and special needs

productive efficiency in education, existing publicly and privately funded voucher programs most often tackle equity or adequacy policy objectives but not efficiency.

Productive efficiency and equity or adequacy may not be mutually exclusive goals; rather, policy generally favors one goal over the other. Policy makers may assume that improved productive efficiency will result from voucher policies designed to improve equity, as low-performing schools are forced to shape up in order to retain students and continue receiving revenue. Later we will discuss whether empirical support exists for this argument.

Voucher programs established by the states of Wisconsin (in Milwaukee) and Ohio (in Cleveland) each provide targeted vouchers for low-income students to attend private religious or independent schools. Similarly, Florida's recently adopted Opportunity Scholarship program targets vouchers to students in low-performing public schools (Gill et al., 2001, p. 7). Where equity and adequacy goals are paramount, participating schools generally are restricted from using competitive admissions criteria and must accept students with special educational needs. Further, voucher-receiving institutions may not charge fees above and beyond the voucher value.

Numerous potential targeted applications of vouchers might improve horizontal or vertical equity for students by income, circumstance, or educational need. Baker and Richards (1998), for example, discuss the possibility of providing wealth-equalized vouchers for gifted low-income children to attend private summer and weekend programming opportunities. Baker and Richards' proposal was in response to dramatic cuts in Northeastern states in public funding for special opportunities for gifted children and a resultant dearth of challenging opportunities in schools with gifted children that serve low-income students. Baker and Friedman-Nimz (2002) more thoroughly documented the imbalance of advanced opportunities in general and gifted programs in particular.

Funds, credits, or subsidies to promote choice currently are provided in at least four ways. First, nonprofit organizations support numerous existing voucher programs through private contributions. Second, states including Arizona and Pennsylvania have recently passed legislation that provides tax credits for individuals and/or corporations who donate funds to nonprofit organizations that sponsor voucher programs. Third, in 2001 Congress passed education savings accounts (ESAs) into law, allowing individuals to tax shelter

funds that may be used for private education. Fourth, and of primary interest in this chapter, are tuition subsidy programs in Milwaukee, Cleveland, and Florida. Tuition subsidy programs are the programs most commonly referred to as *voucher* programs.

Critical elements of a choice program intended to promote equity include the following components: the revenue for the program should be collected via a progressive tax mechanism, and the allocation of vouchers should be such that resources are transferred from wealthier to poorer individuals. On the distribution side, this can be done either by allocating vouchers on a sliding scale according to families' abilities to supplement the vouchers (income), or the vouchers can be targeted, as in Cleveland and Milwaukee, to low-income students. The sliding-scale approach is analogous to foundation aid equalized based on family-level fiscal capacity. In the latter case, it is important to realize that within the targeted group, a range of income and parental education levels and preferences will exist. As such, support for transportation and efforts to inform parents and children of the available choices are critical to achieving equity among the targeted population.

Levin and Driver (1998) point out that implementing an equitable large-scale voucher program would be significantly more costly than current school-funding methods. They estimate the following additional costs of implementing a large-scale, nationwide voucher program in the United States:

1. National cost of adding current private school attendance to vouchers: $16 to $27 billion
2. Record-keeping systems: $43 to $78 per pupil (based on Social Security Administration costs)
3. Transportation costs: $218 to $3,782 per pupil
4. Information dissemination: $38 per pupil per year
5. Adjudication: $1,632 to $5,854 per case (for voucher-related dispute resolution) (Levin & Driver, 1998)

No publicly funded voucher program in the United States possesses regulatory or financing characteristics of a program designed to primarily promote productive efficiency. Voucher programs in Chile and New Zealand, however, do provide choices for all students to attend public or private schools using public subsidies. Chile implemented its national voucher program in 1980, providing parents the opportunity to choose among five different types of public and private schools (Carnoy & McEwan, 2000, p. 215). Public schools were funded by a combination of national vouchers, municipal contributions, and regional development funds and governed either directly by municipalities or by semiautonomous public corporations. Private schools were funded by a combination of national vouchers, private contributions, and church subsidies in the case of religious schools. Later in this chapter, we discuss research findings on the productivity and efficiency of schools in Chile and the implications of those findings for the implementation of large-scale voucher programs in the United States.

Active Privatization

Active Privatization in Theory

Active privatization occurs when local, state, or federal government agencies establish contracts with private individuals or businesses to provide educational or education-related services in the public sector. Potential private service providers include for-profit, nonprofit, and tax-exempt religious institutions. The two major types of private education service providers that currently exist are education management organizations (EMOs) and education service organizations (ESOs). EMOs primarily provide management services, which may encompass school-wide curricular models or may be limited to financial management and business operations management. ESOs provide specific educational service packages to educational institutions, including remedial services, summer school programs, assessments, and test preparation. In addition to EMOs and ESOs, numerous private auxiliary education service organizations (AESOs) exist, which include transportation, food service, and technology support; in addition are the emerging electronic, or Web-based, private providers of educational services (electronic education service organizations, *e*-ESOs).

The economic efficiency benefits of active privatization are contingent on two basic assumptions: (a) that multiple competitors will bid on educational contracts, yielding efficient pricing, and (b) that competitors will be willing (due to competition) to enter into *performance contracts* with governments and public agencies. In addition, public agencies must have access to accurate information regarding available competitors. We differentiate between performance and compliance contracts as follows:

- *Compliance:* A compliance contract includes statements of the minimum service expectations such as meeting basic health and safety requirements and state class size requirements. Compliance contracts may include penalties or an *out* clause for contractors failing to meet compliance guidelines.
- *Performance:* A performance contract includes guidelines for evaluating a contractor's performance on critical outcomes, such as student achievement value added. Performance contracts may or should tie rewards to exceeding performance objectives and should assess penalties for failing to meet those objectives.

School district or state officials, for example, should be able to establish a performance contract with an ESO to provide remediation services where the contract would include specific expectations of student achievement outcomes (e.g., achieving grade-level performance within *x* weeks or months). The ESO would then be bound, contractually, to achieve those objectives or forgo payment.

Hannaway (1999) identifies 10 key contractual clauses that schools must address in establishing the public agency/private provider relationship:

- *Responsibilities and relationships of the contracting parties.* Who (district, charter, or provider) is responsible for what? Curriculum? Code compliance? Facilities? Personnel decisions?
- *Payment.* Based on fee for service? Cost savings? Performance expectations?
- *Duration.*
- *Renewal.* What are the terms for renewal? Will there be renegotiation? Opportunities for other bidders?
- *Performance and performance incentives.* How will performance be measured? What incentives/sanctions will be attached to performance?
- *Asset ownership.* When private providers invest capital in facilities or equipment, who maintains ownership? Hannaway notes that this was an issue of concern in a contract between Education Alternatives Inc. (EAI) and the Hartford, CT, public schools. EAI had invested substantial capital into technology improvements in the district, but the contract was dissolved before it assumed management responsibilities.
- *Intellectual property.* Some contractors may also invest in, for example, development of curricular materials.
- *"No compete" clause.* If a contractor has control over personnel decisions, can a school board break

the contract with the provider but keep the staff it hired? Some contractors may require that the school may not employ the contractor's personnel for a set period after contract termination.

- *Termination agreements.* Specific conditions must be set for contract termination. Conditions may involve expected activities and practices of the contractor, performance outcomes, or financial condition (e.g., contractor declares bankruptcy).

- *Arbitration.* Specifies procedures for dispute resolution (Hannaway, 1999).

Richards, Shore, and Sawicky (1996), in *Risky Business: Private Management of Public Schools*, suggest that the economic theory of contracting may not necessarily be a good fit for public education systems. They identify the following three problem areas:

- The education contract is not between parents and school authorities only. The public interest in educating each child can outstrip the motivations of parents in two respects: Universal education provides both society-wide economic benefits and citizenship/values benefits that may be of little immediate concern to parents.

- Defining the nature of education for purposes of contracting is difficult. The nature of the educational product is inherently complex and difficult to define in terms useful in writing contracts or formulating productivity incentives.

- Necessary regulation of the educational process undermines the rationale for contracting out. Because its outcome is difficult to define, the manner in which education is provided becomes a point of interest and implies some degree of regulatory oversight. Insofar as the contractor must be regulated (i.e., managed from without by public officials), there is less distinction between the contractor and a public agency and less rationale for using an outside organization. (Richards, Shore, & Sawicky, 1996, p. 8)

Active Privatization in Practice

Original attempts to introduce private, for-profit management into public education involved urban school districts contracting with private providers to manage low-performing schools. Perhaps the earliest example is the case of EAI and the city of Baltimore, MD. In the summer of 1992, the Baltimore City School District contracted out the management of nine of its lowest-performing schools (eight elementary and one middle) to EAI, an upstart Minneapolis-based for-profit EMO promoting its yet-to-be-tested ability to turn around underperforming schools while providing cost savings.

At the outset of the project, Baltimore allocated EAI a total budget for the nine schools according to the following guidelines: The district determined a per-pupil allowance relative to the district's total budget and full-time equivalent (FTE) population. The budget included a 15% payback to cover administrative and support costs provided by the district's central administration. The district allocated the resulting per-pupil allowance to EAI to generate a total budget of $23,937,770. (This approach is quite similar to how some states presently approach funding for charter schools, which we discuss later in this chapter.)

Original EAI/TESSERACT Contract
(Office of the President of the City Council, Mary Pat Clarke)

$5,918	per-pupil allowance
− $888	(15% "payback")
$5,030	per pupil
× 4,759	pupils at 9 EAI-run schools
$23,937,770	total funds to EAI

In March of 1994, the Baltimore City Public Schools (BCPS) and EAI modified the contract to reduce the administrative payback to 7.5%, resulting in an 8.8% increase ($2.1 million) in EAI's total budget (after payback).

EAI Formula Modified March 23, 1994
(Office of the President of the City Council, Mary Pat Clarke)

$5,918	per-pupil allowance
− $444	(7.5% "payback")
$5,474	per pupil
× 4,759	pupils at 9 EAI-run schools
$26,050,766	ADJUSTED total funds to EAI

$26,050,766	March 23, 1994 Contract
− 23,937,770	Original EAI Contract
$2,112,996	**Refunded to EAI**

Table 12.2 School-Level Expenditures per Pupil of Baltimore City Public Schools

Grade Level	Average Expenditures	Percent Above EAI	Percentage Below EAI
All BCPS elementary	$4,338	9%	91%
All BCPS middle	$4,026/3,969[a]	0%	100%
Comparison school, elementary	$4,464	14%	86%
Comparison school, middle	$3,808	0%	100%

BCPS, Baltimore City Public Schools; EAI, Education Alternatives Inc.
[a]Second figure represents adjusted mean determined by removal of outlying schools in sample (see charts #2 and #3). Average school-level spending per pupil is reduced when special schools are removed from the calculation. See Richards et al. (1996).
Source: Data from Richards et al. (1996).

Richards, Baker, and Cilo (1996) analyzed the financial arrangement between EAI and the BCPS and found the contracted per-pupil allotment to be misrepresentative of actual school costs in the district. Table 12.2 presents some of their findings. Compared to the EAI contract value of $5,474 per pupil for both elementary and middle schools, BCPS elementary schools spent, on average, $4,338 per pupil, and BCPS middle schools spent, on average $4,026 per pupil. Only 9% (9 total) BCPS elementary schools spent more per pupil than the EAI allotment, and no middle school spent more than the EAI allotment. Richards et al. (1996) selected 9 BCPS schools for comparison with EAI schools based on similarities in size and student demographics. Only one of the comparison elementary schools spent more than the EAI allotment.

Table 12.3 summarizes the estimates by Richards et al. (1996) of the amount that BCPS overpaid EAI for their contract. The table displays a comparison between EAI's contracted budget and a potential EAI budget determined by using Baltimore's average ex-penditures per pupil by school type. Calculating EAI's allowance by this method would have resulted in a total savings of $4.3 million (21%) to EAI elementary schools and $1.4 million (26%) to EAI middle schools per year. Conversely, EAI's total losses per year would exceed $5.7 million. From the fall of 1994 through the end of the term of the contract, the district's total savings would have exceeded $17 million.

Confusion over appropriate contract cost, resulting in apparent significant overspending, made it difficult, if not impossible, to measure whether EAI could accomplish its espoused objective of improving performance at lower cost. Quite simply, the schools were operating at higher cost. In addition, no one was collecting or analyzing performance data. Richards et al. (1996) concluded the following regarding the EAI contract with BCPS:

- Current spending on elementary and middle school students in Baltimore is significantly less than the average spending on education for all students in Baltimore.

Table 12.3 What-If Analysis; If EAI Were Allocated Funds According to Average Expenditures (by School Type) for All Non-EAI Schools

Grade Level	Full-Time Equivalent Enrollment	EAI Average PPE	EAI Total Budget	Non-EAI Average PPE	Revised EAI Budget	$ Excess (Percent)
Elementary	3,790	$5,474	$20,746,460	$4,338	$16,441,020	$4,305,440 (21%)
Middle	969	$5,474	$5,304,306	$4,026	$3,901,194	$1,403,112 (26%)
Total	4,759		$26,050,766		$20,342,214	$5,708,552 (22%)

EAI, Education Alternatives, Inc. PPE, per-pupil expenditure.
Source: Data from Richards et al. (1996).

- The method used for determining "fair contract value" for the EAI allowance was not necessarily appropriate.
- The BCPS could have achieved substantial savings over the term of the EAI contract had they utilized alternative methods of calculating per-pupil allowance.
- Spending inequities may invalidate the validity of the performance comparisons between EAI schools and the selected comparison schools.

Richards et al. (1996) express significant concerns over the numerous apparent oversights in the establishment of the contract between the BCPS and EAI. Because this was the first such relationship to be established on a large scale, multiple competitors did not exist, and competitive bidding for price setting was not an option. Second, the one competitor bidding for the project had no available track record to present to the district. Third, the contract did not include clear stipulations regarding expected performance outcomes. And finally, BCPS made little or no effort to measure and evaluate the effectiveness of the relationship. As such, while EAI's contract with BCPS provided some valuable learning experiences regarding contract formulation, the EAI/BCPS endeavor yielded no substantive evidence regarding the economic efficiency of privatized management.

Hannaway (1999) reviewed 11 contractual arrangements between public and charter schools and EMOs and ESOs. Hannaway indicates that while much of the interest in private providers remains centered on the ideal that private providers may be performance contracted and held to outcome standards, few contracts clearly specify educational performance outcomes and associate specific incentives or sanctions with those outcomes. Hannaway notes "In some of the so called *educational performance* contracts, it is difficult to find the *educational* purpose of the contract, even though that is the presumed central purpose of the venture" (p. 5). Hannaway describes the Sylvan Learning Systems, Inc., approach as "what many people have in mind when they think about contracting in education" (p. 6):

> SYLVAN guarantees that each student in the SYLVAN program who receives the "required number of hours of direct instruction" will attain at least +2 NCEs growth in that student's primary subject (reading or math) . . . NCE growth will be measured by the appropriate subtest of the MAT-7 . . . SYLVAN will, at no charge or cost to CCSD, provide 12 hours of primary subject instruction to each student who does not attain the

growth guaranteed above. . . . (Sylvan–Charleston contract excerpt 4, p. 5, quoted in Hannaway, 1999, p. 6)

In the spring of 2002, the City of Philadelphia embarked on a project similar to that in Baltimore. The project involved shifting control of 42 schools to private for-profit and nonprofit management and to local universities. Philadelphia contracted management of 20 schools to Edison Schools (www.edisonschools.com). In spite of this apparent major success by Edison, by July 2003 amid numerous challenges to Edison's accounting of its annual revenues coupled with plummeting stock prices (greater than 98% decline), Edison went private.

In the aftermath of the financial failings of Edison as a publicly traded stock (which followed the similar financial failings of Education Alternatives, Inc., previously EAI, also publicly traded), significant questions remain regarding the profitability of the education management industry. Nonetheless, between 1998 and 2004, Molnar, Wilson, and Allen (2004, p. 9) identify an increase in the number of companies privately operating public schools from 13 to 51 and an increase in privately managed schools from 135 to 463. Apparently, the less-than-outstanding but limited track record of private management companies has had minimal influence on the interest of either providers or consumers.

Industry analysts and EMO corporate leaders long argued that public education funding was sufficient enough that private operators could manage schools, achieve better student outcomes, and still have room for a profit margin. They have banked on the assumption of economies of scale—management of large numbers of schools—to cut costs of teacher training, administration, purchasing, and so on, in order to widen the profit margin dramatically with growth. As we have discussed in previous chapters, economies of scale do exist in public education, but scale-related costs are driven primarily by the costs of configuring core instructional staff and much less so by administrative overhead, purchasing, or staff development. (We address resource allocation differences by scale in Chapter 15.) Emerging technologies may, or may not, provide private or public managers with increased flexibility in core instructional staffing costs and greater possibility of widening profit margins with scale. (We also discuss resource allocation among schools of different types and sizes more extensively in Chapter 15.)

In recent years, EMOs have become increasingly active in the management of charter schools, a reform we discuss more extensively in the following section. Bulkley and Fisler note that in Michigan, for example, 70% of charter schools contract with EMOs (2002, p. 3). Molnar et al. (2004) indicate that 81% of privately managed public schools are charter schools. As we will show in the next section, private for-profit management of charter schools adds to the complexity of schooling organizations.

Where Do Charter Schools Fit?

Charter schools present interesting dilemmas in our attempts to classify market mechanisms in education. Some suggest that handing control of public funds over to private individuals to run schools, even where those schools are governed directly under state-accountability systems, constitutes privatization. Bettinger (1999), for example, in the opening line of his evaluation of the effects of charter schools on charter and public school students, defines charter schools as "public schools contracted out to the private sector." Within our framework, Bettinger's definition of charter schools is one of active privatization, where the charter serves as the contract between the state and private individuals. Others contend that charter schools are analogous to voucher programs that exclude religious schooling options. Under this model, assuming charter schools are run by private individuals rather than public agents, charter schools would be a form of passive privatization. Where charter schools lie in our framework depends largely on specific state charter school policies.

While we are not necessarily willing to classify charter schools themselves as passive or active privatization, we recognize that the degree of active privatization of educational management and other services that occurs in the charter school context is significant and likely much greater than in traditional public schools. One view is that the authorizers of charter schools, by establishing a contractual relationship with the state, become agents of the state in a manner similar to public school administrators and/or teachers when signing a contract with a local board of education. As such, competition among charter schools and between charter schools and public schools creates a form of government-regulated marketplace, where the entities involved may play by quite similar or quite different rules.

Wherever they fit in, charter schools continue to expand nationally. According to Bulkley and Fisler, in a brief prepared for the Consortium for Policy Research in Education, by 2002, "more than 2,300 schools [served] over 575,000 students in 34 states and the District of Columbia" (2002, p. 1). In addition, "more than half of these schools are concentrated in a few states—Arizona has over 400 charter schools, and California, Florida, Michigan, and Texas each has more than 150." By 2003, nearly 3,000 charter schools were in operation nationwide serving more than 680,000 students. In Washington, DC, alone 43 charter schools served over 10,000 students, more than 15% of the district's student population.

Table 12.4 shows that states including Arizona, Michigan, Delaware, and Colorado already have sizable shares of their total student populations enrolled in charter schools. Even large states including California, Florida, and Texas have approximately 2% of their student populations enrolled in charter schools. As such, understanding the financial dimensions and productivity and efficiency effects of charter schools is becoming increasingly important. Arguably, charter schools have already surpassed the pessimistic forecasts of some that charters will be yet another blip on the education reform movement radar and one of relative insignificance in the long run.

As we discussed previously with respect to voucher programs, charter school policies include both regulatory and financial dimensions. Gill et al. (2001), from the RAND Corporation, laid out the elements of the regulatory and financial dimensions for charter and voucher policies. We include their framework in this section because we find most of the elements of the framework to be more pertinent to charter school policies than voucher policies (see Table 12.5). (We presented our own adaptation of this framework in the previous section.)

Regulatory Dimensions

Whether discussion of charter schools belongs primarily in this chapter or Chapter 14 (government intervention strategies) depends on whether accountability is primarily in the hands of consumers and the competitive marketplace or in the hands of state accrediting agencies. That is, do schools sink or swim by virtue of their ability to attract students or by virtue of their performance on state assessments? And to what extent are the two connected? Further, must charter schools

Table 12.4   Charter Schools Across the States in 2002–2003

State	Charter Schools		Public Districts		Charter Share
	Schools Operating	Enrollment	Districts	Enrollment	
Alaska	20	2,682	55	134,364	2.0%
Arizona	491	73,542	524	973,108	7.6%
Arkansas	11	1,486	316	450,985	0.3%
California	500	153,935	1060	6,245,981	2.5%
Colorado	93	25,512	185	751,862	3.4%
Connecticut	16	2,526	191	572,823	0.4%
Delaware	13	5,262	30	116,342	4.5%
Florida	258	53,350	73	2,541,478	2.1%
Georgia	36	15,117	185	1,501,288	1.0%
Hawaii	26	3,301	1	183,829	1.8%
Idaho	13	2,694	114	248,585	1.1%
Illinois	30	10,309	975	2,084,562	0.5%
Indiana	17	1,275	308	1,003,874	0.1%
Iowa	0	—	371	482,210	0.0%
Kansas	31	2,568	309	470,987	0.5%
Louisiana	16	4,631	87	730,464	0.6%
Maryland	0	—	24	866,743	0.0%
Massachusetts	50	14,013	376	982,989	1.4%
Michigan	210	60,236	793	1,785,912	3.4%
Minnesota	95	12,269	452	849,535	1.4%
Mississippi	1	334	162	492,645	0.1%
Missouri	27	12,130	525	926,648	1.3%
Nevada	14	2,851	17	369,498	0.8%
New Hampshire	0	—	166	208,260	0.0%
New Jersey	52	18,081	641	1,367,449	1.3%
New Mexico	37	4,234	93	331,359	1.3%
New York	51	10,954	776	2,914,574	0.4%
North Corolina	94	21,030	214	1,343,778	1.6%
Ohio	142	28,446	746	1,838,682	1.5%
Oklahoma	12	2,197	546	625,862	0.4%
Oregon	43	2,107	207	556,151	0.4%
Pennsylvania	103	33,656	621	1,816,747	1.9%
Rhode Island	8	914	43	159,000	0.6%
South Carolina	19	1,235	91	696,565	0.2%
Tennessee	4	—	139	908,573	0.0%
Texas	241	74,129	1236	4,259,261	1.7%
Utah	19	1,259	53	484,983	0.3%
Virginia	9	1,440	134	1,178,551	0.1%
Washington	0	—	299	1,014,798	0.0%
Washington, DC	43	11,530	35	76,166	15.1%
Wisconsin	147	26,797	442	881,231	3.0%
Wyoming	1	110	58	86,448	0.1%

Sources: Data on numbers of and enrollment in charter schools from Center for Education Reform, *Fast Facts. Charter Schools.* Retrieved from http://www.edreform.com/index.cfm?fuseAction=stateStats&pSectionID=15&cSectionID=44. Updated figures for 2006 available at http://www.edreform.com/_upload/CER_charter_numbers.pdf. Data on public school district enrollments 2002–2003 from the National Center for Education Statistics, *Local Education Agency Universe Survey of the Common Core of Data.* Retrieved from www.nces.ed.gov/ccd.

Table 12.5   RAND Regulatory and Financial Dimensions of State Charter School Policies

Regulatory	Finance
• Eligible schools • Number of schools/students permitted • Deregulation of existing schools • Student eligibility • Student admissions • Students with disabilities • Family contribution • Teacher certification • School performance requirements • Student testing requirements • Information dissemination • Curriculum requirements • Fiscal accountability • Facility standards	• General operating funds • Facilities • Startup • Special needs • At-risk adjustments • Grade-level adjustments • Transportation

Source: Based on Gill et al. (2002).

comply entirely with certification requirements and other curriculum requirements adopted by state bureaucracies, or may they recruit those employees they believe are best suited to getting the job done and implement curriculum in ways they deem appropriate?

This chapter's appendix summarizes charter school policies across the states. Some states strictly limit the numbers of charter schools that may run concurrently or may be chartered in a given year, and some states regulate whether existing private schools and/or existing public schools may *convert* to charter status. Some states, such as Kansas, only allow charters to be granted to schools within existing districts with approval of local boards of education, eliminating the market competition aspect of charter schools. States also vary widely in their curricular and teacher certification requirements for charter schools. (See Appendix, "Charter School Policies Across the States," at the end of this chapter.)

Financing Dimensions

An intriguing side effect of state charter school policies is that they have advanced the movement toward school-based, rather than district-based, state school finance formulas. The concept of school-based funding formulas has increased in popularity with the increased interest in the measurement of school-based "input" adequacy (e.g., the Wyoming prototypes discussed in Chapter 7).

State-funding mechanisms vary substantially but generally fall under one of two prototypes (see Figure 12.1). In one model (Missouri approach), states require local districts to transfer an allotment per pupil to charter schools for each student who lives in the district but attends that charter school. States use this type of model when they wish to require local districts to use locally generated revenue to pay a portion of students' charter school tuition. This approach may be a fiscal necessity for state legislators in states where local funding still makes up a substantial portion of aid to education. In Missouri, for example, local revenues still make up a substantial portion of school funding. Often in this type of model, districts retain an "overhead" fee, which, in theory, supports costs that the district incurs for providing support services to the charter school. In reality, these overhead fees exist primarily as a political concession, because districts rarely provide substantial services to charter schools not directly under their governance. States may also include other paybacks to or withholdings by the local district. Missouri's charter school funding law reads as follows:

Missouri's Charter School Funding Law

160.415. 1. For the purposes of calculation and distribution of state school aid under section 163.031, RSMo, pupils enrolled in a charter school shall be included in the pupil enrollment of the school district within which each pupil resides. Each charter school shall report the names, addresses, and eligibility for free or reduced-price lunch or other categorical aid, of

Figure 12.1   Alternative Approaches to Charter School Funding

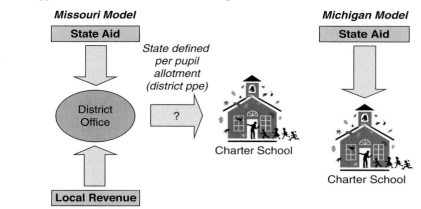

? = district retained share to cover
administrative overhead

PPE, per-pupil expenditure.

pupils resident in a school district who are enrolled in the charter school to the school district in which those pupils reside and to the state department of elementary and secondary education. Each charter school shall promptly notify the state department of elementary and secondary education and the pupil's school district when a student discontinues enrollment at a charter school.

2. (1) A school district having one or more resident pupils attending a charter school shall pay to the charter school an annual amount equal to the product of the equalized, adjusted operating levy for school purposes for the pupils' district of residence for the current year times the guaranteed tax base per eligible pupil, as defined in section 163.011, RSMo, times the number of the district's resident pupils attending the charter school plus all other state aid attributable to such pupils, including summer school, if applicable, and all aid provided pursuant to section 163.031, RSMo.

(2) The district of residence of a pupil attending a charter school shall also pay to the charter school any other federal or state aid that the district receives on account of such child.

(3) The amounts provided pursuant to this subsection shall be prorated for partial year enrollment for a pupil.

(4) A school district shall pay the amounts due pursuant to this subsection as the disbursal agent and no later than twenty days following receipt of any such funds.

(5) The per-pupil amount paid by a school district to a charter school shall be reduced by the amount per pupil determined by the state board of education to be needed by the district in the current year for repayment of leasehold revenue bonds obligated pursuant to a federal court desegregation action.

The second approach involves the state's establishing a per-pupil allotment that the state provides directly to charter schools. Under this model, all public funds that the charter school receives are state funds. The general approach to charter school funding in Michigan, for example, is for the state to provide a foundation allotment per pupil to authorizers of *Public School Academies* (charter schools). In Michigan, charter schools receive a per-pupil allotment equivalent to that of the district in which they are geographically located. In the early 1990s, when Michigan adopted its charter school law, the legislature had already made a commitment to reducing the role of local property tax funding of public education. As a safety valve to cover the increased potential state burden as students shift from local property tax-funded districts into charters, the legislature set a threshold whereby districts with 25% or more students enrolling in charter schools would be required to submit to charter school authorizers the appropriate proportion of locally generated property tax revenues (State School Aid Act of 1976).

In most cases, state funding of charter schools is limited to general operating funds. While charter schools must have access to facilities, and must maintain and operate those facilities, states rarely provide facilities aid. In addition, while charter schools may not exclude children with special needs from attending, charter schools do not all receive additional funding to meet those needs. As we discussed in Chapter 6, facilities aid for traditional public schools continues to vary widely across the states, with several states leaving facilities funding in the hands of local taxpayers. Unlike traditional public schools, however, charter schools do not have taxing authority to make up for revenues not provided by the state.

Table 12.6 presents a summary of the financing dimensions of charter school and voucher programs (Gill et al., 2001). Of the state charter and voucher programs included in the RAND study (Gill et al., 2001), charter schools in Pennsylvania, Colorado, and New Jersey received from 60% to 95% of public school per-pupil expenditure levels; and charter schools in Florida, Michigan, Washington, DC, and Wisconsin received the approximate equivalent of public school revenues per pupil. The RAND study indicated no support for facilities in Pennsylvania and New Jersey but did indicate either substantial direct support for buildings (including lease support) or bonding authority in Colorado, North Carolina, Washington, DC, Minnesota, and Florida.

Alternative Revenues in Charter Schools

Because charter schools receive primarily operational support through public tax dollars and lack local taxing authority of their own, charter schools have developed substantial alternative revenue streams. As we discussed in Chapter 3, Pijanowski and Monk (1996) explain how alternative revenue sources had become increasingly important to traditional public schools before the rapid emergence of charter schools.

In some rare cases, mostly in states limiting taxing authority, traditional public schools may rely on significant annual private contributions, but these cases remain rare. Private, independent schools (schools not receiving church subsidies), typically fund from 10% to 30% of their operating expenses from annual giving campaigns (capital campaigns bring in larger sums of money, but in long-term rather than annual cycles).

In many ways, charter schools function more like private nonprofit educational institutions than traditional public educational institutions, in that charter

Table 12.6   Financing Dimensions of Choice Programs

	Level of Public Subsidy		
Dimension	Low	Medium	High
General operating funds	<60% of public-school PPE: Cleveland (1/3 of district PPE)	60%–95% of public school PPE: Milwaukee (state share), PA (70%–82% PPE), CO (minimum 80% PPE), NJ, FL	Equivalent to full PPE in existing public schools: FL, MI, DC, WI
Facilities	None provided: Milwaukee, Cleveland, FL, PA, NJ	Limited funding available: CA and many other charter states	Substantial funding available: Bond funding in CO and NC, buildings in CO and DC, lease payments in MN and FL
Startup	None (except federal grants): Milwaukee, Cleveland, FL, CO, MI, DC	Available: Charters in AZ, CA, MA, MN	
Special needs	No additional funds available: AZ	Some supplemental funds provided: Cleveland, FL, MA, NC	Funding based on severity of disability: MN, AZ, DC, CA
At-risk adjustment	None: Milwaukee, Cleveland	Additional Funding: CO, MI, TX	
Grade level	None: Milwaukee, Cleveland, PA, MI, TX	Varies by grade level: AZ, DC, MN	
Transportation	None provided: Milwaukee, MI, MN, AZ, CA Prop 38	Subsidized or provided: Cleveland, CT, DC	

PPE, per-pupil expendiures.
Source: Adapted from RAND report by Gill et al. (2001).

schools derive a significant portion of their annual revenue from tax-exempt contributions. Government funds play a role equivalent to tuition for private schools. Many charter schools have aggressively developed foundations and undertaken campaigns to build endowments. That charter schools must survive in many cases on charitable contributions raises questions as to how a charter school could ever be run as a successful for-profit venture. Better to just drop that one.

Figure 12.2 displays the mean annual revenues for the 19 Washington, DC, charter schools reporting to the IRS for fiscal year 2000. Some variations in reporting occurred as to whether government-allocated, per-pupil aid constituted aid for "program services" or "government grants." Some schools reported only competitive, supplemental, and/or targeted government grants as government grants and reported aid per pupil as program services, while other schools reported all aid received from the government as government grants. Thus, it is easier just to aggregate the two for this discussion and note that government sources ("government grants" and "program services" in Figure 12.2) accounted for 85% of DC charter school revenue. Private contributions accounted for a surprisingly large portion.

Despite the relatively healthy level of average private contributions, 6 of the 19 schools in this sample ran annual operating deficits. Of the 6 running deficits

in 2000, two attempted to operate on public support alone, and 2 others attempted to operate with only approximately $10,000 in private contributions in 2000. Perhaps one reason EMOs are an appealing option for charter schools is that they bring with them the necessary capital (often generated by the sale of company stock) to cover critical start-up expenses, relieving the necessity to aggressively seek and then manage private contributions. This benefit to charter school operators, however, may be a disadvantage to private management firms hoping to eventually make profits on school operations.

To the best of our knowledge, while some states provide start-up support for charter schools, none provide additional support for charter schools on the basis of lacking economies of scale. Yet, many charter schools operate for several years if not indefinitely at relatively inefficient scale (elementary less than 300 to 500 students, or secondary less than 600 to 900 students). Further, charter schools autonomous from public school districts incur a variety of central administrative expenses that may not be fully accommodated by charter school aid. That is, on the surface charter schools appear to be a money-losing venture for private managers.

Table 12.7 summarizes the financial structure of four charter schools in Kansas City, Missouri. Under state policy, these four schools should be similarly funded. Revenue listed as program service revenue primarily consists of state aid and local transfer funds from the Kansas City school district. Notably, University Academy also generates substantial "direct public support," or charitable gifts. Urban Community Leadership Academy appears to generate the least additional revenue beyond program service revenue, as such, spending less per pupil than the others and running an annual deficit (at least in 2003). By contrast, University Academy generates the most revenue per pupil and has relatively high, though not the highest, expenditures per pupil. Benjamin Banneker Academy has very high per-pupil spending, and runs a deficit despite high revenues, in part because the school remains relatively small.

Interestingly, many charter schools hold IRS tax status as 501 (c) (3) organizations—or nonprofit organization status. In some cases (Washington, DC), nonprofit status and nonprofit financial reporting are required of charter school operators. In many cases, these nonprofits hold management contracts with for-profit EMOs, increasing the layers of complexity in

Figure 12.2   Revenue Sources of Washington, DC, Charter Schools

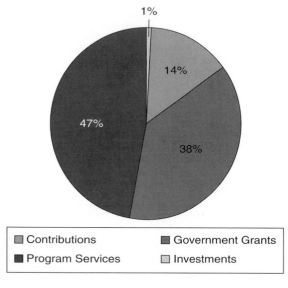

Source: Compiled from 19 Washington, DC, charter schools reporting IRS Form 990. See www.guidestar.org.

Table 12.7 Revenues and Expenditures of Kansas City, Missouri, Charter Schools

	Westport Allen (FY 2002)	Urban Community Leadership (FY 2003)	University Academy (FY 2003)	Benjamin Banneker (FY 2003)
Revenue (IRS 990)				
Direct public			$867,759	$221,466
Indirect public grants	$14,079	$22,925		
Program service revenue	$4,534,422	$1,808,351	$2,508,604	$1,494,071
Interest	$9,966			$1,184
Other	$162,547	$320	$15,338	$12,010
Total Revenue	**$4,721,014**	**$1,831,596**	**$3,391,701**[a]	**$1,728,731**
Current Expenditures (IRS 990)	$4,667,025	$2,011,475	$2,963,308	$2,073,709
Enrollment (DESE)	431	213	273	157
Revenue per Pupil	**$10,954**	**$8,599**	**$12,424**	**$11,011**
Expenditures per Pupil	**$10,828**	**$9,444**	**$10,855**	**$13,208**

[a]Excludes losses from special events (approx. $50k).

Source: Financial data retrieved from each school's IRS form 990 (not-for-profit tax return) available from http://www.guidestar.org. Enrollment data from the Missouri Department of Elementary and Secondary Education. Retrieved from http://www.dese.mo.gov/schooldata/ftpdata.html

schooling organization. For example, in Kansas City, Missouri, Southwest Charter School is a nonprofit organization with a school management contract with Chancellor Beacon Academies, a for-profit EMO. (At the time of this writing, Southwest Charter School had just lost its university sponsorship and was seeking a new sponsor.) Like the Washington, DC, charter schools, in 2000, only 65% of the Southwest Charter School's annual operating revenue came from direct government support (per-pupil aid), and 2.3% came from charitable gifts. In that same year, 6% of expenses were allocated directly to private management with a total of 33% of expenses allocated to management-related functions. In Chapter 15, we discuss more extensively the factors that influence how/where schools and districts spend their money.

Despite the apparent shortcomings of charter school aid per pupil, charter school aid is usually much more substantial than aid provided to private schools through voucher programs. Further, charter school aid is generally not limited to specific student populations, except perhaps by geographic boundary. As such, where both voucher and charter options exist, financial incentives are stronger for schools to participate under charter school policies. To participate as a charter school, however, schools must typically agree (a) not to charge tuition over and above

government aid allocations, (b) not to selectively admit students, and (c) not to provide religious curriculum. Interestingly, Green and Mead (2004) point out that while charter school policies may govern whether religious curriculum may be taught, states might encounter problems if they were to attempt to exclude religious organizations from becoming charter school authorizers.

Do Market-Based Policies Improve Productivity and Efficiency?

In this section, we summarize briefly what is known and not known about whether market-based policies applied to public education systems promote improved productivity and efficiency. Three areas of research along these lines include (a) comparisons of U.S. public and private school productivity and efficiency, assuming that private schools function in a market economy; (b) performance comparisons and demographic analyses of public school students, private school students receiving vouchers, and charter school students in the United States; and (c) international analyses of large-scale voucher programs.

Are Market Approaches More Productive?

Patrick McEwan (2000a) provides one of the more comprehensive reviews and critiques of existing literature on experimental and nonexperimental comparisons of student performance in public and private schools, including studies of students on vouchers. McEwan concludes the following:

> Based on recent experimental evidence, it finds that Catholic elementary schools have modest effects on the mathematics achievement of poor, minority students in grades 2 – 5 (but not in grades 6 – 8 or among non-black students). The evidence on elementary reading achievement does not show consistent effects on achievement. The evidence on attainment is strikingly consistent, indicating that Catholic schools increase the probability of high school completion and college attendance, particularly for minorities in urban areas. (McEwan, 2000a, p. 1)

A recent research brief from the RAND Corporation titled, *What Do We Know About Vouchers and Charter Schools? Separating the Rhetoric From the Reality,* also based on a review of existing literature, similarly concluded, as follows:

> Small experimental, privately funded voucher programs suggest that African-American students may receive a modest achievement benefit after one or two years in the programs. The exact reasons for this benefit, however, remain unknown. Children of other racial groups in voucher schools have shown no consistent evidence of academic benefit or harm. (Gill et al., 2001)

The RAND research brief noted the following regarding charter school performance:

> Charter-school achievement results are mixed. In Arizona, charter schools seem to be outperforming conventional public schools in reading and possibly in math. In Texas, charter schools that focus specifically on students at risk for poor academic performance show an achievement advantage over conventional public schools, but other charter schools perform slightly worse than conventional public schools. An examination of newly opened charter schools in Michigan indicates no difference from conventional public schools in terms of achievement effects in one tested grade (grade 7), while conventional public schools outperform charters in the other tested grade (grade 4). Meanwhile, the studies in both Arizona and Texas suggest that achievement effects in charter schools improve after the first year of operation. (Gill et al., 2001)

An analysis of Texas charter schools, by Texas A&M economists Timothy Gronberg and Dennis Jansen (2001), concluded:

- In general, at-risk charters seem to be performing well. Estimates from individual student fixed-effect regressions, which represent a best attempt to control for the impact of individual student characteristics on test score performance, indicate that at-risk charter schools have a positive value-added effect relative to traditional public schools. The opposite results hold for non-at-risk charters.
- Following cohorts through time, rather than taking 1-year looks, indicate that test score improvements of continuing charter students track those of traditional public schools, and that continuing at-risk students in charters improve their test scores at greater rates than their at-risk traditional public school comparators.
- Students moving into a charter often exhibit a first-year drop in Texas Assessment of Academic Skills (TAAS) test scores, an effect that might be compounded when students move into a newly opened charter. The charter industry has been growing rapidly, and new entrants into charter schools make up a large share of all charter students in any given year. A 1-year look at average changes in test scores for charter students will mainly capture the decline in performance of the new entrants. (Gronberg & Jansen, 2001, pp. 1–2)

Another assumed benefit from school-choice models is that not only will the students choosing to go to private or charter schools benefit but that the students remaining in conventional public schools will benefit as a result of competitive pressures for those schools to improve. In a review of 41 separate studies of the effects of competition on educational outcomes, Levin and Belfield (2002) find, "A sizable majority of these studies report beneficial effects of competition across all outcomes, with many reporting statistically significant correlations" (p. 2).

Through a series of general equilibrium-model simulations, Thomas Nechyba (2003a) finds that modest levels of school vouchers may increase overall school quality and reduce variance in quality.

Little or no evidence indicates whether active privatization—private management—has any specific effect on educational productivity, positive or negative. In terms of productivity for investors, the outlook remains skeptical.

Are Market Approaches More Efficient?

Based on a review of existing literature, Patrick McEwan (in another occasional paper for the National

Center for the Study of Privatization in Education) suggests that private schools show no efficiency advantage in studies that controlled for selection bias regarding who attends private schools and for the relationship between private school enrollments and public school quality (McEwan, 2000b). In an analysis of Chile's nationwide voucher program, McEwan and Carnoy (2000) found that nonreligious private schools were more efficient by virtue of producing academic achievement at a lower cost (probably as a result of lower wages and constraints on resource allocation). The relative efficiency of public and Catholic schools was similar, but Catholic voucher schools were somewhat more effective than public schools (McEwan & Carnoy, 2000).

Few studies have attempted to measure directly the relative efficiency of charter schools in producing educational outcomes. Recall our concerns with the state of efficiency measurement in Chapter 11. Gronberg and Jansen (2001) in their analysis of Texas charter schools, performed both "average efficiency" analysis (comparing predicted and actual costs of charter and public schools) and stochastic frontier analysis to compare the average inefficiencies of charter schools and public schools. Their major findings follow:

- Charter schools are relatively cost-efficient. On average, they achieve a given level of student performance at a lower expenditure per student than would be predicted for a comparable traditional public school district.

- Compared to traditional public schools, a disproportionately large percentage of at-risk students, minority students, and economically disadvantaged students choose to attend charter schools. A meaningful evaluation of the performance of charter schools must recognize and account for these facts.

- Overall, charters allow innovative approaches, they are cost-efficient as a group, and they often achieve student performance levels for at-risk students that rival those of traditional public schools. Judging Texas's experiment with charter schools on all of these grounds, this is an experiment worth continuing, an experiment that will likely lead to new insights in delivery of educational services. While it is far too early to know the final results of this experiment, the initial indications, although certainly mixed, contain many positive signs. The charter industry will likely continue to challenge the traditional public school districts to be more effective, more efficient, and more innovative in their own delivery of educational services.

While executives of education management companies promoted their ability to achieve better outcomes at lower costs, little or no evidence suggests that this has actually been the case (Richards, Baker, & Cilo, 1996). Anecdotal evidence from individual contractual arrangements such as that between the city of Baltimore and EAI suggests that in general, private management companies have spent more, not less in their operation of schools (Richards et al., 1996). Recent evidence regarding raw productivity though not productive efficiency, suggests that private management experiences in Philadelphia have produced mixed results at best (Gill, Zimmer, Christman, & Blanc, 2007).

Policy Recommendations (From RAND)

The RAND brief (Gill et al., 2001) arrives at the following three major recommendations regarding the implementation of voucher and charter programs:

- To ensure that voucher and charter programs will be academically effective, program designers should include existing private schools, enforce requirements for student achievement testing, and actively inform parents about schools and their effectiveness. Some of the most favorable evidence comes from programs that include existing schools rather than relying largely on new start-ups. School choice is also more likely to be effective if parents have complete information about school quality.

- To ensure that voucher and charter programs benefit the students who remain in conventional public schools, policy makers should require that all participating schools practice open admissions to prevent "cream skimming" of the best students into elite schools. They should also encourage the performance of conventional public schools by giving them the autonomy they need to perform in a newly competitive educational market.

- To ensure that voucher and charter schools serve low-income and special-needs students, policy makers should require open admissions, provide generous funding (including supplemental funding for students with special needs), and target specific students. Moreover, policy makers should fund choice programs through direct grants rather than income-tax subsidies, which favor middle- and upper-income families.

Equity and Adequacy Effects

Increasingly, econometric analyses suggest that the ability to send one's child to another district of higher quality reduces the capitalization of schooling quality in housing values. That is, districts with "good schools" experience less benefit in the form of capitalization in a state or metropolitan area where choices are available. At the same time, the adverse effects on housing values in neighborhoods with poor schools are not as strong. These findings create a dilemma for those who prefer to advocate both local control via local taxation and school choice (Reback, 2002).

The upside of disrupting the linkage between residential location and schooling quality is that choice among schools may lead to improved equity of opportunity, assuming certain conditions are met. Nechyba (2004) uses general equilibrium modeling to test the effects of a variety of school finance policy options on the distribution of educational opportunities to children. Policies tested include matching aid, guaranteed tax base, foundation aid formulas, and the school-choice policies. Nechyba (2003b, 2004) finds the distribution of housing to be a significant barrier to achieving equity or adequacy through finance policy alone.

SUMMARY

In this chapter, we have discussed market-driven reforms and their relationship to productivity and efficiency in the delivery of educational services to American children. To date, what we know about market-based reforms is that they change the organizational dynamics of schooling in expected and unexpected, desired and undesired ways serving both conservative and liberal political agendas. In general, poor and minority children do appear to benefit from the opportunity to attend private, predominantly Catholic inner-city schools (McEwan, 2000a). However, the practicality of applying this policy solution nationwide is questionable (Levin & Driver, 1998; McEwan, 2000b). Some evidence also suggests that charter schools, in some states (most notably Texas), may be producing outcomes more efficiently than comparable public schools (Gronberg & Jansen, 2001). Yet, policy makers in many states have established systems of financing charter schools that effectively financially starve these schools, leading them to rely heavily on charitable contributions, capital outlay support from private management firms, and most likely extensive unpaid overtime from start-up staff dedicated to the missions of their schools (Green & Mead, 2004). The ability to replicate charter schools' efficiency gains across public schooling or as charter schooling expands remains questionable. Further, due to the extent of unmeasured inputs of charter schools, estimates of charter schools' current efficiency is also questionable (see private contributions analysis in this chapter).

Choice and market mechanisms can play key roles in improving educational quality for some but probably not all children, most likely at a break-even on efficiency. Quite simply, as Henry Levin discussed in the 1980s (Levin, 1983), a fair and equitable program of school choice most likely costs more, not less, than schooling provided on the basis of residential location. What researchers must evaluate is whether the advantages of choice are worth the costs. Among the clearest advantages of interdistrict, public, and/or private choice is the potential erosion of often politically divisive school district boundaries that serve to (and often were originally designed to) perpetuate disparities in schooling quality associated with neighborhood wealth. Second is the opportunity to relax degrees of regulation on some schooling inputs and processes in an attempt to experiment with new strategies of improving educational outcomes. In Chapters 13 and 15, we discuss how the dominant recipients of voucher students in the United States, urban Catholic schools, are perhaps the most like the public schools from which those students came. Charter schools, on the other hand, are more likely to experiment with different approaches to school personnel and finance.

REFERENCES

Baker, B. D., & Friedman-Nimz, R. C. (2002). Determinants of the availability of opportunities for gifted children: Evidence from NELS '88. *Leadership and Policy in Schools, 1*(1), 52–71.

Baker, B. D., & Richards, C. E. (1998). Equity through vouchers: The special case of gifted children. *Educational Policy, 12*(4), 363–379.

Bettinger, E. (1999). *The effect of charter schools on charter students and public schools.* Occasional Paper #4. National Center for the Study of Privatization in Education. Retrieved from http://www.ncspe.org/publications_files/182_OP04.pdf

Bracey, G. W. (2002). The *war against America's public schools: Privatizing schools, commercializing education.* Boston, MA: Allyn & Bacon.

Bulkley, K., & Fisler, J. (2002). *A decade of charter schools: From theory to practice.* Philadelphia: Consortium for Policy Research in Education, University of Pennsylvania. Retrieved from http://www.cpre.org/Publications/rb35.pdf

Carnoy, M., & McEwan, P. (2000). The effectiveness and efficiency of private schools in Chile's voucher system. *Educational Evaluation and Policy Analysis, 22*(3), 213–239.

Chubb, J. E., & Moe, T. M. (1990). *Politics markets and America's schools.* Washington, DC: Brookings Institution Press.

Friedman, M. (1962). *Capitalism and freedom.* Chicago: University of Chicago Press.

Gill, B., Timpane, M., Ross, K., & Brewer, D. (2001). *Rhetoric vs. reality: What we know and what we need to know about vouchers and charter schools.* The Rand Corporation. Santa Monica, CA. Retrieved from http://www.rand.org/publications/MR/MR1118/MR1118.ch2.pdf

Gill, B., Zimmer, R., Christman, J., & Blanc, S. (2007). *State takeover, school restructuring, private management, and student achievement in Philadelphia.* Santa Monica, CA: The RAND Corporation.

Green, P. C., III, & Mead, J. (2004). *Charter schools and the law: Establishing new legal relationships.* Norwood, MA: Christopher Gordon Publishing.

Gronberg, T. J., & Jansen, D. (2001). *Navigating newly chartered waters: An analysis of Texas charter school performance.* Austin, TX: Texas Public Policy Foundation.

Hannaway, J. (1999). *Contracting as a mechanism for managing education services.* Philadelphia: Consortium for Policy Research in Education.

Heise, M., & Nechyba, T. (1999). *School finance reform: A case for vouchers.* New York, NY: Manhattan Institute, Center for Civic Innovation.

Hill, P. T., Pierce, L. C., Guthrie, & J. W. (1997). *Reinventing public education: How contracting can transform America's schools.* Chicago: University of Chicago Press.

Hoxby, C. M. (1996). Are efficiency and equity in school finance substitutes or compliments? *Journal of Economic Perspectives, 10*(4) 51–72.

Hoxby, C. M. (2000, December). Does competition among public schools benefit students and taxpayers? *American Economic Review,* 1209–1238

Levin, H. J., & Belfield, C. (2002). *The effects of competition on educational outcomes: A review of U.S. evidence.* Working Paper. National Center for the Study of Privatization in Education. Retrieved from www.ncspe.org

Levin, H. M. (1983). Educational choice and the pains of democracy. In *Public Dollars for Private Schools.* Philadelphia: Temple University Press.

Levin, H. M., & Driver, C. (1998). Estimating the cost of an educational voucher system. In W. Fowler (Ed.), *Selected papers in school finance.* Washington, DC. National Center for Education Statistics.

McEwan, P. J. (2000a). *Comparing the effectiveness of public and private schools: A review of evidence and interpretations.* Occasional Paper #3. New York: National Center for the Study of Privatization, Teachers College, Columbia University.

McEwan, P. J. (2000b). *The potential impact of large scale voucher programs.* Occasional Paper #2. New York: National Center for the Study of Privatization, Teachers College, Columbia University.

McEwan, P. J., & Carnoy, M. (2000). The effectiveness and efficiency of private schools in Chile's voucher system. *Educational Evaluation and Policy Analysis, 22*(3), 213–240.

McMillan, R. (1999). *Competition, parental involvement and public school performance.* Retrieved June 1, 2006, from http://www.chass.utoronto.ca/~mcmillan/ntadoc.pdf

Molnar, A., Wilson, G., & Allen, D. (2004). *Profiles of for-profit education management companies: Sixth annual report.* Education Policy Studies Laboratory: Commercialism in Education Research Unit. Arizona State University.

Nechyba, T. (2003a). Introducing school choice into multidistrict public school systems. In C. Hoxby (Ed.), *The economics of school choice* (pp. 145–194). Chicago: University of Chicago Press.

Nechyba, T. (2003b). School finance, spatial segregation and the nature of communities. *Journal of Urban Economics, 54*(1), 61–68.

Nechyba, T. (2004). Prospects for achieving equity or adequacy in education: The limits of state aid in general equilibrium. In J. Yinger (Ed.), *Helping children left behind: State aid and the pursuit of educational equity* (pp. 111–146). Boston: MIT Press.

Niskanen, W. A. (1968). The peculiar economics of bureaucracy. *American Economic Review, 58*(2), 293–305.

Pijanowski, J., & Monk, D. H. (1996). Alternative revenues for public schools: There are many fish in the sea. *School Business Affairs, 62*(7), 4–10.

RAND Corporation. (2001). *What do we know about vouchers and charter schools? Separating the rhetoric from the reality.* Retrieved from http://www.rand.org/pubs/research_briefs/RB8018/index1.html

Reback, R. (2002). *Capitalization under school choice programs: Are the winners really the losers?* Working Paper, Department of Economics, University of Michigan. Retrieved from http://www.econ.lsa.umich.edu/~reback/capitalization.pdf

Richards, C. E., Baker, B. D., & Cilo, M. R. (1996). *Is privatization more efficient? The case of Education Alternatives, Inc. in Baltimore, MD.* Paper presented at the Annual Meeting of the American Educational Research Association, New York.

Richards, C. E., Shore, R., & Sawicky, M. (1996). *Risky business: Private management of public schools.* Washington, DC: Economic Policy Institute.

State School Aid Act of 1979. Retrieved from http://www.michiganlegislature.org/documents/mcl/pdf/mcl-388-1620.pdf

Tiebout, C. (1956). A pure theory of local public expenditure. *Journal of Political Economy, 64*(5), 416–424.

U.S. National Commission on Excellence in Education. (1983). *A nation at risk: The imperative for educational reform.* Washington, DC: U.S. Government Printing Office.

Chapter 12 Appendix

Charter School Policies Across the States

State	Authorizer	Restrictions	Per-Pupil Funding	Other Sources
Alaska	Local school boards, with approval from the state board of education	60	The local school board provides the charter school with an annual program budget, determined by applying an indirect cost rate approved by the state dept. of ed. The amount generated by students enrolled in the charter school is determined in the same fashion as it is for a pupil enrolled in another public school in that school district.	None.
Arizona	Local school board, state board of education, and state board for charter schools	None.	A charter school that is sponsored by a local board is included in the district's budget calculations and is funded pursuant to the school district budgeting and financial assistance formula. A charter school that is sponsored by state board of ed. or state board for charter schools is funded pursuant to the state's small school district aid formula.	A charter school stimulus fund provides funding to charter school applicants and charter schools for start-up costs and costs associated with renovating or remodeling existing buildings.
Arkansas	Local school board and state board of education must approve applications for conversion and enrollment charter schools.	24: The state board of education could grant no more than 4 charters per congressional district in 2005–2006; no more than 5 charters per congressional district in 2006–2007; and no more than 6 charters per congressional district in 2007–2008.	An open-enrollment charter school receives funds equal to the average local and state revenue based on average daily membership. A conversion charter school receives funds equal to the amount apportioned by the district from state and local revenue per average daily membership.	None.
California	Local school boards or county board of ed. The state board of ed. may authorize charter schools operating in multiple sites statewide. If the sites are located within one county, then that county is the authorizer.	1,050 in 2006–2007. Additional 100 in each successive year.	Charter schools receive general-purpose entitlement funding, derived from a combination of state aid and local funds. The entitlement is based on average school district daily attendance.	A charter school revolving loan program funds charter school start-ups. A charter school may obtain multiple loans pursuant to the program, but the total amount may not exceed $250,000. A facility grant program provides up to $750 per pupil, but no more than 75% of the charter school's annual facilities rent and lease costs.

(*continued*)

Charter School Policies Across the States *(continued)*

State	Authorizer	Restrictions	Per-Pupil Funding	Other Sources
Colorado	The state charter school institute may authorize a charter school where the school district has not retained exclusive authority to authorize charter schools. Three types of school districts automatically receive exclusive authority to authorize charters: (1) school districts with total enrollment < 3,000 pupils; (2) districts whose percentage of pupils who are eligible for free or reduced lunch and who are enrolled in charter schools authorized by the districts is greater than the percentage that is 1% below the overall percentage of pupils eligible for free and reduced lunch in the school district; and (3) districts that annually certify to the state board that the total number of students allowed to be enrolled in the charter schools, or the maximum number of students allowed to be enrolled pursuant to charter school contracts entered into by the school district, whichever is greater, divided by the district per pupil enrollment for that budget year, reflected a percentage, exceeds by more than 3 percentage points the percentage of students enrolled in charter schools statewide.	No.	Each institute charter school receives at a minimum 95% of per-pupil revenues from the school district in which the school is located. The state dept. of ed. may deduct up to 2% for administrative costs, and the charter school institute may deduct up to 3% for administrative costs. Each district charter receives at least 95% of per-pupil revenues from the school district (with up to 5% subtracted for district administrative costs), except that a district charter school located in a district with 500 or fewer students may receive at a minimum 85% of per-pupil revenues.	Capital construction bonds may be issued to qualified charter schools.

338

State	Authorizer	Restrictions	Per-Pupil Funding	Other Sources
Connecticut	Local or regional boards of ed. and the state dept. of ed. must approve local charter schools. The state board of ed. must approve state charter schools.	No state charter school may enroll more than 250 students (in the case of a K–8 school, more than 300), or 25% of the enrollment of the school district in which the state charter school is to be located, whichever is less. However, a state charter school with a demonstrated record of achievement may, upon approval by the state board of education, enroll up to 85 students per grade, if funding is available.	For local charter schools, funding is determined in the charter. For state charter schools, the state pays $8,000 per student.	Grant program to assist state charter schools in financing school building projects.
Delaware	Local school boards authorize conversion charters. Local school boards and state board of ed. grant new charters.	No.	Charter schools receive state and local funds, but they do not receive additional funds for facilities.	
District of Columbia	District Board of Public Education and District Charter School Board.	20 per year. Each chartering authority may authorize 10 per year.	Each charter school receives funds based on the District of Columbia's funding formula.	The New Charter School Fund provides payments during a fiscal year to public charter school whose total audited enrollment is greater than the pupil enrollment used to determine the school's annual payment for the year. One of the goals of the Facilities Revitalization Program is to provide long-term funding for capital and maintenance of facilities.
Florida	Local school boards, and state universities. Community colleges may grant charters to charter school technical career centers.	No.	Students enrolled in a charter school are funded as if they were in a basic program or a special program, the same as students enrolled in other public schools in the school district. Laboratory charter schools receive their funding based on the county in which the lab school is located and the General Appropriations Act.	The Comissioner of Education must provide capital outlay funds for eligible charter schools as set out by state law.

(continued)

Charter School Policies Across the States (*continued*)

State	Authorizer	Restrictions	Per-Pupil Funding	Other Sources
Georgia	Local school board and state board of ed. must approve application.	No.	The local school board distributes funds to local charter schools on the basis of the state's Quality Basic Education (QBE) formula. The local school board distributes QBE formula earnings, applicable QBE grants, applicable non-QBE state grants, and applicable federal grants to state-chartered special schools. A state-chartered special school is included in the local school board's equalization grant only if the voters of the local school board have approved the use of revenue from local taxes and local bonded indebtedness to support the school.	A charter school facilities fund was created for (1) the purchase of real property; (2) the construction, purchase, leasing, renovation, and maintenance of school facilities; and (3) the purchase of school transportation vehicles.
Hawaii	State board of education.	23 start-up schools.	The per-pupil allotment for each charter school is based on (1) the actual and projected enrollments of each charter school; (2) a per-pupil amount for each regular education and special education student, which is equal to the total per-pupil cost based on average enrollment in all cost categories, including school support services but excluding special education services, and for all means of financing except federal funds; and (3) fringe benefits.	

State	Authorizer	Restrictions	Per-Pupil Funding	Other Sources
Idaho	Both local school boards and the state charter school commission may authorize new public schools. Only local school boards may approve conversion charter schools.	The charter school statute places the following limitations on the number of charter schools that may open in any given school year: (1) no more than 6 schools may open in 1 year, not including the transfer of a charter for a school already authorized in accordance with section 33-5205A of the state code; (2) no more than 1 new charter school may open within a school district during the school year, not including public virtual charter schools approved by the charter school commission; (3) no school district may convert into a charter district or have any configuration consisting of only charter schools.	The calculation of support units for each charter school is computed according to schedules established within the state code.	The board of directors of a charter school, operating as a nonprofit corporation, may borrow money to finance the purchase or lease of facilities. The board may use the facility as collateral for the loan.

(continued)

Charter School Policies Across the States (*continued*)

State	Authorizer	Restrictions	Per-Pupil Funding	Other Sources
Illinois	Local school boards. Also, 5% or more of the voters of a school district or districts named in a proposal petition the school may order a referendum to determine whether a charter school may be established. If the majority of the voters support the referendum, then the state board of ed. will serve as the school's chartering authority.	60. Chicago may have 30 public schools. The Chicago suburbs may have 15 charter schools (with no more than 1 charter school that has been started by a local board of ed., or by an agreement among boards of ed., functioning at any one time in the school district in which the charter school is located). The rest of the state has 15 charter schools (with no more than 1 charter school that has been started by a local board of ed., or by an agreement among boards of ed., functioning at any one time in the school district in which the charter school is located).	Charter schools and local boards of ed. negotiate funding, but charter schools must receive 75%–125% of the school district's per capita tuition multiplied by the number of pupils living in the school district who are enrolled in the charter school.	The state board of ed. must provide transition impact aid to school districts that approve charter schools. The state board of ed. must also provide grants to charter schools for their start-up costs, not to exceed $250 per pupil enrolled in a charter school. A charter school revolving loan fund is a special fund in the state treasury. The fund is available for the costs associated with establishing charter schools in the state.
Indiana	Local school boards, public universities that offer a 4-year baccalaureate degree, and the mayor of a consolidated city. Also, before bestowing a charter under which more than 50% of the pupils in the school district will attend a charter school, the local school board must obtain the approval of the state dept. of ed.	The mayor of a consolidated city could sponsor no more than 5 charters during the 2001 calendar year. During each calendar year after 2001, the maximum number increased by 5. However, no accumulation occurred from Jan. 1, 2003, to Dec. 31, 2005.	Charter schools receive 100% of the per-pupil funding that traditional public schools receive.	

State	Authorizer	Restrictions	Per-Pupil Funding	Other Sources
Iowa	The local school board and state board of ed. must approve a charter school application.	The state board may approve no more than 10 charter school applications. The state board may approve no more than 1 charter school application per school district. However, if the state board received 10 or fewer applications by June 30, 2003, and 2 or more of the applications received by that date were put forward by one school district, the state board might approve any or all of the applications submitted by that district.	A charter school is part of the school district wherein it is located for purposes of state school foundation aid.	None.
Kansas	The local school board and the state board of ed. must approve a charter school application.	No.	Funding is at the discretion of the school district.	
Louisiana	Local school boards and the state board of ed.	42.	Locally approved charter schools receive funding from the local school board based on average daily membership of the charter school. Charter schools approved by the state board of ed. receive funding from the state dept. of ed. The per-pupil allotment for all charter schools is equal to the per-pupil amount received by the school district in which the charter school is located.	The Louisiana Charter School Start-Up Loan Fund, which is created from the state treasury, provides no-interest loans to help both existing and new charter schools with start-up funding as well as the administrative and legal costs associated with operating charter schools.
Maryland	Local school boards. Under certain circumstances, the state board of education may be the chartering authority for a restructured school.	No.	The local school board must provide charter schools with the same amount of local, state, and federal funding that other public schools located in the district receive.	The local board or the state board of ed. may provide charter schools with surplus educational materials, supplies, furniture, and other equipment.

(continued)

Charter School Policies Across the States (*continued*)

State	Authorizer	Restrictions	Per-Pupil Funding	Other Sources
Massachusetts	Commonwealth charter schools are authorized by the local board of education. Horace Mann charter schools are authorized by the local board of ed., the local teachers union, and the state board of ed.	120, of which 48 may be Horace Mann charter schools and 72 may be Commonwealth charter schools. No less than 3 new charter schools per year may be located in a district whose overall student performance is equal to or falls below the statewide average on the statewide assessment in the year before the application. The state board of ed. may approve only one regional charter school application of any Commonwealth charter school in a school district in which the overall student performance on the statewide assessment is in the top 10% in the year before the application. The state board may not approve a new commonwealth charter school in any community with a population of less than 30,000 unless it is a regional charter school.	If a student attending a charter school resides in a district with a "positive foundation gap," as defined by state statute, the state must pay a tuition amount to the charter school equal to the average cost per student in the district. If the student resides in a district that does not have a positive foundation gap, as so defined, the state must pay a tuition amount to the charter school equal to the lesser of (1) the average cost per student in the district and (2) the average cost per student in the district where the charter school is located.	The state board of ed. must establish a discretionary grant program that assists in the development of charter schools.

State	Authorizer	Restrictions	Per-Pupil Funding	Other Sources
Michigan	Local school boards, intermediate school boards, community college boards, and state university boards.	State universities may authorize 150 charter schools. Further, the total number of charters issued by any state public university may not exceed 50% of the total number authorized by state universities.	A district must pay to the authorizing body of a charter school located in the district for forwarding to the charter school an amount equal to that local school operating revenue per membership pupil for each resident pupil in membership other than special education students in the charter school.	
Minnesota	Local school boards, intermediate school boards, cooperatives, nonprofit organizations, private colleges, community colleges, and state public universities.	No.	A charter school receives general education revenue as though it were a district, but a charter school may not receive money from levies.	A charter school may apply to the commissioner for building lease aid, amounting to the lesser of 90% of approved cost or $1,200. During its first 2 years of operation, a charter school is eligible for start-up cost aid equal to the greater of $50,000 per charter school or $500 times the charter school's pupil units for that year.
Mississippi	State board of ed.	6: 1 charter school for each congressional district and 1 charter school for the Mississippi Delta region. At least 3 charter schools must be located in school districts with accreditation levels of ≤3 at the time that the school submits its initial petition.	Charter schools may receive the same funding as other public schools.	The state board of ed. may give charter schools preference when distributing grant funds other than state funds for alternative school programs, classroom technology, school improvement programs, mentoring programs, or other grant programs created to improve local school performance.

(continued)

Charter School Policies Across the States (*continued*)

State	Authorizer	Restrictions	Per-Pupil Funding	Other Sources
Missouri	(1) Kansas City and St. Louis school boards; (2) a public 4-year college or university located in, or adjacent to, the Kansas City or St. Louis school districts, with an approved teacher education program that satisfies regional or national accreditation standards; or (3) community colleges located in the Kansas City or St. Louis school district.	Charter schools may open only in Kansas City or St. Louis. Also, a maximum of 5% of operating public schools may convert to charter schools.	A charter school receives 100% of the state aid formula for a school district, reduced by the per-pupil amount the district needs to repay leasehold revenue bonds pursuant to a federal court desegregation decree.	None.
Nevada	Local school board or state dept. of ed.	No.	A charter school receives the same level of per-pupil funding that other schools receive.	A revolving loan fund has been created in the state treasury.
New Hampshire	Local school board and the state board of ed. must approve the charter school application. The state board of ed. also may approve charters through a pilot program.	Through a pilot program, the state board of ed. may grant 20 charter schools between July 1, 2003, and June 30, 2013. Pursuant to this pilot program, no more than 10% of the resident pupils of any grade may transfer to a charter school in any school year without approval from the local school board.	Charter schools that are approved by the local school board and the state board of ed. receive at least 80% of the district's average cost per pupil. Funding for charter schools approved pursuant to the pilot program is calculated by adjusting for the annual percentage rate of inflation based on the U.S. Dept. of Labor's Consumer Price Index.	An appropriation establishes charter schools. Eligible charter schools must match state funds through private contributions in order to receive funding that surpasses the state's average per pupil cost for the grade-level weight of the pupil.
New Jersey	The state commissioner of education.	No.	90% of state-mandated per pupil funding.	
New Mexico	Local school boards.	No more than 15 start-up schools per year. The charter school slots remaining in a year are transferred to the succeeding years up to a maximum of 75 start-ups in any 5-year period.	98% of the school-generated program cost.	A charter school stimulus fund provides financial support for initial start-up costs and the costs associated with renovating or remodeling existing buildings.

State	Authorizer	Restrictions	Per-Pupil Funding	Other Sources
New York	Local school boards and the Chancellor of New York City may approve conversions and start-ups. The State University of New York and the State Board of Regents may approve start-ups. The State Board of Regents is the only entity with the authority to issue a charter.	100 total. 50 start-ups approved by the State University of New York and 50 start-ups approved by the State Board of Regents. Charter school conversions have no limitations.	School districts must pay charter schools 100% of state per-pupil funding. However, the amount a charter school receives may be reduced pursuant to an agreement between the charter school and charter entity.	A charter school stimulus fund has been established. In 2006–2007, charter schools could receive awards of up to $200,000 in facilities costs, and $5,000 for start-up costs.
North Carolina	Local school boards, the University of North Carolina, or the state board of ed. The state board of ed. must give final approval for all charter applications.	100, with a limit of 5 per school district per year.	The state board of ed. must allocate the following to each charter school: (1) the average per-pupil allotment for daily membership from the school district's allotments in which the charter school is located, except for the allotment for children with special needs and children with limited English proficiency; (2) an additional amount for children attending the charter school with special needs; and (3) an additional amount for children with limited English proficiency, derived from a formula used by the state board of ed. Further, the school district in which the child lives must transfer to the charter school an amount equal to the per-pupil local current expense appropriation to the local school district for the fiscal year.	None.

Charter School Policies Across the States *(continued)*

State	Authorizer	Restrictions	Per-Pupil Funding	Other Sources
Ohio	Local school boards, boards of vocational school districts, board of educational service centers, state universities that have been approved by the state dept. of ed., and federal tax-exempt entities. New charter school start-ups are prohibited in "Big Eight" school districts (Cleveland, Cincinnati, Columbus, Akron, Canton, Youngstown, Dayton, Toledo) and Pilot Project Area districts (Lucas County) unless the district is in academic watch or emergency. If an authorizer is not in compliance with its duties, the state dept. of ed. may assume sponsorship.	No.	Charter schools are funded through a statewide base cost formula. Ohio provides funds to charter schools by subtracting the funds from school district allotments and distributing them to charter schools.	A classroom facilities loan guarantee fund has been established. The state legislature has also established a revolving loan fund for charter school start-ups. A start-up may receive more than one loan from this fund, but the cumulative amount is limited to $250,000.
Oklahoma	Local school districts or technology center school districts.	Charter schools may open only in districts with a membership of 5,000 or more and in which all or part of the district is located in a county having more than 500,000 or technology center school districts that serve such school districts. No charter school may be chartered in School District I029 in County No. 14 and School District I027 in County No. 9.	Charter schools receive at least 95% of state-aid formula funding.	The Charter School Incentive Fund provides financial support for start-up costs and costs associated with facilities.

State	Authorizer	Restrictions	Per-Pupil Funding	Other Sources
Oregon	Local school boards or the state board of education.	No.	Charter schools that are sponsored by local boards receive at least 80% of the school districts' general-purpose grant fund per weighted average daily membership (ADMw) for K–8 and at least 95% of the districts' general purpose grant fund for 9–12. Charter schools that are sponsored by the state board of ed. receive at least 90% of the districts' ADMw for K–8 and 95% for 9–12.	None.
Pennsylvania	Local school boards. Two or more boards may form regional charters. Dept. of ed. authorizes cyber-charters.	No.	The district of residence for each student pays the charter school its average school district per-pupil budgeted expenditure of the prior year. Charter schools receive additional funding for special needs students from their districts of residence. Charter schools may request additional funding from the intermediate unit in which the charter school is located for special needs services at the same cost that it charges constituent districts of the intermediate unit.	The secretary of ed. is required by state law to provide grants for start-up funding. State law also provides funding for facilities assistance. The secretary of ed. computes an approved rental charge for leases of buildings approved on or after July 1, 2001. The reimbursement annual rental rate for such leases is the lesser of (1) the annual rental rate to be paid under the lease agreement or (2) the enrollment times $160 for elementary schools, $220 for secondary schools, and $270 for area vocational-technical schools.
Rhode Island	Board of regents, after local school board or state commissioner of elementary and secondary education recommends approval of the charter.	20, serving no more than 4% of the state's school-age population. At least 10 charters are preserved for applications designed to increase educational opportunities for at-risk students.	Charter schools receive 100% of school districts' operating costs, minus 5% of state revenue that is designated for indirect cost support to the pupil's school district. Charter schools and school districts may negotiate costs for services provided by the districts.	School districts may access state aid for reimbursement of school housing costs for charter schools sponsored by school districts. Charter schools that are not sponsored by school districts may apply for 30% reimbursement of housing costs on the basis of need.

(continued)

Charter School Policies Across the States (*continued*)

State	Authorizer	Restrictions	Per-Pupil Funding	Other Sources
South Carolina	Local school boards.	No.	The school district distributes state, county, and school district funds to a charter school in accordance with the state funding formula.	None.
Tennessee	Local school boards.	50, 20 of which must be located within a home-rule municipality of a county with a population greater than 897,400, and 4 of which must be located within a county with a population greater than 897,400.	The local school board must allocate 100% of state and local ed. funds to the charter school on the per-pupil expenditure of the school district. The per-pupil expenditure is based on the prior year average daily membership of the school district.	None.
Texas	State board of education for open-enrollment charter schools and university charter schools. Local school boards for home-rule district charters and campus program charters.	215 open-enrollment charter schools. No limits on home-rule district charters or campus program charters.	Open enrollment charter schools are entitled to foundation aid as if it were a school district without a Tier-I local share and without local revenue. Cost of education adjustments and the district enrichment tax rate are based on statewide averages. Funding for district-approved charters is negotiated and specified in the charter.	None.
Utah	Local school boards or state board of ed.	No.	A conversion charter school that is authorized by a local school board is funded through the school district and in the same manner that it received funding before conversion to charter school status. A charter school that operates in district facilities without paying reasonable rent is funded through the school district in the same manner as other schools in the district. All other schools receive their funding in the same manner as a school district.	The state superintendent of public instruction may distribute grants for both start-up and ongoing costs. A Charter School Revolving Loan Program has also been created. Charter schools may take out only one loan at a time. The maximum amount per loan is $300,000.
Virginia	Local school boards. Two or more school boards may authorize regional charter schools.	10% of the school division's total number of schools or two charter schools, whichever is greater.	Charter schools may negotiate funding with local school districts.	None.

State	Authorizer	Restrictions	Per-Pupil Funding	Other Sources
Wisconsin	Outside of Milwaukee, local school boards and the University of Wisconsin-Parkside. In Milwaukee, Milwaukee City Council, University of Wisconsin-Milwaukee, Milwaukee Area Technical College Board, and the Milwaukee School Board.	None, except that the University of Wisconsin-Parkside may sponsor only one charter school.	Funding for charter schools that are authorized by a city council, city school board, universities, and technical colleges is provided through state statute. Such funding is paid directly to the charter school. Funding for charter schools approved by local boards is determined in the charter.	None.
Wyoming	Local school boards.	No.	100% of foundation program, based on average daily membership of the charter school, minus specific adjustments.	No.

Source: Education Commission of the States. (2003)

TEACHER LABOR MARKETS AND SCHOOL FINANCE POLICY

Introduction

Teacher labor markets are an emerging area of interest in education policy, with significant implications for school finance policy goals of achieving equity and adequacy. Determining where the discussion of teacher labor markets belongs in a school finance policy text is difficult. Yet, we strongly believe that understanding teacher labor markets is critical to developing finance policies that will improve educational equity and adequacy. Because competitive labor market forces influence individuals' career choices, we first introduce teacher labor market behavior in this chapter. We then consider some of the intended and unintended interactions between school finance policy and teacher labor market behavior.

Hanushek and Rivken (2000) identify two major changes in the wider U.S. labor market since the latter half of the 20th century that have significantly influenced teacher labor markets. First, they note the expanded access for women to the broader professional labor market and the dramatic improvements in salary equity by gender in noneducation professions. This two-pronged expansion and equalization to professional careers has increased the competitive pressures such that "schools have found it more difficult to attract and retain highly qualified women, who had formed the bulwark of the teaching profession for many years" (Hanushek & Rivken, 2000, p. 8). Second, the authors note the paradoxical effect that substantial increase in the demand for and wages paid to highly educated workers results in both an increased value placed on education and increased cost in providing education (Hanushek & Rivken, 2000).

Consideration of teacher labor markets is important to school finance for a variety of reasons. Education is a profession highly dependent on human capital for the transfer of knowledge and skills, and teachers are the primary human capital resource that schools use to accomplish their educational mission. It thus follows that teachers consume, by far, the largest share of fiscal resources in the school budget. Another important factor is the recent emergence of school finance policies intended to influence teacher labor markets, including a movement among states and urban school districts to introduce a new version of merit pay policies: *paying teachers for what they know and do*. Finally, school finance policies and other education policies that have financial consequences can also have a significant effect on teacher labor market behavior.

It is both too simplistic and idealistic to assume that individuals choosing to teach are driven entirely by altruism, and that those individuals will continue throughout their careers to strive to be the best possible teachers they can, solely as a function of intrinsic motivation. If this were indeed the case, no relation would exist between school finance policy, teacher career choices, and the distribution of quality teaching. Indeed, the entire school system would be run by talented volunteers! We assume teachers are idealistic, and that they enter teaching with high degrees of intrinsic motivation. Does it therefore follow that monetary rewards cannot be a useful policy lever for improving the productivity of education? We think the research evidence provides some useful opportunities to rethink salaries, benefits, and incentives. In Chapter 14, we discuss emerging evidence regarding teachers' responses to extrinsic motivators while discussing school-based performance rewards.

In addition to the specific extrinsic motivators we discuss in Chapter 14, substantial empirical evidence discussed throughout this chapter indicates that competitive labor market forces, both internal and external to education systems, influence who chooses to teach, where they choose to teach, and whether they will stay in teaching. Competition between education systems and other sectors influences teacher supply; and within education systems, schools, districts, and states compete actively to attract and retain the best teachers. This competition among schools and districts for the best teachers has yielded uneven distributions of high-quality teachers.

The current challenge may be stated as follows:

How can school finance and regulatory policies promote an equitable distribution of high-quality teachers across students of varied needs in varied educational settings?

A more rigorous version of this question consistent with our previous discussions of vertical equity and adequacy might be:

How can school finance and regulatory policies promote a distribution of high-quality teachers such that the children with the least extra-school advantages and the highest needs get the best teachers?

Focusing on increasing supply and redistributing teaching quality raises a number of interesting questions.

How Do We Measure Teacher Quality?

Researchers, policy makers, and administrators can measure teacher quality in at least two dimensions: (a) in terms of *inputs* (teacher attributes) or (b) in terms of *outcomes* (teacher performance). Input-based evaluation of teacher quality is useful for determining the types of individuals who should be encouraged to enter (or at least not discouraged from entering) teaching as a career. The objective of much empirical research discussed in this chapter has been to establish some statistical linkage between teacher attributes and student outcomes.

Attributes commonly considered in research include teacher certification status, education level, academic performance, major area of study, and undergraduate institution quality. Outcome-based evaluations of teachers may be most helpful for identifying those teachers who should be encouraged to continue teaching and may also be a basis for interdistrict competition for teachers. That is, districts may wish to lure teachers who have proven themselves in other districts. Outcome-based evaluation of teachers, however, is controversial because it involves evaluating teachers directly on the academic performance of their students.

How Do We Measure the Equitable Distribution of Quality Teachers?

While we have extensive statistical tools for measuring the equitable distribution of financial resources to schools and districts (discussed in Chapter 5), we have yet to develop tools for measuring the distribution of quality teaching. A primary difficulty in doing so relates back to the first question—how to measure teacher quality. Even if precise, valid measures of teacher quality were available, the difficult question of equitable distribution of teachers would remain. For example, applying the notion of horizontal equity, we might assume that similarly situated students should have access to similar-quality teachers, or perhaps teachers with similar qualifications/attributes (certification status, degree level, etc.). Applying vertical equity standards, we might assume that students with special needs require teachers trained to meet those needs, which in some cases might involve more extensive training, leading to more costly teachers. However, we might extend the notion of vertical equity by including student outcomes and suggesting that students either with greater learning difficulties or who simply are further behind when they enter school require higher-quality teachers to bring their performance back in line (as measured by the outcomes they can produce). That is, an equitable distribution of quality teaching might be one in which higher-quality teachers are disproportionately found in districts with more underperforming students.

How Is School Finance Policy Associated With Equitable Teacher Distribution?

What can or should school finance policies do to influence the level of teaching quality and distribution of quality teachers? How far should those policies go? In this section, we address policies that arguably have had adverse effects on teaching equity and/or adequacy, including large-scale class-size reduction efforts and the general emphasis on teacher quantity over teacher quality. We also raise questions about current finance strategies intended to (a) influence teacher labor markets by improving supply and distribution and (b) provide extrinsic motivators to improve teacher performance. We also present future possibilities for more aggressively redistributing teaching quality.

How Do We Raise the Status of Teaching So That It Is Competitive With the Most Competitive Professions?

Clearly, the size and quality of the teacher labor market itself establish the extent to which it will be relatively more or less difficult to redistribute teachers based on their quality once they are in the labor market. Also, teacher redistribution is likely to increase attrition to the extent that teachers are required to work in schools where they would prefer not to work.

Teacher Wages in Economic Context

The "undersupply" of teachers is a frequently expressed concern of state policy makers in recent years. Yet, while data exist on teacher shortages, especially in some curricular areas, comparisons are rarely made with labor market supply in other sectors. Does the teacher shortage differ from shortages in other sectors, or is the supply of eligible workers simply not keeping up with demand for eligible workers across fields? This type of information is critical to understanding whether education systems are remaining competitive.

Researchers often blame the noncompetitiveness of teacher salaries for the lagging quality of the teacher workforce, and it is a frequent point of debate (Allegretto, Corcoran, & Mishel, 2004; Corcoran, Evans, & Schwab, 2004; Greene & Winters, 2007).

If teachers are simply underpaid, the simple solution is to provide more funding to school districts to raise teacher salaries. Existing data paint another picture. Figure 13.1 presents average annual salary data from 1997 for the freshman undergraduate class of 1992–1993, based on the National Center for Education Statistics (NCES) *Baccalaureate and Beyond* dataset (Henke, Chen, & Geis, 2000). The report finds that, in terms of annual salary, not adjusted for hours or days worked, those who became teachers fare poorly compared to their peers in other professions.

Figure 13.2 presents hourly wage data comparisons for teachers and other workers with a bachelor's degree or higher from 1980 to 2005, using data from

Figure 13.1   Salaries in 1997 of the Freshman Undergraduate Class of 1992–1993

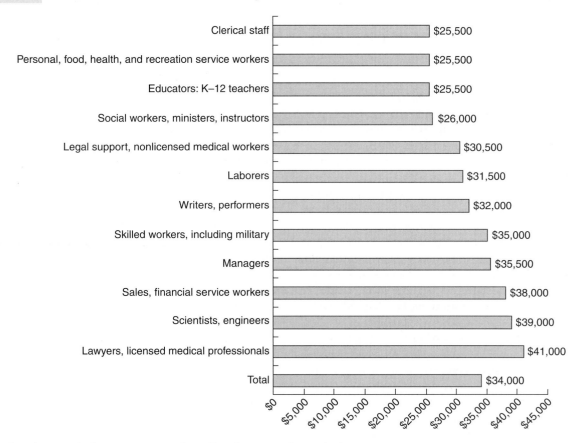

Salary data do not take into account number of weeks or months worked per year.

Data source: U.S. Department of Education, National Center for Education Statistics, *1993 Baccalaureate and Beyond Longitudinal Study.*

Figure 13.2   Elementary and Secondary Teacher Wages and Other Occupations 1980 to 2005[a]

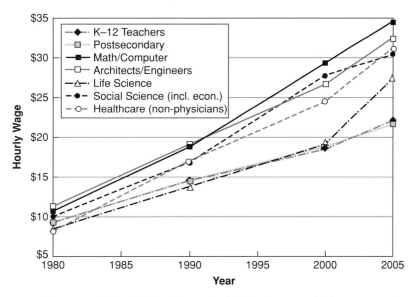

[a]Includes individuals between the ages of 25 and 40 holding a bachelor's degree or higher.

Source: Data from Integrated Public Use Microdata System, Decennial Census 1980, 1990, and 2000, and American Community Survey 2005. Hourly wages determined by dividing income from wages by hours worked per year (usual hours per week times week per year). Ruggles, S., Sobek, M., Alexander, T., Fitch, C. A., Goeken, R., Hall, P. K., King, M., & Ronnander, C. 2004. *Integrated Public Use Microdata Series: Version 3.0* [Machine-readable database]. Minneapolis, MN: Minnesota Population Center [producer and distributor], 2004. Data retrieved June 7, 2007.

the Integrated Public Use Microdata System (IPUMS). Hourly wages are calculated by dividing wage income by the estimated hours worked per year, based on usual hours per week and weeks per year. On an hourly basis, teacher pay appears relatively low and seems to have fallen further behind over time.

Figures 13.1 and 13.2 alone are insufficient to establish whether low salaries in teaching professions are necessarily a primary cause of undersupply (assuming undersupply truly exists). Much debate remains among scholars regarding both the appropriate data sources and methods for comparing teacher and nonteacher wages, and whether teacher wages are competitive with other sectors. Corcoran and Mishel (2007), for example, provide a useful discussion of problems with attempting to compare hourly wages of teachers with other sectors using Bureau of Labor Statistics data.

In addition, the competitiveness of teacher salaries shows significant geographic variation by state. Also teacher salaries in rural areas and small towns are more comparable to nonteacher salaries in those same areas for similarly educated individuals. Teacher salaries tend to lag further behind other professions in major metro-

politan areas. For example, in Washington State, after controlling for age, degree level, occupation, and industry, weeks worked per year and hours per week, researchers found that teachers in the Seattle metropolitan area earned only 78% of their peers' earnings (Conley & Rooney, 2007). Meanwhile, teachers in rural regions of the state earned approximately the same as their peers in other professions.

It is critically important to understand that wages and wage differentials play several roles in education systems. First, increasing the competitiveness of teacher wages with other sectors can influence who chooses to teach. Everything else equal, highly skilled and capable individuals who have many possible career options would be more likely to choose teaching. Second, teacher salary schedules and job security (tenure) may influence whether individuals elect to stay in teaching. This, of course, is a double-edged sword, because wages tied only to experience levels of teachers (or other attributes not necessarily associated with teaching quality) encourage both strong and weak teachers to stay in teaching. Third, teaching itself does not have a career ladder. Advancement usually entails moving into a supervisory or managerial position within education systems. This, too, can be a double-edged sword, in that teachers who are highly effective in the classroom may find that pecuniary rewards are available only by reducing their contact with students. Fourth, school systems in states with highly unequal per-pupil expenditure levels (and therefore highly unequal salary structures, benefits, and working conditions) encourage the best teachers to move from resource-poor districts to wealthy districts. Finally, salary differentials based on type of certification, level of expertise, or demand may serve as incentives to improve performance, seek additional qualifications, or pursue teaching careers in mathematics and science. This is just a short list of the kinds of influences and interactions that might influence individual decisions to participate in teaching. Policy makers have a variety of tools at their disposal for influencing teacher labor markets both locally, regionally, and nationally.

Changes in Teacher Quantities Over Time

Figure 13.3 indicates that from 1986 to 2003, pupil-to-teacher ratios have declined from over 17:1 to under 16:1. As one might expect, as schools have hired more personnel to serve students, spending has increased over time as well. Since the late-1990s, pupil-to-teacher ratios

have leveled off somewhat, and so have increases in per-pupil spending. It is important to recognize, however, that a decline in pupil-to-teacher ratios does not necessarily indicate a decline in average class size. In particular, since the 1980s, schools and districts have hired increasing numbers of specialists and instructional support staff that did not previously exist and who may or may not participate directly in classroom instruction. Patterns vary widely by state, but this trend can be found nationally using longitudinal data from 1986 to 2003 from the National Center for Education Statistics *Common Core of Data, Local Education Agency Universe* and state nonfiscal surveys. For example, between 1994–1995 and 2004–2005, instructional aides increased from 9.6% to 11.7% of total staff.

Measuring Teacher Quality

In our discussion of cost-effectiveness in Chapter 11, we reviewed the class-size research with respect to student performance, which measures teacher quantities in terms of average class sizes or pupil-to-teacher ratios. Indeed, research indicates that teacher quantity, measured by class size, positively influences student outcomes, but is also quite costly (Brewer, Krop, Gill, & Reichardt, 1999; Finn & Achilles, 1999).

Figure 13.3 The Trend Toward More Personnel in Schools

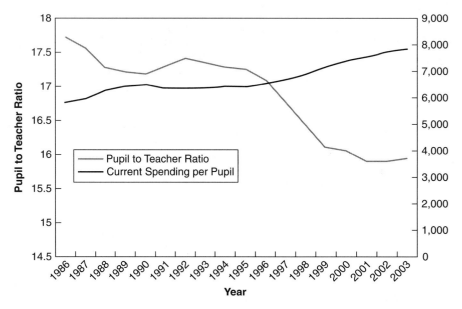

Sources: Data from National Center for Education Statistics. (1986–2004). *Local Education Agency Universe Survey* (enrollments and full-time equivalent teachers) and *Survey of Education Finances* (F-33) of the U.S. Census Bureau and National Center for Education Statistics.

Teacher-to-student ratios answer the question of quantity, but how important is teacher quality, and does it matter whether we measure that quality in terms of inputs or outcomes? In a review of literature for a study on the distribution of teaching quality in New York State, Hamilton Lankford, Susanna Loeb, and Jim Wyckoff note the following:

> Rivkin, Hanushek and Kain (2000) attribute at least seven percent of the total variance in test-score gains to differences in teachers and they argue that this is a lower bound. Sanders and Rivers (1996) find that the difference between attending classes taught by high-quality teachers (highest quartile grouping) and attending classes taught by low-quality teachers (lowest quartile grouping) is huge, approximately 50 percentile points in the distribution of student achievement. They also find residual effects of teachers in later years. That is, having a high quality teacher in grade three increases learning not only in grade three but also in grades four and five. (Lankford et al., 2002, p. 56).

Rivken, Hanushek, and Kain's (2000) research focuses on teacher attributes, while Sanders and Rivers's (1996) research focuses on student outcomes, using the statewide Tennessee Value Added Assessment System (TVAAS) (see, e.g., Wright, Horn, & Sanders, 1997). Both groups find teaching quality to be of significant importance, with the student-outcome-based research (Sanders & Rivers, 1996) revealing substantial differences in student performance over time attributed to exposure to different teachers between grades 2 and 8.

From both research and policy perspectives, understanding which teacher attributes are most associated with improved student performance is important for refining teacher recruitment and preparation policies. Lankford et al. (2002) indicate that *teacher test scores* and *quality of undergraduate institution* (often measured by competitiveness of admissions) are consistently associated with higher student outcomes (Ehrenberg & Brewer, 1994). A substantial number of studies of education production have also considered the role of *teacher degree level* and *content area* of degree. For example, Hedges and Greenwald (1996), in their meta-analysis of production–function studies (see Chapter 11), suggest that teacher education level generally has positive effects on student outcomes. Most often, school- or district-level analyses of education production focus on percentages of teachers with master's degrees as their measure of teacher education level. Research by Monk and King (1994) and by Goldhaber and Brewer (1997) indicates the importance

of *teacher content area* qualifications. That is, secondary teachers with degrees in their content areas (noneducation majors), especially in math and science, appear to yield higher student performance outcomes.

Considerable debate in recent years has taken place regarding the role of teacher certification in education production. Much of this debate was stimulated by an analysis of data from the *National Educational Longitudinal Study of 1988* (NELS) performed by Dominic Brewer and Dan Goldhaber, which indicated no systematic positive effect attributable to teacher certification (Goldhaber & Brewer, 2000). Focusing specifically on high school math and science performance, Goldhaber and Brewer (2000) concluded:

> Contrary to conventional wisdom, mathematics and science students who have teachers with emergency certification credentials do no worse than students whose teachers have standard teaching credentials. (p. 129)

Goldhaber and Brewer's (2000) article elicited a hostile response from Linda Darling-Hammond, Barnett Berry, and Amy Thoreson (2001) of the National Commission on Teacher and America's Future (NCTAF), an organization that strongly advocates more substantial, national teacher certification requirements. Darling-Hammond et al. raise concerns regarding the appropriateness of the NELS sample for the analyses performed by Brewer and Goldhaber, and she points to other, much smaller-scale studies that have found positive effects of certification. Other research by Darling-Hammond (2000) attempts to relate state-certification policies to state-aggregate student outcomes, arguing that states with more aggressive certification regulations produce higher student outcomes than other states. Findings of statistical significance in state-aggregate research, however, are strongly influenced by the type of aggregation bias addressed by Hanushek, Rivkin, and Taylor (1996), discussed in Chapter 11.

In a variation of studies related to certification, Laczko-Kerr and Berliner (2002) studied the performance outcomes of students taught by early career teachers in Arizona with conventional certification and those without conventional certification, including recent college graduates participating in Teach for America (TFA), a program that recruits college graduates with noneducation degrees to teach in high-need areas. With a matched sample of 109 pairs of teachers, the authors found that students of certified teachers outperformed students of undercertified teachers on state assessments.

Laczko-Kerr and Berliner's (2002) study of participants in TFA emphasizes the issue of *undercertified* TFA participants compared to their matched peers. They conclude benefits to conventional teacher certification, at least in the context of Arizona policy. More recently, Decker, Mayer, and Glazerman (2004), in a nationwide randomized controlled study, found that teachers participating in TFA yielded greater gains in student mathematics achievement than their control-group peers. Student reading gains were comparable between control and TFA teachers. TFA participants in the study were more, not less (as in the Arizona study), likely to have held teaching certificates than their novice teaching comparison group but were less likely on average than the entire comparison group. The most notable difference between TFA participants and control group teachers was that 70% of TFA participants had attended highly selective or most-selective undergraduate colleges, compared to only 3.7% of their novice teaching peers (Decker et al., 2004). The finding that these teachers of stronger academic backgrounds yielded better student outcomes is consistent with numerous previous studies.

Some recent analyses, however, suggest that a substantial portion of the advantage gained from teachers with stronger academic backgrounds is offset by the higher turnover rate of these teachers and the necessity to continuously replace them with less-experienced teachers. For example, Boyd, Grossman, and Lankford (2005) show an 85% attrition rate for TFA teachers in New York City by year 4 in contrast with a 37% attrition rate for conventionally certified teachers. In response to these findings, the authors cast doubt on the usefulness of recruiting such teachers, indicating a policy preference for traditionally prepared teachers. We might argue that, rather than advocating the status quo, researchers need to determine how to retain these teachers who show significant positive effects on math performance but who appear far more likely to leave in their first 4 years.

Perhaps the most important issue raised by the teacher-certification debate is that qualification for teacher certification varies among states. Thus, it is difficult to imagine that certification status across states can have uniform, positive effects on student performance without understanding who gets certified and under what conditions. It is also important to understand that the most common undergraduate degree field of currently practicing teachers who are not certified to teach in their primary assignment is elementary education. That is, most *uncertified* teachers are actually those

who've been trained to teach, but lack content preparation for the courses or grade levels that they presently teach (NCES, 2003). Increasingly, states and/or local school districts are focusing attention on National Board Certification (NBC) as a valued teacher attribute. Several states and/or local school districts now provide financial incentives for teachers obtaining NBC. Research from the Consortium for Policy Research in Education at the University of Wisconsin indicates the following:

- *State of North Carolina:* 12% increase to base teaching salary for the life of the certification.
- *State of Ohio:* $2,500 stipend each year for the life of the certification; an additional amount is provided in some districts (e.g., Cincinnati teachers receive an additional $1,000 from the district).
- *Hammond (Indiana) School District:* Provides a salary increase of $2,000 or placement in a doctoral program, whichever is greater.
- *Los Angeles School District:* 15% pay differential for life of the certification for teachers who are NBC certified. (Consortium for Policy Research in Education, 2002)

States and local districts, however, have generally taken this leap of faith with little evidence that NBC is tied to improved teaching performance, or higher-quality teaching. In a recent policy brief, the National Board for Professional Teaching Standards (NBPTS) attempted to validate the importance of NBC by suggesting that NBC teachers surveyed indicated that their students were more engaged and performing better. A separate NBPTS study observed the practices of a sample of 31 teachers who had completed NBC and compared those practices to 34 teachers who tried but failed. In a blind review, qualitative observations favored the teaching styles and practices and student products of teachers who had received NBC. This sample, however, is very small, relative to the 4,808 teachers who had already been awarded NBC and 9,353 in the pipeline as of October of 2000 (Blair, 2000).

A separate unpublished analysis used student data from the TVAAS to compare the performance of 16 NBC teachers in Tennessee to statewide value-added benchmarks. The study found that "The 16 NBPTS certified teachers for whom TVAAS data is available cannot be considered exceptionally effective in terms of their ability to bring about student achievement" (Stone, 2002). The obvious major shortcoming of this study is the very small number of teachers involved. An independent panel of reviewers discounted many of the study's findings primarily on the basis of the limited number of participants and insufficient descriptive information on participants (Zehr, 2002; see also Stone, 2002). More recently, a study in North Carolina suggests that more highly skilled teachers may be more likely to obtain NBC, but it did not necessarily conclude specific benefits of NBC itself (Goldhaber & Anthony, 2004). In other words, well-educated, highly motivated, and competitive students select themselves into NBC, but as yet we have no independent data on whether NBC itself adds value in terms of student outcomes above that which teachers of comparable motivation and ability would accomplish through the usual routes to certification.

The Consortium for Policy Research in Education (CPRE) at the University of Wisconsin is among the many organizations that would appear to endorse the inclusion of NBC as a basis for awarding fiscal incentives. Under the direction of Carolyn Kelley, a researcher with the Teacher Compensation Project and UW-Madison faculty member, the Project presently is conducting a large-scale survey of teachers who went through the certification process in 1999–2000. If policies providing NBC-based incentives continue to proliferate, a body of research on the costs and effects of NBC will no doubt emerge.

One particularly promising area of research focuses on evaluating teachers in terms of their students' value-added outcomes (Wright et al., 1997). As noted by Lankford et al. (2002), a collection of studies based on the TVAAS reveals substantial student performance differences among teachers. These studies do not, however, seek correlational evidence between teacher attributes and their students' performance. That is, while TVAAS has been used to identify high and low performers, researchers using TVAAS have not yet attempted to identify the *attributes* of high-performing teachers. In the TVAAS study, high-performing teachers were identified based on teacher evaluations.

Research on the TVAAS indicates that students with the highest-performing quintile of teachers achieve substantially greater annual achievement gains than students with the lowest performing quintile of teachers and that positive effects are greater for lower-achieving students (Sanders & Rivers, 1996). Presumably, if a teacher-evaluation system based on student outcomes were formalized, teachers could use their student outcome ratings as leverage for pursuing more desirable teaching positions, and schools and districts could respond by providing financial incentives to attract or retain high value-added teachers.

Teacher Supply

In this section, we briefly discuss the evidence on the individuals who enter teaching as a profession and alternative arguments regarding ways to change the flow of the teacher pipeline. Table 13.1 presents findings from the NCES report *Progress Through the Teacher Pipeline*, which followed the undergraduate class of 1992–1993 (Henke et al., 2000). Table 13.1 presents standardized test scores (SAT) of the group based on their career choices by 1997. While the NCES report discusses teacher demographics and other characteristics, we limit

Table 13.1 Characteristics of College Graduates Entering Teaching and Not Entering Teaching

Characteristics	Scores Available	Average of Those With Available Scores		
		Verbal	Math	Composite
Total	44.7	545	544	1,089
Status in teacher pipeline, 1997				
Pipeline-eligible, but did not enter pipeline	46.4	549	551	1,100
Considered teaching or applied to teach	44.3	541	538	1,078
Taught but not prepared	55.9	566	554	1,120
Prepared but had not taught	37.6	534	526	1,061
Prepared and had taught	37.9	522	513	1,035

Source: Reprinted from *Progress Through the Teacher Pipeline: 1992–93 College Graduates and Elementary/Secondary School Teaching as of 1997.* NCES 2000-152. Office of Educational Research and Improvement, National Center for Education Statistics. Washington, DC: U.S. Department of Education. Retrieved from http://nces.ed.gov/dasolv2/tables/index.asp#pse_students

our discussion to teachers' prior test scores in this section, because those scores are the only attribute addressed in the report that the researchers assumed (based on empirical research) to be associated with student outcomes.

The striking and bothersome finding in Table 13.1 is that individuals who were both prepared to teach and pursued a teaching career had by far the lowest verbal and math scores, even lower than those who taught without teacher preparation and lower than those who prepared to teach but chose not to teach. These data confirm the findings of numerous previous reports that indicate that America's best and brightest tend not to pursue teaching as a career. Several differing views explain this finding. One argument is that teaching lacks professional status and that *professionalization*, coupled with commensurate increases in salary, might shift career choice patterns of highly capable undergraduates. The counter argument is that current educator certification standards serve as a barrier to more highly able candidates entering teaching.

Who Stays, and Who Leaves?

Focusing on college entrance exam (CEE) scores, Table 13.2 compares those who stay in teaching with those who leave teaching in New York. Again, somewhat disheartening is the fact that teachers performing least well on CEEs are most likely to stay in teaching, and teachers performing best on CEEs are least likely to stay in education. However, one factor not revealed by the NCES *Progress Through the Teacher Pipeline* (Henke et al., 2000) report is whether individuals with higher CEE scores are more likely to switch careers in general (within or outside of teaching).

Similar to the NCES *Teacher Pipeline* report, Lankford et al. (2002) observe that less-capable individuals are more likely to stay in teaching:

Those who leave teaching in New York public schools altogether are somewhat less likely to have failed the certification exams, 60% more likely to have received their BA from a most or highly competitive college, and somewhat less likely to have graduated from the least competitive college. (p. 50)

Jennifer Imazeki (2001) explored factors associated with teachers' leaving teaching altogether and teachers' moving among districts. She notes that the decision to leave teaching is distinct from the decision to switch districts and finds that younger teachers are much more likely to leave. She also finds the greatest problems of attrition occur in urban and rural districts, but for different reasons; urban districts lose teachers as a result of working conditions, and rural districts lose teachers as a result of low pay. She estimates that reducing attrition in urban and rural districts "to the same levels as in an average district would require wage increases from fifteen to thirty percent" (Imazeki, 2001, p. 30). Similarly, Loeb, Wyckoff, and Lankford (2004) find that for a teacher to take a job in a school with 1 standard deviation more minority students (30% more in the sample studied) would require a compensating differential of nearly $11,000, against an average starting wage in their sample of approximately $32,000.

Factors Influencing Entry Into the Profession

In general, empirical research in economics supports the contention that higher salaries influence the quality of teaching and ultimately, student outcomes. For example:

1. Murnane and Olson (1989) find that salaries affect the decision to enter teaching and the duration of the teaching career.
2. Figlio (1997, 2002) and Ferguson (1991) find that higher salaries are associated with better-qualified teachers.

Table 13.2   Who Stays and Who Leaves Teaching in New York State

Quartile on College Entrance Examination	Stayers	Leavers
Top quartile	68%	32%
Middle half	79%	21%
Bottom quartile	84%	16%

Source: Data from *Progress Through the Teacher Pipeline: 1992–93 College Graduates and Elementary/Secondary School Teaching as of 1997* (p. ix). NCES 2000-152. Office of Educational Research and Improvement, National Center for Education Statistics. Washington, DC: U.S. Department of Education.

3. Loeb and Page (1998, 2000) find that raising teacher wages by 10% reduces high school dropout rates by between 3% and 6% and increases college enrollment rates by 2%.

Policies may also inhibit entry of high-quality teaching candidates into the profession. Both Imazeki (2001) and Figlio and Reuben (2001) find that state-imposed limitations on local taxation may have unintended consequences on teaching quality, in terms of both overall level of quality and distribution. Figlio and Reuben (2001) find,

> The average relative test scores of education majors in tax limit states declined by ten percent as compared to the relative test scores of education majors in states that did not pass limits. This relationship is strengthened if we control for school finance equalization reforms or examine tax limits passed in two different periods. (p. 49)

Imazeki (2001), in a study of Wisconsin teachers, finds that statewide limits on local tax increases prohibit Milwaukee public schools from paying competitive wages and attracting quality teachers.

Teacher Sorting Within the Profession

The sorting of individuals into and out of education systems has significant implications for the adequacy of teaching in our public schools. The sorting of teachers within our public education systems raises equity questions. In the beginning of this section, we addressed only the potential role of teacher salaries for attracting

individuals into teaching, or recruiting teachers from one district to another. Yet, substantial and increasing empirical evidence shows that a variety of factors in addition to salary influence career choices within education. Hanushek, Kain, and Rivkin (2001), in a study of teacher mobility within and between Texas school districts note:

> The results indicate that teacher mobility is much more strongly related to characteristics of the students, particularly race and achievement, than to salary, although salary exerts a modest impact once compensating differentials are taken into account. (p. 1)

Table 13.3 presents a snapshot of Lankford and co-workers' (2002) findings on teacher mobility within and between school districts in New York State between 1993 and 1998. Table 13.3 presents the characteristics of the sending and receiving schools and reports whether differences in characteristics of sending and receiving schools are statistically significant.

Table 13.3 shows clear patterns of "upward mobility," especially for teachers moving between districts. Teachers who changed jobs between 1993 and 1998 within New York State public education tended to move to districts with fewer low-income students, fewer students with limited English language proficiency (LEP), fewer minority students, smaller class sizes, and higher salaries. For within-district moves, similar patterns exist, but only the difference in number of low-income students is statistically (though marginally) significant.

The equity consequences of these mobility findings depend largely on who moves. If both high- and low-quality teachers can make between-district changes, then

Table 13.3   Attributes of Sending and Receiving Schools for 1993 Teachers in New York State Who Transferred by 1998

		Proportion Poor	Proportion With Limited English Proficiency	Proportion Nonwhite	Class Size	Salary Schedule	Actual Salary
Within district	Sending school	0.549	0.11	0.639	24		
	Receiving school	0.506	0.108	0.621	24.2		
	Difference	**−0.043***	**−0.002**	**−0.018**	**0.2**		
Between district	Sending school	0.381	0.062	0.404	23.5	$33,237	$31,685
	Receiving school	0.192	0.034	0.231	21.7	$34,535	$36,482
	Difference	**−0.189***	**−0.028****	**−0.173***	**−1.8****	**$1,298***	**$4,798***

*p < .10. **p < .05. ***p < .01.
Source: Adapted from Lankford, Loeb, and Wyckoff (2002, Table 10, p. 51)

sorting will not necessarily have adverse effects on teaching quality for low-income students. Lankford et al. (2002) find, however, that:

> New York State teachers who began their careers in 1993 and transfer to a different district or quit teaching have stronger qualifications than those who remain in the same district. Teachers transferring to a different district are half as likely to have failed either the NTE General Knowledge or NYSTCE Liberal Arts and Science certification exam. They are 35% more likely to have received their BA from a highly or most competitive college and they are about half as likely to have received their BA from the least competitive colleges. (p. 50)

Given this finding, the implication is that, over time, districts serving more minority, low-income, and (LEP) students lose their more qualified teachers to districts serving fewer minority and low-income students. The authors go on to display the resultant disparities in teacher quality (as measured by attributes) across district types.

Lankford et al. (2002) (using data on New York schools), like Hanushek et al. (2001) (using data on Texas schools), find student population characteristics to exert relatively strong influence on teacher sorting. Loeb (2000) and Boyd, Loeb, Lankford, and Wyckoff (2003), however, attribute some of the insensitivity of teacher mobility to wages to the present lack of sufficient compensating differentials needed to recruit highly capable individuals into teaching to begin with, and further, to encourage high-quality teachers to take jobs in low-performing, "difficult" schools. That is, significant "combat pay" might be required to offset adverse working conditions. Loeb (2000) concludes:

> Targeted salary increases and/or targeted improvements in working conditions are needed to draw high-quality teachers to low-performing schools and to alleviate the inequities we see in the quality of the teacher force across the state (NY) and across the country. (p. 1)

As mentioned previously, Imazeki (2001) identifies compensating differentials ranging from 15% to 30% to retain teachers in poor urban districts compared with average districts (in Wisconsin), and Loeb and colleagues estimate compensating differentials near and exceeding 30% to draw teachers into poor urban schools (based on New York State data).

In summary, teacher labor market research suggests that salary adjustment can be a useful tool for improving equity in the distribution of quality teachers. That is, paying substantially higher salaries in poor urban districts competing for teachers with neighboring wealthy suburban districts may help to balance teaching quality disparities. Further, using fiscal resources to improve working conditions that influence teacher sorting may also help.

State-by-State Comparisons of Supply and Distribution

Tables 13.4 through 13.6 provide some state-by-state comparisons of K–12 teachers' academic preparation. A common thread across most recent economic analyses of teaching quality is the interest in teachers who themselves scored well on tests of academic achievement or teachers who attended more selective undergraduate colleges. One might then characterize the overall quality of a state's teacher pool by the test scores or undergraduate institutions of teachers in a state. Further, one might characterize equity in the distribution of teachers by the differences in test scores or differences in undergraduate preparation of teachers in high- and low-poverty, urban and rural, or high- and low-resource districts.

Table 13.4 provides a summary, by state, of the percentages of teachers who attended different categories of colleges, by selectivity as rated in *Barron's Guide to the Most Competitive Colleges* (2003).[1] Data are from the National Center for Education Statistics, *Schools and Staffing Survey of 1999–2000* (NCES, 2003; analysis by authors). Note that the percentage of teachers attending the highest two categories of selectivity—highly or most selective—is predominantly a function of within-state supply of such institutions (Baker & Dickerson, 2006).

---

[1]Factors that Barron's used in determining the category for each college included the following: median entrance exam scores for the 2001–2002 freshman class (the SAT 1 score used was derived by averaging the median verbal reasoning and the median mathematics reasoning scores; the ACT score used was the median composite score); percentages of 2001–2002 freshmen scoring 500 and above and 600 and above on both the verbal reasoning and mathematics reasoning sections of the SAT I; percentages of 2001–2002 freshmen scoring 21 and above and 27 and above on the ACT; percentage of 2001–2002 freshmen who ranked in the upper fifth and upper two-fifths of their high school graduating classes; minimum class rank and grade-point average required for admission (if any); and percentage of applicants to the 2001–2002 freshman class who were accepted.

Table 13.4 Percentages of Public School Teachers Receiving Their Bachelors' Degrees From Selective and Less-Selective Undergraduate Institutions by State

State	Percentage of Teachers From Top 2 vs. Bottom 4 Categories in Barrons'			Percentage of Teachers in Top 3 vs. Bottom 3 Categories in Barrons'		
	Less Selective (0 to 3)	Highly or Most Selective (4 & 5)	Rank	Less Selective (0 to 3)	More Selective (3 to 5)	Rank
Alabama	98.6%	1.4%	41	92.0%	8.0%	47
Alaska	93.2%	6.8%	21	75.5%	24.6%	21
Arizona	96.5%	3.5%	33	87.9%	12.1%	41
Arkansas	98.6%	1.4%	40	81.6%	18.4%	27
California	87.1%	12.9%	5	73.1%	26.9%	13
Colorado	91.9%	8.1%	18	73.1%	26.9%	20
Connecticut	87.3%	12.8%	6	67.6%	32.4%	24
Delaware	96.7%	3.3%	35	47.8%	52.2%	2
District of Columbia	94.7%	5.3%	27	88.2%	11.8%	43
Florida	81.5%	18.6%	2	61.0%	39.0%	9
Georgia	95.4%	4.6%	29	75.3%	24.8%	26
Hawaii	93.3%	6.7%	22	31.5%	68.5%	1
Idaho	91.1%	8.9%	16	82.9%	17.1%	34
Illinois	90.5%	9.5%	14	76.7%	23.4%	33
Indiana	98.4%	1.6%	39	78.5%	21.5%	30
Iowa	99.2%	0.8%	49	72.7%	27.3%	15
Kansas	98.6%	1.4%	42	86.0%	14.0%	36
Kentucky	99.2%	0.8%	48	90.4%	9.6%	46
Louisiana	98.2%	1.8%	38	82.3%	17.8%	35
Maine	92.5%	7.5%	19	86.2%	13.8%	37
Maryland	90.1%	9.9%	13	54.8%	45.2%	4
Massachusetts	82.6%	17.4%	3	65.4%	34.6%	5
Michigan	96.2%	3.8%	32	78.2%	21.8%	22
Minnesota	93.3%	6.7%	23	66.9%	33.1%	8
Mississippi	99.1%	0.9%	46	96.5%	3.5%	50
Missouri	90.9%	9.1%	15	73.5%	26.5%	12
Montana	97.9%	2.1%	36	93.6%	6.4%	48
Nebraska	99.1%	1.0%	45	91.2%	8.8%	45
Nevada	92.5%	7.5%	20	67.2%	32.8%	11
New Hampshire	89.4%	10.6%	12	78.6%	21.4%	32
New Jersey	87.9%	12.1%	7	66.4%	33.6%	10
New Mexico	95.1%	4.9%	28	88.2%	11.8%	42
New York	88.0%	12.0%	8	72.0%	28.0%	17
North Carolina	88.1%	11.9%	9	82.6%	17.4%	38
North Dakota	99.9%	0.1%	51	75.7%	24.3%	29
Ohio	98.7%	1.3%	43	73.9%	26.1%	25
Oklahoma	96.6%	3.4%	34	73.2%	26.9%	18
Oregon	95.6%	4.4%	30	69.4%	30.7%	6
Pennsylvania	93.9%	6.1%	26	69.9%	30.1%	14
Rhode Island	88.7%	11.3%	10	85.0%	15.0%	40
South Carolina	91.5%	8.5%	17	71.7%	28.3%	16
South Dakota	99.1%	0.9%	47	95.7%	4.3%	49
Tennessee	98.8%	1.2%	44	87.7%	12.3%	39
Texas	93.4%	6.6%	25	76.9%	23.1%	31
Utah	69.3%	30.7%	1	66.2%	33.8%	7
Vermont	89.0%	11.0%	11	75.9%	24.1%	28
Virginia	84.3%	15.7%	4	73.0%	27.0%	23
Washington	93.4%	6.6%	24	57.5%	42.5%	3
West Virginia	99.3%	0.7%	50	97.3%	2.7%	51
Wisconsin	98.0%	2.0%	37	71.9%	28.1%	19
Wyoming	96.2%	3.8%	31	90.8%	9.2%	44

Note. 0 = noncompetitive, 1 = less competitive, 2 = competitive, 3 = very competitive, 4 = highly competitive, 5 = most competitive.
Source: Data from Tourkin, S. C., et al. (2004). *1999–2000 Schools and staffing survey (SASS) data file user's manual* (NCES 2004–303). Washington, DC: U.S. Department of Education, National Center for Education Statistics. Ongoing research of Bruce D. Baker and Jill Dickerson on the distribution of teachers by specific quality indicators in public, private and charter schools, under different state policy and supply contexts. Data used for preparing this table may be accessed by special restricted use license from the National Center for Education Statistics and may not be furnished directly by the authors. Undergraduate institution selectivity drawn from *Barrons' Guide to the Most Competitive Colleges, 2003.*

For example, Massachusetts, a state with many highly selective undergraduate colleges, ranks third in the percentage of teachers who attended such institutions. Interestingly, Utah ranks first because its state university falls into this category, and few other institutions in the state prepare teachers. Our rating criteria reveal unfortunately little about the selectivity or rigor of Utah's teacher-preparation program and students relative to those choosing other majors in the same university. Low-ranking states include states with few or no selective institutions, and/or states with large nonselective teachers' colleges.

Table 13.5 provides the mean percentage poverty of schools in which teachers from more- and less-selective colleges taught. For example, the mean percentage poverty of Alabama schools in which teachers from less-selective colleges taught was 21.7%. The mean percentage poverty in schools in which teachers from highly or most selective colleges taught was 16.4%, or 5.2% lower. Alabama ranked last in this regard, having the largest such gap among states.

Table 13.6 provides the average current expenditures per pupil for districts in which teachers from more- and less-selective colleges taught. In most states, average spending was higher in the districts of teachers from more selective undergraduate colleges. In general, teachers from stronger academic backgrounds teach in schools with fewer children in poverty and more resources.

Differences Between Public, Private, and Public Charter School Teachers

In this section, we discuss briefly some of the statistical differences in the attributes of teachers of different types of schooling organizations. Figure 13.4 shows that in 1999, 92% of all teachers in the United States taught in conventional public schools or school districts. The next largest group, 5%, taught in church-affiliated Catholic schools (diocese dependent), and 1% each in private independent, other religious, and public charter schools.

Figure 13.5 reveals striking differences in the percentages of teachers holding certification in their primary fields of teaching. In public schools, 95% were certified, while in public charter schools and Catholic schools, only 74% to 76% were certified. Most different, were private independent schools, with only 40%

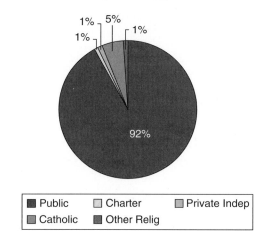

Figure 13.4   Distribution of K–12 Teachers in the United States by School Type

Source: Data from *NCES Schools and Staffing Survey 1999–2000.* Retrieved from http://www.nces.ed.gov/surveys/sass/

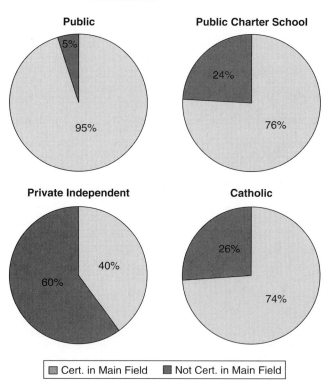

Figure 13.5   Distribution of Fully Certified and Uncertified Teachers

Source: Data from *NCES Schools and Staffing Survey 1999–2000.* Retrieved from http://www.nces.ed.gov/surveys/sass/

Table 13.5 Mean Percentage Poverty of Schools in Which Teachers From Less- and More-Selective Undergraduate Institutions Teach, by State

State	Differences in District-Level Poverty Rates by Teacher Background				Differences in School-Level Poverty Rates by Teacher Background			
	Less Selective (0 to 3)	More Selective (3 to 5)	Poverty Gap (District)	Rank	Less Selective (0 to 3)	More Selective (3 to 5)	Poverty Gap (School)	Rank
Alabama	21.7%	16.4%	5.2%	49	47%	38%	9.1%	50
Alaska	13.5%	14.1%	−0.6%	6	39%	38%	0.9%	10
Arizona	19.2%	19.9%	−0.7%	5	47%	42%	5.1%	36
Arkansas	22.2%	18.7%	3.5%	45	48%	43%	4.5%	32
California	18.8%	18.4%	0.4%	17	47%	43%	4.5%	31
Colorado	13.5%	10.6%	2.9%	41	29%	18%	11.3%	51
Connecticut	11.1%	9.6%	1.5%	31	24%	22%	2.3%	18
Delaware	12.9%	11.4%	1.4%	30	32%	30%	2.4%	23
District of Columbia					70%	70%	−0.1%	8
Florida	17.5%	18.4%	−1.0%	3	43%	43%	0.5%	9
Georgia	21.8%	20.3%	1.6%	32	46%	39%	6.6%	43
Hawaii					37%	39%	−2.0%	6
Idaho	14.0%	13.4%	0.6%	19	36%	35%	1.6%	14
Illinois	12.8%	13.0%	−0.1%	10	31%	34%	−3.6%	4
Indiana	11.9%	11.6%	0.2%	14	25%	24%	1.0%	11
Iowa	12.1%	10.6%	1.6%	33	28%	26%	2.3%	19
Kansas	14.5%	12.6%	1.9%	36	33%	28%	5.6%	38
Kentucky	20.2%	18.5%	1.6%	34	43%	42%	1.2%	12
Louisiana	21.0%	20.8%	0.2%	12	57%	55%	2.4%	22
Maine	12.4%	11.5%	0.9%	22	32%	27%	4.6%	33
Maryland	11.1%	12.4%	−1.3%	2	27%	33%	−5.6%	2
Massachusetts	13.8%	10.4%	3.4%	44	26%	19%	7.8%	46
Michigan	14.6%	15.1%	−0.5%	8	29%	25%	3.5%	29
Minnesota	11.3%	8.6%	2.7%	39	29%	26%	3.4%	28
Mississippi	21.5%	20.6%	0.9%	23	61%	55%	6.3%	42
Missouri	14.5%	13.4%	1.1%	27	34%	34%	−0.2%	7
Montana	18.0%	18.0%	0.0%	11	36%	33%	3.4%	27
Nebraska	10.0%	8.6%	1.3%	28	32%	30%	2.6%	24
Nevada	12.5%	12.2%	0.4%	16	34%	41%	−6.5%	1
New Hampshire	8.0%	7.1%	1.0%	25	17%	12%	4.9%	34
New Jersey	9.6%	12.1%	−2.5%	1	24%	21%	3.2%	26
New Mexico	26.3%	23.8%	2.5%	38	66%	57%	8.3%	49
New York	19.2%	15.4%	3.7%	47	37%	31%	5.2%	37
North Carolina	16.3%	15.9%	0.4%	15	41%	33%	7.7%	45
North Dakota	15.6%	14.8%	0.8%	21	34%	32%	1.8%	15
Ohio	12.2%	11.1%	1.0%	26	27%	30%	−2.3%	5
Oklahoma	22.0%	19.0%	3.0%	43	50%	42%	7.8%	47
Oregon	13.2%	12.7%	0.4%	18	37%	34%	2.4%	21
Pennsylvania	13.4%	9.8%	3.7%	46	28%	22%	6.2%	41
Rhode Island	15.0%	15.9%	−0.9%	4	30%	28%	2.0%	16
South Carolina	19.7%	18.7%	0.9%	24	43%	35%	8.3%	48
South Dakota	15.2%	15.7%	−0.5%	7	40%	44%	−4.2%	3
Tennessee	16.0%	14.7%	1.3%	29	44%	42%	2.3%	20
Texas	20.2%	16.4%	3.8%	48	46%	40%	5.6%	39
Utah	10.4%	9.6%	0.7%	20	31%	27%	3.6%	30
Vermont	9.7%	10.1%	−0.4%	9	25%	22%	3.0%	25
Virginia	15.5%	12.7%	2.8%	40	34%	29%	4.9%	35
Washington	14.2%	11.9%	2.3%	37	36%	29%	6.9%	44
West Virginia	21.0%	18.1%	2.9%	42	47%	45%	2.3%	17
Wisconsin	9.9%	9.7%	0.2%	13	21%	20%	1.5%	13
Wyoming	12.2%	10.4%	1.8%	35	31%	25%	5.9%	40

Source: Data from Tourkin, S. C., et al. (2004). *1999–2000 Schools and staffing survey (SASS) data file user's manual* (NCES 2004–303). Washington, DC: U.S. Department of Education, National Center for Education Statistics. Ongoing research of Bruce D. Baker and Jill Dickerson on the distribution of teachers by specific quality indicators in public, private and charter schools, under different state policy and supply contexts. Data used for preparing this table may be accessed by special restricted use license from the National Center for Education Statistics and may not be furnished directly by the authors. Undergraduate institution selectivity drawn from *Barrons' Guide to the Most Competitive Colleges, 2003.*

Table 13.6 Comparison of Current Expenditures per Pupil (1997) and Distribution of Teachers by Undergraduate Selectivity (Districts With School-Aged Population Exceeding 2,000)

State	Less Selective (0 to 3)	More Selective (3 to 5)	Expenditure Gap	Rank
Pennsylvania	$6,294	$6,892	9%	51
Virginia	$5,574	$5,983	7%	50
South Dakota	$4,750	$5,088	7%	49
Montana	$5,028	$5,306	6%	48
Missouri	$5,165	$5,445	5%	47
Georgia	$5,274	$5,538	5%	46
Tennessee	$4,663	$4,889	5%	45
Illinois	$5,576	$5,842	5%	44
North Carolina	$4,949	$5,161	4%	43
New York	$8,658	$9,027	4%	42
New Mexico	$4,478	$4,663	4%	41
Ohio	$5,408	$5,630	4%	40
Kansas	$5,216	$5,418	4%	39
Nebraska	$5,422	$5,614	4%	38
Massachusetts	$7,015	$7,262	4%	37
Delaware	$7,157	$7,381	3%	36
Louisiana	$4,543	$4,681	3%	35
New Hampshire	$5,739	$5,910	3%	34
Kentucky	$5,454	$5,612	3%	33
Michigan	$6,469	$6,641	3%	32
Oregon	$5,789	$5,894	2%	31
California	$5,426	$5,512	2%	30
South Carolina	$5,067	$5,142	1%	29
Iowa	$5,390	$5,464	1%	28
Maryland	$6,374	$6,460	1%	27
Idaho	$4,286	$4,337	1%	26
Wisconsin	$6,623	$6,691	1%	25
Alabama	$4,655	$4,698	1%	24
Florida	$5,144	$5,185	1%	23
Connecticut	$8,282	$8,347	1%	22
Colorado	$5,102	$5,132	1%	21
Washington	$5,641	$5,658	0%	20
District of Columbia	$8,048	$8,048	0%	18
Hawaii	$5,774	$5,774	0%	19
Arizona	$4,379	$4,376	0%	17
Rhode Island	$7,478	$7,450	0%	16
Wyoming	$5,686	$5,656	−1%	15
Indiana	$5,993	$5,959	−1%	14
Maine	$6,206	$6,169	−1%	13
Texas	$4,957	$4,927	−1%	12
Oklahoma	$4,502	$4,428	−2%	11
Mississippi	$4,074	$3,998	−2%	10
Nevada	$5,080	$4,979	−2%	9
Arkansas	$4,688	$4,589	−2%	8
Utah	$3,901	$3,813	−2%	7
Alaska	$7,563	$7,376	−2%	6
Vermont	$7,366	$7,160	−3%	5
Minnesota	$5,732	$5,568	−3%	4
North Dakota	$4,358	$4,167	−4%	3
West Virginia	$6,043	$5,733	−5%	2
New Jersey	$9,607	$9,059	−6%	1

Source: Data from Tourkin, S. C., et al. (2004). *1999–2000 Schools and staffing survey (SASS) data file user's manual* (NCES 2004–303). Washington, DC: U.S. Department of Education, National Center for Education Statistics. Ongoing research of Bruce D. Baker and Jill Dickerson on the distribution of teachers by specific quality indicators in public, private and charter schools, under different state policy and supply contexts. Data used for preparing this table may be accessed by special restricted use license from the National Center for Education Statistics and may not be furnished directly by the authors. Undergraduate institution selectivity drawn from *Barrons' Guide to the Most Competitive Colleges, 2003.*

holding teaching certificates. This category includes most of the nations' most elite private academies. This finding provides some support for the deregulationist arguments that certification, if worthwhile, even if not required (as in most independent schools), would be favored by schools seeking the best teachers. In fact, it is quite surprising that such a large share of teachers in independent schools do hold teaching certificates without regulatory compulsion. This finding may be partially a function of state accreditation requirements imposed on private schools.

Following the previous information in this chapter regarding teacher attributes associated with student outcomes, Figure 13.6 summarizes the selectivity of the undergraduate institutions of teachers in each type of school. It is generally assumed that graduates of the most selective colleges are simply uninterested in en-

tering teaching either as a temporary or permanent profession. Data on public school teachers support this assertion, with only 8% of teachers coming from highly or most selective colleges. This number increases to 12% in charter schools. Catholic schools are similar in distribution to public schools. Again, teachers in private independent schools are strikingly different, with 37% having attended highly or most selective colleges.

A number of factors are at play in this difference in distribution of teachers from highly or most selective colleges. Perhaps first and foremost is the likelihood that graduates of private independent schools go on to attend more selective colleges and return to teach in the private independent school sector. More generally, cultural awareness of and interest in independent schools is likely to be higher among graduates of selective colleges. Finally, a notably different feature of the labor market for teachers in private independent schools is that it is national, such that the presence of teachers from selective colleges is much less contingent on the local or within-state presence of selective colleges (Baker & Dickerson, 2006).

Figure 13.7 shows that average teacher salaries are highest among public school teachers and lowest among teachers in private religious schools. This figure, coupled with the previous ones, provides some support for the contention that teachers value nonpecuniary factors in their employment sector choices. However, the experience distribution among certain types of schools also differs, as shown in Figure 13.8.

Figure 13.8 displays the average years of experience of teachers in different types of schools. Not only are teachers in Catholic and other religious schools poorly paid (relatively speaking), but also, they are poorly paid with significant years of experience. Similarly, teachers in private independent schools have average experience exceeding public school teachers but are paid less. Teachers in charter schools are the least experienced, perhaps due partly to the newness of charter schools as well as the potential risks entailed in working in an upstart public academy.

Finally, Figure 13.9 displays the percentage of teachers with master's degrees or higher by school type. Master's degrees are least prevalent among teachers in other religious schools and most prevalent among teachers in public schools and in private independent schools.

Figure 13.6   Selectivity of Undergraduate Institutions

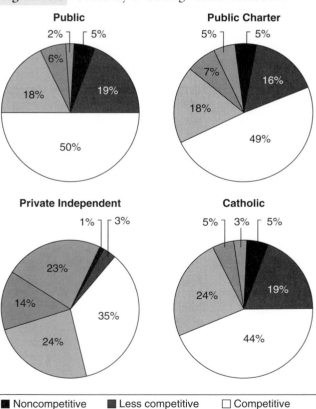

Source: Data from *NCES Schools and Staffing Survey 1999–2000.* Retrieved from http://www.nces.ed.gov/surveys/sass/

Figure 13.7 Average Teacher Salaries

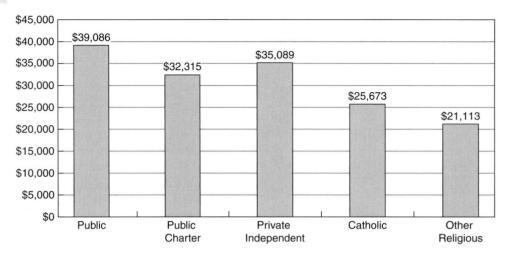

Source: Data from *NCES Schools and Staffing Survey 1999–2000.* Retrieved from http://www.nces.ed.gov/surveys/sass/

Figure 13.8 Average Years of Teacher Experience

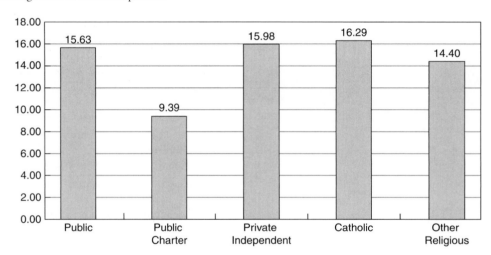

Source: Data from *NCES Schools and Staffing Survey 1999–2000.* Retrieved from http://www.nces.ed.gov/surveys/sass/

Finance Policy and Teacher Labor Markets

Improving the overall level and equitable distribution of teacher quality involves establishing policies to promote the following objectives:

1. Increase the supply of high-quality teachers.
2. Create sufficient incentives for high-quality, highly capable teachers to stay in teaching, while creating disincentives for low-quality teachers to stay.
3. Create incentives for continuous improvement among those who choose to stay.
4. Create sufficient pecuniary and nonpecuniary incentives for high-quality teachers to teach in schools with underperforming students.
5. Avoid those school finance and finance-related policies that have unintended, adverse effects on the level or distribution of teacher quality.

Just as for the previously discussed market-based strategies, policy makers must approach each of these

Figure 13.9   Percentages of Teachers With Master's Degrees or Higher

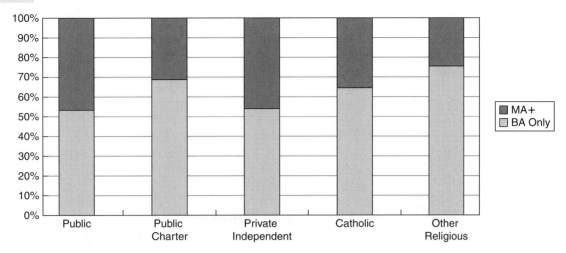

Source: Data from *NCES Schools and Staffing Survey 1999–2000.* Retrieved from http:/www.nces.ed.gov/surveys/sass/

objectives with both financial and regulatory policy tools. In most, if not all cases, we have little compelling evidence regarding the effectiveness of proposed and existing strategies.

As of yet, we do not know the necessary wage levels or compensation structures with respect to external labor markets necessary to attract highly able individuals into teaching. Most recent attention has focused on the regulatory dimension of the recruitment objective, where bitter philosophical differences remain. Economists Ballou and Podgursky (1998b), among others, suggest deregulation, allowing greater mobility into and out of teaching, removing barriers to potential high-quality candidates. Ballou and Podgursky, in particular, suggest that if teaching credentials, including degrees in teacher education and certification, are valuable attributes related to student outcomes, then the market should continue to favor those qualifications.

Ballou and Podgursky (1998a) further argue that teacher certification is a major barrier to entry for high-quality teaching candidates, because teachers in unregulated private schools typically attended more competitive undergraduate institutions, have more extensive background in their content areas, and have little or no formal education training. Ballou and Podgursky's evidence is consistent (in the sense that more competitive undergraduate institutions are more likely to require higher CEE scores) with that of the NCES *Teacher Pipeline* report (Henke et al., 2000) on those who taught but were not prepared, compared with those

who taught and were prepared. Deregulation advocates tend to favor policy strategies that reduce requirements for obtaining teacher certification, typically through alternative route programs. Because this is a school finance policy text, we will not delve more deeply into those policy options at this point. Some recent evidence suggests that less-regulated charter schools are more likely to hire teachers with stronger academic backgrounds than traditional public schools in the same metropolitan area (Baker & Dickerson, 2006). The counter argument remains that education might be made more like medical and legal professions by increased regulation, but little evidence indicates that this strategy would be effective. Specifically pertaining to professional licensure exams, Boyd et al. note:

> Overall, research suggests that requiring certification exams does not result in a higher proportion of "good" teachers' being selected but does reduce overall participation in teacher preparation. (2007, p. 59)

Quite simply, professionalization to the extent that exists in medicine and law has not been tried, and sufficient financial incentives fail to exist for those pursuing teaching careers. Recent research generally indicates that increased barriers to the profession of teaching, especially where those barriers have high costs, tend to reduce rather than improve teaching (Angrist & Guryan, 2003; Reback, 2002). Changing the compensation structure of the profession might mitigate such problems.

In recent years, policy makers have shown increased interest in financial strategies, most often with the primary goal of retaining high-quality teachers, but also with the secondary objective of making teaching a desirable profession for higher quality candidates. State policies that provide financial incentives for groups of teachers whose students perform well, or state performance contracts with schools where teachers receive direct pecuniary incentives may fall into this category in that individuals better prepared to compete may begin to see education as a more desirable profession. Increasingly as well, examples of performance contract arrangements between local boards of education and individual teachers (as represented by their local associations) have been negotiated. Most such examples, as we discuss later in this section, presently focus on teacher input rather than outcome characteristics.

Continuous improvement of "stayers" is important for stayers of all quality levels, but particularly for lower-performing stayers. Ideally, systems should be in place to promote attrition of lower-performing teachers for whom continuous improvement is infeasible. Eric Hanushek has long criticized the lack of built-in incentives for performance enhancement in education. Hanushek (1997) presents the following example:

> Learning how to use a computer can be frustrating and time-consuming in general. Learning how to use one effectively in instruction is more difficult. But there is little help and even less incentive for a teacher to develop a computerized component of instruction because improved student performance is not generally rewarded and the use of computers might even operate to lessen the demand for teachers. Even though much of policy about technology in the classroom is discussed as if the primary shortage is one of hardware, unopened and unused computers in schools around the country suggest that the incentive structure (and related training) of teachers could be much more important. If computers are truly advantageous in learning and if teachers had direct incentives to improve student achievement, we might see more productive use of computer technology than we do now or can expect in the near future. (Hanushek, 1997, p. 305)

One might argue that the school-based performance incentives discussed earlier in this chapter promote continuous improvement of stayers, by getting teams of teachers to work together to improve student performance. Opportunities to pursue individual incentives through school or district performance-based pay plans may also stimulate continuous improvement of stayers but only when policy makers link incentives to direct achievement of improved student outcomes or input characteristics legitimately associated with improved student outcomes (e.g., professional development tied to improved performance).

We have not found any state school-funding models that are aggressively designed to redistributing high-quality teachers to disadvantaged students. One might argue that geographic cost indices (see Chapters 8 and 9) that fully account for harsh working conditions provide some support for poor urban or remote rural districts to attract higher-quality teachers. One might similarly argue that aggressive economies of scale weighting similarly advantage remote rural districts that otherwise might have significant recruitment disadvantages; however, given the higher average costs those districts face for their current labor pool and district operations, we have seen no evidence they have sufficient reserves to leverage teacher quality upward.

District performance contracts with teachers that reward legitimate input characteristics or performance-outcome characteristics may also affect redistribution, depending on which districts choose to establish such contracts and how they balance rewards associated with performance and rewards associated with longevity. If poor urban districts sufficiently reward performance over longevity, they may attract high-quality teachers from surrounding, more-affluent districts that reward longevity over performance. They may also increase the flow of individuals from other professions into public education systems, but only where regulatory barriers are not substantial. Policy makers still lack sufficient knowledge regarding the required "combat pay" differential to attract such teachers into generally less desirable teaching conditions, but certainly, the salary would have to exceed the salary and benefits teachers currently receive in their suburban positions.

Teacher Input- and Process-Based Policies: Paying Teachers for What They Know and Do

An increasingly popular strategy in district performance contracts with teachers is the concept of knowledge- and skill-based pay, or paying teachers for what they know and do. We address this topic with some reservations, because little empirical support demonstrates that the "knowledge and skills" typically addressed in these compensation systems are associated with improved productivity. Nonetheless, knowledge- and skill-based pay systems represent one of the first, politically palatable major departures from historical approaches to teacher compensation.

The approach comes from the work of Allan Odden and Carolyn Kelly (no date) at the Consortium for Policy Research in Education at the University of Wisconsin under the title *The Teacher Compensation Project*. Odden and Kelly suggest that a district-level knowledge- and skill-based pay plan should adhere to the following basic principles:

- Include clear and specific descriptions of the knowledge and skills teachers are to develop, and organize these skills into related sets or levels. Directly relate the skill blocks or standards to the needs of a particular school or district, and provide then in writing with clear performance expectations. The standards could be designed locally or could be based on national standards developed by subject-matter associations.

- Include an objective, sound, and credible assessment system that involves teachers and administrators. The assessment system should include multiple sources of information. In the long term, a state or national teaching standards board could assess expertise in core curriculum and instructional skill blocks, as is done in many other professions.

- Align the knowledge- and skill-based pay plan with other human resources functions, such as evaluation, recruitment, and professional development (Odden & Kelly, no date; see also Odden & Kelly, 1997).

In September of 2000, the Cincinnati, Ohio, teachers union came to agreement with the district on a knowledge- and skill-based pay system. The new system would be designed and implemented by the fall of 2002. The system relied on a combination of teacher-input criteria and teaching process criteria as elicited through peer and supervisor observations. The plan became one of the first to shift salary differentiation dramatically toward knowledge and skills and away from longevity.

The Cincinnati plan established four domains across which teachers would be evaluated and assigned one of five status levels within the district. The four domains included: planning and preparing for student learning, creating an environment for learning, teach-

ing for learning, and professionalism. Each domain then included a series of rubrics, or benchmarks, to guide evaluators. Noticeably absent were any direct measures of student learning. By moving from one career level to another, teachers could gain substantial financial advantage. Teachers declining in career status would have 2 years to improve before salary reduction. Teachers with more than 22 years in the district would have the option to remain on the experience-based contract or participate in the new contract.

Table 13.7 displays the requirements, contractual issues, and salary ranges across the five career stages in Cincinnati. The system does provide the option to release early career teachers who do not surpass novice status, essentially extending the more common probationary period from 3 years to a maximum of 7 years (2 years as apprentice, 5 years as novice) and specifying the requirements of achieving tenured, or career, status.

Minor modifications were proposed for the Cincinnati model for 2002–2003, but ultimately, the union rejected the plan in a May 2002 vote (Odden, 2003).

What Do We Know About Financing Professional Development?

Sadly, we know very little about (a) how much schools currently spend on staff development, or (b) whether those expenditures lead to changes in teaching practices that ultimately have positive effects on student learning. A handful of recent studies have attempted to shed some light on these questions. Killeen, Monk, and Plecki (2002) find that on average, school districts allocate approximately 3% of their budgets to professional development, with very few spending either more than 5% or less than 2% on professional development. The authors also found that urban districts tended to spend more on staff development than other districts, likely due to supply of staff-development opportunities, including higher education institutions.

More thorough case analyses of four states (North Carolina, New York, California, and Washington) reveal significant variation in state efforts to support staff development in the 1990s (Monk, Plecki, & Killeen, 2003). For example, North Carolina, in 1997, established a program of teacher mentoring and recruitment (North Carolina Teacher Fellows Program), to which the state allocated $14.2 million, or $11.40 per pupil, in 2000–2001. In contrast, the state of Washington provided a package of opportunities

Table 13.7   Structure of Cincinnati Knowledge- and Skill-Based Pay System

	Apprentice	Novice	Career	Advanced	Accomplished
Experience	New teachers				
Licensure	Minimum temporary license	Must pass Ohio's teacher licensing test (Praxis 3)			
Rubric ratings		Must have 2s or better in all domains	Must have 3s or better in all domains	Must have 4s in Teaching for Learning domain and at least one other domain; must have at least 3s in other domains	Must have 4s in all domains
Contract status	Nonrenewal at end of year 2 if novice status not attained	Nonrenewal or terminated at end of year 5 as a Novice if career status is not attained	May remain in category throughout career	May remain in category throughout career	May remain in category throughout career
Salary	$30,000	Range: $32,000 to $35,128 (BA)	Range: $38,128 to $49,250 (BA)	Range: $52,500 to $55,000 (BA)	Range: $60,000 to $62,500 (BA)

Source: Data from Cincinnati Public Schools. Retrieved from http://www.wcer.wisc.edu/cpre/conference/dec00/cincinnati.pdf

ranging from support for National Board Certification to mentoring and beginning teacher assistance (TAP) totaling $102.91 per pupil in 2000–2001 (dropping to $85.44 per pupil the next year). California provided a package of opportunities including support for time buy-out, beginning teacher assistance, National Board Certification, education technology, and other programs totaling $170.06 per pupil in 2000–2001.

Rice (2003) mined the *National Educational Longitudinal Study* for insights on the extent of teacher involvement in staff development, predictors of involvement, perceptions of the influence of staff development on teaching practices, and relationship between teacher staff development and student value-added achievement outcomes. Most importantly, the study found limited effects of staff development on student value-added outcomes but did find a positive association between "school system workshops" (the dominant form of staff development in the study) and student math outcomes. The relationship was stronger for novice teachers. While actual outcomes were mixed, teachers generally perceived staff development to positively influence their teaching.

Policies With Unintended Labor Market Consequences

Arguably, a major reason researchers and policy makers have become more aware of the relationship of school finance and other education policies with teacher labor market behavior is that we have been able to observe, over time, the unintended and adverse effects on teacher labor markets of well-intentioned policies. In particular, we have seen how policies intended to promote greater equity in schooling have often led to greater inequity in the distribution of quality teaching. Following are three examples of policies and policy objectives that have had the unintended consequence of reducing equity in teaching quality:

1. *Teacher Quantity-Based Policies, Including Statewide Class-Size Reduction:* Implementing class-size reduction as a statewide policy objective increases overall demand for teachers. Typically, class sizes are larger in poorer districts, but where class-size reduction objectives are low enough such that even wealthier districts must reduce class sizes in order to comply, higher-quality, or at least more qualified, teachers tend to migrate toward the

more desirable teaching positions. One end result is that while students in poorer districts end up having smaller classes, larger proportions of students in poorer districts end up being taught by less-qualified teachers. The extent to which this outcome is problematic, however, depends largely on whether teacher quantities (class size) are more or less important than teaching quality.

2. *Teacher Wage and Geographic Cost Indices in School Finance Policies that Worsen Rather than Improve Teacher Quality Distribution:* Recall that the intent of input price or cost indices is to equalize school districts' ability to purchase comparable educational opportunities. Typically, as in the previous scenario, input price or cost indices place greater emphasis on quantities of resources, which are more easily measurable than quality of resources. As discussed in this chapter, research is just beginning to reveal the extent of teacher preferences to work in school districts with more desirable working conditions, that is, districts with fewer low-income students and smaller class sizes. Yet existing teacher wage and geographic cost indices are rarely if ever progressive enough to provide poorer, urban districts the opportunity to overcome their working conditions. In some cases, due to the economic factors that influence wage index construction, including income and housing unit values, wage indices favor districts that already have a working condition advantage.

3. *Uniform, Labor Market–Insensitive, Revenue and Spending Limits:* The best available example of this policy is the role of state-imposed limitations to local property taxation. Such limitations are problematic in equity terms when they prevent poor urban districts from providing competitive wages. Cost-sensitive aid formulas and cost-sensitive tax limitations that account for necessary compensating differentials may reduce this problem. Limits to growth in spending on education may also render the education sector less competi-

tive with other labor market sectors, lowering the overall quality of teaching force.

The bottom line is that school systems must design policies with consideration for teacher labor market behavior, including both influences on entry to and exit from the profession and distribution among institutions within the profession. School systems might mediate the potential adverse equity effects of class-size reduction policies by targeting class-size reduction to high-need schools. However, any increase in demand for teachers created by policy is associated with the potential for dilution of the talent pool. Policy makers also might couple class-size reduction policies with policies providing wage differentials for teachers to take positions in high-need schools. Imazeki (2003) notes:

> The key issue is that the way in which California's CSR policy is financed does not take into account differing salary costs and hiring needs across schools and districts. By giving the same grant per pupil to all, and by beginning implementation for everyone at the same time, such a policy could exacerbate inequities in the distribution of teacher quality. (p. 173)

Finally, we have some concerns regarding the long-term effects of state school finance policies built too rigidly on resource-cost analyses, like the Wyoming block grant approach to funding schools. While seemingly ideal for creating input-based adequacy for all students, state policies that "fix" the price of educational goods and services may have dire long-term consequences for teacher recruitment and retention. State control over all public school employees' wages may reduce the responsiveness of those wages to local economic conditions, both limiting the competitiveness of teacher labor markets and potentially having adverse effects on local economies where education system employees represent a large component of the local labor market. That is, insufficiently supported, state-controlled fixed-price education may, in some cases, serve to depress local economies.

SUMMARY

In this chapter, we have provided an overview of teacher labor markets. Teachers are undeniably the most important and the most costly resource currently used in the delivery of K–12 education. The quality of teaching varies widely among states and school districts. Until policy makers can leverage school finance and regulatory policy to change the distribution of teaching quality, true equality of educational opportunity will continue to be evasive.

This chapter provides some insights into just how expensive it may be to employ school finance policy as a mechanism for redistributing teachers, yet the knowledge base on teachers' response to financial incentives remains limited. This chapter also provides some insights into other expensive policies, such as statewide class-size reduction, that may have unintended adverse equity consequences—concentrating higher-quality teachers in schools serving students with fewer special needs.

Not addressed in this chapter, but still critical to improving the level and distribution of teaching quality across states, is the teacher-production pipeline. The quality of teacher production varies widely across states, leaving some states with few if any teacher candidates who would be considered high quality by metrics identified in labor economics literature. The nation's most competitive undergraduate colleges continue to produce relatively few graduates who go on to teach in public schools, and those colleges are highly concentrated in certain regions of the country (Reback, 2002). According to related research on teacher hiring and selection, school leaders more often prefer weaker than stronger academic candidates, and rarely cast their recruitment net beyond their local vicinity, resulting in a perpetuating cycle of disparate teacher quality (Strauss et al., 2000). As a result of these and other forces, schools systems ultimately will need more than money to resolve disparities in teaching quality across districts.

REFERENCES

Allegretto, S. A., Corcoran, S. P., & Mishel, L. (2004). *How does teacher pay compare? Methodological challenges and answers*. Washington, DC: Economic Policy Institute.

Angrist, J., & Guryan, J. (2003). *Does teacher testing raise teacher quality? Evidence from state certification requirements*. NBER working paper #9545. Cambridge, MA: National Bureau of Economic Research.

Baker, B. D., & Dickerson, J. (2006). Charter schools, teacher labor market deregulation and teacher quality: evidence from the schools and staffing survey. *Educational Policy, 20*(5), 752–782.

Ballou, D., & Podgursky, M. (1998a). The case against teacher certification. *The Public Interest, 132*, 17–29.

Ballou, D., & Podgursky, M. (1998b). Teacher recruitment and retention in public and private schools. *Journal of Policy Analysis and Management, 17*(3), 393–417.

Barron's Educational Series. (2003.) *Barron's guide to the most competitive colleges*. Hauppauge, NY: Author.

Blair, J. (2000, October 25). National certification found valid. *Education Week*. Retrieved from www.edweek.org

Boyd, W., Goldhaber, D., Lankford, H., & Wyckoff, J. (2007). The effect of certification and preparation on teacher quality. In S. Loeb, C. Rouse, & A. Shorris (Eds.), *The future of children*. Washington, DC: The Brookings Institution.

Boyd, W., Grossman, P., & Lankford, H. (2005). *How changes in entry requirements alter the teacher workforce and affect student achievement*. Working Paper. Teacher Policy Research. Albany, NY: State University of New York at Albany. Retrieved from http://www.teacherpolicyresearch.org/AboutTPR/tabid/113/Default.aspx

Boyd, D., Loeb, S., Lankford, H., & Wyckoff, J. (2003). *Analyzing the determinants of the matching of public school teachers to jobs: estimating compensating differentials in imperfect labor markets*. Working Paper. Teacher Policy Research. Albany, NY: State University of New York at Albany. Retrieved from http://www.teacherpolicyresearch.org/AboutTPR/tabid/113/Default.aspx

Brewer, D., Krop, C., Gill, B. P., & Reichardt, R. (1999). Estimating the costs of national class size reductions under different policy alternatives. *Educational Evaluation and Policy Analysis, 21*(2), 179–192.

Conley, D., & Rooney, K. (2007). *Washington adequacy funding study*. Eugene, OR: Education Policy Improvement Center.

Consortium for Policy Research in Education. (2002). Data retrieved from http://www.wcer.wisc.edu/cpre/tcomp/research/ksbp/certification.asp

Corcoran, S. P., Evans, W. N., & Schwab, R. M. (2004). Changing labor market opportunities for women and the quality of teachers, 1957–2000. *American Economic Review, 94*(2).

Corcoran, S., & Mishel, L. (2007). Review of Jay Greene and Marcus Winters *How much are public school teachers paid?* Tempe: Education Policy Studies Laboratory, Arizona State University. Retrieved from http://epsl.asu.edu/epru/ttreviews/EPSL-0702-229-EPRU.pdf

Darling-Hammond, L. (2000). Teacher quality and student achievement: A review of state policy evidence. *Education Policy Analysis Archives 8*(1). Retrieved from http://epaa.asu.edu/epaa/v8n1/

Darling-Hammond, L., Berry, B., & Thoreson, A. (2001). Does teacher certification matter? Evaluating the evidence.

Educational Evaluation and Policy Analysis 23(1), 57–78.

Decker, P. T., Mayer, D. P., & Glazerman, S. (2004). *The effects of teach for america on students.* Mathematica Policy Research, Inc. Retrieved July 8, 2004, from http://www.mathematica-mpr.com/publications/pdfs/teach.pdf

Ehrenberg, R. G., & Brewer, D. J. (1994). Do school and teacher characteristics matter? Evidence from High School and Beyond. *Economics of Education Review, 13*(1), 1–17.

Ferguson, R. (1991). Paying for public education: New evidence on how and why money matters. *Harvard Journal on Legislation, 28*(2), 465–498.

Figlio, D. N. (1997). Teacher salaries and teacher quality. *Economics Letters, 55,* 267–271.

Figlio, D. N. (2002). Can public schools buy better-qualified teachers? *Industrial and Labor Relations Review, 55,* 686–699.

Figlio, D. N., & Reuben, K. (2001). Tax limits and the qualifications of new teachers. *Journal of Public Economics, 80*(1), 49–71.

Finn, J. D., & Achilles, C. (1999). Tennessee's class size study: findings, implications, misconceptions. *Educational Evaluation and Policy Analysis, 21*(2), 97–109.

Goldhaber, D., & Anthony, E. (2004). Can teacher quality be effectively assessed? Seattle: Center for Reinventing Education. Retrieved from http://www.crpe.org/workingpapers/pdf/NBPTSquality_report.pdf

Goldhaber, D., & Brewer, D. (1997). Evaluating the effect of teacher degree level on educational performance. In W. J. Fowler (Ed.), *Developments in school finance, 1996* (pp. 197–210). Washington, DC: National Center for Education Statistics, U.S. Department of Education.

Goldhaber, D., & Brewer, D. (2000). Does teacher certification matter? High school teacher certification status and student achievement. *Educational Evaluation and Policy Analysis 22*(2), 129–146.

Goldhaber, D., & Brewer, D. (2001). Evaluating the evidence on teacher certification: A rejoinder. *Educational Evaluation and Policy Analysis, 23*(1), 79–86.

Greene, J., & Winters, M. (2007, Jan. 31). *How much are public school teachers paid?* New York: The Manhattan Institute.

Hanushek, E. A. (1997). Outcomes, incentives, and beliefs: Reflections on analysis of the economics of schools. *Educational Evaluation and Policy Analysis, 19*(4), 301–308

Hanushek, E., Kain, J., & Rivken, S. (2001). *Why public schools lose teachers.* Working Paper 8599. National Bureau of Economic Research.

Hanushek E., & Rivken, S. (2000). *Teacher quality and school reform in New York.* Paper presented at the Symposium on Teacher Labor Markets, Rockefeller School of Government. SUNY Albany.

Hanushek, E. A., Rivken, S. G., & Taylor, L. (1996). Aggregation and the estimated effects of school resources. *Review of Economics and Statistics, 78*(4), 611–627.

Hedges, L., & Greenwald, R. (1996). Have times changed? The relation between school resources and student performance. In G. Burtless (Ed.), *Does money matter?* (pp. 74–92). Washington, D.C. The Brookings Institution.

Henke, R. R., Chen, X., & Geis, S. (2000). *Progress through the teacher pipeline: 1992–93 college graduates and elementary/secondary school teaching as of 1997.* P. Knepper, Project Officer. NCES 2000–152. Washington, DC: U.S. Department of Education, National Center for Education Statistics.

Imazeki, J. (2001). *Moving on or moving out? Determinants of job and career changes for teachers.* Working Paper, Department of Economics, San Diego State University.

Imazeki, J. (2003). Class-size reduction and teacher quality: Evidence from California. In M. Plecki & D. H. Monk (Eds.), *School finance and teacher quality: exploring the connections: 2003 yearbook of the American Education Finance Association* (pp. 159–176). Larchmont, NY: Eye on Education.

Kelley, C. (no date). *Teacher compensation project.* Madison: University of Wisconsin. Retrieved from http://www.wcer.wisc.edu/cpre/tcomp/research/standards/board.php

Killeen, K., Monk, D. H., & Plecki, M. (2002). school district spending on professional development: Insights from national data. *Journal of Education Finance, 28*(1), 25–50.

Laczko-Kerr, I., & Berliner, D. C. (2002, September 6). The effectiveness of "Teach for America" and other under-certified teachers on student academic achievement: A case of harmful public policy. *Education Policy Analysis Archives, 10*(37). Retrieved from http://epaa.asu.edu/epaa/v10n37/

Lankford, H., Loeb, S., & Wyckoff, J. (2002). Teacher sorting and the plight of urban schools: A descriptive analysis. *Educational Evaluation and Policy Analysis 24*(1), 37–62.

Loeb, S. (2000). *How teachers' choices affect what a dollar can buy: Wages and quality in K–12 schooling. Working Paper.* Education Finance Research Consortium. Rockefeller Institution of Public Policy. State University of New York at Albany.

Loeb, S., & Page, M. (1998). *Examining the link between wages and quality in the teacher workforce.* Unpublished manuscript. Department of Economics, University of California, Davis.

Loeb, S., & Page, M. (2000). Examining the link between teacher wages and student outcomes: The importance of alternative labor market opportunities and non-pecuniary variation. *Review of Economics and Statistics, 82,* 393–408.

Loeb, S., Wyckoff, J., & Lankford, H. (2004). *Analyzing the determinants of matching of public school teachers to jobs: Estimating compensating differentials in imperfect labor markets.* Retrieved May 9, 2005, from http://www.

teacherpolicyresearch.org/Matching%20of%20Public%20School%20Teachers%20to%20Jobs%20-%20July%20211.pdf

Monk, D. H., & King, J. (1994). Multi-level teacher resource effects on pupil performance in secondary math and science: The role of teacher subject matter preparation. In R. G. Ehrenberg (Ed.), *Contemporary policy issues: Choice and consequences in education* (pp. 29–58). Ithaca, NY: ILR Press.

Monk, D. H., Plecki, M. L., & Killeen, K. (2003). Examining investments in teacher professional development: A look at current practice and a proposal for improving the research base. In M. Plecki & D. H. Monk (Eds.), *School finance and teacher quality: exploring the connections: 2003 yearbook of the American Education Finance Association* (pp. 137–156). Larchmont, NY: Eye on Education.

Murnane, R. J., & Olsen, R. (1989). The effects of salaries and opportunity costs on duration teaching. Evidence from Michigan. *Review of Economics and Statistics, 71*(2), 347–352.

National Center for Education Statistics. (2003, May). *Schools and staffing surveys of 1999–2000*. Washington, DC: U.S. Dept. of Education.

Odden, A. R. (2003). An early assessment of comprehensive teacher compensation plans. In M. Plecki & D. H. Monk (Eds.), *School finance and teacher quality: exploring the connections: 2003 yearbook of the American Education Finance Association* (pp. 209–228). Larchmont, NY: Eye on Education.

Odden, A. R., & Kelly, C. (1997). *Paying Teachers for what they know and do: New and smarter compensation strategies for teachers*. Thousand Oaks, CA: Corwin Press.

Odden, A. R., & Kelly, C. (no date). *The teacher compensation project*. Madison: University of Wisconsin, Consortium for Policy Research in Education. Retrieved from http://cpre.wceruw.org/tcomp/background. php

Reback, R. (2002). *The impact of college course offerings on the supply of academically talented public school teachers*. NBER working paper. Cambridge, MA: National Bureau of Economic Research.

Rice, J. K. (2003). The incidence and impact of teacher professional development: Implications for educational productivity. In M. Plecki & D. H. Monk (Eds.), *School finance and teacher quality: exploring the connections: 2003 yearbook of the American Education Finance Association* (pp. 111–135). Larchmont, NY: Eye on Education.

Rivken, S., Hanushek, E., & Kain, J. F. (2000). *Teachers, schools and academic achievement*. National Bureau of Economic Research, Working Paper 6691. Cambridge, MA: National Bureau of Economic Research.

Sanders, W. L., & Rivers, J. C. (1996). *Research project report: Cumulative and residual effects of teachers on future student academic achievement*. University of Tennessee Value-Added Research and Assessment Center. Retrieved from http://www.mdkl2.org/practices/ensure/tva/tva_2.html

Stone, J. E. (2002). *The value-added achievement gains of NBPTS-certified teachers in Tennessee: A brief report*. Retrieved from http://www.education-consumers.com/briefs/stoneNBPTS.shtm

Strauss, R. P., Bowes, L. R., Marks, M. S., & Plesko, M. R. (2000). Improving teacher preparation and selection: Lessons from the Pennsylvania experience. *Economics of Education Review, 19*(4), 387–415.

Wright, S. P., Horn, S. P., & Sanders, W. (1997). Teacher and classroom context effects on student achievement: Implications for teacher evaluation. *Journal of Personnel Evaluation in Education, 11*, 57–67.

Zehr, M. A. (2002, October 2). ECS review discounts study critical of teaching board. *Education Week*. Retrieved from www.edweek.org

Additional Readings

Plecki, M. L., & Monk, D. H. (2003). *School Finance and Teacher Quality: Exploring the Connections, 2003 Yearbook of the American Education Finance Association*. Larchmont, NY: Eye on Education.

Teacher Quality

Ballou, D., & Podgursky, M. (1998). The case against teacher certification. *The Public Interest, 132,* 17–29.

Ballou, D., & Podgursky, M. (1998). Teacher recruitment and retention in public and private schools. *Journal of Policy Analysis and Management, 17*(3), 393–417.

Ballou, D., & Podgursky, M. (2000). Gaining control of professional licensing and advancement. In T. Loveless (Ed.), *Conflicting missions? Teachers unions and educational reform* (pp. 69–109). Washington, DC: The Brookings Institution.

Darling-Hammond, L., Berry, B., & Thoreson, A. (2001). Does teacher certification matter? Evaluating the evidence. *Educational Evaluation and Policy Analysis, 23*(1), 57–78.

Decker, P. T., Mayer, D. P., & Glazerman, S. (2004). *The effects of Teach for America on students*. Mathematica Policy Research, Inc. Retrieved July 8, 2004, from http://www.mathematica-mpr.com/publications/pdfs/teach.pdf.

Ehrenberg, R. G., & Brewer, D. J. (1994). Do school and teacher characteristics matter? Evidence from high school and beyond. *Economics of Education Review, 13*(1), 1–17.

Ehrenberg, R. G., & Brewer, D. J. (1995). Did teachers' verbal ability and race matter in the 1960's? Coleman revisited. *Economics of Education Review, 14*, 1–21.

Goldhaber, D., & Anthony, E. (2004). *Can teacher quality be effectively assessed?* Seattle: Center for Reinventing Education. Retrieved from http://www.crpe.org/workingpapers/pdf/NBPTSquality_report.pdf

Goldhaber, D., & Brewer, D. J. (2000). Does teacher certification matter? High school teacher certification status and student achievement. *Educational Evaluation and Policy Analysis, 22*(2), 129–145.

Goldhaber, D., & Brewer, D. J. (2001). Evaluating the evidence on teacher certification: A rejoinder. *Educational Evaluation and Policy Analysis, 23*(1), 79–86.

Gordon, G. (1999). Teacher talent and urban schools. *Phi Delta Kappan, 81*(4), 304–307.

Laczko-Kerr, I., & Berliner, D. C. (2002, September 6). The effectiveness of "Teach for America" and other under-certified teachers on student academic achievement: A case of harmful public policy. *Education Policy Analysis Archives, 10*(37). Retrieved from http://epaa.asu.edu/epaa/v10n37/

Podgursky, M. (2003). *Improving academic performance in US schools: Why teacher licensure is (almost) irrelevant.* American Enterprise Institute for Public Policy Research. Retrieved from http://www.aei.org/docLib/20031023_podgursky.pdf

Rivken, S., Hanushek, E., & Kain, J. F. (2000). *Teachers, schools and academic achievement.* National Bureau of Economic Research, Working Paper 6691. National Bureau of Economic Research.

Sanders, W. L., & Rivers, J. C. (1996). *Research project report: Cumulative and residual effects of teachers on future student academic achievement.* University of Tennessee Value-Added Research and Assessment Center. Retrieved from http://www.mdkl2.org/practices/ensure/tva/tva_2.html

Stone, J. E. (no date). *The value-added achievement gains of NBPTS-certified teachers in Tennessee: A brief report.* Retrieved from http://www.education-consumers.com/briefs/stoneNBPTS.shtm

Strauss, R. P., Bowes, L. R., Marks, M. S., & Plesko, M. R. (2000). Improving teacher preparation and selection: Lessons from the Pennsylvania Experience. *Economics of Education Review, 19*(4), 387–415.

Strauss, R. P., & Sawyer, E. (1986). Some new evidence on teacher and student competencies. *Economics of Education Review, 5*(1), 41–48.

Teacher Mobility

Angrist, J., & Guryan, J. (2003). *Does teacher testing raise teacher quality? Evidence from state certification requirements.* NBER working paper #9545. Cambridge, MA: National Bureau of Economic Research.

Baker, B. D., & Cooper, B. S. (2005). Do principals with stronger academic backgrounds hire better teachers? Policy implications for high poverty schools. *Educational Administration Quarterly, 41*(3), 444–479.

Ballou, D. (1996). Do public schools hire the best teachers? *Quarterly Journal of Economics, 111,* 97–133.

Ballou, D., & Podgursky, M. (1995). Recruiting smarter teachers. *Journal of Human Resources, 30*(2), 326–338.

Boyd, D., Loeb, S., Lankford, H., & Wyckoff, J. (2003). *Analyzing the determinants of the matching of public school teachers to jobs: Estimating compensating differentials in imperfect labor markets.* Working Paper. Education Finance Research Consortium. Rockefeller Institution of Public Policy. State University of New York at Albany.

Ferguson, R. F. (1991). Paying for public education: New evidence on how and why money matters. *Harvard Journal of Legislation, 28,* 465–498.

Figlio, D. N. (1997). Teacher salaries and teacher quality. *Economics Letters, 55,* 267–271.

Figlio, D. N. (2002). Can public schools buy better-qualified teachers? *Industrial and Labor Relations Review, 55,* 686–699.

Hanushek, E. A., Kain, J. F., & Rivken, S. G. (1998). *Teachers, schools and academic achievement.* NBER Working Paper 6691. Cambridge, MA: National Bureau of Economic Research.

Hanushek, E. A., Kain, J. F., & Rivken, S. G. (1999). *Do higher salaries buy better teachers?* NBER Working Paper 7082. Cambridge, MA: National Bureau of Economic Research.

Hanushek, E. A., Kain, J. F., & Rivken, S. G. (2001). *Why public schools lose teachers.* Working Paper 8599. Cambridge, MA: National Bureau of Economic Research.

Imazeki, J. (2001). *Moving on or moving out? Determinants of job and career changes for teachers.* Working Paper, Department of Economics, San Diego State University.

Imazeki, J. (2001). *School revenue limits and teacher salaries: evidence from Wisconsin.* Working Paper. Department of Economics. San Diego State University.

Lankford, H., Loeb, S., & Wyckoff, J. (2002). Teacher sorting and the plight of urban schools. *Educational Evaluation and Policy Analysis, 24*(1), 37–62.

Loeb, S. (2000). *How teachers' choices affect what a dollar can buy: Wages and quality in K–12 schooling.* Working Paper. Education Finance Research Consortium. Rockefeller Institution of Public Policy. State University of New York at Albany.

Loeb, S., & Page, M. (1998). Examining the link between wages and quality in the teacher workforce. Department of Economics, University of California, Davis.

Loeb, S., & Page, M. (2000). Examining the link between teacher wages and student outcomes: The importance of alternative labor market opportunities and non-pecuniary variation. *Review of Economics and Statistics, 82,* 393–408.

Murnane, R. J., & Olsen, R. (1989). The effects of salaries and opportunity costs on duration teaching. Evidence from Michigan. *Review of Economics and Statistics, 71*(2), 347–352.

Papa, F., Lankford, H., & Wyckoff, J. (2002). *The attributes and career paths of principals: Implications for improving policy.* State University of New York at Albany.

Reback, R. (2002). *The impact of college course offerings on the supply of academically talented public school teachers.*

NBER working paper. Cambridge, MA: National Bureau of Economic Research.

Strauss, R. P. (2003). *The preparation and selection of public school administrators in Pennsylvania: Supply and demand and the effects on student achievement.* Paper presented at the annual meeting of the American Education Finance Association. Orlando, FL.

CHAPTER 14

PROMOTING PRODUCTIVITY AND EFFICIENCY
GOVERNMENT INTERVENTION STRATEGIES

Introduction

This chapter addresses government-regulated approaches to stimulating changes in productivity and efficiency of schooling. Much has been said about the lack of positive incentives for improving productivity within the current structure of public schooling. Significant reservations remain about the ability of market-based policies to reduce inefficiencies across all types of school districts in all types of settings. For example, for the thousands of schools and districts outside of major metropolitan areas, market competition among schools and districts likely will never be sufficient and the numbers of private providers bidding on educational management and service contracts likely will never be sufficient. As such, state governments concerned with productivity and efficiency in local public school districts must find ways to either stimulate or regulate improvement via nonmarket mechanisms.

As we discuss throughout this text, interest in local public schools by the states has increased dramatically since the mid-1970s (perhaps coincident with the states' increased role in funding school districts and extensive litigation challenging the equity and adequacy of their financing schemes). The following paragraph from a Task Force report to the Governor of Kansas exemplifies the types of changes that have occurred across states in recent decades and the current view of the linkage between the increased state role and the increased state interest in schooling productivity:

> With adoption of the School District Finance and Quality Performance Accreditation Act in 1992 and subsequent amendments, the state became the primary funder of Kansas public schools, with a shift away from the historical reliance on the local property tax. The

Task Force affirms the importance of respecting local decision-making on specific educational matters. However, since the state now serves as the primary funder, Kansas should maintain a significant interest in the performance of the schools in which it invests. Thus, the Task Force seeks to balance its support of local control with a new linkage among funding, accountability, and student achievement in order to ensure the productive and efficient use of state revenues and to achieve the goal of *financing for results.* (Brant, Baker, Ballard, Jones, & Vratil, 2000, p. 1)

In this chapter we discuss two approaches taken by states to either stimulate or directly manage performance improvement of schools. First, we discuss outcome-based policies, or policies that focus on the performance outcomes of teachers, schools, or districts, rewarding performance outcomes with fiscal incentives. Next, we discuss state strategies to intervene in local district practices, notably, local district resource allocation, in order to more directly guide performance improvement.

Outcome-Based Policies

Outcome-based policies, as the name implies, focus on the outcomes attained by the organizational unit under observation (classroom, school, or district). Teachers and administrators retain control over educational processes, as long as they can produce sufficient outcomes at the given price. Outcome-based relationships between government agencies (state to district, district to school, state to charter school) are analogous in some ways to the performance contracts between public agencies and private providers discussed in Chapter 12. That is, that the contractor should stipulate both compliance and performance requirements, and financial incentives should be sufficient to improve performance.

One major difference between public–private contracting and state–local government performance contracts, however, is that competitive bidding does not establish the relationship between government agencies. That is, public schools do not compete, through a bidding process, to obtain contracts with the state to serve the state's children. Such a mechanism might be attempted with charter schools. That is, charter school authorities might bid for contracts with states, providing states the opportunity to contract with authorizers promising to produce higher student outcomes at lower bid prices (per-pupil allotments).

Performance contracting *within public education systems* falls into two categories:

School-Based (or District-Based) Performance Incentives: School-based performance incentive plans are performance contracts between states and schools. State legislatures and departments of education establish performance and compliance guidelines to be met, and provide for lump-sum financial incentives, from funds set aside by the legislature for this purpose, to schools meeting those requirements.

Performance-Based Pay: Performance-based salary schedules are contracts between local school districts and teachers. Statewide teacher contracts are an exception. Typically, performance-based pay systems are arrived at via negotiation between local boards of education and local teachers associations, with the intent of stimulation competition among individual employees.

States may play some role in stimulating local districts to adopt performance-based pay systems, but we contend that performance-based pay systems are primarily a local policy option. Further, unlike school-based incentives (with the possible exception of charter schools noted earlier), districts may use performance contracts with teachers as a negotiating tool for districts competing with one another to contract the "best" teachers. That is, competitive bidding may occur among job-seeking teachers for the best teaching jobs, and in turn, districts may competitively bid for the best teachers via performance contracts.

Input-Based Policies

Input-based policies involve state intervention in school and district operations, including curricular mandates, contact hour mandates, staffing ratios, shares of state funding that must be spent on teachers, and other state interventions in the resource allocation practices of local school districts. In this chapter, we focus on state interventions in fiscal and human resource allocation, which have become increasingly popular methods for reforming underperforming schools and districts. Examples include the New Jersey legislature's attempt to mandate the use of new funding to implement whole-school reforms that involve specific resource configurations and California's state aid targeted for class-size reduction.

Performance Contracts Between States, Districts, and Schools

School-based performance reward programs have picked up momentum in recent years. School-based performance reward programs can be broadly defined as state policies that provide financial incentives to local school districts, or individual local schools based on performance outcome measures. Such policies are a form of "performance contract," where the state assumes the role of the contractor or agent primarily responsible for accomplishing the task at hand, the education of all children in that state. The state then provides financial resources to local districts contingent on performance outcomes established by the contractor. States including Texas, Kentucky, South Carolina, and California have adopted such programs.

This section draws on existing incentive funding policies and research on those policies to derive a set of recommendations for states considering incentive funding programs. We place particular emphasis on the evaluation of school performance and the behaviors promoted by alternative incentive schemes. Given the limited empirical evaluation of current state policies, and the policy variations that exist from state to state, this section draws heavily on our own personal views regarding the optimal design of school-based performance reward systems. We fully recognize that our views on this topic are at times highly speculative, as well as idealistic.

Designing School Performance Measurement Systems

Most existing incentive funding programs use broad portfolios of performance measures including, but not limited to, academic achievement. For example, King and Mathers note that the South Carolina incentive reward program included measures of student achievement, student attendance, teacher attendance, and dropout rate; the authors also note that the Kentucky system included student achievement, performance assessments, student attendance, dropout rate, retention rate and transition from high school (King & Mathers, 1997, p. 153).

Measuring School Performance

Few if any well-developed frameworks exist for designing a performance measurement and monitoring system and/or deciding on a collection of measures to be included in a performance portfolio. As such, present policies across the states are idiosyncratic. Development of a performance measurement system should begin with an understanding of the basic types of measures that should exist in such a system. Measures may be classified as (a) compliance benchmarks, (b) performance benchmarks, and (c) performance path marks.

Compliance Benchmarks: Maintaining a specific level of teacher attendance or student attendance is an example of meeting a compliance benchmark. Compliance benchmarks are things that should simply be expected to happen if teaching and learning are to occur. For the most part, compliance benchmarks measure schooling inputs and processes. Compliance benchmarks alone are not sufficient for performance-based evaluation.

Performance Benchmarks: Performance benchmarks measure important outcomes rather than inputs or processes and may measure those outcomes at a number of performance levels. For example, many state assessments systems test whether students achieve a minimum level of competency in academic achievement across subject areas, while other state systems include multiple levels of competence. Further, states have become more explicit in recent years in defining minimum performance expectations and designing specific assessments related to those standards. Regardless of the number of levels of performance outcomes measured, "standards-based" assessments measure student abilities against static benchmarks.

Performance Path Marks: Finally, performance path marks are measures of rate of gain, or rate of gain relative to an expected or indexed rate of gain (norm-referenced rate of gain). For example, if a series of performance benchmarks exists across grade levels, a student must be expected to achieve a certain, measurable rate of gain to successfully surpass those benchmarks within an appropriate time frame. Individual student gains may be "path marked" against the expected trajectory (Richards, 1988).

Considerations for Measuring Outcomes

Because student academic achievement is more difficult to measure than attendance or dropout rates, and because the meaning of academic achievement measures is often questioned, caution is warranted in the design of the appropriate academic performance index. This, however, does not mean that use of academic achievement measures should be abandoned. Many have argued for abandonment of achievement measures as a basis for fiscal incentives on the grounds that (a) schools are about more than just academic achievement and (b) rewarding schools for academic achievement will simply induce teachers to "teach to the test." The responses to these concerns are quite simple. First, although it is true that schools are about "more than academics," it would be foolish to argue that academic achievement is not at least a significant part of schooling that, as a result, analysts should consider when measuring the performance of schools. Second, if a test or battery of tests is a "good test" that reliably and validly measures students' academic knowledge and skills that have been deemed important by the state, then the harm in teachers' tailoring their practices for students to better understand likely test material is questionable. That is, it may actually be desirable to "teach to the test."

Any academic achievement measure selected as a partial basis for incentive funding will be highly scrutinized. Perhaps to expedite adoption or to develop easily explainable measures, several states have created performance measurement systems that have significant potentially adverse effects on specific student populations. A critically important question that must be asked regarding any academic achievement index follows:

> What teaching/instructional behaviors or practices does this policy promote at the classroom level, for different types of students?

While only a handful of states have adopted performance-based incentive policies, most states have developed or expanded programs for evaluating student and school performance over the past decade, and all states will be compelled to do so under new federal policies. Current academic performance assessment systems can be roughly classified into systems that measure (a) school or district-aggregated proportions of students passing performance benchmarks or performance standards; (b) norm-referenced student assessments that report student's individual *levels* of performance, usually aggregated to school or district means; and (c) individual student rate of achievement gain over time (value-added assessment), which can be aggregated to school or district mean rates of gain.

Standards-Based and Achievement-Level Approaches

In an era of standards-based reforms, performance measures that consider numbers of students passing performance benchmarks have become dominant. In some cases, a single standard is set, and school-level "success" is based on numbers of students who surpass that single externally imposed standard, or "bar." This was the case, for example, in the Texas Successful Schools Award System (TSSAS) and in the reporting of aggregate school performance measures in numerous other states (www.tea.state.tx.us).

In minimum bar systems, the primary motivation of school leaders is to get as many students as possible over the minimum bar to generate the highest aggregate performance value. That is, the goal is to *maximize minimum performance*. In Massachusetts, for example, if 80% of students in a school are minimally proficient and less than 5% receive failing scores, the school is rated in the top (of six) performance categories.

In other cases, including California's Academic Performance Index (API), a system may be norm-referenced (internally generated standards) and contain multiple levels, but have similar implications for students across ability levels. In California's API, for example, schools report the numbers of students who fall at different performance levels (percentile categories) in each curricular area tested (Table 14.1).

Next, percentages of students in each bin are multiplied by weighting factors. For example, the proportion of students surpassing the 80th percentile receives a weight of 1,000, the 60th percentile receives a weight of 875, and so on, according to Table 14.2. Points are summed for each curricular area. The curricular areas receive separate weights, and an aggregate API score is determined for the school.

On the surface, California's API seems quite logical, and more refined than methods considering students surpassing only a single bar. Unfortunately, any system based on the distribution or movement of groups of students across benchmarks may have serious consequences at the classroom level for individual students. Such consequences are magnified when

Table 14.1 Calculation of the California API: Tabulation of Student Performance

		Reading	Math	Language	Spelling
5	80–99th NPR	20	20	20	20
4	60–79th NPR	20	20	20	20
3	40–59th NPR	20	20	20	20
2	20–39th NPR	20	20	20	20
1	1–19th NPR	20	20	20	20
	Number of Students	100	100	100	100

NPR, national percentile rank.

Source: Data from California Department of Education. Retrieved June 2004 from http://www.cde.ca.gov/ta/ac/ap/

Table 14.2 Calculation of the Academic Performance Index: Performance Weighting Factors

| | Stanford 9 | | Reading | |
	A	B	C	D
	Performance Bands	Weighting Factors	Percent of Pupils in Each Band	Weighted Score in Each Band (B × C)
5	80–99th NPR	1000	20%	200
4	60–79th NPR	875	20%	175
3	40–59th NPR	700	20%	140
2	20–39th NPR	500	20%	100
1	1–19th NPR	200	20%	40
			TOTAL	655
				30%
				197

NPR, national percentile rank.

Source: Data from California Department of Education. Retrieved June 2004 from http://www.cde.ca.gov/ta/ac/ap/

measurement systems apply either high stakes for minimum performance or fiscal incentive policies. In a system with a single bar to surpass, for example, if the bar is set in the middle (50th percentile), the incentive at the school and classroom level is to focus effort predominantly on the bottom half of the student population. No incentive exists to challenge even slightly above-average students who will surpass, or perhaps have already surpassed, the bar, and arguably no incentive exists to work with students perceived to have no chance of clearing the bar at all.

One might argue that the Texas standards-based assessments (Texas Assessment of Academic Skills, TAAS, replaced in 2004 by the Texas Assessment of Knowledge and Skills, TAKS) have induced schools to classify large numbers of low-ability students with special needs to exempt them from the test. Moving the bar up or down merely changes the proportions of the student populations "lopped off" at each end but retains a constant sum of those populations.

California's API is only a moderate improvement in that it "lops off" only the students above the 80th rather than 50th percentile. Goertz, Duffy, and Le Floch (2001) indicate that 37 states used assessment systems like California's API in 1999, involving 4 to 5 performance levels.

Pseudo Value-Added Measurement (Grade-Level Change and Cohort Gain)

States often use "percent passing" systems to generate year-to-year "gain" indices. That is, states evaluate schools based on the number or proportion of students who move from below the bar(s) to above the bar, or the number of students who shift into higher bins in a multilevel system such as the API. Numerous complications can occur with this method. First, schools often give standardized tests at particular grade levels, rather than annually. In schools that give math assessments at the fourth- and eighth-grade level, for example, states may judge elementary schools annually on the percentages of their fourth-grade students passing math standards. Unfortunately, such comparisons are likely to measure the changing makeup of fourth-grade cohorts in a school as much as, if not more than, the quality of math instruction in the school. We provide a statistical example of this phenomenon later in this section.

Student-Level, Value-Added (Repeated Measures) Assessment

True value-added learning occurs at the level of the student, in the form of additional knowledge and skills gained, ideally measured on an annual basis. Only a handful of states presently implement a statewide, comprehensive student-level, value-added assessment system. The most referenced, applauded, and criticized example of such a system is the Tennessee Value-Added Assessment System (TVAAS). Dr. William Sanders, a statistician from the University of Tennessee, initially developed the system in the late 1980s (Sanders, 1995; Sanders & Horn, 1998; Sanders & Rivers, 1996). Tennessee implemented the TVAAS as part of the Tennessee Education Improvement Act of 1992 (see Morgan, 2004).

TVAAS tracks the annual rate of achievement gain of all Tennessee students in grades 2 through 8 (Sanders, 1995; Sanders & Rivers, 1996; Wright, Horn, & Sanders, 1997). States may attempt to assess individual student value-added achievement in systems that test students in only fourth and eighth grade, but it is unlikely that one could attribute individual student gains over this 4-year time frame to one particularly successful school, in that most students change schools at least once between fourth and eighth grade.

A system that annually tracks individual student value-added achievement, may aggregate data to determine classroom, school, or district mean value-added indices, providing useful information at each level of the system. Note that with a standards-based approach, which begins with the aggregate, one can derive no useful information about individual performance. Student-level value-added data provide powerful opportunities to evaluate the effectiveness of organizational units (schools and districts) and instructional staff throughout a system. William Sanders and colleagues have used TVAAS extensively to study cumulative teacher quality effects on student performance (Sanders & Rivers, 1996; Wright, Horn, & Sanders, 1997). While developing a student-level, value-added assessment system has numerous advantages, including the opportunity to monitor and evaluate teacher performance, the advantage of such a system in the context of performance-based incentive funding is in the teaching behaviors such a system promotes. Unlike standards-based systems, which set arbitrary "bars" for all students, individual value-added systems promote teaching practices that maximize the value-added achievement of all students. That is, teachers are best served by achieving that maximum average rate of achievement gain across all students in their class, and a school is best served by achieving a maximum average rate of gain across all classrooms.

Student-level, value-added assessment of academic achievement is the most promising performance path

mark for inclusion in a comprehensive, statewide school performance assessment program. Value-added path marks may be used in conjunction with standards-based benchmarks to ensure that state standards are met and that appropriate individualization occurs at the classroom level. Systems that evaluate numbers of students surpassing benchmarks (whether a single minimum bar or multiple levels) and compare numbers of students passing benchmarks from one year to the next in order to generate "improvement" measures are not value-added assessment systems.

Caveats on Student-Level Value-Added Assessment and TVAAS

A few important cautions are in order. TVAAS, while among the more refined approaches to statewide student performance measurement, is still far from perfect. Concerns regarding TVAAS in the context of school performance comparisons are similar and related to the concerns we noted in Chapter 11 regarding the measurement of school district efficiency. Recent research on the statistical method used in TVAAS indicates that the approach may not produce reliable rankings of school performance, in part, because teacher quality within schools varies substantially (Lockwood, Lewis, & McCaffrey, 2002). A 1996 independent review of TVAAS prepared for the Tennessee legislature made several recommendations for improving the reliability of the assessments used in TVAAS but supported the general design of the system (Bock, Wolfe, & Fisher, 1996).

Numerous critiques have been levied about certain underlying assumptions of TVAAS. Perhaps the most common critique is that TVAAS and Sanders and colleagues endorse the notion that controlling for prior performance of students alone allows one to ignore socioeconomic factors when comparing teacher, school, or district performance (Sanders, 1995; Sanders & Horn, 1998; Sanders & Rivers, 1996). That is, students' family backgrounds influence only their starting point in school, and teachers and schools should be able to achieve comparable rates of value-added education regardless of population demographics. Researchers have repeatedly shown that student socioeconomic factors are related to teacher and school ratings that might be generated under TVAAS itself or similar testing systems (Kuppermintz, 2003; see also Figlio, 2004). Student-level, value-added analysis therefore may not be a panacea. Figlio (2004, p. 98) notes, "Given the correlations often found in the data between student test score gains and background

Figure 14.1 Factors Influencing the Production of Outcomes

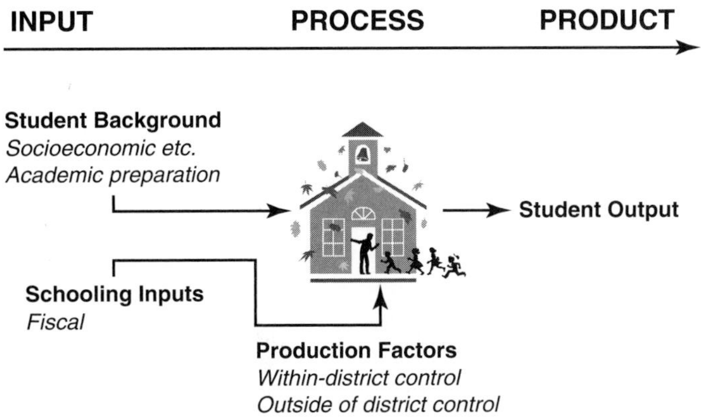

characteristics, empirically controlling for student body attributes may be warranted."

Leveling the Playing Field[1]

The necessity for "apples-to-apples" comparisons is nearly always interjected into conversations around school performance assessments. The most basic comparison method is, of course, to consider all schools as being on the same playing field and to require all schools to meet the same compliance and performance standards in order to obtain shares of the incentive funding pool. This approach generates several concerns. Where states expect schools to achieve given levels of performance, or performance benchmarks, some schools clearly have an advantage over others. Systems that allocate funds to schools achieving and sustaining high-performance levels without consideration for other criteria are at risk of simply rewarding *traditionally successful schools* and not stimulating improvement among schools that believe that they cannot compete. This is not to suggest that schools that maintain a record of success should not have access to the incentive resource pool; however, at least one objective of incentive funding—improving lower performing schools—is sacrificed when requiring all schools to meet the same compliance and performance standards is the sole method of comparison.

It may be useful at this point to refer back to the education production process and the various factors that influence production discussed in Chapter 11. Recall that production of student outcomes is a function of stu-

dent inputs, schooling inputs, and production factors within and beyond the control of local school officials. Ideally, the objective of a performance comparison system is to influence the production factors within the control of local school officials. That is, to make them play harder! To extend the sports analogy, it is only likely that teams will attempt to play harder, if they believe that they are on a level playing field. Leveling the playing field for education production involves either equalizing all factors outside of the control of local schools, or making appropriate adjustments. Unlike professional sports, equalizing external factors can be difficult if not entirely infeasible in public education systems. For example, one would have to begin by randomly assigning students of different socioeconomic backgrounds and prior performance characteristics to schools. One would then have to ensure that all schools have access to comparable production technologies (schools of similar size, with comparable facilities, materials, supplies, and equipment). Equalization of production technology comes along with complete equalization of fiscal inputs, such that schools have comparable ability to recruit and retain high-quality teaching faculty. Unless each of these conditions exists, school systems must make appropriate adjustments (see Figure 14.1).

Adjusting for Prior or Current Performance
One adjustment is to judge school-level current performance, given prior performance. That is, school systems can use the battery of compliance and performance benchmarks to classify schools into competitive brackets. Where student-level, value-added assessment is used, this approach would involve comparing prior mean value-added with current mean value-added achievement (e.g., change in rate of achievement gain). Schools

---

[1]For an exceptional alternative discussion of this topic, see Figlio (2004).

may then compete on these measures with other schools performing at comparable levels. School systems may award high performers in each bracket points toward incentive funding. The behavioral outcome of such an approach should be an upward ratcheting of performance within competitive brackets. Movement among brackets can be stimulated (or at least not deterred) with high-performance maintenance funds awarded by bracket status (performance benchmark). School systems should consider performance path marks and award points separately because, by measuring annual rate of change, performance path marks continually update and account for prior performance of each student.

Adjusting for Student Population Differences

Adjustments for student socioeconomic characteristics are also important unless school systems can achieve randomized assignment. Richards and Sheu explored a South Carolina policy that created "comparison bands" of schools based on socioeconomic criteria and compared those schools by performance gain rather than level:

> Grouping schools into SES [socioeconomic status] bands to compete for incentive awards has important distributional and policy implications. Most importantly, using school gain scores and SES bands together effectively eliminates the impact of SES on the distribution of incentive awards. (Richards & Sheu, 1992, p. 71)

Despite the apparent fairness of comparing similar student populations, however, South Carolina discontinued the approach (King & Mathers, 1997, p. 153). Indeed, substantial evidence shows that schools with higher proportions of low SES students perform relatively poorly on school aggregate outcome measures. In the context of school performance measurement systems, researchers continue to find that schools serving higher than average socioeconomic populations tend to perform better, even when using value-added measures, and when adjusting for measurement error (Ladd & Walsh, 2001).

Adjusting for Local Discretionary Input Differences

Finally, consideration of schooling resource and production technology (scale, facilities, etc.) differences beyond administrative control is important. Regarding schooling resources, the most level playing field would be achieved by using a cost function to estimate the fiscal resources required for each school to achieve a given set of outcomes (at average efficiency), given their student population characteristics and other factors outside the control of local administrators. To maintain the level playing field, no school or district should have more or less revenue than the prescribed amount. While logistically feasible, such an approach may not be politically feasible, because higher-wealth communities may rebel against limitations to local control and taxing authority. If the state legislature concedes on local taxing authority, allowing revenues to vary across districts beyond variance in cost of producing comparable outcomes, then the performance-comparison system must include adjustments for resource differences. It would be foolish and unfair to assume, for example, that districts able to raise more revenue, provide higher-quality facilities, and pay higher salaries are on a level playing field with less fortunate districts, even if all other factors were equal (or adjusted for). Further, such a system would perpetuate fiscal input inequities by rewarding those districts that can spend more to achieve higher outcomes.

In effect, making adjustments for student background characteristics, production characteristics beyond administrative control, and fiscal input differences means comparing schools or districts on the basis of efficiency, rather than production alone. That is, the goal of teachers, administrators, and other school staff should be to get the most from the students they are given, with the resources available. Unfortunately, data on fiscal inputs tend to be available only at the district rather than school level. Further, it can be difficult to account for nontraditional revenues received by schools or districts, including privately raised funds or nonmonetary gifts.

Allocating Financial Rewards

In existing incentive funding programs, states generally allocate financial rewards to schools or districts meeting performance guidelines. States generally allow determination of the use of financial rewards, or allocation within schools, to occur at the school level, with some restrictions imposed by states. In Kentucky, most school-based rewards were allocated to teachers and other school staff as salary bonuses, while neither Texas nor Indiana policies allowed for salary bonuses (King & Mathers, 1997).

Generally, the amount of funding available for incentive rewards has not been substantial. For example, the most aggressive reward program, Kentucky's, allocated bonuses of only $2,500 biannually. In South

Carolina, rewards amounted to $2,500 to $63,000 per school in 1996–1997, and in Texas, $250 to $30,000 per school in 1994–1995. Further, funding for incentive programs has been sporadic and unpredictable (King & Mathers, 1997, p. 152).

Competing for Rewards

How should states allocate incentives to induce desirable competitive behaviors and ultimately improve student outcomes? The first important question is one of competing units, or "who is competing with whom?" We partially addressed this in previous sections dealing with appropriate comparisons in the evaluation of student outcomes. Ideally, the school—not the pupil, classroom, or district—is the unit to be recognized for performance and rewarded accordingly in a state-governed incentive program. Districts may, and should, by negotiation with local unions, develop separate local systems for rewarding individual teacher performance, knowledge, and/or skills (Odden & Kelley, 1999). While incentive funding policies are state contracts with schools, individual performance pay programs are *local* contracts between boards of education and teachers, though a state may play a role in stimulating districts to pursue such arrangements. In the case of school incentive reward programs, the objective is to stimulate competition to improve among schools, promoting team unity and focus among teachers and administrators in each unit.

Some policy makers presume that state-governed fiscal reward programs are unlike market-based reforms, such as vouchers and charter schools, because state-governed fiscal reward programs (a) do not promote competition between schools because they may set absolute rather than relative standards and (b) because those programs may reward all who reach those standards. But because fiscal reward pools must be finite, competition must exist. This is not a negative attribute of such programs. First, if all districts were winners, there would be no higher level toward which to strive, no additional personal benefit to extract. Further, competitive behavior among schools may yield a positive ratcheting of performance outcomes over time.

Despite education policy makers' desires to de-emphasize between-school comparisons and promote external standards, an effective incentive funding program must involve some relative comparisons, or at least norm-referenced cut-offs. That is, there can only be so many winners. It is arguably more important for individuals in competing agencies to know the reward they are competing for than to know the desired level of performance they are attempting to achieve. Not knowing the absolute level of performance required forces the team to shoot as high as possible. Admittedly, teams may become disenchanted with the system if they show substantial performance improvement but still do not make the cut. However, under the alternative, where resources are finite, if a performance benchmark is used and is set too low, the reward pool will be substantially diluted and ultimately disappointingly low, reducing extrinsic motivation for coming years.

Efficiency Questions Regarding Fiscal Incentives

A potential concern regarding incentive funding is that such programs add resources to schools already performing well with existing resources, and by virtue of the fact that the state's resource pool is limited, such programs reduce available resources for schools performing less well. An extension of this argument is that the addition of resources to high-performing institutions may reduce the efficiency of those institutions, presuming resources are increased, but the same high-performance level is only maintained, not necessarily increased.

The efficiency concern provides further support that performance incentives should be tied to value-added performance rather than absolute-performance levels. As resources are increased, performance must increase commensurately, such that efficiency is at least break-even. Ideally, states could set the marginal increase in resources (incentive funding) at levels less than otherwise expected to achieve a given marginal increase in performance. That is, states may set reward levels at efficient levels, where performance improvements tied to those reward levels exceed performance improvements expected from those reward levels, given average district efficiency. While ideal, however, this approach may be technically infeasible, given our present inability to accurately measure efficiency, and it may yield reward levels that are insufficient extrinsic motivators.

Within-School Distribution of Funds

The point of incentive funding is to provide sufficient extrinsic motivation to teachers, administrators, and other potentially relevant players for hard work that leads to successful student outcomes. Consistent with this purpose, incentive resources should ideally go to individual teachers rather than school supplies or some other schooling input enhancement as dictated by some state policies (Texas and Indiana), unless a school system can show that providing a teacher with additional money to purchase classroom supplies motivates comparably to handing that teacher a check for the same amount. Admittedly, supply money may result in personal savings for many teachers in fiscally strapped districts. Providing incentives to individuals for performance rather than increasing schooling inputs both reduces the possibility that incentive funding will decrease schooling efficiency and arguably increases the efficacy of the extrinsic motivator.

Some pecuniary benefit may result from increasing instructional resources in low-resource, low-outcome schools showing improvement. In such cases, school systems may allocate additional instructional resources such that both resources and outcomes increase while maintaining efficiency. Incentive funding programs, however, should generally be adopted as supplements to well-equalized basic funding formulas, where it should be highly unlikely that any low-performing, inadequately funded district exists. It is much more likely in such a system for several higher-spending, yet still low-performing, districts to exist.

Overview of Existing Accountability Programs

In this section, we review recent summaries of state accountability systems. Researchers are paying increased attention to attributes of accountability systems in attempts to tie those attributes to student outcomes. In a framework similar to that which we presented, Hanushek and Raymond (2002) describe the different approaches that states use to evaluate schools and districts. Hanushek and Raymond classify state accountability systems as measuring the following:

Status Only: Status models involve measuring students' average test scores, or percentages of students passing a specific benchmark at a given grade level in a given year.

Status Change: In a status-change model, one might, for example, compare the average performance (or percentage passing a specific benchmark) of students in a specific grade in a school, to students in that same grade, the next year.

Grade-Level Change: Grade-level change models are an extension of status-change models, but focusing specifically on changes in performance of cohorts over time, at specific grade levels, rather than aggregating data to school averages (e.g., rather than combining 3rd-grade status change and 6th-grade status change measures to evaluate a K–6 school).

Cohort Gain: Cohort gain analysis involves comparing the average performance of a cohort of students at one point in time with the average performance of that same cohort at a later point in time. For example, comparing the average scores of 3rd-grade students in year 1 with the average scores of 7th-grade students in year 5.

Individual Gain: Individual gain scores are based on measuring the changes in individual students' scores from one point in time to the next. School systems can use individual gain scores for measuring school or district performance by first calculating individual students' gains, then aggregating the gain scores for individual students to the school level (Bock, Wolfe, & Fisher, 1996; Sanders & Horn, 1998; Wright, Horn, & Sanders, 1997).

Table 14.3 summarizes Hanushek and Raymond's (2004) classification of state accountability systems. Hanushek and Raymond, like others, including Carnoy and Loeb (2002), find that state accountability systems are dominated by systems that cross-sectionally evaluate the average level of student performance at the school level. Hanushek and Raymond levy the criticism, which we will display with examples from Kansas, that systems based on status alone primarily measure socioeconomic conditions of schooling, and minimally if at all address actual schooling quality. Recall, however, that while student-level, value-added analysis is a vast improvement, it offers no perfect solution.

In a recent article finding that state accountability systems do influence student outcomes, Martin Carnoy and Susanna Loeb (2002) develop a strength index for state accountability systems. The strength of accountability systems depends primarily on two factors. First, does the accountability system have significant incentives and/or sanctions tied to good or bad school performance? Second, does the accountability system hold students themselves accountable by having them take tests to progress from one grade level to the next, or by having them take a high school exit exam? Table 14.4 summarizes Carnoy and Loeb's (2002) rankings of state accountability systems. Note that in comparing Table 14.4 with Table 14.3, a handful of examples of states have strong-to-moderate accountability to schools but status-only measurement of performance (including Texas and California). Yet,

Table 14.3   Hanushek and Raymond's Framework for Classifying Student Performance Assessment in the Context of State Accountability Systems

Cross-Sectional Approaches		Student Change	
School-Status Model (or Status Change)	Grade-Level Change	Cohort Gain	Individual Gain Score
Arkansas	Alaska	New Mexico	Tennessee
Alabama	Colorado	North Carolina	Massachusetts
California	Delaware		
Connecticut	Florida		
Georgia	Kentucky		
Mississippi	Louisiana		
Maryland	Oklahoma		
Michigan	Rhode Island		
Nevada	Vermont		
New Hampshire	Wisconsin		
New York			
Ohio			
Oregon			
South Carolina			
Texas			
Virginia			
West Virginia			

Source: Data from Hanushek, E., & Raymond, M. (2004). *Does school accountability lead to improved student performance?* Retrieved June 2005 from http://edpro.stanford.edu/Hanushek/admin/pages/files/uploads/accountability.jpam.jounral.pdf

systems with arguably better measurement of school performance (Tennessee and Massachusetts) have not strengthened the accountability tied to those systems.

Overview of Existing Financial Incentive Programs
Table 14.5 displays a state-by-state summary of school-based performance reward policies. According to Goertz et al. (2001) in a report by the Consortium for Policy Research in Education (CPRE), by 1999, nineteen states either included or planned to include some form of rewards within their school-accountability systems. Table 14.5 summarizes the policies of 15 states, primarily generated from data compiled by Catherine Seilke et al. (2001) for the National Center for Education Statistics (NCES) report, *Public School Finance Programs of the United States and Canada.*

Table 14.5 shows that the majority of states allocating fiscal incentives provide those incentives to schools as competing units and measure performance at the school level. This is notable because, typically, fiscal relationships have been established between states and school districts rather than states and individual schools, with the emerging exception of charter schools. Each of the incentive funding systems includes some form of

academic achievement measure, and a handful of the incentive funding systems include other measures, such as student and teacher attendance rates and dropout rates. Goertz et al. (2001) note that, overall, 39 states include average daily attendance, 37 states include dropout rates, and 27 states include high school graduation rates in their state accountability reporting systems. Goertz et al. (2001) also indicate that 33 states use some form of student achievement measure as the primary measure of school and district performance.

A handful of states, including New Mexico and Massachusetts, take the approach of comparing school performance against demographically adjusted expectations, the approach abandoned by South Carolina in previous years (King & Mathers, 1997).

As discussed previously, many states continue to focus on maximizing minimum performance. That is, schools may achieve "excellence" and receive incentives by raising large numbers of students to minimum proficiency levels. Florida, for example, gives a grade of A or B to schools where at least half of the students reach Level 3 ("the student has partial success with the state standards") on the state assessment (Goertz et al., 2001, p. 20).

Table 14.4   States With Strong-to-Weak Strength Indices and School Accountability

State	Carnoy and Loeb Strength Index	Student-Level Accountability	Strength of School Accountability
Florida	5	Yes	Strong
North Carolina	5	Yes	Strong
New Jersey	5	Yes	Strong
New York	5	Yes	Strong
Texas	5	Yes	Strong
Alabama	4	Yes	Strong
California	4	No	Strong
Kentucky	4	No	Moderate
Maryland	4	Yes	Strong
New Mexico	4	Yes	Strong
West Virginia	3.5	No	Strong
Indiana	3	Yes	Moderate
Louisiana	3	Yes	Moderate
Mississippi	3	Yes	Moderate
Ohio	3	Yes	Moderate
South Carolina	3	Yes	Moderate
Illinois	2.5	No	Moderate
Oregon	2.5	Yes	Weak
Arizona	2	Yes	Weak
Georgia	2	Yes	None
Massachusetts	2	Yes	None
Minnesota	2	Yes	None
Virginia	2	No	Weak
Wisconsin	2	No	Weak
Missouri	1.5	No	Weak
Nevada	1.5	Yes	Weak
Tennessee	1.5	Yes	Weak
Alaska	1	Yes	None
Arkansas	1	No	None
Colorado	1	No	None
Connecticut	1	No	Weak
Delaware	1	No	None
Hawaii	1	No	None
Idaho	1	No	None
Kansas	1	No	None
Maine	1	No	None
Michigan	1	No	Weak
Montana	1	No	None
North Dakota	1	No	Weak
New Hampshire	1	No	None
Oklahoma	1	No	Weak
Pennsylvania	1	No	Weak
Rhode Island	1	No	Weak
South Dakota	1	No	None
Utah	1	No	Weak
Vermont	1	No	Weak
Washington	1	No	Weak
Wyoming	1	No	Weak
Iowa	0	No	None
Nebraska	0	No	None

Source: Data from Carnoy, M., & Loeb, S. (2002). Does external accountability affect student outcomes? A cross state analysis. *Educational Evaluation and Policy Analysis, 24* (4), 305–331.

Table 14.5 State Incentive Funding Policies

State	Compliance Outcomes	Performance Outcomes	Unit of Performance Measurement	Type of Measurement	Unit Receiving Reward	Form and Use of Reward	Amount of Average Award
Colorado	Graduation Attendance	Student achievement Community satisfaction Effective practice	School	Level	School		Plaque, flag, and $1,000/school
Connecticut		4th-, 6th-, & 8th-grade achievement	District	Level	District to school	Monetary: Targeted to schools most responsible for district improvement	Share state pot of $1 million
Delaware		Student achievement	School	Ranking based on performance level, performance gain, and group relative gain	School		Symbols of recognition
Florida (Excellence in teaching)	Teacher national board certification		Teacher	National board teacher certification		Cost of certification, bonus, and salary enhancement	
Florida (Merit)		Student achievement	School	Sustained performance or performance improvement	School	Monetary	
Florida (Performance incentive)	Graduation rates Attendance	Student achievement	School				
Georgia			School	Meet 80% of self-prescribed objectives	Teachers (whole school)	Monetary	$2,000 per certified faculty member
Indiana	Attendance Graduation	Achievement	School	Growth in student performance	School	Not for salaries, bonuses, or athletics	
Kentucky	Dropout rates	Achievement	School	Improvement toward meeting standard	School	Monetary	
Maryland			School		School	Monetary	

(continued)

Table 14.5 State Incentive Funding Policies (*continued*)

State	Compliance Outcomes	Performance Outcomes	Unit of Performance Measurement	Type of Measurement	Unit Receiving Reward	Form and Use of Reward	Amount of Average Award
Massachusetts			School	Meet or exceed expectations	School		
New Jersey		Achievement	School	"Absolute success" (90% passing) or "significant progress"	District	Monetary	
New Mexico		Academic performance	School (adjusted for LEP and free lunch)	High improving and high performing	School	Monetary (top 10% improving) and certificate (top 25% level)	Minimum $1,000 per school
North Carolina		Achievement	School (based on expected growth)	Exceeding 100% or 110% expected growth	Teachers and administrators (per school)	Salary bonus	$750 + benefits for exceeding 100%; $1,500 + benefits for 110%
Oregon		Achievement	School	Classification as "successful school" by application process	School	Teacher salary bonuses	$1,000 per teacher
Pennsylvania	Attendance	Achievement	School	Separate awards for effort (compliance) and achievement	School	50% must be used on planning educational program, 25% may be used on salary bonuses	$7.50 to $37.50 per student
Texas	Dropout rates	Achievement	School	Percent passing level (groups)	School	Monetary or certificate Not for athletics or other presently budgeted items	$500 to $5,000 per school

LEP, limited English proficiency.
Source: Data from Seilke et al., 2001.

Goertz et al. (2001) point out that several state accountability systems include measures of "closing the achievement gap" as measures of performance improvement (Delaware, Illinois, Kentucky, Missouri, Rhode Island, Wisconsin). We have significant concerns over any accountability system where success is more easily achieved by reducing the value-added achievement of any group of students. Closing the achievement gap, like closing the per-pupil spending gap, is most easily achieved by both raising the floor and lowering the ceiling.

Of those states providing fiscal incentives, most of the incentives are nominal, and in some cases those incentives are accompanied by a symbol of recognition such as a letter or plaque. Incentives in Georgia, North Carolina, Oregon, Pennsylvania, and Texas appear more substantial but may still be too low to act as sufficient extrinsic motivators. In some cases, all or some of the incentive funding must be allocated to things other than teacher salary bonuses, with unknown effects on motivation.

Effects of Standards and Accountability, and School-Based Performance Rewards

Accountability Systems in General

Recent research finds significant positive effects on student outcomes of strong accountability systems. For example, in a recent, multistate analysis of the effects of state accountability systems on student outcomes, Carnoy and Loeb (2002) constructed an index of the strength of state accountability systems, ranging from 0 for no accountability to 5 for strong accountability, and tested the relationship between accountability system strength and student outcomes. In general, Carnoy and Loeb found that states having strong accountability systems are reaping significant benefits in terms of student outcomes. In particular, Carnoy and Loeb found:

- "Our results indicate a positive and significant relationship between the strength of accountability systems and math achievement gains at the 8th-grade level across racial/ethnic groups" (2002, p. 320).
- "The 8th grade achievement gains associated with stronger accountability are large. A two-step increase in the accountability scale corresponds to approximately one half a standard deviation higher gain in the percent of students that achieve at least

the basic level; and the effect sizes for gains at the proficiency level are even higher" (2002, p. 320).

- "[S]tates with stronger accountability saw significantly greater gains in the percent of 4th grade Black students that achieved at least the basic level on the math NAEP (more than a third of a standard deviation increase associated with a two-step increase in accountability; and marginally significant greater gains in the percent of 4th grade Hispanic students that achieved at least the basic level on the math NAEP (approximately a quarter of a standard deviation increase associated with a two-step increase in accountability)" (2002, p. 320).

Hanushek and Raymond (2002) also find that the strength of state accountability systems is associated with improved student performance on the National Assessment of Educational Progress (NAEP). (The authors' results pool data on NAEP math gains over both the 1992–1996 and 1996–2000 periods.) In particular, Hanushek and Raymond find:

> The typical student in a state without an accountability system of any form would see a 0.7 percent increase in proficiency scores. States with "report card" systems display test performance and other factors but neither provide any simple aggregation and judgment of performance nor attach sanctions and rewards. In many ways, these systems serve simply as a public disclosure function. Just this reporting moves the expected gain to 1.2 percent. Finally, states that provide explicit scores for schools and that attach sanctions and rewards (what we call "accountability" systems) obtained a 1.6 percent increase in mathematics performance. In short, testing and accountability as practiced have led to gains over that expected without formal systems. (Hanushek & Raymond, 2002, p. 3)

Increasingly, researchers are providing more detailed explanations for why accountability systems seem to matter in terms of student outcomes. Two recent studies published in *Educational Evaluation and Policy Analysis* indicated that increased graduation requirements and related accountability mechanisms are associated with students' taking more rigorous courses. In one study, Schiller and Muller (2003) find that "students in states with more graduation requirements tended to enroll in higher level mathematics courses as freshmen and persist to take more advanced level courses. Similar trends were also found for students in states that link test performance to consequences for schools" (p. 299) (see also Teitlebaum, 2003).

These findings are consistent with numerous previous studies that relate teachers' classroom standards to student outcomes. Figlio and Lucas (2000), for example, find that teachers' classroom grading standards positively influence student outcomes. Taken together with studies of state accountability systems, the implication is that state systems of standards and accountability may simultaneously influence the standards that teachers impose in classrooms, and at the secondary level, especially where student-level accountability is employed, standards may encourage students to pursue more rigorous course work.

School-Based Performance Rewards

Unfortunately, little evidence shows the positive effects of extrinsic motivators such as salary bonuses on teachers and school leaders. Many suggest that teachers are primarily driven by intrinsic and altruistic desires to help children succeed in school and in life. Milanowski's (2000) research indicates that teachers in Charlotte-Mecklenburg and Kentucky rate "receiving a bonus" as a comparable motivator to "personal satisfaction from improved student performance" and the "receiving funds for school improvements." However, Milanowski (2000) also notes that bonuses ranged only from $1,000 ($700 after taxes) in Charlotte-Mecklenburg to $1,250 ($2,500 biannually) in Kentucky. Further, it might be argued that teachers, in today's public education environment, would be highly likely to overemphasize their altruistic attributes and de-emphasize any desire to attain personal benefit. Some evidence, however, shows that performance-based incentive programs, coupled with programs to help underperforming schools, are having positive effects. Carolyn Kelley (1998), in a study of Kentucky's program, notes:

> District differences were found between award and non-award-winning schools. Alignment of school goals and resources, including curriculum, professional development, and principal leadership were key enabling conditions associated with award schools. The state intervention strategy for helping initially unsuccessful schools enabled these schools to develop organizational conditions associated with award-winning schools. The data suggest a model of teacher motivation that builds on previous research in education and on empirical research on employee motivation. (p. 305)

Kelley (1998) indicates that Kentucky's declining and low-performing schools intervention program is perhaps one of the more effective features of the Kentucky Education Reform Act. Kelley notes,

"Statewide, 53 schools were in decline after the first award cycle and consequently had a distinguished educator assigned to them. Remarkably, 31 of the 53 were in rewards in the second cycle; the remaining 22 schools were improving or successful. These statistics, and the comments of teachers at the two decline/reward schools, suggest that this type of intervention can make the difference for 'stuck' schools" (p. 313).

Simultaneously Improving Input- and Outcome-Based Adequacy

Senate Bill 856 in the state of Maryland proposed a somewhat creative approach for simultaneously improving the adequacy of fiscal inputs and student outcomes for Maryland schools (Fiscal Note to Senate Bill 856, 2002). Having recently completed a series of studies of the cost of providing an "adequate" education in Maryland schools, the legislature faced proposing a "phase-in" plan to bring districts to their newly calculated adequate spending levels. Fearing reduced efficiency resulting from districts consuming the new resources, but not yielding commensurate performance improvements, the legislature set out to establish a plan for monitoring and managing the rate at which both the input gaps and outcome gaps should be closed. That is, with respect to both inputs and outcomes, the goal is not to close a gap between high- and low-spending schools and high- and low-performing students, but to close an input gap between low and adequate spending and outcome gap between low and adequate performance.

The plan involves relating a district's "adequacy gap," the difference between current expenditure and "adequate" expenditure levels, to its "MSPAP gap," the difference between the district's current level of performance on the Maryland State Performance Assessment Program (MSPAP) and the desired, or adequate performance level of 70%. Figure 14.2 displays the relationship between MSPAP and Adequacy Gaps across Maryland districts. Somewhat surprisingly, a relatively consistent relationship exists between current "underspending" and current "underperformance." This finding may, in part, be a function of the county level of aggregation of data, typical in Southern states where school districts are organized by county. (Recall from Chapter 11 that Hanushek, Rivkin, and Taylor found that high levels of aggregation tended to inflate the apparent relationship between resources and achievement.)

Figure 14.2 Relating the Adequacy Gap and MSPAP Gap for Maryland School Districts

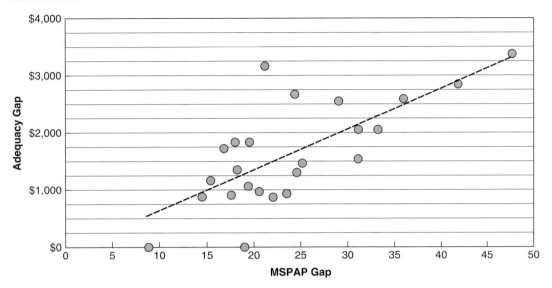

MSPAP, Maryland State Performance Assessment Program.

Source: Exhibit 2, p. 2 of Senate Bill 856 (2002). Retrieved from
http://www.marylandpolicy.org/html/research/documents/sb0856.pdf

One might expect substantial variation among schools within districts, far more outliers, and more significant outliers from the trend line in Figure 14.2.

It is also important to bear in mind that Figure 14.2 fails to fully consider the plethora of student demographic and district structural factors that may influence performance levels, though the figure gives some consideration to student need in the calculation of input adequacy. As we discussed in Chapter 7, the Maryland legislature relied on a combination of "successful schools" and "professional judgment" analysis for establishing "adequate" funding levels. The successful schools approach fails entirely in considering the cost of achieving a given set of outcomes across varied student populations, and the professional judgment approach relies on speculation that a given set of input resources should produce a given set of outcomes across varied student populations.

With those caveats in mind, this framework provides the Maryland legislature the option to develop creative indices of progress toward both input and outcome adequacy. Presently, the emphasis of Senate Bill (SB) 856 is on the development and review of district comprehensive master plans. Further, emphasis is on sanctions for low performance rather than incentives for high performance. The bill stipulates that "The State Board of Education may withhold funding from a school system that fails to demonstrate progress towards State standards and fails to develop an adequate plan" (SB 856, 2001, p. 8).

The tools we provided in Chapter 5 on the dynamics of equity might be useful for developing combined indices of input and outcome gap convergence. For example, one might construct ratios of outcome gap reduction rates (GRRs) to input gap reduction rates:

$$GRR_o/GRR_i = GRE$$

GRR_o refers to the GRR of outcomes, perhaps the 3-year average percentage change rate of convergence between a district's actual and desired performance levels. GRR_i refers to the GRR of inputs, perhaps the 3-year average percentage change rate of convergence between a district's actual and desired revenue or spending levels. GRE refers to the gap reduction efficiency. If performance improvement exceeds revenue increases, efficiency improves, and the GRE will be greater than 1.0. If, on the other hand, revenues, or inputs, increased more quickly than outcomes, the district is declining in efficiency over time. Note that this example remains grossly oversimplified. One significant issue not addressed by the GRE ratio as expressed above is "what is a reasonable lag time for expecting improvements in performance to result from increased inputs?"

Figure 14.3   Reducing Input and Outcome Gaps

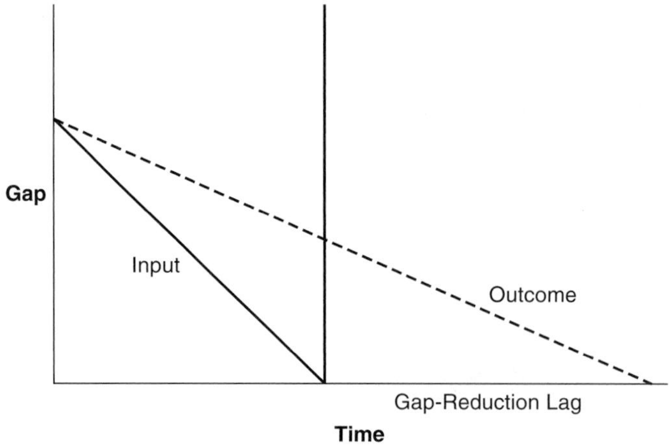

Alternatively, one might approach this problem by calculating gap reduction horizons for both inputs and outcomes, and subtract the input gap horizon from the outcome gap horizon to create an expected outcome lag, or gap reduction lag (see Figure 14.3). The expected outcome lag would be the number of years beyond input-adequacy achievement that outcome adequacy could be expected. Testing such a model would be required for establishing reasonable policy targets for outcome lags. Alternatively, one might use the actual system lag to expect outcomes following increased spending. That is, if a test is given to fourth graders, then we can assume that a 5-year lag occurs between the resource increase and the multi-year benefit received by a cohort of students moving through the system, grade level by grade level. Students 1 year ahead of the cohort would have only four-fifths of the benefit (assuming the gains are proportional). Of course, in all policy analysis, we make simplifying assumptions. We need to be wary, however, that our simplifications don't combine to eliminate all of the variation and causal relationships we were seeking in the first place.

SUMMARY

In this chapter, we have discussed the active role state governments may play in stimulating the improvement of productivity and efficiency in public schooling. In particular, we have focused on the management and regulation of student and school outcomes. Given the present research base, policies across the states, and other views we have presented in Section IV, we recommend the following guidelines for development of new, experimental school-based performance reward programs:

- A school-based performance reward program should measure performance according to a portfolio of (a) compliance benchmarks, (b) performance benchmarks, and (c) performance path marks, where each type of measure focuses on productive efficiency.

- A school-based performance reward program should offer opportunities for accomplishing equity goals as well as efficiency or performance goals.

- A school-based performance reward program must be sufficiently and consistently funded such that rewards provide sufficient extrinsic motivation and are predictable.

- A school-based performance reward program should allocate reward grants by a method that optimizes competitive behavior among schools, promoting team collaboration among teachers and administrators.

- A school-based performance reward program should be linked to a program of sanctions and support mechanisms for underperforming schools, with both supported by a common evaluation framework.

On the first point, the present emphasis of incentive funding programs arguably has been on compliance measures, such as attendance rates, with one or two performance benchmarks added. Even then, one might argue that performance measures set at minimum levels constitute compliance, not performance. Perhaps the most critical element, and presently most underdeveloped element, of such programs for ensuring appropriate treatment of individual students with diverse abilities is the development of efficient, precise, value-added assessment systems such as TVAAS. Under present models, we risk the possibility of denying many children in our public schools the opportunity to learn something new every day.[2]

Richards (1985), in a discussion of merit pay plans, notes, "Incentive plans are most likely to be successful when the technologies are clearly specified, the labor contract is such that productivity is easily separable and measurable in individual units, and when employees clearly understand the terms of the reward structure" (p. 188). However, these requirements are very difficult to meet in practice, and we conclude that on balance, school-based incentives are more likely to meet with teacher enthusiasm and, therefore, the voluntary increased effort required to raise student performance—but only when matched with external support for improvement. The extrinsic motivation that Milanowski (2000) discussed cannot exist without sufficient, predictable extrinsic motivators, and that extrinsic motivation is unlikely to be fairly distributed across teachers in all schools if a basic opportunity to teach does not exist. That is, general resource equity is prerequisite. On the last point, we refer back to Kelly's (1998) finding that Kentucky's declining and low-performing schools intervention program was one of the more effective features of the Kentucky Education Reform Act.

REFERENCES

Bock, R. D., Wolfe, R., & Fisher, T. H. (1996). *A review and analysis of the Tennessee value added assessment system. Final report.* Prepared for the Office of the Comptroller. State of Tennessee.

Brant, D. (chair), Baker, B., Ballard, B., Jones, D., & Vratil, J. (2000). *K–12 education: Financing for results.* In G. Sherrer (chair), *Governor's Vision 21st Century Task Force.* Topeka, KS: Governor's Office, State of Kansas.

Carnoy, M., & Loeb, S. (2002). Does external accountability affect student outcomes? *Educational Evaluation and Policy Analysis, 24*(4), 305–332.

Figlio, D. N. (2004). Funding and accountability: Some conceptual and technical issues in state aid reform. In J. Yinger (Ed.), *Helping children left behind: State aid and the pursuit of educational equity* (pp. 87–110). Cambridge, MA: MIT Press.

Figlio, D. N., & Lucas, M. (2000). *Do high grading standards affect student performance?* Working Paper #7985-2000. Cambridge, MA: National Bureau of Economic Research.

Fiscal Note to Senate Bill 856, Maryland General Assembly, 2002 Session.

Goertz, M., Duffy, M., & Le Floch, K. C. (2001). *Assessment and accountability systems in the 50 states.* Consortium for Policy Research in Education. University of Pennsylvania.

Hanushek, E., & Raymond, M. (2004). *Does school accountability lead to improved student performance?* http://edpro.stanford.edu/Hanushek/admin/pages/files/uploads/accountability.jpam.journel.pdf

Hanushek, E. A., Rivken, S. G., & Taylor, L. (1996). Aggregation and the estimated effects of school resources. *Review of Economics and Statistics, 78*(4), 611–627.

Kelley, C. (1998). The Kentucky school-based performance award program: school-level effects. *Educational Policy, 12*(3), 305–324.

King, R. A., & Mathers, J. K. (1997). Improving schools through performance-based accountability and financial rewards. *Journal of Education Finance, 23*(Fall), 147–176.

Kuppermintz, H. (2003). Teacher effects and teacher effectiveness: A validity investigation of the Tennessee value added assessment system. *Educational Evaluation and Policy Analysis, 25*(3), 287–298.

---

[2]Former special and gifted education lobbyist for the Council for Exceptional Children Jay McIntyre frequently presented his mission for public education as "each child learning something new every day."

Ladd, H., & Walsh, R. (2001). Implementing value-added measures of school effectiveness: Getting the incentives right. *Economics of Education Review, 21*(1), 1–17.

Lockwood, J. R., Lewis, T. A., & McCaffrey, D. F. (2002). Uncertainty in rank estimation: Implications for value-added modeling accountability systems. *Journal of Educational and Behavioral Statistics, 27*(3), 255–270.

Milanowski, A. (2000). School-based performance award programs and teacher motivation. *Journal of Education Finance, 25*(4), 517–544.

Morgan, J. G. (2004). *The Education Improvement Act: A progress report*. Retrieved June 2007 from http://www.comptroller.state.tn.us/orea/reports/educimproveact.pdf

Odden, A. R., & Kelley, C. (1999). *Paying teachers for what they know and do: New and smarter compensation strategies to improve schools*. Thousand Oaks, CA: Corwin Press.

Richards, C. E. (1985). The economics of merit pay: A special case of utility maximization. *Journal of Education Finance, 11*(2), 176–189.

Richards, C. E. (1988). A typology of educational monitoring systems. *Educational Evaluation and Policy Analysis, 10*(2), 105–114.

Richards, C. E., & Sheu, T. M. (1992). The South Carolina school incentive reward program: A policy analysis. *Economics of Education Review, 11*(1), 71–86.

Sanders, W. L. (1995). *An overview of the Tennessee value-added assessment system (TVAAS) with answers to frequently asked questions*. Knoxville, TN: The University of Tennessee Value-Added Research and Assessment Center.

Sanders, W., & Horn, S. (1998). Research findings from the Tennessee value-added assessment system (TVAAS) database: Implications for educational evaluation research. *Journal of Personnel Evaluation in Education, 12*(3), 247–256.

Sanders, W. L., & Rivers, J. C. (1996). *Cumulative and residual effects of teachers on future student academic achievement*. Knoxville, TN: The University of Tennessee Value-Added Research and Assessment Center.

Schiller, K., & Muller, C. (2003.) Raising the bar and equity? Effects of state high school graduation requirements and accountability policies on students' mathematics course taking. *Educational Evaluation and Policy Analysis, 25*(3), 299–318.

Seilke, C., et al. (2001). *Public school finance programs of the United States and Canada*. Washington, DC: National Center for Education Statistics. Retrieved from www.nces.ed.gov/edfin

Senate Bill (SB) 856. (2002). Bridge to Excellence in Public Schools Act. Maryland legislature.

Teitlebaum, P. (2003). The influence of high school graduation requirement policies in mathematics and science on student course-taking patterns and achievement. *Educational Evaluation and Policy Analysis, 25*(1), 31–57.

Wright, S. P., Horn, S. P., & Sanders, W. L. (1997). Teacher and classroom context effects on student achievement: implications for teacher evaluation. *Journal of Personnel Evaluation in Education, 11*(1), 57–67.

ALLOCATING RESOURCES TO PROMOTE PRODUCTIVITY AND EFFICIENCY IN SCHOOLS AND SCHOOL DISTRICTS

Introduction

In this final chapter, we address the topic of district and school resource allocation because of the intuitive notion that schools' and school districts' resource allocation and spending make a difference for students. Presumably, the decision to build a new football stadium over a new science laboratory has consequences for student outcomes. If resource allocation decisions matter for student outcomes, then it follows that local, state, and federal policy makers have a role in influencing and perhaps even controlling the decision-making behavior of schools and school districts in how they allocate scarce resources. Finally, we point out how our discussion of school and district allocation decisions depends heavily on research and concepts we have explored more deeply in previous chapters. Thus, in this chapter, we seek to integrate a good deal of what you have learned previously in our consideration of resource allocation decision making, and we will necessarily refer to the literature in previous chapters.

Although resource allocation decisions occur throughout all levels of the hierarchy of public schooling—from federal guidelines down to individual children—the emphasis in this chapter remains on the relationship between states and public school districts, and the methods that states use to allocate fiscal resources to public school districts. Resource allocation practices at other levels of the hierarchy are no less important, but in many cases they are somewhat less defined and/or formalized. From the district level, fiscal and human resources must be allocated to schools. Within schools, resources must be allocated to particular program areas and classrooms. In addition, schools must spend resources on utilities, and maintenance, and operations of school facilities.

Economic theory suggests that school leaders should be able to optimize the allocation of resources within schools to maximize outputs. That is, for any given level of financial inputs to schooling, an optimal mix of human and material resources and educational processes exists that school leaders can implement to achieve maximum student outcomes. As we discussed in Chapter 11, this is the concept of technical efficiency of production. Unfortunately, as illuminated by our discussion of factors influencing productivity and efficiency in Chapter 11, we still have a great deal more to learn about the best ways to combine and use educational resources toward producing higher outcomes.

Combining the various bodies of productivity research we have discussed thus far, we might argue that low-income and minority children would be best served in environments with relatively small classes (in the range of 15 to 20), with teachers from selective undergraduate colleges with degrees in their content areas (especially secondary teachers). Unfortunately, we know little about how well these resources would combine to yield improved student performance in this somewhat awkward, prototypical setting.

Production and efficiency research like that discussed in Chapter 11 has most often focused on the importance of individual resources to education production, paying less attention to the question of optimal resource mix, given a finite set of fiscal inputs. Production function studies have attempted, for example, to determine whether teacher level of education or class size influences production but have not typically addressed the optimal mix of class size and teacher education. Harris's cost-effectiveness analysis discussed in Chapter 11 is one exception. Further, numerous production function studies relate resource levels to outcomes, focusing specifically on instructional, rather than total, expenditures, and other studies estimate whether shares of spending on functions such as administration influence education production (Brewer, 1996).

Insofar as we know, no research has yet combined all of these potential sources of leverage into a single set of experiments to determine the total combined effects on increased student achievement.

The scrutiny on educational productivity and efficiency in the late 1980s and early 1990s beginning with *A Nation at Risk,* brought about increased attention not only to outcome accountability, as discussed with respect to outcome-based strategies later in this chapter, but also input accountability, or accountability for the use of education dollars. Two issues of primary interest to researchers at that time follow:

1. Identify how much of the education dollar was making it to the classroom.
2. Create more transparent financial reporting methods for schools and districts.

The latter issue arose from the former. That is, as researchers began to attempt to study where the education dollar goes, they began to realize that standard fund-accounting procedures of public school districts did not necessarily yield educationally useful information.

One team of researchers responded by heading into the schools, hand counting the people, space, time, and materials (recall Levin's 1983 *ingredients* or the *resource cost model*) used for the delivery of education, while another team worked on the development of a computer software tool for re-organizing expense data from a school district's general ledger.[1]

As a result of increased attention to "where the money goes" in the 1990s, we now know much more about how resources are organized in public schools and districts of various types and sizes, but still know very little about the relationship between the organization of resources and productivity and efficiency.

Resource Allocation: Concepts and Measurement

As we discussed in Chapter 7, researchers can measure adequacy in terms of financial inputs to schooling or human and material inputs to schooling. That is, one can study either where the dollars go in schools, or where specific human resources such as teachers and aides are assigned in schools. The choice of approach can produce significantly different results. For example, School A may appear to have significantly higher classroom-level costs than School B, simply because School A has a higher proportion of senior teachers than School B; hence, the average salaries of the teachers in School A are also higher, leading to higher average costs. However, both schools could have the same number of teachers per pupil. The dollar method shows apparent inequality, while the resource approach suggests equality. Notice that neither method tells us which group of teachers is of higher quality. They simply have different structural costs.

Financial resources are most often categorized according to standard accounting classifications within the fund accounting system of public education. Financial resources may be categorized either in terms of the *function* they serve in schools (instruction, instructional support, operations, debt service) or the *objects* that are purchased with those resources (salaries, benefits, materials and supplies, equipment). Figure 15.1 displays a breakdown of the average school district expenditures by function, and Figure 15.2 displays a breakdown of the average school district expenditures by object, focusing specifically on salaries and benefits as a share of total district budgets. Observe that the function "instruction" in Figure 15.1 is about 62% and that the object Salaries and Benefits for all employees in Figure 15.2 is about 56%.

In the 1990s, Bruce S. Cooper of Fordham University in New York, in collaboration with Coopers and Lybrand, a New York accounting firm, developed an accounting-type model, the Financial Analysis Model (FAM), for studying education resource allocation that included six dimensions, as summarized in Table 15.1 (Speakman et al., 1996).

---

[1] These are broad characterizations of the research of David Monk and colleagues, who took a resource-based approach in New York schools while Dr. Monk was on faculty at Cornell University in the 1980s and 1990s, and Bruce S. Cooper, along with Sheree Speakman at Coopers and Lybrand, who developed the Financial Analysis Model for analyzing where the education dollar went in New York City Schools. See, for example, Brent, Roellke, and Monk (1997) and Speakman et al. (1996).

Figure 15.1   National Average Expenditures by Function

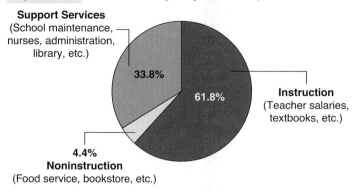

Source: Data from National Center for Education Statistics. (2001–2002). *Common core of data, local education agency universe survey, school district finances.* For updated figures, see: http://www.nces.ed.gov/edfin/graphs/topic.asp?INDEX=3

Figure 15.2   National Average Expenditures by Object

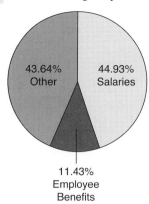

Source: Data from National Center for Education Statistics. (2001–2002). *Common core of data, local education agency universe survey, school district finances.* Retrieved from http://www.nces.ed.gov/edfin/graphs/topic.asp?INDEX=13

The goal of the FAM (later developed into a software product known as IN$ITE, packaged within a product known as Class Act) was to provide a framework for making educational sense of school district budget data. The software worked by coding a school district's general ledger such that analysts could import data on all expenses in a given year into the software and reorganize it according to the analytical dimensions provided in the software.

Under the FAM framework, aggregational analysis involved identifying all costs associated with the operation of a public school district, both annual operating costs and debt obligations. Often, nonoperating costs are excluded from analyses of schooling resources. Structural analysis involves identifying the level in the organization to which resources are allocated, for example, which resources are consumed by the central office of a district, and which resources are handed down to schools. Some state accounting systems for public education include codes that identify school-level allocations, while others require that districts aggregate all expenditures. For example, instructional expenditures across all schools in a district might be reported under a single aggregate function classification—instruction.

FAM varies most from conventional financial reporting models for public schools in the final three dimensions: typological, programmatic, and contractual. The typological frame allows analysis of expenditure patterns by grade level, across schools, and the programmatic frame allows expenditures to be attributed to specific educational programs. The intersection of these frames then allows expenditures to be attributed to specific educational programs by grade level. Finally, the contractual frame allows teacher and other personnel contracts to be disaggregated into contact and noncontact time with students. One potentially valuable use of such a model is for identifying expenditures associated with specific programs in conjunction with performance data on those programs for conducting cost-effectiveness analyses as described in Chapter 11.

FAM is a fiscal resource allocation, or accounting method of analysis, modified to be more educationally useful than standard accounting methods. One can take either a financial accounting approach or resource-based approach for studying inputs to educational systems. Analysts most often study human resource allocation in terms of programmatic allocations (content area, grade level, advanced, regular, or remedial) or by contractual assignment (teacher, aide, support staff). For example, Brent, Roellke, and Monk (1997) study the allocation of high school teaching staff across advanced, regular, and remedial classes by content area for a group of high schools in New York State. We discuss the findings of Brent et al. (1997) later in this section.

Human resource allocation analyses typically generate estimates of fiscal resource allocation across program areas or assignments by assigning prices (either

Table 15.1   The Financial Analysis Model (FAM)

Frame	Focus	Application
1. **Aggregational** • Budget allocations and spending • Fringe benefits • Pensions • Debt obligations	Brings together the obvious and hidden costs of education: purpose is to attribute all possible costs to their sources.	Need to capture all related costs to give a realistic picture of what education is costing taxpayers and government.
2. **Structural** • Hierarchy of costs: central, district, school, and classrooms	Differentiates central, district, and schools on the basis of the structure of the school system. Costs parallel the structure of the system.	Without a clear sense of the relationship between structure and costs, it is difficult to trace resources to teachers and students.
3. **Functional** • Management • Operations • Support • Instruction	Determines the costs of performing various functions in the system; focus is on direct classroom instruction—requiring the isolation of functional expenditures using a model.	Separating instruction from other related costs. Budget allocations model.
4. **Typological** • Elementary school • Middle school • High school • Nonschool	Costs follow the categorization of schools, from elementary through high school. May also show those costs that are not allocated to schools but should be, or that are allocated there but occur elsewhere.	Costs may be attributable to the particular needs and structures of a category or type of school.
5. **Programmatic** • All programs • Special education • Bilingual education • Categorical education • Regular/base education	Tracing costs by program because some programs, as mandated, are more expensive than others. Differentiates among federal, state, and local programs.	Use of average per-pupil cost may obscure the actual resources reaching students, particularly those students without mandated and special services, which are most costly.
6. **Contractual** • Actual teaching time • Planning time • Supervisory periods • Compensated time (2 or 3 of 8 40-minute work periods)	Contracts with teachers and other groups stipulate the number of contact hours ("up time") and other administrative, supervisory, planning, and lunch periods.	Contact minutes per day may not reflect actual time spent with students in conferences, extracurricular activities, etc.

Source: Speakman et al., 1996.

within or across district average prices) to teachers. Researchers may use within-district average prices to study resource concentration within districts across program areas.

Table 15.2 displays national averages (weighted by district enrollment) for numbers of staff per 1,000 pupils and for staffing shares, calculated as numbers of staff in each category with respect to total numbers of staff. As we will discuss later in this section, significant variations in human resource allocations occur across districts, many of which can be explained by understanding differences in district structures and state policies.

Although attaining a better understanding of resource allocation within districts and schools is important, equally, if not more important, is attaining a better understanding of the following:

1. The association between different patterns of schooling resource allocation and improved efficiency and/or productivity

2. Identifying the factors, including state policies, that are associated with differences in resource allocation patterns within schools and districts

Figure 15.3 presents a schematic diagram of the research agenda regarding district and school resource

Table 15.2 National Average Staffing Levels and Shares, *Common Core of Data,*
1999–2000

Resource	Mean	Standard Deviation
Staffing Levels		
Classroom teachers per 1,000 students	61.37	11.43
Support staff per 1,000 students	45.73	13.95
Central administrators per 1,000 students	1.10	1.12
Total administration and administrative staff per 1,000 students	11.79	4.30
Staffing Shares		
Classroom teaching staff share	52.05	5.44
Support staff share	37.76	6.07
Central administrative staff share	3.98	2.41

Source: Data from National Center for Education Statistics. (1999–2000). *Common core of data, local education agency survey.* Retrieved from www.nces.ed.gov/ccd

allocation. The ultimate objective is to develop a better understanding of the relationship between resource allocation levels and productivity and efficiency levels and the relationship between changes in resource allocation practices and changes in productivity and efficiency (i.e., "schooling outcomes," the link furthest to the right in the figure).

Internal allocation of resources is not entirely at the discretion of local district officials, and constraints on

internal allocation of resources are not necessarily entirely embedded, or explicitly stated in policies. Many input accountability and outcome accountability policies naturally assume that allocation of resources within schools and districts is entirely at the discretion of school and district leaders. A handful of researchers have shown how district structural characteristics, most notably total district enrollment, are associated with different patterns of internal resource allocation. Further,

Figure 15.3 Areas for Investigation in Resource Allocation

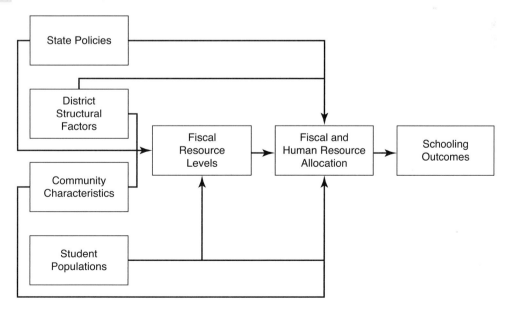

community characteristics, including preferences for particular educational programs and local fiscal capacity, may influence resource allocation practices. Student demographics might influence the need for specific educational programs or might allow the district to receive additional restricted state or federal revenues. Arguably, increased shares of restricted state and federal revenues might increase a district's administrative burden regarding compliance activities. Assuming resource allocation influences efficiency and productivity, it becomes important to understand the factors that both intentionally and unintentionally influence resource allocation. We have portrayed Figure 15.3 as a linear flow model to simply show the basic elements of the model. We are acutely aware, however, that over time schooling outcomes influence community characteristics, and these in turn have strong feedback consequences for all of the inputs, processes, and outcomes in the model.

Perhaps the most difficult aspect of performing empirical analyses of the missing link between resource allocation and schooling outcomes is differentiating between resource quantities and resource qualities. Doing so might be easier if resource prices were more highly associated with resource quality. That is, it might be easier to study the teacher quality/quantity tradeoffs from a resource allocation perspective if higher-quality teachers were to systematically come at a higher price. In this case, district officials might be able to directly substitute teacher quantity (class sizes) and teacher quality and perform more straightforward cost-effectiveness analyses than can presently be performed.

Because teacher salaries are only weakly associated with student outcomes, and teacher salaries and benefits are still the largest single expenditure on education, developing a compelling resource allocation model will not be feasible until we create either a much tighter linkage between cost and quality or much better measures of teacher quality independent of its price.

Where the Money Goes

The study of resource allocation in schools has most often been a descriptive exercise, addressing where the money goes within schools and districts. Studies of where the money goes have focused on both equity and efficiency questions. Equity questions in resource allocation include the following:

1. What is the extent of resource equity between schools within districts, and how does that compare with equity between districts?

2. How equitably distributed are specific curricular and/or co-curricular opportunities across schools and districts?

3. How do changes in district equity influence within-district use of resources?

It is entirely possible, for example, that a state could equalize educational spending per pupil perfectly among school districts in the state only to find that similar schools within the districts have highly unequal access to resources. Many researchers therefore have shifted their attention to school- and classroom-level equity analysis. Efficiency questions in resource allocation research tend to be focused on those elements long assumed (though not necessarily validated) to contribute to efficient education—primarily, the amount and percentage of education funding spent in the classroom or on direct instruction.

Resource Equity Within and Across Districts

One area of major concern has been that while states attempt to promote equity of funding between districts, the dearth of information and lack of systematic approach regarding where the money goes within districts have made it difficult to measure equity of resources between schools within districts. Several studies conducted in the 1990s found significant disparities in resources within districts (Burke, 1999; Hertert, 1996).

Sarah Burke (1999) in particular shows how Gini coefficients estimated to resource distributions at the school rather than district level reveal significant intradistrict disparities that in some states exceed interdistrict disparities (Illinois and New York; Burke, 1999, p. 452).

Stiefel, Rubenstein, and Berne (1998) analyzed school-level data from four large urban districts (Chicago, Fort Worth, New York, and Rochester) in an effort to measure within-district disparities in resources. Using school-level data, they estimated horizontal equity statistics including coefficients of variation, vertical equity statistics based on percentages of students in poverty in each school, and equal opportunity measures, including correlations between available resources, teachers' salaries, and school racial composition. Regarding horizontal equity, they found coefficients of variation for total school resources exceeding .15 in Rochester, New York. Regarding vertical equity, they generally found higher levels of total resources available in schools with more students in poverty, but relationships were not consistent across the four districts, or across schools of different grade levels within the districts. For example, Rochester middle schools showed stronger positive relationships between poverty and resources than Rochester elementary or high schools. They raised the greatest concerns over their finding that teacher salaries tended to be lower in schools serving more poor and minority students but note an apparent tradeoff between teacher quantities and teacher salaries.

Another area of emerging interest is the equity and neutrality of the distribution of specific educational opportunities, as defined by resources, rather than total per-pupil revenues or expenditures, across schools and districts. For example, Brent et al. (1997), in their human resource allocation studies in New York mentioned previously, found that the "small poor" district in their sample of case studies allocated no resources to advanced programs in any of five content areas and allocated comparable resources per pupil to regular and remedial programming in English, social studies, math and science. In contrast, their "small wealthy" district allocated substantial resources to advanced programming in four of five content areas and no resources to remedial programming in two of those four (English and social studies) program areas (Brent et al., 1997, p. 220). This finding raises some concerns regarding horizontal equity and fiscal neutrality of the availability of advanced programming opportunities across New York high schools.

In a national analysis based on data from the National Assessment of Educational Progress (NAEP) *Trial State Assessment*, Raudenbush, Fotiu, and Cheong (1998) found that minority students and students whose parents had less formal education had significantly less access to eighth-grade algebra programs. They also noted that the degree of social and ethnic inequality in access varied significantly across states (p. 253).

Baker and Friedman-Nimz (2002) used data from the *National Educational Longitudinal Study of 1998* to explore the availability of gifted and talented programming across schools and districts in relation to student socioeconomic status (SES), finding that schools with higher mean SES levels were significantly more likely to offer such programs.

Baker (2001), using district-level data from the state of Texas, also found that districts with greater fiscal capacity and larger school districts were more likely

to provide programs for gifted children, and they tended to allocate more personnel and time to gifted programming.

Where the Education Dollar Is Spent

With the emergence of criticisms regarding schooling inefficiency in the late 1980s and early 1990s, research focused on finding out just how many dollars were making it to the classroom proliferated rapidly. One might characterize this period and this research as the "fiscal input accountability" period. The basic assumption behind this research was that dollars that make it to the classroom are more likely to produce higher-level, or improved, student outcomes. Studies on large urban districts, including New York, revealed that as little as 21.9% of total expenditures were making it to the classroom (Speakman et al., 1996).

Considerable debate remains over just what constitutes "instructional" or classroom expenditures. For example, Bruce S. Cooper and colleagues (Speakman et al., 1996), who had revealed the disturbingly low classroom spending in New York City using the FAM, were criticized for subtracting teacher planning time and benefits to arrive at the 21.9% figure. In an effort to standardize the measure of instructional expenditures, the National Center for Education Statistics (NCES) (www.nces.ed.gov) has developed a definition for what it refers to as "core instructional expenditures."

> Core instructional expenditures are only the current expenditures for instruction, student support services (health, attendance, guidance, and speech), and instructional staff support services (curricular development, in-staff training, and educational media, including libraries). The use of the term "core" is designed to reflect the central purpose of the local education agency, which is to educate children. Some users who philosophically differ with this interpretation may wish to add expenditures for student transportation, or food services, or school administration, if they believe these functions would be included in the central purpose of the local education agency. (Parrish, Matsumoto, & Fowler, 1995)

On average, in 1995–1996, school districts spent approximately 62% of current expenditures per pupil[2] on core instruction.

---

[2]Current operating expenditures are expenditures for the categories of instruction, support services, and noninstructional services for salaries, employee benefits, purchased services and supplies, and payments by the state made for or on behalf of school systems. This does not include expenditures for debt services and capital outlay, or property (i.e., equipment); or direct costs (e.g., Head Start, adult education, community colleges, etc.); or community services expenditures.

NCES gathers public school district financial data annually and compiles the data as part of the *Common Core of Data* (www.nces.ed.gov/ccd), which includes census demographic data and enrollment and staffing data in addition to district revenue and expenditure data. As a result, it has become much easier to compare school district revenues and expenditures, and resource allocation patterns in recent years. NCES provides a web-based tool for comparing peer school districts' revenues and expenditures (http://www.nces.ed.gov/edfin/search/search_intro.asp).

Table 15.3 presents a peer-group comparison using 1997–1998 expenditure data for a group of districts that are members of the Council of the Great City Schools (www.cgcs.org). We calculated core ratios by dividing core per pupil expenditures by current per pupil expenditures. These ratios are not provided in the original peer comparison (definitions in footnotes). Note that for this group of very large districts, core expenditures as a percentage of current expenditures are somewhat higher than national averages.

As Table 15.3 shows, the average per-pupil expenditure was $6,526. Of that amount about $4,540, or about 70%, was spent on core instruction in 1997. Again, it is interesting to note that the Great City Schools had a rather substantial variation in per-pupil expenditure, with Newark, New Jersey, spending over $12,100, and St. Paul, Minnesota, spending about $4,300. It is difficult to imagine that Newark faces costs that are 300% higher than St. Paul. Table 15.3 also shows that administrative costs as a percentage of per-pupil costs vary from a high of 21.3% in the District of Columbia, to a low of 8.1% in Boston. Yet again, note that these data do not indicate which system is more cost-effective.

Changes in Resource Allocation Over Time

Arguably, school districts' allocation of financial resources have changed little over time. In general, approaches to resource allocation over time across districts and states have arguably become more similar. Margaret Goertz and Gary Natriello studied resource allocation patterns of school districts in New Jersey, Kentucky, and Texas before and after school finance reforms in those states. In general, they found that in the wake of school finance reforms, despite differences in school contexts, resource allocation patterns tend to become more similar across districts (Goertz & Natriello, 1999, p. 127).

Hannaway, McKay, and Nakib (2002) found similar results. First, they found that in general, instructional spending levels and shares changed little across districts from 1992 through 1997. Second, focusing specifically on four states identified as implementing significant reforms in standards and accountability (Kentucky, Maryland, North Carolina, and Texas), Hannaway et al. found no consistent pattern of changes in resource allocation that could be attributed to the reforms.

One area where significant changes in resource allocation have occurred over the long run (20 to 30 years) is in special education finance and the relative balance of special to general education spending. Hamilton Lankford and James Wyckoff (1999) studied special and general education expenditure patterns for New York school districts from 1980 to 1992. The authors found that while most of the overall increases in educational expenditures could be attributed to teaching expenses, special education teaching expenses had far outpaced general education teaching expenses.

Rothstein and Miles (1995) similarly note that from 1967 to 1991, in a sample of eight representative districts, special education expenditures grew from 4% to 17% of total expenditures, while general education decreased from 80% to 59%. (Much of our summary is derived from the literature review of Stiefel, Rubenstein, & Berne, 1998.)

Factors Associated With Different Patterns of Resource Allocation

Questions regarding factors that influence how districts and schools allocate resources are usually divided into the following:

1. What differences exist in resource allocation across districts of different structures, under different conditions, serving different student populations, and achieving different outcomes?

2. What factors influence how resource allocation patterns change over time within schools and districts?

Factors that influence district and school resource allocation may be divided into those factors that are within and those that are beyond the control of local school districts. Factors beyond the control of local school districts can be further subdivided into policies imposed at higher levels of governance and other

Table 15.3 Core Expenditures per Pupil for Peer Districts (Great City Schools) in 1997–1998

District Name	Current Expenditures per Pupil	Core Expenditure per Pupil	Admin. Ratio	Core Percentage
Albuquerque Public Schools	$4,841	$3,686	8.40%	76.14%
Salt Lake City School District	$4,470	$3,399	8.20%	76.04%
Providence Sch Dist	$7,861	$5,933	9.90%	75.47%
NYC-Chancellor's Office	$8,106	$6,102	5.60%	75.28%
Baltimore City Pub Sch System	$7,298	$5,485	9.80%	75.16%
Boston School District	$10,293	$7,594	8.10%	73.78%
Des Moines Independent Comm Sc	$6,554	$4,796	9.40%	73.18%
Los Angeles Unified	$6,010	$4,374	9.80%	72.78%
Nashville-Davidson County SD	$6,346	$4,609	11.50%	72.63%
Long Beach Unified	$5,262	$3,821	9.90%	72.61%
San Diego City Unified	$5,917	$4,285	17.70%	72.42%
Minneapolis	$8,488	$6,146	11.00%	72.41%
Memphis City School District	$5,349	$3,869	9.10%	72.33%
Anchorage School District	$6,547	$4,723	15.30%	72.14%
Oakland Unified	$6,115	$4,386	12.00%	71.73%
Norfolk City Public Schls	$5,638	$4,038	9.50%	71.62%
Fresno Unified	$5,398	$3,865	13.40%	71.60%
Milwaukee Sch Dist	$8,067	$5,756	13.50%	71.35%
Sacramento City Unified	$5,465	$3,899	11.00%	71.34%
Dallas ISD	$5,309	$3,780	12.60%	71.20%
Buffalo City SD	$8,994	$6,373	9.30%	70.86%
City of Chicago School Dist 29	$6,617	$4,674	9.80%	70.64%
Guilford County Schools	$5,805	$4,095	10.90%	70.54%
Charlotte-Mecklenburg Schools	$5,657	$3,979	12.20%	70.34%
Orleans Parish School Board	$4,986	$3,498	13.50%	70.16%
San Francisco Unified	$6,031	$4,201	12.60%	69.66%
Rochester City SD	$8,791	$6,122	13.60%	69.64%
Birmingham City Sch Dist	$5,098	$3,546	15.60%	69.56%
Fort Worth ISD	$5,343	$3,710	11.90%	69.44%
Columbus City SD	$6,822	$4,721	13.70%	69.20%
Dade County Sch Dist	$5,952	$4,118	11.60%	69.19%
Atlanta City School District	$7,545	$5,213	11.80%	69.09%
Cleveland City SD	$6,403	$4,411	12.60%	68.89%
Orange County Sch Dist	$5,292	$3,619	13.90%	68.39%
Broward County Sch Dist	$5,453	$3,722	14.70%	68.26%
Seattle	$6,865	$4,684	14.40%	68.23%
Omaha Public Schools	$5,560	$3,792	15.10%	68.20%
Houston ISD	$5,340	$3,638	12.30%	68.13%
Hillsborough County Sch Dist	$5,484	$3,736	14.70%	68.13%
Richmond City Public Schls	$7,550	$5,123	11.40%	67.85%
Philadelphia City SD	$5,702	$3,852	14.50%	67.56%
Newark City	$12,105	$8,162	14.90%	67.43%
Denver County 1	$5,739	$3,863	13.10%	67.31%
Detroit City School District	$7,326	$4,928	13.20%	67.27%
Clark County School District	$5,108	$3,430	15.50%	67.15%
Tucson Unified District	$4,783	$3,208	18.70%	67.07%
Toledo City SD	$6,562	$4,400	11.70%	67.05%
Indianapolis Public Schools	$8,056	$5,391	11.10%	66.92%
Pittsburgh SD	$8,550	$5,693	17.40%	66.58%
Tulsa	$5,075	$3,359	12.70%	66.19%
Jefferson CO	$5,880	$3,878	14.10%	65.95%
St. Paul School District	$4,288	$2,803	16.50%	65.37%
District of Columbia Pub Schls	$8,474	$5,486	21.30%	64.74%
St. Louis City	$7,330	$4,687	17.40%	63.94%
Dayton City SD	$7,657	$4,795	14.30%	62.62%
Portland Sch Dist 1J	$7,904	$4,865	11.90%	61.55%
Group Averages	*$6,526*	*$4,541*	*12.70%*	*69.58%*

Source: Data from National Center for Education Statistics. (1997–1998). *Common core of data, local education agency universe survey, school district finances.* Retrieved from www.nces.ed.gov/edfin

exogenous conditions, generally beyond the control of all federal, state, and local policy makers. Finally, policies imposed at higher levels of governance may have direct and intentional effects on local district resource allocation or indirect and/or unintentional effects on local district resource allocation.

District Structural Factors

District scale, as measured by enrollment, is one exogenous factor that strongly influences how school districts allocate their resources. Monk and Hussain (2000) and Baker (2002) each constructed statistical models to test how district characteristics influence resource allocation.

Monk and Hussain (2000), as well as Baker (2002), find that smaller schools and districts tend to have greater numbers of teaching staff per 1,000 pupils and greater numbers of central administrators per 1,000 pupils. Further, smaller districts tend to have greater staffing shares of central administrators. That is, while both the numbers of teachers and numbers of administrators are greater in smaller schools (on a per-pupil basis), numbers of central administrators increase more rapidly than numbers of teachers. Numbers of school administrators, to the contrary, are actually slightly higher in larger districts.

Table 15.4 displays the human and fiscal resource allocation patterns across districts nationally using data from the NCES *Common Core of Data* (www.nces.ed.gov/ccd). Note that districts with less than 500

students have far more classroom teachers per 1,000 pupils than districts with greater than 10,000 students. They similarly have far more instructional support staff and central and total administration staff. Because administrative staffing increases disproportionately in smaller districts, percentages of resources allocated to core instruction tend to be lower and percentages of resources allocated to administration tend to be higher in smaller districts.

District Financial Factors

Researchers have taken alternative routes to studying the influence of district capacity on resource allocation. On the one hand, Brent et al. (1997) and Monk and Hussain (2000) study whether district property wealth per pupil, an exogenous factor, is associated with different patterns of resource allocation. These authors tend to find, for example, that higher wealth districts, which arguably have greater control over their resources (especially in the New York State context of the analyses), tend to spend more on advanced programs and less on remedial programs than their lower-wealth counterparts. However, because student achievement is highly correlated with district wealth, it may be difficult to determine whether wealthy families with highly successful and well-educated parents produce children who demand a more rigorous curriculum or whether a more expensive curriculum with higher-quality teachers produces students who will benefit from advanced

Table 15.4   Differences in Resource Allocation by District Size

	<500	500–1,000	1,000–5,000	5,000–10,000	>10,000
Staff per 1,000 students (1999)					
Classroom teachers	81.89	70.48	64.13	61.84	58.28
Instructional support staff	56.28	48.19	46.84	46.72	44.05
Central administrators	3.85	2.24	1.50	1.00	0.73
Total administrators and admin. support	17.22	13.29	12.28	11.69	11.28
Expenditure shares (1995–1996)					
Percent to core instruction	76.56	78.48	80.84	81.91	80.98
Percent to central administration	12.62	9.06	5.98	4.20	3.06
Percent to total administration	23.44	21.52	19.16	18.09	19.02
Staffing shares (1999)					
Percent classroom teachers	54.25	53.90	52.28	51.85	51.75
Percent instructional support staff	34.45	35.68	37.47	38.19	38.09
Percent central administrative staff	5.66	4.57	4.13	4.05	3.76
Percent school administrative staff	5.64	5.85	6.12	5.91	6.41

Source: Data from National Center for Education Statistics. (1999–2000). *Common core of data, local education agency survey.* Retrieved from www.nces.ed.gov/ccd

Table 15.5   Differences in Resource Allocation by District Expenditures per Pupil

	<3,000	3,000–5,000	5,000–7,000	7,000–9,000	>9,000
Staff per 1,000 students (1999)					
Classroom teachers	59.88	54.37	61.79	71.59	75.05
Instructional support staff	33.86	40.04	45.67	50.49	49.38
Central administrators	0.83	0.74	1.13	1.41	2.29
Total administrators and admin. support	13.19	10.32	11.60	14.24	16.59
Expenditure shares (1995–1996)					
Percent to core instruction	74.53	81.51	80.58	81.16	80.40
Percent to central administration	12.32	3.85	4.52	5.27	6.67
Percent to total administration	25.47	18.49	19.42	18.84	19.60
Staffing shares (1999)					
Percent classroom teachers	57.19	52.94	51.60	52.33	53.91
Percent instructional support staff	30.81	37.15	38.33	37.23	34.59
Percent central administrative staff	2.03	3.01	3.89	4.89	5.22
Percent school administrative staff	9.97	6.91	6.18	5.56	6.28

Source: Data from National Center for Education Statistics. (1999–2000). *Common core of data, local education agency survey.* Retrieved from www.nces.ed.gov/ccd

programs. Exogenous socioeconomic conditions, such as property wealth or income, may also influence community educational preferences (local politics) and/or the mix of students by educational need. One might expect district median family income to have even more significant effects than property wealth on the distribution of resources to advanced curricular opportunities, because income may be a better measure of SES. Monk and Hussain (2000) address poverty status separately, as we discuss later. Cross-sectional regression analysis does not address the reinforcing feedback cycles of privilege adequately.

Referring to our median voter models of local government spending in Chapters 2, 3, 6, and 11, one might consider property wealth, a tax price measure, to be an indirect measure of district fiscal inputs, depending on the state's approach to providing aid and governing local spending behavior. Baker (2002) and Monk and Hussain (2000) both study how total per-pupil expenditures influence local district resource allocation. One might assume, for example, that districts with higher per-pupil expenditures would be able to spend even greater shares of those expenditures on direct instructional services. Indeed, previous research indicates that districts with more resources per pupil tend to purchase more classroom teachers per pupil. However, districts with more resources per pupil also tend to purchase more central and total administrators per pupil. With the exception of the districts with the fewest resources per pupil, districts with more resources

per pupil tend to disproportionately increase central administrative spending shares.

The oversimplified analysis we present in Table 15.4 is confounded by the fact that district expenditures per pupil and district size, discussed in Table 15.5, tend to be highly related. Smaller districts spend more, on average, per pupil as a function of economies of scale, and very large districts may also be inefficient with higher-than-average costs per pupil. The Great City Schools data in Table 15.3, however, seem to suggest that large schools can also have extreme variance in per-pupil spending and administrative overhead, a subject for further study. We know little, however, about their comparative outcomes, relative productivity, and efficiency.

Student Population Characteristics

Student population characteristics can also influence internal resource allocation practices in a variety of ways and for a variety of reasons. As noted previously, student population characteristics may partially reflect parent/voter population characteristics, and local political pressures may influence district programming/resource allocation decisions. For example, more highly educated parents might pressure local boards of education to offer a wider array of advanced placement courses in high schools or enrichment programs in elementary schools. Student population characteristics may also indicate specific educational programming needs. That is, districts with higher percentages of children in poverty may require more instructional support staff to provide adequate programming. Finally, student population characteristics may influence state and federal aid received by a district and may influence programming requirements tied to funding.

Monk and Hussain (2000) and Baker (2002) find that districts with higher percentages of children in poverty tend to have higher ratios of instructional staff per pupil. Monk and Hussain and Baker also produce similar findings regarding administrative shares and poverty levels. Baker, using a national sample of 1999 district-level personnel data and 1995–1996 financial data, finds that districts with higher percentages of children in poverty tend to have larger shares of staff and fiscal resources allocated to central administration. Baker also finds, however, that districts with more children in poverty purchase more instructional staff but fewer administrators. Similarly, Monk and Hussain, using a sample of 1990–1991 New York State schools, find that schools with higher percentages of children in poverty appear to purchase fewer administrators but do have larger shares of administration with respect to instruction. Both suggest that increased categorical programming associated with increased poverty likely causes increased administrative burden for high-poverty districts. Using an expanded set of student population characteristics, Baker also found that increased numbers of

limited-English-proficient (LEP) students were also associated with increased central administrative expenses.

Indirect State Policy Influences

Here, we focus briefly on a few examples of indirect state policy influences on district resource allocation. Then, in the next section, we give greater attention to direct policy influences on district resource allocation. Perhaps the two most significant and two most studied factors influencing district resource allocation are district scale and district fiscal inputs. As such, one type of state policy that might logically affect internal resource allocation is a state policy that provides compensation to districts lacking economies of scale, or a low enrollment, or other district-size adjustment in state aid. Baker (2002) validates that districts in states providing supplemental funding to small districts tend to spend less on core instruction and more on administration (levels and shares) than districts in states without such policies. Clearly, the decision to compensate small districts with extra support because they face higher average costs is complicated. Some rural districts in very sparsely populated regions of the United States cannot easily further consolidate their schools without subjecting their children to daily bus rides exceeding 2 hours.

Figures 15.4 and 15.5 illustrate this particular policy issue, using data from the state of Kansas, one of

Figure 15.4 Kansas and U.S. per-Pupil Revenues by Enrollment

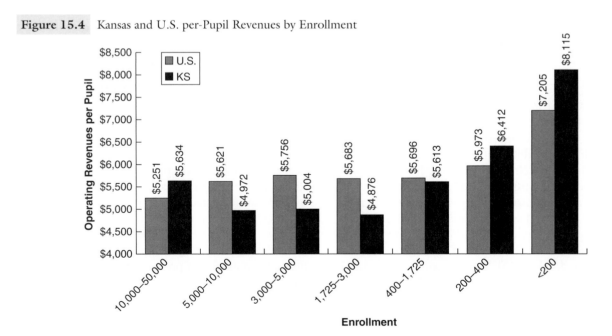

Source: Data from National Center for Education Statistics. (1999–2000). *Common core of data, local education agency survey.* Retrieved from www.nces.ed.gov/ccd

Figure 15.5   Kansas and U.S. Total Administrative Staff by Enrollment

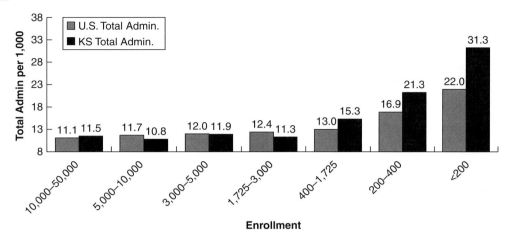

Source: Data from National Center for Education Statistics. (1999–2000). *Common core of data, local education agency survey.* Retrieved from www.nces.ed.gov/ccd

three states with very aggressive economies of scale policies (Kansas, Colorado, and Alaska). Figure 15.4 shows that the smallest districts in Kansas have more fiscal resources per pupil than their national peers, and Kansas mid-sized to larger districts have comparable-to-less fiscal resources than their national peers. As such, because administrative expense is positively related with both size and resources, one might expect that smaller districts in Kansas would spend more on administration than their larger counterparts and more on administration than their similarly small national peers.

Figure 15.5 anecdotally confirms our speculation (focusing on staffing levels), indicating that while the largest districts in Kansas purchase comparable numbers of total administrative staff per 1,000 pupils relative to their national peers, the smaller districts purchase far more total administrative staff per 1,000 pupils than districts of similar size nationally.

Categorical Aid Allocation

State approaches to the allocation of categorical aid may both directly and indirectly influence district internal resource allocation. For example, the explicit intent of a state bilingual education aid program may be to use all state-allocated bilingual education funds to local districts for purchase of human and materials resources to deliver bilingual educational programs to LEP students. The case might be similar for special education, early childhood, and any of the multitudes of targeted aid programs cropping up across states. As

discussed previously, however, in the case of children in poverty, increased categorization of funding can increase compliance demands on local school districts, increasing the need for administrators and additional support staff for those administrators.

Referring back to our discussion of alternative special education funding models in Chapter 8, one might expect to find that funding models including percentage reimbursement or resource-based funding, which entail greater fiscal compliance burdens than block grants or pupil weights, are associated with increased administrative expense. Baker (2002) finds some support for this contention with respect to resource-based special education funding, but he notes that the evidence is still not compelling.

Policies Designed to Influence Resource Allocation

Over the past several years, the Consortium for Policy Research in Education (CPRE) has focused substantial effort on what it refers to as both resource reallocation and school redesign (http://www.wcer.wisc.edu/cpre/finance/reports.php).

In Chapter 7, we discussed an application of this approach in the context of school-funding litigation in New Jersey, where in 1997, the New Jersey court ordered the implementation of specific comprehensive school reform models.

Recall from Chapter 7 that following the most recent round of school finance litigation in New Jersey, the New Jersey court, on the advice of Allan Odden, mandated that schools in the state's "special needs" districts select from a handful of whole-school reform models, where the default model would be Roots and Wings/Success for All. Recall also that it was suggested that most, if not all, schools in special needs districts already possessed sufficient funding to implement any of the prescribed reforms. It would simply be a matter of re-allocating resources to achieve the prescribed staffing configurations (setting aside entirely any mention of staffing qualifications).

Some would argue that if researchers and policy makers can identify effective resource configurations and teaching strategies, then it might be a reasonable state policy either to mandate that schools and districts adopt these resource configurations or to provide incentives for schools or districts to adopt these models or prototypes. This is the rationale underlying present reforms in New Jersey, which is exclusively focused on a subset of urban districts and discussed in Chapter 7. It is perhaps less reasonable, or less politically feasible, to impose such policies statewide. States other than New Jersey have not yet gone to such extremes in managing school-level resource allocation, but increasing numbers of districts across states are attempting reform via model-based resource reallocation. Numerous case studies of such efforts can be found at the CPRE Website (http:// www.wcer.wisc.edu/cpre/finance/reports.php).

These model-based approaches, however, are contingent on the effectiveness and portability of these models, under different circumstances, applied by different individuals, with different groups of students. It might be equally or even more reasonable, however, to draw on the information presented in Chapter 13 on teacher labor markets and teacher attributes linked with student outcomes, to require low-performing schools to hire only teachers who graduated from highly or most selective undergraduate colleges and pay bonuses to both recruit and retain these teachers, assuming they meet performance targets. Either approach involves dictating schooling inputs.

Other, more conventional policies intended to directly influence district resource allocation include the plethora of categorical programs previously discussed, state class-size requirements, and state requirements to spend specific portions of aid on teaching personnel.

Resource Allocation in Private, Charter, and Catholic Schools

Insights into the use of resources in Catholic and charter schools are particularly relevant to today's policy conversations about the opening of the market to other providers of K–12 education. Supporters of vouchers or charter school laws often argue that financing public schooling through private or quasi-public entities necessarily improves the efficiency of public schooling by lowering costs and, at the very least, not compromising outcomes. As discussed in previous chapters, research findings remain mixed regarding whether, overall, Catholic schools are more productive than public schools, when measuring student achievement outcomes. Catholic schools appear to have more positive effects on educational attainment, especially for minority students. Yet, we know little or nothing about the relative efficiency of American Catholic schools because we know so little about their resource use. Similar issues have been addressed in charter school research, with at least one study (Gronberg & Jansen, 2001, discussed in Chapter 11) finding efficiency advantages of charter schools (in Texas).

A common, though not necessarily thoroughly evaluated, perception is that Catholic and charter schools *must* be using their scarce resources much more efficiently than traditional public school districts. That is, by popular perception, more money must be making it to the classroom in Catholic and charter schools. Of course, empirical research has also yet to validate that greater efficiency is achieved when more money makes it to the classroom.

Before we launch into a review of resource allocation in private, parochial, and charter schools, we call your attention to a major problem with research in this field. The entire public–private school distinction is oversimplified and highly politicized. As Rufo-Lignos and Richards (2003) in an article in the *Teachers College Record* have reported, the actual range of interaction along the several dimensions that distinguish public from private schools in the public imagination is much higher than one would think. That is, private schools often have characteristics that one would be inclined to associate with public schools, and public schools often have characteristics that one would associate with private schools. They argue that emerging forms of school organization are developing that are neither distinctly public nor private but have qualities and characteristics that are quasi-public.

In an earlier study, Richards and White (1988) found that special education providers in New Jersey, when compared by whether they were private non-profit or private for-profit, did not differ significantly in resource spending, except that the directors of not-for-profit schools had higher average salaries. The notion that a school is more virtuous because it is not-for-profit is largely an illusion and has more to do with the advantages and disadvantages of its tax status and ability to raise capital, than it is an indication of its commitment to quality education for children. With this caveat in place, we return to our exploration of Catholic and charter schools.

The efficiency arguments presume first that charter schools spend less (per outcome) than their public school counterparts, simply by virtue of their lower (in many cases) tax-dollar-supported aid per pupil. Similarly, Catholic schools are assumed more efficient by virtue of their average tuition charges being less than per-pupil operating expenditures in neighboring public schools. Yet, we have already shown how charter schools often use extensive fiscal resources above and beyond public tax-dollar support, at times to the demise of the for-profit management companies running them! For private schooling, tuition levels, or voucher levels of public subsidy are rarely if ever an accurate measure of actual educational expenditures. For diocesan Catholic schools in particular, church subsidies generated by parishioner tithing generate substantial revenue to offset operating costs, and while decreasing in numbers, church staff, including nuns, have historically played a key role in school operations and delivery of religious curriculum.

Next we present a detailed discussion of the organization of resources in Catholic high schools in the Kansas City metropolitan area, drawn from a recent dissertation at the University of Kansas (Sullivan, 2004) We then provide more anecdotal analyses and comparisons of charter school resource use nationally and in Washington, DC, and Kansas City, MO.

Evidence From Catholic High Schools[3]

In 2001–2002, the sample of Kansas City Catholic high schools in Table 15.6 spent, on average, about $2,660 less per pupil than conventional public school districts. Note that the NCES Geographic Cost of Education Index lists public school geography-related costs (input prices) in the Kansas City metropolitan area at 1.02 (2% above national average). Relative to public school districts, Kansas City Catholic high schools did make do with less. Recall from Chapter 13 that Catholic school teachers nationally are paid relatively poorly compared with their public school teaching peers.

Table 15.6 compares the dollars and shares of Catholic high school budgets across schools, benchmarked against a best-available comparison of similar-size public high school districts. For Catholic high schools, the functional area of "instruction" consumed, on average, from 47% to 52% of school budgets, compared to 60% in public high school districts of similar size. When instruction is combined with instructional support, Catholic high schools spent 65% of their operating budgets on instruction-related expense, compared with a similar expenditure in public high school districts, at 68%. Differences between instruction and instructional support may result from different classifications of expenditures. Also quite similar were expenditures to administration, with Catholic schools at 6% and public high school districts at 5%. Public high school districts spent significantly more on maintenance and operations, transportation and food service, with some major differences occurring in the area of transportation. These differences may occur because of public school districts' obligations to transport and because public high school districts comparable in size to Catholic high schools (especially those with only 400 to 600 pupils) often serve multiple rural communities. Other commitments were a smaller component of public high school district budgets. In general, the resource allocation patterns of Catholic high schools appear quite similar to those of public high schools. Unfortunately, we know nothing of the comparative outcomes and differences in populations served by these high schools, relative to public schools in the same market.

---

[3]This section draws on findings from the doctoral dissertation of Michael Sullivan (2004), *Resource Allocation in Catholic High Schools,* University of Kansas.

Table 15.6　A Comparison of Catholic and Public High Schools Resource Allocation Decisions in Kansas City, 2004: Expenditures per Pupil by Major Function

Functions	Catholic School A	Catholic School B	Catholic School C	Catholic School D	Catholic School Average	9–12 Public HS (400 600 Pupils)[f]
Instruction[a]	$3,818,538	$1,164,391	$775,539	$666,393		
Percent school	52%	48%	47%	48%	49%	60%
Per pupil	$3,031	$2,936	$3,090	$2,742	$2,950	$5,238
Instructional Support[b]	$1,069,820	$309,740.02	$259,679	$286,343.50		
Percent school	15%	12%	16%	21%	16%	8%
Per pupil	$849	$720	$1,035	$1,178	$946	$683
Operations[c]	$1,023,663	$205,119	$145,662	$232,041		
Percent school	14%	8%	9%	17%	12%	22%
Per pupil	$812	$477	$580	$955	$706	$1,892
Other commitments[d]	$689,257	$581,546	$149,932	$65,814		
Percent school	9%	22%	22%	7%	15%	5%
Per pupil	$547	$1,352	$1,430	$408	$934	$445
Leadership[e]	$433,508	$105,589	$92,973	$95,239		
Percent school	6%	4%	6%	7%	6%	5%
Per pupil	$344.05	$245.56	$370.41	$391.93	$338	$448
Total	$7,034,785	$2,366,384	$1,423,785	$1,349,733		
Percent school	100%	100%	100%	100%		
Per pupil	$5,824	$6,179	$6,505	$5,676	$6,046	$8,706
Total pupils	1,260	430	251	243	546	

[a]Includes instructional teachers' salaries and benefits, substitutes, paraprofessionals, pupil-use technology, instructional materials, and supplies.
[b]Includes guidance and counseling, library and media, extracurricular, student health, curriculum development, in-service and staff development, sabbaticals, program development, auxiliary personnel, social workers, therapists, psychologists, and evaluators.
[c]Transportation, food service, safety, school buildings, utilities and maintenance, business office.
[d]Reserves-designated, reserves-undesignated, principal and interest, capital purchases, retiree benefits and other, school management contracts, litigation and settlements.
[e]President salary, principal and assistant principals' salaries, benefits for administrators.
[f]Based on U.S. Census Bureau's *Fiscal Survey—Public Elementary and Secondary Education Finance—2001–02.*
Source: Data from Sullivan (2004).

Table 15.7 provides a comparison of within-high school human resource allocation, using as a baseline the analysis by Brent et al. (1997) of New York State high schools. Sullivan's (2004) analysis calculates costs per pupil of delivering courses in different curricular areas using both "average salaries" (removing variations in salaries due simply to years of experience differences between content-area teachers) and actual salaries. Because dollar values differ between Kansas City in 2002 and New York State in the mid 1990s, Sullivan indexes content area costs around the median cost content area. In general, cost differences by content area in Kansas City Catholic high

schools are not too dissimilar from New York high schools. Primarily as a function of class-size differences by content area, courses in math and English are relatively "average" in cost (near 1.0). Courses in science tend to be more expensive, and courses in music the most expensive. Analysis of the cost of credit hour delivery by field in colleges and universities have yielded similar findings, with faculty costs of delivering credits in the arts and foreign language highest, engineering next in line, and large enrollment courses such as economics, sociology, and psychology being least expensive (Morphew & Baker, 2007).

Table 15.7   Expenditures per Pupil Indexed by Program Area, Compared to Brent, Roellke, and Monk (1997)

Subject	Kansas City Catholic Actual Salary	Kansas City Catholic Average Salary	NY State
English	.93	.92	1.02
Math	1.01	.98	1.09
Science	1.09	1.07	1.35
Social studies	.95	.85	.87
Foreign language	.91	.95	.95
Business	.97	.95	.88
Physical education	.82	.81	.52
Art	1.16	1.26	1.00
Music	1.27	1.17	1.41

Sources: Data on Kansas City Catholic schools from Sullivan (2004). Data on NY State from Brent, Roellke, and Monk (1997).

In summary, resource allocation within the Catholic high schools observed by Sullivan (2004) appears quite similar to resource allocation in traditional public high schools. On average, lower than expected (by conventional thought, not empirically based) levels of resources make it to the classroom in these Catholic high schools. Overall, the Catholic high schools did spend less than the average per-pupil expenditures of public school districts. We caution, however, against trying to draw any broad policy conclusions about these figures other than the possibility that Catholic schools allocate resources surprisingly similarly to conventional public schools.

Research on Charter School Resource Allocation

Because Catholic schools appear to allocate resources so similarly to conventional public high schools and public school districts, one might expect similar behavior in charter schools. Table 15.8 (Charter School Staffing Allocations) begins our analysis by comparing staffing allocations nationally of charter schools and conventional public school districts of similar average enrollment to charter schools. Table 15.8 is based on data from the *1999–2000 Local Education Agency Universe Survey* of the National Center for Education Statistics. In Table 15.8, we compare district independent charter schools (ICSs) with independent public school districts (ISDs) enrolling similar numbers of students. We do not, as we did for Catholic schools, attempt to match by grade level, due to the irregularity

of configurations of charter schools, especially during their start-up year. Our sample had approximately 690 independent charter schools serving 200,000 students. The average enrollment was 670, thus we compare our independent charter schools to traditional public school districts enrolling on average 680 pupils.

We focus on staffing in this example. On average, ICSs had approximately 63 total teachers per 1,000 enrolled students compared to nearly 80 for ISDs of similar size. ICSs appeared to be carrying greater administrative personnel in total numbers per pupil and shares of total personnel.

Table 15.9 displays data from the Washington, DC, charter schools (for which we analyzed revenues in Chapter 12), drawing data from their annual IRS filings. Across all Washington, DC, charter schools, the average administrative expense reported on IRS filings (form 990) was 22%, much higher than might be expected in traditional public schools.

Summary of Findings

Differences between the organizational features of Catholic schools, charter schools, and conventional public schools should not be overlooked. Perhaps the most notable difference that may significantly influence internal resource allocation in these schools is the average scale of production in Catholic and charter schools. That is, due to scale alone, Catholic and charter schools should be expected to spend and allocate more similarly to small rather than average public school districts.

Table 15.8   Staffing Allocations of Charter Schools and Conventional Public School Districts

Variable	Observations	Pupils	Mean	Standard Deviation
Public School Districts				
Enrollment	3,985	1,943,540	683.06	270.77
Teachers per 1,000	3,985	1,943,540	78.53	51.00
School administrators per 1,000	3,985	1,943,540	4.14	3.14
District administrators per 1,000	3,985	1,943,540	3.20	6.04
Percent teachers	3,985	1,943,540	55.6%	14.66%
Percent school administrators	3,985	1,943,540	3.0%	1.70%
Percent district administrators	3,985	1,943,540	2.0%	1.66%
Independent Charter Schools				
Enrollment	690	200,387	668.97	813.46
Teachers per 1,000	690	200,387	63.49	28.70
School administrators per 1,000	690	200,387	4.61	6.28
District administrators per 1,000	690	200,387	4.55	6.91
Percent teachers	690	200,387	58.5%	16.39%
Percent school administrators	690	200,387	4.1%	4.82%
Percent district administrators	690	200,387	3.8%	5.38%

Source: Data from National Center for Education Statistics. (1999–2000). *Common core of data, local education agency survey.* Retrieved from www.nces.ed.gov/ccd

Table 15.9   Expenditures of Washington, DC, Charter Schools

School	Program Services	Administration	Other	Total Expenditures
A	$1,036,994	$189,478	$5,066	$1,231,538
B	$285,300	$85,461	$0	$370,761
C	$1,972,078	$219,122	$0	$2,191,200
D	$1,664,093	$748,733	$0	$2,412,826
E	$515,503	$188,953	$0	$704,456
F	$12,010,483	$6,493,512	$0	$18,503,995
G	$1,024,754	$0	$0	$1,024,754
H	$86,186	$20,106	$0	$106,292
I	$1,023,108	$0	$0	$1,023,108
J	$677,414	$375,995	$0	$999,041
K	$1,188,955	$246,978	$0	$1,435,933
L	$133,856	$2,718	$0	$136,574
M	$3,365,223	$92,505	$138,000	$3,595,728
N	$1,266,636	$99,185	$0	$1,365,821
O	$383,843	$41,526	$0	$425,369
P	$3,080,240	$465,968	$0	$3,546,208
Q	$1,974,153	$89,037	$46,593	$2,109,783
R	$668,968	$79,253	$0	$748,221
TOTAL	$32,357,787	$9,438,530	$189,659	$41,931,608
Percent	77.2%	22.5%	0.5%	100.0%

Source: Data from information and finances compiled from IRS Filings (IRS 990) of nonprofit entities that govern the charter schools, available through www.guidestar.org

A second issue is that private and charter schools are at least perceived to be more autonomous from entrenched bureaucratic governance. This autonomy, while potentially advantageous in terms of creative educational program development, comes with added responsibility and related costs. The primary added cost is that of leasing, purchasing, and maintaining educational facilities. Often, lease payments for charter schools cut into annual operating resources that might otherwise be spent on direct instruction.

A final short-term disadvantage for charter schools in direct comparisons of resource allocation to public schools is the newness of many charter schools and high associated start-up costs. These costs consumed 16% of the 1999–2000 budget for Kansas City's Southwest Charter School. Further, unlike conventional public schools, recruitment of students through marketing may make charter education more expensive or less efficient, unless one adopts the assumption that the best marketing is good performance.

A particularly intriguing finding from this section comparing Catholic, charter, and public school resource allocation and the section of Chapter 13 comparing Catholic, charter, and public school teachers is that Catholic schools appear far more similar to conventional public schools than do charter schools. One might simply attribute these differences to time and assume that given long enough, all schools and districts ultimately revert to the *one best system* (Tyack, 1974).

Due to their religious affiliation, however, the thought of sending public tax dollars to Catholic schools has far less public appeal than supporting charter school legislation. That is, the apparent public willingness to provide financial support to send children to charter schools appears to be a more daring experiment than sending the same children to well-established Catholic schools, yet perhaps more expensive, because Catholic schools have their own facilities and may cost somewhat less on average.

Again, regional differences lead to different policy considerations. In New York City, the Catholic schools play a critical role in supporting K–12 education, enrolling a substantial portion of the city's students. Many of these students are poor, minority, and immigrant, and a very large percentage are not even Catholic. If all Catholic schools were to close, it would create an epic disaster in New York City, because the public schools are currently overcrowded and facing very large and long-term school construction needs.

Research Linking Resource Allocation to Productivity and Efficiency

As we have mentioned, while much research alludes to the linkage between resource allocation and student performance, little research has explicitly tested the relationship between a given resource mix and productivity and efficiency (Speakman et al., 1996). We discuss much of the related research on specific resources such as class sizes and teacher qualifications in Chapter 11. Here, we address a few studies particularly relevant to the question of resource mix and educational productivity and current input-based policy strategies.

Evidence on the Administrative Blob and Inefficiency

As we noted previously, the fiscal accountability movement placed significant emphasis on identifying dollars that made it to the classroom, or instructional spending. Alternatively, administrative expenditures have been perceived as nonproductive expenditures, described by William Bennett in the 1980s as the administrative blob, a component of school budgets growing out of control and hampering educational productivity and efficiency (as discussed by Brewer, 1996). Dominic Brewer (1996) of RAND set out to empirically test the influence of the administrative blob on educational productivity. First, Brewer found that a relatively low proportion of district expenditures (7%) funded building administrative salaries, and an even smaller proportion (4%) funded district administration. Finally, by way of production–function analyses, Brewer found little relationship between noninstructional expenses and student outcomes (Brewer, 1996).

At least three possible conclusions offer themselves here: (a) the districts are already efficient or perhaps have far too few administrators to make a difference in instruction at the school level; (b) Brewer's (1996) study did not have sufficient variance in administrative staffing levels to detect a causal relationship; (c) because districts with the lowest levels did not do any worse than districts with the highest levels, push all district expenses down to the lowest level and redeploy the resources to the classroom, where there is some hope of increasing student achievement.

Effectiveness and Cost-Effectiveness of Comprehensive School Reforms

As districts and states become more enamored with input-management strategies such as CPRE's *model-based reallocation*, it will become increasingly important that researchers and policy makers understand the portability of educational models to different settings and develop a sound research base on the relative cost-effectiveness of those models compared to alternative uses of the same fiscal resources (Odden, 2000). It is beyond the scope of this text to provide a thorough review of all of the proprietary and independent research on comprehensive school reform models. However, Sanders, Wright, Ross, and Wang (2000) find, "The five-year (1995–99) TVAAS [Tennessee Value Added Assessment System] findings are clearly supportive of R&W's [Roots and Wings'] effects in increasing student gains in academic achievement. Taking the results for all 22 R&W schools in the R95, R96, and R97 cohorts combined shows an average pre- to post-reform gain of about 20 points higher than that realized by the control schools" (p. 8). Although the work of Sanders et al. (2000) was not a peer-reviewed, published study, we highlight these findings because they are based on student-level, value-added analyses.

In a more comprehensive analysis of both implementation and effects of comprehensive school reforms in New York City schools, Bifulco, Bordeaux, Duncombe, and Yinger (2002) concluded:

> Overall, our results indicate that whole-school reforms may have small positive impacts on student performance, but low-performing schools should not expect whole-school reform to be a panacea. In addition, any school deciding to adopt a whole-school reform model should recognize that careful, sustained implementation may be necessary for positive program impacts to emerge. (p. 10)

Models investigated included James Comer's School Development Program (SDP), Robert Slavin's Success for All (SFA), and a program called More Effective Schools (MES) (as discussed by Bifulco et al., 2002).

In one recent study, and a second review of existing studies, researchers affiliated with CPRE (which endorses financing based on comprehensive school reforms) and with Johns Hopkins University (former home to Slavin's Roots and Wings/SFA) have claimed decisive evidence that Roots and Wings/SFA is both effective and cost-effective (Borman & Hewes, 2002), and the comprehensive school reforms in general are effective with Roots and Wings/SFA being most effective (Borman, Hewes, Overman, & Brown, 2003). In the first study, the CPRE and Johns Hopkins researchers suggest that "cost effectiveness comparisons to the three prominent interventions (Perry Preschool, Abecedarian Project, and Class Size Reduction) suggest that Success for All is deserving of similar recognition as a sound educational investment that provides strong and lasting educational benefits" (p. 243). Recall, however, from Chapter 11, that class-size reduction, while producing consistent positive effects, may not necessarily be the most cost-effective option. Further, regarding the specific methods employed in the study, Henry Levin notes:

> [The study] suffers from the flaw of both "costless" reallocation and of not considering the costs of resources provided by other agencies such as social workers. It is also based upon the initial replications of the project in Baltimore, the site of the sponsoring institution. The substantial assistance by professional and other staff in implementing the project at those sites is not included in the measured costs in this study. In addition, it is inconsistent in comparing its figures with the putative, full-cost of class size reduction and pre-school programs since each of these could also "reduce" costs through reallocation of resources or through obtaining resources from external sources. Perhaps, the largest bias is introduced by charging the full cost of class size reduction to reading, rather than recognizing that class size reductions also improve mathematics (as in the Tennessee experiment) and other subjects and activities. The pre-school program also is devoted to a wide range of child outcomes. Previous studies have charged one-third of the cost of class size reduction to the improvement of reading (Levin, Glass, and Meister 1987). When this adjustment is made, the cost-effectiveness estimate for class size reduction is superior to that of Success For All by about 2.5 to 1. (Levin, 2002, p. 35)

Borman and Hewes' (2002) comprehensive review and meta-analysis of studies of the effectiveness of comprehensive school reforms includes predominantly proprietary, unpublished research studies and does not include the previously mentioned analysis by Bifulco and colleagues (2002), which was released after the cut-off date used by Borman and colleagues for inclusion in their meta-analysis. As such, even though these two recent articles in prominent educational research journals indicate effectiveness and cost-effectiveness of comprehensive school reforms, particularly Roots and Wings/SFA, we continue to have our doubts about these reforms as a panacea for improving schooling productivity and efficiency.[4]

A Comment on the 65-Cent Solution

An unfortunate diversion in education finance policy that emerged in or around 2005 was a proposal coined the "65 Cent Solution," pitched by an organization called "First Class Education" and financed by the founder of Overstock.com. The 65 Cent Solution essentially requires that all public school districts allocate 65 cents of every operational expenditure dollar to "instruction," as defined by the National Center for Education Statistics. We questioned seriously whether we should dignify this proposal with page space in a school finance textbook. Our initial expectation was that few state legislatures would take this proposal seriously, because (a) little or no evidence supported that allocating 65 cents of every dollar led to improved performance outcomes and (b) this policy represents significant state-level micromanagement of district practices, seemingly against the current wave of granting greater flexibility and holding districts to outcome standards.

Unfortunately, we were wrong, and some states have introduced and adopted variants of this policy from strict requirements to "guidelines." The rationale provided by First Class Education for the 65 Cent Solution is as follows:

> Business schools throughout America teach management techniques called "best practices" and "benchmarking"—determine what the most efficient companies in a given field are doing and apply similar goals for your firm. In the business of K–12 public school education, First Class Education proposes the benchmark of placing 65% of operational budgets in the classroom. http://www.firstclasseducation.org/

The 65-cent recommendation is based solely on the fact that only two states (according to First Class Education) currently exceed 65%, with the national average being between 61% and 62%. Promoters of the plan argue that if the two very different states can put 65% into instruction, then anyone can:

> The diversity of these states shows that a goal of 65% for classroom instruction can be met throughout the nation. In fact, nearly every state has school districts—big, small, rural, urban and suburban—that are performing at and above the 65% goal. Every school district in America may not be able to reach 65%, but every school district should be encouraged to be as efficient as possible and place its classrooms, its teachers and its students as their first funding priorities. http://www.firstclasseducation.org/

They do not, however, explain why anyone should, except to imply that doing so necessarily improves efficiency. Nowhere in the rationale for 65% is any evidence that allocating 65 cents of every dollar is in any way associated with educational improvement.

The recommendation is predicated on the untested and unfounded assumption that the efficient educational institutions are allocating 65 cents of every dollar to instruction. We discussed efficiency analysis extensively in Chapter 11 and discussed here the relationship between inputs and productivity and efficiency. Quite simply, no sound empirical evidence shows that school districts allocating 65 cents of every dollar to instruction are any more or less efficient. Further, we have shown in this chapter how many factors outside the control of local public schools influence school resource allocation patterns. Finally, we are not convinced that codifying the current average behavior of public school districts (65% being slightly above average instructional share) is the best benchmark for reforming K–12 public schooling in America. Rather, we are strong believers in continued experimentation.

The Nexus Between State Aid Policies and Local Opportunity Distributions

One way that states influence local resource allocation practices is through targeting state aid, often to specific categorical educational programs. Often, the goal

---

[4]In their most recent study, class-size reduction advocates from CPRE and Johns Hopkins concluded only that "Students from CSR [class-size reduction] schools had achievement outcomes that were generally equivalent to those for students from matched comparison schools. Under some circumstances, though, LEP students and their English-speaking peers from CSR schools outperformed their comparison school counterparts." The researchers did not compare costs between class-size reduction and comparison schools (Datnow, Borman, Stringfield, Overman, & Castellano, 2003).

of targeting aid to specific programs is to ensure that the programs in question are equitably or uniformly distributed across districts. When state legislatures target aid to specific programs, such as bilingual, early childhood, or gifted education, they are essentially dictating how certain state revenues are to be allocated within districts. As we discussed in Chapter 8, because state revenues for categorical programs rarely cover full costs, district allocation of general education resources may also be influenced by receipt of categorical resources. Where categorical resources are relatively low, district officials may make the conscious decision *not* to allocate resources to that program area, and not to receive the state aid, unless otherwise mandated. This is more often the case in districts with more significant constraints on their resources, resulting from either lower overall resource levels or reduced flexibility due to other mandates. (We first raised this issue under the title "integration" of general and supplemental aid in Chapter 8.)

In Chapter 8, we discussed Baker's framework for evaluating policies intended to promote vertical equity. Recall that the framework involved measures of (a) adequacy, (b) equity, and (c) rationality, and that the framework focused specifically on evaluating the distribution of state aid, a fiscal input to schools. In this section, we briefly address the distribution of opportunities within schools, as reflected by internal allocation of resources. Further, we address the nexus between fiscal input policies and opportunity distributions.

Significant empirical evidence exists regarding inequities in specific opportunities across schools and districts. For example, Brent et al. (1997) found that lower-wealth districts were less likely to offer advanced programming, corroborated by Raudenbush et al. (1998), who found that children from less-educated families were less likely to attend schools that offered eighth-grade algebra and by Baker (2002), and Baker and Friedman-Nimz (2002), who found that schools with lower average SES and districts with lower fiscal capacity are less likely to provide services to gifted and talented children. In subsequent research, Baker and Friedman-Nimz (2004) find similar disparities in states mandating that services be provided and in states providing funding to local districts. Baker and Friedman-Nimz (2004) provide a framework for linking the allocation of targeted state aid, with the distribution of the opportunities of interest. They note that both aid and opportunities can be distributed *neutrally, progressively,* or *regressively* with respect to fiscal capacity indicators. The goal, as they describe it, is to determine the appropriate distribution of aid in order to accomplish the appropriate distribution of opportunities. Assuming student need to be unassociated with fiscal context (a leap in some cases), the ideal opportunity distribution is *neutral* with respect to fiscal capacity.

Figure 15.6 provides one example linking aid distribution to opportunity distribution. Figure 15.6 assumes that general education resources are not perfectly equalized across all districts in a state and assumes that some disparities in general education resources remain associated with local fiscal capacity.

Figure 15.6   Progressive Aid Distribution Toward Neutral Opportunity Distribution

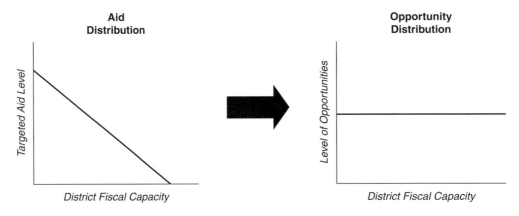

(Context with some fiscal capacity–related disparities.)

Figure 15.7   Neutral Aid Distribution Toward Regressive Opportunity Distribution

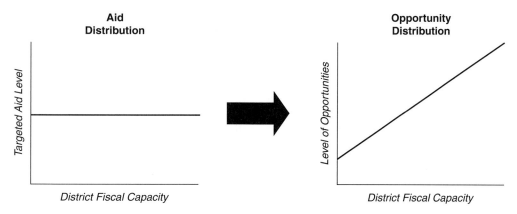

(Context with some fiscal capacity–related disparities.)

Under these conditions, Baker and Friedman-Nimz (2004) point out that states must *progressively* allocate targeted aid to achieve a *neutral* distribution of opportunities. That is, states must provide more aid per pupil to districts of lower fiscal capacity in order to allow districts of varied capacity to allocate comparable resources to the opportunity in question.

While the concept portrayed in Figure 15.6 seems somewhat obvious, recall from Chapter 8 that several states allocate targeted aid as "flat" allocations across districts. The usual assumption regarding flat, targeted aid allocations is, at the very least, that they do no harm to existing equity and neutrality conditions. This assumption is not supported by research. Figure 15.7 displays the relationship between neutral aid allocations and opportunity distributions validated by the research of Baker and Friedman-Nimz (2002), as well as Curley (1991) on programs for gifted and talented students. When states allocate targeted aid in flat amounts across districts of varied capacity, opportunities tend to become even less neutrally distributed than when no targeted aid is provided.

School-Based Budgeting in Seattle

Another movement that followed the wave of scrutiny on productivity and efficiency of district-level financial management was the push for site-based, or school-based, budgeting, especially in large urban districts. Site-based budgeting became popular partly because it was perceived that central office administrators in large urban

districts could not possibly be sensitive to the individual needs of students across all of their schools. The idea was to give school-level administrators increased flexibility over their budgets, including control over staffing, the primary school-level expense. Implementing school-based budgeting meant that large urban districts would have to design funding formulas by which block grants would be allocated to individual schools.

The tendency has been for these formulas to mirror state aid formulas to local districts. That is, states typically provide schools a per-pupil level of foundation aid, accompanied by some form of adjustments to help schools meet the needs of their different student populations. Typical adjustments include pupil weights for special education students, LEP students, and low-income students. Similar to the Education Alternatives, Inc., contract with Baltimore schools and to charter school policies in some states, districts retain some responsibilities, and with them, a cut of the funding. For example, in a district using school-based budgeting, the district might retain responsibility for transportation and/or food service expenses as well as other major facilities expenses.

Perhaps the best-known, and best-documented example of this approach is that of the Seattle Public Schools. In the Seattle public schools, their internal resource allocation formula involves the following components:

> *Weighted Student Allocation:* The weighted student allocation component of the formula uses data on school-level enrollments to

generate funds for general and special instructional purposes. The allocation begins with a Base Funding Factor, which is then multiplied times (a) grade-level weights and (b) student-need weights, including low performance.

Foundation Allocation: Each school also receives an allocation called the foundation allocation, which is intended to cover the administrative overhead costs of running a school of given grade levels and given enrollment.

Table 15.10 shows that the basic funding level per pupil in Seattle for 2006–2007 was to be $4,492 for elementary schools and slightly less for middle and secondary schools. However, the system also allocates, outside of the weighted funding formula, from $600 to nearly $900 in additional per-pupil budgets. That is, for an elementary school of prototypical size, over 26% of funding would be allocated outside of the weighting system as a "foundation" or overhead allotment. Various special education categories of students receive

differentiated weights based on intensity of services. Those weights, like others in the model, are not grounded in actual empirical analysis of the costs of service delivery.

Children from economically disadvantaged backgrounds receive from 9% to 12% additional funding at the elementary level, producing a yield per "need" pupil of about $427. Children with LEP receive a yield per pupil of about $917 at the elementary level, each of these figures being primarily a function of available resources and political will. On average, Baker and Thomas (2006) do find that the Seattle system leads to marginally higher funding in schools with higher versus lower student needs. An elementary school with 100% poverty (measured by free and reduced lunch count) would be expected to receive, on average, nearly 50% more staffing resources per pupil than an elementary school with 0% poverty (Baker & Thomas, 2006, p. 51).

Recently, William Ouchi of the Business School at the University of California at Los Angeles, along with

Table 15.10   Seattle Public Schools Weighted Student Formula, 2006–2007

	Elementary	Middle	High	Nontraditional	Exceptional
Assumed enrollment	250	600	1000	250	250
Foundation allocation		$416,226	$590,368		
Foundation allocation	$217,177	26	68	$217,177	
Foundation per pupil	$869	$769	$590	$869	
Other foundational support					
MS pupil				$431	
HS pupil				$399	
Head start	$300			$300	$300
Negotiated stipend for elementary schools	$1,000			$1,000	1,000
Average per-pupil foundation	$668	$578	$515	$844	$840
Weighted-pupil allocation					
Base-aid amount	$3,392	$3,019	$3,019		
Grade-level factor	1.00	0.89	0.89		
Student needs					
Special ed L2	0.95	0.95	0.95		
Special ed L3	2.64	1.35	1.04		
Special ed L4a	3.78	3.72	3.72		
Special ed L4e	5.25	5.17	0.00		
Special ed. L4b	5.80	5.76	5.76		
Bilingual program	0.27	0.38	0.39		
Free/reduced/lunch	.099 to .126	0.22	0.22		
Dollar value of student need wts					
Bilingual program	$916	$1,289	$1,323		
Free/reduced lunch	$427	$ 740	$ 757		

Source: Data from Baker and Thomas (2006).

co-authors Bruce Cooper of Fordham University and Tim DeRoche, have become strong advocates of decentralized school budget management, coupled with weighted-pupil formulas like that used in Seattle. The authors have presented their arguments for weighted-pupil formulas in popular books and media outlets (see, e.g., DeRoche, Cooper, & Ouchi, 2004). DeRoche et al. (2004) recommend an inclusive political process for the determination of (a) what should be weighted and (b) how much weight should be applied.

Although it is plainly logical to apply weighted funding to schools, just as it is commonly applied in state aid formulas to districts, the same ugly methodological monsters that arise in state weighted-pupil formulas may also rear their heads in district weighted-pupil allocation formulas to schools, especially where political processes are used for setting pupil-need weights.

As we discussed in Chapters 6 through 10, pupil-weighting systems have been around for decades, and the politics of pupil weights have been around nearly as long, with special interests grasping onto specific weights to gain advantage for themselves or their constituents. In fact, in some cases, politics have weighed so heavily on distribution of pupil weights that the end product—weighted-pupil aid—is allocated in inverse relation to actual need. Nonetheless, we believe that school-level pupil-weighting formulas would encourage identification of students with needs, would make more transparent the decisions for allocating resources to schools, and would advance the cause of adequacy by making school-to-school comparisons more feasible. Further, we have suggested some techniques for assessing true needs that would more closely align the development of the weights with the actual costs of offering the services required.

Effectiveness of School-Based Budgeting

In 1997, under Chancellor Rudy Crew, New York City implemented a performance-based, school-based budgeting plan. At the time, six mostly low-income community school districts opted to participate. By 2002, participation had increased to 22 of the city's 32 community school districts. More importantly, however, student "test score data showed that students in the first 61 schools to join the project were outscoring their counterparts elsewhere in the city—and in their own districts—after just three years" (Viadero, 2002, p. 12). Ouchi and colleagues (2004) provide similar anecdotal evidence, but limited rigorous statistical analysis exists regarding the advantages of decentralized budgeting.

Baker and Thomas (2006), in a report to the Hawaii Board of Education, note:

> Indeed many scholars including ourselves believe that decentralization can lead to positive changes [see, e.g., Ouchi, 2003]. But, we are willing to acknowledge that the empirical basis for this assertion remains thin at best, especially as pertains specifically to decentralized city (or state) school systems and weighted student funding. We acknowledge that there exists a wider literature available on school-based management and participatory decision-making. This literature is only tangentially related to the issue at hand, as it mostly pertains to strategies implemented individual (or a small handful of) schools, and not as broader state policy. (Baker & Thomas, 2006)

Rigorous empirical analyses of domestic and international decentralized systems might also provide some guidance, but these analyses tend to find mixed and in some cases negative results (see, e.g., Grosskopf & Moutray, 2001; Gunnarsson, Orazem, Sanchez, & Verdisco, 2004). Internationally, the Chilean experience provides additional mixed evidence and is documented in McEwan and Carnoy (2000). See also related work from Argentina in Galiani, Gertler, and Schargrodsky (2005) and from Nicaragua in Özler and King (2004). Nationally, evaluations of charter school performance and efficiency might provide additional guidance, and some recent studies do find increased efficiency in outcome production in charter schools (Gronberg & Jansen, 2001).

We caution that some, including Ouchi (2003) have substantially overstated the potential efficiency advantages of site-based budgeting, suggesting that decentralization alone can remedy the inefficiencies of urban schooling. Ouchi notes "Today's urban school districts have more than enough money in their budgets to do their jobs well. Now the challenge is to organize them so as to maximize their efficiency and performance" (Ouchi, 2004). We expect that most readers of our chapters on educational adequacy (Chapters 7 to 10) now know better than to assume that large urban districts invariably have sufficient resources to perform well, especially in an era when urban district resources are defined by politics and wealth, rather than the empirics discussed in Chapter 7 through 10. For example, the New York State Supreme Court has found that New York City has been denied the funds required to provide an adequate education to its students, and all parties recognize that *billions* more dollars will be required. The current political infighting over the size, distribution, and use of those funds in addition to who might pay for them is ongoing.

Finally, if we assume charter schooling to represent a reform similar to decentralization, research in the state of Texas (discussed in Chapter 11) suggests modest improvements to efficiency in charter schooling relative to comparable traditional public schools. These modest efficiency gains may serve as a basis for greater experimentation with decentralization, but achieving adequate urban schooling will likely require sufficiently greater (not less) funding than presently exists. One final observation: a very large percentage of the nation's poor, immigrant, and LEP student body resides in very large urban school systems. Thus, both the scope of the problem and its significance are large.

SUMMARY

In this chapter, we have sought to illuminate the continued tensions between two sources and kinds of knowledge: the desire to implement evidence-based strategies gleaned from national and international research that will guarantee success for all children, and the competing desire to decentralize control of schooling including fiscal resource allocation, to let those at the school level—who know best—make all key decisions appropriate to their local circumstances. We have expressed these tensions throughout this textbook in a variety of forms:

- Should states use block grants with wide local latitude in how they are used and control for accountability at the outcome level, or should states prescribe how school districts use the funds at the input and process level?

- Should we let the market determine whether a school survives, or should we protect public schools from market competition?

- Should teacher salary schedules reflect differences in demand for the skill taught, and the quality of the teacher, or should they be uniform and based on educational attainment and years of experience?

These and other similar questions have informed almost all of the research and policy questions we addressed in previous chapters. We think the tensions are healthy, and we certainly do not think the available research has answered them with a definitive statement.

This chapter also highlights just how far we have yet to go in understanding how to optimize resource allocation such as to maximize student outcomes at a given aggregate level of fiscal inputs. It may be that a global maximization formula does not exist. Truly effective schooling is most likely highly adaptive to local context and to the children served. Decentralization and experimentation are to be found not only in site-based budgeting and charter school movements but also in many district-led initiatives. This suggests that the perennial search for a "one best system," described by educational historian David Tyack (1974) in his book of the same name, is an exercise in folly.

At the same time, letting a thousand flowers bloom, without attempting to separate solid practice from utter foolishness, is not an acceptable policy option in a world where 1 year of public schooling for a single child is approaching 25% of the median family income in America.

Lacking sufficient empirical evidence on the productivity and efficiency advantages of centralized versus decentralized policies, it remains difficult to reconcile these dramatically different views on appropriate government intervention strategies. Our take on the inconclusiveness of decentralization reforms is simply that the issue requires more investigation, and that such investigation can occur only if school districts and charter school authorizers are allowed to continue to experiment with alternative approaches to allocating schooling resources and delivering instruction. We expect that, rather than uniform improvement to student outcomes and schooling efficiency, decentralization and experimentation at the school level and *tinkering* with resource allocation patterns will lead to greater variance in schooling productivity and efficiency in schooling—some good and some not-so-good. The key to educational reform is to identify and replicate the good and eliminate and/or remediate the bad.

REFERENCES

Baker, B. D. (2001). Gifted children in the current policy and fiscal context of public education: A national snapshot and state-level equity analysis of Texas. *Educational Evaluation and Policy Analysis, 23*(3), 229–250.

Baker, B. D. (2002). *Do state policies influence the internal allocation of school district resources: Evidence from the common core of data.* Paper presented at the Annual Meeting of the American Education Finance Association. Albuquerque, NM.

Baker, B. D. (2003). State policy influences on the internal allocation of school district resources: Evidence from the Common Core of Data. *Journal of Education Finance, 29*(1), 1–24.

Baker, B.D., & Friedman-Nimz, R. C. (2002). Determinants of the availability of opportunities for gifted children: Evidence from NELS '88. *Leadership and Policy in Schools, 1*(1), 52–71.

Baker, B. D., & Friedman-Nimz, R. C. (2004). State policy influences governing equal opportunity: The example of gifted education. *Educational Evaluation and Policy Analysis, 26*(1), 39–64.

Baker, B. D., & Thomas, S. L. (2006). *Review of Hawaii's weighted student formula.* Honolulu, HI: Hawaii State Board of Education.

Bifulco, R., Bordeaux, C., Duncombe, W., & Yinger, J. (2002). *Do whole school reform programs boost student performance? The Case of New York City.* Smith-Richardson Foundation.

Borman, G. D., & Hewes, G. (2002). The long-term effects and cost effectiveness of success for all. *Educational Evaluation and Policy Analysis, 24*(4), 243–266.

Borman, G., Hewes, G., Overman, L., & Brown, S. (2003). Comprehensive school reform and achievement: A meta-analysis. *Review of Educational Research, 73*(2), 125–230.

Brent, B. O., Roellke, C. F., & Monk, D. H. (1997). Understanding teacher resource allocation in New York State secondary schools: A case study approach. *Journal of Education Finance, 23*(2), 207–233.

Brewer, D. J. (1996). Does more school administration lower educational productivity? Some evidence on the "administrative blob" in New York public schools. *Economics of Education Review, 15*(2), 111–125.

Burke, S. M. (1999). An analysis of resource inequality at the state, district and school levels. *Journal of Education Finance, 24*(4), 435–458.

Curley, J. (1991). Financing programs for education of the gifted in New York State. *Journal of Education Finance, 16*(3), 332–347.

Datnow, A., Borman, G. D., Stringfield, S., Overman, L. T., & Castellano, M. (2003). Comprehensive school reform in culturally and linguistically diverse contexts: Implementation and outcomes from a four-year study. *Educational Evaluation & Policy Analysis, 25*(2), 143–170.

DeRoche, T., Cooper, B. S., & Ouchi, W. (2004, August). When dollars follow students: The political viability, equity, and workability of weighted funding formulas. *The School Administrator,* 14–17. Retrieved from http://www.aasa.org/publications/sa/2004_08/deroche.htm

Galiani, S., Gertler, P., & Schargrodsky, E. (2005). *Helping the good get better, but leaving the rest behind: How decentralization affects school performance.* Working paper. Retrieved from http://www.bu.edu/econ/ied/ seminars/ pdf/Schargrodsky4-24-06.pdf

Goertz, M. E., & Natriello, G. (1999). Court-mandated school finance reform: What do the new dollars buy? In H. Ladd, R. Chalk, & J. Hansen (Eds.), *Equity and adequacy in education finance: Issues and perspectives* (pp. 99–135). Committee on Education Finance, Commission on Behavioral and Social Sciences and Education, National Research Council. Washington, DC: National Academy Press.

Gronberg, T. J., & Jansen, D. (2001). *Navigating newly chartered waters: An analysis of Texas charter school performance.* Austin, TX: Texas Public Policy Foundation.

Grosskopf S., & Moutray C. (2001). Evaluating performance in Chicago public high schools in the wake of decentralization. *Economics of Education Review, 20,* 1–14.

Gunnarsson, V., Orazem, P. F., Sanchez, M., & Verdisco, A. (2004). *Does school decentralization raise student outcomes: Theory and evidence on the roles of school autonomy and community participation.* Working Paper, Dept. of Economics. Iowa State University. Retrieved from http://www.econ.iastate.edu/faculty/orazem/School %20Autonomy%20final.pdf

Hannaway, J., McKay, S., & Nakib, Y. (2002). Reform and resource allocation: National trends and state policies. *Developments in School Finance 1999–2000.* Office of Educational Research and Improvement, National Center for Education Statistics. Washington, DC: U.S. Department of Education.

Hertert, L. (1996). Does equal funding for districts mean equal funding for classroom students? Evidence from California. In L. Picus and J. Wattenbarger (Eds.), *Where does the money go? Resource allocation in elementary and secondary schools* (pp. 71–84). Thousand Oaks, CA: Corwin Press.

Lankford, H., & Wyckoff, J. (1999). The allocation of resources to special education and regular instruction in New York State. In T. Parrish, J. Chambers, & C. Guarino (Eds.) *Funding special education* (pp. 147–175). Thousand Oaks, CA: Corwin Press.

Levin, H. (1983). *Cost effectiveness analysis.* Thousand Oaks, CA: Sage Publications.

Levin, H. M. (2002). *The cost effectiveness of whole school reforms. Urban diversity series No. 114.* ERIC Clearinghouse on Urban Education. Institute for Urban and Minority Education.

McEwan, P. J., & Carnoy, M. (2000). The effectiveness and efficiency of private schools in Chile's voucher system. *Educational Evaluation and Policy Analysis, 22*(3), 213–240.

Monk, D. H., & Hussain, S. (2000). Structural influences on the internal allocation of school district resources: Evidence from New York State. *Educational Evaluation and Policy Analysis, 22*(1), 1–26.

Morphew, C., & Baker, B. D. (2007). On the utility of national data for estimating generalizable price and cost indices in higher education. *Journal of Education Finance.*

Odden, A. (2000). Costs of sustaining educational change via comprehensive school reform. *Phi Delta Kappan, 81*(6), 433—438.

Ouchi, W. G. (2003). *Making schools work: A revolutionary plan to get your children the education they need.* New York: Simon & Schuster.

Ouchi, W. G. (2004, Winter). Academic Freedom. http://www.educationnext.org/20041/21.html

Ouchi, W. G., Cooper, B. S., Segal, L., DeRoche, T., Brown, C., & Galvin, E. (2003). Organizational configuration and performance: The case of primary and secondary school systems. http://www.williamouchi.com/docs/primary_secondary.pdf

Özler, B., & King, E. M. (2004). *What's decentralization got to do with learning? School autonomy and school performance.* The World Bank. Retrieved from http://www.worldbank.org/research/pdffiles/king&boz.pdf

Parrish, T. B., Matsumoto, C., & Fowler, W. (1995). *Disparities in public school district spending 1989-90* (p. E-1). Washington, DC: National Center for Education Statistics. Retrieved from http://nces.ed.gov/pubs95/95300_a.pdf

Raudenbush, S. W., Fotiu, R. P., & Cheong, Y. F. (1998). Inequality of access to educational resources: A national report card for eighth-grade math. *Educational Evaluation and Policy Analysis, 20*(4), 253–267.

Richards, C. E., & White, R. (1988). Quasi-vouchers for private providers of special education in New Jersey. *Journal of Education Finance, 11*(1), 3.

Rothstein, R., & Miles, K. H. (1995). *Where's the money gone? Changes in the level and composition of education spending.* Washington, DC: Economic Policy Institute.

Rufo-Lignos, P., & Richards, C. E. (2003). Emerging forms of school organization. *Teachers College Record, 105*(5), 753–781.

Sanders, W., Wright, S. P., Ross, S. & Wang, L. W. (2000). *Value-added achievement results of three cohorts of Roots and Wings schools in Memphis: 1995–1999 outcomes.* Knoxville, TN: University of Tennessee.

Speakman, S. T., Cooper, B. S., Sampieri, R., May, J., Holsomback, H., & Glass, B. (1996). Bringing money to the classroom: a systematic resource allocations model applied to the New York City public schools. In L. Picus & J. Wattenbarger (Eds.), *Where does the money go? Resource allocation in elementary and secondary schools* (pp. 106–131). Thousand Oaks, CA: Corwin Press.

Stiefel, L., Rubenstein, R., & Berne, R. (1998). Intra district equity in four large cities: Data, methods and results. *Journal of Education Finance, 23*(4), 447–467.

Sullivan, M. (2004). *Resource allocation in Catholic high schools.* Unpublished doctoral dissertation. University of Kansas.

Tyack, D. (1974). *The one best system.* New York: John Wiley.

Viadero, D. (2002, August 7). NYC school-based budgeting linked to test score gains. *Education Week, 21*(43), 12.

CLOSING THOUGHTS

We conclude this textbook on school finance with some major points of synthesis, drawing on the content we have presented in Chapters 1 through 15. As we articulated in the introduction, our goals have been, first, to present an overview of the recent policy history of school finance and, second, to survey the current status of school finance with emphasis on equity and adequacy. We also explored the parallel technical infrastructure of school finance, including the emergence of increasingly sophisticated horizontal equity aid formulas. We then turned to the emergence of adequacy goals, particularly as a legal and strategic effort to supplant equity litigation in those states where equity has been previously unsuccessful (e.g., New York). We then discussed increasingly sophisticated cost-of-education models, used to pursue both adequacy and vertical equity goals. The development of adequacy strategies has necessarily required the field of school finance to rationalize cost analysis and cost-effectiveness in the very cauldron of state political economy. The solutions thus far forged have not been of the highest caliber. We dedicated the latter sections of this text to the topics of educational productivity and efficiency and the policy reforms intended to improve educational productivity and efficiency, some within the state-sponsored educational system and some in the marketplace. Finally, we considered some emerging trends in school organization—largely in response to the perceived ineffectiveness of the dominant paradigm—including charter schools, private for-profit schools, and hybrid forms of schooling that are neither entirely public nor private.

We have covered a lot of ground, but we expect that we have left you with very few definitive answers: Such is the world of social science research in general and school finance in particular. However, it is premature to conclude that all of the work in school finance has resulted in nothing more than technical smoke and mirrors.

The field has made significant progress in some areas and less in others. As we demonstrated in Chapter 1, the United States spends more per child than any other nation, and the vast expansion of state aid during the 20th century has been the determinant factor in reducing within-state inequality of per-pupil expenditure. In addition, co-emergent with the Civil Rights Movement, overt discrimination and segregation in American public education have been generally reduced, though evidence suggests the emergence of re-segregation in more recent years (Orfield, 2001).

Still, children of African-American, Native American, Hispanic-American, and poor children of all races and ethnic groups persistently achieve less in school than children who are not among these reference groups.

We strongly believe that an adequate education by first-world and 21st-century standards includes ensuring the following:

1. All children are safe from abuse and neglect whether at home, in school, or in their communities.
2. All children have a right to healthy food to eat and clean water to drink.
3. All children have a right to regular exercise.
4. All children have a right to caring and highly competent teachers and support staff in their schools.
5. All children have a right to safe and appropriate facilities.
6. All children have a right to appropriate pedagogy and educational materials and supports for their academic learning.
7. All children have a right to be appropriately nurtured, physically, emotionally, mentally, and spiritually in schools such that they anticipate school, not with anxiety or fear, but with happiness and high expectations.

Finally, we are especially dismayed by the relative inattention to funding for high-quality, early childhood education and its positive impact on student achievement, including second-language acquisition.

In addition to the preceding seven fundamental ethical statements we have just advanced, we believe that doing better as a profession requires renewed research and policy debate addressing seven fundamental questions, questions in which school finance must play either a direct or a supporting role.

1. How can the federal government and the states continue to work collaboratively to create better empirical data and, particularly important, time series data, to inform the political debates around school finance policy?

Better data will help us to separate value questions from factual questions. These include better indicators systems at the federal, state, district, school, and child level and better measures of the inputs and processes of education that are strongly supported in the research literature as adding educational value to at-risk children. Politics continues to play too large a role in providing an adequate and reasonably equal education to poor and minority children, and poor data feed unenlightened educational financing.

In Chapters 7 through 10, we explored in considerable detail emerging empirical methods for informing state school finance policy. In Chapters 8 through 10 in particular, we discussed the failures of current political processes in generating *rational* aid formulas, where we define rational as directly related to achieving desired educational outcomes. Quite simply, we need to do better in order to meet our obligation of leaving no child behind. One way to do so is to continue to infuse high-quality empirical information into the political process of designing state school finance policies.

The process of designing and implementing state school finance policy will unquestionably remain a political one. Yet that process is increasingly a collaboration or deliberation negotiated between three branches of state government—executive, legislative, and judicial. Legal theorists have argued that under the No Child Left Behind Act (NCLB) of 2001, states face an increased obligation to ensure that each child, regardless of socioeconomic status (SES), language proficiency, or race (specific points of disaggregation in NCLB) must be provided comparable opportunity to achieve state-mandated outcomes, and all must do so by 2014. Researchers and school leaders must provide courts and legislators with a better toolkit for (a) developing more rational state-aid formulas and (b) evaluating the rationality of current state-aid formulas. The old tools are simply insufficient, and we addressed several new tools in Chapter 10.

Antiquated demurs such as, "there simply are no right answers in school finance policy," are no longer sufficient bases for validating options for policy makers' choices to do whatever they please in the design of state-aid formulas. Indeed, a variety of opinions and policy options may exist on any number of school finance issues. Along the way, one critically important step researchers and policy analysts must take is a strong stand in separating the wheat from the chaff. All opinions and all empirical methods for studying school finance are not created equal. In the current policy context, where opportunity to achieve targeted educational outcomes is the goal, we must continue to develop rigorous statistical methods for evaluating the costs of achieving those outcomes for different groups of students, under different circumstances. Further, as we discussed in Chapter 11, researchers may use complimentary methods to test the efficiency gains and resultant decreases in costs achieved through educational reforms. Most important, from our point of view, is the long-term stability of highly adequate, and ideally, precisely vertically equitable, levels of spending.

While uncertainty characterizes a good deal of social science research, education policy research often seems particularly vulnerable. However, as we have discussed in this textbook, the commonalities of numerous recent empirical analyses of education costs and cost variations far outweigh the differences. Furthermore, they serve the very important function of narrowing the range of acceptable solutions for courts, legislatures, and policy makers.

We now know a great deal about the *shape of educational adequacy* (Chapters 7 and 8) and vertical equity (Chapters 8 through 10), at least in the current policy, organizational, socioeconomic, and demographic context. We have an extensive base of empirical analyses that advocate adjustments for at-risk and/or limited English proficient (LEP) students, ranging from approximately 40% to about 100% additional funding (relative to average costs), with many recent statistical analyses supporting the 100% marginal cost figure. These figures differ dramatically from the 10% to 20% weights often applied in state-aid formulas to artificially low base-aid figures. As a result, we can be quite confident that the costs of achieving desired outcomes in poor urban districts with high concentrations of children needing special education are much higher than the costs of achieving similar outcomes in neighboring suburban districts or in large towns. But we also now know that substantial additional marginal costs are associated with educating children in rural areas.

2. Why is the decay rate of current state school finance policies so rapid?

We must learn to develop, monitor, and maintain sustainable and adaptable state school finance policies. The apparent half-life of state school finance policies appears to be somewhere between 3 and 7 years, where we define "half-life" as a policy with only half its original efficacy. The half-life of modern state school finance policies appears even shorter than those of the past (1970s and 1980s). Half of a short life is less than half of a long life. A variety of factors—both endogenous and exogenous—seems to be destabilizing state aid formulas. Among the endogenous factors is the political manipulation of available policy levers to recapture financial advantages lost by the previous finance reform. Kansas, for example, remains a paradigmatic exemplar: Over the past 15 years in Kansas, policy makers have gradually added loopholes to the strict revenue caps on the aid formula, creating greater inequities over time in a formula designed to improve and maintain equity. When the courts pressured the legislature to increase funding for at-risk programs, it did so marginally but countered with increases for suburban districts with the highest-priced houses (cost of living adjustment discussed in Chapter 9). Other endogenous factors involve tax policy decisions, such as state legislative decisions to limit local district budget growth (Nebraska in the late 1990s) or decisions to shift dramatically tax burdens from one source to another (Michigan in 1994).

Major exogenous factors influencing the cost structure of public education include dramatic changes in the demography of school districts. Often the most dramatic demographic changes occur in small to midsized rural communities that for years had been relatively stagnant. Lexington, Nebraska, now serves a student population that has over 50% of its children in poverty and over 25% LEP children. Yet current Nebraska school finance policies treat Lexington as if it was the second lowest need district, among larger (>2,000 students) districts in the state. In contrast, empirical estimates invariably identify Lexington as the highest need district of greater than 2,000 students in the state.

Many regions of the country are experiencing dramatic suburban sprawl—the exurbs—making the optimization of infrastructure use quite difficult as populations on the fringes of sprawl have more and more children, while the urban and suburban areas mature.

State revenue systems must also adapt to support the increased demands and related costs of public schooling. Arguably, the majority of recent, dramatic decay of state school-funding formulas is a direct function of tax policy decisions leading to insufficient revenues to support otherwise reasonable distribution policies. A major underlying factor has been state legislative disdain for the local property tax in particular and property taxes in general. In Chapter 3, we discussed how scholars dating back to the 1970s proposed the redistribution of property tax revenues as one approach to equity in school funding.

Two states, New Hampshire and Vermont, have based their most recent school finance policies on relatively high statewide property taxes. A balanced portfolio of revenues is critically important for states to sustain their school finance policies. Tax revenues supporting public schooling should include a mix of revenues responsive to economic cycles, such as income and sales tax revenue, and revenues less responsive, such as property tax revenues. In times of economic downturn, property tax revenues provide invaluable stability, while during periods of economic growth, sales and income taxes provide strategic opportunities to leverage the system toward adequacy and equity. Current (2001 to 2003) and future budget shortfalls in New Jersey may destabilize finance equity gains—as has been the recurring pattern in that state for over 30 years. In general, sustainability of state school finance policies requires policies flexible enough to adapt to structural changes in the delivery of schooling and requires state legislatures to consciously address structural and organizational changes in schooling alongside state school finance policies. Arguably, charter schools—the largest ongoing conscious structural change—have been significantly shortchanged in this regard. State school finance policies have only slowly, if at all, adapted to the start-up costs, infrastructure needs, administrative burdens, and scaling up costs associated with decentralizing schooling through charters.

Finally, while legislative sessions occur once yearly, or even biennially, legislators and their analysts must attempt to evaluate the long-term dynamics of state school finance policies, both in terms of their interactions with the available resource base and economic context and in terms of their adaptability to the needs of changing student populations and school structures.

3. What can the U.S. do structurally to uproot the complex overlay of social organization, geography, school district boundaries, and school finance policy that reinforces the vicious cycle of inequities in schooling quality and student outcomes?

Perhaps the most significant barriers to overcome in improving equity and relative adequacy of public schooling in America relate to the deeply embedded, racially and socioeconomically segregated housing patterns and the disconnect between ghettoized communities, civic institutions, employers, and school district organization. Many pundits have criticized as wasteful the expenditure of large sums of money on poor inner-city schools as a result of either desegregation litigation or school finance litigation. The rally cries have recently been amplified by the New York State High Court's decision that the state must allocate substantially more funding to New York City schools (see Chapter 7). Critics most often cite the example of the problems associated with *wasting* money on poor urban schools in Kansas City, Missouri, following the desegregation order in *Missouri v. Jenkins* (see Green & Baker, 2006). They point to the construction of elaborate facilities to be used as magnet schools to attract white children from neighboring suburbs to resolve segregation problems. They point to the fact that Kansas City's schools are now as segregated as ever, are funded among the highest in the state, and continue to perform poorly.

A few important rebuttal comments are in order. First, even though Kansas City, Missouri, public schools do spend higher than state averages, *education cost–function* analysis suggests that Kansas City is still not funded high enough to approach even state average outcomes, given its current student population. (Similar arguments can be made for New York City.) Second, no one seems to ask what *might have happened* in Kansas City had operating revenues remained much lower, and infrastructure existing before the case had been allowed to continue to crumble. It is difficult to imagine that conditions could be even nearly as "good" as they are today.

Finally, and most importantly, the "high cost" of remedying the disparities of poor urban, predominantly African-American and Hispanic schools is largely a function of conscious state and local political decisions. State and local politicians organize neighborhoods, communities, and schools such that poor minority children are concentrated in specific neighborhoods and schools, and policy makers do little or nothing to change these patterns when faced with court orders to improve school quality or integrate schools. State legislatures can reorganize those schools, potentially changing the cost structure of public schooling quite dramatically. It might be cheaper in the long run for states to fully integrate schooling in metropolitan areas. So why don't they? (This is not a naïve question!)

Recall that it is the courts, not legislatures, that are bound by the constraints of *Milliken v. Bradley* that disallow the forcing of predominantly white suburbs from participating in desegregation solutions unless it can be shown that the suburbs intentionally caused the segregation (Chapter 4). State legislatures, such as the Missouri legislature, have made the conscious decision to pay the price to retain segregation, rather than pursuing deeper structural and organizational changes to the delivery of schooling that might reduce total costs.[1]

Lacking court-imposed *Milliken II* remedies, other legislatures such as those in Kansas and Nebraska have opted to retain segregation via the organization of districts *and* to provide lower, not higher, funding to poor, minority districts. Research on the political economy of school vouchers discussed in Chapter 12 confirms that local voters have strong preferences for maintaining the values of their own houses over promoting school choice programs that might lead to more fluid enrollment patterns, greater integration, and reduction in property value disparities (Brunner & Sonsteile, 2003). Deep structural and organizational changes and/or sustained exorbitant public expenditure will likely be required to close racial and socioeconomic achievement gaps in our nation's major and even minor metropolitan areas. Charter schooling has been a very small, positive step in limited ways, but only in states where charter schools are allowed to significantly interrupt racial and socioeconomic geographic boundaries. And only in states where charter school funding levels encourage sustainability (see Chapter 12).

Certainly, radical reorganization of schooling in metropolitan areas could dramatically change the

---

[1]Amazingly, as this book was going to press, Missouri legislators passed legislation (SB 112, 2007) that would change current law requiring bilateral agreement among school districts for annexing territory, specifically, to allow a predominantly white area of Kansas City Missouri School district to annex itself by appeal to the State Board from the district, creating a more segregated KCMSD than has previously existed in any period in the district's history. The bill requires the State Board to approve the annexation if the "sending" district is unaccredited (http://www.senate.mo.gov/07info/pdf-bill/tat/SB112.pdf).

socioeconomic and racial mix in schools, as well as the financial resource base for schooling. In addition, radical reorganization of these districts could dramatically alter teacher labor markets in these metropolitan areas and the equitable distribution of teaching quality. As it stands, suburban districts pay higher wages to attract better teachers, few of whom would arguably choose to teach in the urban core for even lower wages. In addition, substantially less manipulation of expectations would be required for achieving reasonable competitive comparisons on state accountability measures.

4. For the foreseeable future, is school finance litigation the most effective way to achieve educational reform?

Chapters 5 and 7 provide an overview of school finance litigation. As these chapters illustrate, the legal challenges have been controversial and contentious, time-consuming, and expensive. These experiences have led a number of critics to question the effectiveness of school finance litigation. They primarily advance three arguments. First, they assert that courts lack the expertise to develop remedies for inequitable and inadequate school finance systems. As Heise (2002) explains, "The overwhelming majority of judges (and their clerks) are not trained as policy analysts and thus possess little expertise in school finance minutiae. School finance litigation frequently forces judges into unfamiliar technical and policy terrain" (p. 656). Such logic assumes that state legislators, whose terms are often shorter than judges, are more experienced, uniquely qualified, and better informed. Second, they argue that judicially orchestrated school-funding reform is ineffective because courts become mired in multiple rounds of litigation. Critics point to the decades-long legal battles in New Jersey, New York, and Texas as evidence of the failure of school finance litigation. Third, they maintain that increased funding to poor school districts has not resulted in improved educational outcomes for poor school districts. Despite these concerns, school finance litigation will remain a vital part of the educational landscape for the foreseeable future.

Courts may address the first concern by appointing special masters to help them develop remedies to unconstitutional school finance formulas. Special masters have been used in school desegregation cases to help courts develop remedies to *de jure* segregation. In fact, the Arkansas and New Jersey Supreme Courts have appointed special masters to aid in the design of

school finance remedies. Court-appointed special masters may reduce the risk of judicial mistakes by enabling courts to receive technical support from experts in the area of school finance reform.

With respect to the second assertion, it is true that judicial involvement in school finance reform runs the risk of antagonizing state legislatures. However, it is important to consider whether state legislatures would have addressed educational funding disparities if the courts had not become involved. Because of political concerns, it is unlikely that most legislatures would have repaired their school finance formulas without the judiciary acting as a catalyst. Thus, plaintiffs will continue to use the courts to remedy school-funding deficiencies.

With respect to the third concern, we have observed that obtaining equity between rich and poor districts may not achieve equity in terms of educational outcomes. Poor school districts may need more resources to obtain comparable educational outcomes. Chapter 7 explains that future school finance litigation may attempt to obtain these resources by arguing that the failure to provide students from poor-performing school districts with sufficient resources to reach the student performance standards developed by state legislatures may expose states to adequacy claims based on state education clauses and the due process clause. Clearly defined and measurable educational outcomes may also subject future school districts to tort liability when it can be established that districts neglected to teach students literacy and numeric skills.

5. Although a variety of types of inequities exist among school districts (including facilities quality and availability of materials, supplies, textbooks, and computers), what can the U.S. do to overcome the inequity in the distribution of quality teaching, which has been most closely linked to unequal achievement outcomes among students?

We have a great deal yet to learn about teacher labor markets. For example, are teachers more or less qualified today than in 1960? Why or why not? What do we mean by qualified? Can teacher quality be disaggregated into (a) intellectual aptitude, (b) personality factors, (c) pedagogical knowledge and skills, (d) academic content knowledge, and (e) emotional intelligence? If so, which domains of competence are most important at each grade level, and how should we assess competence in each domain (or others that may be deemed important)? We know that suburban districts are culling higher-performing teachers from the general labor market, but even then, we know very little about why they are better, or if these apparent skills are even transferable to urban school settings.

One of the greatest benefits of metropolitan school reorganization as described here would be the corresponding changes to the incentives in major metropolitan area teacher labor markets. Moreover, the costs of bringing more highly qualified teachers into generally more equal schools, at generally more adequate pay, may be significantly less than the costs required to recruit and retain sufficient numbers of high-quality teachers and principals in the current poor urban core and poor urban fringe districts.

In any case, state school finance policies must be sensitive to teacher labor markets. For example, states must provide sufficient incentives such as combat pay to equalize the distribution of quality teaching in districts where legislators shy away from deeper organizational changes that might reduce the necessity for such incentives.

Supply quality and supply quantity cannot be ignored. State school finance policies cannot effectively leverage and distribute teacher supply where the supply pipeline itself is inadequate. State policies must address both the quality and quantity of emerging teachers from conventional production pipelines—schools of education at public colleges and universities—and must also seek alternative pipelines that may expand the available supply of high-quality teachers. Some states, such as Texas, currently offer much higher salaries and benefits than their poorer neighbors, such as Louisiana, and actively recruit teachers educated in Louisiana's university system. In effect, Louisiana pays for the education of Texas teachers.

Finally, even where improving teacher quality is not the central concern of a finance policy decision, teacher labor market dynamics must always be on the minds of policy makers. In Chapter 13, we discussed problems associated with statewide class-size reduction. Similar issues may emerge as states move toward adequacy-based financing, assuming competitive teacher wages/prices based on current conditions of supply and demand, but implementing policies that dramatically alter current conditions. For example, how will the competitive wage for New York City teachers change as demand is dramatically increased by infusion of more financial resources? We might begin a radical experiment by having a state employment agency that determines teacher quality, certifies competency, and then assigns teachers according to need criteria or some combination of need and regional demand but independent of urban–suburban distinctions.

6. What kind of research strategies do we need in order to improve our knowledge base about how to make schools work—and work better?

Decorating the shelves of your suburban Barnes and Noble are likely to be a number of popular titles like *Common Sense School Reform* (Hess, 2004) and *Making Schools Work* (Ouchi, 2003) that propose all-too-simple answers for improving American schools and meeting the standards of NCLB at little or no additional cost. These simple answers range from telling schools and districts precisely what educational model to use, how to organize their staff, and how to deliver a prepackaged curriculum to simply passing budgets along to school-level leaders and letting them achieve outcomes however they may.

In general, we argue for continued experimentation and favor policies that allow for and promote experimentation, while providing appropriate monitoring and analysis to determine exactly what works. Expansion of charter schooling and site-based budgeting and management are two possible options for promoting such experimentation. But the approach is not managed well. American schools would benefit from national demonstration models that provide detailed information about student profiles, per-pupil expenditures, curriculum, organization, hours of instruction, tutoring, and other interventions so that a portrait might emerge of practices and models that are highly effective. We also favor disseminating among school leaders reliable and useful information on strategies that have been tried under specific circumstances and have led to improved performance at comparable or lower cost using more traditional cost-effectiveness audits. Yet productive experimentation accomplished through flexibility, decentralization, and deregulation requires a more knowledgeable, better trained, more creative, entrepreneurial, and quite simply *smarter* labor force of teachers and school leaders.

We approach with extreme caution state policies that would impose one specific solution across varied environments. Indeed, there are "solutions" out there, such as comprehensive school reforms (CSR) or class-size reduction (also CSR, not surprisingly) that have been proposed as the panacea for improved across-the-board school performance, regardless of context, except perhaps—teacher quality. While some modest statistically significant gains for some student populations, under some circumstances may be associated with strategies such as whole-school reform, we take the stand that we still know far too little about not just the effectiveness but, more importantly, about the cost-effectiveness of these strategies (see Chapter 15). Large-scale implementation of such reforms can simply *freeze into place* new inefficiencies in public schooling that are at best marginal improvements over our current "one best system" and are not particularly cost-effective.

7. Are U.S. schools more or less segregated by race and social class in 2007 than in 1960, and has education been an effective means of social mobility in the United States?

Education is widely seen as a vehicle for social mobility. Given the unprecedented amount of money we have spent on public education in the last 40 years, what evidence do we have that it has narrowed social class differences or at least expanded the middle class? Indeed, what are the correlations between the shape of educational production and the shape of the social class structure in the United States, if any?

What is the role of privatization, choice, charter schools, and home schooling in the debate? What alternative forms of schooling organization and delivery appear most promising for the future, and which have failed most miserably in the past? In the United States, we now have over 1 million children home-schooling (Chapter 2). Charter school enrollments have recently reached similar levels (www.edreform.org). We also have a significant use of cyber schooling to meet the needs of children outside bricks-and-mortar school systems. We know virtually nothing of this movement, although it portends to be of critical importance to the future of education and perhaps of even more urgent importance for educational advancement in the developing world

Conclusion

Most graduate students in education leadership, education policy, or economics of education come across a single course in school finance during their program of studies. This course may seek to be comprehensive and address budgeting, capital financing, and even higher education finance. In this textbook, we have purposely chosen the narrow approach and declined to provide a general survey of topics, not because they are unworthy, but because they deserve more attention than we can give them and because the positive trade-off is to provide you with the opportunity to acquire a more in-depth understanding of K–12 education finance. Yet, still we are left with more to say than space and time allow.

We are certain our colleagues in the field have questions of their own, but for the moment these are our questions. We hope that they guide you to make inquiries of your own. We close this book paraphrasing insights put forth by Arthur Wise in 1976 regarding the *then* future of public school finance:

> Some courts, having opened the Pandora's Box of cost-quality research, are willing to close it and are calling for the equalization of educational expenditures—the original objective of school finance reform. Other courts have left the question of equity open and expect educational reform to result from financial reform. It remains to be seen if the strategy of mandating minimum educational adequacy will result in serious educational progress.

Certainly, the cost-quality controversy–with its hyper rationalized view of education–does not deny the possibility of progress. However, the social science controversy poses difficulties to those who wish to challenge a state's total system of school finance. The expectation of demonstrable educational change means that less formidable challenges will be brought. The concept of functional exclusion initiated in *Lau v. Nichols* is particularly potent. The courts are well beyond school finance reform. In how many ways are children functionally excluded from the educational process?

Indeed, we are particularly guilty of having promoted a hyper-rationalized view of school finance policy in this text. Arguably, school finance in the coming decades differs little from that which Arthur Wise foresaw in 1976. While the empirics have improved and state policies evolved, too many children remain functionally excluded from a viable educational process. We would prefer not to rely on the hope that the next 30 years of developments in school finance policy will begin to overcome the deficiencies of the past 30 years. Rather, we hope to rely on a thoughtful and aggressive social agenda in which a well-educated and politically active citizenry succeeds not only in closing the gap but also in raising the bar in educational achievement.

REFERENCES

Brunner, E., & Sonsteile, J. (2003). Homeowners, property values and the political economy of the school voucher. *Journal of Urban Economics, 54*(2), 239–257.

Green, P. C., & Baker, B. D. (2006). Urban legends, desegregation and school finance: Did Kansas City really prove that money doesn't matter? *Michigan Journal of Race and Law, 12*(1), 57–105.

Hess, F. (2004). *Common sense school reform.* New York: Palgrave.

Lau V. Nichols, 414 U.S. 563 (1974).

Orfield, G. (2001). *Schools more separate: Consequences of a decade of resegregation.* Cambridge, MA: Harvard Civil Rights Project.

Ouchi, W. G. (2003). *Making schools work: A revolutionary plan to get your children the education they need.* New York: Simon & Schuster.

Wise, A. (1976). Minimum educational adequacy: Beyond school finance reform. *Journal of Education Finance, 1*(4), 468–483.

SUGGESTED READINGS

Evans, W., Murray, S., & Schwab, R. M. (1999). The impact of court-mandated school finance reform. In H. Ladd, R. Chalk, & J. Hansen (Eds.), *Equity and adequacy in education finance: Issues and perspectives.* Committee on Education Finance, Commission on Behavioral and Social Sciences and Education, National Research Council. Washington, DC: National Academy Press.

Frankenberg, E., & Lee, C. (2002). *Race in American public schools: rapidly resegregating school districts.* Harvard Civil Rights Project. Retrieved from http://www.civilrightsproject.harvard.edu/research/deseg/Race_in_American_Public_Schools1.pdf

Heckman, J., & Krueger, A. (2003). *Inequality in America: What role for human capital policies?* Cambridge, MA: MIT Press.

Hoxby, C. M., & Leigh, A. (2005). *Pulled away or pushed out? explaining the decline of teacher aptitude in the United States.* Retrieved from http://www.educationnext.org/unabridged/20052/50.pdf

Hussar, W., & Sonnenberg, W. (2000). *Trends in disparities in school district level expenditures.* NCES 2000 – 020. Washington, DC: National Center for Education Statistics.

Lukemeyer, A. (2004). Financing a constitutional education: Views from the bench. In J. Yinger (Ed.), *Helping Children Left Behind: State Aid and the Pursuit of Educational Equity.* Cambridge, MA: MIT Press.

Murnane, R. (1996). Staffing the nation's schools with skilled teachers. In E. Hanushek & D. Jorgenson (Eds.), *Improving America's schools: The role of incentives* (p. 247). Washington DC: National Academy Press.

Nechyba, T. J. (2004). Prospects for achieving equity or adequacy in education: Limits of state aid in general equilibrium. In J. Yinger (Ed.), *Helping Children Left Behind: State Aid and the Pursuit of Educational Equity.* Cambridge, MA: MIT Press.

Rothstein, R. (2004). *Class and schools: Using social, economic and educational reform to close the black–white achievement gap.* New York: Teachers College Press.

Rufo-Lignos, P., & Richards, C. E. (2003). Emerging forms of school organization. *Teachers College Record, 105*(5), 753–781.

Wise, A. (1976). Minimum educational adequacy: Beyond school finance reform. *Journal of Education Finance, 1*(4), 468—483.

USEFUL ONLINE RESOURCES

The Civil Rights Project at Harvard University www.civilrightsproject.harvard.edu

National Center for the Study of Privatization in Education www.ncspe.org

Teacher Policy Research Center –Retrieved from http://www.teacherpolicyresearch.org/